Distressed Debt Analysis
Strategies for Speculative Investors

Stephen G. Moyer, CFA

Copyright ©2005 by Stephen G. Moyer

ISBN 1-932159-18-5

Printed and bound in the U.S.A. Printed on acid-free paper
11

Library of Congress Cataloging-in-Publication Data

Moyer, Stephen G., 1957–
  Distressed debt analysis : strategies for speculative investors /
Stephen G. Moyer.
    p. cm.
  Includes bibliographical references and index.
  ISBN 1-932159-18-5
  1. Bankruptcy—United States. 2. Business failures—Law and
legislation—United States. 3. Corporate reorganizations—United
States. 4. Speculation—United States. 5. Investments—United States.
I. Title.
  HG3766.M69 2004
  332.63′2042—dc22   2003027305

Phone: (954) 727-9333
Fax: (561) 892-0700
Web: www.jrosspub.com

DEDICATION

To Tom B. Moyer,
my father,
whose continuing optimism and sense of humor
following a debilitating stroke
have taught me the power of a positive attitude

TABLE OF CONTENTS

NOTES ON STYLE

A few stylistic decisions that were made in an effort to simplify the exposition should be mentioned.

First, in distressed investing, like most aspects of life, if there is a rule, there is almost certainly an exception to the rule. So that the primary point is not lost in a morass of detail, when appropriate, many of these "exceptions" are dealt with in footnotes, as are illustrative examples.

Second, some terminology conventions: "bond" and "note" are used interchangeably, while the word "security" or "securities" can refer to any financial instrument — including bonds, bank debt, and trade claims — even though the latter two may not technically fall within the definition of "securities" under certain laws. Also, the discussion of bond pricing follows the industry trading convention of stating the price as a percentage of par, but with no percent symbol. Thus, if a bond is stated at a price of, for example, 27, it means 27% of the $1000 par amount or $270.

Third, to avoid confusion between references to chapters in this book and the Bankruptcy Code, references to chapters in the latter appear in lowercase letters.

Finally, the following citation conventions are used:

- Bankruptcy Code: The Bankruptcy Act of 1978 as contained in Title 11 of the United States Code, as amended
- BRC: The Bankruptcy Code
- IRC: The Internal Revenue Code of 1986, as amended
- Exchange Act: The Securities Exchange Act of 1934, as amended
- Securities Act: The Securities Exchange Act of 1933, as amended

ACKNOWLEDGMENTS

This book could not have been written without the input and support of many individuals. Their contributions, though different in nature and detail, were all valuable, and thus none shall be highlighted to the exclusion of others. Of course, all errors are the author's alone.

Dana Benson
Andrew Bernknopf
Todd Bolin
Monica Butschek
Connell Byrne
Matt Covington
Andrew Cray
Elizabeth Dobbs
Elizabeth Ellers
Joseph Farricielli
Dan Gechtman
Joe Gechtman
Heather Gift
Mary Gilbert
Larry Gill
Adam Gubner
Susan Hagen
Melissa Henderson
David Hollander
Steve Hornstein

Robert Konefal
Irene Kung
Randy Laufman
Mark Levin
Brian Lieberman
John Martin
Mark Martis
Lauren Kristine Mitte
Menasche Nass
Steven Peterson
JoLynn Pineda
Christopher Provost
Srilata Rao
Tom Salerno
Michael Scaglione
Tom Shinkle
Andrea Smith
Tom Thompson
Richard Waks
Ryan Whitesell

ABOUT THE AUTHOR

Stephen G. Moyer is a Portfolio Manager and Analyst in the Distressed Credit Group at Pacific Investment Management Company (PIMCO). Mr. Moyer has over 20 years of experience in investment analysis and corporate finance. His interest in distressed securities analysis began when he was a member of the High Yield Research Group at Drexel Burnham Lambert. He has also been affiliated with many other leading securities firms and investment managers including Tennenbaum Capital Partners, The First Boston Corporation (now Credit Suisse), Banc of America Securities, Kemper Securities (now Wells Fargo) and Imperial Capital. He began his career as a lawyer at Jones Day and later with Riordan & McKenzie. He is a recognized speaker and writer on the subject of distressed securities and a frequent lecturer at industry events and graduate business programs.

Mr. Moyer received a J.D. from Stanford University Law School, an M.B.A. from the University of Chicago Business School, and a B.A. from Grinnell College. He is a member of the California and Texas bars, holds the Chartered Financial Analyst designation, and has passed the Uniform Certified Public Accounting Examination.

™Web
Added
Value

Free value-added materials available from
the Download Resource Center at www.jrosspub.com

At J. Ross Publishing we are committed to providing today's professional with practical, hands-on tools that enhance the learning experience and give readers an opportunity to apply what they have learned. That is why we offer free ancillary materials available for download on this book and all participating Web Added Value™ publications. These online resources may include interactive versions of material that appears in the book or supplemental templates, worksheets, models, plans, case studies, proposals, spreadsheets and assessment tools, among other things. Whenever you see the WAV™ symbol in any of our publications, it means bonus materials accompany the book and are available from the Web Added Value Download Resource Center at www.jrosspub.com.

Downloads available for *Distressed Debt Analysis: Strategies for Speculative Investors* consist of a due diligence checklist and glossary, sample big-boy letters, confidentiality agreements, participation agreements, and examples of covenant provisions and chapter 11 plans of reorganization.

1

INTRODUCTION

The period from 1999 to 2002 witnessed an unprecedented number of corporate bankruptcies in the United States. A total of approximately 439 firms with assets greater than $100 million filed for bankruptcy during this period. For at least 13 of these firms, it was their second visit to bankruptcy court. For six firms, it was actually their third visit.[1] Fortunately, there appears to be an informal "three strikes and you're out" rule, as each of the so-called chapter 33s appears destined to be liquidated and put out of its misery. The total amount of debt and claims involved in the insolvencies over this period is difficult to precisely estimate, but easily exceeds $400 billion.[2]

For most investors and investment managers, this was a period of significant financial loss. For many investors, however, it was also a period of substantial opportunity. Prescient investors made money "shorting" securities, including debt securities they expected to fall in value. Still others made superior investment returns, adroitly investing in securities of companies in, or at risk of filing for, bankruptcy.

The purpose of this book is to provide the insight and skills necessary to invest successfully in the securities of financially distressed companies. First, we should discuss the subject matter. What is meant by distressed debt and why does it potentially represent an attractive investment? It sounds about as counterintuitive as wanting to invest in "junk bonds," and not surprisingly, the concepts are related. What often surprises many noninvestment professionals is the fact that debt securities — such as bonds and notes, bank loans, leases, and even simple unpaid bills — are traded among institutions and investors much like stocks. They can trade up and down in value, and the general approach to profiting from investment can be summarized by the maxim buy low, sell high.

AN EXAMPLE OF A DISTRESSED DEBT SITUATION

To provide some perspective on the process involved in, and investment return potential of, distressed debt investing, a short case study of Magellan Health Services is presented. The case was selected as being representative of the types of situations that arise and issues that are confronted in distressed debt investing, but was neither the most complicated nor the most lucrative — although the returns, depending on the timing of investment, were certainly attractive.

Magellan is the largest behavioral health managed care provider in the United States. Behavioral health issues, at one time or another, affect over 10% of the population and include a range of ailments from mild depression, to substance abuse and dependency, to more severe pathologies such as paranoia or schizophrenia. In general, Magellan acts as a specialty subcontractor of behavioral health care benefits for larger, full-service health care plans. Thus, if a particular Blue Cross/Blue Shield health care plan, for example, wanted to offer its customers behavioral health coverage but did not want, or did not find it economically feasible, to do the contracting and administration involved in providing such a benefit, it might subcontract with a firm such as Magellan. The very rough economics might be that the cost of providing full health care coverage (which is typically borne by employers) would be $400 per person per month (pp/pm) and the general provider might pay Magellan $5 pp/pm to provide the behavioral health care portion. Magellan might hope to provide that coverage for $4 pp/pm, with the difference representing profit.[3] There are economies of scale in the administration of niche health care benefits; therefore, it might cost the primary provider more than $5 pp/pm to directly provide the behavioral health care benefit on its own. At its peak, Magellan served over 65 million covered lives and had approximately 35% market share.[4]

Magellan grew to become the largest in its niche primarily through acquisition. A pivotal acquisition for the company occurred in 1998 when it purchased the behavioral health care business of Aetna Insurance for $422 million. Payment of the purchase price was structured with $122 million in cash due at closing and five annual cash payments of $60 million (which were subject to adjustment depending on how many covered lives Aetna delivered). Magellan operated on a fiscal year ending September 30. Magellan's revenues grew from $303 million in fiscal 1996 to $1.310 billion in fiscal 1998 (the first full year of the Aetna acquisition) to $1.728 billion in fiscal 2001. In late 1999, Texas Pacific Group (TPG), a well-known private equity investment fund, invested $55 million in the form of convertible preferred stock. When added to previous investments, this raised TPG's fully diluted ownership position to approximately 26%.[5]

In fiscal first quarter 2002, problems began to surface on several levels. On the revenue side, Aetna, which was approximately 23% of Magellan's business, attempted to implement price increases and lost 1.5 million covered lives. In addition, Magellan was notified that it would lose a significant contract for the state of Tennessee. On the cost side, the economic recession, higher unemployment rates, and the aftermath of the September 11 tragedy resulted in higher utilization of behavioral health services, reducing Magellan's margins. In the simple terms outlined above, whereas Magellan had expected the cost of coverage to be only $4 pp/pm, it was perhaps $4.25 to $4.50 pp/pm. Further, Magellan was behind schedule and over budget on a $40 million information system integration project that had a goal of rationalizing 23 separate systems (accumulated during its acquisition phase) into one integrated system and faced additional system demands due to newly mandated patient privacy regulations.[6]

Revenues went from an increasing trend to a declining trend. Cash flow from operations, as measured by earnings before interest, taxes, depreciation, and amortization (EBITDA), began to decline steadily.[7] By June 30, 2002, EBITDA for the last 12 months was $187 million, down from the prior year's rate of $220 million. After a variety of working capital adjustments and special payments, however, true cash from operations was closer to $100–$120 million. While substantial in absolute terms, Magellan had considerable debt and significant cash obligations. Total debt was $1.079 billion, comprised of:

$ Million	Security
144	Secured bank debt and capital leases
250	9.375% senior notes due 2007 (the seniors)
60	Aetna contract payment due March 2003
625	9.00% senior subordinated notes due 2008 (the subs)
1079	Total

Operationally, Magellan faced $88 million in interest costs and required approximately $35–$40 million for capital improvements. In addition, it had to pay the $60 million due to Aetna and needed to replace $22 million of surety bonds that could not be economically renewed with either letters of credit or cash escrow accounts. It was also suspected, but not quantified at the time, that as Magellan's deteriorating financial condition became more well publicized, state insurance regulators might demand increased statutory capital at various insurance subsidiaries. In its 10-Q filing for fiscal third quarter of 2002, management indicated that the company would likely be in technical default of certain covenants in the bank facility on September 30, 2002, and without access to the facility would likely face severe liquidity problems. The price of the seniors fell from 95 on May 15, 2002 to 69 on August 16, 2002. The subs fell from 77 to 30 over the same period.[8]

On October 1, 2002, Magellan announced that it had retained a well-known financial advisor[9] to advise the company with respect to a comprehensive balance sheet restructuring. Prior to this announcement, most observers had expected Magellan to simply try to amend the bank facility and restructure and defer the Aetna payment. The announcement of a "comprehensive restructuring," although recognized as a risk previously, significantly increased the probability of a chapter 11 proceeding. The seniors fell to 65 and the subs to 22. At a price of 22, the market value of the capital structure through the subs was $556 million, which represented 3.0x the last 12 months EBITDA of $187 million; of course, since a bankruptcy might negatively affect Magellan's contracts, making confident estimates of future EBITDA levels was difficult.[10]

Following this announcement, as is often the case, information from Magellan was less forthcoming. On February 23, 2003, Magellan released fiscal first quarter 2003 results that were stronger than the market expected. Although no official word had been released, the market was generally aware that the company was attempting to organize a preplanned chapter 11 reorganization that would likely involve the bank debt, Aetna obligation, and seniors being essentially reinstated, while the subs would be converted into a majority of the equity. This scenario implied that TPG, and other significant stockholders, essentially would be wiped out. The stock had traded from a high of $28 per share in mid-1998 to $0.08 per share. The improved operating results caused the seniors' price to improve to 82, but the subs only improved to 25.[11]

On March 11, 2003, Magellan filed for chapter 11 protection. Included with its petition was a proposed plan of reorganization (the plan) that provided for the senior claims to be reinstated and the subs to receive, before adjustment for certain stock sales in a rights offering, 92.5% of postreorganization equity (with management and certain other unsecured creditors receiving the balance). The plan also contemplated a rights offering (i.e., a right to purchase a share of stock at a specified price) to raise $50 million in new capital. Both the seniors and subs could participate in the offering, the final terms of which had not been determined, and a major hedge fund that had purchased the subs at a significant discount would "backstop" the offering (i.e., purchase any shares not purchased by holders of the seniors or subs). The proposal effectively valued Magellan's equity at $188 million. The seniors improved to 85 and the subs to 28.[12]

Then a bidding war of sorts broke out. On May 28, 2003, Magellan announced that Onex Corp., a private equity fund, had agreed to invest $100 million for 29.9% of Magellan's equity and backstop a $50 million rights offering to the various note classes for 14.9% of the stock. The equity value implied by this transaction was $335 million, with the rights offering tentatively priced at \$18.57 per share. The seniors continued to firm to 99 and the subs rose to 35.[13] On June 30, 2003, in response to more direct negotiations with creditors, a revised valuation, and the potential involvement of other parties, Onex increased its offer to one using an implied equity valuation of \$436 million. This time it offered to invest \$75 million for 17.2% of the equity at a price of \$28.50 per share and backstop a \$75 million rights offering at the same price to creditors. The significance of this adjustment was that it gave the creditors the right to purchase just as much of the equity as Onex. The seniors improved to 101 and the subs (which would receive approximately 60% of the equity directly) jumped to 49.[14] At that point, appreciation in the value of the subs from an October low of 22 was approximately 122%.

Over the next several months, there continued to be fine-tuning, and the final plan of reorganization proposed to give the seniors full recovery (i.e., full face value) in a virtually identical new 9.375% note and a cash payment equal to 9%, for an implied recovery of 109%. From the low of 63, this represented appreciation of 73% over an approximately 15-month period. The subs received 33.1 shares per bond and had the right to purchase an additional 8.5 shares per bond at a price of \$12.39 per share.[15] When the shares began to trade on January 7, 2004, the closing price of \$27 implied a total recovery to the subs (assuming participation in the rights offering) of approximately 102. Factoring in the time periods and the incremental investment required for the rights offering, from the low the total rate of return on investment was approximately 231%. Even if one had waited until July 1, 2003 and purchased the subs at the then offered price of 50, the recovery would have represented 104% of the amount invested.

If at this point you are not quite sure exactly what happened and why — that's all right; you should understand by the end of the book. If you are an experienced distressed investor whose head was nodding because you purchased the subs at 22, good for you, but hopefully you will still benefit from some of the nuances discussed later.[16]

The point of this example is not to suggest that every distressed investment will offer this type of return potential. It is easy to exaggerate returns by choosing low and high prices, although it should be noted that investors had many months to purchase the subs in the 20s and a significant volume of bonds did trade at those price levels. As the Magellan case attests, returns can be very volatile. If an investor had bought at 29 and sold at 20 thinking a mistake had been made, a 31% loss would have been incurred. Of course, someone originally paid 100 for the subs. When the original investors sold, as they must have or there would have been no bonds to trade, they incurred losses. The bigger point of the example, and a main theme of this book, is that distressed debt investing is a process that must be proactively monitored because investment circumstances change. Often these changes can be anticipated and capitalized on to earn superior investment returns.

WHAT IS DISTRESSED DEBT?

There is no universally recognized definition of distressed debt. The most traditional way of categorizing debt is with reference to the ratings systems of the most prominent debt rating agencies: Moody's Investors Service (Moody's) and Standard & Poor's (S&P). While these firms use slightly different ratings notations (see Table 1-1), they have a functionally similar 10-grade scheme ranging from AAA to D. A prominent dividing line is between BBB and BB. BBB and above is classified as investment grade, while BB and below is characterized as speculative grade and was, during the 1980s, pejoratively labeled "junk." S&P's category descriptions paint a grim picture: BB = speculative, B = highly speculative, CCC = substantial risk, CC = extremely speculative, C = may be in default, and D = default. It might be fun to add E = exterminated and F = flushed.

These schemes are only marginally useful for two reasons: first, because the ratings often lag fundamental credit developments, and second, they essentially only attempt to "handicap" the risk of a default. In general, bond ratings do not attempt to provide any information about whether the trading value of any particular bond is appropriate. Indeed, there have been cases where the secured debt of a company in default was technically rated D, but trading at full face value.

One of the more widely accepted definitions of "distressed debt" is generally attributed to Martin Fridson,[17] one of the deans of high-yield bond analysis. Mr. Fridson classified distressed debt as debt trading with a yield to maturity of

Table 1-1. Primary Bond Rating Classification Scheme

S&P	Moody's	
AAA	AAA	
AA	Aa	Investment
A	A	Grade
BBB	Baa	
BB	Ba	
B	B	
CCC	Caa	Speculative
CC	Ca	Grade
C	C	
D		

greater than 1000 basis points more than the comparable underlying treasury security.[18] This approach essentially relies on the "efficiency" of the market, which is presumed to accurately discount all available credit information into trading prices to establish risk parameters. While sound methodologically, the absolute 1000-basis-point benchmark may not be appropriate in all market environments. Historically, average credit risk spreads fluctuate widely. For example, from 1983 to 2000, the average speculative-grade spread was 487 basis points.[19] Excluding the impact of the volatile 1989–1991 period (discussed in Chapter 2), the average spread would have been under 400 basis points. Thus in normal market environments, the 1000-basis-point distressed benchmark basically implies a risk premium of 100–150% of the average risk premium. However, in the third quarter of 2002, the average spread was 1064 basis points. While a great many situations during that period may have been appropriately characterized as distressed, to a certain extent, the descriptive power of the 1000-basis-point benchmark declined.

For the purposes of this book, an exact definition of "distressed debt" is unnecessary. The investment situations examined will generally have a couple of fairly consistent and telling characteristics: the market value of the equity of the "distressed" company will be *diminimus* (e.g., stock trading under $1 per share), and all or some portion of unsecured debt will be trading at a market discount of more than 40%. What this fact pattern generally implies, if not invariably results in, is some type of balance sheet restructuring, in which the creditors eventually own a significant percentage of the company's equity, or a sale of assets and subsequent liquidation. As will be shown later, these balance sheet restructurings and/or liquidations often lead to misvaluations of the company's securities and provide an opportunity for superior investment performance.

The title references debt, but the scope of this book includes a wide variety of investment instruments, including bank loans, bonds of various seniority, leases, trade claims, and even preferred stocks — which, it can be argued, are really very junior debt securities.[20] The fact of the matter is that modern financial markets have created a bewildering array of instruments by which companies can essentially borrow money or finance the purchase of assets, and any of these instruments could have its value affected by the circumstance of financial distress and, theoretically, represent an investment opportunity. The common stock of such companies will, except for its potential as a short-sale or hedge security, generally not receive much attention because in distressed situations it is, more often than not, worthless. The role of shareholders as owners of the equity, although in distressed scenarios this may be more of a technical fact than economic reality, is discussed within the context of chapter 11 bankruptcy reorganizations.

Table 1-2.   **Annual Market Returns for CCC Bonds 1999–2003**[21]

Year	Total Return
1999	−3.0%
2000	−30.6%
2001	−2.1%
2002	−12.7%
2003	50.8%

Source: Credit Suisse First Boston

INVESTING IN DISTRESSED DEBT

Investing in distressed securities can be a risky endeavor. If CCC-rated bonds are, for convenience, used as a proxy for distressed, then the negative market returns for this group over the 1999–2002 period, shown in Table 1-2, illustrate the dangers, while 2003 returns demonstrate the opportunity.

Distressed debt is not a particularly suitable or practical investment for individual investors for at least four reasons. First, as illustrated in Table 1-2, there is significant risk of loss. Second, professional participants in the market could have significant information advantages. Third, the distressed securities market is often fairly illiquid, which means there can be very high transaction costs for individuals investing on a "modest" scale. Such transaction costs increase the relative risk and make it very difficult to earn appropriate risk-adjusted returns. Finally, the size of the average trading unit or block is so large that, except for the most wealthy, it is difficult to have an adequately diversified portfolio — and the risk of this asset class is such that investing should generally be done on a diversified basis. For example, bank debt and corporate bonds generally trade in blocks of $5 million and $1 million, respectively. Thus, though distressed securities may trade at significant discounts, this still implies that to own a diversified portfolio of 20 different companies could require a significant amount of capital. Accordingly, individual investors who want to invest in this asset class are strongly advised to invest through a professionally managed vehicle such as a mutual fund or hedge fund.

The cover of this book depicts a chessboard and two kings: the victorious towering over the vanquished foe. Chess is an appropriate metaphor for distressed investing because, more than any other form of investment, to be successful it requires a well-conceived strategy. As mentioned earlier, a key aspect of distressed debt situations is that a balance sheet restructuring has occurred or may occur. That event, or the risk of that event, introduces a significant level of complexity into the investment process. Just a few of the issues that arise in the context of a restructuring, which this book discusses in detail, include:

- Will the restructuring occur within or outside of a bankruptcy context?
- What is the risk a company could lose economic value if it is forced to go though a formal bankruptcy reorganization because of the loss of key customers, suppliers, or employees?
- How much economic value might be gained through a bankruptcy?
- If the balance sheet is restructured, what will its new composition be, and how will those parts be distributed to existing creditors or other stakeholders?
- What are the tax consequences of a restructuring?
- Does any particular investor have a "controlling" stake that might allow that investor to influence the reorganization process in a way that will affect recoveries of various creditors/investors?

While it could be argued that all investments require a degree of strategic foresight, the degree involved in distressed investing is fundamentally different. Take, for example, the standard stock investment. The investor may take into account management's strategy versus its competition, or have a strategic macroeconomic view that the industry in which the firm participates will benefit from some event or trend, or have an arbitrage-type strategy that the firm will be purchased by another firm. But at the end of the day, the investor chooses a stock and buys it because he or she expects it to go up (or sells short if it is expected to go down). If it is a bond investment, a particular type or maturity of bond might "strategically' be chosen because of some anticipated movement in interest rates.

Without diminishing the difficulty of the analytical process involved in these types of investment decisions, it is less complex compared to the multistep analysis that a distressed debt analyst must undertake. Among the many considerations involved in the analysis of a potential distressed investment are:

- What is the cause of the distress?
- How will the distress be resolved?
- What are the implications of that (or another) resolution on the value of the business and, more specifically, any particular security?
- What actions on the part of bondholders are being assumed to realize any particular outcome?
- Will the price of the instrument being considered simply go up, or will it be exchanged into one or more different securities requiring an analysis of potential market values?

As will be discussed in Chapter 10, it can be useful to construct decision or scenario "trees" to help analyze all of the combinations of events that can affect the investment outcome.

Of course, most games, by definition, also have strategic elements: run versus pass in football, sacrifice fly in baseball, full-court press in basketball. But chess is a particularly appropriate metaphor because it is entirely intellectual, with no element of physical prowess relevant. At most points during the game, there is a relatively wide array of possible moves, and the choice of move necessarily requires an analysis of what the other player may do in response. Accordingly, the best players tend to be better at seeing many moves into the future and planning for many alternative scenarios. However, for the infinite variations possible in a game, each chess piece is governed by a very well-defined set of rules, which can be analogized to the myriad contract, securities, and bankruptcy laws that shape a reorganization.

But there are differences that arguably make distressed debt investing even more strategically challenging than chess. First, chess is between two forces that initially are equal in power with a clear strategic objective: capture the opponent's king. In distressed debt investing, there are many different "players" in the game, many of which have unclear goals that make it difficult to forecast their moves. For example, some participants could be interested in simply minimizing potential losses, which might cause them to sell at times or at levels that later could be second-guessed. Other investors may have a short-term strategy of making a modest investment in a part of the capital structure they think may appreciate in the near future with a view to selling quickly if that occurs. Yet others could have a long-term strategy where they buy the distressed securities with a view that perhaps several years later, following a chapter 11 reorganization, they will be the majority equity holder. Of course, the firm in financial distress is hardly a passive participant. It may be selling key assets to raise cash or using its existing cash to repurchase debt rather than adequately fund its business. Finally, the firm's competitors may also attempt to get involved and use the restructuring or liquidation to strategic advantage.[22]

The complexity brings to mind a chess variation popular in the mid-70s, the "Bobby Fisher" era, where the game is played on three separate boards that are stacked in an offset manner to make visualization of the playing field more challenging. Now imagine that each of the boards has a different set of players and there is imperfect communication between the players on the same side so that there is considerable risk of strategic confusion. Or, in an even more bizarre variation, assume that the players on the middle board, unbeknownst to all the other players, are engaged in a "side game" in which their only strategic objective is to capture an opponent's pawns, regardless of the strategic ramifications for the game as a whole.

While care will be taken to avoid overusing the chess metaphor, and knowledge of chess is certainly not a prerequisite for understanding the material, the basic requirement in chess — that the player think several moves into the future and consider the implications of all the scenarios — is very similar to the analytical process the distressed debt investor must adopt. Accordingly, to reinforce this, and as a hopefully amusing aside to those who may enjoy the game, chess moves are given in standard chess notation at the end of each chapter. These moves recount the fifth game between Bobby Fisher and Boris Spassky in the 1972 World Championship held in Reykjavik, Iceland. A full list of the moves together with a brief note explaining chess notation is provided in the Appendix.

This book is intended to be more of a practitioner's guide than an academic treatise. However, since being effective at distressed debt investing requires knowledge of a number of areas such as bankruptcy law, the trading mechanics of the debt capital markets, and the fundamentals of corporate finance and capital structure, background in, though not a definitive discussion of, these areas is provided. Some of these topics — for example, the implications of a restructuring on the usability of net operating loss carryforwards for purposes of valuing a deferred tax asset — are fairly complex. In approaching these subjects, Albert Einstein's admonition to make things "as simple as possible, but no simpler" was the author's goal.

The organization of the book is from general to specific. First, the scope and nature of the distressed debt market are described. Then a conceptual overview of what it means for firms to be in financial distress and how the distress can be resolved or alleviated through different types of balance sheet restructurings is provided. At the next level, how to recognize companies that are or are likely to become financially distressed, the causes of the distress, and how the cause impacts the investment strategy are reviewed. In this part of the book, some of the more important aspects of the legal intricacies of lending documents or indentures and bankruptcy law are explained because, together, these form the framework or rules within which the restructuring takes place. Finally, with the groundwork laid, the practical aspects of distressed debt investment such as identifying the appropriate opportunity, determining due diligence needs, position accumulation techniques, and negotiation strategies are approached. Throughout the book, references to actual cases will be employed in an attempt to make the book as practical and relevant as possible.

Distressed investing is risky and challenging, but potentially very rewarding. Hopefully, this work will better acquaint the reader with the knowledge, skills, and judgment necessary for success.

The Chess Game Opening Moves

1. Pc4, Pe6

THE DISTRESSED DEBT INVESTMENT OPPORTUNITY

The market opportunity for distressed debt investors has arguably never been greater. While bankruptcies are normally an anathema to most investors, actual or potential corporate insolvency can present a money-making opportunity for distressed investors. During the 2000–2003 period, corporate bankruptcies on a dollar volume basis were unprecedented — over $400 billion. Even when compared historically and weighted by the amount of debt then outstanding, the severity of the recent period was exceeded only twice before: the recession from 1990 to 1991 and the Great Depression from 1929 to 1933.[1]

Since virtually any situation involving financial distress can lead to profitable investment opportunities, this has been an unparalleled environment for investing in distressed securities. Of course, for many of the original investors in what became distressed securities, this was also a period of unparalleled losses. But this didactic is a function of free trading markets, not the fact that it happens to revolve around financial distress. Whenever someone is smart or fortunate enough to sell at the top, it implies someone else made a poor decision. Similarly, when someone buys at the bottom, somebody else had to sell. Perhaps the more important question looking forward, however, is: Will there be comparable opportunities in the future? The future, naturally, is impossible to predict. But many of the elements that appear to correlate with financial distress and restructurings remain in place today. Thus, while there may not be as many situations in the near term, there should be abundant opportunities, depending on the time frame being considered, even if there is a relatively strong economic recovery.

This chapter will put the recently completed period in historical perspective and then suggest the type of opportunity that may lie in the future. First, the size and scope of the recent market for bankruptcies and restructurings will be detailed.[2] Next, to establish that this epoch of financial distress, while significant, is not unique or unrepeatable, some general precursors of financial distress will be developed to help investors identify periods of opportunity in the future. Finally, various inefficiencies in the distressed debt market that should allow skilled investors to earn above-average returns will be reviewed. This will set the stage for the bulk of the book, which will discuss how financial distress is typically resolved and how to identify and profitably invest in such situations.

FINANCIAL RESTRUCTURINGS IN THE 2000–2003 ERA

As a result of all the public press that has been devoted to such high-profile situations as Enron, WorldCom, and Global Crossing, to name just a few, one would need to be the proverbial hermit to be unaware that in the period from 2000 to 2003 the United States witnessed an unprecedented number of corporate bankruptcies and other financial restructurings. Figure 2-1 presents the big-picture summary using Moody's Investors Service (Moody's) data on defaults from 1982 to 2003.

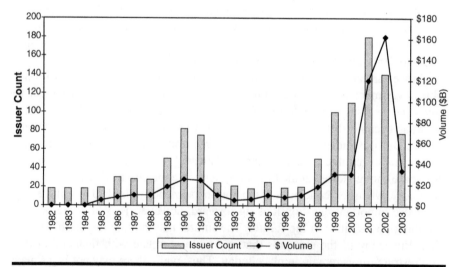

Figure 2-1.   Default Data 1982–2003[3] (Source: Moody's Investors Service)

Moody's defines default broadly to include not just bankruptcies, but also payment defaults, forced exchanges, and other events.[4] From the distressed investor's perspective, this broader definition, relative to simply bankruptcies, is more representative of the number of opportunities that were presented to distressed investors. However, even this understates the "true" number because there are always situations where the financial distress is a risk, which affects securities prices, but ultimately is resolved without triggering any of the definitions of default.[5] The size of the market for defaulted and distressed securities in 2003 was estimated to exceed $800 billion in face amount of securities.[6]

In reviewing Figure 2-1, it should be noted that there was another significant spike in defaults in the 1989–1991 time frame. The magnitude of that spike is somewhat dwarfed by the scale established in 1999–2002, but at the time it was a major financial event that also led to significant investment opportunities. While it is always difficult to prove causation, some of the events which coincided with the 1989–1991 default spike included: (a) a large number of increasingly speculative leveraged buyout transactions in the 1986–1989 period[7] financed by then-record levels of high-yield bond issuance;[8] (b) the implementation by the Federal Reserve of a tight monetary policy designed to quell inflation, which caused interest rates to rise to high nominal levels and resulted in an economic recession in the United States in 1990 and 1991;[9] and (c) the implementation of certain reforms on the then-troubled savings and loan industry, including passage of the Financial Institutions Reform, Recovery, and Enforcement Act of 1989,[10] which effectively required savings and loans to divest their high-yield bond portfolios in an unfavorable market environment.[11]

A better perspective on the distress "cycles" that have occurred in the U.S. economy can be gained by looking at historical default rates. Default rate, as defined by Moody's, is the amount of defaults (either measured by issuers or dollar weighted) during the period relative to the amount of appropriately rated debt outstanding.[12] Figure 2-2 shows default rates during the 1920–2003 time frame. Note that there were four noticeable spikes: 1931–1933, 1970, 1990–1991, and 2000–2002.

Excluding the 1970 aberration,[13] this view shows that the recent spike, while clearly significant, is not without precedent. In fact, as shown in Figure 2-3, on a relative basis, the 1930s and 1990s periods were actually more severe. However, at least three features distinguish the 2000 period from the past: the frequency of previously investment-grade companies defaulting, the average size of default, and the industrial sectors driving the default rates.

The first unique feature of the 2000 period is the number of previously investment-grade-rated companies to default. Chapter 1 discussed the basics of the credit grading scheme used by the major rating agencies. Issuer credit quality is rated from AAA to D. Rating levels above BBB are considered

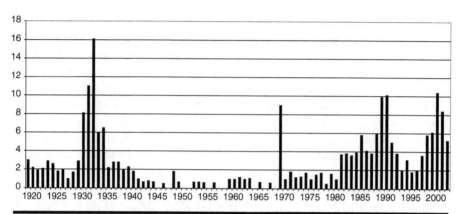

Figure 2-2.   Issuer Default Rates 1920–2003 (Source: Moody's Investors Service)

investment grade, while those below are known either as *below investment grade* or *speculative grade*. The common term for an investment-grade-rated firm that becomes speculative grade is a *fallen angel*. As shown in Figure 2-4, from 1983 to 2000, the percentage of investment-grade issuers falling to speculative grade averaged under 3%, while in 2002, it spiked to over 6% with 171 fallen angels.

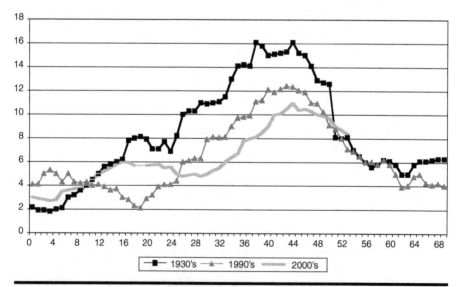

Figure 2-3.   Historical Default Rate Extrema (Source: Moody's Investors Service)

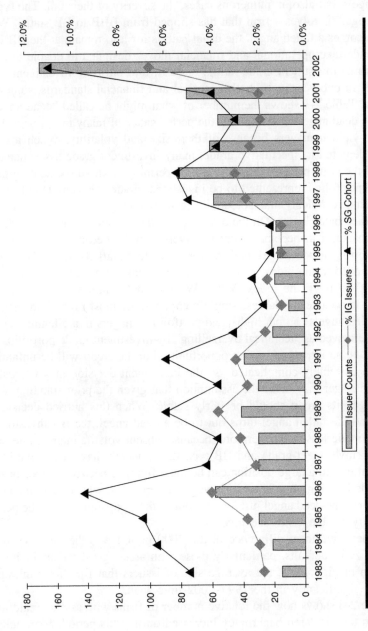

Figure 2-4. Fallen Angel Trends 1983–2002 (Source: Moody's Investors Service)

However, the 2000 period was marked not only by simply the number of fallen angels, but also, in numerous cases, the severity of their fall. The typical "fallen angel" involves a firm that has slipped from BBB to BB status. When a firm becomes a fallen angel, the usual path is for it to remain at the BB level and to undertake operational and financial moves designed to enable the firm to reattain its investment-grade rating. For a firm to fall from investment grade to default in one year is, by both historical and financial standards, somewhat shocking. Table 2-1 shows the number of what might be called "dead angels."

These dead angels severely hurt the performance of many investment-grade and high-yield managers because of their size and volatility. When a fallen angel is demoted to speculative grade, many investment-grade asset managers must sell the issue because they may not be permitted to hold speculative-grade bonds in portfolios represented to be investment grade. This can result in supply–demand technicals that potentially lead to selling at below "fair value," which exacerbates losses. On the other side of the equation, many BB-oriented asset managers can become "forced" buyers. This is because such managers often compare or benchmark their performance to a market index. If the fallen angel is added to the index, managers will often take some exposure (i.e., buy the credit) to track the index. When WorldCom became a fallen angel, for example, it became the largest single component of most high-yield indexes. Large fallen angels can put high-yield portfolio managers in a dilemma. Often, what is perceived as "technical overselling" by investment-grade portfolios can appear to be an attractive buying opportunity, but the credit will be unfamiliar and often extremely complicated. So the investment decision may be rushed, and the manager may make the assumption that given the prior standing of the fallen angel, its credit should be fairly stable. When this hurried decision is wrong, and the fallen angel turns out to be a dead angel, the BB investor can suffer dramatic losses. Furthermore, because, absent volatile interest rate environments, investment-grade and BB-type funds usually have low volatility, a significant loss in a large position can be the difference between outperforming or underperforming competitors. However, the point at which these managers begin selling the dead angel just to get it out of their portfolio can be the perfect opportunity for the distressed investor.

Another significant difference in the 2000 period was the increase in the relative size of defaults, particularly those with assets greater than $1 billion. As shown in Figure 2-5, the average size of issuers that filed for bankruptcy increased significantly in the 1999–2002 time span.

Figure 2-6 shows how the relative number of firms with assets greater than $1 billion that declared bankruptcy increased during this period. More telling, however, is the disproportionate impact these minority of bankruptcies (less than 20% in number in any year) had on assets in bankruptcy, as illustrated in Figure 2.7.

Table 2-1.   Investment-Grade Companies Defaulting Within One Year[14]

Company Name	Rating One Year Prior to Default	Bond Amount ($ Million)
2000 Fallen Angel Defaults		
Armstrong World	Baa1	1,640
Laidlaw	Baa3	3,400
Owens Corning	Baa3	2,675
2001 Fallen Angel Defaults		
Comdisco	Baa1	5,500
Enron	Baa1	13,000
Finova Group	Baa3	11,700
Pacific Gas & Electric	A2	19,300
Southern California Edison	A2	11,400
USG	Baa1	1,000
2002 Fallen Angel Defaults		
AT&T Canada	Baa3	2,960
Banco Commercial	Baa3	220
Banco de Montevideo	Baa3	300
Covanta Energy	Baa2	249
Duty Free International	Baa2	115
Energy Group Overseas	Baa1	500
Genuity	Baa2	2,000
Intermedia Communications	Baa2	3,122
Kmart	Baa3	2,481
Marconi Corporation	Baa2	3,272
MCI Communications	A3	2,640
NRG Energy	Baa3	2,455
NRG Northeast Generating	Baa3	750
NRG South Central Generating	Baa3	800
Petroleum Geo-Services	Baa3	1,460
PG&E National Energy Group	Baa2	1,000
Qwest Capital Funding	Baa1	12,903
Teleglobe	Baa1	1,224
TXU Eastern Funding	Baa1	2,136
TXU Europe	Baa1	150
WorldCom	A3	23,245
2003 Fallen Angel Defaults		
British Energy plc	A3	658
Lumbermans Mutual Casualty	Baa1	700
Northwestern	Baa2	1,294

Source: Moody's Investors Service

From the perspective of the smaller scale distressed debt investor, periods when there are an above-average number of large-scale bankruptcies can be particularly opportune because the larger situations often draw the attention of bigger distressed fund managers, who either overlook, are too busy, or inten-

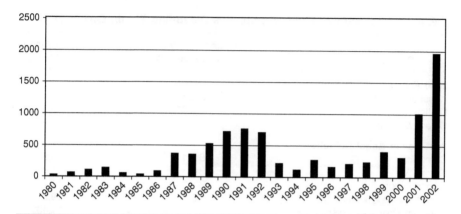

Figure 2-5. Average Asset Size of Bankrupt Firms 1980–2002 (Source: *2003 Bankruptcy Yearbook & Almanac*)

tionally avoid many attractive smaller situations. This can leave a significant number of small and medium-size situations available for smaller institutional investors to play active roles. Table 2-2 shows the trends in the size of bankruptcy filings from 1995 to 2002. Note how the number of bankruptcies involving assets under $50 million was relatively stable compared to many of the other larger asset size categories.

A third difference in the 2000 era was the industry distribution of defaults. As shown in Table 2-3, one of the primary causes of the dramatic increase in

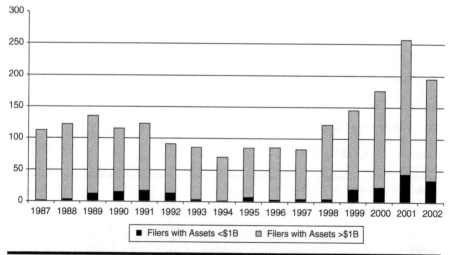

Figure 2-6. Public Bankruptcies by Size (Source: *2003 Bankruptcy Yearbook & Almanac*)

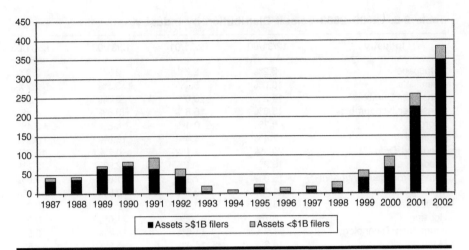

Figure 2-7. Assets of Public Bankruptcies by Size (Source: *2003 Bankruptcy Yearbook & Almanac*)

defaults was the large number of failures in the telecommunications and media sectors. While perhaps a simplification, the telecom defaults were largely a result of the failure of the perceived market for data transmission to develop as projected, resulting in less revenue generation than expected.[15] There was also a "weeding out" of uncompetitive players in the wireless telecommunications sector. When these failures occurred, the losses were often significantly greater than expected because these types of businesses are relatively less well understood and have few "hard" assets that can, as a last resort, be liquidated.[16] How does one sell a mile of "dark fiber" between Austin and Albuquerque or Honolulu and Hong Kong? By comparison, in the 1990 time frame, the retail

Table 2-2. Trends in Bankruptcies by Asset Size 1995–2002

Assets	2002	2001	2000	1999	1998	1997	1996	1995
More than $10 billion	7	5	0	0	0	0	0	0
$5–$10 billion	3	3	4	0	1	0	0	0
$2.5–$5 billion	10	9	5	4	0	1	0	2
$1–$2.5 billion	14	27	13	16	3	3	3	5
$0.5–$1 billion	25	20	18	11	9	4	5	5
$100–$500 million	56	86	65	48	32	22	19	19
$50–$100 million	15	37	22	14	14	11	14	8
Less than $50 million	65	69	49	52	61	41	43	45
Total bankruptcies	**195**	**256**	**176**	**145**	**120**	**82**	**84**	**84**

Source: *2003 Bankruptcy Yearbook & Almanac*

Table 2-3.   2000–2003 Default Distribution by Industry

Industry	12/31/00	12/31/01	12/31/02	12/31/03
Aerospace	3.2%	2.7%	12.7%	2.9%
Chemicals	10.0%	5.4%	3.5%	3.7%
Consumer Durables	14.2%	0.0%	0.0%	0.0%
Consumer Nondurables	13.8%	15.8%	8.8%	4.4%
Energy	0.7%	0.4%	4.8%	3.4%
Financial	7.4%	14.4%	16.8%	0.6%
Food and Drug	20.9%	4.1%	0.7%	10.7%
Food/Tobacco	16.9%	4.1%	3.0%	2.2%
Forest Products/Containers	18.0%	7.1%	1.6%	1.0%
Gaming/Leisure	1.1%	0.3%	0.0%	4.3%
Health Care	4.5%	0.4%	2.1%	10.5%
Housing	6.7%	3.2%	1.6%	0.5%
Information Technology	1.3%	11.6%	15.4%	5.5%
Manufacturing	14.6%	14.4%	5.3%	2.5%
Broadcasting	3.9%	3.7%	2.8%	NA
Cable/Wireless Video	6.0%	15.1%	24.1%	NA
Telecommunications	17.0%	47.0%	11.8%	NA
Wireless Communications	11.5%	7.8%	19.1%	NA
Diversified Media	10.1%	4.8%	4.2%	NA
Metals/Minerals	17.8%	15.8%	6.7%	5.0%
Retail	11.8%	1.9%	1.1%	2.4%
Service	7.2%	3.7%	2.7%	3.0%
Transportation	15.3%	8.3%	4.1%	3.2%
Utility	2.1%	4.5%	14.4%	8.0%
# Industries ≥ 10%	13	7	7	2

Note: Aggregate media/telecom default rate was 4.73%. Subsector data not available.
Source: Credit Suisse First Boston

sector was the primary driver of the default spike. Retailing was readily familiar to everyone and had assets that could, albeit at sometimes significant discounts, always be readily liquidated.

When default rates are adjusted to exclude the skewing impact of large fallen angels and the industries most severely impacted by that particular economic cycle, a more normalized or systematic default rate can be identified, as illustrated in Figure 2-8.

PRECURSORS TO DEFAULT

As a historical matter, it may be nice to know that the hunting field for distressed investors has never had more game, but the important prospective issue

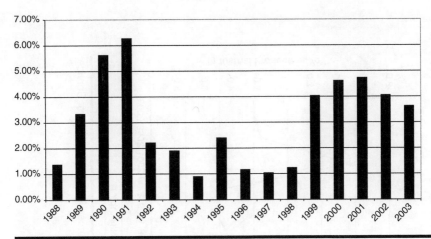

Figure 2-8. Default Rate Excluding Fallen Angels and Recession Industries[17] (Source: Credit Suisse First Boston)

is how good the hunting will be in the future. This, of course, is impossible to predict with certainty. But there are a number of factors — economic performance, relative quantity of lower rated bonds, and capital market liquidity — which appear related to default rates that will be explored and compared within the current environment.[18]

The good news, again from a distressed investor's perspective, is that even if overall theories of causality cannot be statistically proven, history seems to suggest that, inevitably, there will always be instances of financial distress or defaults. Even in the 1993–1998 time period, a remarkable stretch of economic growth and stock market prosperity, on average 29.3 companies with public bond debt outstanding defaulted annually, resulting in an average of $5.4 billion in defaulted notes.[19] This figure does not include bankruptcies where the firm only had bank debt or instances of financial distress that did not involve bankruptcy, which together would likely increase the number significantly.

Economic Performance

Perhaps the factor most logically related to financial distress is a sustained period of general economic weakness. Intuitively, if the economy is weak and the demand for goods and services is soft, many businesses will have difficulty increasing either unit growth or prices, which can lead to reduced cash flow. As a result, it should not be particularly surprising, as shown in Figure 2-9, that there appears to be a correlation between default rates and industrial production.

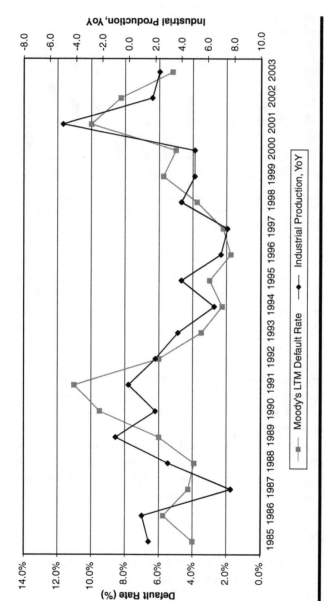

Figure 2-9. Default Rates Versus Industrial Production 1985–2003 (Source: Moody's Investors Service, Federal Reserve)

Relative Quantity of Low-Rated Bonds

Although perhaps not the first factor to come to mind, there appears to be a significant correlation between the amount of low-rated bonds (i.e., B or less) and future defaults. The intuition behind this observation is simple: lower rated bonds have a higher probability of default; thus, the relatively greater the amount outstanding, the relatively greater the amount of defaulted debt that should be expected. Table 2-4 indicates the correlation between ratings and default. It shows that if between 1994 and 2003 Moody's rated a bond between Caa and C, it had a 36.84% chance of default within one year and a 64.27% chance of default within three years. In other words, if one purchases a bond in that rating range and holds it for three years, there is a slightly better than 50/50 chance that it will default. Part of the reason for the relatively high default rate for C-rated bonds, particularly in the first year, is that as credits begin to deteriorate, the rating agencies naturally adjust their ratings. Thus, as the likelihood of default increases, the rating agency will tend to systematically downgrade the issuer to the lowest rating categories, such as Caa or lower. This is akin to the statistical concept of adverse selection.

There are two ways that the quantity of low-rated bonds can increase: downgrades and new issuance. During the 1997–2000 period, the relative number of downgrades increased significantly, as shown in Figure 2-10.

The increased level of downgrades, which is presumably related, at least in part, to the deteriorating economic environment during this period, helped cause an increase in the absolute dollar amount of B or lower rated bonds, which increased from approximately $373 billion at December 31, 2000 to $431 billion at June 30, 2003.[20] However, even though U.S. economic growth increased significantly in the second half of 2003, Table 2-5 shows that at year end 2003,

Table 2-4. U.S. Cumulative Dollar-Weighted Default Rates 1994–2003

Years of Rating Seasoning	1	2	3	4	5
Aaa	0.00	0.00	0.00	0.00	0.00
Aa	0.00	0.00	0.00	0.00	0.00
A	0.65	1.23	1.74	2.19	2.75
Baa	1.04	2.34	3.57	5.06	5.86
Ba	1.09	3.56	6.71	9.17	11.30
B	6.91	17.32	25.27	30.67	33.84
Caa to C	36.84	54.52	64.27	68.58	69.59
Investment Grade	0.58	1.18	1.73	2.32	2.80
Speculative Grade	8.47	16.65	23.06	27.28	29.84
All Corporates	2.12	4.24	6.06	7.55	8.57

Source: Moody's Investors Service

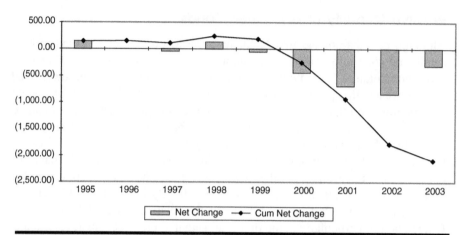

Figure 2-10.   Net and Cumulative Downgrade Activity 1995 –2003 (Source: Moody's Investors Service)

Table 2-5.   Sectors Still Likely to Be Downgraded

Moody's Ratings Outlook for Selected Sectors at Year End 2003

Sector	On Review for Downgrade	Outlook Negative	Total
Aerospace/Defense	0.0%	21.7%	21.7%
Airline	12.5%	70.8%	83.3%
Automotive	3.4%	37.6%	41.0%
Building Materials	4.6%	23.1%	27.7%
Capital Goods	1.7%	18.6%	20.3%
Chemicals	6.0%	24.5%	30.5%
Consumer Products	5.2%	19.3%	24.5%
Forest Products	8.1%	37.8%	45.9%
Life Insurance	0.0%	29.5%	29.5%
Media Entertainment	4.0%	20.6%	24.6%
Metals & Mining	2.1%	29.8%	31.9%
Nonlife Insurance	3.6%	27.7%	31.3%
Other Nonfinancial	5.8%	29.2%	35.0%
Other Transportation	6.3%	15.6%	21.9%
Packaging	0.0%	20.7%	20.7%
Real Estate and Construction	3.1%	28.1%	31.2%
Retail	1.4%	23.6%	25.0%
Technology	3.1%	32.0%	35.1%
Telecom	1.5%	18.9%	20.4%
Utilities	4.7%	28.0%	32.7%
All Sectors*	**3.4%**	**18.8%**	**22.2%**

* All sectors total includes less distressed sectors not listed.

Source: Moody's Investors Service

Table 2-6. Default Rates by Rating at Time of Original Issuance

Year	BBB	BB	B	CCC	NR
1993	0.00%	1.84%	2.40%	0.87%	1.24%
1994	0.00%	1.16%	1.50%	0.84%	0.88%
1995	0.00%	0.34%	1.87%	2.91%	3.70%
1996	0.00%	1.28%	1.68%	1.49%	29.73%
1997	0.27%	0.70%	1.40%	2.48%	1.04%
1998	0.30%	0.55%	1.66%	3.51%	0.24%
1999	0.21%	1.80%	5.06%	3.51%	9.85%
2000	0.73%	1.62%	4.37%	3.28%	14.35%
2001	2.07%	2.33%	10.45%	8.11%	18.46%
2002	4.32%	8.03%	12.66%	11.06%	23.40%
2003	1.76%	1.90%	3.46%	8.99%	6.54%
Average	0.88%	1.96%	4.23%	4.28%	9.95%

Source: Credit Suisse First Boston

20 sectors of the corporate bond market still had negative rating outlooks on more than 20% of the issuers in those sectors. Of course, not all of these will lead to situations of financial distress, but it certainly suggests that there is the potential for many distressed situations in the future.

Besides downgrades, a second source of new low-rated bonds is new issuance. In attempting to access the impact of newly issued bonds on default rates, the default rates in Table 2-4 cannot be used because of the adverse selection problem. To control for the effect of adverse selection, the default history based on the rating at the time of issuance, as shown in Table 2-6, should be used. These data, which were compiled by Credit Suisse First Boston on the basis of combined ratings of different rating agencies and thus do not represent the "track record" of any particular agency, show that the predictive power of initial ratings is generally a good predictor of default rates, although one might have expected a larger increase between the B and CCC categories. However, bonds that were "not rated"[21] clearly had significantly higher rates of default. Although these default rates clearly indicate there is more risk in lower rating categories, the extra risk (excluding the not-rated bonds) is not of an order of magnitude so high that pricing cannot be adjusted to make expected risk-adjusted returns positive.[22]

As shown in Figure 2-11, in the 1996–1999 period, there was a significant increase in B and lower rated debt issued relative to BB high-yield issuance.

Returning to default rate trends, the lagged correlation with this spurt of arguably lower quality new issuance, as shown in Figure 2-12, is fairly clear. Unfortunately, it is difficult to draw any firm conclusions from Figure 2-12 because of the problem of autocorrelation (what portion of the default rate increase is appropriately attributed to the weakening economy, as illustrated in

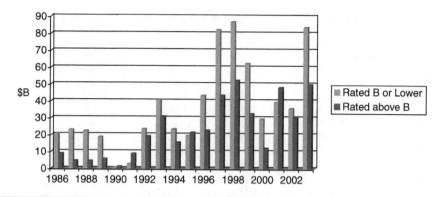

Figure 2-11. New Issuance of Bonds Rated B or Lower (Source: Credit Suisse First Boston)

Figure 2-9, which likely contributed to the increase in downgrades reviewed in Figure 2-10) as opposed to the impact of poor quality issuance. This is a statistical question beyond the scope of this book.

Taken together, these data present a fairly persuasive case that by monitoring rating migration and new issuance trends, it may be possible to forecast periods when default activity is likely to be relatively higher.

Capital Markets Liquidity

A third variable, which likely also contributes to default rates, is the relative ability of speculative-grade quality companies to access the capital markets. As will be discussed frequently later, a common source of financial distress is a firm's need to pay back its existing debt in accordance with its contractual obligations. In most instances, relatively highly leveraged companies cannot accumulate sufficient funds from free cash flow to repay significant debt maturities as they come due. To make such payments, they are usually dependent on having access to the capital markets to refinance the obligation.

For example, assume Debtdue Corp. issues a $100 five-year bond in 1996 and uses the proceeds to expand its operations and/or perhaps make a few modest acquisitions. Debtdue's revenues and cash flow increase during the 1996–2000 period, but in 2001 it does not have enough cash on hand to repay the $100 bond maturity. All things being equal, if Debtdue's operations had improved sufficiently, it should be able to issue another $100 bond, perhaps even at a lower cost since Debtdue may be more creditworthy, to pay off the old bond. But what if all things were not equal? What if a recession was in progress, and despite excellent execution by management, Debtdue's operations, and hence creditworthiness, deteriorated? Or what if Debtdue's operations

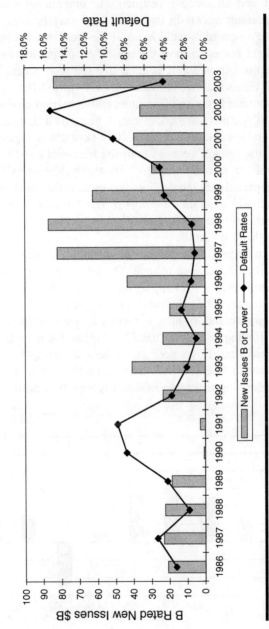

Figure 2-12. Comparison of Issuance Activity and Default Trends (Source: Credit Suisse First Boston)

were relatively stable, but for whatever reason, investors began to avoid the high-yield market and allocated investments to other asset classes (perhaps because of rising default rates)? In that case, there may be very few investors willing to purchase a new high-yield issue. If the stock market had also weakened, Debtdue might not even have the option of attempting to sell stock.

These are situations in which it is generally said that access to the capital markets is limited. Firms that need to raise funds in order to pay off obligations coming due may default because of an unreceptive market environment; even though, by some objective standard, it might be agreed that the firm would usually be able to raise capital. The 2000–2002 period was arguably an inhospitable capital-raising market because both the high-yield and equity markets were weak. One of the primary reasons[23] for the weakness in the high-yield market during this period was the decline, and even withdrawal, of new investment funds. Figure 2-13 examines the flow of funds into and out of high-yield mutual funds from 1993 to 2003. Note that in 1999 and 2000, there were significant net outflows of funds.

As illustrated in Figure 2-14, periods of declining or negative fund flows correlate with declines in issuance volume. The intuition behind this correlation is the simple economic principle of supply and demand. When money flows into funds, portfolio managers need to invest that money and therefore have a demand for new bonds. This demand, in turn, is met by investment banks that "manufacture bonds" by finding issuers in "need" of capital. Demand for investments begets supply. When fund flows decline, so does demand.

Of course, economic theory would also suggest there should be adjustments in price. While addressing this topic in detail is well beyond the scope of this

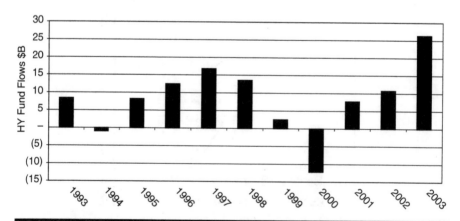

Figure 2-13. Annual High-Yield Mutual Fund Flows 1993–2003 (Source: AMG Data Services)

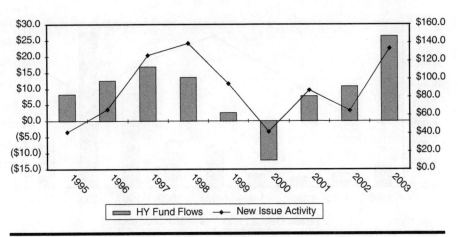

Figure 2-14. Comparison of High-Yield Mutual Fund Flows with New Issuance 1995–2003 (Source: Credit Suisse First Boston and AMG Data Services)

work, Figure 2-15 presents data on the relative cost of capital, as measured by spread to treasuries, during the 1995–2003 time frame. The yield spread (which is the difference between the yield or expected investment return on a given bond and the yield for a similar maturity U.S. Treasury note) can be largely attributed to the premium demanded by investors to purchase a bond of a particular credit risk. From the issuer's perspective, the yield spread is the cost of credit risk.[24] From the investor's perspective, it is the "fee paid" to assume

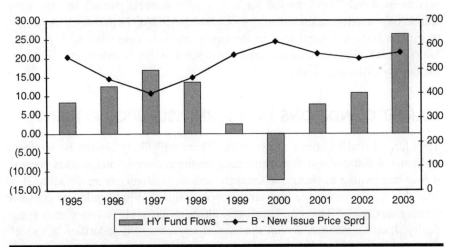

Figure 2-15. Analysis of New Issue Yield Spreads 1995–2003 (Source: Credit Suisse First Boston and AMG Data Services)

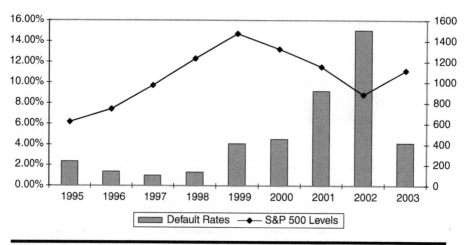

Figure 2-16. Comparison of Default Rates with S&P 500 Index 1995–2003 (Source: Credit Suisse First Boston)

credit risk. Note that in the 1999–2000 time frame, yield spreads, adjusted for rating category, tended to increase in conjunction with a withdrawal of funds from the market. This is evidence that the effective cost of capital was higher during this period. Thus, there was less capital available and it was more expensive.

A weak equity market compounded the dilemma faced by issuers unable to access the high-yield market. The 2000–2002 time period, as is generally known, was an extremely weak period for U.S. equity markets overall and the more technology- and telecommunications-oriented NASDAQ in particular. As shown in Figure 2-16, this weakness in the equity markets coincided with peak defaults, which suggests that the equity market was likely often unavailable to financially distressed firms.

MARKET CONDITIONS THAT PERMIT SUPERIOR RETURNS

Thus far, all that has been shown is that there will likely always be instances of financial distress and that, depending on the economic and market context, it may be possible to predict when there will be relatively more defaults. How does that lead to profitable investment opportunities? Why should one continue reading this book? The simple answer, although difficult to prove in a statistically rigorous manner, is that the market for distressed securities is less efficient than other markets, enabling skilled investors to earn superior risk-adjusted returns.

While this book is intended as a practitioner's guide, rather than an academic treatise, it is important to briefly review the academic concept of the efficient market, although for a thorough review more specialized sources should be consulted.[25] The *efficient market hypothesis* (EMT) essentially states that trading prices reflect all available information and therefore no investor can consistently outperform the market.[26] In what is known as the strong form of the hypothesis, the notion is that markets are so efficient that they reflect all known information. However, this form of the hypothesis has generally been criticized with the observation that inside traders often seem to be able to "beat" the market in particular situations; thus the unique information held by these "investors" apparently had not previously been reflected in prices. The semi-strong form of the hypothesis argues that the market accurately reflects all publicly available information. Proponents of this form of the theory note that while new information clearly can impact prices, price changes are almost instantaneous and thus prolonged inefficiency cannot exist. Under the semi-strong version of the EMT, the market is viewed as a "random walk" — no one can really know whether, at any given time, prices are more likely to go up rather than down. It is a classic coin toss. A monkey throwing darts at the stock market page should do as well as the most knowledgeable and experienced investor. This is a fairly distressing assertion for investment professionals because it implies their services are worthless.

Technically, the EMT is just that — a hypothesis or testable statistical assertion about the stock market. Almost since the day the EMT was proffered, academics have been engaged in competing statistical studies of stock market returns in an effort to prove or disprove the proposition. While it is probably fair to say that the academic jury is still out on whether the EMT accurately describes the stock market, a simple examination of the basic assumptions or preconditions of the EMT shows that it has dubious applicability to the distressed debt market. This is important to establish because if one believed that the distressed debt market was perfectly efficient, there would be no need for this book; knowledge and skill would be irrelevant. However, if the distressed market is "inefficient," superior investors can and should enjoy superior performance.

There are three key assumptions on which the EMT is based: equal access to information, rational behavior, and low transaction costs.

Equal Access to Information

The first assumption is that all investors have access to all available information. Most investors tend to view investment through the prism of equities, where there is often significant analyst and press coverage of events, and each trade is instantaneously reported and disseminated publicly on a tape or other information service. In such cases, it is reasonable to assume that all available information is generally accessible with minimal cost or effort and, therefore, internalized in market prices. This information environment simply does not exist for much of the distressed debt market, particularly for medium- or small-capitalization issuers and bankruptcies. There are literally hundreds of high-yield bond issuers that have no in-depth analyst coverage. In addition, most distressed debt trades in privately negotiated over-the-counter transactions in which prices are not disseminated to the public. Whereas typically every issuer in the equity market is required to file periodic reports with the Securities and Exchange Commission (SEC), in the high-yield market, many issuers have no public equity and, by virtue of having a relatively small number of securities holders, are often exempt from the reporting requirements of the Exchange Act. In those cases, what information, if any, the issuer discloses might only be readily available to holders.

Further, when companies file for bankruptcy protection, even large-capitalization companies, they often discontinue SEC reporting or have lengthy delays in making required filings. Information about events in bankruptcy court is normally a matter of public record, but it often requires significant effort to locate. You should ask yourself whether or not you know how to find a monthly operating statement for a company that has filed for bankruptcy in Louisiana.[27] Even if you do know, you should next ask how much longer it will take to obtain the statement than, for example, AT&T's most recently filed 10-Q. Through the numerous financial information services that are available, an active investor in AT&T could, with minimal effort, monitor every public news story that is reported during the course of the day. In contrast, an investor in WorldCom, which filed for bankruptcy, would be able to do little else if he or she truly wanted to monitor and read every filing made in the case.[28]

Lastly, as will be discussed later in more detail, in a high proportion of distressed debt situations, there will be two different levels of information access: restricted nonpublic information and publicly available information. Banks and bondholders involved in negotiations with the issuer will, after signing appropriate confidentiality agreements, be given material nonpublic information such as more detailed operating data or management projections. Investors with this information are allowed, with proper notice,[29] to continue to transact in the securities. And while most investors who sign confidentiality agreements take their obligations seriously, it would be rather naive to believe that no other party ever gets a hint or a wink here or there.

In sum, in many high-yield and distressed debt situations, the assumption that all investors have easy, equal access to all available and relevant information is simply not true. In some situations, only a limited number of investors will have access to all available information. Even in situations where the

information may theoretically be available, accessing it often requires a significant commitment of time, effort, and out-of-pocket expense.[30] When an investor
buys shares of IBM, he or she typically would not pause to speculate whether
the seller knew something material the investor does not. However, as of this
writing, if that same investor were purchasing the substantially discounted bonds
of Cray Research, a manufacturer of high-end workstations, he or she might
very well pause and wonder whether the seller knows something significant that
the investor did not.

Rational Behavior

A second assumption of the EMT is that investors act rationally. This assumption has recently been broadly challenged by the emerging behaviorist finance
school, which suggests that classic concepts of rationality do not explain the
tendency of the market to engage in periods of speculative excess and other
ostensibly irrational acts.[31] These criticisms may be valid and, to the extent they
are valid in equity and certain other areas, may have validity in distressed
securities. However, there is another entirely separate reason for questioning
whether all transactions in the distressed marketplace are rational: forced or
coerced selling.

One precondition for rational choice is "free will," which in this context
means making purchase and sale decisions solely on the investment merits. To
the extent that the portfolio manager's decision is not based on an independent
view of how to maximize portfolio returns, it is, to some extent, coerced. And
just as coerced confessions often have little to do with truth, coerced sales have
little to do with an efficient market.

What are the sources of these so-called "coerced sales"? Several are fairly
common and widely recognized. First, sales by banks to manage various portfolio quality statistics are often not based on an opinion of fair value. Senior
bank executives typically identify certain performance benchmarks as being
important to either regulators' or investors' perceptions of the bank's health. For
example, a common goal is for the nonperforming asset ratio (generally defaulted assets/total earning assets) to be below a certain target level. In addition,
senior bank executives may want to minimize the risk that bank regulators will
question the adequacy of loss reserve levels. In assessing reserve adequacy,
regulators analyze loan portfolio quality using, among other things, the ratings
issued on nationally syndicated bank loans by the Shared National Credit (SNC)
program.[32] Banks will often want to manage the amount of their loan portfolio
carrying low SNC ratings.[33]

One of the primary tools used to attain portfolio objectives is a loan sale.
These sales will almost certainly occur at a discount to the loan's face amount,

but this discount may already have been "reserved" for, in which case there is no current impact on the income statement (i.e., loss), just a reduction in nonperforming or classified SNC assets. The important point, however, is that such sales are not necessarily motivated by a "rational" view of the value of the loan.[34] It is a rational, or at least voluntary, sale if the thought process of the portfolio manager is: "I don't like this credit anymore. This is the best bid I've seen in a long time and it's approximately equal to my best-case recovery analysis. I'm going to hit the bid and eliminate my exposure." On the other hand, the portfolio manager may think: "I have to sell $60 million in nonperformers to make budget. The bid for this loan is 10 points lower than what the loan is worth, but it is about where the loan is marked. I better hit the bid while it's there." In this case, the sale is not completely voluntary because the portfolio manager is responding more to his or her nonperforming asset goal instead of maximizing portfolio returns. The purchaser of the loan is arguably receiving a windfall. Recognizing the regulatory dilemma of banks, bidders, especially hedge funds for which SNC ratings and nonperforming asset ratios are irrelevant, may lower bids, anticipating that, under the right circumstances, certain banks may be motivated sellers.[35]

Irrational sale pressure can, alternatively, come from a desire to generate earnings. Consider a situation where the bank (this could also easily apply to an insurance company investor) holds nonperforming Loan Y, but it has been written down to zero.[36] Charge-offs or write-downs to zero or very low levels often occur, particularly for loans with the lowest SNC rating of "loss" or unsecured or undersecured loans of bankrupt entities. Assume that in a subsequent period, management is seeking to achieve certain earnings goals, and Loan Y is selling in the market for 20. Management may believe Loan Y is worth 40, but by selling now can recognize gains (because it is carried at 0), enabling management to reach its earnings goal. Here again, a loan sale at less than an objectively "fair" or "rational" price can occur because of considerations other than portfolio return maximization.

Banks, however, are not the only entities that confront portfolio management requirements not strictly related to profit maximization. Most structured investment vehicles, such as collateralized bond obligation (CBO) trusts, collateralized loan obligation (CLO) trusts, and collateralized debt obligation trusts (generically referred to as CDOs[37]), also frequently face purchase and sale pressures not driven by return maximization. A detailed discussion of how these entities function is beyond the scope of this work,[38] but essentially CDOs are entities that seek to make above-average returns by making leveraged investments in a portfolio of high-yielding bonds or highly leveraged loans. The basic strategy is to use debt (usually multiple classes or tranches of debt with different credit ratings and risk of loss will be issued), with a relatively low average cost, to

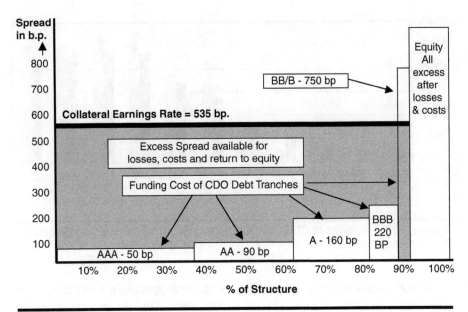

Figure 2-17. Economics of CDO Structure

finance 85–90% of the purchase of a diversified portfolio of high-yield collateral. Equity, or the equivalent, will be used to finance the 10–15% difference. Figure 2-17 illustrates the basic economics of a CDO. In the example illustrated, the collateral has an average yield to worst spread of 535 basis points. The CDO is funded 87% by investment-grade bonds (i.e., AAA to BBB rated) with a weighted average funding spread of approximately 88 basis points. The BB/B tranche is expected to cost 750 basis points. This is a *negative arbitrage*[39] to the collateral, but increases the overall funding cost to only a weighted average of approximately 110 basis points. This implies a net interest spread of 425 basis points that, after losses and costs, will be available to the 10% equity tranche.

For a CDO to make economic sense, it must be done when the borrowing cost relative to the collateral yield provides sufficient spread or arbitrage to permit an adequate risk-adjusted return on the equity component.[40] The CDO will typically be organized in conjunction with an experienced and recognized high-yield asset manager who will often have either a direct or indirect interest in portfolio performance. If the manager can keep portfolio losses significantly below the earnings spread, the equity investors can earn attractive returns. This is the power of leverage. Of course, the equity investment can quickly be lost if portfolio losses are greater than the earnings spread.

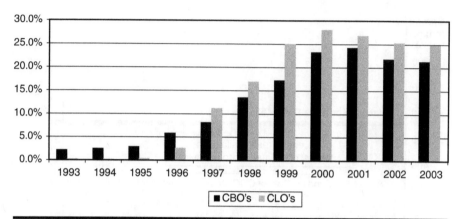

Figure 2-18. Holdings of CBOs and CLOs (Source: Credit Suisse First Boston and Loan Pricing Corporation)

CDOs hold significant percentages of the leveraged loan and speculative-grade bond markets. Figure 2-18 shows that since 1993 the percentage of the low-rated corporate loan and bond market held by CDOs has increased from approximately 3% to over 20%.

The relatively low cost of borrowed funds that CDOs can enjoy is largely due to the fact that one or more rating agencies will rate a significant portion of the debt investment grade.[41] However, to obtain the rating agencies' "backing," the CDO manager will be subject to a highly negotiated set of operating rules (CDO-ORs) that will limit the freedom of the manager's choices. CDO-ORs will, among other things, limit portfolio concentration in any particular credit, industry, or credit quality.[42] In certain circumstances, the CDO-ORs effectively will "compel" the manager to engage in "irrational" transactions. For example, CDO-ORs typically limit the percentage of the CDO's portfolio that can be rated in the lowest rating categories. When an investment in the portfolio is downgraded to B– or CCC, the manager may be forced to sell something (again without regard to the portfolio manager's view of fair value) to remain in compliance with the CDO-ORs.

A third significant source of involuntary or "irrational" selling comes from the liquidity management requirements of high-yield mutual funds. In an open-ended mutual fund, which is the typical structure of most high-yield mutual funds, investors are allowed to redeem their interests on a daily basis at the net asset value of the fund. This means that when sentiment against a particular asset class changes and investors choose to withdraw their funds, the fund manager must have cash on hand to honor such redemptions, which may require selling securities. As noted in Figure 2-13, in 1994 and 2000 high-yield mutual funds actually experienced net outflows of funds. This outflow was not uniform across all funds; thus some funds — especially if their performance had been poor — experienced fairly high percentage withdrawals, requiring their managers to liquidate holdings at precisely the weakest period of the market.

In sum, a large cross-section of holders of high-yield instruments, the primary source pool for distressed investments, at various times are required to make sale decisions for reasons other than the investment merits. This investment "irrationality" can be a significant source of opportunity to distressed debt investors and significantly undermines the applicability of the EMT to the distressed sector.

Low Transaction Costs

Finally, the EMT assumes no, or very low, transaction costs. The intuition behind the need for this assumption is fairly obvious: if investor profit-maximizing behavior is the engine that drives pricing to the precise point of efficiency, then costs cannot be so high that they preclude an investor from engaging in transactions that would make prices optimal. For example, assume an investor believes the value of stock X is $21 per share, when the market price is $20. Efficient market proponents would argue that in a world of no borrowing or transaction costs, the investor would purchase shares of stock X until his or her purchasing activities drive the price up to $21.[43] Similarly, if the price for whatever reason reaches $21.25, the investor might want to sell shares (because in the investor's view they are overvalued) until either his or her position is gone or the price falls to $21. But if it costs the investor $2 per share in transaction fees (an exaggeration to help illustrate the point), clearly he or she would not purchase shares at $20 just because they were theoretically $1 cheaper, because, adjusting for transaction costs, the net cost of the shares would be $22. Similarly, on the sale side, the net proceeds from the sale at $21.25 per share would only be $19.25.

There are at least two sources of transaction costs faced by an investor. One is the settlement fee, which represents the direct transaction cost, including commission to the broker. The other cost is what will be called the "unwind" fee, which represents the bid–ask spread in the market. For an investment to be profitable on a price appreciation basis, the minimum market movement required is an amount greater than the two transaction fees (buy and sell) and the unwind fee. Table 2-7 presents a representative set of costs for several types of transactions.

In most markets, the settlement fee, including brokerage commissions, for institutional-size transactions is fairly nominal. As illustrated in Table 2-7, to purchase 100,000 shares of, say, IBM at $100 per share for a total investment

Table 2-7. Comparative Analysis of Representative Transaction Costs

Transaction Type	Investment ($)	Transaction Cost (%)	Unwind Cost ($) Market Bid	Unwind Cost ($) Market Offer	Unwind Cost	Unwind %	Minimum Market % Move to Profit
Stock Shares	10,000,000	0.05	99.97	100.00	0.03	0.03	0.13
Bonds							
High Grade	10,000,000	0.00	998.50	1000.00	1.50	0.15	0.15
Speculative Grade	10,000,000	0.00	997.50	1000.00	2.50	0.25	0.25
Distressed	3,000,000	0.00	290.00	300.00	10.00	3.33	3.33

of $10 million might involve a transaction or "ticket" cost of only $0.02–$0.05 per share. For a stock of IBM's liquidity, the bid–ask spread per share may be $0.10 or less; thus the minimum price appreciation required to cover all transaction costs and allow a capital gain is only 0.13%. All together, this cost represents a fairly minimal amount that would not unduly impede the free operation of the market. Purchasing $10 million face of investment-grade-rated IBM bonds would likely involve an estimated 0.28%, whereas a standard high-yield bond, trading at a quarter-point bid–ask spread, would include an estimated 0.50%. While these costs may be slightly above those of a highly liquid equity, they are still fairly nominal.

However, consider the potential costs involved in trading a distressed bond. While the transaction fee is reasonable, just enough to handle execution costs,[44] the unwind costs can be significant. In Table 2-7, the bond is assumed to trade in a 29-bid/30-offer context, making the unwind cost effectively one point. This spread will vary widely depending on the liquidity of the particular bond. For a large, actively traded fallen angel, the bid–ask spread, or unwind cost, could be as narrow as an on-the-run high-yield bond. However, for less liquid bonds with few known, or at least active, holders, the bid–ask spread could be several points, which on a lower price security can be fairly large in percentage terms. In any case, with the exception of the most liquid situations, distressed securities generally have significantly higher transaction costs than most other traded securities. These higher costs mean that the quick in-and-out trading on which the EMT depends to internalize all market information into prices may not occur due to the real-world existence of potentially significant transaction costs.

In summary, the vital assumptions or preconditions necessary for efficient markets to exist do not appear to be present in the distressed securities market. First, not all information in the market is easily and freely available to all investors. Second, many investors are often required to sell in poor market conditions with knowledge that they are receiving potentially suboptimal pricing because of the existence of other, noninvestment criteria. Lastly, the distressed securities market may have significantly higher transaction costs, making it impossible for the market to fluidly grind to the "efficient" price.

Each of these factors makes it possible for the skilled distressed investor to earn superior returns. The fact that not all investors can easily acquire all relevant information means that the diligent distressed investor can have an information advantage. The fact that many investors will at times be forced sellers implies that the astute distressed investor, either anticipating such periods or detecting them as they are happening, can potentially accumulate positions at below "fair" value levels. Finally, while the higher transaction costs of the distressed market are a burden on the distressed investor just like anyone else, they also serve as a potential barrier to participation in the market by other investors — and typically a key to superior performance is to be one of a limited number of players.

SUMMARY

The U.S. marketplace is so vast and diverse that at any given point in time, regardless of how strong the economy, a significant number of firms, even if relatively low on a percentage basis, will inevitably encounter some form of financial distress. This distress may lead to an outright bankruptcy, a violation of lending agreements (placing the firm in technical default), or simply a circumstance where there is significant risk the firm might default. In any of these cases, there may be extreme price volatility in the distressed firm's securities, which, either before or after the fact, could give rise to profitable investment opportunities.

Although substantial capital has gravitated to the distressed debt marketplace over the last several years, and many more investors are knowledgeable about the market than was the case in 1998, the distressed market is still very diffused and inherently inefficient. Unlike the more liquid and visible equity markets, information in the distressed market is difficult to obtain, and thus not everyone is always on equal footing. Similarly, many holders of distressed debt are frequently compelled to sell certain of their holdings during unfavorable market environments, which can create attractive purchasing opportunities for the distressed investor.

This suggests that skilled distressed debt investors will always have opportunities to make profitable investments. The rest of this book is about acquiring the knowledge and skills necessary to be a successful participant in this vibrant but complex field.

This Chapter's Chess Moves

2. Nc3, Bb4
3. Nf3, Pc5

CONCEPTUAL OVERVIEW OF FINANCIAL DISTRESS AND THE RESTRUCTURING PROCESS

In the labyrinth sometimes referred to as Generally Accepted Accounting Principles or GAAP, it is easy to get lost in what happens when firms get into financial distress and how restructurings resolve the problem. The conceptual underpinnings of financial distress and the restructuring process are surprisingly simple. In this chapter, a conceptual framework for financial distress and restructurings is developed and explained so that when the accounting minutia of case studies is developed later on, it can be related to general principles more easily.

A SIMPLE MODEL OF THE FIRM

Figure 3-1 is a simple geometric representation of an economic entity. Perhaps the most readily familiar way to think of this is the purchase of a house. The house is purchased for $100, and it is financed with a mortgage of $80 and a down payment of $20. This is essentially a picture of the owner's balance sheet.

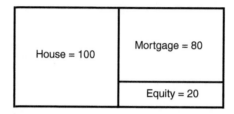

Figure 3-1. Illustration of Home Financing

A firm can be represented in exactly the same way — all that needs to be done is add a bunch of zeroes to the numbers. Similar to the standard accounting presentation of a balance sheet, the box on the left represents the economic value of the firm's assets. On the right side are the firm's liabilities and the owner's equity. The firm will imaginatively be called Boxco. Accountants should like this depiction because the left and right sides are the same size, just the way Boxco's balance sheet should balance.

In the real world, the size of the boxes is never really known. The GAAP balance sheet will always balance, but no accountant, finance professor, or investor would seriously argue that the GAAP presentation represents economic reality. Although perhaps an oversimplification, one could argue that the key to successful investment — not just distressed debt investment — is to have a clear understanding of the sizes of these three "simple" boxes.

To better understand this, two sets of boxes are needed. In Figure 3-2, two depictions or valuations of Boxco are presented. On the left is the original GAAP presentation; on the right is a hypothetical market valuation. The primary difference between the GAAP and market valuation approach is the use of the trading values of a firm's securities — both bonds and equity — to determine the size of the equity and liability boxes.

This market framework typically includes several simplifying assumptions. First, firms have many types of liabilities other than contractual debt obligations. For example, they have accounts payable to vendors for raw materials received but not paid for, accrued expenses for wages earned by employees but not yet paid, and so on. To make things easier, initially, all forms of liabilities in the liability box will simply be referred to as debt. Second, the market value of the debt will be assumed to be equal to its principal amount as long as the market value of the equity is significantly positive. Finally, since conventional wisdom as encapsulated by the efficient market hypothesis (EMT)[1] is that the market is always correct, the left box (asset value [AV]) will be stretched to fit the size of the boxes on the right, to maintain the fiction of balance.

This last simplification — that the assets equal the sum of liabilities and equity — is not a fair characterization of the methodological underpinning of

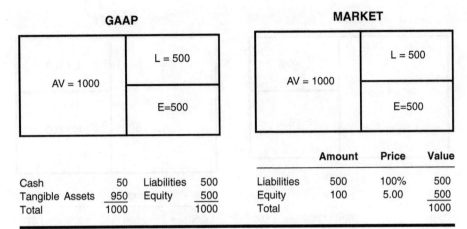

Figure 3-2. Firm Where Market Value Equals GAAP Value

the EMT. The EMT essentially postulates that the market value of a security (it is easiest to think of this within the context of a share of stock) represents the collective valuation judgment of all participants in the market who are assumed to know and analyze properly all available information about the firm. The common trading adage is: No one knows more than the market.

Methodologically, what this implies is that the market has divined the size of the asset box and then adjusted the equity box to fit. So instead of the formula Assets = Liabilities + Equity, it should be more properly thought of as Equity = Assets – Liabilities. However, as a practical matter, only the market price of a share of stock is known, so it is easier to reverse the equation and impute the size of assets.

In the initial case shown in Figure 3-2, the boxes are the same size. This implies that the market's perceived value of Boxco happens to coincide with its GAAP asset value. Therefore, the product of the market-trading price of Boxco's shares times the number of outstanding shares equals GAAP equity. This neat solution exists only in textbooks.

EXTENSIONS OF THE BASIC MODEL

Two common financing transactions that Boxco might engage in will be discussed, along with how they would be represented within this framework. This will later allow for a simple graphical depiction of financial distress and thereafter the ameliorative correction of a restructuring.

One of the most common ways to obtain financing for a firm is to sell stock. In general, managements tend to do this only when they think the market is

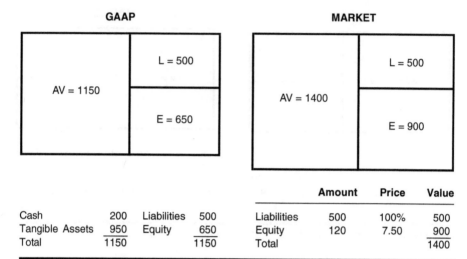

					Amount	Price	Value
Cash	200	Liabilities	500	Liabilities	500	100%	500
Tangible Assets	950	Equity	650	Equity	120	7.50	900
Total	1150		1150	Total			1400

Figure 3-3. Boxco Following Equity Offering

valuing their stock "fairly"; this simply means that they want the highest price possible. In Figure 3-3, it is assumed that Boxco issues an additional 20 shares of stock at a market-determined price of $7.50 per share. Why the market might choose to value Boxco's stock at greater than book value has been discussed at length elsewhere.[2]

How this transaction would be depicted in the GAAP and market frameworks is fairly straightforward. Under GAAP, the $150 Boxco received from selling the stock would be added to the asset cash, and equity would be increased by the same amount. On the market value side, a few additional adjustments would be required. The equity box must be resized to equal 900 (120 shares × $7.50 share) and the asset box stretched to balance. Relative to the scenario in Figure 3-2, the market now views Boxco as being worth more, which is indicated by the increase in the stock price.

Following its stock offering, Boxco announces that it will use the proceeds toward the intuitively obvious money-making proposition of laying glass threads on the ocean floor to facilitate more efficient data and voice telecommunications.[3] Sensing that Boxco's glass fibers would soon be generating boxfuls of cash, the equity market pushes its stock to $10 a share. This would result in the boxes being adjusted as illustrated in Figure 3-4.

Another very common transaction is to buy another company. For example, Boxco's management might get the bright idea to diversify its telecommunications bet and get into the satellite-based wireless communications business. But

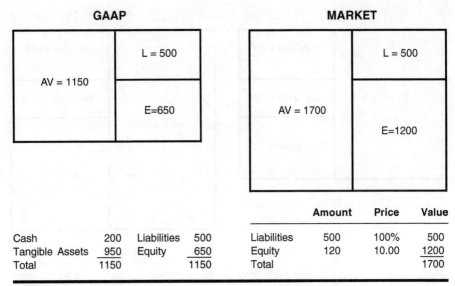

	Amount	Price	Value
Cash	200	Liabilities	500	Liabilities	500	100%	500

GAAP

AV = 1150

L = 500

E=650

MARKET

L = 500

AV = 1700

E=1200

					Amount	Price	Value
Cash	200	Liabilities	500	Liabilities	500	100%	500
Tangible Assets	950	Equity	650	Equity	120	10.00	1200
Total	1150		1150	Total			1700

Figure 3-4. Boxco Following Stock Value Appreciation

management does not have much experience in the sector and wants to avoid competition, so for $200 Boxco purchases the leading company in the field, Dead Star, Inc. However, although Dead Star might have been a "leader," it had just begun its operations recently and had physical assets only worth $20. To finance the purchase, Boxco sells $200 of subordinated ("sub") debt. Assume that the market loves Boxco's strategy and moves the stock price to $15 a share.

This scenario is more complicated, but raises some important nuances of accounting and market behavior. Figure 3-5 illustrates the adjustments.

Within the GAAP framework, the issuance of the sub debt increased liabilities by $200. The prior $500 in debt is now characterized as senior debt. On the asset side, the $200 in cash that was raised from the sale of bonds was used to buy Dead Star, so there is no change in cash. However, that acquisition presents the accountants with a modest problem: $200 was spent, but only $20 in assets was acquired. That does not balance, which makes accountants uncomfortable. Initially, accountants restored balance by creating a fictional "plug" asset referred to as *goodwill* to represent or explain the asset shortfall. When this rule was first developed, premiums were typically only paid for existing businesses, so the notion was that existing customer or vendor relationships — hence goodwill — must justify the higher than book value price. In the last 20 years, a host of acquisitions (like Dead Star, a money-losing start-up) forced the accountants to be more candid. Now the shortfall is simply labeled purchase

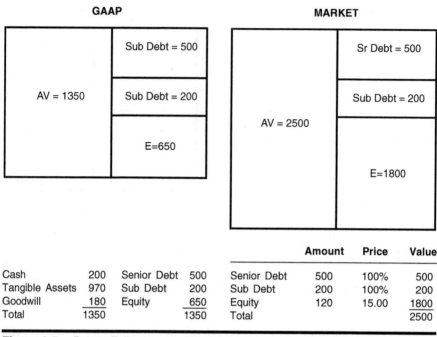

		Amount	Price	Value
Cash	200	Senior Debt	500	Senior Debt	500	100%	500
Tangible Assets	970	Sub Debt	200	Sub Debt	200	100%	200
Goodwill	180	Equity	650	Equity	120	15.00	1800
Total	1350		1350	Total			2500

Figure 3-5. Boxco Following an Acquisition Financed with Debt

cost in excess of assets acquired.[4] So "tangible assets" is increased by $20 and a new "plug" asset of $180 is created.

The market value framework is fairly straightforward. On the liability side, debt is increased by the $200 of sub debt. Equity, of course, is market derived: 120 shares with a market price of $15 a share equals $1800. Liabilities and equity total $2500, so that must be what the assets are worth. There is no need to worry about a tedious attribution of value to "goodwill" here; indeed, a significant percentage of the asset value can no longer be tied to tangible assets, because much of the change was simply imputed from the rising equity valuation.

While fictional, the preceding scenario was "inspired" by many actual company histories that occurred in the 1997–2000 market bubble. It is worth pausing for a moment to reflect on some of the financial implications of the above-outlined events. First, note that in the beginning (Figure 3-1), GAAP and market equity were supported by tangible assets. The ratio of debt/tangible assets was a fairly high 80%, but if the asset value is considered stable (real estate here), this is manageable. In the Boxco example in Figure 3-2, the debt to tangible asset ratio was reduced to 50%, which is representative of many below-investment-grade corporate capital structures. By the time this evolves to the stage of Figure 3-5, debt has increased to $700, with a debt/tangible asset ratio of approximately 60%. Depending on the stability of the business, this might be considered high. However, at the time of the sub debt sale, the pro-forma *market* debt/total capital (i.e., debt + market capitalization of equity) ratio has declined from 50% to 28% ([500 + 200]/2500). On a market basis, it appeared that Boxco's credit had substantially improved.

A CONCEPTUAL VIEW OF FINANCIAL DISTRESS

What "made" Boxco in the preceding example was an optimistic market equity valuation. But as was very clear in the period from 2000 to 2002, during which the Dow Jones Industrial Average and NASDAQ lost, from peak to trough, 37.8% and 77.9%, respectively:[5] what the market gives, the market can take away.

For purposes of illustration, assume that the market changed its view on Boxco's prospects. With the benefit of hindsight, it is clear that companies that invested in fiber optic and satellite-based wireless telecommunications systems in the late 1990s miscalculated the demand for those services. In relatively short periods, the market valuations of many firms in those sectors declined by billions of dollars.

Imagine that one morning you read in the newspaper that Boxco's stock is trading at 10 cents per share with its senior debt at 50 and its sub debt at 20 (recall that when bond trading values are discussed, the number represents the percentage of face value, so the sub debt is trading at 20% of face, or 20 cents on the dollar). The first thing to note is that Boxco's bonds are trading at a discount. As noted above, when a firm's equity has significant value, it is generally assumed that, barring unusual interest rate environments or certain structural abnormalities, the firm's liabilities should be valued at face. The underlying assumption is that since equity is junior to or "below" the debt, if there is a significant risk that the bonds will not be repaid, the value of the equity is questionable. Since Boxco's sub debt is trading at 20 rather than its 100 claim, this suggests that some lenders/investors are so skeptical about how much, if anything, would be recovered that they are willing to sell their claims at substantial discounts. Of course, the investors buying those claims at 20 would presumably only do so if they believed ultimate recoveries would allow them to enjoy an adequate risk-adjusted return on investment.

It may be worth pausing to note that the market appears to be sending contradictory signals when the debt is selling at a significant discount but the stock is still trading at positive, albeit *de minimus,* values. As is discussed later, if Boxco were to ultimately go bankrupt and reorganize or liquidate, it is probable (assuming the market value of the sub debt of 20 is rational) that its stock will receive nothing.

While studies of this apparent market anomaly have been undertaken,[6] there is no consensus explanation. An EMT adherent might argue that equity holders could justify believing that the stock should trade at a positive value by asserting that it continues to have "option value."[7] But in many of these situations, it is difficult to believe that a knowledgeable investor could sincerely believe there are scenarios which could occur, with sufficient probability to merit serious discussion, where the equity could have fundamental value (i.e., that the firm's asset value will actually exceed the face amount of all its liabilities).

The EMT adherent might also argue that at such low values, various market trading rules and transaction costs might prevent the market from operating efficiently. For example, if an investor had strong conviction that a stock was, in fact, worth zero, one would suppose that even at a price of 10 cents per share it would make economic sense to sell the stock short. But various market restrictions on short selling[8] and the relative transaction costs could, as a practical matter, make it difficult to execute this investment strategy. Thus, the EMT proponent might suggest that the normal market process of arbitrage cannot drive an efficient solution. This is more persuasive than the "option value" rationalization, but one might ask why short sellers are needed to drive the market to efficiency. Why wouldn't the vast majority of existing equity holders simply admit they made a mistake and sell the stock at whatever positive value could be realized? This would be particularly true if the sale would allow the investor to recognize a tax loss that could potentially offset other taxable income and create an economic benefit.

Furthermore, one could argue that there are situations where although there can be no rational expectation that the stock has any fundamental equity value (again this refers to a scenario where the value of the firm's assets is less than the face amount of its liabilities), the stock might have economic value based on nonfirm-related sources. A common example of this might be potential recoveries from lawsuits brought by shareholders against negligent or deceitful management where the expected source of payment is an insurance policy issued to protect directors and officers of the firm. This would be a rational reason supporting a positive trading price, but market professionals seldom[9] report discussions about distressed stocks, particularly those selling for less than $1 per share, where the investment rationale is based on such recoveries. Furthermore, if this were truly the rationale, there would be very little basis for daily fluctuations in stock values because there is seldom any new information to cause rational investors to painstakingly reassess expected recovery values on a daily basis.

A final possibility is that the market is just wrong. Perhaps this is because not enough investors understand the restructuring process — which validates the purpose of this book. Perhaps it is because some investors have psychological difficulty in admitting that they made a bad investment decision and therefore do not sell out of a sense of denial. Who knows? But the reality, based on the observation that many reorganizations have left stockholders with no recovery and yet the stock trades at positive values very late into, if not at the conclusion of, the reorganization, is likely to be that they were simply wrong.

This may seem like a rather lengthy digression on an arcane point. The reason for trying the reader's patience is to introduce, early on, the dilemma frequently confronted in distressed securities investing by the market's pricing of various securities within a single firm's capital structure. In the Boxco example, it was assumed that the senior debt was trading at 50 and sub debt at 20. As will be discussed in significant detail in the chapters that follow, generally, under basic contract law or the absolute priority rule of chapter 11 reorganizations, the sub debt would not be entitled to any recovery unless the senior debt is paid in full. If no investor is willing to pay more than 50 for the senior debt, it suggests the market has significant doubt that the senior debt is likely to receive a full recovery. Yet the sub debt is trading at 20. On its face, this appears paradoxical. Similarly, if the sub debt is at 20, does that not imply that the stock is worth zero? Probably so, but the stock is assumed to be (and in the real world normally would be) trading at a positive value. Otherwise, one could apply the logic in reverse and ask: if the equity really has positive value, isn't the implication that the bonds (both senior debt and sub debt) should recover 100? These inconsistencies — the fact that the price of one security appears to imply that the price of another security is wrong — are a practical reality of distressed securities investment that often leads to interesting investment opportunities.

Returning to the plight of Boxco, Figure 3-6 illustrates the impact of the new market price information. On the GAAP format, there is no change because market values are generally irrelevant.[10] In the market value framework, because the debt is trading at a significant discount, the small equity value is ignored; the implied asset value is only $290.[11]

Unlike equity securities that can fluctuate wildly with no particular immediate implications to the underlying firm, debt securities contractually obligate the firm to pay the full amount of the claim. Combining this contractual reality with the market reality, Figure 3-7 can be developed. It is a conceptual depiction of a firm in financial distress. Notice that to maintain symmetry, a fictional item called "negative equity" has been developed. It would probably be more accurate to label this as "unrealized loss."

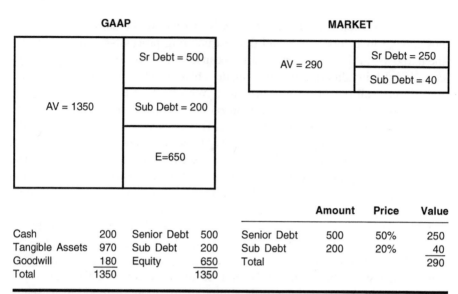

	Amount	Price	Value
Senior Debt	500	50%	250
Sub Debt	200	20%	40
Total			290

Cash 200 Senior Debt 500
Tangible Assets 970 Sub Debt 200
Goodwill 180 Equity 650
Total 1350 1350

Figure 3-6. Boxco Following Market Value Decline

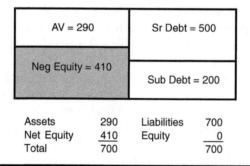

Assets	290	Liabilities	700
Net Equity	410	Equity	0
Total	700		700

Figure 3-7. Boxco in Financial Distress

HOW RESTRUCTURINGS ATTEMPT TO "FIX" THE DISTRESS

The basic "problem" in Figure 3-7 is that the firm's financial value is now less than the debt component of the capital structure. There are two obvious solutions to this problem. First, the asset value could be increased. The way to do this usually is not readily discernible; otherwise, management would presumably have already pursued this strategy. But it is worth noting because, from a legal perspective, there may be no "problem" in the sense that a decline in the market value of a firm hardly ever, by itself, gives rise to a breach of a typical financing contract such as a bank loan agreement or a bond indenture (these will be discussed in more detail later). Thus, as long as the firm has sufficient liquidity (looking back at Figure 3-6, Boxco still had $200 in cash, so operating losses aside, it should be able to make interest payments on its debt for some time) to remain current in its obligations, management theoretically has the option of attempting to increase or restore perceived asset value.

The alternative solution is to reduce the amount of liabilities to reflect current asset value. This, in its simplest sense, is a restructuring. Conceptually, a financial restructuring can be thought of as the process of transforming a firm's capital structure to better fit the current and/or future circumstances of the firm.

When the restructuring process begins, the approach to valuation reverses and focuses on an independent assessment of the value of the firm's assets. Referring back to the early equations, the thought process becomes Assets − Liabilities = Equity. There are at least two reasons why the market-value-based equation — Market Equity + Market Liabilities = Assets — is discarded. The first has already been discussed: in complex capital structures, the market pricing of various securities, particularly the allocation of any positive value to equity, can create confusion as to the appropriate value of any part of the liability or equity side of the balance sheet. Second, the very fact that the firm has become financially distressed and may require a balance sheet restructuring creates an uncertainty that investors will demand to be compensated for in the form of a risk premium. This risk is legitimate and will negatively impact the market value of the capital structure, but it is completely independent of the firm's "true" asset value.[12]

Thus when a restructuring process begins, whether through a voluntary out-of-court process or in a formal chapter 11 bankruptcy proceeding, the threshold question is: What is the firm worth? As discussed in detail later, this ultimately entails an analysis of the firm's future cash-flow-generating capability. If the firm has negative operating cash flow, as is frequently the case with start-ups, and no one is prepared to advance more cash (either through a loan or an equity infusion) to finance the business until it achieves positive operating cash flow, then the conclusion may be that the firm has no positive value and cannot be restructured.[13]

From a graphical perspective, Figure 3-8 presents the resolution options discussed above. Note that in the resized capital structure option, the debt/total capital ratio is a more conservative 34%.

SUMMARY

This chapter has provided a conceptual overview of one-half of the distressed investment story: what it means to become financially distressed. The basic

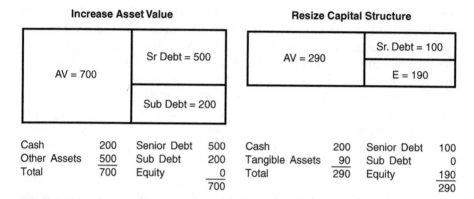

Figure 3-8.   Resolution Options for Boxco's Financial Distress

concept conveyed through the series of box diagrams is that, in many if not most cases, the value of assets is typically quite uncertain and often subjective. In general, the EMT posits that the market can be relied upon to accurately assess the value of assets, and thus, one can infer that value from the market's valuation of the firm's securities (i.e., stocks and bonds). But as numerous well-known real-world cases attest, the market seems capable of making dramatic reassessments, both negative and positive, of these values, often when very little has fundamentally changed about the use or composition of the assets. This can be easily accommodated if the capital structure is made up of equity, but declines in asset value create a problem when the capital structure contains a significant component of debt. There are basically only two solutions: increase the value of the company or "resize" the capital structure. Increasing the value of companies involves basic issues of strategy and operations that are beyond the scope of this book but are the subject of many other works.[14] This book focuses on the process and implications of resizing the capital structure and the investment issues and opportunities involved in that process. The next chapter provides a legal overview of how "resizing" is accomplished through the restructuring process.

This Chapter's Chess Moves

4. Pe3, Nc6

5. Bd3, Bxc3

4

LEGAL OVERVIEW OF DISTRESSED DEBT RESTRUCTURINGS[1]

In the last chapter, the concept of a balance sheet restructuring was introduced as an integral part of the process of distressed debt analysis. Put simply, since a restructuring of some type will very often be a part of the resolution of a firm's financial distress, the implications of that restructuring must be part of the investor's investment calculus.

The process can be analogized to purchasing a rundown home in a foreclosure sale. The investor might believe that expanding and remodeling the property could result in a substantial profit. However, before bidding, the prudent buyer would check, among other things, zoning regulations to see if an expansion were permitted and inspect the foundation to make sure it could be supported. Similarly, a distressed debt investor must always assess how the restructuring process could impact the investment.

In this chapter, the most common methods used to effect a restructuring will be reviewed, along with some of the considerations that go into the choice of options. The concept of restructuring developed earlier was to "fit" the liability side of the balance sheet to the firm's asset value. There are an almost infinite number of ways a specific restructuring can be arranged, but there are basically only two approaches to the process: in-court or out-of-court. In-court refers to the formal process of a chapter 11 reorganization[2] (or occasionally a chapter 7 liquidation). Out-of-court relates to voluntary agreements between the financially distressed firm and certain, but generally not all, of its creditors. Although this chapter is titled legal overview of distressed debt restructurings, in fact, there is relatively little legal "structure" to the out-of-court restructuring. The only real limit imposed on the participants is the fact that if an out-of-court restructuring cannot be achieved, the distressed company may be forced into bankruptcy; thus what tends to guide or control the process are the practicalities of forging a consensual agreement within a context that often involves bitterness and financial loss.[3]

OUT-OF-COURT RESTRUCTURINGS: THE PREFERRED OPTION WHEN EFFECTIVE AND FEASIBLE

As a general proposition, chapter 11 cases are time consuming, administratively expensive, and carry the risk of harming the business because key customers and/or vendors may perceive there are risks in having commercial relationships with a bankrupt business.[4] Thus, an out-of-court restructuring, when it can effectively resolve the financial distress, is generally preferred.

The Financial Effects of an Out-of-Court Restructuring

In an out-of-court restructuring, the firm and its most significant financial creditors typically either negotiate a change in the terms of existing obligations or complete a voluntary exchange of financial interests.[5] Consider what could be done with Boxco as of Figure 3-6, shown as Figure 4-1, with the simplifying assumption that all of the debt is one class (which class, senior or subordinated, does not really matter since it is the only debt) trading at 41. Given the extent by which the face amount of debt exceeds assumed asset value ($700 debt versus $290 asset value), a renegotiation of terms (i.e., lowering the interest rate, extending the maturity) will not be effective to solve the problem. Thus, some type of exchange will need to be arranged. An exchange is just what the word implies: a trade where the original bond is exchanged for new consideration that could include a combination of a bond with a reduced principal amount, some type of equity security, and/or cash. For example, Boxco and the bondholders could agree to a voluntary exchange in which the bondholders reduce the amount of their debt in exchange for all the equity. This would be a fairly plausible offer (despite the loss to existing shareholders) since it would be the most likely outcome of a bankruptcy (as discussed later). Thus, if the desired postreorganization capital structure was $100 of debt and all the stock in the possession of existing bondholders, each $1 of old Boxco bonds ($700 face) would receive approximately 14 cents in a new Boxco bond and an arbitrarily large number of common shares, say 10 shares. Assuming all the

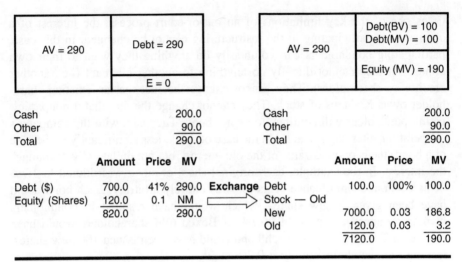

			Amount	Price	MV
AV = 290	Debt = 290				
	E = 0				
Cash					200.0
Other					90.0
Total					290.0
Debt ($)			700.0	41%	290.0
Equity (Shares)			120.0	0.1	NM
			820.0		290.0

		Amount	Price	MV
AV = 290	Debt(BV) = 100 / Debt(MV) = 100			
	Equity (MV) = 190			
Cash				200.0
Other				90.0
Total				290.0
Debt	100.0	100%	100.0	
Stock — Old				
New	7000.0	0.03	186.8	
Old	120.0	0.03	3.2	
	7120.0		190.0	

Exchange ⟹ Stock — Old

Figure 4-1. Exchange of Boxco Debt

Boxco bonds participated in the exchange, afterward Boxco would have $100 (700 bonds × 14.2%) in total debt and 7120 (7000 new shares + 120 old) outstanding shares, 98.3% of which would be held by Boxco bondholders.

A couple of points should be made about this hypothetical restructuring. First, the postreorganization capital structure is in many ways arbitrary. The example assumed approximately $100 in debt and the rest in common stock. The $100 amount was fairly arbitrary. If Boxco had ended up with $150 in debt, it might have been perfectly capable of flourishing. Similarly, nothing was specified about the terms of the debt: $100 of 15% debt that matured in 2 years might be much more challenging for Boxco to manage financially than $150 of 4% debt with a 20-year maturity. Taking things a step further, there is no "requirement" that there be any debt. It could have been negotiated that Boxco's best chance for success was to have no debt and thus the bondholders would have received only stock in exchange for their bonds. An all-equity exchange would not change the hypothetical economic recovery of the bondholder (the "asset" value has not changed; theoretically each share of stock has just increased in value). A complete "equitization" or debt-free solution is often advisable for firms that are not generating stable cash flow or are likely to require additional capital infusions in the future; if there is no other debt, it is much easier to borrow this additional capital.

Second, a stated "goal" of the bondholders in the restructuring was that they would hold all of the outstanding stock. The proposed restructuring did not technically achieve this because existing stockholders retained an interest representing about 1.7% of the equity. Trivial as this interest may seem, it illustrates one of the key limitations of an out-of-court process; the interest of a claimant not participating in the restructuring cannot be changed. In this case, participating bondholders can voluntarily do anything they want to their own bonds, but they cannot directly do anything to another claimant (i.e., another creditor or shareholder). They cannot change the fact that an existing shareholder owns X shares of stock. They cannot change the fact that a nonparticipating bondholder will continue to own a bond. They can, with the company's cooperation, alter (significantly in the case of stock, less significantly in the case of a bond) the economic value of the old interest, but not unilaterally "expunge" the interest. In the example, each original share of stock was diluted to 1.7% of its economic significance. This too was entirely arbitrary. Each bond could have been given 5 new shares, which would have resulted in bondholders owning an aggregate stake of 96.7% of Boxco (old shareholders would have retained a 3.3% interest), or each bond could have been issued 100 new shares, leaving old shareholders only a 0.2% stake.

Lastly, it should be noted that the restructuring can involve payments of cash instead of an exchange of securities. While it may seem counterintuitive that a firm in financial distress would have cash available for such purposes, there were in fact many cases in the 2000–2003 restructuring cycle where this occurred.[6] The typical scenario involved a technology or telecommunications firm that had raised significant capital that was earmarked for deployment in the business at a later date. When the market crashed and/or market fundamentals deteriorated, these companies were left with a strategic decision. They could continue to invest the cash that had been raised in their business and hope that in the future the business would attain a valuation that would allow the company to support or refinance its capital structure, or they could use their cash to restructure by immediately repurchasing their debt at a significant discount.

For example, in Figure 4-1 Boxco still has $200 in cash on its balance sheet. The company could decide that rather than effectively eliminating the interests of its equity holders in a dilutive exchange offer, it would be better to repurchase its bonds at a discount. At the current market price of 42, if it used all $200 of its cash for such repurchases, it could buy back $475 in face amount of debt. This would reduce the outstanding balance to $225, which is higher than would be accomplished in the debt exchange, but existing shareholders would still control the company. Of course, the problem is that Boxco arguably needs that cash to fund its currently money-losing operations. However, many of Boxco's bond investors might prefer to receive cash of potentially less than 42. In the scenario in Figure 4-1, much of the "recovery" is in stock with a very uncertain future, and if exchanging bondholders wanted to sell it, there could be legal restrictions[7] or their sales could depress the price. Thus, Boxco could conceivably be successful in offering bondholders a choice for their bonds: Option 1 is 30 cents in cash and option 2 is 14 cents in new bonds plus 10 shares of common stock.[8]

The Out-of-Court Restructuring Process

Chapter 9 examines in more detail the considerations that go into the structure or terms of any particular exchange proposal; the goal here is to understand the basic mechanics and challenges of the process. The out-of-court restructuring typically begins with a negotiation that ultimately leads to an agreement by the participants on the terms of a deal which is thereafter implemented or at least attempted to be implemented. The key practical points about the process to emphasize are that it is a "negotiation" with "key participants." From an organizational perspective, this presents a conundrum akin to the chicken or egg problem. An effective negotiation cannot take place until the proper parties are involved, yet there is no reason to go through the exercise of identifying the proper parties until a reason for a negotiation has been identified. It may be more effective to first understand who will be involved in the negotiation on the creditor/investor side. Then, how the process typically begins will be explored, along with the mechanisms to implement any proposed changes.

Parties Involved

In cases where a significant part of the debt capital structure is comprised of bank debt, determining who will negotiate on behalf of the creditors is fairly straightforward. If the loan is made by a single or small group of lenders, the relevant participants are self-evident. In the case of a large syndicated loan, the loan agreement will specify an "agent," who receives special compensation, to perform such duties, although other holders can also get involved.

In the case of bonds, the representative will typically be a small group of significant bondholders who form an informal bondholder committee.[9] Although the technical legal representative of the bonds is the indenture trustee, as a legal matter the indenture trustee (typically a bank acting in a custodial capacity) will only act when it believes it is acting on behalf of all or a specified percentage of the bonds. Thus, for most situations other than a payment default, the bondholders must independently "organize" and reach some type of consensus before the trustee can act. As a practical matter, indenture trustees are very "risk averse" and thus will tend to only do what they are clearly obliged to do under the indenture. Indenture trustees are not proactive.

Accordingly, usually a large bondholder will take the initiative to contact other significant bondholders and solicit their participation in an informal bondholder committee to negotiate on behalf of the overall bondholder group. There are no "rules" about who can be on such a bondholder committee, and those on the bondholder committee have no fiduciary duties to either other bondholder committee members or noncommittee creditors. There is no vote or ratification of the members by the bondholders at large. It is essentially several significant, and typically fairly experienced, bondholders getting together and agreeing to get involved in a process best characterized as "self-appointment." The "political check," so to speak, in the process is that for management to recognize the "legitimacy" of the bondholder committee as a group "worth dealing with," the committee must represent a significant percentage of the bonds. Since the bondholder committee will have relatively more negotiating leverage as the amount of bonds its members hold increases, it will generally want to represent as many bonds as is practically feasible without the bondholder committee's size becoming logistically cumbersome. In practice, management will usually not want to work with a bondholder committee whose members do not own at least 25% of the bonds.

The motivations of the bondholder committee members can vary, although the common self-interest of maximizing the value of the investment tends to align everyone's goals. However, sometimes certain investors will have a particular strategic agenda to pursue and will seek bondholder committee participation to try and realize a particular goal. For example, in the Boxco case, some prospective bondholder committee members might believe that the market is misvaluing Boxco and that ultimately its equity could become very valuable. For these investors, the restructuring could present an opportunity to "acquire" an equity position inexpensively. Alternatively, another investor could have just as much conviction that Boxco is a worthless enterprise with bad management whose only worthwhile asset is its cash. This investor would press for Boxco's liquidation. A conflict such as this can be difficult to resolve in a consensual process (see the discussion on holdouts later in this chapter); the two-option exchange proposed above, while appearing to accommodate both positions, is seldom done in practice and could have significant workability problems.

Bondholder committee participation as a "job" can be viewed very differently depending on the orientation of the investor. For example, for a hedge fund investor making an investment with a very focused strategic plan in mind (perhaps to acquire the equity of Boxco), it may be a very key part of the process. Alternatively, for a mutual fund or insurance company that acquired the bonds in the initial distribution and now finds itself with an embarrassing "loss," bondholder committee work may be viewed as a necessary evil. The process can often be fairly time consuming, and investors (either the firms or the individuals involved) typically do not receive any special compensation. Thus, while there is ego gratification associated with being in a position to exercise influence on an important financial event, many participants on the bondholder committee will have only indirect financial interests involved in the outcome.

Once the bondholder committee is formed, its members will directly interact with management or its representatives. Often the bondholder committee will negotiate an agreement with the firm so that it can, at the company's expense, retain legal counsel or financial advisors for advice or to conduct the negotiation on the bondholder committee's behalf.

However, it is important to emphasize that the bondholder committee per se has no legal authority to bind either member or nonmember bondholders.[10] The bondholder committee's purpose is to act as a proxy for all the bondholders. The bondholder committee's role is to perform an analysis of the company's business and financial circumstances (which usually involves receiving confidential, nonpublic information, discussed below) and then negotiate a "solution" that presumably represents the best "achievable" alternative to maximize the value of the bondholders' interests. The more credible the bondholder committee's members, legal counsel, and, where applicable, financial advisor, the better the chance that any "deal" reached between the bondholder committee and the company will be viewed as the legitimate "best available" solution and voluntarily embraced by nonmember holders. The operating assumption of nonmembers is something like: "The people on the bondholder committee are experienced and have a lot at stake; they've seen the inside numbers, they negotiated the best deal they can for themselves, and they are participating. We cannot expect to do better."

Strategic Considerations in Participating on the Bondholder Committee

Given that the bondholder committee can influence the course of the out-of-court restructuring, on the face of it, apart from the lack of compensation, it appears always to be advantageous to try to participate in the process. Otherwise, the investor, in most cases, must passively wait to review the outcome. However, there are at least two important strategic issues that must be considered before making an investment with the goal of participating on the bondholder committee.

First, if an investor has a strategic goal of participating in the process, which is the goal of many aggressive hedge fund investors, this dictates that the investor must accumulate a significant quantity of the bonds. Bondholder committees typically include only members with relatively significant holdings because the logistical problems in scheduling meetings and/or the challenge of reaching a consensus increases with the number of participants. Thus, someone contemplating an investment with a strategy of reducing investment risk by participating on the committee must effectively increase risk by accumulating a sufficiently large block so that he or she can be a credible candidate for the committee. Again, as mentioned above, there are no formal rules about who participates on the bondholder committee (unlike official committees formed during a bankruptcy[11]), so there is very little an investor can do, outside of accumulating a large block of bonds, to enhance one's candidacy.

The bondholder committee process can present slightly different considerations to an existing large holder, such as, for example, the much-maligned mutual fund or insurance company that purchased a large block of bonds in the initial offering and now finds itself in a losing position. The portfolio manager may conclude that even though he or she does not particularly like the situation, he or she is effectively "stuck" because to sell one's holdings, even over time, might cause market levels to decline substantially. Furthermore, mutual funds that hold large positions in distressed companies often see it as the fund's "fiduciary duty" to participate in the restructuring process to protect investor interests. Such a large holder may not need to accumulate more bonds to be eligible for the committee, but may choose to add to holdings if bonds can be purchased at attractive values — to increase its negotiating leverage or to prevent another holder that might have a different agenda from accumulating a stake.

The second strategic issue associated with joining a bondholder committee is that it often requires the investor to accept and review material nonpublic information about the debtor. Procedurally this requires each member to execute a *confidentiality agreement* (a form of which is available for download at www.jrosspub.com) at the beginning of the bondholder committee process. This is generally referred to as signing "confi" and can result in the holder becoming "restricted." The practical implication of becoming restricted is that the holder cannot discuss the nonpublic information with nonrestricted persons and cannot legally purchase or sell securities of the firm without disclosing to the other party the possession (but not the actual content) of such information. This can be a strategic disadvantage because it can significantly limit the investor's ability to trade; on the other hand, it gives the investor access to the best information available.

Bondholder committee members usually must become restricted at some point because in order to negotiate a financial restructuring with the firms's management, the bondholder committee members must assess the financial and operational circumstances of the firm. This generally involves reviewing management's internal forecasts and other detailed financial and operational data, all of which are nonpublic. To maximize the time period members remain unrestricted, the receipt and analysis of confidential information initially can be limited to the financial advisors and counsel, who will then be in a position to advise the bondholder committee members when they become restricted at a later date. The quality and amount of information received by the members are usually a function of how long the bondholder committee is willing to become restricted. However, once members receive nonpublic information, they will become restricted and cannot become unrestricted until the information becomes public, usually through the filing of a Form 8-K, 10-Q, or 10-K, or the information becomes nonmaterial. Thus, where the bondholder committee indicates that it would like the option of becoming unrestricted at a time in the reasonably near future, there will typically be a negotiation concerning the scope of information that will be made available and then later disclosed. Another option which many institutional investors are now pursuing is to establish internal "ethical walls"[12] so that the receipt of confidential information by designated individuals (the representative on the bondholder committee) who agree to not disclose such information to co-workers will not necessarily taint other fund personnel.[13]

Once a holder is in receipt of material nonpublic information (which is essentially presumed if one has signed a confi), the holder cannot buy or sell securities of the company without disclosing to the counter-party that he or she has "nonpublic" information. To engage in transactions without such disclosure could be a violation of the "insider trading" rules of U.S. securities law.[14] This could potentially expose the restricted party to criminal liability and would also give the counter-party the right to "unwind" the transaction and bring an action for damages.[15]

Because of these risks, restricted holders are careful to make sure that the counter-party to any trade is aware that the holder has nonpublic information. To document this, the counter-party must execute what is generally known as a *big-boy letter*[16] (a form of which is available for download at www.jrosspub.com). A big-boy letter generally contains two features: (1) an acknowledgment by the nonrestricted party that he or she is aware that the counter-party is in possession of nonpublic information and (2) a waiver of claims the nonrestricted party might otherwise have under securities laws because of the restricted party's possession of nonpublic information. The execution of a big-boy letter is typically arranged by a broker-dealer intermediary to protect the identity of the two persons involved in the trade. The letter does not contain any nonpublic information or otherwise restrict the counter-party, but it provides a document trail that the restricted party has disclosed his or her status and thus may reduce or eliminate the restricted party's legal liability.[17]

The requirement that a restricted holder must disclose his or her status (i.e., request a "big-boy" letter) can have a detrimental impact on that party's ability to engage in securities transactions. Consider the following situation. Assume that a group of bettors are at an off-track betting salon segregated in a room where there is no information about the outcome of any races. A man walks into the room and announces that he has just watched the third race at Santa Anita and offers to sell his winning ticket on the number six horse for 50% of the amount of the wager. Would anyone be foolish enough to buy it? Of course not. The seller undoubtedly knows that the number six horse did not win the race and that the ticket is worthless. Similarly, when a restricted party indicates that he or she wants to buy or sell, potential counter-parties often will reassess their investment decision.[18] As a result, the decision to join a bondholder committee and sign a "confi" can significantly limit an investor's ability to change an investment. It presents a particular dilemma to the large proactive investor who ideally would like to influence the restructuring process but also desires to continue to increase his or her position in order to gain more power. Because of this potential limitation on market access, many investors will make a strategic decision to forgo access to material nonpublic information and the ability to influence the course of a restructuring.[19]

The risk of restriction also arises when investors purchase bank debt, because bank debt lenders are typically entitled to nonpublic information under the terms of the loan agreement.[20] Investors who choose to remain unrestricted can usually request not to be given such information, but if they are inadvertently informed of something (e.g., an employee of the agent bank indiscreetly mentions that the debtor is close to selling a major asset), they technically become restricted (at least until the nonpublic information is made public). Such "public-side" bank debt holders may also feel at a disadvantage when asked to vote on a waiver or forbearance. However, a request to avoid becoming restricted is usually not an option within the context of working on a bondholder committee, because the review and analysis of such information is a key aspect of the bondholder committee's function.[21]

Beginning the Process

Since an out-of-court process requires the voluntary participation of creditors, there is almost always a negotiation. The process will sometimes begin with what appears to be a unilateral action by the debtor (for example, a tender offer); however, as a practical matter, such actions are usually preceded by, or will lead to some level of, informal or formal negotiation.[22]

The precise impetus for the negotiation can vary. Where the debt is primarily bank debt, it usually begins because the borrower is in or approaching technical default of some provision of the loan. This may give the lender(s) the theoretical right to accelerate if the default is not cured or waived. In such cases, the borrower's chief financial officer typically initiates the process with a call to the agent bank's responsible officer. Once the process begins,[23] it can take any number of courses, as will be discussed later, but the most typical conclusion is a restructuring of the bank loan, which is accomplished via preparation and execution of a legal amendment of some variety. This over-simplifies what will often be a very lengthy, expensive, and arduous process, but that is the essence.

If the debt is primarily in the form of bonds and there is no or minimal bank debt, then how the process begins can vary widely. If the debtor has virtually any public profile, then chances are that any of a myriad of investment bankers, restructuring advisors, turnaround specialists, and other professionals will have discerned that the company may be in financial distress. Often this will involve little more than monitoring trading prices of the company's equity or debt. These professionals then begin soliciting management to retain their services and, in the process, start to educate management. Management often will stub-bornly insist that the problem will be resolved by an upturn in business or a simple refinancing,[24] which potentially exposes management to liability since the fiduciary duties of the board of directors and officers expand to include the interests of creditors when the firm enters the "zone of insolvency."[25] Typically, however, management will ultimately be persuaded by legal counsel, accoun-tants, or another third party that an eventual day of reckoning is at hand and will either retain a specialist for advice or begin formulating strategies inter-nally. Since very few operating management teams are likely to have had experience in the restructuring process, management usually is well advised to retain a specialist sooner rather than later. Generally, an underestimation of what is involved or the prospect of significant professional fees often delays the decision. In the end, however, the company will almost always retain external advisors.

Once an advisor has been retained, the company's options will be reviewed and some strategic alternatives developed. If an out-of-court restructuring ap-pears feasible, the company has essentially one of two options: invite creditors to organize a bondholder committee so that a negotiation can begin or propose a restructuring without prior consultation.

If the first approach is chosen, then typically what occurs is that the company's advisor will identify a few of the largest bondholders and approach them with a request to organize a bondholder committee together with an offer to pay for any professional advisors, or at least lawyers, the bondholder committee may need. The bondholder committee will then form, as described above, and the company will provide the bondholder committee and its advisors with relevant financial information. A negotiation will then begin.

Occasionally, the debtor will decide that it is in its best interests to propose a restructuring without consulting or negotiating with a bondholder committee. This can only be done in the context of public bonds through a process involving a tender or exchange offer.[26] In contrast, bank debt restructurings can only be accomplished through negotiation. As a practical matter, most proposals that are made without the formation of a bondholder committee are in fact preceded by informal discussions between the company's financial advisor and several significant holders. Thus, in the Boxco example, Boxco in conjunction with its financial advisor may have developed the exchange proposal depicted in Figure 4-1. The financial advisor might thereafter discuss the acceptability of a similar "hypothetical" transaction[27] with several significant holders. If the holders indicate that such a transaction might be acceptable, then Boxco might proceed directly with the offer in order to avoid the time delay and cost associated with forming and negotiating with a bondholder committee. This type of "expedited" approach will often be used where, as is the scenario in Figure 4-1, the company is essentially giving all the economic value of the enterprise to the bondholders anyway.

In certain fairly unusual circumstances, a firm may perceive that it is not to its advantage to have any dialogue with bondholders. Because they are unusual, it is difficult to provide general principles about when such situations arise. One scenario in which this "nonnegotiation" strategy may be used is when management is trying to preserve value for the equity, and the firm perceives that it can "coerce" acceptance.

Returning to Boxco, consider what might happen if, instead of the two-option approach that was developed, Boxco unilaterally made a cash tender offer of 25 for each bond (an even more draconian version of option 2). This offer could present a dilemma for bondholders. On its face, the offer does not appear attractive because the example assumed Boxco's bonds were trading at 42. Any holder that wanted cash should sell the bond to the market for 42 rather than tender (which is essentially a sale to the company) for 25. But Boxco's value, implicit in the trading price of the bonds, may be dependent on it being able to fund its operations with cash. If the cash is depleted with the tender offer, then what remains for any bonds that do not tender could be worth materially less. In other words, the offer is coercive because it threatens to diminish the recovery of bondholders who do not participate. It also has the effect of, at least on the face of it, leaving the existing equity holders intact — which distressed debt holders typically object to on general "fairness" grounds. Of course, although under this approach the equity may not be diluted, it does not appear to have much value. Further, if cash is required to operate the business, the dilution may simply be postponed until the financing that raises the needed capital.[28] If Boxco wants to pursue this strategy, it may perceive that it has nothing to gain by having a dialogue with a bondholder committee. In fact, Boxco could arguably be worse off if it engaged in a negotiation because the process would tend to deplete its cash, and the information it would normally give the bondholder committee might be used to block or enjoin the tender offer.[29] Thus, in a limited set of cases, a firm may have a better chance of achieving its objective by not working with bondholders.[30]

Bondholders can also initiate the restructuring negotiation. This is less common because unless there is some type of breach of the loan instrument pending or imminent, the creditor has no bargaining power with the firm. Management can simply refuse to have a dialogue by not accepting the call. In fact, as a technical matter, in the case of bonds, the only entity that the firm has a legal relationship with and that can formally pursue a legal action is the indenture trustee. As a result, outside of calling management to ask questions and/or offer to sell their securities to the firm at a discount, there is very little the "minor" creditors can do. So often they do not bother.

The dynamic is different when one holder has accumulated a significant block of the debt. If there is no default, such a party still has only modest bargaining leverage. But management will usually at least meet with the creditor, recognizing that, at some point in the future, the creditor may have more leverage. At that point, it may be beneficial to have established a constructive dialogue since the creditor could end up controlling the business and effectively being the "boss."

Implementing the Restructuring

How the restructuring will be implemented will be a function of the type of debt involved and the nature of the restructuring. If the debt is in the form of a bank loan, implementation is relatively easy and usually consists of an amendment of the loan agreement signed by some or all of the bank debt holders. Most bank loans allow holders of a majority of the debt to execute amendments of most provisions that are binding on all of the lenders. However, loan agreements uniformly require 100% consent to make certain types of amendments, including extension of the maturity date, reduction in principal amount or amortization rate, reduction in interest rate, and change in collateral security.

If the debt is in the form of bonds and the restructuring can be accomplished with a transaction involving only the participants on the bondholder committee, then implementing the agreement can again be fairly easy and will usually be accomplished with a relatively simple private exchange. However, since restructurings typically involve some "sacrifice" (usually by changing the form or reducing the amount of the claim) by those participating, the participants will want virtually all of the bondholders to participate and thus share the sacrifice. To solicit the participation of other, noncommittee investors will usually require a formal exchange or tender offer in compliance with various requirements of the Exchange Act.[31]

Feasibility: The Holdout Problem

The next issue is feasibility. Because out-of-court exchanges are based on voluntary participation, they are often not feasible because of a lack of cooperation. This is referred to as the "holdout" problem: those not participating in the exchange may be better off than those that do, but if too many hold out, all will be worse off.

This is the general game theory problem known as the "prisoner's dilemma."[32] Consider the Boxco exchange in which the $700 in face debt will exchange into 14 cents in new debt and 10 shares of stock per $1 of debt. The bonds will have a 98.3% stake in an equity with a value of $190. Bondholders that participate in the exchange will receive a 14.3% recovery in a new bond plus shares of stock, for a combined aggregate value, assuming full participation, of approximately 41 (287/700). What if one bondholder with 50 bonds does not participate (i.e., holds out)? The transaction would probably still be effective at resolving Boxco's financial distress (total debt would still be a potentially manageable $143 versus $100 if all participated), but the lone holdout would be materially better off. The holdout would still have a full 100-cent-on-the-dollar claim which, because Boxco's financial distress has presumably been resolved, would now trade at a substantially higher market value, perhaps 100. In contrast, holders that participate have securities that are only worth 36.5. One might argue that the exchanging bondholders have equity upside: if Boxco performs well, stock appreciation could result in recoveries greater than 100. This may be true, but presumably the holdout bondholder could purchase Boxco shares and participate in the same extraordinary performance and still retain the full bond claim.

What if there are too many holdouts? In the worst case, Boxco's voluntary restructuring is not successful in resolving its financial distress, requiring it to file for bankruptcy. In that scenario, assuming there are few other benefits from the chapter 11 process other than the ability to bind the holdouts through either approval by the class or the operation of the Bankruptcy Code's "cram-down" provisions[33] (discussed below), recoveries are inevitably lower. All that the bankruptcy does is add costs that ideally could have been avoided. For example, assume that bankruptcy administrative expenses and lost customer relationships reduce Boxco's value from $287 to $215. If the same restructuring is implemented, bondholder recoveries will fall from 41.0% (287/700), had a voluntary exchange enjoyed 100% participation, to 30.4% (215/700) in the bankruptcy scenario.[34] Everyone is significantly worse off.

There are two general approaches to managing the holdout problem. The first can be thought of as "moral" coercion, but it really relates to the threat or ability to apply economic leverage at some point in the future. For better or worse, morality does not play a particularly large role in distressed debt investing. However, as outlined in Chapter 2, the major distressed debt players are a relatively small community that are known to each other. They are involved with each other in multiple transactions over time, and thus they consider the ramifications of what they do in one deal within the context of the future. The executives of the "regulars" form personal relationships (or in some cases animosities) with each other. Thus, although each investment or restructuring is structurally independent of all others, the overall market involves a process where "players" will work with or oppose each other in a series of transactions.

It is because of the probability of future contact and the risk that the financial leverage positions might be different in a future situation that groups can "coerce" cooperation. However, as in poker, which is analogous because the "multiple-hand" format of the game is similar to the series of transactions in the distressed marketplace, to be effective one must have a credible "bluff." In economics, a bluff is an intentionally irrational act engaged in to create uncertainty. A poker player who is known to raise only when he or she has good cards will not be successful. Thus even beginning poker players learn to lose a hand (this requires staying in until someone calls and showing cards) with weak cards to establish their bluffing credibility. Similarly, investors may occasionally act in a manner seemingly against their immediate best interests with an eye on future deals.

The second approach to managing holdouts is through coercive structural devices. These are more applicable in the context of attempting an exchange offer for bonds as opposed to the bank debt scenario just reviewed. In the context of an exchange offer for bonds, there is seldom a "leader," like an agent bank, that has sufficient "leverage" to informally force cooperation. The most common coercive tactic is to "strip" the covenant protections of nontendering bonds. To implement this, the exchange offer will include a provision that tendering bonds will be deemed to have voted to authorize an amendment to the indenture of the original bonds, which effectively deletes all protective covenants. Thus, if a majority tender, holdouts will have a significantly less attractive bond. A second technique used when a bankruptcy reorganization is the only clear alternative is to combine an exchange offer with a solicitation of support for a prepackaged chapter 11 filing (discussed in more detail below and in Chapter 12). This accomplishes two things: First, it legitimizes the threat of bankruptcy to the holdouts (the holdout should have no doubt about the firm's commitment to follow through with the threat, given that an extensive bankruptcy filing has already been prepared). Second, in the event a chapter 11 filing is required, it minimizes the related costs and expedites the time the firm is in bankruptcy. Prepackaged bankruptcies can be completed in less than 45 days.

Another structural feature commonly included in all exchange offers (but not necessarily cash tender offers) is a high minimum tender participation rate requirement. Typically, an exchange offer would include a provision to the effect that no tendered bonds will be accepted for exchange unless at least 90%[35] of all bonds tender. This "signals" to the market that (a) if the deal is completed, there is minimal risk that the financial distress will not have been resolved and (b) the benefit holdouts receive will be limited to only a small group. It also puts pressure on all holders to participate because they will realize that even a relatively small amount of nonparticipation will result in all being worse off. In fact, because it is often the case that in a public bond context some small portion of the bonds will not be aware of the offer, the "conscious" participation rate must make up for certain "innocent" holdouts.

However, if relative to a bond's current trading price the loss in the event of a bankruptcy is small compared to the substantial gain which might be captured from holding out, the temptation is still great. Furthermore, although tender offers do typically contain minimum participation requirements, the tendering firm usually retains the unilateral right to waive the requirement without notice. This can be justified by the need to retain the flexibility to facilitate the completion of a value-enhancing transaction where there is, say, only 89.5% participation. But bondholders cannot protect themselves from the risk that the tendering firm completes the transaction, even though the holdout rate is much higher (e.g., only 60% tender).

The general difficulty of the holdout problem escalates with the complexity of the capital structure. Thus if multiple levels of debt (as was the case with Boxco in Figure 3-5, which is why the example was simplified) must all consent to exchanges with varying terms, the holdout problem is often perceived to be so insurmountable that a voluntary exchange is not even attempted.[36]

Summary

Given the relative simplicity of the out-of-court restructuring, one might well wonder why it is successfully employed less than 10% of the time.[37] As the subtitle to this section suggests: it can be accomplished only when it is "effective" and "feasible." Effective means that the restructuring successfully solves the financial distress. As will be discussed in the next section and in more detail in Chapter 12, there can be many significant benefits to a chapter 11 process, particularly a bankruptcy court's authority to reject and resolve various liabilities. Thus, if the firm's financial distress is due to significant actual or contingent nonfinancial liabilities (e.g., pension or asbestos claims, above-market leases, or uneconomic contracts), then a chapter 11 process, in which these types of claims can be better managed, may be the only viable choice. Feasible alludes to the challenge, when the debt to be restructured is held by more than a handful of investors, of minimizing holdouts, which in a desire to maximize their individual returns will often frustrate the cooperative spirit of a majority and end up reducing everyone's recovery.

IN-COURT RESTRUCTURINGS: AN OVERVIEW OF THE BANKRUPTCY PROCESS

Besides the fact that a lot of lawyers will make a lot of money, there are probably at least two "universal" truths about a bankruptcy. First, it is hardly ever a surprise when a firm files for bankruptcy protection. As will be discussed in later chapters, basic financial analysis coupled with various market indicators make it simple to identify firms where the probability of a bankruptcy is fairly high. Even more explicitly, it is now common for firms to send many signals or warnings to the market preceding a bankruptcy filing. These can include candidly discussing the risk of bankruptcy in public securities filings or announcing the retention of a law firm or financial advisor generally associated with the bankruptcy process.

The second truth is that some or all of the original creditors will usually incur some amount of financial loss. This second truth is why this book was written. If there were no losses, no creditor would ever sell its claim for a significant discount. Because original creditors fear losses and want to mitigate them or avoid the bankruptcy process, they are willing to sell those claims, often at substantial discounts. This opportunity gives rise to distressed debt investing. So while the second universal truth is an unfortunate reality for some, it is a source of opportunity for others.

The point to emphasize here is that adroit distressed debt investors must be able to identify early on which firms are likely to end up in financial distress or bankruptcy and what that implies for the value of any particular claim. This gives the investor more opportunities to identify potential misvaluations or accumulate strategically important stakes — but proper execution also requires having a strategic plan or view that is focused many months or, depending on the investment objective, even years in the future.

One's intuition might be that, in the case where a bankruptcy will be required to resolve the financial distress, all that matters is to estimate when the filing will be made and then assume that the best time to buy is close to or immediately after the filing. This is naïve for at least two reasons. First, since few bankruptcies are a surprise, market prices will typically have adjusted to reflect the likelihood of bankruptcy well before the filing. Often, the actual filing of the bankruptcy petition is a noninformation event.[38] Second, even if this were the "bottom" price point, the illiquidity of the market often makes it very difficult to acquire stakes at the moment of the investor's choosing. If the investor wants to accumulate the bank debt, for example, he or she may find that it has already traded to someone else who realized that very few holders might be inclined to sell and that amassing a significant position was worth accumulating stakes at above what might be the bottom price point. Hoping to be able to buy everything at the "bottom" is simply not realistic.

The key is not necessarily to time the "bottom" but rather to buy what is available for less than it is worth. Although perhaps an overbroad generalization, in most cases, by the time of the bankruptcy filing, the "game" is often already over; the major strategic investors have already accumulated their positions and are ready to start carving up the cadaver.[39]

There are many sources of detailed information on the bankruptcy process.[40] The more the distressed investor knows about the process, the better, of course, but the practical reality is that from the perspective of analyzing a specific situation at some point in the future, the lack of information the investor is likely to have about the debtor will tend to limit how much detailed analysis can be done.[41] Thus, the point of this discussion is to review the basic framework of the process. In later chapters, a variety of provisions of the Bankruptcy Code that can have very important implications for recovery values are discussed in more detail, but even that discussion will be designed to alert the investor to what issues bear more investigation, rather than definitive guidance on how any particular issue will be resolved. Nothing in this book is intended to be legal advice on any particular issue.

The discussion in this section is intended to provide a brief overview of the bankruptcy process so that a minimum threshold of understanding can be assumed in later chapters. This tour, however, will not be completely chronological. First, the process of filing for bankruptcy protection and the initial procedural steps are reviewed. Then the end of the process — the creation and effect of a plan of reorganization — is discussed to help the reader understand the goal of the process. What will be apparent is that the outcome of a bankruptcy can be fairly similar to what is achievable in an out-of-court reorganization. With the start and finish established, the often long process of moving between the two is outlined.

Declaring Bankruptcy

Legally, a bankruptcy case begins when an appropriate petition is filed with a bankruptcy court.[42] In the vast majority of cases, this petition is filed by the debtor and is known as a "voluntary petition." In a few cases, three or more creditors may have grounds for filing an "involuntary petition,"[43] but the debtor confronted with such an action is likely to file its own petition and be granted control of the case.[44]

The petition will typically seek protection under the provisions of chapter 11 of the Bankruptcy Code, but chapter 7 is also a possibility. The primary difference between the two is that chapter 11 contemplates allowing the existing management to reorganize the debtor as a going concern,[45] while chapter 7 anticipates that a court-appointed trustee will supervise the liquidation of the debtor's assets. Both management and creditors tend to prefer chapter 11. From a cynic's perspective, the management would prefer chapter 11 because the executives are allowed to keep their jobs and at times can even extract premium wages on the theory that they must be provided extra incentives to remain in a higher risk business. Creditors generally prefer chapter 11 because they expect that the assets will be worth more as a going concern or if sold through an orderly disposition process than if liquidated in a fire-sale auction. However, where there are multiple classes of creditors, there may be differences of opinion or motivation. For example, if there is a secured class that could recover its claim in a quick liquidation, it may push for this option as the fast resolution, regardless of whether such a move would maximize returns for other creditors.

Jurisdiction of Filing

Like most legal actions, there will be strategic thought given to the jurisdiction in which the bankruptcy filing is made.[46] If the debtor has already reached a consensus with the major creditors about how the firm should be reorganized (such preplanned or prepackaged bankruptcies will be discussed later), a jurisdiction with a reputation for expediting the bankruptcy process may be favored. Alternatively, if management wants to remain in control and anticipates a contentious fight with creditors, it may choose a jurisdiction that it perceives to be more "debtor" or "home-town" friendly. The key issues for the distressed investor to consider are the relative level of bankruptcy planning that has occurred or may be possible, the probable jurisdiction of filing, and what this implies for the timing of the resolution and the potential effect on the treatment of various claims.

Timing of Filing

The timing of the bankruptcy filing will, when possible, also be carefully planned. The key issues here will be the debtor's effort to control the jurisdiction of filing and maximize liquidity. To maintain control of jurisdiction, the debtor will typically choose to file before it is in material breach of an agreement (e.g., failure to make an interest payment) that would give creditors a right to make an involuntary filing. Even if the debtor is usually able to change this after the fact as just discussed, it is a risk that is typically avoided.

The liquidity aspect of the strategy is twofold. First, if the debtor has faced the reality that a bankruptcy reorganization is inevitable, then any payments it makes to creditors will represent a drain of assets from the firm, particularly if the payment is to an unsecured creditor. This consideration will often lead firms to begin delaying payments to vendors (i.e., "stretching the trade") to conserve cash. A particularly common focal point for a filing will be the requirement to pay a large interest payment on a bond issue, especially unsecured bonds (which are the vast majority). If the debtor has a large bank loan on which it is in technical default,[47] the lender will usually have the power, through what are known as blockage provisions, to prevent such an interest payment.[48] Even if the debtor can make the interest payment (perhaps there is no bank loan or the borrower is in full compliance), it may choose to file for bankruptcy just to avoid making the payment and conserve cash.[49] Second, unless the firm has significant cash on hand, it will take steps to improve or ensure its liquidity. One common strategy, which is particularly damaging to banks, is for a firm to draw down all available capacity on revolving facilities in advance of a filing.[50] Alternatively, or in addition, a firm may also arrange for postbankruptcy financing, a subject discussed later. These timing considerations often make it fairly easy to predict the approximate date a firm will choose to file for bankruptcy.

The actual date of filing is significant because it forms a bright line in the debtor's operations. Everything that occurred before that date, including all liabilities incurred, is considered "prepetition"; all liabilities incurred after are "postpetition" and are effectively senior to most prepetition unsecured claims. Thus, if one were to go into a financially distressed grocery store, slip on a banana peel, become injured, and subsequently win a million-dollar damage verdict, it would be significant whether the injury occurred the day before the filing or the day after. If after, one would likely recover everything; if before, the claim would be a general unsecured claim, and potentially only a fractional recovery might be received. The filing date also sets look-back periods relating to the permissibility of certain transfers and may establish the valuation date,[51] for certain purposes, for a secured creditor's collateral. Finally, unless the debtor is solvent (which is fairly unusual), it tolls the accrual of interest on unsecured and undersecured claims.

In most cases, the debtor's management continues to operate the businesses after the filing of the bankruptcy petition. When the management operates the debtor postpetition, it does so as a fiduciary of the creditors, much like a de facto trustee. This relationship is connoted by the recognition of a fictional entity called the *debtor in possession*.[52] The management's scope of authority is limited to managing the day-to-day affairs of the business. Any transaction outside of the ordinary course of business (e.g., a major asset sale) requires the approval of the bankruptcy court.[53] Creditors will often be skeptical about the abilities of the management (who will generally be blamed for the events that resulted in the bankruptcy) and/or will believe the management misled them in the past about the company's financial circumstances. Thus, creditors often view the debtor's management as either incompetent or untrustworthy. Occasionally, the resignation of one or more senior executives will occur almost simultaneously with the bankruptcy filing. In cases of management turnover, outsiders with experience in corporate turnarounds and the bankruptcy reorganization process often fill the positions. Since the bankruptcy process can consume much of senior management's time and requires knowledge and a skill set that many executives have not previously had occasion to develop, turnaround consultants are often retained even when the management stays in place. Sometimes creditors will request an examiner be appointed to review management's supervision of the business.[54] In rare cases, usually involving gross mismanagement or fraud, the creditors may press for the appointment of a trustee to administer the day-to-day affairs of the estate instead of the previous management.[55]

Another organizational event that occurs at the outset of a chapter 11 process is the creation of the *official committee of unsecured creditors*. This committee is appointed by the U.S. Trustee and under the Bankruptcy Code is supposed to consist of the seven largest creditors who are willing to serve,[56] but the U.S. Trustee has reasonable discretion to form committees of different sizes and with a creditor group appropriate for the case. In large cases involving complicated capital structures and creditors with conflicting interests, multiple committees may be formed, but to minimize the burden of multiple sets of professional advisors to the committees, the bias is toward one committee with representation from each of the various unsecured creditor constituencies. Even though committee members may have conflicting individual economic interests, once they accept a position on the committee they have a fiduciary duty to represent the interests of all unsecured creditors. The committee is empowered to examine the business of the debtor, help formulate a plan of reorganization or liquidation, and, in conjunction with the trustee and debtor, oversee the administration of the estate.[57] The committee is allowed to retain, with court approval and at the estate's expense, lawyers, accountants, and financial advisors for assistance and counsel.

Secured creditors are grouped in classes according to the collateral by which the claim is secured. In cases where the secured creditor is oversecured, it will usually be entitled to have the fees and expenses of its own counsel and, when appropriate, financial advisor paid for by the estate.[58] In the case of syndicated credit facilities, the agent bank typically represents the entire bank group in the negotiation process.

Equity holders, although the last in line, are legally entitled to participate in the bankruptcy process and, in certain cases, vote on the acceptance of any plan of reorganization.[59] In situations where there is sufficient asset value that equity holders will potentially be entitled to some recovery, a separate equity committee may be formed to represent their interests. However, in the more typical case, equity holders will receive nothing and the proponent of the plan will presume, for confirmation purposes, that they object and not even bother to solicit their acceptance.

The Goal: The Plan of Reorganization

The term *plan of reorganization,* or plan, has been used a number of times, but not yet clearly described. The plan is basically a legal document that comprehensively discusses what will happen to the debtor, its assets, and all constituent liabilities, including equity interests, upon the debtor's exit from bankruptcy.[60] From the distressed investor's standpoint, its most important provisions relate to the determination of the status of various claims against the debtor and a description or analysis of how those claims will be treated or "paid."[61] As part of the process to solicit creditor acceptance of the plan, a disclosure statement is prepared, which is expected to provide sufficient information about the debtor, its business, and the effect of the plan to allow creditors to make an informed decision when they vote on whether or not to accept the plan.[62] It is similar to the process of soliciting shareholder votes via a proxy statement.[63] When the disclosure statement is approved, the proponent of the plan can then begin to solicit approval by creditors and equity holders. Opponents of the plan are also allowed to solicit rejections.[64] If the plan is accepted (by all or at least one "impaired" class), which involves complicated voting rules that will be discussed in more detail later, then the plan may, if it meets certain criteria or tests, be "confirmed" by the bankruptcy court.[65] Confirmation of the plan is the pivotal legal event. Confirmation has the powerful effect of instantaneously altering, often with significant uncompensated loss, preexisting legal relationships such as lending agreements, leases, and other contracts.[66]

The Role of Exclusivity and Prefiling Coordination

Similar to the out-of-court restructurings discussed above, the plan of reorganization typically is the result of a negotiation between and among the debtor and the creditors. However, in the context of chapter 11, the process is fairly structured. A literal reading of the Bankruptcy Code suggests that it contemplates a rather confrontational approach to the "negotiation" of the plan, but in practice the process is usually fairly fluid. Upon filing, the debtor is granted the exclusive right to propose a plan within 120 days of filing.[67] The bankruptcy court will typically, upon the request of the debtor, extend the exclusivity period virtually indefinitely so long as the debtor appears to be making a good faith effort to develop a plan. After exclusivity (which from a creditor's perspective will seem to continue indefinitely) has elapsed, the creditors or any other interested party can propose a plan.[68] Sometimes the debtor and certain creditors will each propose competing plans that will essentially force creditors and other interest holders in the debtor to make a choice.[69]

The process of allowing the debtor time to fashion a plan which is then offered for "acceptance" to the creditors may seem rather genteel. But if the investor is holding unsecured debt and perceives that management is potentially eroding the value of the investor's recovery by taking longer than necessary and incurring significant costs or operating losses, the issue of exclusivity can become emotionally charged. In fact, the general theory behind a finite period of exclusivity is to give the debtor an incentive to propose a plan in a timely fashion or risk losing control of the case to the creditors.[70] How the actual process evolves in any particular situation is difficult to predict and can depend upon the personalities involved as well as business exigencies. In general, the more the business is likely to deteriorate while it is in bankruptcy, the greater the incentive creditors and management have to forge a constructive relationship so that the time period in bankruptcy is minimal.

In cases where there is significant cooperation, the management and creditors work out a tentative plan and essentially have it ready to be voted on at the time of the filing of the bankruptcy petition. This is referred to as a "prenegotiated" chapter 11 filing.[71] In particularly well-planned cases, the creditors will vote on the acceptability of the plan prior to the filing of the petition.[72] This is called a prepackaged plan and can reduce the time needed to complete a reorganization to less than 45 days.[73]

At the opposite end of the spectrum, when the bankruptcy filing is abrupt or done in a context where no consensus has been reached, it is often referred to as a "free-fall" chapter 11. From an investor's perspective, a "free-fall" process is a warning sign that the reorganization process may be unusually lengthy (e.g., 1–3 years) and expensive. Furthermore, if the reason for the lack of preparation is a confrontational dynamic between creditors and management, it may also imply that the reorganization will involve a change of management. While in some cases this may be a positive development for the firm, it always introduces an additional element of investment risk.

Content and Structure of the Plan

The term "plan of reorganization" may sound rather ominous, but conceptually it is reasonably simple. There are fundamentally two operative parts to the plan.[74] The first identifies all the various claimants and then assigns them to various classes for purposes of voting and priority. The basic rule for classification is commonality of interest. Each individual class must be comprised of claims that are similar in nature. "Similarity" in this context mostly means having similar priority against the debtor; unsecured bank debt, bonds, and even tort claims can all be put in the same class. Secured claims are classified separately from unsecured claims and grouped based on the collateral in which they have an interest and their lien priority. The amount of the secured claim is limited to the lesser of the amount of the claim or the value of the creditor's collateral. To the extent a secured creditor has collateral worth less than its claim, this deficiency becomes part of the pool of general unsecured claims. This means that a creditor secured by a second lien on collateral may find that its claim is deemed to be entirely unsecured if the amount of the claim secured by the first-priority lien exceeds the value of the collateral. Unsecured creditors can be combined together or separated into different classes, depending on the objectives of the plan and whether or not the creditors consent to the proposed treatment. Classifications of unsecured claims can become particularly important, and contentious, in complicated corporate structures involving distinct legal entities (i.e., parent and subsidiaries). In some instances the plan may propose to recognize the legal identities of the various entities, while in other situations it may seek to join all the entities through a substantive consolidation. Structural issues can dramatically affect expected recoveries because, as will be discussed in Chapter 7, claims at a holding company are generally structurally subordinated to similar claims at an operating subsidiary. Thus claims, including trade claims, at a subsidiary with assets may enjoy a much higher rate of recovery.

The second part of the plan provides for what, if anything, each class will receive in the reorganization. All claims grouped within a class must be treated similarly. Sometimes in recognition of the fact that different creditors desire different types of recoveries, claims that are of similar priority will be grouped in different classes so that the recovery can be modified. For example, senior debt holders and trade claims are pari passu in terms of priority but can have very different desires in terms of recoveries. Trade creditors tend to prefer cash, even amounts substantially discounted to their claim, as opposed to new securities in the reorganized debtor. Alternatively, senior debt holders, particularly if they happen to be hedge funds that have purchased the debt as a vehicle to gain an ownership interest in the debtor, may prefer common stock. Thus, sometimes these otherwise equal claims will be grouped in two classes, although it is also possible to group them in one class and offer an election on the preferred form of recovery.

Returning to the Boxco example, a hypothetical plan of reorganization, sans the legalese, might read as follows:

Class 1: Administrative Claims. These claims shall include all postpetition fees and costs of all lawyers, accountants, and other professional advisors involved in the administration of the bankruptcy including the bankruptcy trustee. The claims total $5 and shall be paid in full in cash upon confirmation of the Plan.

Class 2: Secured Claims. These claims represent all amounts extended under the DIP (Debtor in Possession) line. These amounts total $3 and will be paid in full from the proceeds of a new working capital facility entered into at confirmation.

Class 3: Priority Claims. These claims represent a portion of the allowed amounts payable to employees relating to prepetition expenses. These amounts total $0.50 and shall be paid in full in cash upon confirmation.

Class 4: Senior Unsecured Claims. These claims represent all prepetition claims of trade creditors and senior unsecured note holders. These claims total $700 and shall receive $150 in new senior notes and all 100 shares of newly created common stock of Boxco.

Class 5: Equity. These interests represent the equity interest of prepetition shareholders. These interests shall receive nothing, and all previously outstanding common stock of Boxco will be canceled.

This represents a fairly simple plan, but is representative of how plans operate and are described. An excerpt from an actual plan of reorganization is available for download at www.jrosspub.com. Note that the hypothetical plan contemplates a capital structure that is very similar to that proposed in the out-of-court restructuring (except for the effect of the extra $5 in costs associated with the bankruptcy process). This is because, in the Boxco case, there was no particular advantage to the chapter 11 process (such as the rejection of uneconomic leases and so on, which will be reviewed shortly), so it represents a situation where everyone would have been better off had the restructuring been completed voluntarily. There is no magic to chapter 11, nor is it a mysterious black box. The distressed investor should view chapter 11 as a controlled system to enforce a restructuring that could not be voluntarily implemented. The key is to understand the process and how it affects potential investment returns and strategies.

Operating Under Chapter 11

Now that the beginning and end of the chapter 11 process have been reviewed briefly, it is time to discuss the process of getting between these two and some of the advantages and/or trade-offs chapter 11 brings to the debtor and certain creditors.

Once a bankruptcy process starts, there are essentially four main objectives: (1) to stabilize the firm's operations and provide for its immediate liquidity needs so that it can operate effectively on a postpetition basis, (2) to develop a going-forward business plan to maximize the value of the firm or its assets, (3) to determine the "legitimate" liabilities of the firm and their relative priority, and (4) in the case of a reorganization, to create and allocate a new capital structure. Although simple to state, the process involves many parties, each of which has its own self-interests. Accordingly, it is often a contentious, zero-sum game where one party's gain necessarily implies another party's loss. Thus, each of the above four "phases" in the process can significantly affect the recoveries of various parts of the capital structure and thus investment returns.

Stabilizing Operations

Following the filing of a chapter 11 petition, the *automatic stay* comes into existence.[75] The automatic stay prevents any claimants from pursuing an action that could have been commenced prepetition against the debtor except with the permission of the bankruptcy court. This essentially freezes all creditors in their prepetition position. From a distressed investor's perspective, the implications of the automatic stay will depend on the investor's position in the capital structure. The automatic stay significantly limits the leverage of secured lenders and thus can be viewed as protecting the estate for unsecured creditors. However, it can also benefit secured creditors to the extent it results in their collateral retaining going-concern valuations, rather than what might be recovered if the debtor were forced to liquidate.

For the debtor, the primary benefits of the automatic stay are "breathing room" and some financial flexibility. For example, imagine the debtor is a Mississippi River barge operator in default of a loan secured by its boats. The secured lender is threatening to foreclose and repossess the barges. If the lender were allowed to take control of the barges, the debtor's business would be destroyed. Upon filing, the automatic stay would prevent the creditor from repossessing the barges without the bankruptcy court's permission, thus giving the debtor a period[76] to use the barges, subject to certain protections for the secured creditor,[77] and to analyze its options and develop an operating plan in a more organized manner.

Another event that typically occurs at the commencement of a reorganization is the execution, with the approval of the bankruptcy court, of a lending relationship, typically referred to as a debtor-in-possession or DIP facility. Borrowings made postpetition, including normal trade credit, are characterized as administrative claims and thus have priority over prepetition unsecured liabilities.[78] However, even with such priority, many lenders will be unwilling to extend credit to a debtor on anything other than a secured basis. This often presents a problem because it is likely that the debtor has already pledged all of its assets — including cash, accounts receivable, inventories, real estate, etc. — to prepetition secured creditors.[79]

To deal with this issue, the Bankruptcy Code allows the debtor, with bankruptcy court approval, to grant the DIP facility lender a super-priority interest in previously encumbered assets of the debtor so that the lender can have greater assurance of repayment. This is sometimes called *priming*. In order to not unduly impair the original secured creditor's position, the granting of the super-priority lien will require the debtor to show that the original creditor is adequately protected. Adequate protection is a term of art that refers to the right of the creditor to insist that it be protected against any loss in value of an interest in property it has (such as a security interest) as a result of the bankruptcy. Despite the adequate protection provisions, to avoid the risk of being primed, many prepetition secured lenders will offer to become DIP lenders. One benefit of becoming a DIP lender is that the prepetition lenders are sometimes able to effectively convert their prepetition claim into a postpetition claim in a process commonly referred to as a *rollup*.

However, often the prepetition secured lender will have more than sufficient collateral to ensure the repayment of its loan. This, of course, was the lender's intent — to have more than adequate collateral. For example, the lender may be owed $65 but have $150 of accounts receivable as collateral. In such cases, the bankruptcy court may conclude that a proposed $75 DIP facility may be given a super-priority interest to the extent of $75 of the collateral (leaving $75 to cover the $65 owed) and still find the prepetition creditor adequately protected. On the other hand, if the prepetition creditor had a lien on the gasoline in a debtor gas station's underground tanks and the debtor was allowed to sell the gas and use the cash to pay employee wages, then the creditor's rights might be compromised and debtor's actions blocked. However, allowing the debtor to sell the gas so long as the proceeds were used to buy more gas might bridge this conflict. Thus the "tool" of adequate protection can allow a bankruptcy court to (1) allow a debtor to use its working capital to fund its ongoing operations (the gas example) and (2) allow the secured creditor's collateral to be used to raise additional capital (the accounts receivable example) and thereby potentially enhance or preserve the value of the debtor's estate while still protecting the secured creditor's rights.

Providing for operating liquidity is often an essential near-term need, especially where the debtor has little cash on hand at the time of filing.[80] Although a chapter 11 filing can in some ways improve operating liquidity by reducing the debtor's cash outflows related to the payment of postpetition interest on unsecured or undersecured debt[81] and defer or reduce the payment of prepetition amounts owed to vendors, these curtailments are not complete and other factors often offset these benefits. For example, secured lenders will often receive postpetition interest and other payments designed to provide them with adequate protection (discussed below). The debtor may also view certain vendors as so essential to the business that management will ask the bankruptcy court permission, in what is known as a *critical vendor motion,* to pay such vendors their prepetition claims in order to ensure their ongoing affiliation with the debtor. While payment of prepetition claims may be withheld from noncritical vendors, those parties that previously may have sold merchandise to the debtor with 30-day terms may insist on cash on or before delivery for all postpetition business. Finally, customers of the debtor that would normally pay within the ordinary payment cycle may withhold payments while they study the debtor's situation.

Operating stability also requires the continued commitment of employees. Senior executives and others who are critical to the organization may require new contracts to induce them to stay with the troubled business. This is particularly true where a significant portion of their compensation was in the form of equity-related incentives. Accordingly, these employees often will be offered an incentive called a key employee retention program (KERP). While no one would dispute the need for a firm to have effective leadership during the reorganization process, creditors will occasionally oppose KERPs on the grounds that they are unnecessary or too generous. Being skeptical for a moment, it is important to recognize that oftentimes the inept management that caused the business to fail and need to file for bankruptcy protection will attempt to use such KERPs as a way to perpetuate its tenure, often at inflated salary rates. Because of concerns about prior management, creditors often will press for a crisis or turnaround manager (sometimes titled the chief restructuring officer) to be brought in from outside the organization. The chief restructuring officer will generally have significant experience in guiding organizations through the restructuring process and can be important in restoring management's credibility with creditors. Finally, of course, the firm must have sufficient liquidity to pay nonessential employees their going-forward wages on a current basis.

On paper, the exercise of stabilizing the debtor's operations can seem rather clinical, but its practical effect cannot be overemphasized. Although it is often overlooked, a surprising amount of business depends on trust and cooperation. A supplier sends widgets to a manufacturer, trusting that it will get paid. When it gets paid, it will pay the bill of its supplier that provided the raw material from which the widgets were made, and so on. When the chain breaks down due to, say, the bankruptcy of the manufacturer, the business can unravel very quickly. The buyer of the widget worries that the manufacturer may not replace defective items, so it withholds payments. The manufacturer needs cash, so it requests that future payments be made COD. A competitor of the manufacturer asks the buyer why it wants to depend on a bankrupt business and offers the buyer more favorable credit terms. All of a sudden, the bankrupt manufacturer can lose an important customer relationship that may have taken years to develop. Thus tremendous value erosion can occur rapidly if the debtor's day-to-day operations cannot be continued.

Developing a Going-Forward Business Plan

After the debtor's day-to-day operations are stabilized, the next goal of the reorganization process is to develop a new business plan or strategy for the firm. This is largely within the control of the debtor's management and its advisors, particularly during the exclusivity period. However, since bankruptcy court approval must be obtained for any transactions out of the ordinary course of business and creditors can oppose such actions, the debtor will typically consult with the official committee of unsecured creditors as it develops its strategy and implements any steps relating thereto. Common actions that can be taken during this phase include downsizing the labor force, closing unprofitable facilities, selling noncore lines of business or assets, and renegotiating various types of contracts. About the only thing that is not common is to make a significant acquisition, although nothing in the Bankruptcy Code technically prevents this.

In most cases, creditors will have little quarrel with management's actions, particularly in the cost-cutting and cash-generating realm, other than they are not fast or radical enough. Probably the most common area of dispute will be size and scope of the postreorganization entity. As mentioned above, creditors will often be skeptical of management's abilities and thus may conclude that the best way to maximize the value of the estate is to sell relatively more of the debtor's assets to other firms with better managers. This creates more cash to pay off claims and minimizes the risk that the debtor's "poor management" can further harm the business. In the extreme, creditors may potentially oppose management's business plan and instead propose that all of the business assets be auctioned as ongoing business units, thus essentially providing for an orderly liquidation. This approach can be offered as a competing plan of reorganization if the debtor's plan of reorganization exclusivity period ends.

The risk of "radical" creditor proposals is an additional reason why management has an incentive to include the creditors in the formulation of the business plan. Management will need to convince the creditors that a going concern under the direction of the existing management is the best approach to maximize recoveries.

Determining the Assets and Liabilities

While the business plan is being developed, the debtor and the creditors will also be focusing on the composition of the estate's assets and liabilities. Ostensibly, one would assume that if the debtor had been regularly audited, this would be reasonably straightforward. However, the picture of the debtor rendered by a Generally Accepted Accounting Principles balance sheet at the time of the filing may have very little resemblance to what will be presented when the plan of reorganization is confirmed. Some of the issues involved in this process will be discussed in more detail in Chapter 12; here the discussion will be general.

On the asset side, there are at least two major areas of concern. The first is whether certain distributions or transactions that occurred before the bankruptcy filing should be unwound and any assets transferred in connection therewith brought back into the estate. The largest class of such transactions is called *voidable preferences*. Voidable preferences involve payments or other transfers (such as grants of liens) in payment of antecedent debts owed to creditors in the period immediately prior to the filing.[82] The relevant "look-back" period is 90 days unless the creditor is an insider,[83] in which case the period is one year. The basic goal of the rule is fairness by preventing the debtor from paying creditors that it, for whatever reason, "preferred," to the detriment of other creditors. If the transfer is found to be a voidable preference (and whether the debtor had a subjective preference for the creditor is irrelevant; only the timing of the transfer matters), then the benefited creditor, which could assert a variety of defenses,[84] must return whatever property was received, typically cash, and join the rest of the creditors in seeking recovery.

Another type of transaction that can be "unwound" is a *fraudulent conveyance*. An action for fraudulent conveyance is essentially a general tort claim that is codified in the Bankruptcy Code and under state law.[85] The issue is frequently, although not exclusively, considered in leveraged buyout situations that fail.[86] The essence of a fraudulent conveyance claim is that the debtor did not receive fair value in the transaction in question and at the time or as a result of the transaction was insolvent. For example, Boxco might argue that the acquisition of Dead Star (Figure 3-5), which the sub debt was issued to finance, was a fraudulent conveyance. Boxco might claim that despite its stock market value and ample liquidity, Boxco was insolvent after the acquisition and that what was purchased (the $20 in physical assets) was not worth the consideration (the $200 paid). If such an action succeeded (and the Boxco/Dead Star fact pattern has potential), the sellers of Dead Star could be required to return the purchase price and Boxco would return the Dead Star assets. This would clearly benefit the estate.

Fraudulent conveyance actions are frequently discussed but only rarely actually litigated. One of the main challenges in winning a fraudulent conveyance action is that it is standard procedure in most significant acquisition transactions that a recognized financial expert issue a formal opinion, usually referred to as a fairness opinion, that the transfer is for fair value and that the purchaser is solvent. Thus the sellers of Dead Star would have probably insisted that an investment bank issue an opinion that the transaction was fair and Boxco was solvent when the deal was completed. This is essentially viewed as the purchase of "fraudulent conveyance insurance."[87] Thus, even though Boxco might appear to have a meritorious case, the management and certain creditors may decide that it is not worth the time (such actions could theoretically delay the bankruptcy process for years, although increasingly, as discussed in Chapter 13, litigation claims are simply transferred to postconfirmation litigation trusts that allow the debtor to efficiently conclude the reorganization) and legal expense to pursue. However, as will be discussed in Chapter 12, the sub debt holders could possibly use the issue to "extort" value in the pie-splitting negotiation.

In addition to assets arising from inappropriate transfers or transactions, another potential source of assets relates to lawsuits that the debtor or the official committee of unsecured creditors can bring.[88] Perhaps an affiliated party acted unscrupulously and should be sued.[89] Perhaps the former directors and officers defrauded or breached their duties to the firm and should be sued[90] in order to collect under a director and officer liability insurance policy. More recently, it has become fashionable to blame the auditors for the debtor's problems.[91] There are often many potential legal claims that can be pursued and either litigated or settled for significant amounts of money that can enhance the estate.

On the liability side, the Bankruptcy Code provides debtors with powerful tools to eliminate or minimize liabilities. Chief among these is the power to reject executory contracts and unexpired leases.[92] In general, an executory contract is one in which there is sufficient performance remaining by both parties such that if either defaults, it would be a material breach.[93] For example, Boxco may have contracted with a third party to lay several more expensive undersea cables that it now appears Boxco no longer needs. This contract would impose a liability on Boxco in return for an asset that would be worth less than the cost of performing under the contract. Boxco can reject this contract. Of course, this rejection would constitute a breach entitling the cable layer to damages, but these would be unsecured prepetition claims. The most commonly rejected executory contract is an unexpired lease. For example, Boxco may have an expensive, long-term lease for palatial office space that it no longer needs. This lease, which again could represent a significant future liability to pay rent, can be rejected and Boxco can move out. In the case of a real estate lease, however, the Bankruptcy Code has specific provisions limiting allowed claims for damages generally to no more than three years of rent.[94]

The debtor can petition to reject a contract based on its business judgment that the enterprise will be better off in the future.[95] The request to reject or assume must be approved by the bankruptcy court,[96] which should consider the totality of the circumstances of the rejection as well as principles of equity in making its decision.[97] Several important types of contracts, including collective bargaining agreements and retiree benefits plans, are subject to a higher standard for rejection.[98] As a result, collective bargaining agreements, and the pension plan obligations that they often entail, cannot be rejected in many cases even where it would advantageous for the debtor to do so.

Another important power conferred by the Bankruptcy Code relates to the ability to consolidate and effectively value "tort" liabilities. The most prominent recent example involves asbestos liability, which has resulted in the bankruptcies of at least 60 firms since 1979.[99] In general, tort claims against debtors are the result of actions taken by the debtor prior to the filing of the bankruptcy. They are therefore prepetition obligations. The bankruptcy court has the power to consolidate these claims and use an expedited process to "value" the compensatory liability. The consolidated claim is then recognized as an unsecured claim and resolved within the plan of reorganization. A common technique to manage this liability in cases involving significant, indeterminate future claims is to establish a trust for the benefit of past and future claimants, to which the debtor contributes a majority of its postreorganization stock together with cash or an obligation to make a series of ongoing payments.[100] This type of settlement, particularly the obligation to give the trust beneficiaries a majority of the equity, clearly reduces recoveries to other creditors. However, the important point, from the perspective of the debtor and financial creditors, is that the debtor's tort liability is finally capped instead of the seemingly endless stream of claims that existed before the bankruptcy.

Determining the Valuation and the New Capital Structure

A critically important part of the formulation of a plan of reorganization is the development of a valuation. As part of the confirmation process (which occurs after the plan is voted on by the creditors) and typically included in the disclosure statement, there are usually two valuations prepared: a liquidation analysis, prepared for purposes of analyzing the "best interests" test, and a going-concern enterprise valuation, prepared to justify the appropriateness of the treatments in the plan.[101] The liquidation analysis generally does not play a very important role. The concept of the "best interests test" is that no creditor should receive less in a reorganization than it would have in a liquidation[102] — which is usually easily satisfied since the test typically is prepared using very conservative "fire-sale" liquidation assumptions.[103]

The going-concern valuation often will be a subject of intense debate because it has significant implications for the "pie-splitting" exercise that occurs later. The primary developer of the valuation is typically the debtor's financial advisor. The financial advisor will use standard methodologies in deriving a valuation opinion (primarily a combination of discounted cash flow or cash flow multiple techniques). However, as will be discussed in more detail in Chapter 5, there is sufficient latitude within these approaches that different valuation professionals can often arrive at widely divergent values for the same business.

The reason the valuation can critically affect the allocation of recoveries can be made clear by returning to Boxco at the stage of Figure 3-7. In Figure 4-2 that presentation is slightly modified to help illustrate the issue.

Notice that the original $290 asset value "assumed" in Figure 3-7 has been characterized as the "low" value and that an alternative "high" value of $600 has also been proposed. The reality is that Boxco's postconfirmation "value" will be what it will be, and such future value will be a function of management execution and outside factors that cannot be controlled. The valuation is an estimate that is irrelevant to the future reality, although it should be noted that it is the most common benchmark initially used by the marketplace.

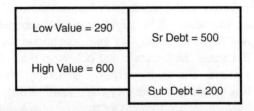

Figure 4-2. Recoveries for Boxco Creditors Under Alternative Valuations

The valuation is, however, extremely relevant to the treatment of the various creditors. If the low value is used to determine the future capital structure, there is nothing available for the sub debt. Under the low valuation, the capital structure in Figure 3-8 might be adopted ($100 new debt/$190 equity), with all of the debt and equity being allocated, pursuant to the concept of absolute priority, to the senior debt. Alternatively, if the high value is used, then different capital structures can be considered and the sub debt will be entitled to participate in the recovery because there is more than enough value to cover the senior debt. Consider the implications if the capital structure for the high valuation was composed of $400 in debt and $200 in equity. Assume all of the debt plus $100 of the equity is given to the senior debt to satisfy its $500 claim.[104] The remaining $100 in equity would then go to the sub debt. This implies that the equity could be split 50/50 between the senior debt and the sub debt.

As has been indicated earlier, it is important to understand that the valuation and/or the structure and allocation of the capital structure are essentially negotiated. The rules within the Bankruptcy Code provide a structure that significantly defines the negotiating leverage of the various parties, but usually a number of parties have some degree of leverage. In the example above, if the debtor proposes a plan of reorganization (this is likely to be an informal circulation of a draft plan to the members of the official committee of unsecured creditors, not a formal filing with the bankruptcy court) that reflected the valuation and capital structure presented in Figure 3-8, the sub debt would essentially be wiped out. In addition, as will be discussed shortly, even though the sub debt will be entitled to vote[105] and may reject the plan, it could still be confirmed (i.e., approved by the bankruptcy court and hence "imposed" upon the sub debt) over such rejection.

But the sub debt may not be powerless. Those involved could argue to the bankruptcy judge that the valuation was incorrect and offer an alternative, higher valuation that, if accepted as accurate, would make the proposed treatment of claims under the plan inappropriate (because it would allow the $500 senior debt claim to recover $600). As discussed in Chapter 12, to the extent the senior debt feels there is a risk that the sub debt can convince the bankruptcy court to consider an alternative valuation or otherwise successfully object to plan confirmation, the senior debt might offer the sub debt some level of recovery, perhaps 10% of the equity, to gain its support for the plan.

This starkly illustrates the dynamic that occurs in the valuation/plan treatment negotiation phase. The senior creditors generally have an incentive to argue for a very low valuation so that they can "hoard" a disproportionate share of the recovery for themselves. Remember that the plan valuation can be very different than the actual future value. If the $290 valuation was used to justify allocating all of Boxco's value to the $500 senior debt claim, but subsequently the senior creditors sold Boxco for $600, they would keep the $100 "windfall profit." Alternatively, junior creditors have an incentive to argue for high valuations and, generally, relatively more debt so that they can grab relatively more equity. In subsequent chapters, the risk/reward trade-off of adding debt and the sources of negotiating power of the various constituents will be discussed in more detail, but the above example should make it reasonably clear that it is a dynamic process. Furthermore, it should reinforce the potential strategic benefit of being a sufficiently large holder that one can obtain a position on the committee and thus be an active participant in the process.

Voting on and Confirming a Plan of Reorganization

As illustrated above, substantial negotiation and gamesmanship can occur in the development of a plan of reorganization. An experienced investor with control of a senior class can wield significant leverage. The ultimate constraint on that power is the plan voting and confirmation process.

Procedurally, after the plan has been prepared, a disclosure statement, which describes, among other things, the debtor, the financial advisor's valuation of the debtor, and the plan, is drafted for use in the vote solicitation process. Except in "prepackaged" bankruptcies, in which solicitation and voting occur before the bankruptcy filing, the bankruptcy court must approve the disclosure statement before it can be sent to creditors.[106] This approval process can be rather pro forma or, when certain creditors are stridently opposed to the plan, the beginning of the battle to prevent its confirmation. Using the Boxco example, were the disclosure statement to include the low valuation, representatives of the sub debt might argue that it was misleading because it was materially inaccurate. However, the bankruptcy court's scope of review at this phase is limited to whether the disclosure statement contains sufficient information to permit a hypothetical creditor to make an informed vote on the plan. The bankruptcy court typically does not decide the merits of various challenges such as valuation until the confirmation process, although the bankruptcy court may refuse to approve a disclosure statement if the plan it describes is facially unconfirmable. In addition to the disclosure statement, the bankruptcy court will also approve the ballot, which will be part of the solicitation package sent to creditors.

Once the solicitation package is approved, it will be sent to all holders of impaired claims and interests. As mentioned above, classes of claims left unimpaired (i.e., paid off or complete reinstatement) are deemed to accept and are not solicited. Classes of claims or interests receiving no recovery under the plan are generally simply deemed to reject. The classes of claims that do vote are basically those that are receiving some type of recovery but are impaired.

For a class to accept the plan, more than 50% in number of claims representing at least 66 2/3% in amount must vote in favor. These thresholds are based on those participating in the voting process, not the full class size. If a class votes to accept and the plan is confirmed, then all creditors in the class are bound by the plan's treatment, subject to the satisfaction of the "best interests test" discussed below. By establishing this voting standard, the developers of the Bankruptcy Code were trying to prevent a "tyranny of the majority," whether in number or amount, in the voting process. Of course, as with any voting process, it essentially involves the creation of various, to a certain degree arbitrary, classes; therefore the process is susceptible to manipulation through gerrymandering. Bankruptcy courts are mindful of this risk and keep a watchful eye for such situations.

Once the votes are tallied, the stage is set for the all-important confirmation hearing. The Bankruptcy Code specifies a number of factors that the bankruptcy court must conclude are satisfied before it can confirm a plan.[107] Most of the requirements are essentially procedural and thus only occasionally come into play from the perspective of the distressed debt investor:

- The plan of reorganization complies with the Bankruptcy Code
- The proponent of the plan is appropriate
- All fees paid to the professionals in the case are found to be reasonable
- The plan discloses the identity of postconfirmation officers and directors
- Administrative and priority clams are treated appropriately
- Any required regulatory approval has been obtained
- U.S. Trustee fees are provided for
- Retiree benefits are appropriately addressed

In addition to these, there are four additional "tests" that represent either minimum standards for the treatment of claims or more general standards that provide a court with discretion and thus may be a source of leverage by creditors unhappy with their treatment.

Best interests of creditor test: This requirement, mentioned above, provides that if a creditor votes against the plan of reorganization (it cannot be raised by a creditor that votes in favor even if the overall class rejects), the proponent of the plan must establish that the dissenting creditor's proposed recovery under the plan must be at least as great as if the debtor had been liquidated under chapter 7 of the Bankruptcy Code. This test can present some complicated issues when the creditor involved is a secured creditor, but is generally not much protection for unsecured creditors because the standard of reference will typically be a very conservatively prepared "fire-sale" liquidation analysis that will often indicate nothing will be available for unsecured creditors.

Good faith test: The Bankruptcy Code requires that the plan of reorganization be proposed in good faith — but then fails to define the term. The vagueness of the words can give opponents of a plan fairly broad grounds to challenge any particular provision, but in reality, the case law indicates that it is fairly difficult to use this provision to upset plans because it is fairly easy for the proponent to establish some minimum threshold of good faith.

Feasibility test: The bankruptcy court must find that confirmation of the plan of reorganization will most likely not result in a subsequent liquidation or further reorganization. There will often be significant challenges to feasibility, and this is often the most contentious part of the confirmation hearing because any single creditor can raise a challenge. Also, it can be used by different classes to argue different ends. For example, in the Boxco case, if the plan came out with the low valuation, the sub debt might try to use the feasibility requirement to raise issues about Boxco's proposed strategy (e.g., if Boxco is only worth $290, perhaps it is too small to be a viable competitor in the telecommunications sector and should instead be sold in an auction to a larger competitor) in an effort to cause delay and perhaps a better treatment from the senior debt. On the other hand, if the high valuation is used, a senior debt holder might argue that too much debt is being placed on the new firm.

Consent or cram-down: Cram-down is the process by which a plan or reorganization is imposed on an impaired class that has voted to reject the plan. The Bankruptcy Code basically requires that for a plan to be confirmed on a rejecting class, the plan comply with the Bankruptcy Code and be approved by at least one impaired class (not including insiders). Since the Bankruptcy Code includes the doctrine of absolute priority, a key practical effect of the cram-down provision is to force the debtor to garner the support of all impaired classes if it attempts to provide any type of recovery to an out-of-the-money junior class without paying all more senior classes in full. For example, if a debtor wants to give any type of value to its equity (regardless of how minimal), then it must obtain the consent of, or provide full recoveries for, all impaired creditors or the plan will fail because it is in violation of the absolute priority rule. As discussed in more detail in Chapter 12, this can give junior creditors leverage on the debtor to negotiate provisions that they favor. However, if the plan does not provide for the allocation of any value to a junior claim, the creditors' threat to oppose the plan may not be that strong. In the Boxco example, assuming for a moment that the low valuation was used and the sub debt rejected the plan, the absolute priority requirement would not have been a source of leverage to the sub debt since nothing was being given to a more junior class. The cram-down provisions also specify certain minimum payment or recovery amounts which must be given to objecting secured creditors.

The confirmation process is the ultimate point at which any particular creditor's leverage has effect. To the extent that creditors are able to raise objections that cause the bankruptcy court to deny confirmation, they gain valuable leverage. This leverage will normally be used to force the proponent to "recut the deal" to give more value to the obstructing class in an effort to gain their consent. Of course, depending on why the bankruptcy court refused confirmation, the plan proponents may attempt a slightly different structure that they believe will be confirmed which does not involve sharing any more value with the obstructors, but this strategy can be risky and time consuming. However, if junior creditors are going to receive nothing under the plan, they have nothing to lose, other than professional fees, in fighting confirmation by, for example, arguing about valuation. Thus, the cost of strictly enforcing priority rights can be increased delay. But delay almost always hurts the investment rate of return; thus, typically, it will be in someone's best interest to share a little value in order to obtain an expeditious confirmation.

Summary

If a consensual restructuring cannot be arranged or will not be effective in resolving the primary source of distress, a chapter 11 reorganization may be the only feasible alternative. Bankruptcy restructurings are complicated endeavors that often involve significant negotiation and gamesmanship. The distressed investor must therefore gain an appreciation for both the other participants in the process and everyone's source of negotiating leverage. Particularly when contemplating investments in unsecured claims, especially legally or structurally subordinated claims, there may be significant risk that if secured creditors are able to "work with" the debtor's management to proceed with a conservative valuation, the challenge of getting a "fair" recovery will be an uphill fight. Secured claims are likely to have greater assurance of recovery, but will have commensurately lower return potential. In addition, they may have to share recoveries to which they typically would be entitled with junior classes in order to complete a reorganization expeditiously.

Thus far, the concept of value has been used, but always assumed and never defined. In the next chapter, the process by which the investor determines the value of a business and its related debt instruments is discussed.

This Chapter's Chess Moves

6. Pxc3, Pd6
7. Pe4, Pe5
8. Pd5, Ne7

5

OVERVIEW OF THE
VALUATION PROCESS

Up to this point, the concepts of firm value and capital structure have been discussed without worrying about how they are derived. The ever-present Boxco behaves like so much Silly Putty: its asset value box expands and then shrinks, and then the boxes on the other side (debt and equity) are stretched or chopped down to conform. This is a conceptually sound construct because, as a general proposition, capital structure must, in the long run, bear some relation to asset value. The dependence or causality is from asset value to capital structure, not vice versa.

In Chapter 3, this construct was used to depict the concept of financial distress and how it will often force a restructuring of the capital structure: the asset box shrinks, so the liability and equity boxes must be chopped down to conform (review Figure 3-8). As was discussed in Chapter 4, whether this restructuring is done through a voluntary agreement among the creditors or under the auspices of a bankruptcy proceeding, the basic notion of matching the capital structure to the asset value is the same.[1] But for this exercise to have practical relevance to the distressed debt investor, it must advance from concept to concrete. Bonds trade at prices. To assess whether a bond should be bought or sold at any given price requires the development of techniques to estimate the size of the asset box and, having derived that, decide if the size of the debt box implied by a given price is appropriate or workable.

In this chapter, the basic concepts of firm valuation are reviewed. Chapter 6 develops various principles for what a firm's "value" implies about its capital structure. The discussion is not intended to be comprehensive, and you may want to supplement your understanding by reviewing more specialized texts.[2] The treatment here, though more basic, should be helpful, however, in that it approaches the topics from the perspective of the distressed debt investor. Specifically, it employs a "bottom-up" approach that starts with determining asset value and then looking at the appropriateness of the capital structure. First, the basic concept of value as derived from expected cash flow generation is reviewed. Then, the rationale behind and limitations of the most widely used proxy for cash flow — earnings before interest, taxes, depreciation, and amortization (EBITDA) — are discussed. Next, "multiple"-based valuation and comparable company analysis are reviewed. Finally, the chapter concludes with an overview of the most common alternatives to multiple-based analysis.

THE BASICS OF CASH-FLOW-BASED VALUATION

It is a fairly universally held principle that the value of a firm is the sum of all discounted future dividends or cash flows.[3] Valuations based on this principle, typically called discounted cash flow (DCF) analysis, however, are complicated and time consuming. Furthermore, since they are based on projections of the future, their accuracy is inherently constrained by forecasting uncertainty.

In practice, most distressed debt investors use a simplified approach to valuing firms: the cash flow multiple methodology using EBITDA as a proxy for cash flow. This is generally referred to as the EBITDA multiple approach. For example, if a firm generated $10 in annual EBITDA and was valued using a multiple of 5 (how the appropriate multiple is chosen is discussed below), it would be worth $50. Because of their widespread use in practice, EBITDA multiples will be used as the general valuation metric in this book. An example of how to develop a DCF valuation based on a detailed cash flow projection is available for download at www.jrosspub.com.

Using EBITDA as a Measurement of Cash Flow

Although EBITDA is a fairly common term or concept, it is worth reviewing the basics of how it is derived. Table 5-1 shows a sample income statement and the related calculation of EBITDA.

Note that this calculation did not use the precise order of the acronym (the reverse order, in which the items typically are presented on an income statement, was used), which has been adopted as convention for ease of pronunciation, but this does not affect the result. Although most people involved in finance on a daily basis simply accept EBITDA as a reasonable measure of cash flow, it may not be intuitively obvious why it is used more readily than net income (or earnings), which is the accounting number most frequently used to judge a firm's performance and the most common basis for equity valuations.

Table 5-1. Derivation of EBITDA

Income Statement		EBITDA Calculation	
Sales	200	Net Income (Loss)	(8)
Cost of Goods Sold	120		
Gross Margin	80	Taxes	3
Sales, General, and Administrative Expense	40		
Depreciation and Amortization Expense	30	Interest Expense	15
Interest Expense	15		
Pretax Income (Loss)	(5)	Depreciation and Amortization Expense	30
Taxes	3		
Net Income (Loss)	(8)	EBITDA	40

The basic reason for the broad use of EBITDA is to improve the comparability among firms. Anyone reasonably familiar with investing in stocks has probably heard stocks compared to each other based on the price as a multiple of earnings, or P/E ratio. The common-sense notion is that if two firms, A and B, in the same industry (hence comparable competitive risks, cycles, etc.) earn $1 per share but A's stock sells for $15 per share (P/E = 15) while B's sells for $12 per share (P/E = 12), the P/E ratio may be an indication of relative value. Perhaps B is cheap or A is overpriced, but it seems odd to pay a different price for the "same" $1 of earnings. While much could be criticized about this simplistic approach, one can find this type of analysis in virtually any stock research report.

Table 5-2 illustrates that making an investment decision on the basis of simple P/E comparisons can be very difficult. Which of the three firms in the table, all of which are in the same industry, is the better value?

The reader, of course, will likely presume there is a "trick." Each firm's stock sells for $12 a share. The firms are obviously of different scale based on the significant difference in sales levels. It is also fairly easy to deduce that the debt levels are proportionately different given that A has lower revenues than B but higher interest expense. Since C has no interest expense, it apparently has no debt. Beyond these observations, however, most readers likely will be reaching for their calculators (or, heaven forbid, exercising their brains) to attempt some additional analysis, which is exactly the point: net income and P/E ratios provide only limited information about these firms.

Understanding and Adjusting EDITDA

The next step is to examine each firm on an EBITDA basis. But before jumping straight to the numbers, it is worth spending a moment on the rationale behind

Table 5-2.   Limitations of P/E-Based Investment Analysis

	Firms		
	A	B	C
Income Statement			
Sales	1000.0	3000.0	2000.0
Cost of Goods Sold	560.0	1740.0	1200.0
Gross Margin	440.0	1260.0	800.0
Sales, General, and Administrative Expense	270.0	870.0	520.0
Depreciation and Amortization Expense	80.0	125.0	50.0
Interest Expense	71.9	54.3	0.0
Total Expense	421.9	1049.3	570.0
Pretax Income	18.1	210.8	230.0
Taxes	(6.3)	(73.8)	(80.5)
Net Income	11.7	137.0	149.5
Earnings per Share	0.84	0.72	1.00
Share Price	$12.00	$12.00	$12.00
P/E	**14.3x**	**16.6x**	**12.0x**

the use of EBITDA, because in any particular case adjustments to the basic formula may be required, and without some sense of the rationale behind or goal of EBITDA, it will be difficult to determine such adjustments.

The goal of an EBITDA-based valuation analysis is to estimate the result of a future cash flow projection. Each component of the formula should be viewed from that perspective. The first component is net income, the standard accounting measure of a firm's performance. If the operating results being reviewed include items that are not representative of expected future performance, an adjustment may be needed. The most common, nonformula adjustments that need to be considered arise if earnings include charges for restructuring operations (such as the cost of severance associated with reducing the scale of operations) or to discontinue operations.[4] These will usually be easily identifiable line items. However, there occasionally will be less obvious adjustments buried within regular line items such as charges to write off obsolete inventory within cost of goods sold. To identify when these may be present, it can be helpful to review operations on a percentage of revenue basis and look for sudden deviations from historical norms. Usually the occurrence of such "one-time" events will be discussed in the "Management's Discussion and Analysis of Operations" section of Securities and Exchange Commission (SEC) filings, but they may not be, in which case the investor may have to contact the company to see if it will explain the abnormality.[5] When it is decided that an adjustment to EBITDA should be made because of such items, the amount of the adjustment is added to or subtracted from the previously calculated EBITDA to derive an adjusted EBITDA. It may not be appropriate to make adjustments for everything that management chooses to characterize as one-time in nature. In making these judgments, investors may want to consider management's track record in taking such charges and operating trends at comparable companies.

The rationale for adjusting earnings for interest expense is that such expense reflects a decision to use debt in the capital structure, and the firm's value is independent of capital structure. This goes back to our basic observation that the size of the asset box is independent of the historical liabilities and equity. In the example above, based on the interest expense line, it can be deduced that Firm C has no debt, whereas Firm A has significant leverage. Thus, to make the results of firms with varying amounts of debt comparable, one must adjust for interest expense. Another adjustment that is frequently made to reflect differences in capital structure decisions is to adjust for rent expense. Consider two fast-food restaurant chains, FF-O and FF-R, each with 100 restaurants or stores. FF-O owns all its stores and financed the development and/or purchase cost with a $100 million, 10% bond issue. FF-R rents all of its locations at an average annual rate of $90,000 per store, or $9 million in total. The rent expense will normally be included in sales, general, and administrative expense. All other things being equal, FF-O will appear to generate more EBITDA and have a better operating margin. To reduce this distortion, analysts often will adjust for the rent by "capitalizing" the obligation. There are two aspects to this adjustment: EBITDA and long-term liabilities. On the EBITDA side, annual rent expense is added back to (i.e., increasing it similar to adding back interest expense) the standard EBITDA calculation. This is usually referred to as EBITDAR. On the long-term liability side, the amount of on-balance-sheet debt will be increased by an estimate of the capitalized value of the operating leases, which is the financial equivalent to using future rent expense to calculate the present value of an annuity. A precise estimate of this value requires a projection of rent expense and the derivation of the appropriate discount rate;[6] in practice, analysts who are in a hurry will usually just multiply the annual rent by a cap factor of from 7x to 11x depending on the firm's unsecured cost of capital. Thus using a midpoint of 9x, FF-R's debt would be increased by $81 million (9 × $9 million annual rent).

The general rationale for adjusting earnings for depreciation and amortization is that both these expenses are "noncash" accounting entries; therefore, including them understates cash flow. This is literally true, but in the case of depreciation[7] the stronger rationale is that firms should be compared independent of historical capital investment decisions. For example, what if Firm B had an old plant that, because of the then existing technology, required lots of equipment for different processes that needed to be upgraded to keep up with the evolution of the final product? Firm B's plant also happens to have been built domestically in a region with relatively high wage rates, high energy costs, and strict environmental standards. In comparison, Firm A built its plant with the newest technology (which, although more expensive per machine, greatly reduced the number of processes) in a third-world country with lower wages and environmental standards.[8] The depreciation expense of Firms A and B could be very different. Both firms' depreciation charges are noncash and distort cash flow, and thus adjustments should be made if trying to measure cash flow. But the larger point is that historical decisions on capital investment are fairly irrelevant in determining the value of Firm A or B. In our example, Firm B has a larger investment in property, plant, and equipment, but Firm A's plant could have much more cash-generating potential.

The same is true of many of the sources of amortization charges. Until recently, the biggest distortion to comparability caused by amortization charges was the result of differences in the accounting treatment of acquisitions. As was briefly discussed in Chapter 3, if an acquisition was accounted for as a "purchase" and the price exceeded the fair market value of the assets acquired, an entry called "goodwill" was recorded and amortized over time.[9] Amortization is also used to expense the historical cost of intangible assets, which often is irrelevant to the current value of a firm. Finally, amortization can also arise from the expensing of deferred financing costs associated with debt.[10] Since these once again relate to decisions pertaining to capital structure composition, they are irrelevant to current firm value.

The final adjustment relates to taxes. Taxes, unfortunately, generally do require cash payments and thus affect cash flows. However, for two identical firms (putting aside the issue of different tax jurisdictions), the tax load will be equal. The problem is that taxes are based on pretax income, which reflects the impact of interest expense and depreciation and amortization.[11] Since the goal is to establish comparability independent of historical capital investment and capital structure, taxes should be added back. It is not uncommon for firms experiencing financial distress to also report negative earnings and thus possibly qualify for refunds of taxes previously paid. Such refunds can represent important sources of cash flow. Furthermore, operating losses can have substantial value by "shielding" future tax payments; these are often referred to as *net operating loss (NOL) carryforwards*. When there is a significant likelihood of future earnings and the magnitude and timing of the "tax savings" from NOL carryforwards can be reasonably estimated, a deferred tax asset will be recognized under Generally Accepted Accounting Principles (GAAP).[12] Such tax assets can have significant value, but, as will be discussed in Chapter 11, this

Table 5-3.   Use of EBITDA in Analysis of Firms' Valuation

	A	B	C
Balance Sheet			
Current Assets	40.0	150.0	120.0
Property, Plant, and Equipment	800.0	2000.0	1000.0
Total Assets	840.0	2150.0	1120.0
Current Liabilities	25.0	125.0	35.0
Debt	685.0	775.0	0.0
Equity	130.0	1250.0	1085.0
Total Liabilities and Equity	840.0	2150.0	1120.0
Shares	14.0	190.0	150.0
EBITDA Calculation			
Net Income	11.7	137.0	149.5
+ Taxes	6.3	73.8	80.5
+ Interest Expense	71.9	54.3	0.0
+ Depreciation and Amortization	80.0	125.0	50.0
EBITDA	170.0	390.0	280.0
Selected Data			
EBITDA/Revenue %	17.0%	13.0%	14.0%
Debt/EBITDA	**4.0x**	**2.0x**	**0.0x**
EBITDA/Share	**12.14**	**2.05**	**1.87**
Interest Rate	10.5%	7.0%	5.0%
Tax Rate	35.0%	35.0%	35.0%
Revenue/Assets	119.0%	140.0%	179.0%
Prior Data — Summary			
Revenue	1000.0	3000.0	2000.0
Net Income	11.7	137.0	149.5
Earnings per Share	0.84	0.72	1.00
Share Price	$12.00	$12.00	$12.00
P/E	14.3x	16.6x	12.0x

value can be negatively impacted if the ownership of the firm changes significantly. Accordingly, it is recommended that recognition or weighting of this value should be done outside the context of the EBITDA multiple valuation discussed here. In other words, develop a firm valuation using a normal valuation process and then decide whether to adjust that value to reflect specific tax attributes.

Now that the "why" behind the EBITDA metric has been explained, it is time to return to the analysis of the relative values of Firms A, B, and C. In Table 5-3, the analysis of these firms is expanded to add basic balance sheet information, together with a calculation of EBITDA and certain other performance metrics.

Reviewing the data in Table 5-3 adds significant, although certainly not dispositive, information to aid in comparing the three firms. Among the more important points to notice are:

- Firm A has relatively more debt, as measured by debt/EBITDA.
- Firm A is the most efficient in generating EBITDA from sales, as illustrated by the EBITDA/revenue margin.
- Firm A generates significantly more EBITDA per share.

Again, the point behind using EBITDA is not that it is a magical, "one-number-tells-all" figure, but rather that it enhances comparability by removing the influence of historical capital investment, capital structure, and taxes (which are impacted by capital structure among other things). There are many other things to consider before declaring one firm the "best value," but the data in Table 5-3 should illustrate that whereas Firm C clearly is the "least expensive" on a P/E basis, it may not be the obvious choice when the valuation is more closely tied to cash flow.

Limitations of EBITDA

While EBITDA is a useful and widely used metric for cash flow generation, it has a number of significant limitations and must be used cautiously and adjusted frequently.[13] Some of the more significant limitations of EBITDA as a measurement of cash flow are as follows:[14]

- EBITDA fails to reflect changes in working capital. Thus, if during the period the company consumes cash by building either inventory or accounts receivable or paying down previously stretched accounts payable, actual cash generated will be lower.
- EBITDA does not reflect the need to make capital expenditures (CAPX). Depreciation (and sometimes amortization) is a noncash accounting entry designed to reflect the "cost" of using a capital asset, like a machine, during the period. Those assets must be replaced or maintained. However, EBITDA calculations discount this on the theory that during any particular period, such costs are discretionary and can be deferred. Thus, depending on the capital intensity of the business, analysts may prefer to use EBIT (earnings before interest and taxes) or EBITDA-CAPX.
- EBITDA, as discussed above, often needs to be adjusted to reflect "one-time" charges. Particularly in the context of a firm in financial distress, these charges can cover a broad variety of things, such as severance costs of laid-off workers or charge-offs of unsaleable inventory or un-

collectible accounts receivable. These charges often represent a cash cost to the business (either immediately or in the future) but, arguably, are out of the ordinary course. Thus, unless EBITDA is adjusted, it may understate the company's cash-flow-generating ability.

■ If the conditions in which the firm has operated over the last 12 months (the typical period of analysis) are considered likely to be unrepresentative (for financially distressed firms such results are usually below the firm's "capability"), it may be appropriate to rely on an estimate of "normalized" future EBITDA rather than historical data. This will be particularly true if, because of its distressed circumstances, portions of the business have been closed or sold.

Despite these limitations, in practice, EBITDA or an appropriate variant thereof is the standard proxy for cash flow.

Comparing Discounted Cash Flow and EBITDA Multiple Approaches

As discussed at the outset of the chapter, although the theoretically correct value of a firm is the present value of all future cash flows (also referred to as the DCF approach), in practice, most investors use a methodology that involves multiples as a shortcut for the tedious, and ultimately inexact, process of developing such cash flow forecasts. There are several reasons why the multiple methodology is used, including simplicity, familiarity, comparability, and practicality. It involves the simple multiplication of two numbers — EBITDA × multiple, which is familiar to most analysts because it is similar to estimating the potential value of a stock by multiplying earnings per share × P/E ratio. It is also very practical because the data to perform the estimate are readily available, which allows basic analysis to be performed quickly and investors to make decisions in often fast-moving markets.

Mathematically, multiples can be a very close substitute for the actual DCF process. In Table 5-4, a sensitivity analysis is provided which shows the present value of a 25-period series of cash flows divided by the initial cash flow amount. These figures were derived using the following variant of the standard DCF equation:

$$\sum_{1}^{25}[CF * (1 + g)^n * 1/(1 + DCR)^n]/CF$$

where CF = initial cash flow amount, g = growth rate %, DCR = present value discount rate, and n = period.

Table 5-4. Multiple for Various Growth and Discount Rates

Discount Rate	Growth Rate				
	0%	2%	4%	6%	8%
10%	9.1x	10.6x	12.6x	15.1x	18.4x
12%	7.8x	9.0x	10.5x	12.4x	14.9x
15%	6.5x	7.3x	8.3x	9.7x	11.3x
18%	5.5x	6.1x	6.8x	7.8x	8.9x
20%	4.9x	5.5x	6.1x	6.8x	7.7x
25%	4.0x	4.3x	4.7x	5.2x	5.7x
30%	3.3x	3.6x	3.8x	4.1x	4.5x

What this table shows is that if, for example, a firm's cash flow were, over the long term, expected to grow at 4% (slightly above the historical growth rate of the U.S. economy), and the firm's risk profile merited a 20% discount rate (i.e., the required investment return), the valuation multiple would equal 6.1x. The risk associated with investing in distressed debt is relatively high; thus, most investors tend to require returns of between 15 and 25% and will, to be conservative, assume relatively low (i.e., 0–4%) growth rates. This implies a multiple range of between 4.0x and 8.3x depending on the circumstances. Of course, this implicitly assumes a fairly stable, long-term business. Adjustments will need to be made if initial growth rates are expected to be higher (which is often foreseeable or expected if a firm has been constrained by financial distress) or if the time horizon (the example assumed 25 periods) is shorter. However, as illustrated in Figure 5-1, the percentage addition to the present value for incremental periods of cash flow beyond 15, depending on the discount rate, is relatively low. In other words, to add an additional period of cash flow beyond the 15th period would change the present value (i.e., valuation) by less than 2% at a 20% DCR.

The point of this discussion is to demonstrate that using the multiple approach can fairly effectively replicate the results of using the more theoretically correct, but extremely time consuming, approach of long-term projections. This is a particularly important point when one considers the practical difficulty, if not impossibility, of being able to forecast the future results of financially distressed firms with any degree of certainty.

Comparable Company Analysis Based on Enterprise Value

The basic premise of EBITDA multiple-based valuations is that by using the EBITDA metric, it is possible to estimate the enterprise value (EV) of a firm by multiplying the appropriately derived EBITDA by a multiplier. The key is

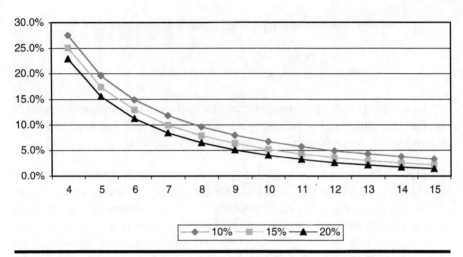

Figure 5-1.   Percentage Impact of Incremental Periods of Cash Flow

to choose the appropriate multiplier or multiple. Unfortunately, this is not an exact science that can be accomplished by simply writing out a formula. It takes judgment, experience, and knowledge of the marketplace. The process begins with the development of an array of comparable company multiples. To develop this array, the investor selects a group of companies that are in the same industry. The companies need to be publicly traded so that the investor has access to both the companies' financial data as well as security prices determined by the trading market. Access to data relating to private companies that have recently been purchased or sold can also be very useful. Ideally, some of the companies in the comparable universe will be of approximately the same size as the target company in terms of revenues.

Once the universe is identified, the investor should assemble the key operating, balance sheet, and valuation data about the firms. What is relevant will vary from industry to industry, and thus a basic understanding of the industry in question is an essential prerequisite to performing a competent valuation. Among the most important data points in this analysis are the EBITDA and EV figures.

Calculating Enterprise Value

The concept of EV has not yet been defined. EV is the market-indicated value of a business adjusted to consider debt and cash.[15] The value is typically derived as follows:

Equity value (market price of stock × shares outstanding)
+ Debt
− Cash balance
= Enterprise value

However, as with everything else in financial analysis, this formula must be applied thoughtfully. The following are some basic issues that need to be considered when developing EVs for comparable companies.

Equity — If the firm being analyzed is in financial distress, the threshold issue is whether it is relevant to even consider the equity. As discussed in Chapter 3, the market equity value for financially distressed companies may be fairly meaningless when it trades at a very low nominal value (e.g., less than $1 per share) or the debt in the capital structure trades at a significant discount. If the debt is trading at a discount, it may be more accurate to use the market value of the debt to estimate EV. Assuming equity is to be counted, which would be the typical case, the number of shares to include in the calculation should be considered. Most of the time, it will be appropriate to use the number of shares outstanding, but if there is a significant disparity (i.e., greater than 10%) between the primary and fully diluted share figures, the investor may need to adjust the share number for common share equivalents (CSE).[16] A typical example would be warrants or options with exercise prices considerably below current market values. When adding such securities to the share count, it is common to adjust EV to reflect the amount the firm would receive as a result of their exercise.[17] Preferred stock should be treated as a debt security and valued at its aggregate liquidation value (with appropriate adjustment for accrued but unpaid dividends).

Debt — Debt typically should be valued as shown on the GAAP balance sheet. There are at least three exceptions to this rule. First, if the debt is convertible, it should generally be valued as a debt (this applies to convertible preferred stock as well) unless the security's conversion feature is "in the money" (i.e., the current market price is above the effective conversion price), which will be fairly rare in the case of a financially distressed firm. In that case, it may be more appropriate to treat it as a CSE, but care should be taken to ensure there is no double counting of shares if the CSE method has been used as a result of using the fully diluted share count. Second, and this is a very limited exception, if the debt is the obligation of a firm that has previously gone through a chapter 11 reorganization and is accounted for using "fresh-start" accounting principles (which value the debt at a discounted rate),[18] then the face or full principal amount of the debt is more appropriate. Finally, as mentioned above, if the firm is in financial distress, then it may be more appropriate to value the debt using market prices as opposed to its balance sheet value. Thus, if there is $200 in debt but it is trading at 40, then it may be more appropriate to value it at $80 instead of $200.

Special care should be taken when the debt in question was structured and issued as discount debt. Discount debt is a debt obligation that is intentionally structured with a coupon rate (which can be payable for a specified portion or the entire life of the bond) significantly below the yield required by the market for the bond to trade at par. Because of the below-market coupon (which can often be 0% or less than 5% for a credit that might require a coupon greater than 10%), the bond is initially sold at a discount (the discount determined by the appropriate "market" interest rate) but is paid off at par.[19] Such debt structures are frequently used in start-up companies that are not expected to generate sufficient cash flow in their early years of operation to pay interest at market rates. It has also been popular for established companies to issue long-maturity, deep-discount 0% coupon convertible securities that are often initially sold at steep discounts (e.g., 40%) to face.[20]

Under GAAP, discount debt initially is carried on the balance sheet at approximately the price sold and then "accretes" to par value based on the internal rate of return represented by the original issue discount adjusted by the coupon, if it is greater than 0%.[21] Discount securities are typically structured as 0% coupon for life or a specified number of years, after which the bond begins paying interest at a higher "market" rate. This latter structure is known as a "step-up" or "split-coupon" bond. A hypothetical 10-year split-coupon bond might pay no interest for the first 5 years and then pay 12% interest for the last 5 years (split coupons such as this are often designated "0/12"). This bond is likely to have been issued at a price equal to the present value of $1000 (standard bond denomination) discounted by 12% for five years or $567, representing a trading value of 56.7. At the end of two years, it will be carried on the issuer's balance sheet at an amount representing the present value discounting for three years (the time remaining until it turns "cash pay"), or 71.2. Table 5-5 illustrates the basic accounting treatment of the 0/12 split-coupon bond just described.

Table 5-5. Accounting for 0/12 Split-Coupon Bond

Period	0	1	2	3	4	5	6	7	8	9	10
Balance Sheet Carrying Value	56.7	63.6	71.2	79.7	89.3	100.0	100.0	100.0	100.0	100.0	100.0
Interest Expense Accrued		6.8	7.6	8.5	9.6	10.7					
Interest Expense Paid							12.0	12.0	12.0	12.0	12.0

When valuing discount securities, for the purpose of estimating EV or otherwise, it is important to note that the market trading convention is to quote the trading price as a percentage of face or full principal value. Thus, if after two years the 0/12 was trading at 65, this would mean it was trading at $650 or 65% of the $1000 face amount. Its accreted or carrying value was calculated to be 71.2, and thus its trading price as a percentage of accreted value is 91.3%. The trading price as a percentage of accreted value is important to note because, as in this example, it can give important insight as to whether the debt is trading as if the firm is in financial distress. Here the debt had a market price of 65, which would normally be an indication of financial distress. However, when viewed relative to its accreted amount (i.e., 65/71.2 = 91.3%), it suggests it is trading at only a modest discount and the firm is apparently not perceived as being in financial distress. For purposes of determining EV, a discount bond should be valued at accreted or carrying value if it is not in financial distress and at market value if the issuer is considered distressed.

Cash — A final consideration in estimating EV is the treatment of cash or cash equivalents such as short-term investments. Particularly if a firm has recently completed a financing and not yet deployed all the proceeds into the business, it may hold large cash reserves. This was commonplace in the late 1990s when firms, especially in the telecommunications and biotechnology fields, raised large amounts of capital in a favorable market environment to prefund large capital expenditure programs or projected start-up operating losses. In cases like these, an investor might, adjusting for scale, find a firm with $300 in debt and $500 in market capitalization of equity, implying an EV of $800 but $250 in cash equivalents. The conceptual issue is whether the market is valuing the core enterprise at $800 or as an enterprise worth $550 with $250 in cash. The usual convention is to be conservative and assume the latter; thus the indicated EV is typically reduced by "excess" cash.

Even when the excess cash is not the result of a recent financing, it is standard practice to reduce EV by cash. The rationale for this is that the decision by the firm to hold cash rather than pay down debt is a strategic financial decision. For example, consider two firms that, for hypothetical purposes, have exactly the same intrinsic EV. The management of Firm X wants to appear to have strong liquidity and thus holds a large cash balance over the quarter-end reporting date. The management of Firm Y wants to show that it has relatively less leverage and thus uses all available cash to pay down a working capital line on the last day of the quarter. If no adjustment for cash is made, Firm Y would appear to have a higher EV even though, per our assumption, they are equal.

Netting debt by all cash may not always be appropriate, however. First, the practice can be criticized as not being realistic about the practical needs of a

Table 5-6. Calculation of Enterprise Value

	Firm		
	A	**B**	**C**
Equity Market Capitalization	168.0	2280.0	1800.0
+ Debt	685.0	775.0	0.0
– Cash	(40.0)	(150.0)	(120.0)
EV	813.0	2905.0	1680.0
EV/EBITDA	4.8x	7.4x	6.0x
F-EV/Shares*	23.93	8.24	11.20
P/E	14.3x	16.6x	12.0x

* Fixed-mult EV (F-EV) calculated as [(LTM EBITDA × 6 mult) – gross debt]/shares.

business. Firms need ready liquidity to function and pay the bills. Some need this in the form of cash. For example, a fast-food restaurant chain requires cash in its point of sale registers. Second, while most liquidity needs can be handled with a working capital line of credit, such lines are not universally available to all types of businesses and do entail costs. So, just as not using cash to pay down debt can be viewed as a strategic decision, not having a working capital line of credit can be viewed as a strategic decision. In the latter case, there may be no practical option but to maintain a certain amount of working capital in the form of cash. Thus, like most general rules, judgment is required in specific situations.[22]

With these caveats in mind, the EVs of Firms A, B, and C are calculated in Table 5-6. To simplify the presentation, it is assumed that all amounts characterized as current assets are in the form of cash.

Notice that EV can provide significant insight into the issue of relative value among these firms. If a fixed EV multiple (i.e., industry multiple) is used to derive EV (F-EV), an alternative share valuation can be derived. Firm C, which appeared the "cheapest" on a P/E basis, now looks to be appropriately valued with an F-EV/sh of $11.20 per share versus its market price of $12. Firm B is considerably overvalued from an F-EV/sh perspective and should have a share price of $8.24, which would bring its P/E ratio down to 11.2x, which is more in line with Firm C. Firm A, on the other hand, is clearly undervalued with operating metrics that would justify a share price of $23.93.

Determining the Correct Multiple

Obviously, in the simple formula EBITDA × multiple = EV, the validity of any answer is directly dependent on choosing an appropriate multiple. Why is any given multiple appropriate? There is no exact science. As a practical matter, one examines the data developed in a comparable firm analysis and then uses judgment as to how any particular target compares, an exercise that will be done shortly. But the data are not viewed in a vacuum. As was established in Table 5-4, given the relatively high DCRs typically applied to compensate for the inherent risk associated with investing in distressed situations, the range of multiples will likely be within the range of 4x–8x. Values that appear to be materially outside that range should be closely scrutinized.

Another consideration in judging the appropriateness of a given multiple is whether it represents a financial or strategic valuation. The distinction between these two is rooted in the merger and acquisition marketplace, which, as a simplification, is comprised of two types of buyers: financial and strategic. A financial buyer is an entity that purchases a firm solely on the expectation that the investment will provide a satisfactory risk-adjusted rate of return on a stand-alone basis. A strategic buyer is an entity that typically is already involved in the industry and views the rate of return on investment within the context of a larger entity. The basic difference is what has come to be skeptically viewed as "synergy" values. The strategic buyer may believe the entity is worth more to it because it can increase revenues by making it a part of its product line or by using its distribution system or can improve operating profitability by consolidating manufacturing, sales, or administrative functions. Whatever the source of the expected synergistic value, methodologically these can be thought of as an increase in postacquisition expected levels of EBITDA generation.

First, the perspective of the financial buyer will be examined in more detail since this, in practice, forms the bedrock of firm valuations. Financial buyers, as a group, can be thought of as the leveraged buyout firms[23] of the 1980s or the private equity firms[24] of the current period. The financial buyer accepts the proposition, discussed at the outset, that a firm is the present value of future cash flows but solves the equation differently: Given a forecasted series of cash flows, if the purchase requires an investment of X, what is the return on that investment? Financially this is referred to as the *internal rate of return* or IRR of an investment. The IRR is the effective equivalent of the DCR: it is just a function of what are viewed as dependent versus independent variables. The IRR is the dependent variable calculated based on the independent variable price. The present value, or price, is the dependent variable calculated based on the independent variable DCR. Financial buyers tend to think in terms of the price paid (independent variable) and then determine whether the IRR is adequate. The price paid, of course, can be thought of or derived as an EBITDA multiple.

In Table 5-7, the IRR of an investment/purchase is derived for an array of multiples and forecasted EBITDA growth rates. For example, if the base EBITDA was $10, and the buyer conservatively assumed that this would be constant and offered to pay a multiple of 5x or $50, the IRR on the investment would be

Table 5-7. Expected IRRs for Different Growth Rates and Purchase Multiples

| Growth | Purchase Multiple | | | | | |
Rate	2	4	5	6	8	10
0%	50.0%	24.9%	19.8%	16.3%	11.7%	8.8%
2%	52.0%	26.9%	21.8%	18.3%	13.7%	10.7%
4%	54.0%	28.9%	23.7%	20.2%	15.6%	12.6%
6%	56.0%	30.9%	25.7%	22.2%	17.6%	14.6%
8%	58.0%	32.9%	27.7%	24.2%	19.5%	16.5%
10%	60.0%	34.8%	29.7%	26.1%	21.4%	18.4%

19.8%. If the firm could be purchased for 2x EBITDA, the return would be a very attractive 50%, but that level of potential return would be likely to attract higher competing offers. If buyers thought EBITDA was likely to grow at an average rate of 4%, they could pay 6x and still realize an IRR of 20.2%. For investors seeking 20%+ returns, which is a typical return target for financial buyers, purchase multiples in excess of 6x can only be justified if they believe sustained EBITDA improvement is attainable.

In order to boost returns, financial buyers will often employ leverage (i.e., borrow a portion of the purchase price to minimize the equity investment). This can significantly enhance equity returns, but also increase risk. However, there are practical constraints on how much can be borrowed. Lenders, in particular banks, want to see a cash flow forecast that shows the borrower can generate sufficient internal cash flow to repay, or significantly pay down, the loan. In Table 5-8, a forward cash flow projection is developed assuming that: (a) the investor used 80% borrowed money to finance the purchase, (b) EBITDA (which is shown net of maintenance CAPX) is assumed to grow at 4%, (c) the interest rate on the loan is 10%, and (d) the banks require that the loan be paid

Table 5-8. Ability of Firm to Internally Finance Debt Payoff

| EBITDA-CAPX | 10 | Debt Multiple | 4.0x | Amortization Period (Years) | 7 |
| Growth Rate % | 4% | Debt Interest % | 10% | | |

| | Period | | | | | | | | | |
	1	2	3	4	5	6	7	8	9	10
EBITDA-CAPX	10.0	10.4	10.8	11.2	11.7	12.2	12.7	13.2	13.7	13.7
Interest	4.0	3.4	2.9	2.3	1.7	1.1	0.6	0.0	0.0	0.0
Available	6.0	7.0	8.0	9.0	10.0	11.0	12.1	13.2	13.7	13.7
Beginning Debt	40.0	34.3	28.6	22.9	17.1	11.4	5.7	0.0	0.0	0.0
Amortization	5.7	5.7	5.7	5.7	5.7	5.7	5.7	0.0	0.0	0.0
Excess $	0.3	1.5	3.8	7.0	11.3	16.6	23.0			

off evenly over seven years. Although the projection suggests this level of leverage can be managed, there is very little margin for error, particularly in the first three years. If everything works as planned, the investor could earn a very high IRR on investment. However, if performance is somewhat below plan, the borrower could quickly be in default on the loan. Thus, as this illustration justifies, and is in fact true in practice, without a very compelling strategy for EBITDA improvement, lenders, particularly bank lenders, tend to be reluctant to extend credit when total leverage reaches much above 4.0x EBITDA. Banks, even on a secured basis, will often limit lending to 2.5x leverage.

Strategic buyers will often be observed apparently paying above the range of 4x–6x. Their decisions to pay more can be justified on two grounds. First, they may believe that by integrating the target firm into their existing operations, EBITDA can be increased above the target's stand-alone forecast. Thus, if EBITDA is expected to grow relatively faster, a higher purchase price can be justified. Second, the strategic buyer may have a lower targeted return on investment. Typically strategic buyers can justify any acquisition where the IRR exceeds the acquiring firm's cost of capital.[25] Referring back to Table 5-7, if the required IRR is, for example, only 15%, then, particularly in high-growth-rate scenarios, multiples as high as 10x can be rationalized. Of course, no buyer will pay more than it needs to, but if there are several strategic buyers in the market, the competition will tend to drive the price up.

A common strategy is for financial buyers to purchase assets that they think will ultimately have "strategic value" to a strategic buyer and wait for the right opportunity to sell at a higher value. In very simple terms, the financial buyer will opportunistically purchase a company at, say, 5x EBITDA, do what it can to improve operations, and then wait for a stronger point in the market and attempt to sell the firm to a strategic buyer for a higher multiple, say 7x–8x EBITDA.[26] When these strategies are financed on a leveraged basis and work as planned, returns can be very high. However, there is always the danger that when the financial buyer assumes control of a stand-alone company, the incumbent operators in the industry will view the target as a financially frail (because of its leverage) competitor whose market share can be attacked. This can lead to aggressive competitive practices that can diminish the value of the target, wipe out the investment of the financial buyer, and create a distressed debt restructuring opportunity.

Using Comparable Company Analysis

Now that some of the more general considerations that relate to applying comparable company analysis have been developed, it is time to apply what has been discussed to help estimate the value of a target. In Table 5-9, the data on

Firms A, B, and C are represented together with data on a target firm, T, whose stock is trading at $0.50 per share and debt is offered at 25. The goal of the analysis is to decide efficiently whether there is a potential investment opportunity in T.

What can one quickly tell about T? First, it should be recognized that T is the largest firm in the group, with revenues greater than B and considerably

Table 5-9. Preliminary Valuation of Target

Income Data	A	B	C	T
Revenue	1000.0	3000.0	2000.0	3500.0
Net Income	11.7	137.0	149.5	−156.0
Earnings per Share	0.84	0.72	1.00	−0.78
Share Price	$12.00	$12.00	$12.00	$0.50
P/E	14.3x	16.6x	12.0x	NM
Balance Sheet				
Current Assets	40.0	150.0	120.0	20.0
Property, Plant, and Equipment	800.0	2000.0	1000.0	3500.0
Total Assets	840.0	2150.0	1120.0	3520.0
Current Liabilities	25.0	125.0	35.0	20.0
Debt	685.0	775.0	0.0	2400.0
Equity	130.0	1250.0	1085.0	1100.0
Total Liabilities and Equity	840.0	2150.0	1120.0	3520.0
Shares	14.0	190.0	150.0	200.0
EBITDA Calculation				
Net Income	11.7	137.0	149.5	−156.0
+ Taxes	6.3	73.8	80.5	0.0
+ Interest Expense	71.9	54.3	0.0	156.0
+ Depreciation and Amortization	80.0	125.0	50.0	175.0
EBITDA	170.0	390.0	280.0	175.0
Selected Data				
EBITDA/Revenue %	17.0%	13.0%	14.0%	5.0%
Debt/EBITDA	4.0x	2.0x	0.0x	13.7x
EBITDA/Share	12.14	2.05	1.87	0.88
Interest Rate	10.5%	7.0%	5.0%	6.5%
Tax Rate	35.0%	35.0%	35.0%	35.0%
Revenue/Assets	119.0%	139.5%	178.6%	99.4%
Enterprise Value				
Equity Market Capitalization	168.0	2280.0	1800.0	0.0
+ Debt	685.0	775.0	0.0	600.0
− Cash	(40.0)	(150.0)	(120.0)	(0.0)
Enterprise Value	813.0	2905.0	1680.0	600.0
EV/EBITDA	4.8x	7.4x	6.0x	3.4x
F-EV/Shares*	23.93	8.24	11.20	(6.75)

* Calculated as [(LTM EBITDA × 6) − gross debt]/shares.

more assets. (It is unclear what those assets are currently worth, but the GAAP carrying value is $3500.) T lost money during the reported period on a GAAP basis. This is probably due to the fact that its EBITDA/revenue margin was only 5% relative to the peer range of 13–17%. This suggests significant operating issues in addition to whatever problems might be caused by T's very high $2400 debt load. T essentially has no liquidity, with current assets equaling current liabilities. Its EBITDA is positive and exceeds interest expense, so it conceivably could limp along for a while, but if depreciation is representative of maintenance CAPX, then it cannot afford to maintain its plant. On the surface, it would be reasonable to infer that T needs an operational turnaround and a balance sheet restructuring.

Looking at EV, since the stock is trading below $1 per share and debt is trading at 25, the small implied equity value is excluded from the analysis and the debt is valued at its market trading level of 600 (2400 × 25%). No adjustment is made for cash since there is clearly no excess liquidity. This implies an EV of 600, which represents an EV/EBITDA multiple of 3.4x. This multiple is below the multiple range of the peer group, which is between 4.8x and 7.4x. However, as discussed above, C's valuation is probably the most representative; thus the valuation range can probably be narrowed to 5.5x–6.0x.

On a very preliminary basis then, it appears that T could potentially be undervalued. There is certainly not enough known to make an investment decision, but by playing with the spreadsheet one can estimate that if T traded at an EV multiple of 5.5x, the bonds should be worth 40, roughly 60% above current levels. Further, if operations could be improved so that the EBITDA margin was raised to 10%, still below C's 13%, the bonds, still at an EBITDA multiple of 5.5x, would potentially be worth 80. And, absent the existence of significant off-balance-sheet liabilities, it might be reasonable to assume there is limited downside from 25. There are many, many more things to investigate, which will be discussed in Chapter 11, but the preliminary review suggests that an investment in T bonds has sufficient return potential to merit additional due diligence.

ALTERNATIVES TO THE EBITDA MULTIPLE APPROACH

While cash-flow-based multiple valuations are the most common approach to valuation, several alternatives are also commonly used. In this section, four of the most common of these will be reviewed: revenue-based, asset-based, customer-based, and liquidation. The primary reasons for using alternatives are that either (a) actual cash flow experience may not be a very reliable indicator of a firm's potential or (b) data on the purchase or sale of companies, which is frequently considered superior to general market trading-based valuations because the purchaser has presumably done significant due diligence in determining the price paid, are commonly reported on an alternative basis.

Revenue-Based Valuations

Revenue-based valuations are frequently used for both of the rationales listed above. In fact, it is hard to imagine performing a valuation without weighing various operating metrics relative to revenue. At the most basic level, revenue is an indication of breadth of the target's customer relationships or product acceptance, which is among the defining elements of a successful enterprise. In the three-firm example analyzed above, several references were made to the EBITDA/revenue margin. A metric like this can be very useful because it may be a general indication of the quality of management, something for which EBITDA does not adjust. If several firms are fairly similar but one management can achieve a 17% EBITDA margin (Firm A) and another only 5% (Firm T), it is natural to wonder what the potential of the underperforming firm might be under the direction of more successful management. Thus, in many industries where the product or service is fairly generic (e.g., food retailers, low- and mid-price-point restaurants, movie theaters, commercial paper products, commodity industrial chemicals, just to name a few), the fact that a company has significant revenues may itself constitute a significant competitive asset. The potential of those sales under the control of another management team may be more relevant to valuation than what the existing management team has been able to accomplish. In considering the use of revenue-based valuation metrics, EBITDA/revenue or EV/revenue would be the most common approach.

Asset-Based Valuations

Asset-based valuations are most frequently employed where possession of a key asset is a significant competitive advantage. The most prominent examples of this relate to natural resources or real estate that may have some measure of scarcity value. Because of this scarcity issue, the question is not so much whether any particular firm can sell the product, but when and for what margin over cost. In addition, the amount of the scarce resource possessed by the firm, barring new acquisitions or discoveries, puts a cap on its future revenue and cash-flow-generating potential. For example, it would not make much sense to extrapolate 25 years of EBITDA projections based on the last 3 years of history for a gold mine with only one project site that is expected to be exhausted in 3 years. In that case, the amount of gold reserves owned would significantly influence the valuation estimate. Thus in industries where raw material scarcity is an issue, metrics based on the quantity controlled (e.g., proven and unproven reserves in the case of an oil and gas production company) must be factored into the valuation calculus.

Customer-Based Valuations

Similar to the rationale in asset-based valuation approaches, often the critical competitive issue is possession of a customer, particularly where there are economic or regulatory constraints that limit free access to customers.

Perhaps the most prominent example is cable television companies. Prior to the advent of satellite-based television systems, cable companies effectively had a monopoly on the customers within their geographic service area. Accordingly, it was fairly common to measure the potential value of these companies by reference to metrics associated with existing or potential customers. Furthermore, most sales transactions tend to be reported on this basis rather than relative to cash flow.

For example, a cable company might report that it sold a noncore service area for a price equaling $2000 per existing subscriber, but it will be less common to know what the cash flow associated with the sale represented. The purchaser of the assets will presumably base the purchase price on a cash flow basis. However, since often such buyers will be "strategic" in nature, it may be hard to use the price paid to make an inference of what historical EBITDA might have been because the strategic buyer may have a significantly different view of the purchased asset's EBITDA potential within its system. Assume, to continue the example, that the service area sold was a noncore, noncontiguous region that the seller controlled by virtue of an old acquisition. Because of its small scale and location, it may not make economic sense for the seller to make capital investments that would allow it to offer premium or on-demand programming or to offer broadband Internet access in this area. Thus its average revenue per subscriber might be $30 a month, well below the average for upgraded systems. If a cable company with an adjacent service area purchased the remote service area, it might be able to provide upgraded services with minimal incremental capital investment by leveraging its existing infrastructure. If this would allow it to forecast the ability to extract $70 a month per subscriber, then it would likely be willing to pay a price considerably higher than the EBITDA generated by the existing owner based on what the lower monthly revenue might merit.

Wireless communication companies, including radio stations, also are often valued, at least in part, on the size of their existing or potential customer base. This is because part of their competitive advantage stems from the possession of a regulatory license that gives them some degree of customer access monopoly.

Liquidation Valuations

As mentioned in Chapter 4, sometimes businesses simply cannot generate sufficient "value added" to justify their existence as a going concern, and thus the highest and best use of their assets is to be sold in a liquidation. This is particularly true for firms that for either competitive circumstance, inadequacy of physical plant, or poor management simply cannot generate positive EBITDA on a sustained basis. In these situations, historical or potential future EBITDA generation is irrelevant to the firm's value. The investor must attempt to estimate the selling price of the firm's assets (portions of which might be saleable as business units with going-concern valuations). This is a very speculative endeavor because there is typically very little information on the market value of a firm's assets,[27] and it may be unclear whether the liquidation will be conducted on a fire-sale versus orderly basis.

However, this does not mean that good returns may not be available for distressed investors. The very fact that the firm will be going out of business tends to eliminate the interest of many investors — and there is often a positive correlation between disinterest in a situation and the likelihood of misvaluation.[28]

SUMMARY

Perhaps no other skill is more necessary to successful distressed debt investing, indeed investing in general, than valuation. This chapter reviewed the basic principles behind the most commonly used methodology, the EBITDA multiple valuation approach, and how it compares to the more theoretically correct, but time consuming, DCF approach. It also described some of the basic advantages and disadvantages of using the EBITDA metric. Finally, it also discussed several of the more common alternative valuation methodologies and some of the more common contexts in which those alternatives are used. In the next chapter, the concept of credit support and its relationship to valuation is developed.

This Chapter's Chess Moves

9. Nh4, Ph6

10. Pf4, Ng6

11. Nxg6, Pxg6

6

LEVERAGE AND THE CONCEPTS OF CREDIT SUPPORT AND CAPACITY

By definition, the balance sheet has two sides: assets versus liabilities and equity. The last chapter considered the determinants of the size of the left or asset side of the ledger. In this chapter, the discussion shifts to the right-hand side of the picture: the capital structure. More specifically, the considerations that affect the size and structural characteristics of the debt box will be examined. As part of that discussion, the concepts of credit support and credit capacity will be developed. These will be used to help assess the maximum amount of debt that may "prudently" be included in any particular capital structure. Chapter 7 will then address how the capital structure manages and allocates credit risk. Although the basic tenets of cost-of-capital theory will be touched upon, the approach to credit analysis in this and the next chapter attempts to capture the "real-world" way that lending decisions tend to be made, which, one may be surprised to find, are driven much more by judgment and market trends than elaborate quantitative models.

THE INTERRELATIONSHIP OF CREDIT RISK AND CREDIT SUPPORT

Credit risk assessment and distressed debt analysis are similar exercises; it is just a question of when they are performed. By analogy, credit risk is like standing on a dock under tranquil skies and calmly discussing the risk that a boat carrying gold might capsize should an unexpected storm arise; distressed debt analysis is like being on the boat in a hurricane and deciding how much to offer to buy it, recognizing that the boat could sink or it might be necessary to throw some of the gold overboard to survive.

While a discussion of leverage may seem superfluous within the context of distressed debt investing, which implicitly presupposes that there is debt (probably too much) outstanding, the topic is relevant for several reasons: First, the concepts developed here will help investors to identify in advance those situations that may become financially distressed. Second, and perhaps more importantly, an understanding of credit capacity is key to predicting the treatment of any particular debt class in a potential restructuring. Finally, credit fundamentals are essential in devising appropriate postrestructuring capital structures.

In the parlance of the high-yield market, "leverage" is sometimes ambiguously used to mean the quantity or amount of debt. Thus, if someone were to ask how much leverage company X has, the response could be an absolute figure (e.g., $523 million). This book will use the term leverage to indicate the amount of debt relative to the credit support, generally cash flow (e.g., 6.2x last 12 months earnings before interest, taxes, depreciation, and amortization [EBITDA]).

Credit Risk

Credit risk, a term introduced above, is the probability that the contractual payment terms of a loan or bond are breached. Put more simply, it is the chance that principal and interest are not paid when due. Credit risk is a function of three parameters — leverage, priority, and time — all of which are relative. Viewing these parameters in the extreme helps illustrate the continuum. A one-dollar, one-day senior secured loan to an AAA-rated corporation with $20 billion in liquid assets and no other debt has a very high probability of being repaid on time. In contrast, it would be fairly imprudent to make a $100 million, 50-year junior subordinated loan to a company with a stock price of a penny that has no cash, minimal tangible assets, no known intellectual property, and $5 billion in secured[1] bank debt that matures next week. In this chapter, the focus will be on leverage, while the concepts of priority and time will be deferred to Chapter 7, which deals with how companies manage risk through their capital structures.

Credit Support

Credit support refers to the source of the funds used to repay a debt and is typically classified as either collateral or cash flow. As noted in Chapter 5, in general, firms are valued relative to their future cash-flow-generating capability. Any general obligation or full recourse debt of a firm is implicitly backed by a firm's cash flows. Thus, in a simple example, if a firm has $50 in EBITDA and wants to borrow $100, leverage would be 2.0x; the terminology and concepts are fairly similar to the EBITDA multiple analysis used for valuations. If these were the only relevant considerations, a lender might view the probability of recovering the amount of the loan (whether through contractual repayment or otherwise) as reasonably high. Using a multiple-based valuation, the lender might assume that, in the worst case, the business was worth or could be sold to someone for 3x EBITDA, or $150, and thus there should be plenty of value to provide for repayment of the $100 debt.

Often, cash flows either are inadequate, too volatile, or there are too many other creditors to provide a lender with sufficient comfort to make a loan. In such cases, the loan may be conditioned on receiving an adequate pledge of collateral. This is similar to a mortgage on a house. Lenders can essentially have any asset pledged as collateral and, as mentioned in Chapter 4, sometimes will take broad liens against all of a firm's assets. Thus, while a bank might not be willing to make a "cash-flow"-type loan to a new start-up with unproven revenues, it might be willing to lend money to finance 60% of the cost of a new machine with the machine as collateral. The credit judgment might be that even if the company failed, the lender could recoup the loan by foreclosing on and selling the machine. Similarly, lenders often provide working capital lines of credit that are secured by accounts receivable and inventories. Such loans have what are called *borrowing bases,* which define how much credit will be extended relative to available collateral. A typical structure might define the borrowing base as 50% of inventory and 75% of eligible receivables. The basic theory of such loans is that the collateral should always be sufficient to repay the loan regardless of what happens to the borrower.

Credit Capacity

Determining how much debt a firm can prudently incur involves an analysis of the firm's credit capacity.[2] Credit capacity is a concept typically used within the context of unsecured lending; in other words, how much debt can be supported by the firm's operating cash flows alone. This cannot be answered in an absolute sense because the concept of credit capacity is relative to risk. This latter point is clear if one frames the issue as how much one can lend to a hypothetical Company A and have 50% versus 99% confidence of recovering the loan. To have a higher confidence level, one would naturally lend less. This reflects the rather obvious point that the more that is lent to any particular firm, the relatively higher the risk of default.

The concept of credit capacity also applies to loans made on the basis of collateral support (i.e., secured lending), but in that context, the analysis turns on the appraised value of the collateral and a judgment as to the stability of that value. At the upper limit, the question is what percentage of the collateral's market value can be advanced prudently. If the collateral is readily saleable and fairly stable in value, the advance rate may be 90% or more. As the stability of the collateral's value or its liquidity declines, so will the advance rate.

Even if there is sufficient appraised asset value, a company's ability to service the debt must be considered. For example, consider a land development company that wants to borrow money collateralized by unimproved property to purchase raw land. A lender would be shortsighted to focus only on the adequacy of the collateral support and not consider how the loan will be serviced until such time that the land can begin to generate cash.[3]

There is no universally accepted method of determining credit capacity based on cash flow as the credit support. Since it relies on a view of the future, which is of course uncertain, it is more a matter of judgment than science. Forecasting the magnitude and stability of cash flows, which can vary both positively and negatively relative to recent history or expectations, is the critical factor in judging a firm's credit capacity. If a business is highly competitive and cyclical, it may only be prudent to lend it a very low multiple (e.g., 1.0–1.5x) of its EBITDA. Where the cash flow is more certain, lenders may feel safe lending relatively more. For example, an electric utility with long-term contracts for its source fuel might be considered stable. Utilities (particularly in regions that have not deregulated) generally have a monopoly in their service areas. Electricity, although a commodity, is an essential item with few substitutes, so demand is generally stable or increasing. Thus, if the cost of the fuel (e.g., coal or natural gas) is "locked in," providing the utility with a relatively certain operating margin, a lender might feel comfortable lending a larger amount, perhaps 3.0–3.5x EBITDA.

Implicit in characterizing a particular leverage multiple as acceptable is an underlying measure or criterion for debt capacity. Why might leverage of 3.5x be "inappropriate" for a borrower with relatively uncertain cash flows but acceptable for the hypothetical utility? As mentioned above, there is no absolute answer because it is largely a function of risk tolerance. In general, the most common considerations used to assess a borrower's debt capacity are the ability to pay interest, meaningfully repay the principal balance over time, refinance the debt at maturity, and maintain asset value greater than the amount of the loan. The weight placed on any particular one of these considerations will vary depending on the lender and the type and structure of the loan or bond.

CREDIT CAPACITY AS MEASURED BY DEBT REPAYMENT ABILITY

Of the criteria just mentioned, the most stringent, and not accidentally the most often employed by banks, is the ability of the borrower to fund the repayment of a loan from internally generated cash flow.[4] Banks, because of the nature of their business model and regulatory constraints, are fairly risk averse (see sidebar on the next page). Not only will they usually insist on having collateral as credit support well in excess of the amount of the loan, but, on a pure cash flow basis, they will also look for substantial cash flow support. This "belt and suspenders" approach to lending has more to do with the issue of priority, discussed in the next chapter, than a notion of "double" credit support. If one thinks practically for a moment, there is no "double support" because, in most businesses, were one to foreclose and sell all the assets held as collateral, there would no longer be a business to generate cash flow.

Because banks are risk averse, they typically require periodic amortization or partial principal repayment of a loan. Regular principal amortization[5] both reduces the lender's exposure over time as well as minimizes the risk that there will be a default if the borrower needs to refinance at maturity and cannot access the capital markets. This is quite different from the structure of most corporate bonds where there is seldom any amortization[6] and repayment is often premised on a company's future ability to raise more capital (generally by selling more bonds) to fund the repayment of the original bonds. There seems to be an implicit optimism in bond financing that companies will always grow and thus have stronger credit profiles when the bonds mature. Bankers, whose compensation is typically more closely tied to the credit performance of their loan portfolios than bond fund managers,[7] tend to be more conservative.

To analyze debt capacity from the perspective of internal debt retirement ability, scenarios involving stable and cyclical cash flows will be reviewed.

Stable Cash Flow Scenarios

Table 6-1 sets forth a cash flow model that shows the borrower's ability to repay a loan under some well-defined scenarios. The model assumes that all cash flow (defined as EBITDA) after the payment of interest expense and capital expenditures (CAPX) is used to retire debt (taxes are ignored in the interest of simplicity). CAPX is held constant across time and EBITDA is assumed to be highly predictable, growing at a specified growth rate (2%) across the time horizon. This scenario shows that if leverage (defined as a multiple of EBITDA) is only 2.0x, the borrower is able to repay the loan in its entirety within the five-year forecast period with internally generated funds.

Bank Risk Aversion

Since banks, as a class, are heavily involved in the corporate debt market and by default (or, perhaps more accurately, through default) the distressed debt market, it is worth reviewing for a moment why banks are relatively risk averse. The basic reasons are their business model and regulatory oversight. As a great simplification, banks make money by borrowing money at a low rate from depositors and relending it at a higher rate to individuals and businesses. For example, a bank may offer 4% interest to borrow money under a one-year certificate of deposit and then relend that money to a company at 7%. This results in an "interest margin" of 3%. If the bank's operating expenses are 1% of loans outstanding, this implies a pretax, precredit expense (i.e., risk of loan loss) margin of 2%. Although the absolute interest levels fluctuate, these relative spreads are actually fairly representative.

Relatively speaking, 2% is not very much. In Chapter 2 it was noted, for example, that the long-term inflation-adjusted historical return on equity investments was approximately 13%. Thus, to offer sufficient returns to attract equity investment, banks must employ high leverage. In other words, they must borrow and relend many multiples of their equity capital. Consider the following simple example. A bank has $10 in equity, takes in $60 in deposits, and then makes $70 in loans. If it makes 2% net of operating costs on the amount of the loans, this would equal $1.40, which represents a 14% pretax, precredit expense return on its $10 in equity. So, assuming away taxes, the bank will have a competitive equity return as long as it does not have any loan losses. This could be characterized as a low-margin, low-risk, high-financial-leverage (6:1) business model.

The model is viable, but only if loan losses are well managed. If our hypothetical bank has a loss rate of 1.2% on loans, [8] it would have to increase its interest margin to 4% (through a combination of lowering its borrowing cost and increasing its loan rates) to still achieve a 14% pretax return on equity. Thus, banks as a financial proposition tend to avoid making loans that have a very high risk of loss.

In addition, bank regulators (i.e., the government) monitor the risk profile of bank loan portfolios. The government's regulatory interest is twofold: first, budgetary, because the government, through the Federal Deposit Insurance Corporation (FDIC), insures most deposits and thus might have to pay out money if a bank has large losses and fails; second, economic, because large-scale bank failures could hurt investor and consumer confidence and thus do broad harm to the economy. Together, regulatory scrutiny and a low-margin business model tend to make banks fairly risk averse.

Table 6-1. Debt Capacity with Stable Cash Flows and 2.0x Leverage

	EBITDA Stable Scenario				
	Year				
	1	2	3	4	5
EBITDA	250.0	255.0	260.1	265.3	270.6
Interest Expense	50.0	42.5	33.8	23.6	11.9
CAPX	125.0	125.0	125.0	125.0	125.0
Available for Debt	75.0	87.5	101.4	116.7	133.7
Beginning Debt	500.0	425.0	337.5	236.2	119.5
Amortization	(75.0)	(87.5)	(101.4)	(116.7)	(119.5)
End Debt	425.0	337.5	236.2	119.5	0.0
Debt/EBITDA	2.0	1.3	0.9	0.5	0.0
EBITDA/Interest Expense	5.0	6.0	7.7	11.2	22.7
Interest Rate	**10.0%**	**10.0%**	**10.0%**	**10.0%**	**10.0%**
EBITDA Growth Rate		**2.0%**	**2.0%**	**2.0%**	**2.0%**

However, as illustrated in Table 6-2, if the scenario is changed to increase the leverage to 3.0x, even with a higher growth assumption of 4% per year, only 56% ([750 − 330]/750) of the loan can be retired.

Table 6-2. Debt Capacity with Stable Cash Flows and 3.0x Leverage

	EBITDA Stable Scenario				
	Year				
	1	2	3	4	5
EBITDA	250.0	260.0	270.4	281.2	292.5
Interest Expense	75.0	70.0	63.5	55.3	45.2
CAPX	125.0	125.0	125.0	125.0	125.0
Available for Debt	50.0	65.0	81.9	100.9	122.2
Beginning Debt	750.0	700.0	635.0	553.1	452.2
Amortization	(50.0)	(65.0)	(81.9)	(100.9)	(122.2)
End Debt	700.0	635.0	553.1	452.2	329.9
Debt/EBITDA	3.0	2.4	2.0	1.6	1.1
EBITDA/Interest Expense	3.3	3.7	4.3	5.1	6.5
Interest Rate	**10.0%**	**10.0%**	**10.0%**	**10.0%**	**10.0%**
EBITDA Growth Rate		**4.0%**	**4.0%**	**4.0%**	**4.0%**

Table 6-3. Sensitivity of Debt Repayment Ability to Leverage and Growth Rate

Leverage	Growth Rate				
	0.0%	2.0%	4.0%	6.0%	8.0%
2.0x	92%	100%	100%	100%	100%
2.5x	61%	70%	79%	89%	99%
3.0x	41%	48%	56%	64%	73%
3.5x	26%	33%	39%	46%	53%
4.0x	15%	21%	27%	33%	39%
4.5x	7%	12%	17%	22%	28%
5.0x	0%	5%	9%	14%	19%

The trade-off between leverage and assumed growth rate in the ability of the hypothetical firm to retire its debt can be more generally seen in the sensitivity analysis provided in Table 6-3. In this analysis, the percentages in the table represent the percentage of loan repayment for a given leverage (vertical axis) and EBITDA growth rate (horizontal axis) scenario.

Note that for the particular assumptions of this case, even at a fairly high 8% growth assumption, if initial leverage is 3.0x EBITDA, only 73% of the loan can be repaid over the five-year horizon. The primary determinant of this result, as you may have realized, is the CAPX assumption of $125 per year. This consumes almost 50% of EBITDA (although such a percentage is not at all uncommon). If leverage were measured on the basis of EBITDA-CAPX (a common adjustment discussed in Chapter 5), leverage would be 6.0x. Thus, although this example should not be taken as leading to any general conclusions, it does help illustrate the correlation between duration of debt repayment and leverage.

Volatile Cash Flow Scenarios

This initial example, however, assumed highly stable cash flows — a simplifying assumption that in the real world the lender makes at its peril. Next, the effect of cash flow volatility on debt capacity is considered. In Table 6-4, the EBITDA assumption for the company has been changed to make it cyclical. This can be easily seen by looking at the EBITDA growth rate line that tracks the change in EBITDA.

Focusing on just the future EBITDA assumption, Figure 6-1 charts the scenario in Table 6-4. The modeled scenario illustrates the most dangerous environment for the lender in a cyclical business: at the time of the loan, the borrower is on a cyclical upswing, looking forward to another year of improving fundamentals; thus the lender might feel comfortable lending $750, or 3.0x

Table 6-4. Debt Capacity with Volatile Cash Flow and 3.0x Leverage

	EBITDA Volatile Scenario					
	Year					
	1	**2**	**3**	**4**	**5**	**6**
EBITDA	250.0	262.5	210.0	189.0	207.9	228.7
Interest Expense	75.0	70.0	63.3	61.1	60.8	58.6
CAPX	125.0	125.0	125.0	125.0	125.0	125.0
Available for Debt	50.0	67.5	21.8	2.9	22.1	45.1
Beginning Debt	750.0	700.0	632.5	610.8	607.8	585.7
Amortization	(50.0)	(67.5)	(21.8)	(2.9)	(22.1)	(45.1)
End Debt	700.0	632.5	610.8	607.8	585.7	540.6
Debt/EBITDA	3.0	2.4	2.9	3.2	2.8	2.4
EBITDA/Interest Expense	3.3	3.8	3.3	3.1	3.4	3.9
Interest Rate	**10.0%**	**10.0%**	**10.0%**	**10.0%**	**10.0%**	**10.0%**
EBITDA Growth Rate		**5.0%**	**−20.0%**	**−10.0%**	**10.0%**	**10.0%**

EBITDA. Then the corrective part of the cycle begins, and EBITDA trends down for two years before rebounding.

It is beyond the scope of this book to debate the inherency of either industry or economic cycles, but whatever their causes they seem to recur with sufficient regularity that the prudent lender must consider them, depending on the past history of the industry.[9] The above pattern may seem quite severe, but many high-fixed-cost businesses can experience such volatility because it is difficult

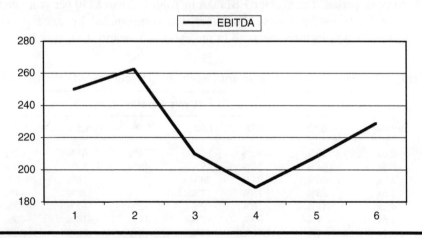

Figure 6-1. Cycle in EBITDA Volatile Scenario

for them to adjust costs when revenue weakness occurs. Examining the debt/ EBITDA (i.e., leverage) line in Table 6-4 reveals the dilemma of the lender. Initially, leverage is falling as debt is reduced, but in years 3 and 4 EBITDA has fallen so much that leverage has risen even though the absolute amount of debt is lower. If the loan had a minimum amortization requirement (e.g., $50 per year), the borrower would be in default, and since neither the borrower nor the lenders know with certainty in year 3 that there will be a rebound in year 5, everyone is likely to be quite nervous. Fortunately, the rebound comes, and at the end of the six-year horizon the loan has been reduced to $540 and leverage has fallen to a "manageable" 2.4x.

In Table 6-5, the sensitivity of loan repayment capability (the percentages in the table again represent the relative amount of loan repayment over the six-year horizon) to leverage and EBITDA is calculated. Unlike the constant growth model in Table 6-1, the EBITDA parameter in this case (shown on the horizontal axis) represents the severity of the cyclical swing. The level illustrated in Table 6-4 corresponds to a severity factor of 1 in this scale (think of this as the average cycle). Thus, relative to the hypothetical average cycle, the percentage change in EBITDA at level 1.5 is 150% as much: the severity factor essentially amplifies the pattern. What the analysis illustrates is that EBITDA volatility can lower a firm's debt repayment capacity. Notice that the most favorable scenario shown — 2.0x leverage and a cycle severity of 0.5 — is the only case in which the loan is repaid.

The negative values in the table indicate that, under the given assumptions, the firm would have been a net borrower of funds rather than have the ability to reduce the original balance. From a mathematical perspective, the simple explanation for the uniformly lower credit capacity is the average EBITDA over the forecast period. The average EBITDA in Table 6-1 was $270 per year versus $225 in Table 6-4; however, the effect was compounded by extra interest expense that was incurred because in the cyclical scenario there was less free

Table 6-5.   Sensitivity of Repayment Capability to Cycle Severity and Leverage

Leverage	Cycle Severity					
	0.50	0.75	1.00	1.25	1.50	1.75
2.0x	99%	90%	80%	71%	61%	50%
2.5x	64%	56%	49%	41%	33%	25%
3.0x	40%	34%	28%	21%	15%	8%
3.5x	23%	18%	13%	7%	2%	−4%
4.0x	11%	6%	2%	−3%	−8%	−13%
4.5x	1%	−3%	−7%	−11%	−16%	−20%
5.0x	−7%	−10%	−14%	−18%	−22%	−26%

cash to pay down the loan in the early years. Nonetheless, the point should be clear: the greater the expected volatility in cash flow, the more difficult it is to assess a borrower's debt capacity.[10]

DEBT CAPACITY UNDER ALTERNATIVE CRITERIA

To judge debt capacity exclusively by the projected ability to fund repayment internally would be to overlook or underweight the presence of other important factors. After all, how many people could purchase a house if the mortgage had to be repaid in five years? Thus it is one criterion that needs to be weighed in conjunction with other factors. In the case of an unsecured loan, the ability to fund repayment internally may be viewed as important. In the case of a secured loan where the value of the collateral is deemed adequate and fairly stable, it is less essential. The key is whether the lender can be comfortable that, in a fairly broad range of probable scenarios,[11] the value of the borrowing firm exceeds the value of the debt. The reason why the ability to fund debt repayment internally is a desirable credit attribute, to state the obvious, is that as the amount of the loan declines through repayment, the likelihood that the value of the firm exceeds the remaining balance generally increases.

Asset Coverage

The notion that the bottom-line lending/investment criterion is that the borrower's value should exceed the loan value explains why the chapter on firm valuation preceded this discussion. This concept is generally referred to as "asset coverage." At one level, asset coverage is very similar to collateral support. The difference is that the term collateral always implies that the assets comprising the collateral have been effectively set aside (legally, not physically) for the exclusive benefit or credit support of a particular creditor. The term asset coverage, as used here, denotes the more general concept of the value of the borrower, using the concepts reviewed in Chapter 5, relative to debt.

In terms of Boxco, asset coverage means that the asset box needs to be larger than the debt box. If it is not, this violates the fundamental tenet developed earlier, that capital structure is driven by asset value. As discussed in Chapter 3, when nominal debt exceeds asset value, the market eventually recognizes this and lowers the market value of the debt to a point of equality. Until this happens, it could represent a short-sale opportunity for the distressed investor.

Asset coverage would seem like such a basic principle that it would never be violated. But it frequently is, as numerous bankruptcies in the 2000–2003 period attest. The analysis provided in Table 6-4, which discussed debt capacity in volatile cash flow scenarios, should suggest a common cause — failure to achieve projected performance. In periods of general economic expansion (such as in 1995–1999), it seems that lenders/investors can often be seduced by management's optimism about the future. One can easily imagine that the lender in Table 6-4 could have been convinced that it was instead looking at a Table 6-3 scenario of consistent upward trending cash flows. The lender might have modeled the loan on a 2% growth assumption and viewed the 5% growth realized in year 2 (in the Table 6-4 scenario) as validation of its conservatism.

To illustrate what can often happen, the scenario in Table 6-4 will be modified. It will be assumed that early in year 2, with results running ahead of year 1, the company obtains the bank's permission to issue $200 of subordinated debt to fund prospective growth opportunities. The bank might go along because it views more cash coming into the firm as a positive development, particularly from a subordinated capital source. During the process of marketing the subordinated debt, projections similar to those set forth in Table 6-6 might have been presented. The 5% growth rate would have been an extrapolation of early year 2 results. The 9.5x enterprise value (EV) multiple may seem high, particularly by the criteria discussed in Chapter 5, but during the late 1990s valuation multiples of this magnitude might actually have been viewed as conservative. Here it will be assumed that the valuation was driven by a healthy market equity valuation (recall that during this period there were numerous companies with greater than $1 billion valuations that had no positive operating cash flow[12]).

As Table 6-6 illustrates, much can be rationalized when the economy and markets are favorable. Here, based on the assumed 5% EBITDA growth rate, the bank debt is completely paid off during the period of the projection despite the additional interest expense burden produced by the $200 of subordinated debt. Further, it may be noted that because of the interaction of the growth and EV assumptions, asset coverage of total debt is perceived as high at the beginning of year 3 as when the first loan was made in year 1. It is no wonder the bank was amenable to the borrower taking on a "relatively small" amount of new debt (<10% of EV) and why the subordinated debt was easily (it will be assumed) sold in the market: under the assumptions, there was arguably no particular increase in the credit risk. Standing on the dock with the sun shining, it looked like smooth sailing.

But, of course, the forecast was wrong; instead of the gentle breeze to the back of Table 6-6, the hurricane of Table 6-4 (with a severity factor of 1.5) came out of nowhere. Cash flow turned out to be as volatile as the churning seas, and because the market was undoubtedly disappointed and perhaps "frightened"[13] by the sudden storm, the equity value collapsed. Table 6-7 charts the new course.

Table 6-6. Debt Added When Outlook Positive

	EBITDA Scenario = Stable Growth						
	Year						
	1	**2**	**3**	**4**	**5**	**6**	
EBITDA	250.0	262.5	275.6	289.4	303.9	319.1	
Interest Expense	50.0	68.5	61.6	52.7	41.5	27.8	
CAPX	125.0	125.0	125.0	125.0	125.0	125.0	
Available for Debt	75.0	69.0	89.0	111.7	137.3	166.3	
Beginning Bank Debt	500.0	425.0	356.0	267.0	155.3	17.9	
Debt Paydown	(75.0)	(69.0)	(89.0)	(111.7)	(137.3)	(17.9)	
End Bank Debt	425.0	356.0	267.0	155.3	17.9	0.0	New
Subordinated (Sub) Debt	0.0	200.0	200.0	200.0	200.0	200.0	◄— sub
Total Debt	425.0	556.0	467.0	355.3	217.9	200.0	debt
Bank Debt/EBITDA	2.0x	1.4x	1.0x	0.5x	0.1x	0.0x	
Interest Rate — Bank	10%	10%	10%	10%	10%	10%	Growth
Interest Rate — Sub Debt	0%	13%	13%	13%	13%	13%	allows
Total Debt/EBITDA	1.7x	2.1x	1.7x	1.2x	0.7x	0.6x	◄— debt to
EBITDA/Interest Expense	5.0x	3.8x	4.5x	5.5x	7.3x	11.5x	decline
Asset Value (EV)	2381	2500	2625	2757	2894	3039	
Total Debt Coverage	560%	450%	562%	776%	1328%	1520%	
Bank Debt Coverage	560%	702%	983%	1775%	16155%	—	
Sub Debt Coverage*		1072%	1179%	1301%	1438%	1520%	
EV Multiple	9.5x	9.5x	9.5x	9.5x	9.5x	9.5x	High
EBITDA Growth %		**5%**	**5%**	**5%**	**5%**	**5%**	EV

* Coverage is calculated as (EV – bank debt)/sub debt. This follows the principles of absolute priority but can lead to a distorted view when the denominator is relatively small. For example, note that initially the bank debt appears to have less asset support.

Note that with the decline in EBITDA and the EV multiple, asset coverage of the subordinated debt declines to under 100%. The bank debt continues to be covered, but by a much narrower margin than the lender desired. These presumed adjustments might seem draconian. In particular, the reader may deem the EV contraction from 9.5x to 3.0x as unrealistically severe. But when cash flow rapidly erodes, there is considerable uncertainty. Assuming one could accurately forecast year 4 EBITDA in year 3, EV in year 3 would be 3.5x year 4 EBITDA. Also, of course, no one could know with certainty in year 3 that a rebound would happen in year 5. If the business deterioration were perceived to give rise to near-term liquidity issues (perhaps a breach of a bank covenant), then the risk of a default rises, which could further snowball into significant erosion of EV. Assuming the firm survives to year 5 and EBITDA rebounds, one could probably expect an expansion in the EV multiple at that time.

Table 6-7. Deterioration in Asset Coverage During Down Cycle

Year	1	2	3	4	5	6	
EBITDA	250.0	262.5	183.8	156.2	179.6	206.6	EV multiple
							contracts with
Asset Value (EV)	2381	2500	551	469	718	1033	EBITDA decline
Total Debt Coverage	560%	450%	99%	79%	120%	177%	
Bank Debt Coverage	560%	702%	154%	120%	180%	269%	Asset coverage
Sub Debt Coverage*		1072%	96%	40%	159%	324%	of sub debt falls
							Cyclical
EV Multiple	9.5x	9.5x	3.0x	3.0x	4.0x	5.0x	EBITDA pattern
EBITDA Growth %		5%	−30%	−15%	15%	15%	emerges

* Coverage is calculated as (EV − bank debt)/sub debt. This follows the principles of absolute priority but can lead to a distorted view when the denominator is relatively small.

Hopefully, the reader would have recognized that the sinking ship story just discussed is simply a replay, with slight variations in the numbers, of Boxco's parable in Figures 3-5 and 3-6 in a slightly different context. In Figure 3-6, it was simply posited that the stock market sold off, leading to the decline in apparent asset coverage. With the basic principles of valuation and leverage now developed, it is possible to discuss the situation from a more numeric, as opposed to conceptual, perspective.

Ability to Refinance

Outside of the distressed investment perspective, the goal of lenders generally is to have a loan repaid on time with interest. No one starts a lending relationship planning to recover the loan principal out of the proceeds of a liquidation auction. If the amount of leverage is such that the debt cannot be repaid through internally generated funds during the life of the loan, this effectively means the unpaid balance must be refinanced at maturity. In the case of bank loans, it will usually be the case that if the borrower has performed as expected, the bank would want to renew the facility. Banks make money by having performing loans on their portfolio; thus once a bank develops a relationship with a borrower that pays regularly, it tends to want to maintain the relationship.

In the bond context, however, there can be no expectation, in the absence of a *de facto* restructuring, of a renewal by the existing holders. When a bond matures, it must be paid. If the bond is a material part of the capital structure, it tends to require some type of refinancing. Unlike the bank loan market, even if the firm has performed well, some type of capital-raising transaction will be required to refinance the maturing issue, although original holders may choose to reinvest. The same may be true even in the bank loan context if the lead bank has syndicated the loan to other participants (particularly collateralized loan obligations) or if the loan has changed hands in the secondary market.

The ability to foresee a capital-raising event is another significant reason why asset coverage is a critical element in considering credit capacity. Outside of the secured context, it is generally very difficult (and certainly very expensive) to borrow additional money when there is a perception that asset value is insufficient to cover a firm's total debts. It is also generally very difficult to raise equity in such circumstances because if debt is greater than asset value, there is arguably no equity.

But even when there is sufficient asset value, it can often be difficult to refinance for other reasons that effectively constrain debt capacity. The most general reason a refinancing may not be feasible even when there is sufficient asset value is if there is a significant near-term liquidity constraint. For example, consider what the refinance outlook would be in Table 6-7 if the bank debt matured in year 4 and the subordinated debt in year 5. When it was time to refinance the bank debt, there was still sufficient asset value to cover the outstanding balance, but who would want to lend given the risk that there is likely to be a default in year 5, when the subordinated debt would need to be refinanced (as it turned out, theoretically there would be sufficient asset value to refinance the subordinated debt when it matures in year 5, but this could not be known with any level of certainty in year 4).

Interest Expense Coverage

A final constraint on debt capacity is the ability to pay interest. From a cash flow perspective, it is fairly obvious that there is a significant risk of an interest payment default if the interest on aggregate debt equals or exceeds EBITDA. This level of debt service basically implies that the firm will have no cash for working capital fluctuations, to make capital investments, or to pay taxes.[14] The slightest shortfall in performance could lead to a default on an interest payment.

The reader may well wonder how there could be situations where there could be debt capacity from an asset coverage or refinancing perspective, but not from an interest payment standpoint. When would interest payment ability be a separate and unique constraint? As a practical matter, if EBITDA is less than projected interest expense, it would be fairly unusual for there to be positive asset coverage. One could conceive of situations where the borrower had significant assets that were not generating much cash (for example, proven but undeveloped reserves of a natural resource), but this is generally not the way this constraint comes into play. The more typical way interest coverage becomes a constraint is when lenders decline to lend because the risk of an interest payment default in the future becomes all too real and therefore unacceptable. Thus, if a lender is looking at a situation where EBITDA/interest expense = 2.0x and (EBITDA − CAPX)/interest = 1.2x, the lender may quite legitimately perceive the risk that if there is any negative volatility in cash flow, the borrower could either default on interest payment or suffer an erosion in its cash-generating capability by foregoing potentially necessary capital investment. Even assuming the lender were offered collateral sufficient to reasonably assure that its loan would be repaid regardless of a default, only the most aggressive lenders would choose to extend funds where there was a high risk of a default on an interest payment.

As discussed above, most lenders, particularly banks, just want their money back with no hassles. If there is significant risk of a default on interest or principal, they tend to avoid such situations. Even if there is collateral support, the profitability of the loan is typically insufficient to make up for the extra management effort or time delay associated with recovering a defaulted loan. However, in a free market, there are always those that, for the right compensation, are willing to undertake such risks so one will see situations where secured lenders become involved in high-default-probability situations.[15]

CAPITAL INSTRUMENTS DESIGNED TO "AVOID" CREDIT CAPACITY CRITERIA

The prior discussion has essentially set forth a group of general rules or principles that most traditional lenders follow in assessing whether a particular borrower has the capacity, independent of collateral, to repay a loan. Those rules can be set forth as follows:

- The safest loans are those that the borrower can entirely or substantially repay from internally generated funds during the term of the loan.
- Positive asset coverage should be expected to exist throughout the term of the loan.
- Constraints on the ability to refinance maturing obligations should be manageable.
- Liquidity, whether through operations or available assets, should be sufficient to fund intermediate-term capital costs.

But show a rule to a team of creative lawyers and investment bankers and they will often figure out a way to push the "capital structure envelope" to seemingly avoid the rule. Thus, over the years a number of capital instruments have been developed that appear feasible for a firm to offer, although the form, even if slightly recast, would be likely to violate one or more of the principles discussed above. Distressed investors should be aware of these instruments so that the nature of the risks they present can be appropriately analyzed.

Exchangeable Preferred Stock

One common way to add "debt" when there is insufficient asset coverage is to characterize the new capital as preferred equity. Thus, there are a variety of examples of instruments denominated as preferred stock that have features allowing them to be converted, at the issuer's option, into "true debt."[16] These preferred stocks usually have mandatory redemption features (i.e., a requirement that they be repaid) that blur the line with debt. However, the legal argument that is advanced is that it is not "true debt" because a failure to make a dividend or redemption payment will only have limited repercussions. Often the issuer's tax circumstances are such that the structure can be justified on tax grounds (if the company has no taxable income and significant accumulated losses, the economic value of the interest expense deduction on additional debt is limited), but the practical reality is that such instruments are generally issued when the effective leverage is very high.

Convertible Bonds

Convertible bonds are bonds that have a feature allowing the holder to convert the face amount of the bond into a specified number of shares (this is referred to as the "conversion ratio") of the issuer's common stock. The conversion ratio effectively implies a share price that generally is 18–25% above (the "conversion premium") the share price at the time the bond is issued.[17] These bonds tend to skirt general credit rules because the whole premise of why they are issued is that the issuer's stock is expected to appreciate above the effective conversion price and debt will be converted into equity; therefore, it is easy to dismiss such issues as "temporary debt." In fact, the typical "pitch" to corporate management to issue such securities is that they effectively represent the "forward sale" of the issuer's stock at a premium price to the current market. Of course, if the issuer's stock declines in value, then the convertibility options become meaningless but the debt aspect becomes very real. Such securities are referred to as *busted converts* and they often represent significant opportunities for distressed investors.

Discount Notes and Payment-in-Kind Notes

When the capacity constraint is interest expense coverage ability, the primary technique to avoid this is to design securities that allow the payment of cash interest to be deferred. The most common structures used to accomplish this are discount notes (described in Chapter 5), split-coupon notes, and payment-in-kind notes (each of which is described in the glossary available for download at www.jrosspub.com). Under Generally Accepted Accounting Principles, interest expense is still recorded on the income statement, but each structure essentially allows the cash payment of the interest to be deferred until the maturity date. At that time, it is optimistically assumed that the borrower would have grown sufficiently that it will be able to fund repayment of the maturing principal and accumulated coupons by raising additional debt or equity.

SUMMARY

The goal of this chapter was to explain the considerations that go into the determination of how much debt any particular firm can "prudently" manage. The concept of credit support was discussed within two general contexts: collateral support and cash flow support. The notion of cash flow support was further developed to show how it can be measured with reference to the ability of a firm to fund repayment of an obligation internally and how the risk of cash flow volatility complicated that assessment. Asset coverage, a notion which builds upon the valuation concepts developed in Chapter 5, was presented as the ultimate determinant of credit capacity, but other considerations such as the ability to refinance and interest expense coverage were also reviewed. Finally, several capital securities that were designed, at least in part, to seemingly avoid traditional credit principles were discussed.

Hopefully, the chapter also provided the relatively novice reader with a good sense of how much he or she has advanced. In Chapter 3, the notions of leverage and financial distress could only be discussed graphically with reference to Boxco. This was akin to cartoon finance. In this chapter, the same general concepts were fully reconstructed in numerical terms. If you fully understood the analysis in this chapter, you are reasonably prepared for the more detailed discussion that follows.

One might ask how, in a free market, leverage is allowed to exceed prudent limits. As alluded to in this chapter, the basic answer lies in the acceptance of optimistic assumptions about the future. If all lending in the late 1990s had been done based on the application of traditional credit capacity metrics applied to historical, as opposed to projected, EBITDA, then the bankruptcy rate in 2001 and 2002 would have been a fraction of what was actually experienced. But the rampant optimism that prevailed in the equity markets similarly infected the debt markets, and investors purchased deals that in most credit cycles would never have been possible. Although they would probably not want to admit it, such investors may have based much of their lending decisions on the assumption that since the market had placed a large value on the borrower's equity, there must be substantial asset coverage. Among other reasons, that is also why significant opportunities in distressed debt continue to be present.

> ### This Chapter's Chess Moves
> 12. Pxe5, Pxe5
> 13. Be3, Pb6
> 14. 0-0, 0-0

7

CAPITAL STRUCTURES AND THE ALLOCATION AND MANAGEMENT OF CREDIT RISK

In Chapter 6, the concept of credit risk was defined and attributed to three sources of risk: leverage, priority, and time. From the notion of relative leverage, the concept of credit capacity was developed to provide a quantitative foundation for the perhaps intuitively obvious propositions that (1) as debt increased, credit risk increased and (2) there is only so much debt that any firm can prudently assume. In this chapter, the other sources of credit risk — priority and time — are discussed within the context of how capital structures allocate and manage credit risk.

Every investment, with the theoretical exception of U.S. Treasury bills (and in an era of escalating deficits, sometimes one may be skeptical of even these), involves credit risk. In the most basic sense, if a firm's capital structure has both debt and equity components, it is because of the general proposition that investors with different risk preferences seek investments with appropriate risk/return characteristics. However, the distinctions are finer than simply debt or equity. Perhaps the more appropriate way to consider a capital structure is as a risk continuum. Figure 7-1 depicts such a view.

On the right, a hierarchy of different capital structure instruments is given that, from top to bottom, suggests a least-to-most-"risky" order. Although each instrument is aligned with a leverage metric, there should be no inference that a particular metric is appropriate to a particular instrument. A precise descrip-

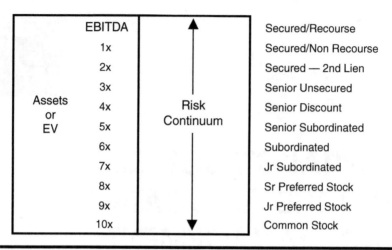

Assets or EV	EBITDA	Risk Continuum	Secured/Recourse
	1x		Secured/Non Recourse
	2x		Secured — 2nd Lien
	3x		Senior Unsecured
	4x		Senior Discount
	5x		Senior Subordinated
	6x		Subordinated
	7x		Jr Subordinated
	8x		Sr Preferred Stock
	9x		Jr Preferred Stock
	10x		Common Stock

Figure 7-1.   Capital Structure Continuum

tion of each of these instruments will not be attempted because the title of a security tells one very little about its true economic value;[1] everything is situation specific. As will be discussed below, a senior unsecured bond with a negative pledge clause may be as "safe" as a secured bond. A subordinated note at an operating subsidiary may have effectively higher priority than a senior secured note at a holding company. However, the depiction of the continuum is valuable in visualizing risk as a function of leverage and priority, and how capital structures "allocate" risk. A tenet of modern portfolio theory is that in an efficient market, as the risk of any particular security increases, the expected return must correspondingly increase or investors will simply choose an alternative investment with more attractive risk/reward attributes.[2] Thus one would generally expect that in complex capital structures with multiple classes of securities, prices would adjust to provide investors with higher returns commensurate with perceived increased risk. However, as has been argued above, the distressed securities market may not always be efficient; therefore, the task of distressed debt analysis is to identify situations where securities may be misvalued, allowing astute investors to realize attractive risk-adjusted returns.

The basic technique of credit risk allocation is related to one of the three identified sources of credit risk — priority. Each of the different instruments listed in Figure 7-1 arguably could have a different priority, but as alluded to above, the mere title is relatively meaningless. The key is the specific terms of the documents creating the obligation relative to other obligations in the capital structure. Another important aspect of such documents is what limitations, if any, they place on management in changing the credit characteristics of the firm after the loan is made. A lender/investor might feel very comfortable making an investment in a firm that owned casinos, but, if a month after the loan is made, management sells all the casinos and reinvests the proceeds to start an airline, the investor might feel deceived. The investor's only protection against such after-the-fact changes (absent faith in the character of management, which unfortunately is generally not very high as of this writing) is contractual restrictions, called covenants, contained in the loan document, whether it be a bank credit facility or bond indenture.[3]

The way in which a capital structure allocates and manages credit risk is of critical importance to the distressed investor because these mechanisms determine claim status, negotiating leverage, and recoveries. The reader has been spared references to the chess analogy made in the introduction, but at this point enough background has been developed to help tie various elements together. As is hopefully clear by now, distressed investing involves a strategic thought process similar to chess, but in many ways much more complicated. The game of distressed restructurings has essentially two phases — prebankruptcy and postbankruptcy — although the latter phase does not necessarily have to be played. There are many players, not all of whom have the same goals. In the prebankruptcy phase, the contest is generally between the company and the creditors/investors. The investors are generally passive players making moves based primarily on market prices. The company's power during the prebankruptcy phase is largely determined by lending covenants. These elements, in a very real sense, define the "moves" the company can make. This also means that, unlike chess, the rules in every game are somewhat different because no two capital structures are the same. If the game advances to the bankruptcy phase, which is generally the company's choice (although bankruptcy can also be forced if the investors can move the "default piece"), then the contest involves much more internecine conflict among the creditors, with the bankruptcy laws governing what the creditors can do to the company and each other.

USING CORPORATE AND CAPITAL STRUCTURES TO ALLOCATE CREDIT RISK

As mentioned, the primary method by which credit risk is allocated within a capital structure is through the use of prioritization mechanisms. Priority, within the credit context, basically indicates or controls the order of repayment. As discussed in Chapter 4, in a bankruptcy these priorities control the application of the all-important absolute priority rule, which is applied before a plan of reorganization can be confirmed. There are four primary techniques for distinguishing priority: grants of collateral, term structure, contractual provisions, and corporate structure.

Grants of Collateral

In the previous discussion on leverage, collateral as a source of credit support was reviewed. In corporate lending, collateral rights are generally granted through a separate *security agreement* that will be referenced in and made a part of the primary lending agreement. The primary purpose of the security agreement is for the borrower to grant a security interest, within the meaning of the Uniform Commercial Code,[4] in collateral for the benefit of the lender. The lender must still, in many cases, take additional steps to "perfect" its security interest in order to ensure its effectiveness. As will be discussed in Chapter 12, failure of the lender to precisely comply with the complex rules associated with "perfection" will often give unsecured lenders important negotiating leverage in the workout process.

The reason that collateral is especially useful as an identifiable source of credit support is based on the notion of priority. The secured lender is first in line to collect the proceeds of the collateral, regardless of what other claims are against the debtor. Without a valid security interest to give priority, a lender would just have a claim against the estate and would have to share the value of any assets with all the other claims of similar seniority. Thus, when a lender has a broad lien on all of the debtor's assets, the lender has pretty much assured itself that no other claim will be honored before the secured lender is fully repaid.

Contractual Provisions

Perhaps the most straightforward way to assign priority is via contractual provisions such as subordination, a legal provision contained in the indenture or loan document of the instrument in question. It is important to note that legal subordination can only occur through an express provision in the bond being subordinated. A typical provision might be: "The Notes are subordinate in right of payment to all Senior Debt." It is not possible for one bond to attempt to assert its seniority over other claims. For example, consider the following hypothetical provision:

> These Super-Duper Senior Notes shall have first priority on all distributions, including those in bankruptcy, and no other claim of the Issuer, including plain old Senior Notes, shall receive any recovery until these Super-Duper Senior Notes are paid in full.

Such a provision would not be effective, by itself, to give the super-duper senior notes any priority over any other instrument. Essentially, the law assumes that all liabilities of a firm are equal unless the holders of those liabilities explicitly agree to reduce the priority, or subordinate their claim.

In reviewing subordination provisions, it is important to analyze carefully to what specific claims the obligation in question has agreed to become subordinate. Notice that our example of the subordination provision read "subordinate in right of payment to all Senior Debt." By capitalizing senior debt, the implication is that this is a specifically defined term in the note's indenture. That definition could make the scope fairly broad: "Senior Debt shall mean all obligations of the Company not expressly subordinate to Senior Debt." This would be fairly atypical. Usually the definition will be narrower: "Senior Debt shall mean the Bank Loan and the 10% Senior Notes and any renewal or extension thereof." A key issue to consider is whether the obligation in question is subordinate to nondebt claims, generally called *trade claims* of the issuer. Normally, the subordinate note investor will insist on a fairly narrow provision that will limit subordination only to other debt, but the investor should always review the language carefully rather than make an assumption.

When a capital structure contains liabilities that are subordinated to some, but not all, claims (as would typically be the case in narrowly drafted subordination provisions), the mechanics of calculating recoveries become more difficult. This is because the subordinated obligation will be counted as a claim, but any recovery that it is entitled to will be payable to the benefited claim. Figure 7-2 provides an example. Assume, to keep things simple, that Dead Co. is liquidating. It has only $75 in assets versus $200 in unsecured claims. The sub note claim is subordinated to the Bank Debt but not to the trade claims.

Ignoring the subordination issue for a moment, the assets represent 37.5% (75/200) of claims. However, since the sub notes are subordinated to the bank

Dead Co.	
	$50 Bank Debt
	$50 Trade Claims
$75	$100 Sub Notes
	Equity

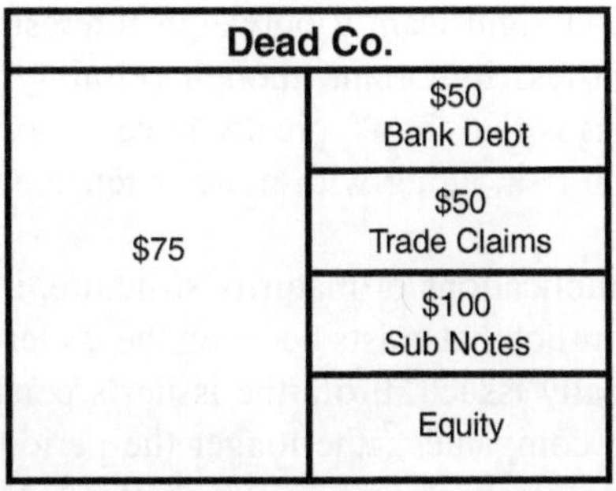

Figure 7-2. Dead Co. Capital Structure

Table 7-1.   Effect of Subrogation on Recoveries

Assets		Pro Rata Recovery	Effect of Subrogation	Adjusted Recovery	Recovery %
Bank Debt	50.00	18.75	31.25	50.00	100.0%
Trade Claims	50.00	18.75	0	18.75	37.5%
Sub Notes	100.00	37.50	−31.25	6.25	6.3%
Total Claims	200.00	75.00		75.00	

debt, anything they are entitled to will go to the bank debt until the bank debt is paid in full. Table 7-1 illustrates the adjusted recoveries. Note that from the perspective that all claims are generally equal, the trade claim recovery is neither harmed nor benefited by the existence of subordination. The bank debt, however, generally would have been entitled to a recovery of only $18.75 (37.5% × 50) on its claim, but because of subrogation is paid in full. After the sub notes cover the deficiency in the bank debt, they recover a small amount. Had the sub notes been subordinated to both the bank debt and trade claims, then each of those claims would have benefited from subrogation and had a total recovery of 75% (75/[50 + 50]).

Maturity Structure

Maturity structure is generally a more important consideration when analyzing the investment characteristics of bonds than bank loans. When analyzing investment-grade bonds, which typically have fixed coupon rates, time to maturity is a paramount consideration because the longer the term of the bond, the greater the volatility of price movement to changes in interest rates. If one holds a 10-year bond and long-term interest rates decline, the bond will appreciate in value significantly more than a 2-year bond. This is technically known as the concept of duration.[5] However, when dealing with below-investment-grade bonds, credit risk considerations[6] can significantly outweigh interest rate risks. The reason maturity structure is a less important, though certainly not irrelevant, consideration with bank loans is that they typically have floating interest rates, which minimizes the duration risk, along with more extensive covenant protection to manage credit risk.

In analyzing the implications of maturity structure, it is important to understand the tension or conflict that exists between the issuer and the bond investors when the bond is initially issued. From the issuer's perspective, particularly in the case of high-yield companies,[7] the longer the period before funds must be raised to pay off a maturing obligation, the better.[8] Although the longer the maturity the higher the interest rate,[9] most chief financial officers of below-investment-grade companies would be happy to pay the higher rate for the increased stability of the funding source. Conversely, since uncertainty increases with time, bond buyers typically want a shorter maturity to reduce the length of time they are exposed to adverse credit developments. To go back to our extreme example, a 1-day loan to a AAA-rated company is hardly risky at all, although a 50-year loan to the same entity can have considerable risk.[10]

This tension, when combined with the principle of priority mentioned above, often creates financing challenges for companies with complex capital structures. As a general rule, senior lenders will not want relatively junior loans or bonds to mature or otherwise be repaid prior to the repayment of the senior loan. This is because the senior creditor never wants an erosion of credit support. Consider Figure 7-2 again, but this time it will be assumed that Dead Co. is still operating and the sub debt consists of two $50 bonds, one which is payable this year and the other in five years. The bank debt is not due for two years. At the end of the year, the borrower pays out $50 to the maturing sub debt, reducing its assets to $25. Four months later, it encounters a liquidity crisis and files for bankruptcy. Because the payment to the sub debt significantly eroded the bank debt's credit support, the bank will now recover significantly less.[11]

In fact, the "priority" issue raised above can be an issue even with pari passu obligations. For example, in the scenario just discussed, the same credit issue would have been present if the obligation maturing in one year had been a senior note instead of a subordinated note. The point is that the early-maturing note recovered its principal first and therefore had a significant advantage relative to the obligations maturing at a later date.[12]

However, occasionally, capital structure anomalies arise which can present opportunities for the alert distressed debt investor. Consider the following hypothetical situation. A start-up company has $100 in cash but is expected to have EBITDA-CAPX in the range of negative $20–$25 per year for the next two years until it reaches profitable operating scale. Its primary liability is a $75 senior bond that is payable in seven years. But it also has a subordinated loan of $5 (presumably from an early round of financing) coming due in one year. On these facts alone, the company appears to be heading for distress unless cash flow turns around after the two-year horizon. Depending on the market's optimism of a turnaround, the senior bond could trade at a significant discount. However, the $5 subordinated loan probably has a fairly high probability of repayment since the company is expected to have at least $75 in cash left when the loan matures in one year.[13] Interestingly, rating agencies tend to disregard term structure. Thus, in this example, the junior debt (if rated) would probably carry a lower credit rating than the senior bond even though the probability of its repayment is higher (of course, were the firm to go bankrupt prior to the junior loan's repayment, the junior debt's recoveries would be adversely affected if it were subordinated to the senior bond).

Corporate Structure

Another technique for distinguishing priorities among instruments is their placement in multitier corporate structures. Up to this point, the examples have been fairly simple entities where the implicit assumption is that all firm activities occur within a single corporate shell. In fact, most firms conduct their operations through multientity structures in which a nonoperating holding corporation owns, directly or indirectly, a variety of nonoperating and operating subsidiary corporations. There are many reasons for dividing up operations this way, including limiting liability, taxes, financial reporting, organizational accountability, and so on. Additionally, it is used to create or reinforce capital structure priority differences. Figure 7-3 provides a simple illustration of a firm with a two-tier subsidiary structure.

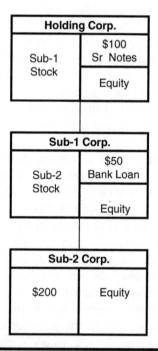

Figure 7-3. Multiple-Subsidiary Corporate Structure

Consolidated	
$200	$50 Bank Loan
	$100 Sr Notes
	$50 Equity

Figure 7-4. Consolidated View of Multiple-Subsidiary Structure

This structure assumes that the only assets of value are located in, or are the legal property of, Sub-2 Corp., which can be thought of as the primary operating subsidiary. Holding Corp. holds only Sub-1 Corp. stock as an asset and has issued $100 in senior notes. Holding Corp.'s equity is what the shareholders of this conglomerate ultimately hold. Sub-1 Corp. holds only Sub-2 Corp. stock as an asset and has a $50 bank loan. It is presumed that Holding Corp. contributed the $100 it received from the senior notes to Sub-1 which then contributed that cash plus the proceeds of the $50 bank loan to Sub-2 as equity. Perhaps the "motive" for this structure was that it was important for Sub-2 Corp. to be able to present itself to other parties as debt free.

On a consolidated basis, this conglomerate would appear as shown in Figure 7-4. Had there been just a single corporation and the bank loan demanded, as a condition of funding, that it be entitled to the first-priority recovery, it would be necessary (setting aside the issue of collateral) for the senior notes' indenture to contain express subordination language in favor of the bank. But if the senior notes were already outstanding when the bank loan was needed, adding the subordination language would, as a practical matter, be very difficult.[14]

By layering the financing into multiple subsidiaries, technically the bank loan does not need the priority via explicit subordination language in the Holding Corp. senior notes because they are "structurally" subordinated to all claims of any lower tier subsidiary. This occurs as the result of standard bankruptcy rules of liquidation. Consider what would happen if all the entities file for chapter 7 bankruptcy liquidation (ignoring, for simplicity, the potential issue of substantive consolidation discussed in Chapter 11). Sub-2 Corp. would liquidate. It has no liabilities, so its $200 in assets would belong to its sole shareholder, Sub-1 Corp. In Sub-1 Corp.'s liquidation, the bank loan would be paid out of the liquidation proceeds of Sub-2 Corp., and anything remaining (i.e., $150) would belong to Sub-2's sole shareholder, Holding Corp. In Holding Corp.'s liquidation, the senior notes would be paid their $100 claim and the remainder ($50) would be distributed to Holding Corp.'s equity holders. By operation of law, value flows up in accordance with stock ownership. If, for some reason, $190 in assets had been at Holding Corp. and only $10 at Sub-2, the bank loan could suffer a loss of $40.[15]

Not surprisingly, whenever possible, sophisticated lenders seldom allow the operation of the principles of law to control the outcome of events. They prefer that all foreseeable scenarios be governed by contractual provisions that either reinforce or, depending on the circumstance, "override" the normally applicable legal rules.[16] Subordination is a common "override" provision that supplants the general rule that all liabilities are equal or pari passu. Grants of security interests can similarly be viewed as provisions to override the general rule that property in an estate is shared pro rata among creditors.

Another common "override" provision that has only been mentioned in passing is the *guaranty*. A guaranty is a contractual promise to pay the obligation of another. It essentially has the legal effect, depending on the terms, of making the guaranteeing party a co-obligor. Thus, in the example in Figure 7-3, as a practical matter, the bank would probably be unwilling to make the loan to an "empty" intermediate holding company, Sub-1 Corp., without receiving a contractual repayment guaranty from, at the very least, Sub-2 (the recipient of the loan proceeds). The bank is likely also to request a guaranty from Holding Corp., but whether this would be given would depend on a variety of factors. If the bank had guaranties from both Sub-2 and Holding Corp., then it would effectively be protected even in the scenario where $190 was at Holding Corp. However, as a fine point, this would not be protected as a result of having a priority claim relative to the senior notes. As a general rule, the guaranty by Holding Corp. of the debt of Sub-1 would technically be a pari passu obligation to the senior notes, unless they expressly were subordinated to such a guaranty. Again, subordination is only effective when it is explicitly a term of the instrument being "disadvantaged." No guaranty by Holding Corp. can unilaterally change the priority status of the senior notes.

The opposite of a guaranty is a "nonrecourse" provision. A nonrecourse provision (typically only found in secured loans) states that in the event of a default on the loan, the lender has no right to attempt to recover from certain persons. Such loans are more common with individuals and small businesses as opposed to large corporations. The most common context for a nonrecourse loan is a mortgage on income-producing real estate. The no-recourse loan terms state that in the event of a default, the lender can foreclose on the property, but has no right to pursue the owner for any deficiency. It is an explicit "nonguaranty" of an obligation.

Within the corporate context, a common situation in which recourse must be considered is asset-backed, off-balance-sheet financings. Prior to recent changes in accounting requirements,[17] companies would seek borrowing structures that would technically not have to be included on the balance sheet of the entity (i.e., off-balance-sheet) effectively receiving the benefit (i.e., cash) of the loan. A typical context involves the financing of accounts receivable or loan portfolios. For example, CreditCard Co. is in the business of making short-term loans to consumers. CreditCard Co. may be able to borrow funds to finance these loans, but as it grows, its "on-balance-sheet," debt will become very high, potentially causing deterioration of its credit rating. To avoid financing on-balance-sheet, CreditCard Co. will "sell" the receivables to Special Purpose Finance Sub Co. (SPFS). SPFS will then borrow money to finance the "purchase" of the receivables with the explicit understanding that the loan is non-recourse to CreditCard Co. This structure might appear to isolate CreditCard Co. from SPF's credit risk, except that SPFS's lender will typically require CreditCard Co., even if the loan is nonrecourse, to provide "support" in various ways, such as ensuring that all the loans sold to SPFS are good collateral. It is easy to see how fuzzy the line can get to say that the loan is "nonrecourse" to CreditCard Co. but simultaneously commit CreditCard Co. to contribute or substitute loans (which, of course, costs CreditCard Co. money) to SPFS if necessary. Among other reasons, this is why it is now more difficult under GAAP to achieve off-balance treatment of such structures.

HOW CAPITAL STRUCTURES MANAGE CREDIT RISK

The prior discussion reviewed how capital structures allocate credit risk, primarily through the technique of credit layering. However, as mentioned earlier, even if one has senior secured standing, one could still be exposed to substantial credit risk if borrowers had unfettered power to make changes that either directly or indirectly materially change the capital structure. Consider the position of the bank loan to Sub-1 Corp. in Figure 7-3, but strengthen the bank's credit position by making the "real-world" assumption that it would insist on a senior guaranty from Sub-2 Corp. Its $50 claim looks well protected (4x coverage) by Sub-2's $200 in assets. But what if Holding Corp. decides to make a $2000 acquisition using $2000 in newly borrowed funds which it causes Sub-2 to guaranty? Subsequently, it is determined that the acquired entity is worthless. Now what is the position of the bank loan? Because of Sub-2's two guaranties, its $200 in assets now back $2200 in claims, implying a recovery of approximately 9%. This illustrates the basic need for the ongoing management of credit risk after a loan has been made.

The basic tools of credit risk management are restrictive contract provisions, generally called *covenants*. Covenants are detailed contractual provisions contained in lending documents or bond indentures. Covenants are intensely negotiated and often the most difficult aspect of the lending document upon which to agree. Lenders want as much protection as possible. From the lender's perspective, it is looking at the borrower at a point in time and making a credit decision based on the borrower's current circumstances and the management's stated plans for the future. Experienced executives know the right things to say to make lenders comfortable. Lenders know that executives know this. Lenders worry that once the borrower has the money, it will do something other than what has been represented or planned. Borrowers, on the other hand, want as much freedom as possible to adapt their business to changing circumstances.

As a general rule, the weaker the credit profile of the borrower, the more extensive the covenants. Indeed, in most bond indentures of investment-grade firms, particularly those rated single A or better, there will generally be no "restrictive" type of covenants.[18] Lenders would, of course, prefer the protection of covenants when lending to an investment-grade company; however, in a free and competitive market, the borrower is able to shop for the best deal available, and covenants, just like prices, are negotiable. Thus, if one lender offers a loan but requests restrictive covenants, while another lender offers a similarly priced loan with few or no covenants, borrowers will naturally choose the one that offers more flexibility. This is also true for high-yield borrowers, and in strong credit cycles, such as the valuation bubble period of the late 1990s, lenders and underwriters often competed via relaxed covenants[19] as a way to offer more attractive deals without having to reduce prices.

However, as credit risk is perceived to increase, borrowing options usually decline, and few lenders are willing to extend credit without certain basic protections. At the extreme, when there is significant credit risk and the borrower is perceived to have few options, lenders will use their leverage to impose extremely comprehensive covenants. An example of a fairly comprehensive set of covenants for a below-investment-grade company is available for download at www.jrosspub.com.

It should not be surprising that the need or inspiration for most covenants can, either directly or indirectly, be traced to the three sources of credit risk — leverage, priority, and time — discussed previously. Next, how covenants try to manage each of these sources of risk will be discussed. This review will not attempt to analyze different covenant structures exhaustively, but rather will take what is far too often, at least in the view of most nonlawyers,[20] an unnecessarily turgid and impenetrable mass of legalese-laced verbiage and explain why it exists and what it is attempting to accomplish. Hopefully, although there can be no guarantee, this will make deciphering these provisions easier. Chapter 11 further discusses covenants from a due diligence perspective and reviews some nuances of covenants that distressed investors will want to factor into their investment analysis.

Leverage

Leverage is concerned with the amount of debt relative to the available credit support. When this was first discussed in Chapter 6, it was hypothesized that a $100 loan to a firm with $50 in earnings before interest, taxes, depreciation, and amortization (EBITDA) was reasonably safe because the firm was probably worth at least $150 (3x EBITDA) and thus enterprise value covered the loan by at least 1.5x.

This implicitly assumed that $50 was the only debt. Lenders need to protect against the risk of the borrower later going out and borrowing additional money and increasing the risk of default. The typical provision to protect against this is called the *leverage covenant,* which is usually structured to limit debt to a specified multiple of EBITDA. The covenant may also condition new borrowings on the maintenance of specified pro forma interest coverage. In complex multitiered capital structures, the leverage test may only address the layer in question. Thus a senior loan may specify that senior debt will not be more than, for example, 2.5x EBITDA, but may be silent on how much total debt is allowed.

Violation of a leverage covenant typically is not an event of default which might give rise to a right of acceleration. The usual "penalty" for violating the provision, which usually occurs because of a decline in operating performance, is to prohibit the issuer from incurring additional debt. Although this may seem rather innocuous, if a firm's operating performance is such that it is experiencing negative cash flow, the inability to borrow to obtain liquidity is effectively a death sentence.

Priority

The basic issue in the area of priority is to limit or prohibit the erosion of credit support before the loan in question is repaid. Relative to the magnitude issue, ensuring priority can be much more complicated and typically involves a variety of covenants or restrictions. Again, putting oneself in the shoes of the lender (which are the shoes the distressed investor wears), one would want restrictions that prevent the borrower from doing anything that tends to increase the risk that the existing assets of the firm are not available to repay the current loan. There are two basic priority-related covenants: restricted payment provisions and negative pledge clauses.

Restricted Payments

Lenders naturally want all the assets of the borrower to stay in the firm as available credit support. This is the purpose of the restricted payment test. It is designed to limit the firm from distributing its assets to third parties to the detriment of the creditor. The worst-case scenario for the lender is to lend money only to have the borrowing company give a multimillion-dollar dividend to shareholders (coincidently, also the senior managers) who subsequently take up residence in a country that has no extradition treaty with the United States.

Of course, borrowers want the maximum degree of flexibility. If a lending agreement restricted all third-party distributions (which would include wages to employees, payments to suppliers, and so on), the firm would not be able to function. Also, borrowers will argue that assets added after the loan is made that increase the credit support should be treated differently than the assets that were part of the original credit support. For example, after a loan is made, assume that the borrower uses its stock to acquire another company that has, among other assets, large cash reserves. Should the lender be entitled to restrict this newly acquired cash?

These can be complicated issues. Restricted payment provisions are negotiated and structured to balance the needs of the borrower with the risk to the lender. As a practical matter, restricted payment provisions are usually structured to (a) identify those parties to whom distributions, in the lender's view, will be likely to erode credit support (since the distressed investor shares this perspective, these parties will be pejoratively characterized as "leeches") as opposed to those parties that further the legitimate value and credit-support-enhancing functions of the business (like employees, suppliers, etc.) and (b) define what assets or activities of the borrower should be restricted.

Who or what are leeches? The size and character of leeches evolve not through the process of Darwinian survival, but rather the imagination of lawyers. From the perspective of the lender, a leech is any party to which the borrower gives money or other assets, and as a result, the lender's credit support, if an immediate liquidation is performed, is weakened. As the earlier, perhaps extreme, multimillion-dollar dividend example illustrated, a major concern is any payment to shareholders and junior creditors as well as extraordinary payments to managers (although if the shareholders and managers deal at arms length, the shareholders' interest will normally act as a check against this risk). Lawyers can be very clever in the way such payments are "disguised" so that the provisions must restrict not only straightforward transfers such as dividends but also securities repurchases (perhaps the leech issued himself stock) and loans to affiliated companies (perhaps the leech set up a sham company). The list is much longer, but the reader should now understand the issue.

An additional concern arises in the context of multisubsidiary corporate structures. Lending documents usually will require all or as many subsidiaries as possible to become parties to the lending agreement (and thus become joint and several obligors) or at least provide guaranties of the loan. However, often, the borrower will object, arguing that to make a particular subsidiary an obligor to the loan would have adverse tax consequences[21] or prevent the subsidiary from being able to develop credit relationships it needs to conduct its specific mission. A good example would be a multinational corporation with foreign subsidiaries involved in the manufacture and/or distribution of its products. Often a foreign government will offer incentives to entice a firm to locate in its country to create jobs for local citizens. These incentives may be in the form of favorable tax packages or financing facilities.[22] However, the foreign lender would not want the subsidiary to be legally burdened by the entire amount of the parent's obligations (which it could be if, for example, it issued a general guaranty).

To overcome this conflict, such a subsidiary will be "carved out" of the parent's loan agreement. This is typically accomplished by creating classes of subsidiaries described as "restricted" or "unrestricted." Unrestricted subsidiaries are generally not bound by the terms of the loan agreement in question and, analytically, are not part of the credit support for the loan. They are, therefore, potential leeches. Restricted subsidiaries, in contrast, are bound by the loan agreement. Thus, from the perspective of the parent's loan agreement, unrestricted subsidiaries can borrow money, lend money, make dividends, and do anything they want — they are unrestricted. However, the loan agreement will treat these unrestricted subsidiaries as essentially unaffiliated third parties, thus preventing the parent from activities such as lending or advancing money to them, providing guaranties on their behalf, and so on. Figure 7-5 provides a visual depiction of the common areas of concern in restricted payment provisions.

A final general area of concern deals with payments to junior creditors. From the senior lender's perspective, junior creditors are still leeches, but their claim on funds is "legitimate" and the consequences of preventing their timely payment is a default, which seldom makes anyone better off.

The approach to dealing with payments to junior creditors varies significantly between secured bank loans and senior unsecured bonds. A secured bank loan will often have fairly restrictive performance covenants (discussed below) that are breached when the borrower begins to experience financial distress. This usually gives the bank the right to prevent interest payments due on unsecured (even senior unsecured) debt, even when the borrower has the cash to make the payment. This is referred to as *blocking*.

Blocking an interest payment, of course, is a payment default that, if not cured within the typical 30-day "grace period,"[23] will give the bondholders the right to accelerate. Acceleration of the principal repayment obligation, in turn, is likely to force the borrower to file for chapter 11 protection. Thus, if the bank

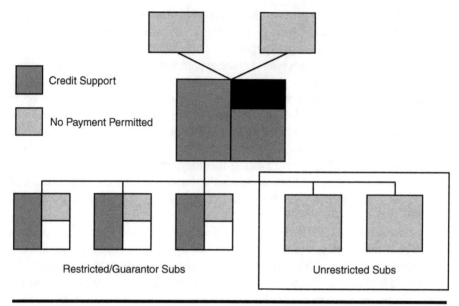

Figure 7-5.   Diagram of Areas of Concern in Restricted Payment Provisions

loan holder blocks an interest payment, it is essentially signaling that it is perfectly willing to force a bankruptcy, so the borrower and unsecured creditors need to act quickly (assuming they want to avoid an immediate bankruptcy) to figure out a way to appease the banks.

If the bank loan is well secured, trading at a price above 90, and still controlled by banks or collateralized debt obligation (CDO) trusts, then an accommodation is relatively more likely since a bankruptcy has disadvantages to the bank loan holders. For the banks, the disadvantage is a potential require-ment to characterize the loan as a nonperforming asset. For CDOs, the disad-vantage is that the loan usually will need to be carried at a discounted value (i.e., they effectively recognize a loss, regardless of the expected recovery of the loan). However, if the loan has been bought at a discount in the secondary market by an aggressive distressed debt investor, then the borrower/unsecured creditors have less leverage because the distressed investor may be perfectly willing to go through the chapter 11 process on the assumption that he or she will get a 100% recovery (because of the apparent adequacy of collateral) in a reasonable time frame.

If instead of a bank loan the context is a bond, then the restricted payment provision typically will allow all interest payments to junior debt, but there will often be restrictions to the repayment of principal. Perhaps the more common approach[24] is to prohibit any principal payments prior to maturity (unless from the "basket" discussed shortly) and then require that at maturity the principal be financed with the proceeds from offerings of new junior debt or equity securities. This completely protects against erosion of credit support, but also exposes the borrower to significant capital markets risk if the markets are relatively hostile at the time of maturity. It also prevents the borrower from making early redemptions of the junior debt. If the junior debt is trading at a significant discount, this eliminates an important strategy the borrower might have to reduce its leverage. More liberal restricted payment provisions will be structured to allow the borrower flexibility to use any funds available to manage the repayment of principal at maturity and, in some cases, specify an amount of money that can be used for early redemptions/discount repurchases. This definitely creates a risk of erosion, but reduces the risk of a default for non-payment.

The distressed debt investor has no absolute preference about the structure of the restricted payment provision because his or her outlook will depend on the security being considered for investment. For example, if the distressed investor has taken a position in the junior debt, he or she might benefit from a "liberal" provision that allows repurchases by the firm (which could cause price appreciation of the junior bonds held by the investor) at the expense of senior holders. The key, therefore, is to do a thorough analysis and frame an investment strategy properly. For example, Chapter 11 reviews a situation involving Aames Financial where a "loophole" in the restricted payment test in the senior notes was exploited and the subordinated notes (as well as the equity) significantly benefited.

However as was noted above, even with respect to leeches, borrowers have a compelling argument that not all cash should be restricted forever. If this were true, then dividends in the ordinary course of business would never be permitted for large classes of companies, and junior securities, as noted above, would frequently be defaulted on and therefore impossible to issue. The traditional approach to determine what assets are appropriate to restrict essentially involves taking a snapshot of the credit support at the time the loan is made. To the extent that the borrower has enhanced the amount of credit support, some or all of the excess is generally allowed to be used to make distributions that would otherwise be restricted. The implicit theory here is that the lender is no worse off.

The general mechanism for tracking what amounts are available for restricted payments is a lengthy formula that describes additions to and reductions from what is called the *basket*. A typical basket formula, stripped of the legalese, would be constructed as follows:

Following the end of the fiscal quarter in which the loan is made, restricted payments may only be made in the following aggregate amount:

$5 million (general carve-out)

Plus:
50% of all net income earned
100% of proceeds from the sale of common or preferred stock
100% of the proceeds from the issuance of any junior debt securities

Less:
100% of all net losses
100% of all amounts distributed as dividends
100% of all amounts used to repurchase common or preferred stock of the company
100% of all amounts contributed or loaned to (or amounts guaranteed on behalf of) unrestricted subsidiaries
100% of all amounts defined as restricted payments not otherwise covered above

A complete, "unsimplified" version of a restricted payment test is contained in the sample covenants available for review in the previously referenced download at www.jrosspub.com.

Negative Pledge Clauses

A second manner in which a senior lender's priority can be compromised, particularly if unsecured, is by giving other creditors liens or security interests in certain assets. As discussed above, the major advantage of having a collateral pledge is that it gives the secured borrower first priority over any proceeds from the sale or liquidation of the pledged asset. That is great for the secured lender, but a potentially tremendous disadvantage to an unsecured lender. Thus, when a lender provides unsecured credit to a firm that has not previously given collateral pledges (other than perhaps mortgage loans on owned real estate or liens associate with lease financings), it essentially does so on the assumption that, in addition to the firm's cash flow, its existing assets are generally available to all unsecured creditors as credit support.

But imagine that sometime later the borrower's credit has deteriorated and new financing is only available on a secured basis. If the borrower, for example, enters into a new working capital line of credit secured by all inventories and accounts receivable, the credit support of the previous unsecured creditors will be substantially compromised. To protect against this scenario, unsecured lenders will request a negative pledge provision, which essentially states that if the borrower gives a security interest in any of its assets to any other lender, it must include the existing unsecured debt as beneficiaries of that pledge.

Time

The basic issue posed by time is uncertainty; specifically, the risk that credit support will deteriorate due to unforeseeable events that occur in the future. A lender may analyze a firm at the time of the loan and consider the credit support to be adequate, but if the financing in question is a 10-year bond, the circumstances of the borrower could materially change over time. Of course, a borrower will understandably be reluctant to effectively issue guarantees that "nothing bad" will happen in the future because it makes planning difficult and is something that in many cases (for example a natural disaster, change in regulatory climate, or technological development) management cannot control. Over time, however, four provisions (strictly speaking, only one of them can be considered a covenant) have become increasingly common techniques used by lenders to manage future risk.

Performance Covenants

Often, a bank loan will be made where cash flow is the primary credit support on the premise that management has a workable plan to significantly improve operations. From the lender's perspective, the loan would probably not be made if recent operating trends were representative of future cash-flow-generating potential. In such cases, lenders — and this is almost exclusively limited to bank lending situations[25] — may require affirmative performance milestones to be achieved. An example of such a milestone might be: "EBITDA for the third fiscal quarter will exceed $X." This is a very different type of provision than the restrictive covenants previously discussed. With a restrictive covenant, if the borrower's financial situation declines, the covenant may prevent it from taking some specific action (such as borrowing more money or making a dividend payment), but the deterioration in performance is not, by itself, generally grounds for a default. However, where performance covenants are included, failure to comply with the requirement is a default.

The basic purpose of these covenants is to control the lender's risk and to give it more say in the management of the business when things are not proceeding as planned. Essentially, the lender is giving management a chance to execute its business plan. If management does, then the lender is happy (because improved operations have presumably reduced credit risk) to passively wait to be repaid. But if management does not execute, then the lender will have the right to revisit the plan and renegotiate the deal. Lenders seldom summarily declare a default and force the borrower into bankruptcy, but they do want leverage over management to enforce changes, and they will certainly use the default as an opportunity to extract more fees and/or increase pricing.

Put Rights

A second method to limit the risk of uncertainty of long-term financings is to provide for interim milestones when lenders can decide whether or not they want to remain in the deal. If they do not, the borrower must repay the loan. These are basically just put options[26] given to the lender that, one could argue, obviate the purpose of negotiating a long-term loan. Nonetheless, these securities are fairly commonplace. One very common structure is a zero coupon accretion note with a stock convertibility option.[27] The structure provides that on each five-year anniversary, investors will have the right to require the issuer to repay the note at the then accreted value, provided that the issuer has the option of paying in either cash, stock (at the current market price, which can be highly dilutive), or a combination thereof.

Another common structure used on straight (i.e., nonconvertible) bonds involves what is called a remarketing feature.[28] This feature requires a remarketing agent (usually the original underwriter) to remarket (i.e., find a new interest rate at which the bonds will sell at par) and make a tender offer for the bonds at that price. If bondholders tender, the remarketing agent will sell them to new investors. If the marketing agent cannot remarket the bonds, then the issuer must buy back all those that have been tendered.

Forced Call in the Event of a Downgrade

Increasingly, credit facilities and bonds issued with investment-grade ratings (i.e., BBB–/Baa3 or higher) will include provisions specifying that in the event either Standard & Poor's (S&P) or Moody's rates the loan or bond below investment grade, the borrower must offer to repay the obligation. These are similar to put rights discussed above, with the exception that their timing is not precisely known, and they only come into play in "falling angel" situations (because they are generally only in bonds originally rated investment grade). However, the distressed investor should carefully consider the impact of these provisions because they can trigger more significant problems. For example, since the precipitating event, a credit downgrade, suggests the firm's finances are on a deteriorating trend, the firm could also be facing diminished availability on its bank lines, which may also contain downgrade triggers. Such a combination could easily lead to a liquidity crisis. For example, at the height of the California energy crisis in January 2001, PG&E Corporation (the parent holding company) and Pacific Gas & Electric Company (the operating utility) (together PG&E) were downgraded by S&P from A to BBB– due to mounting electricity purchase obligations. That downgrade caused the cancellation of an $850 million undrawn credit facility that backstopped maturing commercial paper. When the commercial paper matured and was not repaid, it triggered cross-default provisions in most of PG&E's outstanding debt obligations. If the rating agencies had reduced the rating to below investment grade (i.e., BB+ or lower), this would have set off other triggers. For that and other reasons, PG&E filed for chapter 11 protection in April 2001.[29] PG&E's descent from investment grade to default in three months is among the fastest falls in corporate history.

Performance-Linked Pricing Provisions

A final method of protecting against the risk that adverse performance in the future could cause the value of loans to decline is through provisions that automatically adjust interest rates in the event of credit deterioration. These provisions are not technically covenants and thus operate differently than the performance covenants cited above. In the case of the violation of a performance covenant, a default occurs. With a repricing provision, there is no default, just an adjustment in the interest rate payable. The following is an example of the structure of a typical repricing provision:

If EBITDA/total interest expense (coverage ratio [CR]) is

Ratio	Pricing Margin (in basis points) over LIBOR
CR > 3.0	250
3.0 > CR > 2.5	300
2.5 > CR > 2.0	400
2.0 > CR > 1.5	500

While such provisions cannot prevent deterioration, the interest rate adjustment provides additional compensation to offset the risk, at least partially, and presumably increases the value of the loan. Such provisions typically will include some minimum performance standard below when a default would occur. In the example above, the default trigger point might be set at a CR <1.5.

SUMMARY

Investing in distressed debt, like all investments, involves appropriately gauging the risk and return potential of any particular investment. Capital structures can be viewed as risk continuums, and the risk of any particular instrument in any particular capital structure must be independently assessed. Securities can have titles such as secured debt or subordinated debt, but by themselves these names convey very little information. As was illustrated in several examples, a subordinated note at an operating company level or with a maturity in the near future may be more valuable than a senior bond elsewhere in the same capital structure. On the other hand, a carefully structured senior secured security can wield enormous power over the borrower and other creditors.

This chapter discussed how, primarily through the process of credit layering, capital structures allocate risk. Such risk allocation serves a valuable purpose during the original capitalization of a firm because it allows the matching of investors with different risk preferences with securities of appropriate risk and return profiles. This same principle also applies when a firm becomes distressed: not all distressed debt investors have the same risk preferences. Some distressed investors will prefer less risky (bearing in mind that everything is relative), more stable returns, while others will always be looking for the home run.

However, the initial allocation of risk in a capital structure may be misleading if the issuer has unfettered power to change its risk profile. Accordingly, a second essential function of the instruments in the capital structure is to "manage" changes in credit risk through the use of contractual provisions such as covenants. The analogy was made that just as the Bankruptcy Code constrains the potential moves of investors in the postpetition phase of the distressed investment game, covenants define the moves of management in the prepetition phase. Investors must have a thorough understanding of the role and operation of the specific covenants in all of the instruments in a firm's capital structure to appropriately assess risk and bargaining leverage.

This chapter concludes the overview portion of the book. First, the size and scope of the distressed investment universe were discussed, and a number of factors that indicate why the market is inefficient and offers above-average return potential were reviewed. Next, the notion of financial distress and the role of workouts in resolving that distress were reviewed from both a conceptual and legal perspective. After that, a more detailed discussion of the principles behind firm valuation and leverage were developed so that distressed investors would have a quantitative framework for analyzing investment opportunities. Finally, this chapter focused on the role of the capital structure in allocating and managing risk because such principles are essential to assessing the risk and return potential of any particular security the distressed investor is analyzing. The next phase of the book examines in more detail how to recognize the basic causes of financial distress and their implications for the firm's reorganization and, hence, the potential for investment return.

> ### This Chapter's Chess Moves
>
> **15. Pa4, Pa5**
>
> **16. Rb1, Bd7**
>
> **17. Rb2, Rb8**

CAUSES OF FINANCIAL DISTRESS AND THE RESTRUCTURING IMPLICATIONS

Thus far, financial distress has been simplistically viewed as the asset box becoming smaller than the debt box (see Figure 3-7). Logically, the asset/liability asymmetry can also arise from ballooning liabilities. Moving from the conceptual to the practical, the reasons behind the asymmetries have significant implications for investment analysis. This chapter considers many of the more common causes of financial distress and how they affect the analysis of the investment. First, however, some general indicators of financial distress are described as tools to help identify which situations merit attention. The concept is to first determine which situations are likely to be distressed and then to diagnose the reason for the distress and how that impacts the investment decision. Organizationally, concepts will be developed and then reinforced and built upon with more detailed discussion and examples.

INDICATORS OF FINANCIAL DISTRESS

There are at least three general methodologies the distressed investor can use as a "screening" tool for identifying the firms that are likely to encounter financial distress: debt ratings, predictive statistical models, and market prices. Each of these will be briefly discussed, but it should be noted at the outset that by themselves these indicators have only limited utility to the distressed investor for two reasons. First, the critical investment issue is not whether a firm is in financial distress, but whether the market value of its securities is appropriate relative to its actual or potential asset value. Identifying whether a firm is in distress represents only the first step in the analysis. Second, these indicators, with the possible exception of the predictive models, are not particularly oriented to helping the investor be the first to identify a potential situation. To a certain extent, ratings and price movements just tend to validate that something adverse has happened. Truly forecasting that a situation is deteriorating usually relies on very specific insights into the firm or industry in question and is beyond the scope of this book.

Debt Ratings

The most prominent and easily accessed indicator of financial distress is a deterioration in the credit ratings issued by the major national credit rating organizations: Moody's, Standard & Poor's (S&P), Duff & Phelps, and Fitch. Many investors, particularly in the investment-grade area, rely almost exclusively on ratings to guide investment and securities valuation. It is fairly common to see the pricing of investment grade bonds delineated almost exclusively by rating category (AAA, AA, A, etc.), with no other indices of credit quality (e.g., leverage ratio, coverage ratio, etc.) provided. Given that, as established in Chapter 2, ratings movements are generally fairly correlated with increasing risk of financial distress, this reliance is not totally misplaced. Furthermore, while securities tend to trade in ratings-related bands, the market certainly does not price all A-rated bonds the same, which suggests that other firm-specific factors are also weighed.

Rating agencies ostensibly should be a relatively better assessor of credit than the general market because they have significantly better information. In the process of obtaining a rating, issuers will typically provide the rating agency with extensive nonpublic information about the issuer's operations, provide the representatives of the agencies with tours of their more significant facilities, and make senior executives available for in-depth questioning. While it is increasingly common for management teams to simply decline to answer an investor's question on the basis that such information is not generally disclosed,[1] rating agencies are usually able to obtain any information they request, and the inability or unwillingness of a company to provide such data is likely to be viewed negatively. Since debt ratings directly impact an issuer's cost of funds, management teams have significant incentives to make as favorable an impression as possible.

At least three things should be noted about the major rating agencies. First, these services have an important, but at times awkward, role in the debt capital markets. Debt instruments are not required to "obtain" credit ratings; indeed many bonds are issued and trade on a nonrated (NR) basis. Issuers request and pay for ratings in an effort to minimize the cost of their debt. The higher the credit rating, the lower the interest rate generally demanded/required by investors. The cost of a corporate rating is about $35,000–$40,000 for a $100 million bond issue, plus an annual fee for maintenance of the rating.[2] The fee is the same regardless of the rating, so there is no particular bias inherent in the rating process. Typically, the ratings of both Moody's and S&P are obtained, particularly for investment-grade firms. It is not uncommon for bonds, particularly bonds issued with especially low ratings (e.g., B or CCC) to only have one rating. Often, the reason only one rating is obtained is because the issuer believes that the rating that was not obtained would have been lower than desired. Thus, for example, if an issuer obtains a B rating from one agency but believes that it will receive a lower CCC rating from the other,[3] it may strategically choose to forgo the latter rating, believing that an explicit lower rating will be more harmful than the ambiguity of an NR. The issuer will often attempt to explain away the lack of a second rating as being an "unnecessary" expense and waste of management's time; however, this seldom allays investor skepticism.

Second, the rating from an agency is essentially its best estimate of the probability of default (meaning a failure to make contractually specified interest and/or principal payments) and says nothing about the relative value of the security at any given trading level.[4] Thus, a firm that has a high probability of not being able to meet its financial commitments (which, of course, could lead to a bankruptcy filing) would have all of its debt downgraded to very low levels even though some of it may be well secured with a very high probability of recovering all principal and any pre- and even postpetition interest. Consequently, ratings have a fairly limited role in identifying an investment opportunity for a distressed investor.

Finally, rating agencies are frequently viewed by investors as being slow in adjusting ratings to changes in a firm's financial or economic circumstances.[5] Sometimes this is understandable, as when an unforeseeable event occurs; take, for example, the terrorism of 9/11 and its impact on the airline, travel, and insurance industries. In such cases, the rating agencies typically issue a "rating under review" notice promptly (usually such statement will indicate whether the review has "positive" or "negative" implications) and then issue a more formal change with supporting rationale sometime thereafter. Other times, the ratings simply appear to lag developments. A notable example occurred during the California energy crisis in the 2000–2001 period. California's two major utilities, Pacific Gas & Electric and Southern California Edison, were experiencing staggering operating deficits, estimated as high as $12 billion, as the price of wholesale electricity surged, but the utilities were unable to adjust regulated retail prices to consumers.[6] Industry executives clearly warned that unless the California legislature acted in support of the utilities, defaults were highly likely.[7] Despite the fairly obvious deterioration in economic circumstances, both S&P and Moody's maintained both utilities at investment-grade ratings until Southern California Edison defaulted on a debt repayment obligation.[8]

Predictive Models

Although there have been a number of statistically derived predictive models,[9] the most well known is a set developed by Professor Edward Altman,[10] arguably the leading academic researcher in the field of bankruptcy and distressed debt. Professor Altman first developed a multivariate predictive model in 1968 that he called the *Z-score model*.[11] The purpose of the model was to use various accounting ratios and market-derived price data to attempt to predict future bankruptcy. His original model, which was based on data from 1946 to 1965, was then updated in 1993 to reflect a more complete data set and the implications of the Bankruptcy Act of 1978. The current formulation of the Z-score model, which has since been replaced with an expanded but proprietary Zeta Model, is as follows:

$$Z = 0.012 \ X_1 + 0.014 \ X_2 + 0.033 \ X_3 + 0.006 \ X_4 + 0.999 \ X_5$$

where X_1 = working capital/total assets, X_2 = retained earnings/total assets, X_3 = earnings before interest and taxes (EBIT)/total assets, X_4 = market value of equity/book value of total liabilities, and X_5 = sales/total assets.

Z-scores of <1.81 have been shown as highly predictive of a bankruptcy as long as two years in advance. Z-scores of >3 are generally indicative of reasonable credit stability.

The model has been widely tested by academics and used by practitioners. The set of variables used has clear and intuitive connection to credit metrics. The working capital/total assets variable tests relative liquidity. Retained earnings/total assets is a measure of a firm's cumulative earnings power and dividend policy and has a tendency to favor firms that have been profitable for an extended period of time. Weighted more than twice as much as these variables, the EBIT/total assets variable takes into account the cash-flow-generating capability of a firm. Somewhat surprisingly, the dominant factor, with a coefficient of 0.999, three times as high as the next closest factor, is sales/total assets.

The importance of this variable, and it should be noted that the Z-score was developed for manufacturing firms and not retailers, is to suggest that if a firm can generate above-average sales per dollar of investment in assets, it has a significant credit advantage. Also of interest was that none of these variables, which were chosen for explanatory value from a set of 22 possible variables, directly measure leverage such as a total debt/earnings before interest, taxes, depreciation, and amortization (EBITDA) or total debt/total assets.

The distressed debt analyst will find it useful to calculate a target's Z-score as a factor to be weighed in making an overall credit assessment. However, it should be noted that as with credit ratings, the purpose of the predictive model is to predict bankruptcies, not investment recoveries. Accordingly, if it is clear that a firm is in financial distress, the model will be of little utility in determining the potential returns of an investment in any particular security at a given price.

Market Prices

A final indicator of financial distress, of course, is market trading prices. There have been numerous studies of how well the price of a firm's stock reflects its future earnings outlook.[12] There have not been as many studies analyzing the ability of changes in debt prices to forecast operating deterioration or financial distress,[13] but this may be attributable to the relative difficulty of obtaining reliable market price data on below-investment-grade bonds. The debt markets, at least anecdotally, appear very cognizant of the risk of distress, although the price adjustments are not necessarily correct. Indeed, during the 2000–2001 period there were many situations where the debt of technology and telecommunications companies began trading at levels suggesting significant risk, while the public equity valuations of these same firms were in the hundreds of millions if not billions of dollars.[14] The later stock market performance of these sectors suggests that the bond prices were often more prescient as to the ultimate outcome.

In summary, the distressed debt investor can benefit significantly from the ability to assess the likelihood that a firm will become financially distressed. If one can properly identify the risk of financial distress in advance of others in the marketplace, investment strategies involving short selling the securities can be profitably effected. At the very least, the investor can avoid making long investments in securities that have a high risk of falling prices. Early identification of potential investment opportunities also gives the distressed investor more time to research the target firm and industry thoroughly so that when a market opportunity arises, he or she can act decisively. In addition to recognizing the possible decline, formulating a winning investment strategy also requires an understanding of the cause of the financial distress and how that impacts short- and long-term investment value.

CAUSES OF FINANCIAL DISTRESS

In addition to identifying the fact that a firm is in or will soon be in financial distress, it is essential to properly identify the cause of the financial distress in order to formulate an appropriate investment strategy.[15] Two examples illustrate the point.

Firm X is a specialty retailer of home-improvement-related products such as tile and carpeting. X is reasonably profitable until major national "category-killer" chains such as Home Depot and Lowe's saturate the country. These high-volume, full-line stores have relatively lower operating costs and can undercut X's prices because of their ability to extract larger volume purchase discounts and promotional benefits from suppliers. X begins incurring negative EBITDA and falls into financial distress. What is the investment potential? Obviously, it is very limited. This situation represents a secular change in a market where there is no obvious competitive response by X. No financial restructuring will "fix" the fundamental operating problem. X is destined for liquidation,[16] and thus only investment strategies based on the expectation of bond price declines and/or recovery amounts out of liquidation[17] should be considered.

Alternatively, the plight of the utilities, mentioned above, can be considered. Although California had begun the process of deregulating electricity, it was far from fully implemented, leaving the two incumbent utilities with significant monopoly power for an indispensable product — electricity. The source of their financial distress was a short-run disruption in the supply market, which was compounded by a flawed regulatory system that failed to allow adjustment in prices to consumers. Here, there was no real question that the entities would survive; it was more an issue of who would bear the economic burden of the market dislocation: Californians as consumers, Californians as taxpayers, or the stakeholders of the utilities (which, in many cases, represented Californians as investors). Thus, from an investment perspective, it was a completely different set of issues, including a legal analysis of the entities' capital structures (diversified holding company obligations versus operating utility obligations[18]) and either proper analysis or intuition of market fundamentals[19] and politics. The range of investment strategies included identifying any misvaluations in the capital structure and/or arbitrage hedging possibilities.

Next, the primary reasons for financial distress and implications for investment will be outlined. It should be emphasized that every investment turns on the specifics of that situation and that the guidelines outlined below should be viewed more as considerations than absolute "rules."

Performance Materially Below Expectation

The most common reason that firms become financially distressed is that operating results are different than, typically below, what was expected. However, there are various reasons why operations can be below expectations, each of which can have different investment implications for the distressed investor.

Economic Downturn

Economic history appears to suggest that economic cycles, including economic recessions, are inevitable.[20] It is perhaps more debatable whether there need to be periodic episodes of severe economic contraction or depression, but this may be splitting hairs. Few businesses are completely immune to changes in the economy, although some may be "countercyclical" and benefit from a period of general economic slowdown.

The challenge when analyzing a firm that appears to be in, or approaching, financial distress due to an economic slowdown is to assess whether that is really the essential "cause" of the financial distress. When things get bad, it is always easy to blame the economy. Is the issue the economy or management? Since it is well known that the economy goes through cycles, it may be fair to ask why management allowed the firm to be vulnerable. If it is determined that it is primarily the economy, then the issue comes down to assessing the extent to which operating adjustments, such as downsizing, can "fix" the problem and whether the firm has the financial wherewithal to reposition itself. As a general proposition, if a business is fundamentally a sound business with a value-added, or at least needed, product or service with established customers, then the distressed analyst should focus primarily on whether the performance downturn will in fact lead to distress and then carry out the valuation. If the investor believes that management is also a significant contributing factor, then a variety of other issues (discussed below) need to be considered.

Example — During January 2003, following the release of poorer than expected operating results, AmeriCredit Financial's 9.875% senior notes due 2006 fell from the mid-90s to the mid-50s. As of this writing, AmeriCredit is the largest subprime auto finance company in the United States. The company's basic business is to buy auto finance contracts or loans of car buyers with "poor" credit from car dealers that have such buyers as customers. Interest rates on the loans are fairly high, so if the borrower repays the loan, AmeriCredit makes a significant profit. If the borrower defaults, AmeriCredit repossesses the car, sells it at an auction, and loses money. As with any bank or finance company, the basic business issue for AmeriCredit is to make enough money on loans that generate income to offset losses on bad loans.

The triggering event to the price decline was the disclosure by AmeriCredit that rising unemployment rates resulting from the weak economy were causing the number of loan defaults to increase and that used car prices were at relative lows (attributed to attractive 0% interest rate financing offers by manufacturers on new cars). Thus, AmeriCredit was repossessing more cars than expected and losing more money than projected on each repossession. Large charge-offs were taken, and the company announced that the cash flows it normally received from previously purchased car loans held in its "portfolio" could be significantly curtailed,[21] potentially leading to liquidity shortfalls.

This was clearly not a good situation for AmeriCredit, but it appeared primarily related to the slow-down of the American economy in the 2000–2003 period. The key analytical issues were: (1) whether the business could be adjusted to "work" within the existing economic conditions; (2) if so, whether liquidity was sufficient to allow the company to avoid financial distress; and (3) whether there was adequate asset value to support the existing capital structure. The answer to all three of these questions turned out to be yes.

Shortly after disclosing the "problem," a management reshuffling was announced, along with a downsizing strategy that entailed closing or consolidating 60% of loan production offices, reducing new loan purchases by 50–70%, and cutting 20–25% of staff. AmeriCredit implemented the plan in approximately 60 days. The company had sufficient liquidity (approximately $350 million in cash on March 31, 2003) to "survive" until cash-flow-positive operations could be achieved in the third quarter of 2003. By the time AmeriCredit announced first-quarter results documenting these changes, the 9.875% notes had rallied to approximately 85, an increase of over 30% in about three months. Thus, the deterioration was caused by an economic downturn, but the company had the ability and wherewithal to successfully adapt itself, and those investors who correctly discerned this made handsome profits.

Uncompetitive Product or Service

Business is not static. In an era of relatively rapid technological advancement, perfectly reasonable businesses that satisfy legitimate consumer or business needs in a cost-effective manner quickly can be rendered obsolete by advances in technology. The Pony Express was replaced by the train, which led to rapid hand delivery, which has been replaced by e-mail; trains and passenger steamships were largely replaced by airplanes, which may decline in use because of videoconferencing; lawn rakes were replaced by leaf blowers; slide rules were replaced by calculators and computers; carbon paper by copy machines; records by tape players by compact discs by mp3 downloads; corner grocery, drug, or hardware stores by large-scale "category killers"; Carolina textile makers by Mexican then Chinese textile makers; retail stockbrokers by "on-line" brokerages; the list is endless.

Thus, any time a business begins to decline, one must assess whether the business still has a viable product or service. Since all businesses attempt to evolve with the changing environment, this is not always an easy task. Incumbent managers will acknowledge the new paradigm, but almost invariably have a glib response for how their firm will manage or adjust. The investors' challenge will be to properly assess the basic issue of ongoing viability. If a firm's products and/or business model are obsolete, a financial restructuring will do little to cure the root problem, and investment strategies need to be oriented toward declining asset value situations.

Example — Iridium was an apparently promising satellite-based wireless communications company. During the 1997–1999 time frame, it invested over $7 billion to acquire broadcast spectrum and launch a constellation of 66 low-earth-orbit (LEO) satellites that would be able to receive and relay voice and data communications anywhere on the globe. It partnered with Loral Spacecom, to build the satellites, and Motorola, to design and build the phones and terrestrial infrastructure. Iridium's strategic premise was that in a world of multistandard, incompatible cellular phone systems, users would pay a modest premium for the ability to use one phone anywhere in the world. The concept sounded so promising that, at its peak, Iridium had an equity market capitalization of more than $5 billion.

But then some significant technical problems arose. Despite significant research and development expenditures, Motorola could not develop a light-weight, sleek handset powerful enough to directly transmit and receive signals from the LEO satellites. The technology worked, but required users to carry handsets that were several times the size and weight of other standard cell phones. And because there was limited volume, operating costs required that per-minute charges be prohibitively high.[22] In contrast to Iridium's technological challenges, terrestrial cellular phone usage and capability were growing rapidly. Standards began to converge and the infrastructure build-out was sufficiently extensive that there were few reasonably populated places in either first- or second-world countries where it was not possible to use a cell phone.

Thus, unless one was calling from a ship far out at sea or an Antarctic weather station, there was probably a more convenient, lower cost alternative to Iridium.

In early 1999, Iridium's strategic partners, Motorola and Loral, decided to cut their losses and discontinue further investment. Unable to post results suggesting the business was viable, Iridium filed for bankruptcy in August 1999, with approximately $200 million in cash on its balance sheet.[23] Its system of 66 LEO satellites was deemed so worthless that it appeared that the satellites would simply be decommissioned and forced to endure self-immolation in the earth's atmosphere. However, at the last moment, Iridium sold the system to a private group for $25 million — approximately 0.35% of the cost to build — which subsequently leased it to the U.S. military.[24] Iridium's $4 billion in unsecured bonds faced *de minimus* liquidation recoveries and had fallen to a price less than 5.[25]

Unrealistic Business Plan

Deciding if a business becomes financially distressed because of an "unrealistic business plan" is inherently a judgment call. Presumably the business plan appeared to have merit, or the sponsor would not have been able to convince reasonably sophisticated investors to invest large sums of money in the venture. "Unrealistic" is a very vague concept. Is not every business plan based on an uncompetitive product or service, as discussed above, inherently unrealistic? Probably. If a business plan fails to provide flexibility in case of an economic downturn, couldn't it also be considered unrealistic? Perhaps. Would it be fair to call a business plan "unrealistic" if the firm failed after a protracted economic downturn? Maybe; maybe not. How does one distinguish between an unrealistic business plan and poor management? If the managers were as brilliant as their salaries, they should be able to identify and avoid uncompetitive products and manage through economic downturns.

Recognizing that it is easy to become bogged down in unproductive definitional issues, a general definition will be offered: An unrealistic business plan is one where the firm fails, but the underlying product or service continues to be used or consumed in the target marketplace on a relatively broad scale, and the failure can be largely attributed to growth or margin assumptions in the business plan that could not be realized.

Consider another example from the telecommunications sector. Assume that an early-stage regional cellular phone company (which is affiliated with a nationwide service and brand)[26] is raising expansion capital in the form of high-yield or convertible debt. Its projections call for it to be viable if it can capture 15% market share at a fairly reasonable average revenue per user (ARPU) during a four-year build-out/ramp-up period. On the face of it, everything is quite plausible. But, after the fact, it turns out that there is significant competitive entry, resulting in the firm only being able to capture 12% market share at an ARPU which is 25% below original projection. The firm becomes financially distressed because its business, as it has been able to develop it, cannot support its original capital structure. Going back to the visualization in Chapter 3, ultimately the box on the right side never got as big as the box on the left side.

There are at least three "types" of business plans that are especially prone to being unrealistic:

- **Leveraged buyouts (LBOs):** These were very prominent in the 1985–1990 time frame. Much has been written about whether the phenomenon was the result of tax policies that favored debt versus equity capital structures, or agency issues associated with divergent management/ownership interests,[27] or just opportunistic acquisitions. Regardless, when these fail (and many succeed and produce handsome returns for investors, so there is nothing inherently wrong with the strategy), it is frequently because forecasted expense reductions or profit improvement could not be realized. As briefly discussed in Chapter 6 on leverage, often the financing (particularly the bank debt component) used to make these acquisitions was structured on the assumption that either proceeds from asset sales or internally generated funds based on revenue or EBITDA margin improvements could be used to delever the firm. When these funds did not materialize, the firms became financially distressed.
- **Rollups:** The term "rollup" refers to the strategy of attempting to consolidate fragmented industries through the acquisition and subsequent merger of many local or regional businesses into a large regional or nationwide entity. The strategic premise is that the consolidated entity will have improved economies of scale — in areas such as administration, funding, marketing, and resource utilization — giving it a significant competitive advantage over the remaining "mom and pops." Here again, the concept is perfectly plausible, and several have been reasonably successful. However, there are many challenges associated with the strategy that can often result in the promised economies of scale not being realized. Typically, none of the data/information systems of the acquired firms will be compatible, necessitating lengthy, disruptive, and expensive transitions. Often the acquired business's success is closely tied to the selling entrepreneur, who is either entirely displaced or no longer similarly motivated. The start of one "rollup" can attract others to attempt consolidation, and this leads to a bidding up of the values

of the target small businesses. Alone or in combination, these and other factors can make projected benefits unachievable.

■ **PIGS**: This stands for place in growing sector (an acronym developed by the author that is not yet broadly used) and refers to situations where the viability of a new entrant is premised on a market environment that is perceived as growing so rapidly that there should be room for virtually all early entrants (a variant of the "all ships rise" metaphor). This is basically the fact pattern of the regional cellular phone company example above. The growth of the Internet, and the perceived demand for broadband services associated with it, is probably the most prominent recent example of such a sector. Literally dozens of businesses (such as competitive local exchange carriers, DSL service providers, IP telephony services, long line capacity providers, and many others) entered what was perceived as a "paradigm-busting" economic evolution and failed because, although there was significant demand for the service they attempted to provide, it was not as great (within the assumed time period) or not as high margin as originally expected.

From a distressed investor's perspective, the key issue to focus on in situations involving unrealistic business plans is valuation. By definition, the products or services of these firms are used in the target marketplace; thus there is potential economic value to a firm providing such a product or service. Every situation is different, so it is difficult to prescribe general rules. In many cases, the business is essentially viable and can be fixed by a balance sheet restructuring coupled with managerial/strategic changes. If the firm's securities can be purchased at sufficiently low prices, attractive returns may be possible in a restructuring. In other cases, there can be so much overcapacity that the firm's assets may not be economically efficient on a stand-alone basis. In these situations, the highest and best use may be to be combined with another entity that has sufficient scale to be viable in an excess capacity environment. Thus, for example, in the case of many niche competitive local exchange carriers, their fiber optic infrastructures had a modicum of value, but only when combined with larger entities that had more captive "on-network" traffic.[28] In these cases, the distressed investor may need to approach the investment assuming that there will eventually be either a sale or a liquidation.

Poor Management

As mentioned above, if one starts with the perspective that great management should avoid uncompetitive products, manage through economic downturns, and adroitly effect LBOs or rollups, then all failures can be laid at the feet of incompetent managers. But clearly there are some firms or situations that even very talented executives cannot solve or make prosper. Take, for example, the fairly celebrated case of Gary Wendt, who attempted to turn around troubled Conseco, a diversified financial services firm. Mr. Wendt was widely praised and credited for building GE Finance into a profitable juggernaut. He assumed the helm of Conseco after the firm's senior debt had been downgraded from Baa3 to Ba1, but was unable to make sufficient progress for the firm to avoid filing for bankruptcy in December 2002. He arguably took all the right steps, but the problems were too deep and fundamental for a mere change of management to solve.[29] Thus, to blame management in every case is going overboard and unlikely to be of much use to the distressed investor.

To begin, it is important to note that poor management is a fairly vague term. There are at least two different "poor management" situations that the investor should attempt to distinguish between: incompetent managers and conflicted managers.

Incompetent managers or executives are simply those that do not have a skill set which enables them to manage the multiple demands or requirements of overseeing and directing complex organizations in situations of competitive change or economic turbulence.[30] Such managers are more pervasive than many might expect, although it is impossible to delineate the two or three key qualities that invariably identify them. For obvious liability reasons, no specific examples will be suggested. Some of the signs to look for are high-growth business with no change in management, significant nepotism, board of directors of mediocre experience or quality, high employee turnover, stagnant products or internal processes, failure to respond to a change in the environment, and so on.[31] None of these signs or traits, of course, is suggested as being dispositive. There are always exceptions to the above: entrepreneurs who successfully manage large enterprises and heirs of founders who are great leaders and managers. Similarly, one cannot rely on a board of directors that looks good on paper to make sure management is performing. In forming an opinion, the investor must look carefully at the record, get as much direct contact as possible with the management (which unfortunately is being made more difficult by recent Securities and Exchange Commission regulations), and attempt to elicit the opinions of competitors, suppliers, and industry analysts.

A conflicted manager or executive is one whose self-interest appears to be out-of-line with that of shareholders or creditors. These individuals may be reasonably capable, but improperly motivated. Signs to look for here are high cash and/or benefit compensation relative to firm size or income; failure to have a meaningful stake in the upside, whether through options or direct stock investment; and the presence of nonemployment-related associations with the firm, such as the firm contracting services or renting property from entities in which an executive has an economic stake. These can be strong indicators that management may be quite happy with the status quo or that the firm may be performing at below its potential. Many of the telltale signs of incompetent managers are likely to be present with conflicted managers. After all, it is extremely difficult from the outside to distinguish between an executive who is simply not up to the task and one who may be capable but not motivated. Again, for potential liability reasons, no specific examples will be cited.

How the distressed investor assesses the impact of poor management on the investment decision will turn on a variety of factors. The first is the expected scope of involvement. If the investor is not in a position to play an active role (i.e., acquire control of the firm or at least a stake large enough to get on the bondholder or creditor committee), then the investor cannot really do anything about the problem, so the management issue is simply a part of the valuation calculus, although this may not be true if the investor believes that an activist bondholder, for whom the investor has regard, is involved and can be expected to take the required steps to change management. In that case, the more passive investor may be able to essentially free ride on the efforts of the more active investor (although one must bear in mind the power and self-interest of a controlling activist bondholder).

If the investor intends to take control or at least assume an activist role, then an important issue is whether the creditors have sufficient negotiating leverage to effect a change. For example, if the distressed firm has a bank line that is in technical default, then the lenders (which could include a distressed investor who has purchased an interest in the bank debt) generally have leverage to force management changes, which usually begins with the creditors inserting a turn-around or crisis manager into the distressed firm. Their source of leverage is either the carrot of a waiver or continuing access to the credit line or the threat of acceleration or other remedies. Alternatively, if leverage is more limited, the creditors may deem it in their best interest effectively to bribe the poor manager (who after the bonus or other severance payments will certainly be rich) into leaving so that he or she can be replaced with someone more competent or motivated.

If the investor is opting to take a more passive role, and activist creditors cannot be counted on to effect change, then the investor's valuation approach needs to assume the worst. Management could try to keep itself in place for as long as possible, all the while wasting corporate assets. The reorganization process could be contentious and drawn out. In the case of conflicted management, creditors may have an opportunity to pursue the manager personally for self-dealing to enhance recoveries.

NEAR-TERM LIQUIDITY ISSUES

The most common focal point for a restructuring is an impending liquidity issue. These situations can lead to significant volatility in the trading prices of debt. The three most common contexts for liquidity events are the violation of a bank covenant, the requirement to make a bond coupon interest payment when the firm has very limited cash and/or seeks to draw down on a revolver to make the payment, and a bond or bank debt maturity. At the fundamental level, the basic analysis is essentially an assessment of the probability that the liquidity issue will lead to a bankruptcy or an attempt at an out-of-court restructuring (see Chapter 10 for further discussion of this issue). In analyzing this, it is important to realize that the course of events will vary materially depending upon whether or not the distressed firm has significant bank debt.

Bank Debt Scenarios

If the firm has bank debt, the most frequent potential threat of a liquidity event will be the violation of a technical covenant. This allows the bank to, on threat of acceleration, step in and extract additional fees or waiver payments and/or begin asserting influence on, if not dictating, how management will run the firm — although the bank will be very mindful of the issue of lender liability before asserting its influence too forcefully.[32] If the bank is unsecured, it will use the negotiating leverage presented by the breach to attempt to partially or fully secure itself. If the investor holds bank debt, this is a positive development. If the investor holds unsecured debt (without a negative pledge clause), this can be negative because, as discussed in Chapter 4, being a secured creditor has numerous advantages that can be detrimental to the recoveries of unsecured claims.

Assuming the more typical situation where the bank debt is already secured, some type of waiver will typically be arranged, at least in the early stages of distress. This is true both because banks do not want to be viewed as forcing a bankruptcy over a relatively minor issue and, depending on the perceived risk, may not want to add a nonperforming loan to their balance sheet. In the case of a simple amendment, the process tends to have little effect on trading prices of either the secured or unsecured debt. If, however, the bank deems itself undersecured and concludes that further operations will tend to erode its asset support (this would be true if the firm is operating with negative EBITDA), then the bank has a more difficult decision. Increasingly, however, if a bankruptcy is a reasonably likely event at some point in the relatively near future (e.g., the firm is hopelessly overleveraged), the bank may force a bankruptcy proceeding immediately to protect its collateral value, particularly if the bank has any concerns about management (bankruptcy makes it easier to monitor managerial activities). Thus, for the investor assessing unsecured debt, it is important to analyze the collateral position of the bank. If the bank appears well secured, then covenant violations are not as likely to lead to an immediate bankruptcy. Usually this is a good thing because the investor will continue collecting coupons with the hope the firm can recover. However, if the bank's collateral position is fairly thin and potentially eroding, then any covenant violation could be the pretext for a filing.

A common context for a bank to believe that its collateral protection is being eroded involves the payment of bond coupons. For many distressed firms, coming up with the cash to make a bond coupon is a major event. For a $150 million issue of 12% notes, the semi-annual coupon is $9 million. That can be a lot of money to a firm that is operating at negative or break-even EBITDA. Banks are very sensitive to coupons being paid out to unsecured creditors because, from the bank perspective, such expenditures do nothing to improve the borrower's business. And in the event the firm is planning to draw down on the bank revolver to fund the interest payment, it represents an actual increase in risk to the bank and an inequitable benefit to a junior class. Thus, when cash flow is extremely tight and collateral is thin, unsecured note holders should not take any coupon payment for granted, as each payment is a potential bankruptcy trigger.

No Bank Debt Scenarios

Where there is no bank debt, the near-term liquidity event is more predictable because it will more likely be either a coupon payment or a pending maturity. If the firm is in such distress that coupon payments are questionable, then the bonds are likely to have been discounted by the relatively high probability of a restructuring, and nonpayment may only result in modest price volatility. However, potential coupon defaults can be triggers for an effort to complete an out-of-court restructuring.

The more interesting and potentially volatile situations arise when the liquidity event is an actual bond maturity. If the firm is operating somewhat below plan or the capital markets are relatively tight, this can make the refinancing of the note questionable and lead to interesting investment opportunities.[33]

Example — Orbital Sciences is involved in building satellites and various types of rockets. After an extended period of selling assets and reducing debt, by December 31, 2001 it had only $100 million in convertible notes outstanding, which were due on October 1, 2002. The notes were trading at 70 due to the company's inconsistent operating history (core businesses only marginally profitable), checkered history (including the bankruptcy of two significant subsidiaries), uncertain future, and inhospitable capital markets. In particular, there was concern that, given that the company's largest customer was the U.S. Department of Defense, the company's uncertain financial outlook could jeopardize its ability to retain existing contracts and win new ones.

In the first quarter of 2002, the company was awarded a major government defense contract and core operations showed improved profitability. The company also retained an investment bank to advise it on how to manage the upcoming maturity of the notes, which by that time had traded up to the low 80s. Given the major contract win, it was reasonably clear that the company's value was easily greater than the $100 million balance of the notes.[34] However, when the company filed its 2002 10-K, the audit opinion contained a going-concern qualification because of the uncertainty related to the notes.

By May 2002, the notes had traded to the low 90s. The company announced that it had retained a different investment bank, and there was "market talk" that large existing holders were being approached concerning their interest in participating in an exchange offer that would swap the maturing notes for longer dated convertible notes with a lower conversion price, reflecting the stock's then $6–$7 per share trading price.[35] There was also a disclosure that the company was being sued by the bondholders of one of its bankrupt subsidiaries. The timing of the lawsuit was viewed by some as an effort to force a favorable settlement so that the litigation uncertainty would not impede the efforts to refinance or restructure then maturing notes.

Shortly thereafter, the market talk was that existing holders were not willing to participate in an exchange offer because the market for the company's stock was so thinly traded that the holders could not hedge the more dilutive notes properly (i.e., the holders would not be able to "short" a sufficient amount of stock). The notes fell back to 88, representing a yield to maturity of approximately 40%.

In June 2002, the company announced that it had raised $100 million through the placement of $100 million 12% second secured notes, which were offered together with warrants for approximately 25% of the company's fully diluted stock. It had also arranged a $60 million secured working capital facility. In combination, these financings allowed the company to call the existing $100 million in notes at par in July 2002.[36] Investors that had purchased the notes at 70 in December 2001 captured 42% in price appreciation. Investors that had purchased notes when they dropped back to 88 enjoyed 13.6% price appreciation in approximately two months, representing an annualized rate of return of over 81.6%.

UNEXPECTED LIABILITIES

Sometimes a firm can be well run, profitable, and easily able to manage its debt when a large series of nondebt claims are made against the firm. These can completely change the firm's credit dynamics and result in a material decline in the firm's valuation. In accounting parlance, these are essentially off-balance-sheet contingent liabilities that suddenly become material on-balance-sheet liabilities. The most common sources of these liabilities are tort claims and contract liabilities.

Tort Claims

Tort claims have killed the financial health of many otherwise healthy businesses.[37] The most well-known recent examples include liability associated with silicon breast implants, asbestos, tobacco, and silicosis. Companies felled by tort liability actions include Johns Manville, Armstrong, USG, Halliburton, and Dow Corning, just to name a few. The tobacco industry has weathered lawsuits for many years, but the many recent multibillion-dollar punitive damage suits awarded against Phillip Morris may signal that even these companies may face crippling liability at some point. A more recent addition to the list is claims associated with silicosis, a disease allegedly associated with the mining of silicon, which may at some point threaten the viability of firms associated with the production of that substance.

Based on recent history, it appears that a chapter 11 reorganization may be the only avenue that firms with significant tort liabilities can use to manage their exposure, although recent legislative initiatives by the U.S. Congress[38] in the area of asbestos tort reform may provide some relief for that sector. Within a chapter 11 proceeding, the bankruptcy court can approve a binding claim resolution process to limit the claims of all prepetition and postpetition tort victims. A typical approach is to set up a trust into which the firm contributes cash (either in a lump sum or as periodic payments) and the majority of its stock. All claims of prepetition tort victims, regardless of whether they are asserted before or after the petition, can only be asserted against this pool of assets.[39] This process appears to work reasonably well, and it reduces the legal cost of victims asserting a claim (the company usually concedes the legal issue of liability, making damages the only issue that needs to be determined). Also, since it reduces or eliminates punitive damage awards, it eliminates an important incentive for attorneys. However, class-action plaintiffs' lawyers, having attained a certain expertise in the area, then start searching for other not yet bankrupt companies to sue. Thus firms with increasingly tenuous connection with the underlying tort find themselves defending an increasing series of actions as lawyers hunt for the next "deep pocket."

For distressed investors, such tort liabilities have been very dangerous. Managements usually underestimate the number of potential claims and probable financial liability. This is not because they are necessarily unrealistic, but rather because, in general, claims have tended to exceed all reasonable expectations. Insurance that may be in place to cover such liability is frequently insufficient or the insurer contests coverage. Taken together, to date, it has been very difficult, if not impossible, to estimate the magnitude of claims, whether the firm will ultimately need to file chapter 11, and the implications for recoveries in a chapter 11 process.

As a result of this history, virtually any time a firm becomes associated with potential personal injury tort exposure, even indirectly, the market tends to assume the worst and significantly discount its securities. This can lead to opportunities.

Example — GAF was the distant parent[40] of Building Materials Corporation of America (BMCA). GAF, through a subsidiary, made the fatal mistake of acquiring a company called Ruberoid, which had been involved with asbestos products throughout the 1970s. Litigation associated with Ruberoid forced GAF into bankruptcy in January 2001. Seeking additional sources of recovery, asbestos litigants sought to involve BMCA, which had never been involved in asbestos and was not part of the bankruptcy filing, in the bankruptcy case. BMCA's bonds traded down to the 30s on fears that these consolidation actions might be successful. However, after BMCA prevailed in several court challenges, by September 2001 the bonds had doubled to the 70s.[41]

Contract Liabilities

Contract liabilities can be another source of unexpected liabilities. These are basically liabilities associated with uneconomic or bad contracts. Sometimes these contracts are consciously entered into within the ordinary course of business and appear reasonable at the time, but prove otherwise with a change in circumstance. Other times, such contracts are unwittingly acquired when another company is purchased and the purchaser's due diligence fails to either identify the contract or its significance. Finally, and perhaps more of an issue for the future, is the potential exposure under financial derivative contracts. More and more firms are using derivative contracts to attempt to reduce various risks in their business. For example, an aluminum manufacturer may purchase electricity-related derivatives in order to "lock in" the future cost of electricity so that, in turn, it can enter into fixed-price, long-term delivery contracts with customers. Financial firms often use derivative contracts to manage their interest rate risk. These contracts have a valid place in business, but they are a relatively new phenomenon, and it is easily foreseeable that at some point, a poorly conceived derivative strategy could force a firm into chapter 11 in order to take advantage of the power to reject executory contracts. Over and above the direct risk this might pose to any particular counter-party, one can anticipate that it could negatively affect the valuations of many participants in the markets.

Realistically, it is very difficult as a distressed investor to protect oneself from the possible liabilities associated with uneconomic contracts. For the most part, financial disclosure related to these contracts is fairly limited,[42] and in any case, what typically gives rise to these contracts leading to financial distress is unforeseeable.

On the other hand, there may be significant opportunities to profit from the revelation of an unexpected contractual liability because the market may misvalue the exposure or simply overreact. In these cases, the critical element would be to clearly understand the potential liability under the contract, how that affects the firm's valuation, and how the claim may affect a chapter 11 process.

Example — Washington Group is a construction company (roads, power plants, airports, etc.) formerly known as Morrison Knudson. In July 2000, after over a year of due diligence and contract negotiation, Washington purchased the construction business, including projects in process, of Raytheon Corporation. On March 8, 2001, less than one year after the purchase, Washington disclosed that the cost to complete several of the purchased projects was significantly higher than estimated, perhaps by more than $1 billion, and sued Raytheon for fraud and breach of contract.

At the time, Washington had approximately $400 million in bank debt and $300 million in bonds outstanding. Prior to the revelations, Washington was rated Ba2/BBB– and the bonds were trading in the 90s. After the disclosure, the bonds dropped to the 60s.[43] Uncertain about the company's status and viewing the "new" liabilities as a breach of the loan agreement, Washington's bank lenders restricted access to the facility. Although Washington had approximately $372 million in cash as of September 1, 2000, given the long payment cycle often involved in major construction projects, that amount could quickly be dissipated.

In a somewhat surprising, proactive move, Washington filed for chapter 11 protection on May 14, 2001. The chapter 11 process allowed Washington to reject the contracts with the hemorrhaging cost overruns. As part of the settlement of the Raytheon litigation, responsibility for completion of the projects was returned to Raytheon.

Washington and its creditors correctly focused on the fact that it would be very difficult for Washington to compete for new contracts while it was in bankruptcy. (Who would award a multimillion-dollar construction contract to a bankrupt entity when numerous strong solvent companies were also competing for the business?) Washington proposed a plan of reorganization on September 18, 2001 (fairly fast for a situation with no prenegotiation) which provided that creditors, including the banks, would receive 100% of the company's stock, and shareholders, including the chairman and largest shareholder, would receive only warrants. Following the disclosure of the plan, the bonds rebounded to the low 80s.

There are several lessons to be learned from the Washington example. First, unexpected liabilities can "come out of left field," with fairly devastating results. A company with a credit rating of Ba2/BBB–, an enterprise value of over $1 billion, and cash on the balance sheet of approximately $350 million can be forced to seek chapter 11 protection within a matter of months. Second, to maximize recoveries, it is often necessary for the company and creditors to quickly agree on a plan of reorganization and minimize the time spent in bankruptcy to limit the potential erosion in enterprise value. Third, the nature of the postreorganization recovery will often be dictated by the nature of the company and its business circumstances. Washington arguably could have supported a reasonable amount of debt on its postreorganization balance sheet, but strategically chose to emerge debt free so that it could present as strong as possible an image to the marketplace. Washington's management should arguably receive an "F" for its due diligence in the Raytheon acquisition, but probably deserves an "A" for its handling of the restructuring process.

CRISIS OF CONFIDENCE: FRAUD AND OTHER EVENTS THAT CREATE FINANCIAL UNCERTAINTY

Although, as of this writing, this is arguably the most topical cause of financial distress, looking back on the history of insolvencies over the last 15 years, bankruptcies relating to crisis of confidence events deserve to be placed last on this list. However, there is no question that during the 2001–2003 period, such events have led to considerable price volatility in numerous very large companies and created tremendous trading opportunities. Situations of financial distress that can be attributed to crisis of confidence events include Global Crossing, WorldCom, Enron, and HealthSouth. In aggregate, these four situations resulted in the sharp decline in valuation of over $60 billion in debt instruments. Usually there is little warning preceding the disclosure of the crisis of confidence event, so there is little a distressed investor can do to position himself or herself to benefit from such revelations. However, once the event occurs and price volatility increases, there can be many profitable investment opportunities.

Interestingly, in the four situations highlighted above, the information event that triggered the ensuing crisis of confidence event was a revelation by either the company itself or an insider. For Global Crossing, it was a company disclosure relating to a "revision" of its accounting practices for certain "capacity swaps."[44] For WorldCom, it was a company disclosure relating to a revision of accounting policies that resulted in the capitalization of various costs that should have been expensed.[45] For Enron, it was a company disclosure of various conflicts of interest that were present in the management of certain off-balance-sheet affiliated entities.[46] For HealthSouth, it was the confession of its chief financial officer to complicity in a multiyear fraud designed to overstate revenues and profits.[47] However, this is not always the case. In the Learnout & Hauspie situation,[48] for example, the suggestion that the company's revenue figures might be inflated first surfaced in a *Wall Street Journal* article,[49] which was initially disputed by Learnout management.

The key factors to focus on when the crisis of confidence event occurs are the implications relating to: (1) the reliability of historical financial information and whether such data can be used to form a valuation and (2) liquidity and whether a chapter 11 process will be required. Each of these will be briefly discussed.

Reliability of Historical Financial Data and Valuation Issues

Revelations of fraud and/or the need for accounting restatements clearly make any reliance on historical financial data questionable. Without such information, it is difficult to confidently prepare a valuation, given that once any "number" has been called into question, one should be justifiably skeptical of all the rest. It is important, however, to analyze carefully the nature of the alleged issue to see if there may still be some basis to make a valuation, regardless of how tenuous.

For example, in the WorldCom situation, the alleged misstatement related to the capitalization of certain costs that should have been expensed. In the broader scheme of things, this is manageable. There was nothing to suggest revenues were not reliably stated. In fact, although net income may have been materially overstated, theoretically, operating cash flow as measured by EBITDA-capital expenditures (see Chapter 5) may not have been materially affected.[50] Alternatively, one might have looked at WorldCom's revenue and applied the operating metrics (i.e., EBITDA margin) of comparable companies to develop a valuation.

In the Global Crossing case, the basic accounting issue was the legitimacy of various "capacity" swaps. In these transactions, it is alleged that Global Crossing would "sell" certain excess capacity on its network to a competitor for greater than fair market value and accept as payment "capacity" on the competitor's system, the value of which was similarly overstated. Both parties to the transaction were able to make it appear that they were filling up their networks with profitably priced traffic. EBITDA was overstated because Global Crossing would recognize the revenue from the sale immediately, but amortize the cost of the acquired capacity over time. The bottom line of this technique was that Global Crossing was incurring substantial negative cash flow and the legitimate demand for much of its fiber optic capacity was questionable. Thus, in that case, it was very difficult to have any basis on which to confidently make a valuation.[51]

Liquidity and the Likelihood of Bankruptcy

A second key consideration is whether the information event will lead to a major liquidity crisis or bankruptcy. To assess this, the factors to quickly consider are:

- Cash on hand
- Whether the firm is dependent on a bank line of credit for liquidity and the probability that access to that line will remain in place
- Whether the information event is so severe that it would allow lenders to accelerate or other third parties to terminate material agreements
- The presence and magnitude of an immediate cash need such as a significant coupon payment or bond maturity.

In the case of Global Crossing, when the information event occurred, the company had approximately $2 billion in cash and manageable cash burn, so there was no immediate liquidity event. However, once the magnitude of the EBITDA shortfall became clear, it was fairly obvious that the company was destined to fail. The bankruptcy process began simply because it was in the best interests of the creditors and other constituents.

In WorldCom, the information event again did not portend a liquidity crisis. The company had cash and was substantially EBITDA positive; however, its debt load was so massive ($30 billion) that it required ongoing access to the capital markets to handle normal refinancing demands, and as its debt fell in value, it became obvious that such access was not available.[52]

When the information event is perceived to potentially lead to a liquidity challenge, bond price volatility is likely to be significantly greater, particularly if the capital structure contains subordinated debt. This can present the distressed investor with excellent opportunities if there is a reasonable basis upon which to make a valuation and the bonds fall to attractive levels.

Example — HealthSouth is a diversified health care business. In a totally unexpected development, in late March 2003 the chief financial officer, who was facing the requirements imposed by the new Sarbanes-Oxley Act[53] to personally certify the financials, walked into the Birmingham, Alabama U.S. Attorney's office and confessed to complicity in a four-year scheme to overstate revenues. The total estimated overstatement was approximately $1.2 billion (approximately $400 million per year).

HealthSouth, which was rated Ba3/BB–, had $3 billion in unsecured debt, including $2 billion in senior debt and $800 million in subordinated debt. When the confession was disclosed, the senior debt fell from 90 to 45 and the subordinated debt fell from 96 to approximately 15. HealthSouth's cash position was not precisely known, but it had shown $389 million in cash at September 30, 2002 (its last public filing).[54]

Although HealthSouth had cash and was likely significantly EBITDA positive (even adjusting for the accounting issues), the information event created a crisis because of pending interest and principal repayment obligations. On April 1, 2003, just 11 days after the confession, the company was scheduled to retire $354 million of its 3.25% convertible subordinated notes and pay approximately $44 million in coupon obligations on its other debt. It is likely that the company had planned to draw down on its bank revolver (which was estimated to have $800 million in availability) to fund these payments, but the fraud disclosure constituted a breach which caused the banks to freeze access. However, the bank line was unsecured, and bank lenders generally do not like to be part of unplanned chapter 11 proceedings when they are unsecured. The provisions of the negative pledge clauses in HealthSouth's various senior note indentures were not completely consistent, but a reasonable interpretation was that the existing bank lenders probably could secure up to $300 million in borrowings without triggering the requirement to ratably secure the other senior debt.

This presented a very complex analytical scenario. If HealthSouth did not get access to the bank line, it would default on its April 1 payment obligations. The banks arguably had an interest in helping HealthSouth avoid chapter 11 because they did not want to be in a bankruptcy on an unsecured basis. By making a secured loan, the banks could fund most of the company's liquidity needs on a fairly safe basis. Assuming this scenario, the 3.25s would be paid and investors making a 15 investment could receive 100 in less than a month — a staggering return opportunity.

A few days later, the banks indicated that they would not fund HealthSouth. Well-regarded health care turnaround specialists were brought in to manage the company. On April 1, 2003, HealthSouth failed to meet its payment obligations, but the creditor groups agreed to postpone a declaration of default. With the crisis of confidence managed, the senior notes traded up to 60 and the subordinated notes traded to the low 30s. As of September 2003, although the default of the 3.25s continued, interest on all debt was being paid on a current basis and the 3.25s were trading in the mid-80s, representing over a 500% return from the March low. The 3.25s ultimately were retired at par with the proceeds of a new bank loan in January 2004.

SUMMARY

In analyzing a distressed debt investment, it is critical to understand the reason for the financial distress and how that impacts the investment strategy. When the cause of the financial distress is basically due to the capital structure, either because there is simply too much leverage or the term structure of the debt creates a liquidity challenge, the investor can analyze the investment from the perspective that a restructuring may be feasible. This does not necessarily mean that investment is attractive, but at least the investor can apply his or her valuation skills and knowledge of the reorganization process to estimate the potential for a favorable outcome. On the other hand, if the cause of the distress is that the company has uncompetitive products or is poorly managed, the investor may want to discount the likelihood that the business will be reorganized and evaluate the investment only from the perspective of a sale or liquidation.

These basic distinctions are essential for the investor to clearly identify because each presents a separate set of risks and/or challenges. For example, in the first category, simple deleveraging restructurings might appear feasible, but the investor must accurately assess the amount and composition (cash, new debt, new equity, etc.) of his or her recovery to achieve the desired investment result. In cases requiring the discharge or capitation of liabilities, since the process inherently requires entering chapter 11, there is a higher risk of an extended stay in bankruptcy, with the related risk of deterioration to the debtor's business or long delays in investment recoveries. Lastly, in situations involving flawed businesses, it may be very difficult to identify the problem. Does the firm have a viable business niche but poor management? Is business deterioration a cyclical phenomenon or an incident of secular change? Was the business model ever really viable? The first option might be salvageable, but the latter two are hopeless. It is critical, therefore, to be able to identify the business issue properly.

As a firm approaches financial distress, the investor must bear in mind what moves or actions might be taken by the firm to try to avoid or better position itself for a restructuring. These considerations are discussed in the next chapter.

This Chapter's Chess Moves

19. Rbf2, Qe7

20. Bc2, Pg5

9

OPTIONS FOR ALLEVIATING FINANCIAL DISTRESS: THE COMPANY'S PERSPECTIVE

In Chapter 8, the various sources of financial distress were identified for the primary purpose of helping the distressed investor recognize those situations in which a restructuring could create value and those that were essentially beyond hope. In this chapter, the focus is on analyzing properly the options available to a distressed firm to solve its problem(s). Going back to our chess analogy, this is an analysis of what "moves" the firm can make. The range of moves is fairly narrow — raise new capital or repurchase or restructure existing debt either within or outside of bankruptcy — but always situation specific: that is why it is such a challenging game. The primary determinants of the range of moves are time, liquidity, industry fundamentals, outlook, limitations imposed by the firm's contracts (such as debt covenants), the attractiveness and severability of its business units, the complexity of the capital structure, and the cause(s) of the financial distress.[1] Each of these factors will be discussed below in more detail.

PROPERLY ASSESSING THE DISTRESSED FIRM'S LIKELY ACTIONS IS KEY TO ASSESSING INVESTMENT OUTCOMES

The reason it is important to clearly understand a firm's potential "moves" is to better predict the likely course of events and the expected outcome of the investment. As in chess, a firm can be expected to analyze each combination of available "moves." The investor can also analyze the firm's moves or options and base investment "moves" on an educated guess of what the firm will do. Also, of course, both the firm and the investor should each expect that their moves will be anticipated, thus creating a "feedback" loop.

The process can best be illustrated by a couple of hypothetical examples. In reviewing these, first the firm's circumstances will be discussed briefly, and the "thought process" or options of the firm will be analyzed. Then, given that the investor should be able to anticipate the firm's options (at least that is the goal of this chapter), the investor's thought process will be reviewed.

Example 1: Playing the Waiting Game

Webco is an Internet company with $225 in cash and $1000 in historical investment in various Internet ventures that have modest negative operating cash flow. To mature these businesses to the point that they have value potential will require further investment of at least an additional $150 in aggregate. Webco's only nontrade-credit liability is $200 in 5% subordinated convertible notes maturing in two years. Its formerly high-priced stock (peak value $200 per share) trades at under $1 a share and the notes are trading at 25 because the market is skeptical whether or not the firm's various negative cash flow businesses have value. The notes have virtually no covenants, and Webco's cash position essentially ensures there will be no payment default until maturity. Webco's circumstances are summarized in Table 9-1.

Table 9-1. Summary Information on Webco

		Debt	Amount	Coupon	Maturity	Price	Market Value
Settlement	6/20/03						
Cash	225	Secured Bank Line	0	5.5%		100	0
		5% Senior Notes	200	5.0%	6/30/05	25	50
Required CAPX	(150)	Total	200				50
LTM EBITDA	(10)	Equity	1100				NA

What are some of the potential scenarios? The note holders, in a perfect world, would likely prefer that Webco file an immediate chapter 7 liquidation and, depending on the drag of administrative expenses and trade claims versus the liquidation value of the operating investments, take the $225 in cash for a par recovery.[2] Given the market price of 25, this would be a home run! But, unfortunately, the note holders, absent a default, have no power to force a bankruptcy, and such a scenario does nothing for management and the existing equity.

Management's perfect-world scenario is to continue with the business plan because, given its genius (a.k.a. ego) and the turn in the marketplace that, in management's view, is undoubtedly just around the corner, the market is likely once again to recognize Webco's true potential. When that occurs, the stock will go up, members of management will get rich from the new $1 options they have awarded themselves, and a refinancing or asset sale will be used to repay the maturing debt. The collapse of the stock price may prompt management to consider share repurchases, which would result in an erosion of the notes' asset support, that the note holders will be powerless to prevent because there is no restricted payment covenant in the notes' weak indenture. If management is wrong, Webco will squander its cash and likely will have to file for bankruptcy when the notes mature in two years.

These are two possible (though admittedly polar) scenarios, but assuming management is acting at least semi-rationally in its, and hopefully the shareholders', interests, there are other more probable and mutually beneficial scenarios. Even if management is myopic, the executives should realize that in a bankruptcy, the equity is likely to be wiped out and they will be out of jobs and humiliated. Therefore, unless they have already soaked the firm for enough cash that they are fairly wealthy, or are confident they can dupe the note holders into believing they are truly irreplaceable and obtain perhaps even more lucrative contracts under a key employee retention plan, members of management will want to avoid or at least minimize the worst-case consequences of that scenario.

A fairly obvious strategy is to buy back the notes at a discount. Since the market value of the notes is only $50 ($200 × 25%), there is a strong argument to use some of the $225 in cash to purchase them at the discount — and use the remaining funds for the business plan. Of course, when the market realizes the that firm is engaging in repurchases, the notes' price will rise. Nonetheless, at a 25 price level, a note buyback is compelling. The aggregate amount to spend, the price to pay, and the trade-off versus further investments in the business will be variables in a difficult calculus, but repurchase of notes is a clear first step.

Second, besides focusing on how to spend existing cash, management will be looking to get more. New equity financing is out of the question (a new shareholder might just as well write a check to the notes[3]), so management would probably start exploring asset sales to raise more cash. Monetizing assets, assuming "fair prices" can be realized, would be a desirable course for the notes.

Management may also consider trying to obtain a secured loan. The loan would have to be done on a secured basis because, practically speaking, no lender would make an unsecured loan to a firm where the existing market perception of the borrower's risk is such that its debt trades at 25. Even on a secured basis, it is unclear that any lender would be interested in such a financing unless the primary collateral is the cash.[4] In that case, management would have not have derived much net benefit, spent money and time in arranging the financing, and, given the onerous covenants typically demanded by secured lenders, limited its operating flexibility. From a note holder's perspective, if a secured lender had a pledge of all the assets including the cash, the notes would clearly be worse off. Fortunately, since it is not very obvious why the management or Webco would benefit from such a secured borrowing, the investor could view this risk as an acceptably low probability.

As management looks out to the maturity of the bonds, it should be planning for the probability, or at least the possibility, that unless the market really does rebound, Webco will not have the resources for repayment. In that case, on the basis of the limited facts given, it does not appear that a bankruptcy would add value (through lease rejection, etc.) to the enterprise, and thus its inherent costs would only burden the potential recovery, tenuous as it may be, of the equity. Therefore, in the "no market recovery" scenario, the endgame should be some type of out-of-court exchange proposal in which the notes are given the vast majority of the equity, but the existing shareholders retain a sliver. A well-conceived and well-executed exchange would also give management executives a *de facto* opportunity to make amends with the bondholders in an effort to preserve their jobs. There could, of course, be many other scenarios, but these, which are summarized in Figure 9-1, are the most probable.

The prospective distressed investor might reasonably look at the investment as follows: The investment is at 25. No default is likely until maturity, so I'll receive three coupons totaling 7.5, which should reduce the cash risk to 17.50. Webco has a compelling incentive to buy back the notes, which means the price could be pushed higher, providing at least one profitable outcome. Even if the company doesn't repurchase, the logical approach for management would be to do an exchange in two years,[5] at which point the investment will most likely be converted to equity (unless Webco is generating enough cash to support a modest amount of debt, in which case its market value will likely be much higher than the current perception). There is a risk that Webco's existing assets are worthless, but if any return can be realized on the $150 being invested between now and the maturity of the notes, there should be some downside

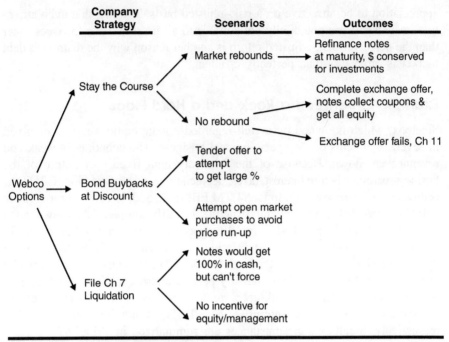

Company Strategy	Scenarios	Outcomes

Figure 9-1. Possible Webco Scenarios

protection. More optimistically, if Webco can buy back a significant percentage of the notes and operations rebound, there is substantial upside. Taking all factors into account, the scenario is buy and hold for two years with the expectation of the notes being converted into equity in the end, unless Webco pushes prices up with repurchases. In that case, there may be an option for an earlier sale. If management botches things, the worst case is Webco goes into chapter 11 and the notes get all the assets. This could result in losses, but after the coupons, only 17.50 in cash will be at risk, and surely all that historical investment (1000 before + 150 prospective) should be worth at least 35 ($200 × 17.5%).

Whether or not this scenario is acceptable to a distressed investor will depend on the investor's investment objectives. In general, investors in bonds trading at 25 will have the mind-set that they are investing in the firm's equity and will have an expectation for equity-like (20–30%) returns. Some investors desire shorter time horizons. Others may want to avoid scenarios that result in a recovery involving potentially illiquid, nonearning assets such as postreorganization/restructuring equity. Other investors, however, might find an investment with a current yield of 20% and an option for potentially significant appreciation to be attractive on a risk-adjusted basis. The fact that even attractive investments are potentially not suitable to all investors due to issues other than the perceived risk-adjusted return is another reason why the distressed debt market is often less than perfectly efficient.[6]

Example 2: Between a Rock and a Hard Place

Steelbox, which is owned by a well-regarded private equity fund, is involved in several segments of the specialty steel business. The economy is weak and revenues are down. Because of the relatively high fixed cost nature of the business, earnings before interest, taxes, depreciation, and amortization (EBITDA) is down even more severely. In fact, LTM EBITDA, $20, is a six-year low (peak EBITDA was $40). The capital structure is fairly simple: $50 drawn on a secured bank revolver and $150 in 12% unsecured senior notes that mature in one year. These notes trade at 50. Liquidity is limited: cash is down to $6 and there is a technical default on the bank line. A $9 bond coupon payment is due in two weeks. Steelbox's three industry peers are also exhibiting weak performance. One has filed for bankruptcy protection. The other two are likely to survive and are trading at enterprise value/EBITDA multiples of 6x and 7x, respectively. Steelbox's circumstances are summarized in Table 9-2.

What are the potential scenarios here? Relative to the Webco case, there are a couple of very clear "big-picture" differences. First, there is no need to

Table 9-2. Summary Information on Steelbox

		Debt	Amount		Maturity	Price	Market Value
Settlement	6/20/03						
Cash	6	Secured Bank Line	50	5.5%		100	50
		12% Senior Notes	150	12.0%	6/30/04	50	75
Peak EBITDA	40	Total	200				125
LTM EBITDA	20	Equity	Private				NA

	Leverage	At Face	Net at Market
EBITDA = 20	Thru Secured	2.5x	2.5x
	Thru Senior	10.0x	6.3x
EBITDA = 30	Thru Secured	1.7x	1.7x
	Thru Senior	6.7x	4.2x
EBITDA = 40	Thru Secured	1.3x	1.3x
	Thru Senior	5.0x	3.1x

speculate on where management will be focused; since Steelbox is owned by a private equity fund, executives of the fund will be proactively involved in making sure management is focused on maximizing the potential value of the fund's investment. Second, the fact that there is a technical[7] default on the credit facility means that the banks have significant influence on the course of events. Third, this is an established, capital-intensive business that undoubtedly has a fair amount of hard assets and is making money. The key challenge here, assuming the banks have sufficient collateral that they have little credit risk over the near term, is the one-year maturity of the notes. Since the notes trade at 50, it is unlikely that they can be refinanced in the ordinary course unless there is enough asset value to support a large secured financing that would refinance both the notes and the bank line.[8] Steelbox has limited cash ($6), so it does not have the internally funded deleveraging option present in the Webco case.

The concentration of ownership in a private equity fund is a key variable. Unlike disparate shareholders that are difficult to coordinate, with fund ownership one can assume that the fund executives and firm management are completely focused on attempting to find an economically rational solution. Furthermore, the fund is likely to have the wherewithal to write a check to "fix" the problem (which is exactly what the bank will be demanding), if the fund deems it a prudent investment. However, unless the fund is wildly more optimistic about the firm's outlook than the market appears to be, it is hard to imagine the fund investing more just to pay off the bonds.[9] Indeed, if the fund really likes the business, it would be far better off buying the bonds at 50 and forgiving them at maturity. Sometimes an investor in the notes needs to be wary of an equity sponsor (i.e., the fund) structuring a capital infusion as a borrowing senior to the notes in question.[10] The equity sponsor could be motivated to do this so as to maximize the recoverability of any incremental investment. This could be a risk in the Steelbox situation, but because the bank probably already has a pledge of all the assets, the best the fund could get would be a second lien. Even if that fund made a loan secured by a second lien, since the potential bankruptcy is within one year (the note maturity), the fund might be at risk of the loan being equitably subordinated,[11] which would be like writing a check to the notes. The fund's lawyers would do the best they could to create various legal artifices to minimize this risk, but there would still be some risk. Therefore, the fund will probably not write a check to fix the problem.

Accordingly, the investor should probably plan on a restructuring. The next question is when. This is effectively at the discretion of the bank. Steelbox is in technical default and apparently needs some money from the bank or the fund to make the $9 interest payment in two weeks. If the bank is extremely well collateralized and management is proposing a credible plan to reduce the bank's exposure (e.g., sell certain assets and use the proceeds to pay off the bank), it might agree to amend the loan (to cure the technical default) and partially fund the interest payment, but this would by no means be certain. The investor would probably want to make the conservative assumption that the coupon will not be paid and thus, if the bond is trading with interest (as opposed to flat), recognize that the real investment will be 56 (because of the accrued interest the investor will pay, which will not be returned in the coupon), not 50. In sum, the worst case is that the restructuring starts in two weeks, and the investor will collect no interest. The best case is that the restructuring is in one year, and the investor collects a coupon.[12]

Next, the investor needs to consider the type of restructuring: in-court or out-of-court. Steelbox has a fairly simple capital structure, so an out-of-court exchange offer would theoretically be feasible. However, if the time line is really only two weeks, there is insufficient time to effect such an exchange. If the fund has a strong view that an exchange is likely to enhance its value relative to a bankruptcy, then the fund might consider giving Steelbox sufficient capital to make the interest payment; this would effectively buy six months of planning time. Of course, the fund would prefer that the bank fund the interest payment on the strength of the collateral. The fund has no direct leverage to coerce the bank into increasing its exposure. However, it might propose that if the bank finances the interest payment, the fund would assure the bank that it would be the debtor-in-possession (DIP) lender (which typically carries very lucrative fees) if a chapter 11 is required despite the exchange offer. On the other hand, if the bank does not cooperate, Steelbox will use another lender for the DIP, and the sponsor might threaten to not use the lender on any of its other deals. If the bank is very comfortable with its collateral position, it may find the proposition attractive relative to the modest size of the advance.

Assume for a moment that the coupon payment is made, allowing Steelbox time to attempt an exchange offer. Should it be attempted? What would be its structure (i.e., what would it offer note holders)? Would it be successful? Would it allow Steelbox to avoid a chapter 11 later? It might be more efficient to start with the last question first: Would it ultimately help avoid chapter 11? Tied with this question is whether chapter 11 should be avoided. This is a difficult question to answer, particularly given the limited information that the prospective distressed investor is likely to have.

While it normally would be beneficial to restructure outside of chapter 11, here the nature of the firm may suggest that there would be benefits to a chapter 11 reorganization. A company in the steel industry typically has many on- and off-balance-sheet liabilities that a chapter 11 process is uniquely able to rationalize. These can include uncompetitive union labor contracts, uneconomic long-term purchase or sale contracts, legacy pension and postretirement benefit expenses, environmental cleanup liabilities, etc. Given that a significant percentage of the steel industry reorganized under chapter 11 protection in the 1998–2002 time period,[13] the note holders may conclude that a chapter 11 is inevitable, if for no other reason than the competitors that emerge from a chapter 11 restructuring are likely to have an advantageous cost structure.

Steelbox's competitive position relative to reorganized competitors will likely be a risk informally debated by note holders when any exchange offer is made. If the risk is viewed as significant, then the exchange offer is likely to fail, unless the note holders are somehow made better off. One possible inducement is to offer note holders an improvement in their claim status. Usually, an exchange offer involves a reduction in the claim. For example, on these facts, Steelbox would typically want to attempt a discount offer: perhaps a package of 60 in new, longer maturity notes and 10 in new common or preferred stock. Relative to the market price of 50, this would appear to offer a premium of 20.[14] It might even appear fair relative to the expected outcome in a bankruptcy because new notes at 60% of claim would imply total debt[15] of $140 ($50 bank + [$150 × 60%]), which would represent a reasonable 4.7x leverage based on a median EBITDA of $30. But if note holders expect that a chapter 11 would be required in the future anyway (because of the legacy costs and other issues), then they would be reluctant to do the exchange because, in the subsequent chapter 11, their senior unsecured claim would only be 60 and their 10 in equity would be subordinated to the multitude of other unsecured claims that are likely to be asserted. And, of course, since holdouts to the exchange would receive 100 at maturity, there is a substantial benefit to not cooperating.

Note holders might be willing to participate in an exchange if it appeared to improve their claim status. For example, if the offer above were made with 60 in second-lien notes (assuming that the bank agreement would allow this), then the note holders might go along despite the risk of a chapter 11 if they perceive that 60 in a second-lien claim is worth more than 100 in an unsecured claim.[16] In other words, they might be willing to participate if they thought that having secured status would allow them to recover 90% or more on the secured claim of 60 (i.e., 55) and potentially receive the benefit of postpetition adequate protection payments, as opposed to the unsecured claim that might recover only 20 because of the substantial dilution of off-balance-sheet claimants. In sum, if note holders perceive a chapter 11 as reasonably likely despite the exchange offer, they would not participate in an exchange (assuming aside the holdout issues) if it results in a decline in their claim, unless, despite the discount, they believe their net recovery will improve.

From the fund's perspective, it would prefer a discounted exchange because it reduces debt. The fund is reasonably indifferent to giving the second lien because its equity interest is junior to both secured and unsecured claims. Moreover, if the fund believes that chapter 11 might be necessary, it has a strong incentive to have the firm proceed with the exchange offer anyway, since the exchange would, if successful, reduce the claims senior to the equity. However, if the fund perceives that a chapter 11 is probable, then it is not likely to make an equity contribution to help fund the pending coupon payment (without which there is no time to attempt an exchange offer).

Where does all this thought lead the investor? It should suggest that Steelbox has very few options (to succumb to the obvious pun, it's in a box), and thus, the range of outcomes is fairly narrow. Given the industry, a chapter 11 process is probably needed to put Steelbox on competitively equal footing with its peers. If a chapter 11 will ultimately be needed, then it makes little sense for Steelbox to pay the pending interest payment, even if the bank is willing to fund it.[17] The prudent investor here would assume an immediate chapter 11. Other outcomes are possible, of course, but here the immediate filing would seem the most logical scenario. In the restructuring, there is likely to be significant uncertainty as to recoveries because the claim pool could be inflated with many nonfinancial claims (pensions, environmental issues, etc.), which tend to lengthen workout proceedings. Since Steelbox does have reasonably significant cash flow, a portion of the recovery is likely to be in debt, but a significant component is likely to be equity. These options are summarized in Figure 9-2.

If the investor perceives that the expected returns at 50 justify the outlook for an immediate, protracted bankruptcy where note holders could easily end up with a noncontrolling stake in the equity, then he or she should go ahead. Mathematically, the decision would be driven by the valuation and claims outlook. If the investor believes the correct value was 7x EBITDA of $30, or $210, the key is the amount of other unsecured claims. A simple calculation is presented in Table 9-3.

Summary

While lengthy, hopefully these examples illustrate the important point that proper analysis of the distressed firm's options is essential in predicting the course of the restructuring. Such analysis may not necessarily define the magnitude of the ultimate recovery, but it can significantly illuminate the course of the process, which is an important factor for an investor to consider. In the Webco case, the probability is to collect coupons for two years and then receive stock. In the Steelbox case, the probability is an immediate, lengthy and uncertain bankruptcy where the recovery will be in new debt and stock.[18] These are very different scenarios; one or the other may not be acceptable to certain investors regardless of the magnitude of the expected return. For example, a collateralized bond obligation[19] could potentially be interested in Webco, but

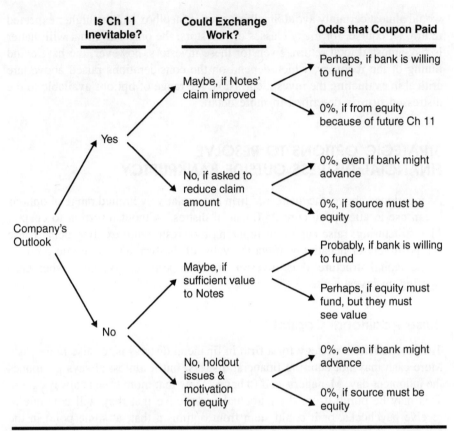

	Is Ch 11 Inevitable?	Could Exchange Work?	Odds that Coupon Paid
		Maybe, if Notes' claim improved	Perhaps, if bank is willing to fund
			0%, if from equity because of future Ch 11
	Yes	No, if asked to reduce claim amount	0%, even if bank might advance
Company's Outlook			0%, if source must be equity
		Maybe, if sufficient value to Notes	Probably, if bank is willing to fund
	No		Perhaps, if equity must fund, but they must see value
		No, holdout issues & motivation for equity	0%, even if bank might advance
			0%, if source must be equity

Figure 9-2. Steelbox Options

Table 9-3. Return Analysis of Steelbox

Estimated Value			210		
Secured Debt			(50)		
BKR and Administrative Claims			(15)		
Net to Unsecured Creditors			145		
Bond Claim	150	150	150	150	150
Other Unsecured	0	50	100	150	200
Total Unsecured	150	200	250	300	350
% Recovery to Unsecured	97%	73%	58%	48%	41%
1-Year Internal Rate of Return on Investment @ 50	93%	45%	16%	–3%	–17%

would almost certainly avoid Steelbox, even if Steelbox had the higher expected return. Of course, for many classes of investors, the only thing that will matter is risk-adjusted total return. Even for these investors, however, the nature and timing of the recovery, which depend on the considerations raised above, are critical in evaluating the investment. Next, the range of options available to the distressed firm is described in more detail.

STRATEGIC OPTIONS TO RESOLVE FINANCIAL DISTRESS OUTSIDE BANKRUPTCY

As mentioned above, the distressed firm has a relatively limited range of options it can use to attempt to cure its financial distress without resorting to chapter 11 restructuring: raise capital or repurchase or restructure existing debt. These can positively or negatively affect the value of the firm and/or certain portions of the capital structure; thus, investors must properly analyze them when considering an investment.

Raise Additional Capital

The most obvious strategy for a firm in financial distress is to raise more cash. More cash may not cure the financial distress, but it almost always postpones the judgment day. Managers tend to have a view that more time is always good. This may be purely from the parochial perspective that they will continue to receive paychecks, or it could stem from optimism that, at some point in the future, business conditions must improve. From the investor's perspective, raising cash has advantages and disadvantages. If it enhances the credit support for the particular piece of debt being considered, it can be a good, if not great, option. If it reduces credit support (e.g., new secured debt would be pledged assets that might previously have been indirectly available to the unsecured debt) or allows bad management more time to erode the value of the business, it is obviously less desirable.

Of course, firms in financial distress, by definition, do not have ready access to capital. In the Steelbox case, it was noted that the presence of a deep-pocketed equity holder could be positive because it was a potential source of capital. This is true, but these investors are not in the business of making eleemosynary contributions to debt holders. They will only make a further investment — which will be seen as potentially throwing good money after bad — if they view the investment as being in their best interest. And since many investment situations are essentially zero-sum games, this means the new capital can effectively come at the expense of creditors.

The two most common ways for a distressed firm to raise additional cash are to sell assets or borrow against assets.

Asset Sales

The concept of an asset sale is fairly straightforward. The type and nature of the assets that can be sold will vary by business. In some cases, it may be a discrete business unit; examples would include a diversified consumer products company selling or licensing a single brand or a media company selling a single property (newspaper, magazine, radio station, etc.). Natural resource companies might have producing or nonproducing properties either inside or outside of their main area of operation. Cable television companies might have pockets of stranded subscribers in noncontiguous service areas that are costly to service. Occasionally, there will be nonoperating assets such as underutilized land or buildings that can be sold. A key feasibility issue, however, is whether a potential purchaser will be willing to complete a transaction with the distressed company in light of the fact that if the seller subsequently files for bankruptcy, the sale transaction could potentially be unwound as a fraudulent conveyance. As discussed in Chapter 12, this factor frequently causes prospective purchasers to insist that the distressed seller file for chapter 11 protection in order that the buyer can purchase the assets in a bankruptcy court-approved transaction.[20]

Whether the asset sale benefits the distressed investor depends on the circumstances. Among the most critical factors, not surprisingly, is price. If the firm receives a good price, then the asset sale is potentially a value-enhancing event, depending on what happens to the cash. For example, if the asset sale is essentially being forced by bank lenders[21] and the cash is used to pay down bank debt, most creditors are generally better off. The holders of the secured debt are happy because they are being at least partially repaid. Holders of the unsecured debt, if any, will generally be happy[22] because the amount of secured debt above them is being reduced, and the probability of getting a decent price on the asset sale may be higher before, rather than after, filing for chapter 11.[23]

Mathematically, whether the debt will be better off turns on the relationship between the multiple of the EBITDA the sale price represents relative to leverage and how the proceeds are used. For example, assume a firm with $50 in EBITDA has $500 in notes trading at 40. This implies that the market-adjusted value of the debt is $200 (500 × 40%) and that leverage-at-face value is 10x (500/50), but only 4x (200/50) at market. Now assume that the firm sells a division that contributes $20 in EBITDA for $120, or 6x. Is this good or bad for the debt?

If the proceeds are used to pay off debt at face value, as they would if all or a portion of the debt was secured bank debt, then the face amount will decline to $380, which represents 12.6x the remaining $30 in EBITDA. Thus, leverage at face value increases. Mathematically, this will happen whenever the sale multiple is less than the leverage-at-face multiple.

What about leverage at market price? This, of course, will depend on how the sale affects market prices. On the one hand, if the old market price implied that the value of the firm was only 4x, then this suggests that since only $30 in EBITDA is left, the value of the firm is $120 ($30 × 4). Since there is $380 (500 – 120) in debt remaining, this would imply its value should decline to 31.5 (120/380). On the other hand, perhaps the lesson from the sale is that the market was undervaluing the firm. Perhaps the remaining $30 in EBITDA should also be valued at 6x. In that case, the value of the firm would be $180, implying that the value of the debt should rise to 47.3 (180/380).

This valuation approach presumes that the cash is used to retire the debt at face value. If the debt is in the form of publicly traded notes (which was the assumption), then the firm is likely to have the flexibility to attempt to buy the bonds in the open market at a discount. If it could invest all of the proceeds in bond repurchases at a price of 40, it could theoretically repurchase $300 (120/0.4) in notes, which would reduce the outstanding amount to $200. This would cause leverage at face to decline to 6.6x (200/30). Even if the remaining EBITDA is only worth 4x, the $120 (30 × 4) in enterprise value would suggest that the remaining $200 in bonds should be worth 60 (120/200). When asset sale proceeds can be used to retire debt at discounted market values, it probably will be accretive to the value of remaining debt. Of course, the fallacy here is the assumption that market prices fail to adjust — presumably the company's repurchase activities will cause prices to increase.

Secured Financings

If a firm has unencumbered assets, cash could also be raised through a secured borrowing of some type. However, the practical relevance of this option, in most cases, is rather limited. In the case of a credit that has always been below investment grade, there is a good chance that a bank lender that has become involved would have already demanded a collateral pledge of virtually all available assets. Even if the lender originally extended credit on an unsecured basis, as soon as operations started coming in below forecast and technical covenant defaults began occurring, a collateral pledge would probably be demanded as part of an early restructuring. Thus, by the time the firm begins to really become distressed, the bank would have already done its best to protect itself at the expense of unsecured creditors.

There are at least three situations that occasionally arise where the potential for a secured financing — which, again, may be adverse to an unsecured holder

— should be carefully analyzed. The first involves fallen angels: investment-grade credits whose credit quality has deteriorated to below investment grade. Typically these are large, often asset-rich companies which, because of their investment-grade status, have historically borrowed on an unsecured basis. Such credits will often have ample unsecured assets, and the primary analytical issue will be the structure of the negative pledge provision (as discussed in Chapter 7) that the existing debt's covenants are likely to contain.[24] Often, negative pledge provisions have fairly significant "carve-outs" that will be stated in either absolute (e.g., $100 million) or relative (e.g., 10% of net tangible assets) amounts. In the absence of other lending provisions that may be constraints (discussed below), these carve-outs essentially define how much cash the firm can raise on a secured basis.

A second group of credits that will often have unencumbered assets is in the technology sector. Technology companies, particularly start-ups in the microelectronics or biotechnology sectors, typically are not deemed good credits by traditional lending standards because they often have minimal, if any, positive cash flow after incurring research and development expenses and/or capital expenditures. However, in the late 1990s, many of these firms were able to raise significant amounts of capital through the issuance of convertible notes. At the time of issuance, most issuers, and investors, expected the notes to be retired through the issuance of appreciated equity, not in cash. When the equity valuation bubble broke in the 2000–2001 period, that expectation vanished and these financings suddenly became cash liabilities. Convertible notes, however, are almost always unsecured and typically do not include any meaningful protective covenants, including negative pledge provisions and limitations on borrowings. Thus, these issuers, when their financial circumstances deteriorate, can conceivably borrow on a secured basis with the only effective limitation being the value a secured lender is willing to ascribe to their assets. For example, lenders would be unlikely to ascribe much collateral value to the patent on a promising drug in Phase III clinical trials that is still at risk of not receiving FDA approval. However, if, instead of research and development, the firm had invested capital in a state-of-the-art drug production facility, then there might be some pledgeable assets.

Lastly, even in situations where secured debt already exists and has been factored into the analysis, it may be necessary to consider the risk that additional second-lien secured debt is layered into the capital structure above the unsecured debt. The practical feasibility of such a financing will turn on several factors. From the prospective second-lien lender's perspective, he or she will have to conclude that there is sufficient collateral value in excess of any existing first-lien debt that a loan based primarily on asset-based credit support is prudent. From the issuer's perspective, the key issues will be whether it is permitted

to incur the loan and grant security interests under its existing lending agreements. While these issues alone or in combination will usually limit the feasibility of such a financing, it has become an increasingly popular structure that
can pose risks for unsecured debt holders.[25]

In most cases, the addition of secured debt to a capital structure does not
enhance the value of existing unsecured credit and thus should be viewed as
a risk. The simple reason for this is that secured lenders always ask for more
than the value of their loan in collateral and, in a worst-case liquidation, are
more interested in liquidating that collateral quickly in a way that eliminates
their exposure rather than in a way that maximizes asset value. To the extent
that asset value is not maximized, this tends to be at the expense of unsecured
creditors. In addition, adequately secured claims usually are entitled to postpetition
payments, either for interest or adequate protection, which further erodes unsecured creditor recoveries.

Sale/Leaseback Financings

A sale/leaseback is a hybrid of the sales and secured financing approaches
discussed previously. In a sale/leaseback, the firm will sell an asset, usually real
property, to a third party with the implicit understanding that the new owner
will simultaneously lease it back to the selling firm. The transaction is advantageous relative to an outright sale because the firm may still need the asset for
its operations. It can offer advantages relative to a secured or mortgage financing in that the lease can be structured as an off-balance-sheet liability; thus, from
a simple GAAP perspective, leverage will appear lower. Furthermore, depending on the terms of the lease, the proceeds advanced may also be higher. For
example, assume a firm has an unencumbered warehouse it uses for distribution.
Given the value of warehouse facilities in that particular location, a commercial
mortgage lender might only be willing to lend $5 million because the lender
will tend to base the size of the loan on the "liquidation" value of the property.
On the other hand, a sale/leaseback can often be structured to capture some
going-concern value. If the firm were willing to enter into a 10-year lease that
provides for annual rental payments of $500,000, the lessor might be willing
to "pay" $7 million for the property. The effective cost of the funds under the
sale/leaseback will likely be higher, but the firm may gladly incur these in
exchange for the higher proceeds.

Equity Sponsors

The presence of a controlling (50%+) institutional equity holder in the capital
structure should generally be viewed as a positive to debt holders, although this

is not uniformly the case, particularly if the legal protections in the lending documents are weak. The reason it is a positive is that such an equity holder can typically only realize value on its equity investment after satisfying the debt claims, and thus there is a strong alignment of interest. This is, of course, always true with respect to equity, but when the equity is widely held by public shareholders, typically no single shareholder either has sufficient incentive to figure out how to solve the financial distress or is willing to let all the other shareholders "free-ride" on his or her efforts. Where the holder is a large institutional holder, such as a private equity or leveraged buyout fund, there is an ideal combination of incentive, sophistication, and wherewithal.

However, as noted above, such investors are very astute and only act when it is in their self-interest. The first thing to understand about the motivations of such investors or funds is that when the firm in which they have invested is in distress, the fund will be perceived as having made a costly mistake. So as an institutional matter, within the fund there is likely to be a certain amount of internal finger-pointing and a general reluctance to appear to be throwing good money after bad.

To put this point in perspective, it may be worth briefly discussing the structure of the typical private equity or leveraged buyout fund. These funds are basically pools of capital raised from other large, sophisticated investors that want investment diversification into an asset class that such institutions internally do not have the expertise to manage. Thus, an insurance company may self-manage a portfolio of mortgage-backed securities, but may outsource to a specialized fund an allocation of capital to a risky, but potentially high-return, asset class such as equity investments in leveraged buyouts. Investments in a leveraged buyout fund will typically be a minimum of $10 million and will be supervised or monitored by fairly sophisticated managers. It is embarrassing, but forgivable, for the managers of a fund to have to go to these investors and explain that they made a mistake — that despite all their expertise, brains, and the exorbitant fees, they lost money in a situation. This is acceptable, to a certain degree, because the investments are viewed as high risk and no one can be perfect all the time. But the level of potential risk to one's professional reputation becomes much higher when it is clear that one has already lost money and now is proposing to put more at risk. These are not naive investors prone to succumbing to the sunk-cost fallacy.[26] If the incremental investment is lost, it is a significantly more embarrassing event, particularly since the fund is likely to have extensive inside information on, if not essential control of, the distressed firm. It is no longer simply a regrettable mistake; it is a serious error in judgment.

Under these circumstances, it is hard to generalize about when an institutional equity sponsor will continue to participate, other than the obvious economic proposition that it will do so when it perceives it to be profitable and a way to enhance the probability of recovering some of its original investment. This latter point is important and bears illustration. Assume Powerfund owns 100% of the equity of Powerco, an independent power generator in a remote region, for which the fund invested $50 and, until recently, believed/estimated was worth $200. Powerco has been growing and recently was earning $100 of EBITDA annually. It has $400 in unsecured debt maturing in two years and a normal $20 coupon payable in two weeks. The firm has $10 in cash and an undrawn $50 bank revolver. Powerco's largest customer, Aluminumco, which buys 75% of Powerco's electricity output, unexpectedly files for bankruptcy, which triggers an event of default in the bank agreement.

Powerco's immediate problem is to arrange the funds for the upcoming $20 coupon; otherwise, it will default and risk being forced into bankruptcy. Powerco's bonds have a $50 carve-out in the negative pledge provision; thus, Powerfund could easily advance money for the coupon on a secured basis. Would Powerfund be likely to make the incremental investment? Even though the loan appears to be very safe, Powerfund's inclination to stay involved is likely to be significantly influenced by the implications for its existing investment. For example, assume that Aluminumco is expected to liquidate, never purchase another kilowatt of electricity, and no substitute consumer of power is available. In that case, Powerfund's equity investment is probably completely gone, and it will have very little interest in ongoing involvement — Powerfund is not in the business of making short-term secured loans, even seemingly safe ones.[27]

Alternatively, assume Aluminumco is expected to remain a profitable customer both during and following its bankruptcy, but if Powerco is forced to file for bankruptcy, then Aluminumco will start purchasing 50% of its electricity needs from another source. In that case, if Powerfund does not make the advance, it will jeopardize its original investment, which likely will continue to be worth something only if Aluminumco continues to buy all of its electricity from Powerco. In that case, it will almost certainly make the advance because it enhances the recoverability of its original investment.[28]

To add a note of realism to the situation, two observations should be made. First, in the event Powerco were forced to file chapter 11, any loan Powerfund makes on a secured basis is subject to the risk of being attacked on an equitable subordination theory. Second, in the typical case, Aluminumco would likely have a well-defined supply contract with Powerco. If Powerco filed for bankruptcy, it probably would be able to reject such a contract if it were in its economic interest to do so. However, Aluminumco would have no comparable right, even if the contract stated that a bankruptcy filing by either party was a default. Aluminumco would likely still have to continue purchasing power.

Reducing Leverage

Another tool available to a distressed company to resolve its financial distress is to take steps to reduce its leverage by purchasing or otherwise acquiring the debt at a discount. In general, there are three typical approaches that can be used.

Open Market Repurchases

The easiest method for a firm to purchase its debt at a discount is open market repurchases. Normally, discount debt repurchases can only be effected with respect to bonds. If the firm has bank debt and the debt is in sufficient distress to cause it to be sold at a meaningful discount, the lenders will be likely to have sufficient power via the lending agreements to require any available cash to be used to repay the debt at face.

To effect a bond purchase, the firm, like any investor, will simply call broker-dealers active in its bonds and make purchases through such dealers at the then current price.[29] The primary strategic consideration the firm will have is keeping its activities secret. Once the market learns the firm is a buyer, market prices for the bonds may increase.[30] The firm would be required (as an accounting matter) to disclose the repurchases in its quarterly 10-Q filings since the purchases affect the balance sheet totals for cash and debt and are likely to have income statement implications. Even purchases made after the end of the fiscal period in question, but before the filing of the disclosure document, are typically disclosed in the filing because they are deemed material subsequent events.[31] However, this leaves a window between the date the firm makes its required filing and when it next announces earnings or makes another required financial filing to affect its repurchases without market knowledge. There is nothing to prevent the firm from continuing to repurchase bonds after it publicly discloses it has been doing so; it is just that market prices are likely to increase to reflect such information.

Direct Purchases from Holders

Besides purchasing bonds from or through broker-dealers, a firm can make direct, individually negotiated purchases from holders. The typical scenario for these purchases is that a holder, anticipating that the firm may be a purchaser, will call the firm and offer to sell the securities. Holders, which could include the distressed investor, will do this on the expectation that they can receive a higher net price since no fee needs to be paid to a broker-dealer intermediary.

Returning to the Webco case study, the following is representative of the negotiating dynamic that might take place. A holder of a significant block of bonds, say $40, or 20% of the issue (if the holder does not have a significant block, it is unlikely Webco would get involved), might call Webco's treasurer and offer the bonds for sale. The holder will have researched the market and received general price indications from several dealers that the bonds are trading in a 24–26 context, but only in small size. The treasurer will know that the firm's bonds have generally been quoted in the mid-20s. The holder may start the process by offering the block at 29. If the treasurer suggests the market had been mid-20s, the holder might respond that the ability to buy a block is worth a premium. The savvy treasurer may feign indifference, or a lack of authority to make the purchase, but say that he or she will check internally and get back to the holder. The treasurer will then, in an effort to be as casual as possible, call a dealer (probably the underwriter of the notes) and ask for a general update, information on any recent trades, etc. The treasurer would be unwise to ask, "What would I need to bid to bring out $40 bonds?" because this would be a significant signal to the dealer. Thus, even though the treasurer might generally trust the dealer, he or she might fear that the dealer would then go out in the market and indicate the company was an aggressive bidder in size or start buying bonds for the dealer's own inventory ahead of the company. If this in fact happened, the market would be likely to adjust the prices upward. It should be noted that, similarly, the holder would never go to a dealer and say the equivalent of "I want out. What's your bid for $40 bonds?" because this would certainly depress prices and hurt the holder's negotiating position.

Thus, a negotiation or dance is started. Webco does not have to buy the holder's particular bonds, nor does the holder need to sell them only to Webco. A voluntary transaction will need to be negotiated. If Webco has made the decision that it wants to start buying bonds, a block of $40 will be attractive, and some premium might be merited. On the facts given, the price would probably work out somewhere between 26 and 29.

Cash Tender Offers

The most public way that bonds can be repurchased in the market is through a tender offer process. In a tender offer, a firm, through a mechanism prescribed by the Securities Act, will propose to purchase bonds in accordance with a very specific set of conditions. These conditions will typically include a deadline by which tenders must be received, the maximum amount that will be purchased (and the pro-ration process if more than the maximum is tendered), and the price. Recently, the price component of many tender offers has been structured as a modified Dutch auction. In a modified Dutch auction, a firm will offer to purchase a specified face amount of bonds at a clearing price within a specified

Table 9-4.   Determination of Clearing Price in a Modified Dutch Auction

Tender Price	Tender Amount	Cumulative
31	45	
30	35	
29	30	105
28	30	75
27	25	45
26	20	20
Total	185	

price range. (The concept of "modified" relates to the specification of price boundaries; in a "pure" Dutch auction, there would be no specific price range).

To continue the Webco example, rather than engage in one-off market transactions, the firm might decide that it would be cost-effective to make a tender offer for a significant portion of its bonds. The terms of the offer might be to purchase $100 face amount of bonds at a modified Dutch auction clearing price between 26 and 31 on a date 30–45 days in the future. If they wish to participate, holders will be directed to submit tenders of their bonds at specified prices by the closing of the tender offer period. At the conclusion of the auction period, Webco will review the tenders and determine the minimum price at which a total of $100 has been tendered. Table 9-4 illustrates how the "clearing" price, in this case 29, in a modified Dutch auction would be determined. All the bonds tendered at a price of 29 or less (potentially subject to pro ration since more than the tender amount was tendered) will receive the clearing price.

The reasons why a firm would choose a tender offer versus open market repurchases largely turn on a variety of practical and strategic considerations. In general, open market purchases are preferred because they are simpler, faster, more discreet, require limited legal and related professional expenditures, and can usually be accomplished without unduly moving market prices. If the re-purchases are going to be relatively modest in scope, say the lesser of 20% of the bonds outstanding or $20 million (which is usually the result of the firm having a limited amount of cash), then open market purchases are probably the preferred approach. If the repurchase is for a large quantity of bonds (on either an absolute or relative basis) or consideration other than cash will be used for some or all of the purchase price, then a tender offer is the more logical alternative.

From the distressed investor's perspective, the primary consideration is how the company's options can affect the investor's objectives. If the investor already has a "full position," then from the simple perspective of making money, any kind of repurchase activity by the issuer is good. At one level, the firm is just another buyer in the market (and unless the firm is doing the repurchase via a tender offer or, for some reason, the firm's repurchase activities have become known,[32] the investor will probably not know that the firm is a buyer), and, if the distressed investor is a holder, that is generally a good thing. If the investor accumulated his or her position at an attractive price and simply wants to realize a holding period gain through a quick sale, then the implicit market "support" of having a large buyer is good. Even if the investor does not want to sell, the fact that the firm is repurchasing its debt at a discount is usually a favorable credit development.

On the other hand, if the distressed investor has not yet accumulated his or her desired position, then the prospect of the firm being a potential buyer has a different set of trade-offs. It may imply that the investor should move quickly to establish his or her position before the firm becomes a competing buyer for the bonds. Or it may mean an investor has a reasonably attractive short-term investment opportunity to buy now on the expectation he or she can sell at a higher price paid by the firm. Or it may mean, in the scenario where the market reflects the fact that the firm is a prospective buyer, market prices are "fair" and future purchases by the firm may not cause significant appreciation. Or it may mean that in complicated capital structures with multiple layers of debt, the fulcrum security that will receive the most relative benefit of a restructuring will change. There is no general guidance that can be given to distinguish one of these possible scenarios (and there are, of course, many more) from another, but these are the types of considerations that the distressed investor needs to weigh in the strategic calculus.

Under what circumstances will a cash tender offer be successful? Two important aspects are (1) that the amount of bonds remaining, even if the tender is successful relative to the remaining enterprise value, should be significant and (2) that holdouts should have a relatively low probability of (or at least significant uncertainty about) receiving a cash recovery of principal in the future. Consider the following hypothetical situation. A technology firm has $200 in cash and $300 in subordinated debt maturing in three years that trades at 40. The firm has an operating cash burn of $25 per quarter. Management says this burn will eventually be reduced and break-even operations are attainable, but given historic performance, there is understandable investor skepticism. The firm makes a tender offer for up to $200 of its bonds at a price of 40 (or it uses a Dutch auction with a range from 38–44). Given these facts, note holders, unless they have significant conviction that the firm's business has significantly more value than the general market believes,[33] would have a strong incentive to tender. Looking at it from the holdout's perspective, if everyone tenders at 40, the firm will spend $80 of its cash, leaving a balance of $120. At a burn rate of $25 a quarter, this implies that the firm will be out of cash in five quarters, potentially leading to a payment default on the remaining bonds. Although the ratio of cash to remaining debt will improve, in general, the posttender offer outlook poses significant risks for the holdouts. Further, given the firm's need to fund its cash burn, the holdouts could not reasonably expect that the firm will come back to the market after the tender and purchase bonds at a higher price. In fact, to completely eliminate holdouts' hopes that higher priced repurchases will occur after the tender, firms have begun including explicit prohibitions against future repurchases in the terms of the tender offer.[34] Under these circumstances, the prospects for a successful tender offer are reasonable.

Exchange Offers

As described above, by repurchasing its debt at a discount, either through open market purchases or a tender offer, a firm can significantly reduce its leverage. However, this requires cash, and in general, firms in financial distress do not have significant amounts of excess cash. There were a relatively large number of cash-rich distressed credits in the 2000–2003 period because firms used the valuation bubble of 1997–2000 to raise capital, but this was a fairly unusual circumstance.

More typically, a firm is in distress because it has limited cash. In these circumstances, repurchasing debt, even at very steep discounts, may not be a practical option. However, deleveraging can be accomplished via an exchange offer using new securities of the distressed firm as consideration. Exchange offers can be structured in many ways, but a useful way of distinguishing them is whether they are coercive or non-coercive, which essentially corresponds with the carrot and stick approach.

Coercive Exchange Offers

Exchange offers are "coercive" when they compel cooperation by exposing nonparticipants to the risk of being made worse off. Returning to the Webco example above, assume that Webco has $90 in cash instead of $200 and that its debt trades at 20. Given its cash burn and investment obligations, it would be fiscally imprudent for Webco to use its cash for debt repurchases since it only has a limited amount of liquidity. But its heavy debt load is almost certainly dooming Webco to bankruptcy if it cannot restructure. The firm could propose, subject to a 90% participation requirement, to exchange each old bond for 25 cents (just to make it appear that a premium is being offered relative to the prior trading price) of a new senior secured note that matures the day before the old subordinated note. Since the new notes are senior secured, they would obviously have a higher priority than the original subordinated notes in the event of a bankruptcy.[35] Thus, old note holders that choose to hold out and not participate would retain their full claim, but would be at risk of receiving very little in a bankruptcy (which, given the facts, is a fairly high risk) due to the subordination. Note that if 100% participate (the 90% condition is a floor, not a cap), debt will be reduced from $200 to $50, an amount that Webco can "afford," and yet still represents a 25% premium from the prior trading level.

Noncoercive Exchange Offers

A noncoercive exchange offer, the reader might anticipate, does not "threaten" to make the nonparticipant worse off as a result of nonparticipation. Instead, the offer attempts to present a comparatively attractive opportunity in order to induce participation. For example, assume that it is 18 months later and Webco has only $30 in cash left and is facing the full $200 note maturity in six months. Now it has relatively fewer options because of the limited amount of time and cash available. The most obvious transaction to attempt is a voluntary debt for equity exchange. Since a default appears to be inevitable, bondholders should already have an expectation that they will ultimately hold equity. Accordingly, a voluntary exchange will facilitate the same result without the need to go through the expense and potential damage to the enterprise of a bankruptcy. Thus, if Webco were to offer note holders a very high percentage of the common stock (e.g., 90% or more) on the condition that 90% or more of the notes are tendered, note holders would effectively own the firm without the value loss entailed in a bankruptcy process. Some might argue that in a bankruptcy, the notes would likely own 100% of the stock. This may or may not be true. For example, Webco might have technology that is very difficult to value. In a bankruptcy, the equity holders might argue that Webco's asset value is greater than the $200 bond balance, regardless of what the market trading values of the securities imply, and the equity should retain a stake. In any case, the rational decision for a note holder is to compare the prospect of owning 100% of Webco after a chapter 11 process versus 90% without. If a bankruptcy could erode enterprise value by more than 10%, then the latter would be preferable, and the exchange has a reasonable chance for success. There will, of course, still be a holdout challenge, but this is an inherent shortcoming of any voluntary process.

CONSTRAINTS ON THE RANGE OF OPTIONS

While the range of options discussed above is theoretically available to any distressed firm, circumstances will make many of them impractical. Thus, the distressed investor can narrow down the range of issues to analyze by looking at the broader circumstances of the firm. The key factors to look for that effectively constrain the firm's choices are as follows.

Liquidity

If the firm has limited excess liquidity, then it probably does not have the ability to make discounted note purchases. This is important since it eliminates the easiest mechanism to reduce leverage and a source of price support or appreciation for the debt.

Time-to-Liquidity Event

After determining the amount of liquidity, the next issue is how much time remains until the firm's next significant liquidity event. The definition of a liquidity event is relative. For example, in the Steelbox case, the firm did not have enough cash to make the next coupon payment; that was the next liquidity event. For Webco, which had $200 in cash, there was no liquidity event for two years. Many things can give rise to a liquidity event, including interest payments, debt principal repayment obligations, negative operating cash flow, pension funding requirements, and litigation judgments. In any distressed situation, the analyst should make a projection, unless it is patently obvious, to estimate the cause and timing of the event.

The time until the liquidity event is critical because many of the options discussed above take time, as a practical matter, to effect. For example, it is difficult to complete the sale of a business unit in two months, but it is a viable option if one has six months or more. Exchange offers typically take at least 60 days to plan and complete. Competent management should be proactive in its efforts to avoid becoming time constrained. However, not all managements are as competent as one would hope. And even competent managers cannot foresee all events. For example, perhaps investment bankers had assured the firm that it could access the capital markets to refinance an obligation, but then an unanticipated event roils the markets. Or perhaps the firm was in the process of selling an asset to raise capital when the buyer backed away or defaulted. Even if the distressed firm believes it has legal recourse against the counterparty in such events, that will not solve the liquidity problem.

For a particularly dramatic real-life example, consider the previously mentioned case of HealthSouth Corporation in March 2003. At the end of 2002, HealthSouth had approximately $3 billion in debt against $600 million in EBITDA and was rated Ba1/BBB–. It had a $400 million subordinated note maturing on April 1, 2003, but it was assumed that this maturity would be funded by drawing down on the company's unsecured bank revolver, which had approximately $1 billion in availability. In late March 2003, an accounting fraud was disclosed and the banks declared a breach of the revolver, preventing any further borrowings. This was 11 days before the company was supposed to write a $400 million check to retire the maturing subordinated notes. HealthSouth's senior notes and subordinated notes fell significantly, and it appeared fairly certain that the company would need to file for chapter 11 protection. Had the next bond maturity been two years away instead of two weeks, the risk of chapter 11 would likely have been manageable because the company was reasonably profitable and arguably would have had a number of options for raising cash, including asset sales or arranging secured borrowings. But given the two-week constraint, it effectively had very few options and, in fact, failed to pay the scheduled maturity. As it turned out, the note holders, apparently seeing no advantage in forcing a chapter 11, did not declare a default and instead began negotiations with the company on what turned out to be a successful consensual resolution.[36]

Magnitude of Problem

The ability of a distressed firm to work out its issues on its own will, in part, be determined by the relative size of the problem. Relative, of course, is a function of time and resources. As suggested by Steelbox, sometimes the problem can be as small as a coupon payment, but if liquidity is constrained and there is very little planning time, small problems can be big problems. Webco had $200 in cash, which was adequate relative to its debt, but obviously would not have been had its debt been $2000 or its operating cash burn been $50 per quarter.

Complexity of Capital Structure

In general, the more layers that exist in a capital structure, the more difficult it will be for the firm to restructure. In particular, if there is a significant amount of secured bank debt, the range of options will likely be significantly constrained because of the onerous covenants usually found in such facilities. If assets are sold, typically the proceeds will need to be applied to reduce the bank debt, not buy back junior debt at a discount. Coercive exchange offers will likely not be able to offer first liens, and there could be constraints on the maturity structure that could be used. Even the free use of cash may be constrained by restricted payment tests. It is essential that the analyst carefully evaluate the provisions of all significant capital instruments when formulating an analysis of the firm's options.

Severability of Business Units

Asset sales can be an important source of liquidity, but only if there are discrete assets that can be sold. Thus, in a diversified business with core and noncore operations, there may be many sale opportunities. On the other hand, where the firm is one single business, such as a casino or a steel mill for example, then there may be no nonessential parts that can be sold.

Cause(s) of Financial Distress

As discussed in detail in Chapter 8, it is always important to understand why the business became distressed. The cause of the distress will often significantly narrow the distressed firm's range of options.

STRATEGIES WHEN BANKRUPTCY APPEARS NECESSARY

If the investor's assessment is that a distressed firm's circumstances are such that a bankruptcy is highly likely or inevitable, he or she will also want to analyze what moves the firm may make as it starts preparing for that process. Many of these issues will be discussed in more detail in Chapter 12, but it is important to anticipate how a firm will provide for liquidity and the potential length of the bankruptcy.

Maintaining Liquidity

When a distressed firm confronts the reality that it will likely need to file bankruptcy, or should at least consider the option, the first issue it will focus on is how to maintain liquidity.[37] When a firm files for bankruptcy, working capital from prepetition sources effectively freezes. If there was a revolving credit line, it will be frozen, together with the cash pledged as collateral. Suppliers that previously extended customary terms will demand payment in cash either on or even before delivery. Customers that would normally pay receivables will likely delay as they assess what will happen to the distressed firm. Accordingly, it should be assumed that the distressed firm will prepare for this reality and factor it into the investment analysis.

There are three common techniques that a distressed firm will likely use to maintain or provide for postpetition liquidity. First, a firm will probably begin stretching its payables. As cash becomes dear, only the most critical invoices will be paid. Payable performance can be monitored as a potential indicator of a firm's distresses. The important strategic consideration on which the investor should focus is how this potentially affects his or her claim. Stretching payables essentially means that the claims of the trade creditors will be relatively greater. If the investor is considering an investment that is junior in priority to the trade claims (for example, because of structural subordination), it may negatively affect the recovery analysis. If the investor is considering secured paper, then it has less effect.

Second, a distressed firm may attempt to draw down on its revolving line of credit. If the firm has been relatively chronically distressed and forced to seek multiple amendments from its bank lenders, this is likely not a significant risk because the lending agreement will give the banks so much power that the borrower's flexibility will be rather limited. However, if the analyst is looking at a situation where, although the firm is deteriorating, it still has relatively free access to a line of credit with significant borrowing availability, more often than not this liquidity will be used as a tool to forestall a bankruptcy. But when financial circumstances change quickly and the firm realizes that bankruptcy is inevitable, it might draw down all available lines to build a cash war chest.

A final liquidity measure a distressed firm will pursue is to prearrange a DIP lending facility. This is fairly standard and thus should be anticipated, whether it is arranged beforehand or put in place after filing. Unsecured investors should almost always assume that a DIP will be put in place and, to the extent they can, factor the implications into their recoveries.

Preplanned Filings

As discussed in Chapter 12, when feasible, it is in the best interest of a firm to prenegotiate a bankruptcy agreement with creditors. To the extent the broad outlines of a proposed plan of reorganization can be agreed to, and sometimes even formally voted on, it can greatly streamline the chapter 11 process. The primary reason the distressed investor will want to focus on this issue is its effect on the timing of the back-end recovery. Where circumstances are such that some level of preplanning is possible, the investor will want to factor that into his or her analysis. For example, suppose a bond facing the likely prospect of a bankruptcy is trading for 25 and has an expected recovery of 35. If the market is pricing the bond on the assumption the chapter 11 will last the normal 15 months, an acceptable 30% internal rate of return is implied, but the investor would not want to chase the bonds much above the 25 level. On the other hand, for the investor convinced that the situation was ripe for a preplanned reorganization that would only last six months, a purchase at 25 would represent an 80% annualized return. Given this outlook, one could aggressively bid the bonds to 29, which likely would allow the investor to accumulate all he or she wanted and, if right, enjoy a 41% annualized return. Therefore, being able to correctly anticipate an expedited chapter 11 process may allow the investor to capture an opportunity that others may decline because they believe it offers inadequate return potential.

SUMMARY

Understanding the potential "self-cure" methods available to a distressed firm is critical to making probability assessments of the likely direction of the workout. In particular, it can tremendously influence deciding when and how to invest. For example, if the investor's analysis of a situation in the early stages of distress is that the firm will ultimately have no options other than bankruptcy, and it will likely steadily deteriorate until forced to file, then, depending on market prices, this could prompt the investor to either short the bonds or delay the timing of a long investment. On the other hand, where a firm has viable options, this must also be taken into account. The investor might inappropriately avoid a situation based on the assumption that the firm would ultimately file for bankruptcy, when in fact a consensual restructuring that boosted bond values might be arranged.

A firm's planning moves can also hurt investment returns. For example, if the investor invests on the premise that a consensual debt/equity exchange will be offered, he or she may be disappointed if, instead, a coercive discounted exchange is launched or, in other situations, if significant amounts of secured debt are added above the investor's bonds.

In the next chapter, the focus turns to the investor's moves. This will allow the valuation calculus previously developed to be melded with a view of the strategies the distressed firm may employ to come up with a variety of investment options.

This Chapter's Chess Moves

20. Bd2, Qe8

21. Be1, Qg6

10

PROFITING FROM FINANCIAL DISTRESS: THE INVESTOR'S PERSPECTIVE

The final portion of this book makes the transition from the fundamentals to strategies. Reverting to the chess analogy, the nature of the playing board and the moves of the players/pieces must be developed before strategy can be meaningfully discussed. Chapter 9 dealt with the "strategies" or "moves" available to the distressed firm. As alluded to earlier, in the first portion of the "restructuring game," the distressed investor is a relatively passive observer, similar to a vulture circling over a distressed gazelle fleeing from a cheetah. As in any "chase," the pursuer must consider the "exit" strategies of the pursued. Chapter 9 reviewed the various options (discount debt repurchases, exchange offers, asset sales, etc.) available to a distressed firm to relieve or escape its financial distress outside a chapter 11 context and how those options might impact the investment decision.

This chapter begins the process of exploring the distressed investor's "moves." Viewed from one perspective, the range of moves is fairly limited: buy, don't buy, hold, sell, sell short. At this level, it would not take an entire paragraph, let alone a chapter, to review the options, but that would be like reducing poker to a game of merely betting or not betting.

Fortunately, there is a little more to distressed investing than merely buying or selling. There are the related questions of what, when, how, how much, and price. Decisions on these choices must be made within the context of the investor's objectives and existing market realities. This chapter begins by first considering the investor's objectives and then reviewing the implications of those objectives to the just-mentioned questions. To a certain extent, that discussion will be premised on the existence of a "perfect world" where it is feasible for the investor to implement the strategy. Of course, there is nothing perfect about the world of distressed investing, so next it is important to apply the practical overlay of the reality of the market environment, which encompasses not only considerations of price but also who else is involved and the distribution of holdings (i.e., the other players and their cards). Finally, the chapter closes with an examination of various hedging strategies distressed investors often utilize.

Since the discussion is turning from theoretical to practical, it will be considerably more numbers oriented. The math involved, however, is fairly basic. The discussion will assume the reader is conversant with the basics of using the earnings before interest, taxes, depreciation, and amortization (EBITDA) multiple method of estimating enterprise valuations (EV) (review Chapter 5) and the basic implications of a firm's EV for the value of its debt and equity securities (review Chapter 6).

DEFINING THE INVESTMENT OBJECTIVES

Obviously, the investment objective is always to have the highest possible risk-adjusted return. Practically speaking, there are constraints on the pursuit of that objective. First, not all investors, even institutional investors, have the same tolerance for risk. Insurance companies and mutual funds tend to be relatively risk averse, while hedge funds usually, but not always,[1] are willing to accept more risk. Second, many institutions simply do not want to deal with the procedural complexity and "hassle" associated with distressed debt reorganizations. Third, the absolute level of risk tolerance will often vary with changes in the macroenvironment and the perception of how "competing" asset classes will perform. In both the 1990–1992 and 2000–2002 periods, for example, when there were a relatively large number of distressed investment opportunities (see Chapter 2), high-yield bonds tended to lead the recovery before equity participated.[2] On a macro basis, investment funds started rotating toward the high-yield asset class, causing all ships to rise with the tide. During such periods, portfolio managers may select situations or securities where expected returns are adequate, but the downside risk is deemed minimal — they want to avoid being sunk by a torpedo. Alternatively, when other asset classes (i.e., equity, mortgage-backed securities, etc.) are also performing well and the manager is competing to get a bigger share of a fixed or shrinking pie, he or she may take more risk in the belief that better returns will be required for his or her fund to remain competitive.

After defining risk tolerance, the basic issues are how the investor expects to exit the investment, the form of recovery, and the level of involvement that will be required to increase the odds of achieving the desired outcome. These will be different for nearly every situation.

TAILORING A STRATEGY TO THE INVESTMENT OBJECTIVES

To help illustrate the issues, variations on the following hypothetical situations involving Chipco, illustrated in Table 10-1, will be referred to in examining some of the more common investment approaches. When potential returns are discussed, in most cases only simple price appreciation will be calculated, rather than total rates of return (TRR). TRR includes both price appreciation and interest income received and is time weighted for the period of investment.[3] While it is a more comprehensive measure of investment return, it also requires fairly detailed assumptions about the period over which the investment is presumed to be held (whether interest payments are actually made, the amount of

Table 10-1. Debt and Leverage Metrics of Chipco at 12/31/02

		Debt	Amount	Price	Market Value	YTM
LTM Period End	12/31/02					
Settlement Date	1/15/03					
Cash	100	Secured Bank Term Loan	150	100	150	5.5%
		9.0% Senior Notes 6/1/04	350	90	315	17.4%
Peak EBITDA	350	9.5% Senior Notes 3/1/09	500	82	410	14.0%
LTM EBITDA	150	6.0% Convertible Sub Notes 2/1/06	250	65	163	22.5%
		Total	1250		1038	
		Equity	200		200	

	Leverage	At Face	Net at Market
EBITDA = 150	Thru Senior	6.7x	5.2x
	Thru Sub	8.3x	7.1x
EBITDA = 250	Thru Senior	4.0x	3.1x
	Thru Sub	5.0x	4.3x
EBITDA = 350	Thru Senior	2.9x	2.2x
	Thru Sub	3.6x	3.0x

LTM = last 12 months. YTM = yield to maturity.

accrued interest at the time of purchase, etc.), which significantly complicates the discussion. Furthermore, to verify TRR results, the reader would have to perform fairly sophisticated modeling, whereas price appreciation calculations are simple division on a hand calculator. The use of simple appreciation versus TRR as the measure of investment return should not alter the basic analytical conclusions.

It is January 2003. Chipco is involved in semiconductor chip manufacturing and board assembly and has highly cyclical operations. In its peak year, it generated $350 in EBITDA, but in the year just ended only $150. At year end 2002, its capital structure and market trading values were as shown in Table 10-1. As the reader by now can hopefully easily identify, the primary credit issue facing Chipco is its ability to refinance the 9.0% senior notes due June 1, 2004 (the '04 seniors).

Non-Chapter 11 Situations

Some distressed debt investors prefer not to become involved in the chapter 11 reorganization process if they can avoid it.[4] They seek investment opportunities that, in their view, are either likely to avoid bankruptcy or can be sold for a profit before any potential filing. Such investments can be done on either a passive or active basis.

Passive Involvement

A passive investment is the simplest, most basic, and most common investment scenario. The investor believes a security is trading at below "fair" value. If purchased, the bond should, over time, rise to its fair value, at which point it will be sold or held until it is paid off at maturity, in either case resulting in an attractive return. This approach is common in both equity and nondistressed bond contexts. The only difference here is that the target is a distressed firm. The reasons why the investor may expect the bond to increase in value can vary. It may be that he or she believes other investors are mistaken concerning certain structural aspects of the bond (e.g., perhaps the bond is depressed because it is unsecured and secured debt has been layered on top of it, but the investor has reason to believe the priority will ultimately be invalidated). It may be that the underlying business is cyclical and the implied "market" valuation fails to take this into account (e.g., Chipco's leverage at face through the debt is 8.3x last 12 months (LTM) EBITDA, but this is cyclically depressed and a more normalized $250 EBITDA figure implies leverage of only 5.0x). It may be that the investor believes the firm will attempt to delever by repurchasing its bonds at a discount and such purchase activity will drive up prices. Many investment rationales for why a distressed bond may appreciate are possible, and in most cases, the rationale will have few, if any, implications for how the investment strategy is implemented. The investor will simply attempt to identify the most advantageous buy-in point, make the purchase, and then monitor the situation to determine the validity of the investment rationale and the opportune sale or exit point.

When the target has a complex capital structure with a variety of investment choices (e.g., bank debt, senior unsecured bonds, subordinated bonds), the investor will want to weigh the risk/reward trade-offs of each security. For example, in the case of Chipco, the investor may view the 2002 EBITDA of $150 as the "trough" and expect it to rebound substantially. The 9.50% senior notes due in 2009 ('09 seniors) are trading at 82, while the 6% convertible[5] subordinated notes due 2006 (sub notes) are trading at 65. The relatively more risk-averse investor may prefer the '09 seniors by reasoning that if his or her investment thesis is right, the bonds may improve to 90 (10% return), but there is relatively limited downside risk given that the bonds are senior. In making the latter assessment, the investor notes that net leverage at market through the senior notes based on last year's low-cycle EBITDA was 5.2x, which, based on a comparable company analysis he or she has performed, should be covered by the value of Chipco.

The more aggressive investor may prefer the sub notes, reasoning that if he or she is right about a rebound in the fundamentals, perhaps they will improve to 75 (23.0% appreciation), and although they are junior and vulnerable in a restructuring (net leverage at market using $150 EBITDA through the sub notes is a relatively high 7.1x), this is an acceptable worst-case risk. The sub notes are particularly interesting because of their near-term maturity (three years), which, because they are trading at a significant discount (i.e., 65), implies a relatively high 22.5% YTM if they are paid off. In addition, if the '04 seniors are successfully refinanced, the sub notes become the next maturity in the capital structure and thus, from a term-structure perspective, are ahead of the '09 seniors.[6]

Table 10-2 summarizes some of the potential investment scenarios available to the passive investor, but it should be used thoughtfully. While the approach used in this table can be helpful in visualizing various strategies, investors are cautioned that these types of analyses tend to imbue too much certainty to selected data points. The investor should bear in mind that estimates of future trading levels represent little more than educated guesses. The better, although more complex, approach would be to use a range of values. Similarly, presenting this analysis in a decision tree framework almost automatically suggests that probabilities can be attached to various outcomes to derive an "expected" result. This type of analysis may seem like a logical and rigorous extension, but

Table 10-2.   Investment Options/Outcomes for Passive Investor

Scenario	Security/ Price	If Refinanced	If Chapter 11	Profit/ Loss	Price Change
Medium Risk	'04 Senior 90	➤100		10	11.1%
			➤80	(10)	−11.1%
Lower Risk	'09 Senior 82	➤85		3	3.7%
			➤80	(2)	−2.4%
Higher Risk	Sub Note 65	➤80		15	23.1%
			➤25	(40)	−61.5%

investors need to remain mindful that there will almost never be an empirical basis from which to derive a probability. Every distressed situation is unique, and hence such probability assessments are essentially the analyst's judgment. Considering the impact of different outcomes and probabilities is useful in considering risk, but there is a great tendency, once data are placed in a spread-sheet and values are calculated, to elevate these "calculated values" to the status of "answers."

Active Involvement

In some situations, the investor may identify an undervalued security but anticipate that in order to realize higher values, active investor participation will be required. The most typical situation is when the investor believes that although the target firm is in financial distress, it has fairly good options (such as note buybacks, private exchanges, or public exchange offers) for avoiding the chapter 11 process. These opportunities, as reviewed in Chapter 9, are most commonly present when the target firm's financial distress is solely a function of overleverage and it has a reasonably simple capital structure (ideally only the distressed debt in question) and/or significant cash. In these cases, even though the target firm must ultimately take the desired action, the investor, through his or her involvement, may be able to increase the probability of a value-enhancing out-of-court resolution.

For example, the investor may believe that he or she can acquire a reasonably large block of the distressed bonds and then, by organizing the other note holders, approach the firm with various restructuring scenarios to reduce leverage. Most management teams are inexperienced in the restructuring process and often in denial about the severity of their circumstances. This was particularly true of the managements of many Internet-bubble companies; they had difficulty confronting the reality that although for a period the stock market irrationally valued their firms at several billion dollars, they were not really worth that much and probably would never be. In these situations, an experienced investor with the appropriate approach may be able to facilitate a successful deleveraging transaction that ends up enhancing the value of the investment.

This strategy can be risky. For the investor to have credibility in working with management or organizing other holders, he or she generally needs to accumulate a fairly significant position. If the investor does so, and for whatever reason the deleveraging transaction cannot be effected, there may be substantial downside risk. While the investor accumulates his or her position and approaches the firm (either alone or, more forcefully, with others), time will pass. The passage of time usually works against distressed firms because their liquidity and the range of options generally decline. Thus the investor, if unsuccessful in fomenting some type of credit-enhancing event, may find himself or herself in a position where the bonds have declined in value because the company's liquidity has deteriorated. The investor may then face the unenviable process of trying to unwind a potentially large position in an unfavorable market environment. This latter problem could well be exacerbated by the fact that the marketplace[7] is likely to realize the investor has a large position (because he or she may have contacted other holders in an effort to coordinate them) and is a possible seller. Where the market is fairly illiquid, this could make it more difficult for the investor to find attractive bids. Accordingly, even where the investor's strategy is to orchestrate an out-of-court value catalyst, he or she will want to carefully analyze the target's ultimate value to properly assess downside risk.

An alternative strategy might be to purchase bonds with the expectation of using them as currency to purchase some of the target firm's assets. For example, assume Chipco had a relatively noncore operation, Ramsub, that was attractive to the investor from a strategic perspective. Perhaps the investor is a private equity fund that owns several businesses in the sector and is seeking to consolidate the industry. Through the fund's other involvement in the sector, it estimates that the value of Ramsub is $100. The fund might reason that at a price of 65 it can buy $120 in face amount of sub notes for only $78 ($120 × 65%) and approach Chipco with an offer to swap $120 in sub notes for a $100 asset — seemingly a win-win proposition.

These transactions are occasionally attempted, but again can be risky. The basic risk is that it is unlikely the investor will have an agreement with the target to sell the asset in question. If the fund attempts to mitigate this risk by approaching the firm and, assuming the firm is interested, negotiating a sale agreement, then the target may have a legal obligation to disclose the proposed sale as a material event. In that case, the fund's intent may be signaled to the marketplace, making it more difficult to purchase bonds at attractive levels. In addition, having negotiated a purchase, the fund is likely to be in possession of nonpublic information about the target.[8] As a restricted party, the fund may need to make its purchases using "big-boy" letters, which again may make purchasing the bonds at attractive levels difficult.

On the other hand, if the fund accumulates the position without having an agreement with the target, it runs the risk that the firm may be unwilling to consider a sale. In particular, the fund faces the basic financial dilemma that if Ramsub is really worth $100, why Chipco would not just sell it for that amount and (assuming away the issue of price changes, bond covenants, etc.) use the cash to purchase $154 ($100/65%) of the sub notes.

Finally, even if the fund miraculously effects the purchase using the bonds purchased at a discount as consideration, in the event the target files for bankruptcy within 90 days of the transaction, the asset for debt exchange might be challenged as either a voidable preference or fraudulent conveyance and be unwound.[9]

The situation presented by Chipco is not a particularly good candidate for an investment premised on the investor being able to add value through proactive involvement. While Chipco arguably has too much leverage given the current operating environment, it would be challenging for it to complete any type of meaningful, voluntary deleveraging transaction. This can be understood by considering the practical implications of Chipco's market circumstances, which are represented in Table 10-3 (same data as Table 10-1).

First, relative to its debt, which has an aggregate market value of $1038, it has a relatively small amount of cash (i.e., $100). This cash, assuming it is "excess" cash not needed to fund operating needs like capital expenditures to remain technologically competitive, can only marginally help with the retirement of the '04 seniors, which have a market trading value of $315.

Second, with three different bonds and two different classes, it is very unlikely that a voluntary exchange offer can be orchestrated, for several reasons:

1. Since the '04 seniors are the bonds causing the liquidity issue, they are the key security that must be restructured or refinanced. Given the current trading price of 90, no holder will accept a deeply discounted offer (e.g., 50), so no meaningful deleveraging can occur.
2. It will be difficult to induce an '04 senior holder to exchange for a pari passu, longer maturity bond because the trading price of the '09 seniors (i.e., 82) implies a market value loss would be incurred (a bond trading at 90 will not willingly exchange into a bond trading for 82).[10]

Table 10-3. Debt Metrics of Chipco at 12/31/02

		Debt	Amount	Price	Market Value	YTM
LTM Period End	12/31/02					
Settlement Date	1/15/03					
Cash	100	Secured Bank Term Loan	150	100	150	5.5%
		9.0% Senior Notes 6/1/04	350	90	315	17.4%
Peak EBITDA	350	9.5% Senior Notes 3/1/09	500	82	410	14.0%
LTM EBITDA	150	6.0% Convertible Sub Notes 2/1/06	250	65	163	22.5%
		Total	1250		1038	
		Equity	200		200	

3. A proposed exchange to a longer dated bond would also be complicated by the risk presented by the sub notes maturing in 2006.

4. A proposed exchange into equity, while offering the investor potentially attractive upside, would put the investor at significant risk in the event of a subsequent bankruptcy, where the equity would be junior to all debt and other claims. Existing shareholders who would be materially diluted might also resist this strategy.

5. Assuming the bank debt has a lien on substantially all assets, Chipco may have limited options to try to structure a coercive exchange offer. As discussed in Chapter 9, in a coercive exchange offer, the offer is structured so that nonexchanging holders are worse off. One technique to accomplish this is to offer an exchange into secured debt. However, if the existing bank debt has a lien on substantially all the assets, there may be little or nothing to offer.[11]

6. Depending on the corporate structure, it may be possible to offer a structurally senior security; for example, if the existing bonds are all at a holding company, the firm could offer new senior unsecured notes at the operating company level. This is not as strong as being secured and may or may not be attractive to holders depending on the estimated trading price of such operating-level debt. There is also the risk, although probably small on the stated facts, that in the event of a subsequent bankruptcy, the existing debt, both the '09 seniors and sub notes, could successfully argue for substantive consolidation (which would effectively negate the structural advantage gained in the exchange).

These risks are summarized in Table 10-4.

In summary, proactive involvement by an investor can often lead to the creation of investment value. However, not every situation is equally conducive

Table 10-4. Summary of Challenges to Voluntary Restructuring

Option	Challenges
Cash bond buybacks to deleverage	$100 cash balance insufficient '04 seniors trading at relatively high levels for meaningful deleveraging
Voluntary exchange for pari passu longer bond	'04 seniors holders would perceive market value decline Maturity of sub notes presents risk
Coercive exchange for secured debt	Bank likely has liens on all assets Second lien may not be of much value
Coercive exchange for structurally senior debt	May not be permitted by bond covenants Risk of substantive consolidation challenge

to an investor's efforts being effective. While theoretically anything can be done on a voluntary basis, practically speaking, Chipco may have too many moving parts, and there may be too few sources of potential leverage to make a voluntary exchange feasible. If the sub notes trading at 65 were the only bond in the capital structure, there might be some options. Realistically, however, if the sub notes were the only bond, they would likely be trading at a price higher than 65.

Chapter 11 Situations

The previous section considered situations where the investor anticipated that the investment would appreciate in value and he or she could exit outside of a chapter 11 context. This section considers those situations where the investor believes that a chapter 11 reorganization is inevitable, but expects that the postreorganization value of the securities being analyzed may be significantly higher.

The first step in analyzing chapter 11 scenarios is to assess the range of outcomes that can occur as a result of the reorganization process. Consider a slightly different perspective on Chipco illustrated in Table 10-5.

It is now one year later, January 2004, and while Chipco's business appears to have rebounded modestly (EBITDA improved from $150 in 2002 to $175 in 2003), there is still very little evidence that a strong rebound is immediately at hand. However, Chipco is now facing the need to refinance the '04 seniors, which mature in five months. While EBITDA improved, cash remained level due to investment in working capital and capital expenditures. The capital markets are showing a more receptive tone, but the investor must wonder why, if Chipco could refinance, it has waited so long to do so. Because of the risk

Table 10-5. Chipco at the End of 2003

Debt		Amount	Price	Market Value	YTM
LTM Period End 12/31/03					
Settlement Date 1/15/04					
Cash	100	Secured Bank Term Loan	150	100	150	5.5%
		9.0% Senior Notes 6/1/04	350	85	298	56.6%
Peak EBITDA	350	9.5% Senior Notes 3/1/09	500	70	350	18.9%
LTM EBITDA	175	6.0% Convertible Sub Notes 2/1/06	250	55	138	40.4%
		Total	1250		935	
		Equity	200		200	

	Leverage	At Face	Net at Market
EBITDA = 175	Thru Senior	5.7x	4.0x
	Thru Sub	7.1x	5.9x
EBITDA = 250	Thru Senior	4.0x	2.8x
	Thru Sub	5.0x	4.2x
EBITDA = 350	Thru Senior	2.9x	2.0x
	Thru Sub	3.6x	3.0x

that Chipco will not be able to refinance and be forced to file for chapter 11, all of its bonds have declined in price. The '04 seniors have declined modestly to 85, but their yield to maturity (YTM), because of the short five-month horizon, is a significant 56.6%, suggesting that the market demands a significant return for investing in the bonds. The probable reason for this is that the pari passu '09 seniors are trading at 70. Thus, an investor in the '04 seniors faces near-term upside of 15 points if the bonds are successfully refinanced and he or she collects 100. However, if Chipco cannot retire the '04 seniors — or complete an out-of-court exchange offer, which it has already been shown is challenging — it will likely be forced to file for chapter 11, in which case the two pari passu senior note issues should logically trade at the same price level.[12] The best indication of this level is the current price of the '09 seniors; thus the '04 seniors have at least 15 points of downside risk.

The revised Chipco situation gives rise to a number of different investment strategies. An investor could have a particularly bullish view on the probable refinancing of the '04 seniors, in which case a simple purchase could be the correct approach. An investor who is reasonably bullish but wants to hedge his or her risk might consider pairing the purchase of the '04 seniors with a short sale, if feasible, of some amount of sub notes on the assumption that the 15-point spread between the sub notes and the '09 seniors would widen in the event

Table 10-6. Bullish Investor's Strategic Options

Scenario	Security/ Price	If Refinanced	If Chapter 11	Profit/ Loss	Price Change
1 Long Purchase	'04 Seniors 85	►100		15	17.6%
			►70	(15)	−17.6%
2 Long Purchase + Short Sale	'04 Seniors 85	►100		15	17.6%
			►70	(15)	−17.6%
	Short Sub Note 55	►65		(10)	18.2%
			►30	25	45.5%
	Net Hedge		►5		
			►10		

of a chapter 11 filing (this will be elaborated on below). The short-term outlook for some of the bullish investor's options is summarized in Table 10-6.

Alternatively, an investor might be skeptical of Chipco's ability to refinance and forecast that a chapter 11 is inevitable. However, the investor may still think there are attractive investment opportunities based on a belief that the market value of the debt is cheap relative to ultimate recoveries. In this case, if the investor had strong conviction that the value of Chipco equaled or exceeded the value of its debt (for example, using a normalized EBITDA of $250 and a multiple of at least 5.0x implies an enterprise value of $1250 [$250 × 5], equal to Chipco's debt of $1250), then attractive investment opportunities would still be present.

When the investment strategy contemplates recovering value in the form of postreorganization securities (e.g., new debt or equity of Chipco), the selection of which security to purchase is critical. The first issue the investor needs to assess is how much risk to take; the second is what type of postreorganization recovery, in terms of new debt or equity, will likely be allocated to the various securities. From a risk perspective, the skeptical investor who expects a chapter 11 is inevitable will clearly avoid the '04 seniors, which are likely to decline in value if there is a chapter 11 filing. This investor more likely will choose the '09 seniors. Assuming all of the senior debt is valued at 70, this implies a value of 4.2x LTM EBITDA of $175. This seems reasonable, but the investor would want to investigate whether this type of business may be vulnerable to a significant value erosion were it to go through a bankruptcy.

If the investor has strong conviction about the $1250 valuation of Chipco, then he or she may see more upside potential in the sub notes. If this conviction is right, they may ultimately be worth 100 and thus a purchase at 55 would be attractive. However, since the sub notes are subordinated to a reasonably significant amount of senior debt ($1000, representing 5.7x LTM EBITDA — in this assessment, face, not market value, is the appropriate metric because of the subordinated status of the sub notes), the investor may need to be prepared for a price decline in the event of a filing. It is not uncommon in a situation where leverage through the senior debt is fairly high for there to be wider than a 21% spread ([70 − 55]/70 = 21%) between the valuation of senior and junior securities. Note that a valuation of 5.5x LTM EBITDA would imply an enterprise value of only $963 (5.5 × 175), which when compared to senior debt of $1000 suggests a 0 recovery to the sub notes. Accordingly, even if the investor ultimately believes the sub notes are "money good," he or she may be wise to postpone some or all of the purchase, expecting that they will fall in value once the probability of a chapter 11 is closer.

The second issue the skeptical investor needs to assess is whether or not he or she has a significant preference in terms of what type of securities (debt or equity) he or she receives on a postreorganization basis. (For a review of the factors that will impact this decision, the reader may wish to review the concepts in Chapter 6.) To evaluate this, the investor will need to estimate what valuation might be used when Chipco's plan of reorganization (plan) is developed; note that this requires forecasting a year or more in the future. This is different than the investor's own view of the issue (in this case, 5 × $250 = $1250). The plan valuation, as discussed in Chapter 4, will, to a certain extent, be an outcome of the negotiation between the unsecured creditors' committee and the management of bankrupt Chipco. As was pointed out before, and will be elaborated on further in Chapter 12, senior creditors tend to have an interest in keeping the plan valuation as low as possible because it will lead to their recovering a disproportionate share of the value upon emergence. Junior creditors and equity claimants, on the other hand, have a bias toward relatively higher valuations.

After the issue of potential plan valuation, the next important question in the restructuring of Chipco will be the appropriate amount of postreorganization leverage. In the event of a filing, since the secured term loan only represents 1x LTM EBITDA, it is reasonable to assume that it will either be reinstated or repaid from the proceeds of a similar postconfirmation facility.

The question is the appropriate amount, if any, of additional debt with which to burden the reorganized Chipco. There is no clear answer, and the investor should realize that the preferences of management and the members of the unsecured creditors' committee may play an important role. For example, if most of the committee's senior note members prefer to have some or all of their recovery in debt (which is more stable and predictable in value and retains its senior claim status), then there may be a reasonable amount of postreorganization leverage. Under the facts, if the committee felt that total leverage of 3.0x normalized EBITDA of $250 was prudent, then in addition to the bank facility, an additional $600 (3 × $250 = $750; $750 [capacity] – $150 [bank line] = $600 [potential additional debt]) in debt might be put in place. This would give the $850 in unsecured senior debt (assuming away the issue of other claims) a 70% recovery in debt, with the remainder in equity. Alternatively, the committee might push for a plan that had no debt other than the bank facility. The committee might reach this decision based on a view that, given the cyclical nature of Chipco, minimizing leverage was more prudent. Or, less selflessly, they might prefer a low-debt plan because it would result in the senior creditors (who would likely be the majority of the committee) receiving a significant, if not controlling, share of the equity postconfirmation.

The various scenarios that could be encapsulated in the final plan would also determine the size and nature of the recovery to the sub notes. Thus, the investor has numerous permutations to consider when analyzing the prospective investment. To simplify the analysis, only two scenarios for each variable will be analyzed: valuation — lower (4.5x)/higher (6.0x), and leverage — lower (secured only)/moderate (3.0x EBITDA).

First, the low valuation scenarios are illustrated in Table 10-7. This analysis assumes that the plan will adopt $250 as the appropriate EBITDA and use a 4.5x multiple, for a total enterprise valuation of $1125. The actual valuation methodology used by Chipco's financial advisor will undoubtedly be significantly more elaborate, but, as reviewed in Chapter 5, in the end, most valuations can be expressed using the EBITDA multiple valuation approach.

Once the valuation is specified, two leverage scenarios are considered. The "low"-leverage scenario assumes that only the bank facility is retained postreorganization; the "moderate"-leverage scenario assumes that leverage equal to 3.0x EBITDA, or $750, is employed, implying $600 of additional, postconfirmation debt (long-term [LT] debt), all of which will be assumed to be distributed to the senior creditors.[13] The valuation has been conveniently selected to fully cover senior claims to avoid adjustments related to the operation of subordination provisions of the sub notes.[14] Note that the valuation determines the absolute recovery of the various classes, especially the $125 recovery to the sub notes and the $0 recovery to the equity. The leverage assumption impacts the composition of recoveries. For example, in the moderate-leverage scenario, the senior creditors receive 67% of the recovery in debt

Table 10-7. Potential Low-Valuation Plan Outcomes

Low-Valuation Scenario

Valuation EBITDA	250	
Valuation Multiple	4.5	Lower valuation multiple
Plan Value	1125	

Low-Leverage/Low-Valuation Plan

Allocation	Claim	Recovery	% Equity
Bank Facility		150	Leverage 0.6x
New Senior Debt		0	Difference in debt
Value of Equity		975	
Senior Debt	850	850	87%
Sub Note	250	125	13%
Equity		0	0%

Allocation of equity impacted by debt assumption

Moderate-Leverage/Low-Valuation Plan

Allocation	Claim	Recovery	% Equity
Bank Facility		150	Leverage 0.6x
New Senior Debt		600	2.4x
Value of Equity		375	
Senior Debt Claim	250	250	67%
Sub Note Claim	250	125	33%
Equity		0	0%

and 33% in equity, whereas in the low-leverage scenario, 100% of the recovery is equity. Notice, too, the obvious implications for the allocation of equity. In the low-leverage scenario, the senior creditors receive 87% of the equity, while in the moderate-leverage scenario they receive only 67%.

Next, the higher valuation scenarios are illustrated in Table 10-8. Here, the same $250 EBITDA assumption is used, but a higher (5.5x) multiple is employed, leading to a $1375 valuation. This valuation allows a full recovery to both the senior and subordinated claims with enough value left over to provide some recovery (i.e., $125) to the prepetition equity interests. In the low-leverage scenario, notice that the senior claims would control 70% of the equity, with the subordinated claims and equity interest receiving 20 and 10%, respectively. Alternatively, under the moderate-leverage scenario, the senior and subordinate claims would have equal 40% allocations of the equity, with the equity interests receiving the remaining 20%.

To summarize the possible outcomes, the investor could construct a matrix such as that presented in Table 10-9. This summary illustrates how the plan formulation process can materially affect the amount and composition of

Table 10-8. Potential Higher Valuation Plan Outcomes

Higher Valuation Scenario		
Valuation EBITDA	250	
Valuation Multiple	5.5	← Higher multiple
Plan Value	1375	

Low-Leverage/Higher Valuation Plan			
			Leverage
Bank Facility		150	0.6x
New Senior Debt		0	0.0x
Value of Equity		1225	
Allocation	**Claim**	**Recovery**	**% Equity**
Senior Debt Claim	850	850	70%
Sub Note Claim	250	250	20%
Equity Recovery		125	10%

Allocation of equity impacted by debt assumption

Moderate-Leverage/Higher Valuation Plan			
			Leverage
Bank Facility		150	0.6x
New Senior Debt		600	2.4x
Value of Equity		625	
Allocation			**% Equity**
Senior Debt Claim	250	250	40%
Sub Note Claim	250	250	40%
Equity Recovery		125	20%

Table 10-9. Matrix of Potential Recoveries

			Low Leverage		High Leverage	
		Recovery ($ Recovery/ % of Claim)	Debt ($ Amount/ % of Claim)	Equity ($ Amount/ % of Equity)	Debt ($ Amount/ % of Claim)	Equity ($ Amount/ % of Equity)
Low	Senior	$850/100%	$0/0%	$850/87%	$600/71%	$250/67%
Valuation	Sub	$125/50%	$0/0%	$125/13%	$0/0%	$125/33%
	Equity	$0/NA	$0/NA	$0/0%	$0/NA	$0/0%
High	Senior	$850/100%	$0/0%	$850/70%	$600/71%	$250/40%
Valuation	Sub	$250/100%	$0/0%	$250/20%	$0/0%	$250/40%
	Equity	$125/NA	$0/NA	$125/10%	$0/NA	$125/20%

postconfirmation recoveries. Again, note that the valuation assumption determines the total amount of recovery, particularly to junior classes. This should reinforce why the issue of valuation is so hotly contested in the plan negotiation. It is usually in the most senior creditors' interest to negotiate a relatively low plan valuation because it will imply that relative to their claim, even if it is fully covered, the senior creditors will get a relatively larger percentage of the value.

That senior creditors will tend to have a bias for low valuations deserves emphasis because one must bear in mind that the "true" value[15] of the firm in reorganization is unknowable at the time of plan formulation and confirmation. The valuation used for purposes of determining creditor recoveries, theoretically, should try to reflect this true value, but in practice, this theoretical aspiration can be compromised by the dynamics of the plan negotiation process (discussed in more detail in Chapter 12). This negotiation dynamic is similar to a zero-sum game in which the gain of one class can only come at the "loss" of another. From the senior creditors' perspective, they will use the unknowability of the true value to justify a low valuation. They will argue that bankruptcy is almost always detrimental to the reorganized entity's value and that their senior status entitles them not to bear the downside risk of loss, should the true value postconfirmation be less than what might be expected in a nonreorganization context.

The junior or more impaired classes will, of course, argue that the low-valuation assumption unfairly reduces the recovery to which they are "entitled," since senior claims are only entitled to recovery of their claim amount — nothing more.[16] The financial underpinnings of their argument are illustrated in Table 10-10. The left column of numbers shows the allocation consequences shown in Figure 10-7 for a low-valuation/low-debt plan of reorganization. The right column shows the implication for recoveries if in fact the true value (assume this was established because Chipco received an acquisition proposal for this amount three months following confirmation) were $1500, or 6.0x EBITDA. Since the low-value/low-leverage plan was adopted, the senior notes were allocated 87% of Chipco's equity. When Chipco turned out to be worth $1500, rather than the $1125 assumed in the plan, the value of the senior notes' equity turned out to be $1177, 38% more than their $850 claim entitlement. And although the undervalued equity resulted in a sub note recovery of 69% of claim, which was higher than the 50% projected in the plan, had the valuation in the plan been $1500, the sub notes would have received 100% of claim. Of course, the biggest losers were the equity holders. Had the plan value been accurate, the equity holders would have been allocated $250 (1500 − 1250) in value. This scenario illustrates the senior claims' considerable incentive to have the plan value be considerably below true value.

While the senior claims are always better off with a lower plan value, the decision on how much debt to include in the postconfirmation capital structure is less clear-cut. If recoveries are such that equity holders will receive nothing (which is typically the case), then management is likely to have a bias toward as little debt as possible to maximize the firm's postconfirmation financial

Table 10-10. Potential "Upside" Resulting from Low Plan Valuation

	PLAN Low Valuation/ Low Leverage	TRUE Value Higher	
EBITDA	250	250	
Valuation Multiple	4.5x	6.0x	
Enterprise Value	1125	1500	Assume TRUE value high enough to cover all debt with some value to equity
Less: Bank Debt	150	150	
Less: LT Debt	0	0	
Equity Value	975	1350	
Senior Note Claim	850	850	
Debt	0	0	Senior notes recover substantially more than their claim due to low plan value
Equity %	87%	87%	
Equity $	850	1177	
Total Recovery	850	1177	
% of Claim	100%	138%	
Sub Note Claim	250	250	
Debt	0	0	Low plan value results in sub notes and equity receiving less than entitled to had plan value been accurate
Equity %	13%	13%	
Equity $	125	173	
Total Recovery	125	173	
% of Claim	50%	69%	
Equity			
Debt	0	0	
Equity %	0%	0%	
Equity $	0	0	
Total Recovery	0	0	
% of Claim	NA	NA	

flexibility. If the existing shareholders or management are receiving an equity allocation, then they may have a modest bias toward more debt because this will tend to increase the proportion of equity allocated to them (compare the 10% [$0 LT debt] versus 20% [$600 in LT debt] equity allocations in Table 10-8).

On the creditor side, the presence and allocation of debt may be significantly influenced by the preferences of the unsecured creditors' committee members and the negotiating dynamics. For example, if many of the committee members prefer holding earning assets (e.g., insurance companies, high-yield mutual funds), they may prefer a capital structure with more debt and that the debt be allocated to their recovery. Alternatively, where investors that want to control the postconfirmation equity dominate the committee, no LT debt may be included in the plan. Another consideration affecting the LT debt decision is the perception of future risk. If all the claims accept equity and postconfirmation Chipco performs poorly, the new equity is at significant risk. Thus, where the

Table 10-11. **Returns with $600 in LT Debt Allocated to Senior Claims**

	–20%	–10%	Plan	10%	20%
True Enterprise Value/Plan Enterprise Value	80%	90%	100%	110%	120%
Senior Recovery % Claim	82%	91%	100%	109%	118%
Sub Recovery % Claim	20%	35%	50%	65%	80%
Equity $ Recovery	$–	$–	$–	$–	$–

outlook is unclear, more risk-averse investors may push for a recovery that includes debt, because this gives them a debt claim (versus an equity interest) should financial distress be encountered later. Tables 10-11 and 10-12 illustrate the impact of debt on returns in the low-valuation scenario shown in Table 10-7 across an array of true values. Table 10-11 shows returns in the high-leverage case, while Table 10-12 show returns in the low-leverage scenario. The –20% column represents returns if true value turns out to be 20% below the plan valuation.

Notice that the inclusion of the $600 in LT debt in the high-leverage scenario tends to moderate the returns of the senior claim and amplify the volatility of the sub claim. In this regard, the effect of leverage is the same prereorganization as postreorganization.

There is no requirement that the debt contemplated by the plan must be allocated to the senior claims. Thus, if the plan valuation was such that value needed to be allocated to junior claims, it is theoretically possible that debt would be allocated to these interests such that the senior claims could control 100% of the equity. More often however, the junior claims have little interest in receiving a trifling amount of illiquid debt. Thus, if it is clear that the senior debt has the inclination and power to maintain control of the equity, the junior claims may prefer that the plan provide for postconfirmation debt financing to bring cash into the estate, which can be used to pay the junior claims their recovery.

To bring closure to this discussion and to provide a sense of the stakes involved, the potential returns of purchasing the various securities at the stated

Table 10-12. **Returns with $0 in LT Debt**

	–20%	–10%	Plan	10%	20%
True Enterprise Value/Plan Enterprise Value	80%	90%	100%	110%	120%
Senior Recovery % Claim	77%	88%	100%	112%	123%
Sub Recovery % Claim	38%	44%	50%	56%	62%
Equity $ Recovery	$–	$–	$–	$–	$–

Table 10-13. Potential Returns for Various Scenarios for Chipco

Security	Price	Returns* at Low Plan Valuation		Returns* if True Value Realized	
		Low Leverage	Medium Leverage	Low Leverage	Medium Leverage
9.0% Senior Notes 6/1/04	85	18%	18%	66%	55%
9.5% Senior Notes 3/1/09	70	43%	43%	101%	88%
5.5% Convertible Sub Notes 2/1/06	55	–9%	–9%	30%	86%

* Returns represent price appreciation over assumed one-year workout period.

prices in the low-valuation scenario are calculated in Table 10-13. Note that in the low-valuation scenario (review Table 10-7), the recovery of $125 for the sub notes per the plan would have resulted in a negative return on investment regardless of the leverage assumption. However, assuming the true value was realized, the sub note investment return would have nonetheless been positive. In fact, the recovery would be a quite attractive 86% in the medium-leverage scenario under which the sub notes would have been allocated 33% of the equity.

FEASIBILITY CONSIDERATIONS

As was mentioned at the outset of this chapter, many strategies may appear feasible in a "perfect world"; unfortunately, however, distressed debt investing must be done in the real world. In the real world, there are a variety of constraints that must be taken into account when considering the feasibility of a strategy, particularly where it entails becoming proactively involved in the restructuring process.

Capital Structure

The first factor a distressed debt investor should analyze is the capital structure and what that structure effectively allows the investor to do. The capital structure is the chessboard: it largely defines what moves can be made.

The investor's first step will be to make an assessment of the amount of leverage represented by the secured bank debt, if any, relative to firm value. The greater the amount of bank debt, the less likely it will be that the investor can get involved in a meaningful way, other than purchasing a large block of the bank facility, which typically does not trade at significant discounts. There are two reasons why a large overhang of bank debt limits an investor's range of options. First, as discussed in Chapter 7, bank debt tends to have all-encompassing covenant packages, including performance covenants. A firm in or bordering on financial distress usually will be in violation of these covenants, giving the banks great influence over the firm under the threat of either cutting off access to a needed working capital line or exercising a contractual right of acceleration — either of which would effectively force the firm to file for chapter 11 protection. Prior to a bankruptcy, banks can use this leverage to extract fees or additional collateral pledges, demand asset sales to fund pay down requirements, block interest payments on unsecured debt — effectively almost anything they want, and often many of these changes can be to the detriment of any unsecured debt in the capital structure.

Second, as discussed in Chapter 12, after a filing, even though the automatic stay prevents the banks from seizing collateral, they are still protected by the powerful concept of adequate protection. The secured creditor's right to demand adequate protection can be used to demand postpetition interest. Adequate protection also can limit what a firm can do with the assets pledged as security (which usually is almost all assets.) Where the bank debt is modest relative to the scope of an enterprise, as is the case in the example involving Chipco, the banks may not have that much postbankruptcy power. However, where a facility is more significant, the banks may have significant leverage over the ultimate shape of the plan of reorganization.

Finally, bank loan agreements designate that the agent bank effectively will serve as the representative of the bank facility — unlike the committee typically found in the unsecured debt context — which, again, limits the influence of a distressed investor. Thus, as a general rule, the greater the amount of secured bank debt, the less the opportunity for the distressed investor to control the outcome of the case unless he or she can purchase a significant block of such debt.

Interestingly, the likelihood of the distressed investor being able to accumulate a significant block of bank debt increases with the distress of the borrower, particularly if the distress is sufficient to cause the bank debt to trade below 70. When this occurs, banks and collateralized debt obligations (CDOs) are much more likely to become sellers, often for nonvalue-related reasons. For banks, this could be a desire to manage the amount of nonperforming loans maintained on the balance sheet. For CDOs, it can be due to the requirements of arbitrary valuation rules. In these situations, opportunities to accumulate bank debt at attractive valuations may exist.

Much more promising are situations when the bank debt, if any, is limited to a working capital facility, which represents only a modest amount of the capital structure relative to unsecured long-term debt. In these situations, it is generally easier to accumulate a position in the unsecured debt and become involved in the restructuring process. Here, the investor first will analyze the probability that the distress could be cured outside of a chapter 11 process; otherwise, the firm will probably need to file. In the former case, the investor will consider the return possibilities, as discussed above, and determine if these are sufficiently attractive to merit either his or her due diligence time or invest-ment. If a chapter 11 is more likely, then the investor will perform the type of analysis reviewed in the prior section to determine how the postreorganization capital structure is likely to be distributed among existing securities and how this distribution matches with his or her investment objectives. To the extent the investor prefers postreorganization debt, he or she may prefer to stay more senior; if the objective is equity, the investor will have to identify the fulcrum class.

Market Versus True Valuation

It is tautological that the key to obtaining superior risk-adjusted returns is to identify securities misvalued relative to their "true" value. It is not enough to identify situations involving a firm in financial distress; one must also find a case of misvaluation. This requires an investor to apply the type of valuation skills discussed in Chapter 5 to filter through possible situations to identify those that are most promising. Often the best chance of finding misvalued securities will be after a significant negative information event. Such an event can lead to exaggerated price movements as sellers, seeking to exit a situation because it has not gone as planned, find a marketplace where buyers want significant price reductions in light of the new uncertainty. Put differently, when the news is very bad, the market often will trade down to the worst-case scenario valuations.[17]

Other contexts in which it is promising to find misvaluations are (1) when the financial distress is primarily driven by significant near-term liquidity re-quirements such as a debt maturity or a large interest payment, (2) when cyclical industries are going through a "down phase" which results in leverage based on cyclically low LTM EBITDA to appear high, and (3) where the total capi-talization is less than $500 million, resulting in relatively less market awareness. This is not to say that every situation within the contexts cited above will be attractive. The market may, from time to time, be inefficient, but it is seldom completely irrational for sustained periods. There is typically a reason why the securities have declined in value. In (1) above, there will always be the risk that if the liquidity crisis forces a filing, considerable franchise value could be lost in the process. In (2), there will always be the uncertainty of whether this is really just a cyclical issue or whether the firm has become uncompetitive. In

(3), the relatively small size may result in an illiquid market where accumulating a position is difficult. As with most situations in the capital markets, if it were obvious, the opportunity would not be there for long.

Market Liquidity/Concentration of Holdings

Closely related to the prior point of market valuation is the issue of market liquidity. An investor might find a situation where, based on market price indications, he or she feels that a misvaluation exists. If the market is illiquid, however, the ability to accumulate the desired position may be difficult. An investor will want to investigate the feasibility of acquiring a position in a cost-effective manner by reviewing data such as the distribution of holdings (which is available on the holdings of mutual funds and insurance companies), how frequently they are quoted on broker-dealers' trading axes, and general market inquiries. In this regard, larger distressed investors may have an advantage over smaller investors because it is easier to disguise their investigative inquiries with broker-dealers as part of their day-to-day market updates. Like an inartful detective doing an investigation in a small town, anyone asking too many questions draws attention. Thus, part of the distressed investor's competitive edge will be an information network that allows him or her to assess the playing field. One of the particularly baffling aspects of the distressed chess game is that in the early stages of the game, not all the players and their pieces are readily apparent. An investor will, to the best of his or her ability, determine the following.

Other Distressed Investors

It is important to know whether significant distressed investors have already become involved. The implications of such involvement will vary depending on an investor's objective. To a relatively small investor likely to be making a passive investment, the presence of a respected distressed investor may, to a certain extent, validate the merit of the investment. In addition, the passive investor may be able to assume that the larger investor will commit the time and energy to negotiate a successful outcome. The passive investor can then just tag along. Finally, the identity and track record of the other distressed investor may also suggest how the restructuring may evolve. For example, if the distressed investor already involved is known to prefer postreorganization equity stakes, it may indicate the direction of the current situation. Alternatively, if an investor had hoped to have significant influence on the course of the restructuring, the fact that he or she is "second at the table" may make it more difficult and expensive to achieve this objective.

Bank Debt

The importance of knowing what is going on in the bank debt, if any is present, will depend on its materiality in the capital structure. To the extent that it is a relatively small facility that primarily provides working capital and would be effectively included in any postreorganization capital structure, it may be fairly irrelevant. Conversely, the larger the secured facility, the greater the need to know who is involved. Is it still the bank group or have other distressed investors accumulated stakes? In most cases, this usually will be a matter of public record because the bank agreement and any amendments thereto will be filed with the Securities and Exchange Commission and the signature pages will reveal the holders. However, this review is not totally reliable because it is possible for a signatory to sell its economic interest to another holder through participation.[18] In a participation agreement (a form of which is available for download at www.jrosspub.com), the buyer purchases the seller's economic interest in and control over the bank debt, but the seller continues to remain the record holder. Often bank debt purchases are structured as participations specifically because the buyer does not want his or her identity known.

Large Block Holders of Public Debt

On the bond side, the process is more difficult. Regulators require mutual funds and insurance companies to disclose their portfolio holdings quarterly and annually, respectively. Thus, these holdings can be identified, but potentially out of date. Hedge funds are private investment pools that at present are subject to very little regulatory oversight and are not required to disclose their holdings.[19] The presence of a significant concentration of holdings among mutual funds and insurance companies has several implications for the distressed investor. Since these institutions, insurance companies in particular, often are "buy and hold"–type investors, it may imply that the general trading "float" of bonds in the secondary market may be fairly limited, thus making it more difficult to accumulate a position. On the other hand, if an investor desires to acquire a meaningful or controlling stake, it could indicate a single source of a large block of bonds. Part of the investment process is the ability to accumulate the desired position. If an investor can artfully determine that one or more of the blocks can be acquired, it significantly reduces the accumulation risk.

HEDGING AND CAPITAL STRUCTURE ARBITRAGE

The prior discussion has, in general, assumed that the distressed investor has a relatively long-term investment horizon and is basing the investment decision on a fundamental view of investment value. While this approach probably describes the majority of distressed debt investing, it certainly is not the only approach that can be used. The increasing liquidity of the distressed market has made hedged investing possible. In hedged investing, an investor seeks to minimize his or her overall risk by having two or more offsetting investments that have negative price correlation to the same systemic risk element. Put more simply, if a particular event happens, like a default, one investment can be expected to go up, while the other is expected to go down. Such transactions can be structured to either take advantage of an expected change in credit fundamentals (either positive or negative) or be credit neutral. Two of the more common techniques for hedging involve capital structure arbitrage or the use of credit default swaps.[20] Hedging can lower risk or volatility, reduce the amount of net capital invested, and increase risk-adjusted rates of return.

Capital structure arbitrage is a type of hedged investment strategy that allows an investor to profit from the identification of a misvaluation in the market between securities in the same capital structure. The concept of arbitrage is a riskless economic return. In a capital structure arbitrage, an investor attempts through the trade combination to "lock in" a "riskless" economic return. The classic example of a capital structure arbitrage is a hedged convertible bond trade. A convertible arbitraguer that arranges a capital structure arbitrage, which is called "putting on the trade," will purchase the convertible bond and then sell short an appropriate amount of stock. The short sale of the stock is designed to "neutralize" the price impact on the convertible bond of changes in the underlying stock price. If the stock falls in value, the long convertible position will decline but be offset by a gain in the short stock position. One goal of such arbitrages is to "lock in" the coupon income with potentially minimal net capital investment (because the proceeds from the short stock sale largely fund the convertible bond investment). The availability of such investment opportunities depends on the target firm's capital structure, market price levels, and liquidity.

Return Potential of Capital Structure Arbitrage

Capital structure arbitrage presents an opportunity for very attractive return potential primarily because the net investment in the transaction can be fairly small. The Chipco situation presented earlier offers a number of potential capital structure arbitrage opportunities, the structure of which will depend on an investor's assessment of what most likely will occur. For ease of reference, Chipco's situation as of January 2004 is restated in Table 10-14.

For example, an investor with the view that Chipco's fundamentals are generally improving and that a refinancing of the '04 seniors is likely may perceive that the sub notes, which are the next maturing security after the '04

Table 10-14. Chipco Six Months Before the '04 Senior Maturity

Debt		Amount	Price	Market Value	YTM
LTM Period End 12/31/03					
Settlement Date 1/15/04					
Cash	100	Secured Bank Line	150	100	150	5.5%
		9.0% Senior Notes 6/1/04	350	85	298	56.6%
Peak EBITDA	350	9.5% Senior Notes 3/1/09	500	70	350	18.9%
LTM EBITDA	175	5.5% Convertible Sub Notes 2/1/06	250	55	138	40.4%
		Total	1250		935	
		Equity	200		200	

	Leverage	At Face	Net at Market
EBITDA = 175	Thru Senior	5.7x	4.0x
	Thru Sub	7.1x	5.9x
EBITDA = 250	Thru Senior	4.0x	2.8x
	Thru Sub	5.0x	4.2x
EBITDA = 350	Thru Senior	2.9x	2.0x
	Thru Sub	3.6x	3.0x

seniors, will enjoy the greatest percentage price movement. Thus the investor will want to be long, or own, that security. However, even though one may be relatively confident in this assessment that Chipco can refinance, an investor should recognize that there is no certainty. Capital markets can be roiled by many unforeseeable events such as acts of terrorism, international crises, etc. Accordingly, the investor may not want to be fully exposed to the risk of what may happen to the sub notes if the refinancing is not successful and Chipco must file for chapter 11 protection. To do this, the investor will want to identify a security that will fall in price in the event of a default. The bond that seems most likely to fall in the event of a default is the '04 senior, which can be expected to fall to the same trading level as the pari passu '09 senior. Accordingly, the investor will want to sell short the '04 senior.

In a "short sale," the investor borrows the security from another holder (this is done through market brokers) and then sells it in the market. At some point in the future — the timing will not always be within the short seller's control as the party that "lent" the security can demand its return at any time — the investor must repurchase the security so that it can be returned to the lender. While "shorting" is common with stocks, many investors may not realize that it also can be done with bonds. An important consideration, however, is the requirement that the short seller pay the security lender all coupons (since the bond has been sold, the lender will not be the record owner and the coupon will be paid to whomever purchased the bond). The lender, who in many cases will not even realize that the securities have been loaned, will expect to receive coupons, and this becomes part of the short seller's investment cost. The short seller of a stock has a similar obligation in the event of a dividend payment on the sold shares.

In setting up the investment, the investor needs to estimate what will happen in various scenarios. In the Chipco example, there are two basic scenarios: the '04 seniors are refinanced, or they are not refinanced and Chipco files for bankruptcy. If the '04 seniors are refinanced as the investor expects, then the investor knows he or she will lose 15 points on the short sale, because the lender of the '04 seniors will be entitled to a redemption payment of 100. However, the investor assumes that the sub notes, which had been trading at 55, will appreciate, perhaps to 75, providing a 20-point profit. On a net basis, before adjusting for interest expense differential, the investor has made 5 points. If the '04 seniors are not refinanced and Chipco files chapter 11, then an opposite return scenario occurs. The '04 seniors can be expected to decline to at least the 70 trading level of the '09 seniors, which implies a 15-point profit on the short sale. However, the sub notes also will be likely to decline in value, perhaps to 40. In that case, the investor will have, again ignoring the interest difference, broken even on the trade. If the sub notes fall to 35, the investor loses 5 points on the trade.

In Table 10-15, the return dynamics of this trade are analyzed. One factor that was dismissed in the narrative above was the differential in the coupon rates between the long and short security. Since the investor is long a 5.5% bond and short a 9% bond, he or she must incur a "negative carry" of 3.5% per year. Thus over the six-month expected time horizon of this investment, and assuming an equal amount of bonds in both the long and the short position, the investor will have to pay out a net 1.75%. This negative carry must be more than made up in the offsetting bond price movements for the trade to be profitable.

Table 10-15 analyzes both the upside (refinance) and downside (bankruptcy) outcomes of the hedged investment. In interpreting the table, it is important to keep in mind the direction of the cash flows. The long position (100 of the 5.5s) is purchased and therefore presents a cash outflow. When it is sold at the end, it represents an inflow. Similarly, but opposite, at the beginning of the short position, the securities are sold, which is an inflow. They must be repurchased at the end, which is an outflow. In the given fact pattern, at the beginning of the trade the investor actually is left with a positive cash balance of $30, because the proceeds from the securities being shorted (i.e., 85) exceed the cost of the long securities (i.e., 55). This balance will be reinvested, in this case a 3% reinvestment rate (or, had it been the opposite, borrow rate), which is shown,

Table 10-15. Return Dynamics of Capital Structure Arbitrage

| | Hedge Ratio | 100% | | Cash Reinvested or Borrowed | | | 3% | |
| | Time Period | 0.5 Year | | | | | | |

	Size	Coupon	Beginning Price	Value	End Price	Value	Carry	% Price Change
Refinance Scenario								
Long	(100.00)	5.50%	55.00	(55.00)	75.00	75.00	2.75	36.4%
Short	100.00	9.00%	85.00	85.00	100.00	(100.00)	(4.50)	17.6%
Net	—			30.00		(25.00)	(1.75)	
Bankruptcy Scenario								
Long	(100.00)	5.50%	55.00	(55.00)	40.00	40.00	2.75	−27.3%
Short	100.00	9.00%	85.00	85.00	70.00	(70.00)	(4.50)	−17.6%
Net	—			30.00		(30.00)	(1.75)	

Summary	Refinance	Chapter 11
Cash After Put On	30.00	30.00
Cash to Close Out	(25.00)	(30.00)
Investment Carry	0.45	0.45
Coupon Carry	(1.75)	(1.75)
Net Return	3.70	(1.30)

in the summary section, to contribute 0.45. This partially offsets the 1.75 negative coupon carry.

The scenario assumes that in the "upside" refinance case, the '04 seniors are paid 100, but the sub notes appreciate to 75; thus the investor nets 5. In the downside bankruptcy case, the '04 seniors fall to 70 and the sub notes fall to 40 — a wash. Thus, netting out the various interest carries, if both scenarios are assumed equally probable, the hedge has an expected positive return of $1.20. And since the investor actually had no cash invested, the rate of return is essentially infinite.

Several factors drove this particular outcome. First was the assumption that the sub notes would appreciate relatively more in the upside scenario (36%) than they would decline in the downside scenario (−24%), whereas the '04 seniors were assumed to have equal volatility (17.6%). The expected ending levels, with the exception of the value of the '04 seniors in the refinance scenario (i.e., 100), are educated estimates. The downside of the '04 seniors in the bankruptcy scenario could be greater than 15 as it is certainly possible that in the event of a bankruptcy both the '09 seniors and '04 seniors would trade down below this level. The upside of the sub notes is difficult to estimate —

at a price of 75, they would have an expected YTM of 26%, which is reasonably attractive, but the price change could be more or less. The downside of the sub notes is perhaps the most difficult to estimate. They are junior to $1000 in senior debt, which suggests there is significant risk. On the other hand, at 40, leverage through the sub notes is a reasonable 4.1x normalized EBITDA of $250, but it would be fairly easy to make a case that they should trade lower. Estimating the probable outcomes of hedged transactions requires a combination of judgment and science.

A second factor that influenced the returns was the decision to use equal face amounts of securities for both the long and the short positions. From a mathematical perspective, this put a higher investment emphasis on the '04 senior notes, the security with the perceived lower volatility. Given the other factors, this actually reduced expected returns. In Table 10-16, the same scenario as depicted in Table 10-15 is shown with the exception that the long and short positions are dollar weighted, rather than based on face. At least three differences between these two scenarios should be noted. First, there is no cash after the trade is put on and hence no reinvestment income. Second, since the dollar value of the higher coupon security is lower, the negative coupon carry

Table 10-16. Hedge Dynamics: Equal Dollar Weight

| | Hedge Ratio | 65% | | Cash Reinvested or Borrowed | | 3% | |
| | Time Period | 0.5 Year | | | | | |

	Size	Coupon	Beginning Price	Value	End Price	Value	Carry	% Price Change
Refinance Scenario								
Long	(100.00)	5.50%	55.00	(55.00)	75.00	75.00	2.75	36.4%
Short	64.71	9.00%	85.00	55.00	100.00	(64.71)	(2.91)	17.6%
Net	(35.29)			0.00		10.29	(0.16)	
Bankruptcy Scenario								
Long	(100.00)	5.50%	55.00	(55.00)	40.00	40.00	2.75	−27.3%
Short	64.71	9.00%	85.00	55.00	70.00	(45.30)	(2.91)	−17.6%
Net	(35.29)			0.00		(5.30)	(0.16)	

Summary	Refinance	Chapter 11
Cash After Put On	0.00	0.00
Cash to Close Out	10.29	(5.30)
Investment Carry	0.00	0.00
Coupon Carry	(0.16)	(0.16)
Net Return	10.13	(5.46)

declines. Finally, the expected value of the transaction, assuming equal probability weighting, increases to 2.34. This last result is due to the relatively greater weight for the security with the higher positive volatility.[21] The equal probability assumption is arguably what is reflected in the stated market prices: the pricing of the '04 seniors at 85 relative to market price of the '09 seniors at 70 implies 15 points of upside to 100 and 15 points of downside to 70 — a 50/50 bet.

But the market's equal probability assessment does not necessarily need to be the investor's assumption. An investor could, based on his or her own judgment and market outlook, believe the refinance outlook is better than 50/50. Even better, maybe the investor's judgment has been informed by a conversation with someone at the bank who indicated that, while no decisions or commitments had been made, the bank would prefer to avoid a chapter 11 and was considering extending a $500 facility, thereby enabling a refinancing of the '04 seniors.[22] Where an investor has a strong belief in the probability of an expected outcome, his or her perceived risk-adjusted outcome could be different than the 50/50 assumption. For example, if the investor felt the refinance/bankruptcy probability distribution was 70/30, the probability-weighted net return would increase to 5.46. It is worth reemphasizing that this is an essentially infinite rate of return since the investor has no cash in the transaction.

However, just to show how minor changes in assumptions can completely change the investment strategy, consider the same fact pattern with only a few adjustments. In the new scenario, the investor, who can be characterized as skeptical, believes the probability that a refinancing will occur is less than 50/50. Indeed, when any bond in the capital structure is trading at a 40.4% YTM, as is true for the sub notes, access to the capital markets may be challenging. Also, this investor believes that in the event of a chapter 11, the sub notes have significant downside risk and certainly should trade at less than 50% of the senior notes' expected trading value, which would imply a price of 35 or less. The investor views 20 as the market's likely valuation, noting that this represents 6.0x leverage based on LTM EBITDA of 175. The skeptical investor believes LTM EBITDA is the more appropriate metric because it may not be easy to materially improve EBITDA once Chipco is in bankruptcy.

Given the skeptical investor's outlook, he or she will make exactly the opposite trade. The skeptical investor will start from the premise that the most misvalued security is the sub notes trading at 55. Given the view that a bankruptcy is likely, the investor believes it is probable that these will fall to 20, making a short sale very profitable. However, given the uncertainties, the investor also wants to hedge his or her position because if the refinancing in fact occurs, the sub notes are likely to appreciate in value, perhaps to as high as 75.

Table 10-17. Dynamics Assuming Bankruptcy Likely

	Hedge Ratio	155%		Cash Reinvested or Borrowed		3%		
	Time Period	0.5 Year						

	Size	Coupon	Beginning Price	Value	End Price	Value	Carry	% Price Change
Refinance Scenario								
Long	(100.00)	9.00%	85.00	(85.00)	100.00	100.00	4.50	17.6%
Short	154.55	5.50%	55.00	85.00	75.00	(115.91)	(4.25)	36.4%
Net	54.55			0.00		(15.91)	0.25	
Bankruptcy Scenario								
Long	(100.00)	9.00%	85.00	(85.00)	70.00	70.00	4.50	−17.6%
Short	154.55	5.50%	55.00	85.00	20.00	(30.91)	(4.25)	−63.6%
Net	54.55			0.00		39.09	0.25	

Summary	Refinance	Chapter 11
Cash After Put On	0.00	0.00
Cash to Close Out	(15.91)	39.09
Investment Carry	0.00	0.00
Coupon Carry	0.25	0.25
Net Return	(15.66)	39.34

To hedge his or her risk, the investor will want to be long on a security that will increase in value if the refinancing occurs (this will offset the expected loss on the short sale of the sub notes). The logical candidate, of course, is the '04 seniors, which will clearly get 100 in the case of the refinancing. So the second investor does the opposite transaction, on a dollar-weighted basis, with a different expectation. Table 10-17 depicts the expected returns from the skeptical investor's perspective.

Note that in Table 10-17 the upside/downside price volatility of the long security (in this case the '04 seniors) is an equally offsetting 17.6%. However, the investor believes that the upside/downside on the 5.50s is considerably negative, which is why the short sale appears attractive. Here the expected return from the transaction, assuming a 50/50 probability, is 11.84.[23]

Common Capital Structure Arbitrage Trades

Depending on the capital structure, there are three common "trades" that can be designed. While many of these trades are useful in the context of distressed debt investing, they also are common strategies for managing other types of securities portfolios.

Pari Passu Securities with Different Maturities

This is a fairly straightforward trade that is possible when there are two bonds in the capital structure that are, or at least are perceived to be, pari passu. In the Chipco example, one could consider a trade between the '04 seniors and the '09 seniors, which are pari passu but trading at a 15 point spread. The trade is usually attractive in two contexts: (1) when there is a near-term maturity that leads to a price discrepancy that may collapse and (2) when two securities deemed pari passu and trading at similar levels are suspected of actually having different claim status and thus the price spread may widen.

The first scenario outlined above is exactly the scenario present in the Chipco example. If it was known with certainty that Chipco would file for bankruptcy, then the two senior securities should trade at the same price — 70 or perhaps lower. However, if there is some chance that the '04 seniors may actually be paid off in six months, then, all things being equal, investors would prefer to have that early redemption "option." If the '04 seniors and the '09 seniors were trading at exactly the same price, this "option" effectively would be free. Everyone would sell '09 seniors and buy '04 seniors. Demand and supply would quickly act to create a price discrepancy, which would represent the premium that investors are willing to pay for the early redemption option. The size of the premium would implicitly reflect the probability that investors placed on the refinancing.

An investor who feels the market has overvalued the early redemption option might consider a trade in which he or she is long the '09 seniors and short the '04 seniors. The investor's thesis might be that if the refinancing occurs (which the investor believes is less than a 50/50 chance), the short will lose 15 points (85–100), but the long security might appreciate modestly in value, say 70 to 75, because the risk of a near-term bankruptcy has been reduced. On the other hand, if the bankruptcy occurs, the two securities should trade at the same level, implying a 15-point profit, regardless of the impact of the bankruptcy on the trading value of the '09 seniors. The trade would be as depicted in Table 10-18.

Based on the investor's assumptions, the trade has an expected payoff of 2.98, assuming a 50/50 probability. If the investor believes the probability of a bankruptcy is 70%, his or her expected return would improve to 7.98. Two details are worth pointing out about this trade. First, since the investor is short the higher priced security (and assuming equal weighting based on face), there again is a positive cash balance (i.e., 15) at the beginning of the trade. Second, because the investor is long the security with the higher coupon (the '09 seniors have a 9.50% coupon versus the 9.00% coupon on the '04 seniors), there is positive coupon carry on the trade.

Table 10-18. Arbitrage Between Pari Passu Securities

| | | Hedge Ratio | 100% | Cash Reinvested or Borrowed | | 3% | |
| | | Time Period | 0.5 Year | | | | |

	Size	Coupon	Beginning Price	Value	End Price	Value	Carry	% Price Change
Refinance Scenario								
Long	(100.00)	9.50%	70.00	(70.00)	75.00	75.00	4.75	7.1%
Short	100.00	9.00%	85.00	85.00	100.00	(100.00)	(4.50)	17.6%
Net	—			15.00		(25.00)	0.25	
Bankruptcy Scenario								
Upside/Downside								
Long	(100.00)	9.50%	70.00	(70.00)	95.00	95.00	4.75	35.7%
Short	100.00	9.00%	85.00	85.00	95.00	(95.00)	(4.50)	11.8%
Net	—			15.00		—	0.25	

Summary	Refinance	Chapter 11
Cash After Put On	15.00	15.00
Cash to Close Out	(25.00)	—
Investment Carry	0.23	0.23
Coupon Carry	0.25	0.25
Net Return	(9.53)	15.48

The second scenario envisioned above (trading as if pari passu but expected to be different) generally only arises in fairly complicated capital structures where debt is at different entities within the corporate family. Acquisitions of entities with previously issued debt can give rise to these situations. Assume Firm P makes a stock acquisition of Firm T and both P and T have outstanding senior unsecured debt. While the combined firm is performing well, the two bonds are likely to trade in harmony as pari passu bonds. Some time after the acquisition, the combined entity becomes financially distressed. The market may trade the bonds equally on the "assumption" that they are pari passu or that in the event of a bankruptcy there will be a substantive consolidation. However, there are reasons why the two bonds may not be pari passu. Perhaps T was never made a guarantor of P, which would be one way to make the securities pari passu, and T has valuable unencumbered assets. In that case, T's bonds may be more valuable. Alternatively, perhaps T's operations are particularly worthless (perhaps P stripped it of all its assets) and P never assumed T's obligations. In that case, P's obligations may be worth more.

One might assume that important legal "details" such as guarantees, agreements to assume, and compliance with covenants would never be overlooked, but occasionally they are.[24] Particularly when the acquiring firm is investment grade, it is easy for various parties/creditors to assume repayment and not sweat the details; when an acquisition is made, there are plenty of other issues that may seem more pressing. Through thorough due diligence, an investor may identify issues that differentiate the credit characteristics of the two bonds. In that case, the investor might put on a trade going long the security he or she feels will be benefited and short the other. If the investor is right, a trading spread between the two securities should develop to reflect the identified benefit and he or she will profit. If, on the other hand, the two securities were ultimately pari passu, the investor's downside risk is limited to transaction costs and cost of carry differences. Of course, if the investor is completely wrong in his or her analysis and the security that was thought to be worth more turns out to be worth less, then substantial losses could be incurred. Recent examples of misvaluations of this nature occurred in the PSI Net and Global Crossing bankruptcies.[25]

A less commonly considered, but potentially attractive, situation in which to do pari passu hedges involves trade claim investments. Trade claims, which will be discussed in more detail in the next chapter, are liabilities of a firm owed to nonfinancial creditors such as vendors. Trade creditors often will sell such claims (which usually are senior, unsecured obligations of the operating company) at discounts because the creditors need the liquidity, prefer not to become involved in bankruptcies, or are relatively inexperienced in the process. Trade claims, which generally are not negotiable instruments, are less liquid than tradable securities and thus usually trade at a discount, sometimes a significant discount, relative to comparable bond claims. Investors in trade claims might, where possible, consider hedging their credit risk by shorting senior unsecured notes.[26] The two claims should have pari passu status, and the hedge effectively allows the investor to capture or lock in the discount associated with the illiquidity of the trade claim. The same trade potentially can also be done with subordinated debt, particularly if it is the only debt in the capital structure, but it is important to carefully analyze the subordination provisions to ensure such debt is a pari passu claim.

Senior Versus Junior Securities

This trade is put on when the trading price difference between a senior and more junior security is deemed inappropriate. The misvaluation can arise in any number of contexts depending on the complexity of the capital structure: senior secured versus senior unsecured (a common relationship between bank debt and senior bonds), senior versus subordinated, and holding company versus operating company. In all these cases, what investors seek is a trading discrepancy that they believe misvalues the actual value or recovery potential. The Chipco-related trades analyzed in Tables 10-15 to 10-18 involving different scenarios of the sub notes versus the senior notes are examples of senior versus junior hedges.

In designing the hedge, the ideal hedge security would provide significant protection if an investor's primary bet is wrong, but only minimally affect returns when the bet is correct. Note that in Table 10-17 when the skeptical investor bet on bankruptcy but hedged himself or herself with the '04 seniors, the loss on the '04 senior long position partially reduced the returns on the profitable sub notes short position. Assume, for purposes of a slightly different scenario, that an investor wants to bet there will be a bankruptcy, but feels the biggest risk of being short is not the refinancing (in fact, the investor is so certain the refinancing will not occur, he or she would be willing to short the sub notes without a hedge) but that Chipco will be acquired by a strategic party (perhaps a customer dependent on Chipco that does not want to risk supply disruptions in the event of a bankruptcy). In the case of an acquisition, which the investor judges is a 20% probability, the risk of being short the sub notes is that they potentially will appreciate to 100 (almost a certainty if they contain a change of control put), a loss of 45. To hedge this risk, the investor would be better off longing the '09 seniors. If Chipco is acquired, the '09 seniors should trade to 100, providing a 30-point offset to the loss on the short. On the other hand, if there is a bankruptcy, then the price decline, if any, in the '09 seniors will have less of an impact on the profit on the short sub notes position. This trade is analyzed in Table 10-19.

In this scenario, the investor assumes that the '09 seniors will trade up 30 if the acquisition occurs, but down only 5 if the higher probability bankruptcy occurs. However, the investor expects much more volatility in the sub notes. If the bankruptcy occurs, he or she expects these to trade down at least 35 points to 20. In the acquisition scenario, they may trade to 100, a loss of 45. Note that the 25/45 upside/downside ratio on the short of the sub notes would make this investment irrational if the scenarios were deemed equally likely; in that case, one would want to be long the sub notes, not short. However, since the investor judges the acquisition scenario to be only a 20% risk, the expected value of the position is 22.8.

Trades between senior and junior debt can be a particularly attractive strategy if an investor has a strong view on the deterioration of credit quality of an investment-grade company. In investment-grade companies, the trading spread between senior and subordinated notes can, at least by distressed standards, be trivial — often only 20–50 basis points in yield spread. However, if the firm is downgraded to below investment grade, the spread typically will widen

Table 10-19. Long '09 Seniors and Short Sub Note Trade

| | Hedge Ratio | 100% | | Cash Reinvested or Borrowed | | | 3% | |
| | Time Period | 0.5 Year | | | | | | |

	Size	Coupon	Beginning Price	Value	End Price	Value	Carry	% Price Change
Acquisition Scenario								
Long	(100.00)	9.50%	70.00	(70.00)	100.00	100.00	4.75	42.9%
Short	100.00	5.50%	55.00	55.00	100.00	(100.00)	(2.75)	81.8%
Net	—			(15.00)		—	2.00	
Bankruptcy Scenario								
Long	(100.00)	9.50%	70.00	(70.00)	65.00	65.00	4.75	−7.1%
Short	100.00	5.50%	55.00	55.00	20.00	(20.00)	(2.75)	−63.6%
Net	—			(15.00)		45.00	2.00	

Summary	Acquisition	Chapter 11
Cash After Put On	(15.00)	(15.00)
Cash to Close Out	—	45.00
Investment Carry	(0.23)	(0.23)
Coupon Carry	2.00	2.00
Net Return	(13.23)	31.78

significantly. In a situation where a firm quickly becomes financially distressed, the widening can be even more material. Of course, in this scenario, the investor may view the downside risk of being short the subordinated note without a hedge as being manageable.

Bonds Versus Equity

This trade is conceptually similar to the senior versus junior trade. In fact, it could be viewed as the ultimate senior versus junior trade. However, there are a variety of trade-offs to consider when trying to hedge credit risk with equity. On the positive side, the mechanics of shorting equity (compared to debt) are generally easier, so the trade may be simpler, and when done with a financially deteriorating firm, it is unlikely there will be any carry associated with dividends. In addition, most companies with public debt will have public equity. Thus, in firms with fairly simple capital structures involving only one debt issue, equity may be the only hedge security available.

On the negative side, equity is usually significantly more volatile than debt. Thus, while the general direction of price movement relative to an event is likely predictable, the magnitude of the price movement can be difficult to estimate. Furthermore, when shorting equity, there is, theoretically at least, no cap on the downside risk. Bonds seldom go materially above 100, so the worst-case scenario is more easily defined. Stocks, of course, have no theoretical limit, although this upside risk is mitigated by the fact that equities are typically more liquid than bonds; thus it can be easier to cover one's position. Lastly, in deteriorating situations, shorting often is difficult because of the "up-tick" rule and other regulations.[27]

As discussed above, the most common context for a bond versus equity trade is hedging an in-the-money convertible bond. In that case, the price dynamics of the bond and stock can be reasonably correlated. However, there are many other contexts in which the trade can be appropriate. In particular, in any capital structure where an investor is considering going long a junior security, the equity, if it can be shorted, effectively may be the only way of managing downside risk.

Consider, for the last time, the case of Chipco and the situation involving the optimistic investor depicted in Table 10-15. In that scenario, the investor went long the sub notes and short the '04 seniors on the investment premise that a refinancing was likely and, if he or she was wrong, the downside risk on the sub notes was 40. Objectively speaking, the riskiest assumption in the investor's outlook may be on the downside of the sub notes. As noted in several other examples, it is very plausible to assume the sub notes could fall significantly below 40, in light of the significant amount of senior debt involved. Thus, while the investor may have a strong belief that refinancing is likely, he or she may want to buy some "insurance" in the form of shorting some equity — if it is possible to do so. If the investor shorts the equity, then he or she can reasonably assume that if the sub notes trade significantly below 40, the equity will be worth 0. In the event refinancing occurs, as the investor expects, there is certainly risk that the equity could appreciate in price, but this may be manageable since the absolute amount of leverage involved should limit the potential equity valuation. It also should be noted that the investor does not have to put the equity short on at the same time he or she puts on the bond trade. He or she could put on the bond trade and then monitor the situation. At a later time, if the investor's perception of the probability of the refinancing has changed, he or she could decide whether to unwind the trade or add the short sale of the stock; of course, in the latter case the investor is assuming the risk that he or she can add the short at the moment of his or her choosing. It is critical when engaged in a hedged investment to constantly monitor all developments and adjust or rebalance the hedge to reflect the revised probability of pending events.

SUMMARY

This chapter has analyzed a few of the strategies or "moves" available to the distressed investor. It should be kept in mind that, like every game of chess, every restructuring is unique and requires independent and creative analysis to be successful. The strategies analyzed above are intended not to be exhaustive, but rather illustrative of the thought process in which the investor must engage when analyzing a distressed investment.

A tremendous simplification that was made in this analysis was to reduce the scenario analysis to a simple two-variable model: an expected event either happened or did not happen. In reality, there are, of course, many more variables. Even when the basic investment premise appears as simple as it was presented for Chipco (whether or not it can refinance a near-term maturity), there always will be many other factors. For example, in the Chipco analysis, the potential impact on recoveries associated with trade claims was, for simplicity, never considered. The various scenarios also assumed that probabilities could rationally be associated with different outcomes; in most cases, at least from a true statistical perspective, no such probabilities can be derived. If it was as simple as presented here, distressed investment would be largely a numbers game of probability, weighting different outcomes and investing in those situations with the highest expected values.

Of course, it is not so simple. The next chapter, which discusses the practical aspects of identifying investment opportunities and then determining the factors that should be considered in making the investment decision, hopefully will give a sense of the actual complexity involved in the process. Investors will never have true certainty about the outcome of an investment. But with an insightful thought process and diligent analysis of the issues, it should be possible to identify and properly assess the risks. Sometimes the uncertainties or unknown elements will be too great, in which case the investment would be unwise. However, in most cases the key factors affecting returns at least can be identified and the risks assessed, allowing the experienced investor to balance projected numerical outcomes with judgment in making an investment decision.

This Chapter's Chess Moves

22. Qd3, Nh5

23. Rxf8+, Rxf8

11

PRACTICAL ASPECTS OF THE INVESTMENT PROCESS AND DUE DILIGENCE

There are a myriad of potential opportunities in the market. Before an investor can implement the strategies developed in Chapter 10, it is necessary to first identify an attractive opportunity. After that, one must do sufficient investigation and analysis to reach an appropriate level of "comfort" or "certainty" that the investment risks and uncertainties have been identified and appropriately weighted. Finally, although the distressed securities market is less efficient than most equity and investment-grade debt markets, it is also more illiquid, which makes it important to accumulate positions efficiently to maximize investment returns.

There will always be uncertainties — whether or not the investor cares to recognize them. The issue is to identify and understand the risks so that they can be appropriately weighed against the return potential. Returning to a scenario that has been discussed before, assume a subordinated note is trading at distressed levels because it matures in one year, the capital markets have been tight, and the firm's operations have been weak, all of which raise the risk that the firm may not be able to pay the bond at maturity. This could compel the firm to either try an out-of-court restructuring or, failing that, file for bankruptcy protection. The investor judges that the risk of the firm not being able to refinance the note maturity is minimal because he or she foresees a turnaround in the industry and believes that, although the firm has a secured working capital facility, it has significant unpledged assets that could be used to support a refinancing using secured debt. The investment is essentially a "bet" that a refinancing will be feasible because of improved fundamentals coupled with the ability to access the senior secured debt market.

Realistically, however, the investor cannot "know" with metaphysical certitude[1] that the firm will be able to access the capital markets in the future, and, mathematically, it is difficult to meaningfully or rigorously "quantify" the risk of refinancing. The investor can make an investment judgment based on an experienced assessment of the environment. However, that investment judgment will be erroneously derived, if the investor fails to uncover that another bond indenture of the firm prohibits the refinancing of the subordinated debt with other than junior securities, for which there may be no market, or that the working capital facility has a lien on all assets, not just the typical accounts receivable and inventory. Those factors were not in the "terms" of the bet. It would be like making a bet on a horse in a given race and then finding out that at the last moment the jockey was being changed or that three very strong horses had been added to the field. To properly calculate the odds, you need all the facts. That is the role of "due diligence."

Most of the procedures reviewed here will reinforce and build upon the fundamentals developed in earlier chapters. First, the practical realities of analyzing an investment or valuing a security and certain "less obvious" extra-financial considerations are discussed, and the steps required to ascertain as much information as is available are reviewed. Then, the trade-offs and mechanics of investing in different types of investments are discussed. Finally, some strategic considerations on accumulating an investment position are explored.

PRACTICAL REALITIES OF THE INVESTMENT ANALYSIS PROCESS

As much as the quantitative approach of financial econometricians would suggest that investing is fundamentally a science, in distressed investing it is more of an art. The challenge, as with all investments, if not life in general, is uncertainty regarding the future. But distressed investing faces even more uncertainty and information challenges than most investments because of the various dynamics previously reviewed. This is why knowledge of the process, experience, and judgment are often more critical to investment success than tedious hours of financial modeling.

Screening Situations to Prioritize Opportunities

An ever-present constraint for the distressed investor is lack of time. This is because when the market conditions are most ripe for misvaluation, which is usually when the supply of distressed investments exceeds available investment capital, there are almost always more situations to analyze than one person, or even large teams, can feasibly dissect. By way of illustration, at the end of 2002, over $100 billion in face amount of debt was trading at prices below 50. In such market environments, it is important to develop "screening" processes to help identify the most promising situations on which to focus. With an average personal computer and simple database, it is now fairly easy to construct data sets and algorithms that can screen or rank potential investments. For example, a simple screen might be to search for all bonds with a rating less than B1/B+, a bond price less than 50, a market equity capitalization greater than $20 million (or perhaps some specified percentage of total debt) and leverage based on last 12 months earnings before interest, taxes, depreciation, and amortization (EBITDA) of less than 6.0x. The "theory" behind this search would be to find significantly discounted bonds where leverage, by recent historical standards, is not too high and the equity markets perceive enough potential enterprise value (contrary to the implication of the discounted bond price) for the stock to trade at more than a diminimus price. If this screen had been run in January 2002, it would have returned over 100 different companies.[2] However, this would have been significantly less than the hundreds that were in financial distress.

Of course, many other criteria could be used depending on what type of situations an investor believes will best identify the most suitable investment candidates. If the investor is large and only wants situations where significant capital can be invested or requires significant liquidity, a minimum bond size threshold (e.g., $300 million) would further limit the potential targets. Alternatively, other distressed investors may believe better opportunities may lie in smaller situations (e.g., less than $150 million in debt) that are intentionally avoided by larger hedge funds. Taken to the extreme, if an investor operates under the theory that the most likely situation to be misvalued is that which is least likely to attract investor interest, then he or she may want to sort using criteria the typical investor would likely seek to avoid.[3]

After screening to develop a set of target opportunities, the investor will likely still need to develop criteria to prioritize the candidates. These will vary for each investor. Some investors have preferences for, or aversions to, certain industries. Sometimes the preferences are based on a fundamental view of the industry's future prospects or risk characteristics. Other times, they can be more psychologically driven; for example, some investors are reluctant to invest in industries where they have previously suffered significant investment losses.

After some additional prioritization, the investor may choose to review research information, when available, from broker-dealers. Often, a 20-minute review of a report or conversation with a "sell-side" analyst can help an investor further refine his or her priorities. The goal is to develop a process that maximizes the percentage of attractive investment ideas developed from limited time investment in company-specific fundamental analysis.

Reacting to Volatile Situations

In addition to the sheer number of potential situations, the market environment can significantly constrain an investor's ability to complete exhaustive due diligence on any particular opportunity. Imagine a situation where new information, which has been interpreted negatively, has caused market values of a firm's securities to decline significantly. An investor learns there is an offering of bonds 20 points below the last trading level, senses opportunity, and begins to do his or her analysis. The investor reaches a very preliminary conclusion that the situation appears misvalued at current prices. He or she will then want to continue the investigation and analysis to develop a higher confidence level, but will always be concerned that another investor may, at any time, begin buying the bonds and perhaps drive up the price. As a practical matter, it is very difficult to know whether a given offering is a single seller that has motivations based on criteria other than investment value or a group of existing holders attempting to exit based on changed fundamentals. If the former is true, then the attractive investment may have a very limited life span. If the latter, then the investor will essentially be catching a live hand grenade thrown by a seller with arguably better insight. Thus, in situations that arise due to sudden market volatility, an investor new to the situation will often feel pressured to act before completing all the analysis he or she would like to perform. This is where experience and intuition are required to help determine how high a confidence level should be attained before acting. However, it is essential to always remain disciplined: someone who likely knows the situation has decided to sell at a reduced price, and other investors, who are already involved and knowledgeable, have not yet bought the offering.

A Time-Efficient Valuation Methodology

Recognizing the reality that time will always be at least a perceived constraint, the analytical approach, other than in hedged trade situations, should be efficient, but disciplined. The conventional wisdom on investment approach is to determine a valuation of a firm, assess the magnitude of liabilities, determine the probable claim priority of the liabilities, and then compare this to the valuation. This probably more accurately describes the thought process used in articulating an investment rationale rather than the actual process. For example, if an analyst presents a summary investment recommendation to a portfolio manager, it would be very logical to organize it as follows: The company is worth at least $300 given my expectation that EBITDA will be $60 and comparable companies are valued at more than 5x EBITDA. The company has total debt of $400, made up of $200 senior and $200 subordinated. The senior notes are trading at 80 and the subordinated notes are trading at 25. The implied value of the subordinated notes is 50. The potential investment return on the subs is 100% and downside risk is limited. We should buy the subs.

The hypothetical analyst who actually performed his or her analysis exactly as he or she presented it could hardly be faulted. However, just as a discounted cash flow model is arguably the "correct" way to value a firm as opposed to an EBITDA multiple, the actual "process" or order of investigation most investors use is probably quite different.

The following outline is an approach that is arguably more representative of the way experienced distressed investors approach the analysis, particularly in situations involving significant market volatility where time may be particularly limited.

1. Analyze the most recent financials to determine the capital structure. Determine total debt and relative priority given the legal (security and seniority) and structural (operating versus holding company) considerations.
2. Value the capital structure given market trading prices.
3. Analyze recent EBITDA trends and determine the relative leverage (on an EBITDA multiple basis) of the various levels of the capital structure at both face and market value.
4. Consider whether, given conservative or appropriate industry valuation metrics, the business is likely worth more than current trading levels.

Of course, this is not enough analysis on which to base an investment decision, but it is a time efficient way to determine the relative attractiveness, and hence time priority, of the opportunity. The reason why experienced analysts in practice rarely start with an estimate of firm value is that a thorough valuation can be extremely time consuming and, ultimately, is uncertain. By starting with the capital structure, an analyst can quickly make a preliminary assessment of a firm's complexity and estimate a threshold for what the minimum firm value needs to be to potentially provide a return on investment. Then, the analyst can examine historical EBITDA and capital expenditure needs to quickly "ball-park" going-concern or enterprise value (EV). The analyst would also quickly review the asset side of the balance sheet to assess whether there are assets that potentially could provide an independent worst-case liquidation source of credit support. In most situations, except the most complex capital structures, an experienced analyst with a preestablished spreadsheet template model can do a "quick-and-dirty" assessment in about 15–30 minutes. Again, this is certainly not sufficient work on which to commit capital; the issue at this point is whether to commit time.

PERFORMING DUE DILIGENCE

Due diligence can be thought of as investment homework. More formally, due diligence is the process of investigating all aspects of an investment in an effort to improve the confidence level of one's risk and return estimation. Those who have been involved in a corporate acquisition will probably be familiar with lengthy, detailed due diligence checklists[4] of documents, contracts, and financial schedules to be obtained and reviewed before a transaction is consummated. These lists contemplate that the target's management cooperates and shares information such as customer lists, detailed product cost and revenue information, all material contracts, asset value appraisals, analyses of litigation, internal projections, etc. These lists are designed to try to unearth every fact relevant to the transaction.

Investors would all prefer to have this comprehensive information, but, as a practical matter, much of it is nonpublic and management may not be compelled to share it with outsiders.[5] The general rationale for restricting the information given to investors (who, at the equity level, are the owners) is that such materials often include proprietary data that could hurt the firm's competitive position *vis a vis* other market participants if they were to obtain it. Thus, investment due diligence typically must be conducted within the context of having significantly less information than is typical in a full-blown corporate acquisition.

Due Diligence Cost-Benefit Analysis

The procedures for, and mechanics of, conducting investment due diligence will depend on the investment objective and circumstances surrounding the timing of the investment. While any investor would prefer to have as much information and insight about a target firm as is feasible to obtain, there are practical considerations that prevent an investor from obtaining this in every situation. If an investor is considering investing several hundred million dollars with a goal of taking control of a major enterprise in a relatively stable price environment, either pre- or postbankruptcy, then a significant, no-expense-spared investment in the due diligence process can be justified. Consultants, including former executives of the target, may be retained to provide detailed insight on the firm's current circumstances, prospects, and valuation. Lawyers may be used to meticulously analyze all relevant corporate governance and lending documents, provide advice on claims that might arise from existing litigation and tax considerations, and outline liabilities (or assets) that might arise in the event of a chapter 11 process. It is easy to imagine $150,000–$300,000 being invested in third-party professional services, not counting the opportunity cost of the analyst's time, if the investment is material enough.

At the other extreme, if an investor is considering paying $600,000 to purchase $2 million face of subordinated notes at 30 in a dynamic price environment, time and expense constraints will limit the detail with which the issues listed above can be explored. Either way, there will likely still be uncertainty, requiring the application of seasoned investment judgment. Additional investment in the due diligence process should lead to better risk analysis, confidence level, and investment performance; however, there is usually a diminishing return on investment. In other words, the learning curve can begin to flatten reasonably quickly.

An early decision an investor must often confront is whether or not to access nonpublic information. As has been discussed several times before, in the ordinary context, there are generally two levels of information:[6] (1) publicly disclosed information that is available to all investors by virtue of a firm's obligation to make specified filings with the Securities and Exchange Commission (SEC)[7] and (2) private information disclosed to bank lenders which can be obtained only after executing a confidentiality agreement. In situations where there is no bank debt, the latter level of information is not available, and an investor has little ability to demand nonpublic information in exchange for a confidentiality agreement. While any investor would prefer to have access to the more detailed "bank level" of information, as discussed in Chapter 4, possessing such information can make it more difficult to engage in the purchase and sale of securities and, hence, has certain strategic disadvantages. It should also be noted that even when investors purchase bank debt in part to have access to nonpublic information, they should be aware that this does not give them the right to ask for all information on the borrower. Thus, prior to becoming restricted, an investor should discuss with other members of the bank group the type and detail of information to which he or she will have access.

Prioritizing the Diligence Issues

To efficiently perform due diligence, it is important to define the investment objective and determine in which security the investor is most likely to invest. Then the most critical, or likely, risks can be identified and the investigation can target those risks. Assume, for example, that an analyst had been asked to take a look at Kmart in January 2002 when its financial distress was well known, the bonds had traded to low levels, and it appeared likely that the company would have to file for chapter 11 protection. Kmart had a very complicated $4.7 billion capital structure with more than 40 different outstanding recourse and nonrecourse debt obligations. To know "everything" that was available to know about Kmart would be a daunting if not impossible task.

Where does one begin? For this discussion, it will be assumed the analyst has been directed to consider specific securities. In addition, significant liberties with the actual facts of the Kmart case, which exited bankruptcy in May 2003, will be taken to simplify the discussion and allow various points to be illustrated.

First, assume the portfolio manager was primarily interested in investing in the secured bank debt, which is trading at 60, a 40-point premium to the unsecured senior debt priced at 20. Logically, since the valuation difference appears to be driven primarily by the pledge of collateral,[8] the analyst first would want to make sure he or she understood the nature of the collateral and all the relevant risks to the collateral either not being available to, or "owned" by, the lender or inadequate to support the loan. Some of the more obvious factors to consider would be:

- What is the estimated value of the collateral and therefore the risk that the secured debt would not receive a full recovery or, in the event of a bankruptcy, might be deemed undersecured and thus potentially not entitled to postpetition interest (very important given the potentially long time period required for a reorganization of the complexity of Kmart)?
- Has the bank properly perfected its security interest?[9] Do other prepetition creditors have priority over the bank's security interest?
- If the bank debt had originally been unsecured but became secured as part of a covenant waiver negotiation, when did that occur and what is the risk that if the company filed an immediate bankruptcy the pledge could be challenged as a preferential transfer?
- If a significant number of stores were expected to be closed, how might this affect the collateral value?

There are many more issues the analyst would want to consider and investigate to home in on the investment value of the secured debt. However, being cognizant of time management, there are whole classes of issues that are of relatively lower priority. For example, whether a trust preferred stock issue in the capital structure had the priority of a subordinated claim or was only an equity interest might be assigned a fairly low priority or dismissed as irrelevant. The resolution of that issue would, in the vast majority of cases, have few implications for the value of the senior secured debt.

Alternatively, assume that the portfolio manager was interested in buying a special-purpose municipal bond secured by a store leased to Kmart. Here the analyst's work would become much more focused on the actual pledged property.

- How is that store performing?
- Is it likely to be closed and have the lease rejected?
- Is the note secured by the real estate or only the lease?
- Are there any maintenance escrow accounts that might have available cash balances?
- If the lease is rejected, what are the prospects for re-leasing the store?
- What would be the approximate claim amount if the lease is rejected, and what, given Kmart's circumstances, is the estimated value of such a claim?
- Is there any plausible argument under the documents that the debt is fully recourse to Kmart or the municipality?

In a lease rejection scenario, a portion of the bond's value would derive from an unsecured claim against the general estate. Theoretically, therefore, all the valuation issues at the corporate level are also relevant. The time it would be prudent to devote to an analysis of those issues would depend on the circumstances. If the store in question is a flagship store in a great location with a low probability of lease rejection, then general corporate credit issues might have little impact on value. On the other hand, if it is an underperforming, poorly located store, with a high probability of the lease being rejected, and the bonds were trading at 3 with the expectation that the only recovery would come from the lease rejection claim against the estate, then, obviously, more consideration of Kmart's overall credit fundamentals would be essential.[10]

Finally, assume that the portfolio manager is interested in a preferred stock trading at 2, and to simplify matters, assume there were no trust preferred issues as referenced above. In many ways, analyzing the potential recovery value of a preferred stock issue is much simpler. The analyst should know, or likely will be able to easily determine, that the preferred stock is junior to all the debt and trade claims of the estate. He or she will not care whether the pledge of collateral to the secured debt can be rejected and will not care if the subordinated debt is pari passu with the trade debt. How those debt claims carve up the pie is generally irrelevant. The preferred stock is only entitled to any residual value. The analyst's primary concern is whether there will be any pie left after the creditors are done carving.

Given the prior discussion in Chapters 4 and 10 about the politics and incentives of the creditors in the restructuring process, the analyst should realize that an "objective" analysis of the company's "true" value, relative to creditors' claims, is of limited value. Particularly if the debt is trading at a significant discount (earlier it was posited that the senior unsecured debt was trading at 20), the creditors will likely be able to make a forceful argument in a bankruptcy proceeding that the value of the estate is materially less than the creditors' claims and, therefore, the preferred stock is worthless.[11] Of course, regardless of the valuation merits, the creditors have a substantial incentive to make such an argument.[12]

As a practical matter, a critical issue is whether there is a colorable valuation argument or other source of negotiating leverage that gives the preferred stockholders a credible threat of interference with the workout process sufficient to extract at least a nuisance value payment. This may be difficult to assess without the involvement of experienced legal counsel. Issues to focus on include:

- What is the possibility that an equity committee will be appointed? This is usually a long shot, but if an aggressive investor has acquired some of the company's common stock and has a sufficiently large stake to justify getting involved, the chances improve. If an equity committee is authorized by the bankruptcy court, then the preferred stock is in an excellent position because the equity committee will typically have company-funded legal counsel and financial advisors[13] to wage a valuation fight or identify other sources of recovery. Of course, the preferred stock is legally senior to the common, so any recovery to the common stock should benefit the preferred.

- Who are the major players on the committee? When one is "betting" on the ability to extract a nuisance value concession, it is important to know with whom one will be negotiating.

- Does the relative size of the preferred class make it inexpensive to "pay off"? If the preferred class is relatively small, say $100 million liquidation preference, then relative to the magnitude of Kmart, it would take a relatively modest allocation of value (which would almost certainly be in new equity or warrants) to buy cooperation. For example, if the value being recovered by the creditors was $4 billion, then a $4 million "tip" to buy the cooperation of the preferreds would be a "rounding error," and yet this could provide a preferred shareholder a recovery that would represent a 100% return on an investment acquired at 2.

This should provide a brief overview of some of the basic considerations that go into forming a time- and cost-effective due diligence strategy. Next, both financial and legal diligence will be discussed in more detail.

FINANCIAL DUE DILIGENCE

Basic Goals of Financial Due Diligence

The basic goal of financial due diligence is to develop a firm valuation and understand the short-term financial issues impacting the firm, which, when used in conjunction with the legal due diligence discussed later, will help develop a valuation or investment strategy related to a particular security within the capital structure. The output or work product of the financial due diligence process should be:

- **A financial analysis of recent historical information**: How far back this analysis should go will depend on the circumstances. For long-standing businesses, particularly cyclical businesses, it can be useful to compile data for the last ten years in order to provide insight on the magnitude of cyclical fluctuations and whether there have been any systemic changes to the industry (e.g., if a competitor's strategy of outsourcing production to lower cost regions has resulted in margin compression). Multiperiod analyses can also aid in assessing long-term capital expenditure requirements. Often, when looking at just the last year or two of results of a firm experiencing financial distress, the reported amount of capital expenditures may be below the true needs of the business, since this can be one of the first areas of cost cutting. As a general rule, capital expenditures should equal or exceed depreciation charges. When a firm provides operating data on different segments, it should be analyzed in an effort to determine whether discrete components of the business can be sold, as well as the potential valuations of such units.

- **A projection of the firm's future operating prospects**: The number of periods that should be projected will depend on the stability of the firm's operating environment. When analyzing a firm that is not operating in bankruptcy, then, at a minimum, the projection should extend to the point where financial distress is predicted, which for these purposes should be defined to mean the point at which a liquidity event could force a bankruptcy filing. For example, a firm may have sufficient liquidity to operate over the near term, but is facing a significant debt maturity in three years that the firm is unlikely to fund through internally generated cash. The analyst would model to the period of the debt maturity in an effort to assess the firm's likelihood of being able to refinance and/or assess the recovery value to the debt at that time. There is a tendency when doing recovery analyses to value the firm as if it were liquidated or sold as of the moment of the analysis, even though it is unlikely such an event will occur in the near term. The better practice is to predict when the liquidity crisis will occur and attempt to assess the distressed firm's options at that time.

- **A corporate organizational chart**: An organizational chart can be very helpful in analyzing relative priorities for securities and potential access to sources of credit support. The chart should identify the corporate location of all key operations and significant liabilities.

- **A valuation analysis of comparable companies**: As discussed in Chapter 5, this is needed to estimate a valuation range for the firm.

- **A liquidation analysis**: This is a "worst-case" type of analysis (see Chapter 5) which assumes the firm's assets are liquidated individually rather than the firm being sold as a going concern. Particularly in the case of multilayer capital structures, it can be useful in gauging downside risk.

- **General industry outlook and analysis of the firm's position**: This may be somewhat more qualitative in nature, but as part of the valuation process, it is critical to understand the larger forces at work in the target's industry. Is it an industry leader or a struggling "also-ran" buffeted by a dominant competitor (e.g., Kmart by Wal-Mart)? Is the industry in technological decline (e.g., pager industry)? Hundreds of questions could be posed, but the basic point is that a valuation cannot be reliably performed without considering the broader industry fundamentals.

Obtaining Publicly Available Financial Information

Fortunately, the wonders of the Internet have made obtaining basic SEC filings a fairly simple matter. SEC filings can be downloaded for no charge at www.sec.gov/edgar. In addition, most public companies will have Web sites that will usually contain links to the firm's SEC filings. While there is no substitute for an analyst carefully reviewing a firm's primary filings, there are third-party data services[14] that allow filed SEC financial data to be downloaded directly into spreadsheets. This can virtually eliminate the need to tediously enter data, although it is recommended that the analyst verify the data for the most recent periods since this information will be the most heavily relied upon.

Most participants in the investment community are fairly conversant with the information in standard SEC filings; therefore, this will not be reviewed in detail here.[15] However, finding and analyzing data associated with a bankruptcy is likely a less familiar process. A bankruptcy is a legal process before a bankruptcy court, with virtually all information associated with the process in the form of filings listed on the case docket of the relevant court. Fortunately, most U.S. courts, including bankruptcy courts, have made it reasonably easy to access their dockets. This is done through the Public Access to Court Electronic Records system, referred to by the acronym PACER, at www.pacer.psc.uscourts.gov. This service does charge fees to access court filings, but they are reasonable, and there are usually few practical alternatives. Some law firms will post on their Web sites (typically access is free) filings related to cases in which they are involved, so it may be worthwhile once counsel (particularly the debtor's primary bankruptcy counsel) has been identified to check that law firm's Web site to see what is available. Also, debtors' Web sites sometimes post major filings (e.g., plan of reorganization, disclosure statement, etc.).

In a bankruptcy of any size or complexity, the number of filings can quickly escalate to almost overwhelming proportions. Therefore, it will likely take the new user some time to efficiently find what he or she is looking for. Of most interest to a distressed analyst will be the initial petition and related schedules and all subsequently filed monthly operating reports. In particular, a required part of the initial filing is the debtor's schedule of the 20 largest unsecured creditors. Reviewing this list can often give insight on the possible composition of the unsecured creditor committee since, as discussed in Chapter 4, this committee is appointed by the U.S. Trustee and is comprised of the seven largest creditors willing to serve. The operating reports can also be useful because, in many cases, bankrupt firms will discontinue making SEC filings. Thus, the operating statements are typically the only source of financial information. The initial operating statement is prospective in nature and requires information[16] relating to the next 30 days on:

- Cash available for operations
- The estimated cost of operations
- The estimated profit and loss
- How the debtor intends to fund operations

Following this prospective statement, the debtor is required to file monthly operating reports covering:

- Operating profitability
- A reconciliation of beginning and ending cash
- An analysis of changes in assets such as inventory or items liquidated to raise cash
- An itemized list of accrued but unpaid liabilities

Unfortunately, in many if not most situations, these statements, while presumably accurate, are far less comprehensive than the reports mandated by the

Exchange Act. In particular, there is often very little balance sheet information. Accordingly, an investor will usually need to network with the unsecured creditors' committee's financial advisors and attorneys and other investors to gain as comprehensive a view as possible of the debtor's ongoing financial condition.

The bankruptcy docket must be monitored constantly because material events can occur which may not independently be announced (i.e., outside of the filing of a document with the court) by the debtor. Important developments such as motions to allow for the preferential payment of certain creditors, to allow for the sale of certain assets, and to reject executory contracts are all filed with the court, and there can be no assurance, particularly in less prominent cases, that the news will be disseminated very quickly. Similarly, actions by various creditor constituencies that can give important insight on their strategies will also be filed, but otherwise not generally announced. In summary, unlike the flow of information that occurs before a bankruptcy, where virtually all public announcements by the firm are broadly disseminated and accessible by simply entering the firm's stock ticker symbol into any of a number of on-line services, bankruptcy developments require proactive monitoring.

Accessing Management

Historically, corporate management has been an essential source of insight into a firm's operations, plans, competitive position, etc. The level of management an investor could access (i.e., CEO versus CFO versus treasurer versus investor relations officer) was somewhat serendipitous, but usually driven by the "status" of the investor or analyst. Institutional shareholders that held significant blocks (i.e., greater than 5%) typically had access to the highest levels, while less well-known investors merely considering an investment were seldom likely to get above the investor relations level.[17] This, of course, was never a written policy, just a practical reality.

However, the introduction of Regulation FD, which became effective October 23, 2000,[18] has significantly changed the nature of the dialogue that management can have with investors and analysts.[19] Regulation FD, which stands for "full disclosure," prohibits companies from selectively disclosing material, nonpublic information to selected individuals, such as influential securities analysts or investors. The rule was intended to combat the practice of executives "leaking" information selectively to analysts, which could result in certain market participants having preferential access to material information. Thus, if a firm's earnings forecast for a quarter was being lowered due to a more difficult competitive environment, rather than issue a general statement that might cause a panic in the stock, executives would "whisper" their more conservative views to favored analysts, who would then spread it in the market such that by the time earnings were reported, the outcome was "expected." The goal of the rule preventing this trickle-down approach was the quite laudable ambition of ensuring that all investors had equal access to information. However, it is possible that Regulation FD may result in an overall decline in the amount of information released to the market. In any event, as a practical matter, the regulation has generally made it more difficult for analysts and investors to gain much incremental insight on a firm through management.

The impact of Regulation FD on distressed investors is more modest than for investors in "performing" firms, because executives of distressed firms have often been relatively less forthcoming with information. Within the context of a performing firm, one of the primary goals of management is to maximize the firm's perceived market value or stock price. Executives are usually eager to "tell their story" to investors. This changes very quickly when their financial fortunes darken. Typically, required financial filings will be made on schedule, but often incremental information or even discussion with investors is curtailed. When an investor begins to see this pattern, it is usually a warning sign that management is unsure what is going on or how to "fix" the problem, or worse, management doesn't know how bad it is, but wants to mask it as much as possible in an effort to maintain trade and other credit relationships.

Of course, sometimes management will view candid disclosure as being in the firm's best interest in order to win the trust and support of creditors. For example, when Southern California Edison defaulted on various debt obligations following the 2001 California energy crisis, senior management participated in almost daily conference calls with investors to provide detailed information on current financial and regulatory developments. This was successful in keeping debt holders from filing involuntary bankruptcy petitions against the company, despite numerous covenant and payment defaults. This type of candor, however, is the exception, not the rule.

If an investor is beginning the analysis after the firm has filed, information barriers can be even more daunting. In many cases, the firm will cease making public financial filings with the SEC.[20] While the code requires the firm to file monthly operating reports with the court, often there will be a substantial period of delay before such filings are actually made. Even when operating reports are filed, they can initially be difficult to assess because they are not particularly comparable with the previously filed SEC statements. Furthermore, the individuals in management typically will be very difficult to contact, as they will have been instructed by their lawyers and financial advisors to minimize such conversations.

Special Valuation Considerations in Financially Distressed Contexts

Chapter 5 reviewed the general process of valuing enterprises and their securities. These concepts will guide the production of the work product outlined at the beginning of this section. It is important, however, as the analyst refines his or her analysis, to attempt to anticipate how a reorganization, particularly one completed within a chapter 11 proceeding, will affect firm valuation. Some issues the analyst may want to consider include the following.

Business Deterioration During a Reorganization

The extent to which a bankruptcy will harm a firm's business outlook is impossible to quantify precisely. Indeed, even management, which has likely never operated a business in bankruptcy before, may not have a very good sense, so essentially everyone in the process is just making an educated guess. As a general rule, a reorganization will likely adversely affect the sales of firms in the business-to-business market because the creditworthiness and stability of the relationship are usually extremely important to the other party in the transaction. It would be easy to imagine an automaker, which likely operates on a just-in-time supply basis, shifting its steel purchases from a distressed to a healthy company in order to ensure consistent supply of a critical element. Apart from basic industries, it can be difficult for distressed technology and software companies to keep and generate new commercial customers for mission-critical systems if the customer perceives a risk the distressed firm will not be around to provide future maintenance and upgrades.[21] Firms heavily involved in the government contract market may also be negatively impacted. As a result of the automatic stay, the government has no power to terminate an existing relationship because of a chapter 11 filing, but future awards of business, almost all of which are put through some type of bid process, could be affected.[22] Loss of future government contracts in particular might be at risk, to be cynical for a moment, if one speculates on whether a performing or bankrupt firm is likely to be a more active campaign contributor. In contrast, consumers tend to be relatively indifferent as to whether they are purchasing their groceries from a bankrupt supermarket, if they are even aware of the firm's status at all.[23] The reorganization process often will also lead to the incurrence of higher operating costs. In particular, a troubled firm will often lose important vendor discounts, which can cause profit margins to deteriorate.

On the more positive side, there can be significant benefits to a bankruptcy reorganization. During the term of the reorganization, interest on unsecured debt can be suspended. Longer term, there is the potentially substantial benefit of being able to reject uneconomic contracts and leases.[24] As a practical matter, however, the analyst typically does not have access to sufficiently detailed information to rigorously analyze these potential savings. The best an analyst may be able to do is compare the firm's prepetition operating margins with those of its peers and, if the troubled firm's margins are lower, consider whether the reorganization process would likely allow it to be more competitive. Frequently, the debtor's public filings will discuss the aspects of its business that are uneconomic. These discussions will usually be cast as: "But for X losing plants or Y underperforming stores, profitability would have been Z." Such disclosures may form a foundation for estimating potential reorganization savings.

Reorganization Costs

Bankruptcy is expensive. Over and above the potential erosion in value to the business and the opportunity cost of executives who will now devote virtually 100% of their time to the reorganization instead of the development of the business, there are substantial professional fees paid for by the bankruptcy estate, including those for financial advisors (at a minimum, one each for the debtor, committee, and secured lender[25]), lawyers (several teams, including the debtor and often several representing different creditor constituencies since there can be conflicting interests among creditors), accountants, and workout experts. As an extreme example, the aggregate professional fees in the Enron bankruptcy are expected to exceed $1 billion.[26]

Costs vary, of course, depending on the complexity of the case, but even in relatively simple cases, one should probably assume a minimum of $5 million in costs. However, this can easily escalate to $10 million. From a valuation perspective, these costs all come in at the level of administrative expenses and are paid in full before any distributions to creditors. In other words, these are a dead weight loss to the firm's value.

Critical Vendor Payments

While the general rule of bankruptcy is that all unsecured prepetition claims are impacted equally by the automatic stay provisions, and thus no payments are made on behalf of such creditors until the conclusion of the case, some bankruptcy courts allow an exception for a creditor deemed to be critical to the ability of the debtor to reorganize and that agrees, if paid, to extend normal credit terms to the debtor postpetition. Although not explicit under the Bankruptcy Code, pursuant to BRC §105(a), a debtor can petition the bankruptcy court to permit the payment of prepetition liabilities owed to vendors deemed to be critical to the debtor's ability to reorganize. If such payments are made,

Table 11-1.   Effect of Critical Vendor Payments in Dead Co. Liquidation

Cash	35	Trade Claim — Critical Vendor	30
Other Assets	40	Trade Claim — Regular Vendor	25
		Unsecured Bonds	100
		Equity	0
Total	75	Total	155
Unsecured Recovery with Critical Vendor			36%
Unsecured Recovery with No Critical Vendor			48%

they arguably, from the perspective of a noncritical unsecured claim holder, represent a preference to one creditor potentially to the detriment of others.

This is true in particular where the case ultimately ends in liquidation. Consider the example illustrated in Table 11-1. Dead Co. files for chapter 11 protection, initially contemplating a reorganization. It petitions the bankruptcy court to permit $30 of trade claims to be paid, asserting that they are owed to critical vendors whose ongoing cooperation is essential to the reorganization of Dead Co. The court allows these claims (trade claim — critical vendor) to be paid, and then sometime later, it is decided that a reorganization is not feasible and Dead Co. is liquidated. Since the critical vendor payment was made, the expected recovery to the remaining creditors (noncritical vendors [trade claim — regular vendor] and unsecured bonds) is 36%. Had the critical vendor claim not been permitted, all creditors would have recovered 48%, a 33% improvement.

If an investor had purchased the bonds at 40 with a view that (a) best case, the reorganized entity is worth considerably more than 75 and the investor's return is potentially significant or (b) worst case, Dead Co. liquidates and the investor recovers (assuming away expenses, etc.) 48, the payment of the critical vendor claims is the difference between making and losing money.

Often, it is very difficult for an investor to estimate in advance how much trade may be deemed "critical." Perhaps the only reasonable way to estimate this is to review bankruptcies of similar companies, if there are any, and determine what happened in those situations.[27]

Creditors can object to critical vendor payments, but critical vendor motions are typically made immediately after the chapter 11 petition is filed, and it can be very difficult for a creditor to have sufficient information to second-guess management. Unquestionably, there are many cases where a vendor's ongoing support is critical. However, the issue is whether the payment is truly necessary to maintain the commercial relationship. If the vendor has the prospect of maintaining the debtor as a profitable customer following the petition, how is it in the vendor's best interest to act in a way that might force the potential customer to go out of business and liquidate? Furthermore, if debtor-in-possession financing (DIP) is in place, it may not be essential that the vendor offer normal credit terms—the firm can use the DIP to pay COD.

On the other hand, management's interests in this issue may not always be aligned with financial creditors. Being cynical, managers may have strong interests in maintaining favorable relationships with vendors with which they might deal at some time in the future at another firm. In contrast, they may actually have animosity toward financial creditors that management may perceive as having been the cause of the bankruptcy due to the creditors' failure to be cooperative. From this perspective, it is very plausible that designating a favored creditor as a critical vendor can be used to accomplish something that a preferential payment made before the filing of the petition could not. Accordingly, financial creditors may have legitimate concerns that critical vendor payments are truly critical, and bankruptcy judges are well aware of management's potential bias.

Practically speaking, there is little that a minor investor can do about the critical vendor issue other than to be cognizant of the potential implications to recoveries. However, larger, more influential investors can influence the process through preparation. In most significant cases, the larger financial creditors will, as discussed in Chapter 4, already have formed an unofficial creditor committee and will usually have retained legal counsel and perhaps a financial advisor. Usually, this committee and the firm will have a constructive working relationship and the committee and its counsel will have been afforded the opportunity to review and comment on all first-day pleadings, including critical vendor motions. When prior review is not provided, the committee and its advisors should anticipate a potential critical vendor request and be prepared to respond.

Cash Accumulation During the Reorganization

When undertaking a valuation of a firm in or expected to commence a chapter 11, often the focus is on estimating a reorganization value based on projected cash flow upon emergence or, in the alternative, liquidation values based on the last available balance sheet. Since the firm was not able to generate sufficient cash to keep itself out of bankruptcy, and it is clear that the bankruptcy process will consume a significant amount of cash, it may be easy to dismiss potential postpetition cash generation as not being very material. However, this can be a mistake. Particularly for companies with a disproportionate amount of unsecured debt (e.g., debt/total capital > 60%), the fact that interest will cease to accrue postpetition can result in a significant source of cash build. Similarly, payments relating to rejected leases and contracts will not be made, also adding to the potential cash pot.

Offsetting these sources of cash, the analyst will also need to consider the extra cash burdens that are confronted in a chapter 11 process. First, there are the significant professional fees, which usually are paid on an ongoing basis. Second, there is the potential investment in working capital that may be required as vendors may have more restrictive credit policies. Finally, there is the likely decrease in operating cash flow that will happen as a normal process of revenues declining during the case.

The analyst will likely never feel he or she has a sound basis for making the estimates contemplated above, but still the exercise must be undertaken, particularly in heavily leveraged situations. Analytically, the part of the accumulated cash that is deemed truly "excess" should be added to the normal EBITDA-based valuation. Strategically, accumulated excess cash can be a valuable tool in crafting a reorganization plan since it is often much easier to obtain creditor cooperation when a meaningful part of its recovery is in cash.

Tax Issues[28]

Tax issues can be a source of significant value in the reorganization process, but they can also be among the most complicated[29] and difficult to properly value as an outside third party. In the discussion that follows, some of the most common issues of which an investor should be mindful will be highlighted. However, the discussion will be general, and the analyst should bear in mind that, most of the time, the detailed information required to assess tax attributes typically will not be available. In many cases, much of the relevant data has never been compiled or analyzed even by the distressed firm,[30] which means that opportunities to preserve valuable tax assets are often missed simply because, in the pressure of trying to keep "the ship afloat," the priority of tax planning often falls somewhere below more immediately pressing issues such as making payroll or keeping the bank from foreclosing. In addition, given the generality of this discussion and the fact that tax rules change frequently, no reader should rely on this discussion in forming an investment decision.

As a general proposition, bankruptcy is not a "tax event" in and of itself. The circumstances that bring a distressed firm to the threshold of bankruptcy may have tax attributes or consequences. The process by which the financial distress is relieved or resolved can have tax consequences. However, with only a few exceptions, the fact that a chapter 11 (or chapter 7) petition has been filed is irrelevant to the tax issues. The taxing authority (whether local, state, federal, or foreign) is essentially just another creditor demanding payment, although, not surprisingly, since the drafter of the bankruptcy rules is a taxing authority (i.e., the U.S. Congress), tax authorities are given certain preferences over general creditors. When undertaking the analysis of a financially distressed firm, there can be many tax-related issues to consider, but this discussion will be limited to three that are deemed to be the most critical from the perspective of valuing a prospective investment opportunity: (1) the immediate liquidity implications of a distressed firm's current tax status, (2) the potential value of a distressed firm's net operating losses (NOLs) going forward, and (3) the priority status of tax claims in a chapter 11 reorganization.

Liquidity Implications of a Distressed Firm's Current Tax Status

Perhaps the first basic issue an analyst should examine is how near-term tax liabilities or potential refunds will affect a firm's liquidity. The relevance of this issue will depend on the facts and circumstances of the firm's financial distress. If the firm is EBITDA positive but its distress is the result of a pending debt maturity that it cannot refinance, then near-term tax payments or potential refunds will be a less critical issue. However, if the distress is because the firm has suffered an operating downturn and its sources of liquidity are declining, then the possibility of a tax refund that could materially improve liquidity is higher and surprisingly is often overlooked.

As most people are generally aware, corporate taxpayers are allowed to use NOLs incurred in one period to offset income incurred in past and, potentially, future periods. Thus, if taxes were paid on previously reported income, a refund of those prior tax payments may be possible. The rules governing NOL carrybacks and carryforwards are generally contained in Internal Revenue Code (IRC) §172, and rules limiting the use of a corporation's NOLs when there is a change of ownership are contained in IRC §382. Together, these are considered among the most complex in the entire tax code.

The basic rule under IRC §172 is that NOLs can be carried back two years[31] and forward 20 years from the year the loss is incurred. Under certain circumstances, NOLs can be carried back additional periods, but these are fairly unusual and would be very difficult for an investor to identify in advance. In the case of a carryback of an NOL resulting in a refund, conceptually what will happen is that the firm will be allowed to amend its previously filed tax return and claim, as a deduction from income, the NOL incurred in the most current period. To the extent tax was paid on the prior-period income, it may be refundable. Consider the example in Table 11-2, again involving Dead Co.,

Table 11-2. Carryback of Dead Co. NOL to Attain Refund

Tax Year	Pretax Income/(Loss)	Tax Paid/(Refunded)	Tax Rate
CY	(70)	(25)	
CY-1	75	26	35%
CY-2	55	19	35%

which, it is assumed, had been earning income but suffered a downturn and incurred an NOL in the most recently completed period.

Generally speaking, under IRC §172, the $70 NOL in the current year (CY) will first be applied against income from the earliest allowed carryback year (CY-2), and then any remaining NOL will be applied against income in the next allowed carryback year (CY-1). Note that in this example, the $70 NOL in CY was not sufficient to completely "shelter" all the pretax income in CY-1 (the $70 NOL first eliminated the $55 of income in CY-2 and then $15 of income in CY-1); thus Dead Co. did not qualify for a refund of all tax paid in CY-1, just $5.25 (35% × $15 NOL) of the approximately $26 paid during the period. In the event Dead Co. incurred another NOL in the next year (CY+1), that NOL can be carried back to qualify for a refund of the remaining $20 (26 − 6) of tax attributable to CY-1. Depending on Dead Co.'s circumstances, the ability to estimate that it might be entitled to a significant refund could greatly impact the liquidity and valuation analysis.

From a due diligence perspective, when the situation warrants, the analyst will want to closely review all tax-related disclosure in a firm's filings. The key figure the analyst will attempt to estimate is actual taxes paid in the two preceding years, which often can be significantly different than the tax accrual on the income statement. Using this figure and the tax rate,[32] the analyst, using simple division, can estimate the operating income in the prior periods and then compare this to the magnitude of NOL he or she expects in the current period. This will allow the analyst to estimate the size of a potential refund.

In many cases, a firm's SEC filings will disclose the potential for a tax refund, and if the application for refund has been filed and its receipt is considered sufficiently probable, it may be reflected on the firm's balance sheet as a tax asset (tax refund due). In this case, the market will likely have already factored the refund into the valuation of securities. However, in some cases, there may not be much discussion, and the market may not be properly factoring a potential refund into a bond's valuation. Management generally has a fair amount of discretion about when and how much to disclose about things that might happen in the future, and its motives to air on the side of conservatism (i.e., not disclose) can vary. For example, perhaps a firm is negotiating a revision to its bank debt amortization, and it is seeking to minimize such amortization by arguing that its future cash flow projections suggest only a certain amount can be afforded. In this case, the firm may not want to highlight the potential for a refund, thus allowing itself more flexibility in how such funds may be used. Normally, a lender could be expected to be mindful of the possibility of a refund, but in practice things are missed. Perhaps a firm would like to repurchase its bonds in the market and would prefer investors not run up prices on the speculation that the firm's liquidity might improve. There can be any number of considerations that can lead management to be conservative and not discuss the possibility of a refund until its receipt is considered virtually certain.

Penton Media, a diversified media company involved in publishing specialized trade magazines and producing trade shows, may be a good example of a potential tax refund not being appropriately valued in the market. Penton enjoyed strong profitability in 1999 and 2000, but suffered a significant downturn in 2001 and 2002 when marketing/advertising expenditures, particularly in the telecommunications and technology sectors, contracted sharply. In November 2002, after the release of Penton's third-quarter results, it was fairly clear that it was going to suffer a significant NOL for 2002.[33] Liquidity was adequate, but in light of the then cautious outlook and Penton's own operating issues, there was skepticism that it would be sufficient to assure that Penton could weather the cycle. Reflecting the outlook, Penton's 11.875% senior bonds were trading in the 50s.[34] However, in March 2003, when it was disclosed that Penton would file for and likely receive a tax refund of $53 million, its 11.875% bonds traded to the mid-90s.[35]

Potential Value from Carryforward of Net Operating Losses

The previous section looked at the potential value and liquidity benefits resulting from the carry back of NOLs to receive tax refunds. Since NOLs usually can be carried back only two years, frequently there will be a significant accumulation of unused NOLs which can have significant value because they can be used as deductions against operating income in future periods. When there are no restrictions on their use, carryforwards can effectively make subsequent earnings up to the amount of the accumulated NOL tax exempt.

While there is a clear "fairness" in allowing NOLs to have future value to a firm and its shareholders who have suffered losses, early efforts to abuse the system, with schemes whereby tax-paying entities would buy companies with NOL carryforwards simply to take advantage of the potential tax shelter, resulted in the implementation of a variety of extremely complex restrictions with a "goal" of limiting the carryforward benefit to the "original" owners and for the business that incurred the loss. So if, for example, one owns a nursing home company that experiences losses but sticks it out and remains in the nursing home business, any NOL accumulated during the difficult years can be used going forward. However, if the nursing home owner sells the business to someone else or decides to sell the underlying properties and open another unrelated business, say for example, a casino, the ability to carry forward the NOLs will be restricted — often so severely as to have no significant value.

Rules under IRC §382 limit the amount of NOLs that can be used per year after a more than 50% change of ownership (COO) of a corporation. It should be noted that, unlike certain other areas of tax and securities law that focus on changes of "control," the concern in IRC §382 is only on COOs. There does not need to be any kind of showing that, as a result of the COO, a change of control occurred, nor can lack of a change of control be raised as a defense to a finding that a COO occurred. The issue of "control" is essentially irrelevant for IRC §382 purposes.

The basic rule under IRC §382 is that whenever the ownership of holders owning more than 5% of a corporation's shares (major holders) in aggregate have their stakes increase by more than 50% relative to any point during the prior three years, a COO has occurred and a limitation may be imposed. For purposes of this test, the aggregate holdings of nonmajor holders in a public company are treated as one major holder.

To help put this abstraction into context, consider the following scenarios set forth in Table 11-3 involving major holders A, B, and C and their holdings in the current year (CY) compared to a period three years earlier (CY-3). Scenario 1 is the classic NOL trafficking problem where major holder C is a profitable corporation that purchases a major stake in the NOL-rich firm in an effort to get the benefit of the NOLs.

Scenario 2 is a somewhat less obvious case. Here, assume that the firm was public (major holder C is the public holders) but got in trouble, and two large shareholders (major holders A and B) made significant new investments to keep the firm afloat. Their stakes in aggregate increase by more than 50%, so a COO has occurred.

Scenario 3 is the classic problem in a reorganization. The firm is public, with major holder B representing the public shareholders. The firm files for chapter

Table 11-3. Analysis of Changes of Ownership Under IRC §382

	Major Holder A	Major Holder B	Major Holder C	Aggregate Change	Scenario
CY	4%	16%	80%	80%	1. Closely held firm does IPO or
CY-3	20%	80%	0%		sells new stock to new owner
CY	40%	40%	20%	60%	2. Major holders A and B infuse
CY-3	10%	10%	80%		new capital and become large holders
CY	0%	0%	90%	90%	3. Company reorganizes and
CY-3	10%	90%	0%		major holder C, the bank, gets 90% of equity under the plan of reorganization

11 protection, and pursuant to the plan of reorganization, the holders of the bank debt (major holder C), who previously had no equity interest, receive 90% of the new equity (the other 10% was allocated to other creditors). Again, a COO has occurred.

This brief overview does not do justice to the complexity of the rules. Since the amounts at stake can be huge, literally billions of dollars, very clever lawyers continue to devise schemes to beat the rules through the use of different entities or instruments such as options, warrants, convertible securities, etc. But the just as diligent, if substantially less well paid, rule writers, when they discover such mechanisms, simply issue additional, complicated regulations in an effort to thwart the new schemes.

There is an important exception to the COO test and the consequences of failing it related to bankruptcy reorganizations, which will be discussed shortly, but first the general "penalty" for the existence of a COO needs to be developed. In general, when a COO occurs, the deductibility of pre-COO NOLs is limited to a statutorily specified rate of return (generally called the §382 rate[36]) on the fair market value of the firm's pre-COO equity.[37] For example, assume P Corp. purchases 80% of the stock of publicly traded N Corp. in a tender offer concluding on April 1. On that day, N Corp. had a market capitalization of $200 and an aggregate NOL of $500. If the §382 rate for April is 5%, the deductibility of N Corp.'s NOLs will thereafter be limited to $10 per year (200 × 5%), which means that over the 20-year carryforward period, the most that can possibly be used is $200. The remaining $300 in NOLs effectively will have been forfeited forever.

Since the absolute amount of the limitation turns on what is deemed the "fair market value" of the equity, this value is obviously another area where there is possibility for manipulation or abuse and hence a significant focus of regulatory attention. In the relatively straightforward case of a publicly traded company, the trading value is considered a compelling indicia of worth. Similarly, if the COO occurs as the result of an arm's-length sale, the sale price will be given heavy weight. The equity value can be positively adjusted to reflect the existence of certain other instruments such as options, warrants, convertible securities, and preferred stock. On the other hand, other adjustments will be made to prevent equity "stuffing" (i.e., consider an 11th-hour preferred equity contribution by the seller which is subject to a mandatory redemption right) and to limit the value of assets held for investment (which, again, could potentially be manipulated to inflate value at any given moment in time). In transactions involving private companies where the NOL carryforward is a critical component of the deal, a third-party valuation opinion often will be obtained.[38]

Another limitation on the ability to carry forward the deductibility of NOLs is the notion of business continuity. Under IRC §382, if the NOL firm fails to continue its primary business for at least two years following the COO, the carryforward deduction amount will be reduced to zero, and worse yet, this will be retroactively applied to the date of the COO. Satisfying the business continuity test usually requires the continuation of at least one major line of business or the ongoing use of "a significant portion" of the firm's pre-COO assets in the ongoing business during the two-year "look-forward" period.[39]

Another consideration is the treatment of unrealized gains existing on an NOL firm's balance sheet at the time of the COO. To pick a simple example, assume that at the time of P Corp.'s purchase of N Corp., N Corp. owned a piece of land with a tax basis of 10, but a fair market value of $200. IRC §382 essentially recognizes that this gain was the property of N Corp.'s original owners and that, had they sold the property prior to any COO, the gain would have been sheltered by the NOL; hence, the economic value of the tax-sheltered gain could have been realized by the original owners. Thus, so as not to force the sale of the asset simply to recognize the gain, the rules allow the amount of the annual NOL deduction carryforward to increase to offset any gain on assets realized during the five-year period following the COO.

One important exception to the COO rule is generally known as the "bankruptcy" exception. The bankruptcy exception essentially looks at the shareholders and the creditors of the debtor as one big happy family and provides that if the COO occurs as the result of a plan of reorganization (the typical problem being that the creditors often will recover a majority of the equity) and as long as ownership stays within the happy family, no limitation will be applied.[40] Thus, in scenario C above, if the bankruptcy exception is used, there may be no limitation assuming major holder 3, the bank that got 90% of the equity, is considered part of the happy family. More precisely, no limitation is applied if after the plan is implemented at least 50% of the stock of the reorganized entity is held by: (1) holders of prepetition shares, (2) trade or ordinary course of business creditors as long as the claim has been continuously held by such creditors, and (3) financial creditors that held their debt claim at least 18 months prior to the filing of the petition.

The third requirement for the bankruptcy exception, the 18-month look-back test (generally referred to as the "old and cold test"), often limits the applicability of the exception because it is fairly common for a substantial amount of the debt to trade either immediately before or after the petition is filed. Accordingly, it is not uncommon for firms to attempt to limit trading in their securities during a reorganization in order to preserve the value of the NOL. There are a number of detailed rules governing a firm's obligation to inquire into creditors' holding periods, exclusions for certain transfers, and presumptions relating to holders of less than 5% of postreorganization equity that occasionally allow plans of reorganization on the cusp to qualify. However, for the classic situation of a vulture investor purchasing the fulcrum debt to achieve control of the postreorganization equity, the exception may not apply and some of the economic benefit of gaining control or ownership of the firm may be lost. It should also be noted that even when a firm qualifies for the exception, any interest accrued or paid during the three years prior to the COO on any debt converted into equity would reduce the amount of the NOL. The theory behind this adjustment is to prevent double dipping — if the creditor got the benefit of the interest payment, it should not get a second benefit because that interest payment increased the NOL.

There is another aspect of the "bankruptcy" exception relating to the post-COO limitation on carryforward deductions that is also very valuable. As previously discussed, the general rule is that the annual NOL deduction will be limited to the pre-COO equity value times the IRC §382 rate. In cases where a firm is reorganized through a formal bankruptcy process but a limitation is imposed because a COO occurs even after application of the broader bankruptcy exception, the amount of the limitation will be based on the post-COO equity value,[41] not the pre-COO value. This can be beneficial because in the typical case of a bankrupt company, the equity value will be zero (almost by definition, liabilities will exceed the value of assets). Thus, a COO would result in complete forfeiture of the NOL (the deductible amount would be zero times the §382 rate). In contrast, since reorganization plans will almost always have positive equity value,[42] under the bankruptcy exception to the carryforward limitation rule, the NOL will have some ongoing value. Notice that the nature of the exception tends to give an incentive, at least from an NOL utilization perspective, for reorganization plans to maximize the amount of postreorganization equity. This can lead to complex planning issues since equitizing certain financial creditor claims can lead to failing the COO test outright. Thus, absent the issues of what it takes to obtain the consent of impaired creditors, from the strict perspective of maximizing the future value of NOLs, there may be pressure for certain creditor classes to take returns mainly in nonequity forms so as to reduce the risk of causing a COO; however, if a COO is inevitable (i.e., where the fulcrum class was acquired postpetition and for business reasons the investor wants voting control of the firm's postreorganization stock), then there are incentives to increase the equity component of the plan of reorganization.

In bringing this discussion to a close, it is important to put the issues discussed above in perspective. Clearly, the tax issues associated with preserving the value of NOLs are very complicated. At best, the discussion above should be viewed as a cursory outline of a subject defined by many pages of dense regulations and case law precedent. Most of the time, unless one is a member of an unsecured creditors' committee, an investor will not have enough information to make any meaningful assessment of the NOL's potential value, which at any point in time could be dramatically affected by a future sale of securities to a new holder or the future composition of a plan of reorganization. Having said this, there are several issues to bear in mind when conducting due diligence investigations. First, because of the bankruptcy exceptions to both the COO definition and calculation of carryforward limitation, there can be significant advantages to effecting a reorganization within a chapter 11 proceeding relative to a consensual reorganization where debt is exchanged for a controlling stake of the equity. Second, if an investor is considering taking a very proactive role in the investment, then maximizing the value of the NOL may have implications for when and what the investor purchases and might cause the investor to press for the imposition of trading restrictions on securities by the bankruptcy court in an effort to prevent a COO.[43] Lastly, where one is aware that significant blocks of securities have been accumulated by one or more relatively new investors, one will want to do a preliminary assessment of whether a COO is likely and thus how the value of the NOL may be affected. As a practical matter, given the uncertainties, most investors tend to heavily discount the potential future value of NOLs.

Priority Status of Tax Claims

Under BRC §507, claims for taxes incurred prepetition are accorded the status of a priority claim and thus are senior to unsecured claims.

LEGAL DUE DILIGENCE

The goal of legal due diligence is, when integrated with the findings of the financial due diligence, to help determine the valuation of a particular security or inform an investment strategy. In many ways, it is difficult to view financial and legal issues separately, and thus putting them in one box versus another is fairly irrelevant. Many financial conclusions are dependent on some underlying legal assumption that the careful analyst will attempt to verify. For example, whether one security has seniority to another is essentially a legal issue, but it obviously has significant financial implications for any valuation. Similarly, forming a conclusion that a transaction can potentially be challenged as a fraudulent conveyance is a legal conclusion, but with potential financial implications.

In most investment scenarios, it is cost prohibitive to retain outside legal counsel to conduct legal due diligence. Accordingly, the task will generally fall to the analyst or portfolio manager, who, particularly in the area of distressed debt analysis, often has legal training. In those cases where the analyst has not had the benefit of formal legal training, the good news is that much of the work involves careful reading and analysis of documents rather than drawing upon some storehouse of embedded legal knowledge. The bad news is that it usually takes time for nonlawyers to become comfortable reading and interpreting what often can be fairly complex agreements. While it is well outside the scope of this book to attempt to teach the reader how to read or think like a lawyer, two thoughts will be provided: First, when reading a document, especially an indenture, understand the defined terms and always read it from the perspective of "Is there any way this can be read or interpreted so that I don't get the result I want?" Second, have a good sense of what you know, and don't know, and get help or a second opinion when you don't know. Distressed debt analysis is complicated and challenging. Only the most experienced investors and analysts are likely to have a thorough understanding, which is why many of the most successful investors have a very collaborative approach.

Obtaining the Relevant Documents

As with financial due diligence, the first step is to obtain and read the relevant documents. Fortunately, for public companies, these documents can be obtained from the same sources as discussed above for SEC filings and bankruptcy documents. Most of the critical credit agreements and indentures will be filed as exhibits to other filings. To find the indenture to a bond issued in 1997, the analyst would search through the EDGAR filings for documents filed in 1997 and 1998 and look for a registration statement relating to the issuance or exchange of bonds. These usually can be found by looking at the index of exhibits to the company's 10-Ks and 10-Qs, which usually will refer to a prior filing (such as an S-1 or S-4) that has the indenture and related documents as exhibits. The registration statement usually will include the prospectus, which will describe the securities but is not the binding legal document governing the bond issue, and it is unwise to rely on the description of the indenture contained in the prospectus. Therefore, it is always important to find and then analyze the actual indenture. If one cannot locate the indenture as an attachment to the relevant registration statement, check filings on Forms 10-K, 10-Q, or 8-K around the time of the offering, as sometimes the indenture will be included as attachments to these filings. The prospectus will also provide pertinent information about the context of the offering, including whether the securities or the issuer thereof has received guarantees from any other entities. Bank loans are not securities which require registration with the SEC; thus they will never be part of a registration statement. However, because they are deemed a material contract of the registrant, they will be filed as exhibits to SEC information filings as material contracts.

Checklist of Legal and Bankruptcy-Related Issues to Consider

When analyzing a distressed debt situation, there are myriad legal issues that can apply to any given context. Legal issues, in this sense, refer to issues arising as a matter of law or contained in contracts or documents relevant to the situation. Bankruptcy issues are those additional considerations that arise exclusively because the debtor has filed or may file for bankruptcy protection. For example, if a debtor pays off the liability of a foreign subsidiary from the proceeds of a newly obtained bank line, it raises a legal issue as to whether such a payment was permitted under the restricted payment provisions of its various financing agreements and indentures. If shortly thereafter the debtor files for bankruptcy protection, creditors might have a claim against a nonguarantor subsidiary relating to the payment. Alternatively, there might, depending on issues apart from the covenant, be voidable preference or fraudulent conveyance issues under bankruptcy law. Accordingly, the context of the situation will dictate the types of issues to consider.

It is very difficult to simply read an indenture. Instead, one must have a question in mind to be answered and then seek the answer in the document. For example, if one were analyzing the indenture of a subordinated note, the first question might be to what exactly the note is subordinated. One might also ask what options the firm has to refinance the subordinated note. As discussed in Chapter 7, however, the answer to this question will not be in the subordinated note indenture; instead one will need to review the documents relating to all other financings since they will be the contracts that will contain the relevant financing constraints.

As a practical matter, it is impossible to anticipate every issue that likely will arise; therefore it is recommended that analysts begin developing checklists of issues to consider. A sample checklist is available for download at www.jrosspub.com. This should be viewed as a good starting point, rather than a definitive document, and analysts should expand upon it as rules change or as the result of personal experiences. In particular, within the bankruptcy context, whether a petition has been filed or is merely prospective, there are at least three issues that always must be considered: voidable preferences, substantive consolidation, and structural advantages.

Voidable Preferences

As mentioned in Chapter 4, under BRC §547, whenever a creditor receives a payment, which can include the grant of a lien, on account of an antecedent debt within a period of 90 days prior to a bankruptcy filing (one year before filing if the creditor is deemed an insider), not allowed under BRC §547(c), the payment may be deemed a voidable preference and is required to be returned to the estate. Thus, whenever a company actually files for bankruptcy, the investor should look at all available information to determine whether significant preferences are likely to be present. One should start with the most recently filed financials, which will disclose material payments made to financial creditors in the cash flow statement and any collateral transfers or material amendments in appropriate footnotes. If one identifies a potential preference, it could present a short-term trading opportunity, as securities of equal priority often trade up on disclosure that the estate or the creditors will seek to recover a preference payment. This is not a situation where the analyst needs to worry about identifying a payment that might be missed in the normal bankruptcy process (preference analysis is one of the highest priority reviews for both debtor's and creditor's counsel), and it is a fairly easy matter to verify by looking at distributions made over the relevant time frames. But if an investor can identify the potential early on, it may lead to a trading opportunity.

Substantive Consolidation

Substantive consolidation[44] is the legal doctrine which states that when different entities within a corporate family have been operated in such an interrelated manner that parent-subsidiary autonomy was not observed — that the two entities were essentially alter egos of each other — then the entities should be treated as a single entity. Since substantive consolidation effectively eliminates the notion of structural priority, it can materially affect the recoveries of different creditors in the capital structure, and thus bankruptcy courts are reluctant to invoke the doctrine unless they feel it is equitable to do so. Unsecured debt or trade claims at an operating level that were considered structurally senior to holding company claims could suddenly find themselves diluted, or vice versa, structurally subordinated holding company claims could enjoy a windfall benefit.

Identifying substantive consolidation situations is not an exact science and is very fact specific. Different jurisdictions use different tests in assessing whether substantive consolidation is appropriate. Two of the most generally considered factors are (1) whether, in practice, the firm failed to maintain the legal and financial separateness of the entities (e.g., using funds of one entity to pay bills of another) or (2) whether the costs of separating the firm's financial affairs outweigh the benefit. If an operating company is held by a passive holding company, the risk is probably minimal. On the other hand, where different subsidiaries within a corporate family engage in significant intercompany transactions, which often can be identified by reviewing the magnitude of affiliated party transactions in the firm's segment operating data, the chances are greater. In such cases, where claims at the different entities are trading at different prices, it may be profitable to put on a hedge trade designed to profit in the event a substantive consolidation makes the two claims pari passu (this would generally involve buying the lower priced bond and shorting the higher priced debt).

Structural Advantages

The analytical issue when looking for structural advantages is similar to that presented by substantive consolidation, except with a different goal — the analyst is looking for a subtle reason why seemingly similar securities should be treated differently. Hidden structural advantages are unlikely to be present in fairly simple capital structures. The most likely context involves a bond issued by a firm that is then acquired by another firm, and the bond remains outstanding. Consider the example presented in Figure 11-1.[45]

Assume Bighold purchased Addon when Bighold had thriving credit fundamentals and/or a large equity market capitalization. Even if the Addon senior notes had relatively standard change-of-control put provisions, holders may not have exercised this right, believing that, as part of Bighold, the Addon senior notes might trade at a significant premium. In this case, notice that Bighold at some point had been able to issue holding-company-level debt with a 6.25% coupon, while Addon had to issue debt with an 11.50% coupon. Depending on

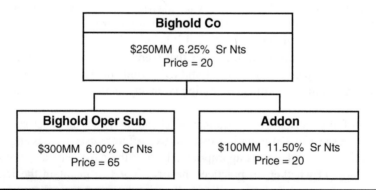

Figure 11-1. Nonobvious Structural Advantages

how much call protection, if any, was left on the Addon notes, investors might have assumed at the time of the acquisition that the notes could trade to a 6.25% yield (assuming the Bighold senior notes were then trading at par), which would imply a substantial premium — well in excess of the 1% premium contained in the typical change-of-control put. Accordingly, the Addon note holders would likely keep their investment and happily join the Bighold family; being acquired by a stronger credit is something akin to nirvana for a bond investor.

However, as indicated in Figure 11-1, times have changed and Bighold's holding company notes (6.25s) are trading at 20, while the operating company debt (6.00s) is trading at 65. The market is valuing the Addon senior notes (11.50s) at 20, perhaps based on the belief that they had similar credit fundamentals to Bighold Co. But this is not necessarily the case. If Addon had any operations, and the covenants of the Addon notes were consistent with what one would expect in a high-coupon senior note, it is likely that the Addon notes would have independent sources of credit support. Even in situations where it appears that Bighold materially altered the operations of Addon in a way that would suggest that little of its former operations remain, Bighold may have caused Addon to distribute assets or engage in other transactions that were in violation of the Addon debt's covenants. Everyone watches things closely when situations are in distress, but when bonds trade above par or are part of a "highly regarded" credit, oversight processes can become relaxed. In this situation, the Addon notes may only have a lawsuit against Bighold Co. for violating the covenants, but this can still provide leverage in a restructuring context. The investment can be made fairly riskless by being long the Addon notes and short the Bighold Co. notes.

Equitable Subordination

Equitable subordination is a legal doctrine that can be used by a bankruptcy court to subordinate one claim to another claim. The principle of equity is generally applied against either insiders or creditors that, through the exercise of substantial influence over the borrower, effectively become an "insider" able to control or affect the borrower's actions, using their influence in a way that is detrimental to other creditors. Injured creditors can petition for the controlling creditor's claim to be subordinated in right of recovery.[46]

The classic context for equitable subordination involves controlling equity holders who are also corporate officers and directors. For example, assume an insider causes a corporation to make a substantial dividend (which, of course, would be to the insider as a shareholder), and then the insider invests the money back into the corporation in the form of secured debt. A little over a year later, the corporation files for bankruptcy. Under these facts, the unsecured trade creditors could find themselves in a significantly worse position than they had been before the attempt by the insider to convert the equity into a secured loan. The trade creditors potentially could bring an action in the bankruptcy court requesting that the insider's secured loan be subordinated in right of payment to the trade creditors' claims.

The doctrine has evolved over the years and has been found to apply to not only classic insiders (i.e., shareholders, officers, etc.) but also senior creditors that exercise substantial influence and use that influence to inappropriately benefit their own interests. Assume a borrower is in technical default on its bank loan agreement. The bank has become worried about its exposure and requires the firm, as part of an amendment negotiated under threat of acceleration, to rapidly liquidate its excess inventories (of which the bank lent only 50% of the value) and other assets (in which the bank never had a security interest) and use 100% of the proceeds to repay the bank loan. The firm complies with these requirements, but subsequently, arguably because its low inventory levels prevent it from satisfying customer orders, files for bankruptcy. In this case, the firm might be able to recover all recent payments as preferences (as discussed above), but the other creditors might argue that the bank's actions constituted an impermissible exercise of control and that, under the doctrine of equitable subordination, the entire loan balance should be subordinated. This is potentially an extremely powerful tool or, at least, a threat that unsecured creditors frequently have *vis-à-vis* secured creditors.

To prevail in a request for equitable subordination, which is now partially codified as BRC §510(c), the petitioner must establish that (1) the creditor must have engaged in some type of inequitable conduct, (2) the misconduct resulted in injury to creditors or conferred an unfair advantage on the party to be subordinated, and (3) subordination of the claim is not inconsistent with the provisions of the Bankruptcy Code.[47] The case law involving equitable subordination and the related concept of *lender liability* is extensive, and it is beyond the scope of this book to review it in detail.[48] From the analyst's perspective of trying to identify those situations where equitable subordination may be an issue, some of the key facts to look for include:

- A significant or controlling interest in the debtor's stock
- Presence of employees or affiliates of the creditor on the debtor's board or in key management positions
- Loan agreement provisions that are nonstandard
- Loan agreements or amendments that may have been negotiated after the debtor was insolvent or in a circumstance where the negotiation is likely to not truly have been at "arm's length"
- The granting of security agreements after the debtor is insolvent

Again, the distressed investor or analyst — unless he or she is on the unsecured creditors' committee, in which case all these issues almost certainly will be discussed in detail by the committee's counsel — likely will never have sufficient information to be able to form a well-founded conclusion. However, one can assess the potential for an equitable subordination claim and include it in the investment calculus.

There are several fact patterns that often arise which present contexts for equitable subordination arguments. One scenario where the potential for equitable subordination should always be considered is where a significant equity sponsor, classically a private equity or leveraged buyout fund, has chosen to put additional capital into the distressed firm but has decided to structure the investment as debt, rather than additional equity. In this case, the "control" aspect of the issue is a given; the viability of the claim will turn more on the other elements of the action: (a) whether another creditor was harmed and (b) whether the conduct was egregious. A second scenario is where the debtor has a particularly involved relationship with the bank lender. Evidence includes such things as multiple credit agreement amendments, issuance of additional security agreements, issuance to the bank of warrants, and signs that perhaps the bank arguably coerced the debtor into materially changing its business plan (e.g., required asset sales to fund amortization payments) or bringing in different executives.

Stepping back for a moment, the analyst should also bear in mind that the doctrine of equitable subordination may also deter actions that might, on their face, seem economically rational. For example, assume that a firm is in financial distress as the result of a near-term debt maturity of some sort, but the firm's circumstances or the capital markets are such that it may not be able to easily raise money from third parties for a refinancing. The firm might have a deep-pocket equity sponsor that could easily advance the funds and, although it was not inclined to do so as equity because such funds likely then would be committed for an extended period, would be willing to provide capital as a bridge loan on commercially customary terms. Even though such a bridge loan might be an objectively good investment — for all parties — the sponsor might be deterred from making the loan out of concern that if the firm was subsequently forced into bankruptcy, other creditors would argue for equitable subordination of the loan (review the Steelbox example in Chapter 9). Thus, there may be times when analyzing an investment where the analyst might assume or consider in the investment calculus that a rational equity sponsor would support the credit rather than allow it to founder over a minor liquidity issue; however, that assessment will need to factor in the risk that the equity sponsor might not provide the support because of the risk of an equitable subordination action.

Zone of Insolvency

Zone of insolvency is an issue that relates to when a distressed firm's board of directors must begin considering the interests of the creditors, in addition to its normal fiduciary obligation to further the interests of stockholders. The issue is a relatively recent development, by the standards of common law anyway, that was first put forward in 1990 in the now well-known Delaware Court of Chancery case of *Credit Lyonnais v. Pathe Communications.*[49] The finding in *Credit Lyonnais* was essentially that boards of directors have a fiduciary obligation to consider the interests of creditors as well as equity holders at such time as the corporation entered the "vicinity" of insolvency. The basic rationale is that when a firm is insolvent, the assets of the debtor are to be held in "trust" for the benefit of the creditors. What was notable about *Credit Lyonnais* was the court's willingness to make a finding of insolvency outside of the bankruptcy context. What constitutes "vicinity," which over time has been rephrased "zone," of insolvency was not specified in much detail in the case and is still fairly ambiguous today, but generally involves the application of either the "balance sheet test" (assets < liabilities) or "equitable insolvency test" (inability to meet obligations in the ordinary course).[50]

It should be noted that *Credit Lyonnais* is not a bankruptcy issue per se, but one of corporate governance. The reason the distressed investor needs to factor this issue into the investment analysis is that it can, in certain cases, impact the pressure that can be brought upon a board of directors in advance of a bankruptcy. To date, the case law has suggested that the burden on creditors is fairly high. However, these case outcomes may understate the impact of *Credit Lyonnais.* While few boards may have been found to have violated the principle, the case clearly increased the visibility of the issue, and it is hard to imagine that any board of a distressed firm is not thoroughly briefed on its obligations. Directors prefer not to be sued; even if they are not that worried about being found at fault, the threat of a *Credit Lyonnais*–type suit may at least give them second thoughts.

Special Considerations When Investing in Claims That Are Not Negotiable Instruments

For simplicity, so far the discussion in this book has focused on bonds, bank facilities, or, occasionally, stock. Passing references have been made to the claim priority of trade creditors and others, but the potential investment opportunities in these other types of claims have not been specifically addressed. This section will discuss the pros and cons associated with investing in such claims, as well as some of the common ways to participate.

There are numerous types of creditors or claims holders other than financial creditors. The largest class of nonfinancial commercial claims is those that arise on account of the provision of goods or services, generally called trade claims. These are generally represented by bills of lading, invoices, purchase orders, etc. These claims are usually characterized as general unsecured claims and thus are equal in status with unsecured debt. Typically, trade claims, to the extent they are available, can be purchased at a discount to the trading levels of more liquid securities, providing the investor in such securities with potentially significant returns. There are several possible reasons why holders of these claims may sell them at discounts to trading levels of similarly ranked claims:

1. The claim is significantly less liquid and thus purchasers often insist on a discount to compensate for this illiquidity.
2. The claim holder may not have the financial wherewithal to wait until the completion of a bankruptcy case to realize full value of the claim and thus is a forced seller.
3. The claim holder may realize that at the conclusion of the bankruptcy he or she most likely will receive stock for his or her claim and would rather have cash sooner.
4. The claim holder is a business, not a distressed debt investor, and prefers to sell rather than become involved in a lengthy, uncertain process.
5. The claim holder is relatively less familiar with the bankruptcy process and may have no idea how to assess the probable value of his or her claim.

As a result of being able to buy such claims at potentially significant discounts to their "market value," distressed investors who specialize in this sector often enjoy significant returns — although it should be noted that the transaction costs associated with acquiring trade claims must be factored into the return calculation.

The financial analysis involved in investing in trade claims is the same as that for unsecured debt; thus the main issues to consider involve a variety of legal differences. The securities that have been the primary focus of this book (bonds, notes, etc.) have the important common characteristic that they are negotiable instruments[51] and as such the investor or purchaser takes the instrument free of a variety of challenges that obligors can raise in other contexts such as with trade claims. A negotiable instrument is an instrument that contains the obligor's, or maker's, unconditional promise to pay the obligation in accordance with its terms. Under state law, which is generally governed by the Uniform Commercial Code, the payer on a negotiable instrument cannot assert against a *holder in due course* defenses to payment that would have been valid against the original payee on the instrument. A holder in due course is a person who acquired the instrument in good faith for value without notice of claims against the instrument or certain types of defects in the instrument.[52]

Trade claims, however, do not qualify as negotiable instruments, and therefore purchasing them carries significantly more risks. The primary risk, depending on when they are purchased, is that in the event of a bankruptcy the purchased claim will not be an allowed claim, which is essential to receiving any recovery. For example, the debtor may object to the claim because the goods or services giving rise to the claim were defective, never ordered, returned, purchased for different price terms, etc. In the usual case, the prospective purchaser of a trade claim will have very little information about the circumstances giving rise to the claim, but as a purchaser essentially steps into the shoes of the original holder.

This "nonallowance" risk can be managed through a variety of mechanisms. The first is to only purchase claims that have been deemed allowed by the bankruptcy court or at least have been admitted by the debtor.[53] The problem with only purchasing allowed claims is that this can involve significant delays since the determination of allowed claims often happens fairly late in the process, often after confirmation of a plan of reorganization. At that point in time, there may be significant market information concerning potential recovery values, reducing the investor's chance of acquiring the claims at a significant discount. The problem with purchasing only claims initially admitted by the debtor is that this pool may be fairly small, and it is not riskless since the debtor can amend its schedules and effectively dispute the claim. For active investors in this area, the more common approach is to seek protections via the purchase agreement. A prospective investor will want to include provisions such as representations and warranties relating to the status of the claim so that in the event it is not allowed, the investor has recourse to the transferor or seller. Often, a contract may even provide for a holdback or escrow of some or all of the funds pending the determination of the claim's allowed status.

A second difference involved in purchasing trade claims is the requirement[54] that notice of any transfer be submitted to the bankruptcy court. Furthermore, the transfer must be approved before the purchaser will be deemed a valid holder. This gives rise to a number of issues. First, the required notice of transfer, although this can vary by court, can require disclosure of the purchaser's identity (which often can be avoided by using a shell corporation as the buyer). Second, if the bankruptcy court does not approve the transfer, the purchaser technically will not have the direct right to vote the claims in the plan of reorganization approval process. Interesting conflict of law issues arise when dealing with the risk that the bankruptcy court will not approve the transfer.

Generally, state law governs the validity of transfers of chattel paper. There is nothing in the bankruptcy rules specifying the effect of a court's failing to officially recognize the new transferee on the legal effect of the underlying transfer. The considered view is that it should not invalidate a transfer otherwise valid under state law.[55] Once again, this risk can be managed with properly constructed purchase documents. The purchase contract should specify that in the event the transfer is not officially recognized, the transferor will vote the claims, and deliver all proceeds received pursuant to a confirmed plan, in accordance with the purchaser's instructions.

Recent Developments Under the Sarbanes-Oxley Act of 2002

Following a series of well-publicized cases (Global Crossing, Enron, etc.) of corporate malfeasance or, worse yet, fraud, Congress enacted the Sarbanes-Oxley Act of 2002,[56] which sought to significantly revamp many aspects of corporate governance. Among the most celebrated provisions of the act is the requirement that a firm's CEO and CFO attest to the accuracy of their financial statements.

Of less public notice at the time was another provision which increases the SEC's power to assess fines against a firm found to have violated federal securities laws and then, in the SEC's discretion, distribute the proceeds of those fines to damaged shareholders. While such a provision definitely has certain populist appeal, it potentially undermines very well-settled principles concerning the subordination of claims relating to damages resulting from the purchase and sale of stock. As a general proposition, lawsuits brought relating to prepetition acts of the debtor are accorded the status of general unsecured claims (i.e., pari passu with unsecured debt, trade claims, etc.). However, where the suit relates to damages arising from the purchase or sale of equity securities, BRC §510(b) reduces the claim status of such suits to the status of the security in question — which would be the claim of an equity interest holder, subordinated to all creditor claims.

The new provision in Sarbanes-Oxley Act could threaten to significantly undermine this principle by essentially allowing the SEC to use its status as a priority administrative claimant to dramatically raise the claim status of equity losses. As of this writing, the only instance where the SEC has used this power for the benefit of shareholders involves a $500 million fine imposed in the WorldCom case.[57] However, the mere existence of the provision suggests that the distressed analyst must additionally consider the likelihood that the SEC may, for whatever reason, intervene and take up the cause of shareholders to the detriment of creditors.

MECHANICS OF ACCUMULATING THE INVESTMENT

One might hope that after all the hard work of identifying an investment opportunity, and then completing the requisite financial and legal due diligence, at least purchasing the investment would be simple. Unfortunately, if one is truly interested in maximizing returns, even this process, depending on the circumstances, must be thoughtfully considered.

As has been noted frequently, one of the sources of opportunity in distressed debt investing is the fact that the securities are often illiquid. Liquidity, of course, is a matter of degree. Since many of the other securities markets commonly invested in by institutions (like listed, or over-the-counter, stocks or government/agencies bonds) are fairly liquid, it is appropriate to take a moment to discuss exactly what is meant by the observation that the market is relatively illiquid. Illiquid, as used here, simply means that at any given moment the demand or supply for any given bond within a fairly narrowly defined price spread, say 2.0%, is limited, perhaps to less than $5 million in face amount. In terms of trading vernacular, this means the bond might be quoted 32/34. This means an investor could sell $5 million at 32 and buy that amount at 34. One might make a bid within the "context" (i.e., 33) to see what happens, but if one wants to buy right then, one must buy the offering at 34. To put this in perspective, in the U.S. Treasury market, if the current clearing price of five-year notes is 98.00, by bidding as little as 98.01 one could easily purchase $500 million or more.

For the reader more familiar with trading stocks, consider the following comparison. In the case of a listed security, an investor that had access to the stock-trading specialist would be able to see, in most cases, a significant array of both bids and offerings made. If the last trade was at $20 per share, the specialist could describe how much was bid for at $19.90 per share, how much more at $19.80 per share, etc. Similarly, a picture of the offered side of the market would also be available. And this would only be the market for investors with "announced" interest; it might be that any number of other investors would enter orders if they observed the price moving to their desired level. In contrast, in many smaller issues within the distressed debt universe, often there may be absolutely no firm bids or offerings in the market, and there may not even be a recent quote.

For the larger distressed credits, those with greater than $1 billion in outstanding debt, the market can be fairly liquid, which means that one could purchase or sell $5–$10 million to or from a dealer within a market spread as tight as 0.25% (a quarter point). However, as shown in Chapter 2, there are a very large number of distressed firms where the outstanding debt is less than $500 million and a significant number with debt less than $200 million. Trading in these smaller situations, depending on how widely held the bonds are, can quite literally be by appointment, which means if the investor is not ready to participate in the market when another investor with the opposite inclination shows up, nothing will happen. Practically speaking, what does that mean? Let's say you identify a security you want to buy, check several dealers for markets, and purchase the best offering, say $1 million at 30. Then you bid 30 for $1 million more. There may be none available — period — unless you are willing to raise the price, perhaps significantly.

Since it is not recommended that individuals directly invest in securities of distressed companies, this discussion will assume the investor is, or works for, some type of institutional investment vehicle with established relationships with several broker-dealers active in the distressed market.[58]

Investment Strategy and Market Environment Drive Accumulation Approach

How an investor approaches the accumulation process largely will be determined by the investment strategy and market environment. For example, the approach required to accumulate a control or at least blocking position in a bond with an issue size of only $100 million obviously is much different than purchasing $50 million of WorldCom bonds (over $10 billion outstanding). Accordingly, an investor should go through the following steps in formulating an accumulation strategy.

First, an investor needs to determine the amount of the issue or facility that needs to be purchased to accomplish the investment strategy or portfolio management objective. This can change over time, but one should know at the outset, for a given price level, how much he or she ideally would like to buy. When the investment strategy dictates accumulating a fairly large percentage of the issue or class in question, then even if the security is reasonably liquid, an accumulation approach will have to be considered to try to minimize the impact on price.

Second, an investor should research, through any of the several holdings services that are available,[59] the amount of the issue owned by publicly disclosed holders. These services, however, only track holdings of mutual funds and insurance companies, which are required by law to disclose their holdings quarterly and annually, respectively. If two or three holders own significant blocks, this could significantly reduce the float. On the other hand, if one sees a significant number of listed holders with relatively small positions, this can be a positive because such holders may be fairly interested in getting out of a position that is immaterial in terms of dollars (relative to the entire portfolio), yet could require significant oversight because it is distressed.

Finally, depending on the amount that needs to be accumulated and the relative liquidity of the issue, an investor should determine how to approach the broker-dealer market. The broker-dealer market is critical to the distressed investor because dealers are the intermediaries for securities purchases and sales; because of the liquidity and transfer of bankruptcy rights issues, the types of electronic trading interfaces that have developed in certain equity and bond markets have not evolved for distressed securities. A key issue is whether the investor's objective is best served by working with one or many brokers. The general advantage of working with one broker is that there is less risk that the investor's interest will be broadly disseminated to the market. If, as is often the case, there are only a few sellers at the current price levels in the market, working with one broker assures that multiple brokers are not bidding, creating the impression of demand. The primary concern in dealing with only one broker is that one has no assurance of getting the best execution. Accordingly, the general rule is that where an investor is accumulating a small position relative to the average trading volume of any particular issue, using several dealers to ensure the best possible execution (i.e., lowest purchase price) is advisable, or a strategy of rotating the buy order on a daily basis to different brokers until securities are bought can be employed. In this context, the risk of dealing with multiple brokers is negligible since the investor's purchase should not technically affect the market, and the investor's identity, even if he or she is relatively well known,[60] will likely draw little notice since almost everyone is involved in the big deals.

However, where the strategy involves accumulating a relatively large amount relative to average trading volume, particularly in smaller issues, then it may be better to work exclusively with one dealer.[61] While it might seem that working with multiple dealers would give an investor the broadest possible canvas of a tight market, the risk is that no one dealer may believe he or she has a high enough probability of executing a trade, and thereby generating revenue, to invest sufficient time to make the trade happen — and in less traded contexts, proactive dealer involvement is often critical to facilitating a transaction. In addition, a buyer only wants holders to hear of potential interest from one source. Since dealers generally cover the same population of institutional investors, if multiple dealers are involved, several people will be calling the same holders inquiring about their position and generally leaving the impression that there are multiple potential buyers for the bonds. This is the opposite effect the buyer is trying to achieve; the buyer is trying to present the picture that he or she is "the only sucker on the planet dumb enough to buy these things; if you miss this bid, the next buyer will pay less." And the buyer may, in fact, drop his or her bid for a day or two and then increase it to reinforce the reality that he or she is the only buyer in the market.

If an investor chooses to work with one dealer, it is critical that he or she select the right dealer. The same dealer may not be right for every situation because not every dealer, practically speaking, has equal "access" to every bond. A dealer who underwrote, or for whatever reason became actively involved in the secondary trading of, a bond has an inherent advantage over a nonactive dealer in knowing the identity and trading history of some or all of the holders. One way to identify which dealers are involved in a particular security of interest to an investor is to survey dealers' distributed "ax" sheets. Ax sheets are lists of securities (bond descriptions followed by bid and offer prices), which dealers typically circulate daily to their customers, in which they quote markets in bonds on a "subject" basis. An investor will be looking to identify who, if anyone, appears to be involved in a security in which he or she is interested. In particular, an investor should research who distributed the securities, as in many cases that dealer will have the best ongoing knowledge of holders of the issue. If the particular security an investor is looking for is not listed on any of these "ax" sheets, it may indicate that the accumulation will be challenging, but also hold out the potential that the security can be accumulated at an attractive price.

An investor will also want to find a dealer who is ethical and willing to commit the time to make the trade happen. Most dealers will, of course, present themselves as knowledgeable, involved, and interested, but if no trade occurs in a few days, dealers tend to stop working and assume that the problem is that the buyer's bid is too low. To be effective, particularly within the context of thinly traded securities, a dealer must view his or her job as getting the parties together to make a transaction happen. That often requires tenacity and patience. Since over time a dealer or, more accurately, a dealer's salesperson will likely be able to discern an investor's strategy, the investor must also feel the dealer/ salesperson is trustworthy. Consequently, over and above what might be indicated by reviewing several days of trading runs and noticing that a dealer has frequently posted markets in a security, the investor will want to weigh his or her prior dealings with the dealer/salesperson as well as the dealer's apparent involvement in the market.

Having said this, an investor should never be naïve about a dealer/ salesperson's interests. The dealer is there to make money. The dealer, unless purchasing the bonds from another broker, will be working with two customers that he or she is seeking to please or at least not anger. The dealer may act as an agent for the investor, but the dealer does not owe the investor any particular fiduciary duty. Of course, the dealer does have a long-term interest in fostering a productive working relationship with the client, particularly if the investor is fairly active, which helps to keep the dealer's and the investor's interests aligned.

To begin a conversation with a prospective dealer in a way that should not give rise to too much suspicion, an investor may want to wait for the relevant salesperson to call him or her, listen to whatever the dealer has to say, and then, as casually as possible, say: "I noticed you had XYZs on your run. Someone told me we should look at it, but I wanted to find out if there was anything to do before I started to work." The goal of the conversation will be to discretely "quiz" the salesperson to determine the dealer's level of involvement. Was the dealer the underwriter? What does the dealer know about the credit? Does the dealer have any research? When was the last time the dealer actually traded a bond? How many of the bonds has the dealer traded in total?

Consummating the Trade

Once an investor has selected a dealer, then the hard part begins: getting the right trade. Trading securities is not for amateurs. The world of trading operates with its own customs and vernacular, and purchases and sales of tens of millions of securities can be consummated with just a few words. Therefore, it is extremely important to understand the trading vocabulary, or one may inadvertently commit to a transaction, or frustrate a dealer such that the dealer will no longer want to do business with the investor.

Most large institutional investors have individuals dedicated to the role of "trading." Traders are responsible for keeping track of all markets for the portfolio securities, pricing or valuing the securities in the portfolio (which for mutual funds must be done daily), and executing the accumulation or disposition of positions. Sometimes, trading will be delegated to the analyst covering the sector on the theory that information in the market flows most quickly through trading channels. Thus, in order to ensure the analyst is aware of all information in the market, whether factual or rumor, it is important for him or her to be in the trading flow. In smaller firms, the trading function often will be assumed by the portfolio manager, because he or she ultimately is responsible for the fund's performance and will want the information flow. Those actively involved in trading will likely have developed their own strategies and have a group of "trusted" relationships through which they prefer to work. The discussion that follows is intended to give non-traders a sense of the thought process and strategies involved in position accumulation, although it is particularly general because almost every situation will have its own market dynamic.

It is important to keep in mind that the distressed securities market is an over-the-counter or negotiated market. There are no ticker tapes or electronic screens showing bids, offers, or last trades.[62] The trading process begins with an investor indicating his or her interest in a particular security. To illustrate the process, a hypothetical trade involving xyz bond will be developed. It is assumed that the investor has done his or her due diligence, determined that $10 million in face amount is necessary to achieve his or her objective, learned that there are very few publicly known holders, and decided to use SureTrade as his or her dealer. To begin the process, the investor, who will be referred to as the buyer, might ask SureTrade for current market color. The question might be phrased, "What's the market in xyz?" or "You had xyz on your ax sheet; what's going on?" The dealer will then check with his or her clients and "the street" to identify if anyone has recently been trading in the securities and the approximate market context of the most recent transactions. The reference to "the street" means that the dealer usually will also consult with "broker's brokers," who act as intermediaries between dealers to hide the identity of active parties. SureTrade might respond in any number of ways depending on the market. Possible responses are:

- "The general context is 28/32" — Translation: The dealer has nothing firm, but his or her best estimate of the market is there are bids at 28 and offers at 32.

- "We are 29/31, 1 by 1" — Translation: The dealer is making a firm market to the investor, who can purchase (at 31) or sell (at 29) $1 million face amount with an immediate response of "I buy" or "I sell." The investor does not have to transact ("Thanks. I'll think about it."), but if he or she hangs up the phone, that particular market is no longer valid. The investor can call back and attempt to "renew" the market, but does not have the right to get off the line and then call back five minutes later (which usually will be spent trying to "shop the bid" with other dealers) and demand a trade at the given prices.

- "There's a 26 bid in the street, but no offering" — Translation: "There may be a 26 bid from another dealer and we can go back and firm that up if you want, but there are no firm or even indicated sellers." Implication: This is a fairly illiquid market on which no one focuses, but to get involved one likely will have to start with a 26 or better bid. SureTrade probably does not have a client working with it on that security (SureTrade may have a relationship with the bidder, but that investor has chosen to work with another dealer on xyz), but another dealer apparently does.

- "We have an offering at 40, but no bid" — Translation: The dealer has a client who has indicated interest in selling xyz at 40. Since no size is indicated, the investor cannot expect to be able to buy immediately, and in any case, the offering is higher than the investor wants to pay. However, it is fairly common, particularly in thin markets, for sellers to start with an above-the-market price.

The investor's next move, of course, is dependent on what type of response was received. The example will be continued for the firm market and "off-the-market" offering scenarios.

Firm Market

Assume the response to the buyer was: "We are 29/31, 1 by 1." This suggests that there is activity in the market, but the buyer must decide how to proceed to get the $10 million he or she wants at the best possible price. Different approaches follow.

The buyer might respond: "I'll buy the 1, and bid 29.25 for $5 million, but don't show that to the street." This does several things: By purchasing the $1 million at 31, the investor is showing that he or she is serious, establishing the reliability of the dealer's market (if the dealer backs away from the offering, it would be a serious breach of protocol) as well as starting his or her position. The investor may have paid slightly more than he or she would like, but now also has bonds in hand with which to strategically test a bid, if he or she chooses. The firm 29 bid for $5 million indicates the investor is a block buyer ready to do something. The dealer will want to respond quickly for fear the buyer will show the bid to someone else and the dealer will miss the trade. The addition of "don't show that to the street" tells the broker not to attempt to find an offering by working with broker's brokers to see what other dealers have; that may only serve to run up the price if existing holders start getting multiple inquiries from different brokers. The buyer wants the dealer to go to his or her own client network, presumably starting with the last seller, and see if a block is available.

Alternatively, the buyer might say: "I'll bid 29 for 10." This approach may appear to be putting all of the investor's cards on the table, so to speak, but the dealer does not know that. The investor would probably not want to make this firm a response outside of a firm market, but once again is signaling that he or she is very serious and wants size. A firm bid for this size should galvanize the dealer's attention. The buyer should not expect this bid to be "hit" (i.e., the response to be "I sell you 10 xyz at 29"). A potential response, after SureTrade talks with the seller, might be some type of firm offer in size: "We can offer you 5 firm at 31."

At this point, the buyer may want to counter at something between 29 and 31, but also has the "right" to "size" the seller. To "size" means to inquire how many bonds the seller is interested in selling at that price. Trading etiquette is generally that one cannot size an offering without having legitimate interest and being willing to make a bid. The reason to ask size is to get a sense of what might happen down the road. If the seller only has 5, that means a second holder must be found to complete the desired position. If the seller has 15, then the buyer should be concerned that: (a) the seller is going to lure the buyer in by filling part of the buyer's order, and then raising the offering price for any other bonds the seller wants, or (b) there may be an offering of the five left over after the buyer is finished, which might push down market levels and require the buyer to immediately record a mark to market loss.

If one asks for size and the seller is responsive, then the buyer, per etiquette, is obliged to make a bid within the context, preferably for the entire offering. For example, assuming the response was "seller has 15," the buyer might respond: "I'll bid 29.5 for all 15." This assumes that the buyer has the resources to buy all 15, but this is only an incremental approximately $1.5 million. And if the buyer liked the situation enough to want 10, usually he or she will be pleased to have even more, particularly below his or her desired price level. The seller will likely want to continue to dicker on price, but usually the "take-out" bid effectively escalates the size of the trade to the block of 15. The seller has made the psychological decision to sell; now it is just a question of the price — which likely will end up being between 29.5 and 31.

No Market or Above-Market Offering

The more likely response when dealing with illiquid distressed securities is: "We have an offering at 40, no bid." A significantly above-market offering (of course, in this case it is not clear there is any market) is really no offering. Wouldn't anyone be willing to offer to sell the ballpoint pen in his or her hand for $10? Of course, they would.

Attempting to accumulate a position when there is no real market can be a source of opportunity, but it can also be frustrating because it may take time to determine if the objective is achievable. This is where it is important for an investor to have allied himself or herself with a dealer with tenacity, because what lies ahead is a lengthy negotiation, which will combine elements of substantive discussion with plain old horse trading. To start the negotiation, the buyer will generally need to put a bid on the table. The buyer may begin with: "Show a 26 bid for 1." This gives the dealer something to take to the potential seller to start a conversation. The gulf between 40 and 26 is fairly large, 54% from the buyer's perspective, which suggests a potentially significant difference of perspective on the credit. A competent dealer will know how to bridge the gap. The dealer may start with the seller and say: "We have a potential buyer, but his bid seems pretty low. What can we tell him about this credit that will help us get him to improve the bid?" More often than not, if the dealer has a good relationship with the seller, the seller will engage in a conversation. And, of course, the buyer may be asked to essentially justify his bid. The dealer will pass responses back and forth in an effort to develop a consensus on the fundamental credit outlook or value. If this can be accomplished, then the horse-trading aspects of slightly raised offers and modestly lowered bids can start.

Although every situation has its own dynamics, often when trying to trade very illiquid situations, a key objective is to complete a trade, even of modest size, just to establish a price context. When a trade occurs, the dealer will, absent a specific understanding with the parties, generally "post" the market. To *post* means that the dealer, and sometimes the parties involved, will disseminate[63] the occurrence of the trade and the price context, but typically not the size and never the parties, into the marketplace. Posting tends to galvanize attention. Investors often will come to the dealer for more information or to confirm the price, because it may have implications for the pricing of their own portfolios. This feedback is useful to the process because it helps the dealer identify other holders and hence additional potential sellers. Accordingly, early on when a dealer has only one prospective seller, he or she may suggest that the seller "let go of a few bonds at a lower price" just to get the buyer "pregnant." The buyer, of course, will want to be cognizant of the process and likely will benefit if a trade can be completed close to his or her desired context, but it is important that the buyer remain disciplined. The distressed investor must always bear in mind that, particularly in illiquid situations, there is no assurance that he or she will be able to accumulate the ideal position at the ideal price.

Settling the Trade

Once the buyer and seller reach agreement, settling the transaction is typically fairly simple as long as the parties have been careful about the details of the transaction. There are four essential information points that should be clear when an investor finalizes a trade with a dealer: (1) the price; (2) whether the buyer will pay accrued interest to the date of settlement (this is the normal convention, but when the market believes it unlikely that the issuer will pay the next coupon, then securities trade without accrued interest, or "flat"); (3) the exact security, which ideally is specified by CUSIP number;[64] and (4) quantity. All of these details should be confirmed at the time of sale, and the investor should realize that the dealer's telephone is being recorded to minimize the risk of misunderstanding. The dealer will typically send an electronic message, called the *confirmation,* confirming the essential terms within 24 hours, which should be carefully reviewed by the investor to ensure there has been no misunderstanding or clerical error. The confirmation sent to the buyer will also include the accrued interest calculation and specify the exact settlement amount.

Trades involving notes or bonds conventionally "settle," which means money is transferred to the account of the seller and record ownership is entered in the name of the buyer, within three days (called T+3) of the verbal agreement. When the settlement is very close to the record date of a distribution (dividend, interest payment, liquidation payment, etc.), it is good practice to clarify at the time of the trade which party is expected to receive the distribution. If a party needs more than the typical three-day period to settle, this should be specified in advance and the counter-party's consent obtained.

Bank Debt

The process of purchasing a position in bank debt is significantly different than that involved in buying a bond. By almost any definition, almost all bank debt is fairly illiquid. Very few dealers, outside of the agent bank on a loan, will actually keep an "inventory" of bank debt; therefore, in the vast majority of cases, the transaction will be an agency transaction. Some of the more relevant differences to be aware of include the following.

Holder Identity

Unlike a bond, where the holders often will be very difficult to identify, the lenders in any particular bank loan are fairly easy to identify because anytime a bank loan is amended, which in the case of distressed firms is actually fairly often, the amendment will be circulated for all of the then participants to sign. Thus, when an amendment is filed with the SEC, a simple review of the signature pages will show the holders, though typically not the amount of the holding.

Settlement

While bonds generally settle in three days with nominal transaction fees, bank debt takes considerably longer because formal assignment documentation must be prepared by lawyers and actually executed by the parties. For loans of healthy borrowers (referred to as the *par loan market*), the settlement convention typically is 10 days (T+10), but modest delays are common. However, when the borrower is distressed, the loan documentation and security agreements typically receive much more careful review, which can extend the settlement process. The settlement convention in the distressed bank debt market is 30 days, but delays (sometimes of up to 120 days) are fairly common. Of course, all of this also involves costs. The typical transfer fee payable to the agent is $2500–$5000, although agents sometimes will waive the fee as an inducement to execute the trade.

Special Considerations for Revolving Loans

Generally speaking, bank credit facilities are structured as either term loans, a revolving facility, or a combination. Under a term loan structure, the entire amount of the loan is funded at the beginning of the loan, and any payment of principal by the borrower permanently reduces the balance. Term loans will typically, but not always, have amortization requirements designed to cause partial repayment of principal over the term of the loan. A revolving facility is fundamentally different because it is generally structured to finance the borrower's working capital needs, which often are seasonal. Under a typical revolving credit facility, the maximum amount the lenders will advance will be determined up front (e.g., $100 million), but the maximum amount that the borrower can borrow, typically referred to as "draw down," at any one time depends on the amount of collateral, or borrowing base, then pledged to support the loan. Revolvers usually are secured by the borrower's accounts receivable and inventory. The amount that can be borrowed will be determined by a borrowing base formula, the terms of which will vary depending on the lender's assessment of the liquidation value of the collateral. A typical formula might be 50% of inventories and 75% of accounts receivable. Accordingly, if a borrower had 70 in accounts receivable and 50 of inventory, the maximum amount that could be borrowed would be 77.5 ([70 × 75%] + [50 × 50%]). If the borrower does not need the capital, then it may not borrow simply to avoid paying interest charges. If the borrower has borrowed the entire 77.5 but the borrowing base declines because accounts receivable decline, then the revolver must be paid down (but presumably the collection of the account receivable provides the cash for this repayment). Thus, unlike a term loan, a repayment of principal does not permanently reduce the amount of the loan.

The structure of the revolver has two important implications for an investor. First, since the revolver can be drawn down at any time by the borrower (provided there is capacity, sufficient available borrowing base, and no default), an investor must be prepared to fund his or her proportionate share of such drawdown virtually instantaneously. Because of this requirement, the terms of the revolving facility will usually limit who can own it to institutions expected to have the ability to comply with the potential funding requirements. At the time of the settlement of a revolver transfer, the purchaser is required to fund the seller's pro rata share of the amount outstanding.

Second, as compensation to the purchaser for undertaking the risk of potentially having to advance additional funds to the borrower, revolvers are sold subject to a rebate called the "net-back." The net-back is a holdback from the purchase price and is calculated as: (1 − purchase price%) × unfunded amount.

For example, assume an investor wishes to purchase $10 of a $100 revolver that is 50% drawn at a price of 80. The purchase price begins with the cost of the funded portion, in this case, 80% × (50% × 10) or 4. This price will be reduced by the net-back, which will be (1 – 80%) × 5 or 1. Thus, the net amount paid will be 3. Essentially the investor received a 25% discount because of the net-back. As a result, it can be fairly advantageous to purchase revolvers that are only partially drawn where it appears the borrower is or will be in breach of covenants preventing any further drawdowns. However, this can also be a risky situation, since borrowers facing distress often will make large drawdowns in anticipation that they may soon lose access to the facility.

SUMMARY

Like most things in business, the devil is in the detail. This overused phrase should have been the subtitle to this chapter. Being an effective distressed debt investor requires strong analytical skills, but also good time management, thoroughness, an appreciation for the most significant legal issues, and finesse. With all the opportunities that will typically present themselves during a promising market phase, an investor should develop screening criteria, which can be used to help identify those situations most suitable for that investor. Those criteria will be different for each investor, and contrarians may find that the most opportunity for misvaluation is in situations that traditional metrics are likely to reject. However, since time and market pressures are always factors, it is also necessary to develop the ability to quickly assess the return potential in any particular situation.

Once a situation passes an investor's preliminary screens or tests, the challenging, and sometimes tedious, work of making sure that all of the pertinent risks have been identified and properly factored into the investment decision calculus begins. This is the role of due diligence, which has both financial and legal components. On the financial side, obtaining company and industry performance information, developing a detailed valuation, and considering how that valuation may be affected by different reorganization scenarios are essential. On the legal side, the rights afforded by the terms of the security under consideration must be thoroughly understood to confirm some of the basic premises of the valuation. In addition, where bankruptcy reorganization is a high probability, consideration should be given to the myriad issues that can arise in that process and how those could impact expected investment returns.

Finally, when an investor has completed his or her homework and feels confident in moving forward to implement the investment decision, he or she must assess the market environment and develop a strategy to actually find and acquire the securities. If the situation involves a large, well-traded capital structure, and the amount of the position is small relative to average trading volumes, then the purchase is simple. In smaller less liquid situations, which is often where the better chance of misvaluation can be found, a more thoughtful and patient approach may be needed to locate the securities and assess whether it is possible to acquire the desired position at desired levels. This is perhaps where the most discipline is required because after investing considerable time and thought in a situation, it is often difficult to "walk away" simply because the market has drifted to higher levels. Of course, no investor has ever bought a bond and not wished the price had been lower; however, the key is to remain realistic about probable returns at any given price and judge whether they are adequate given the risks and the portfolio objectives.

On the assumption that the investor has taken the plunge and is now involved in a situation that is, or will likely become, a chapter 11 reorganization, the mechanics and dynamics of the reorganization process are discussed in the next chapter.

This Chapter's Chess Moves

24. Rxf8+, Kxf8

25. Bd1, Nf4

12

DYNAMICS OF THE WORKOUT PROCESS: THE ENDGAME

The previous chapter discussed practical steps for identifying potential distressed investment opportunities and then developing an appropriate due diligence program so that, to the greatest extent possible, an investor can have confidence in identifying and properly considering all of the relevant risks. Since many distressed investments are premised on a firm resolving its distress within bankruptcy reorganization, this chapter explores the dynamics involved in the process that can affect investment returns: the "endgame" of the distressed investment.

The discussion will proceed in a roughly chronological fashion. First, the primary participants and their roles in the process will be discussed. Next some of the basic approaches to the chapter 11 process (prepackaged or prenegotiated filings, preplanned asset sales, unplanned filings) are discussed, since the type of case can significantly affect the required investment horizon. After this, some of the dynamics of negotiating the plan of reorganization (plan) are considered. These are discussed in the context of winning bankruptcy court approval of the disclosure statement, as well as confirmation of the plan. Since each reorganization will be shaped by the facts and circumstances of the case, the discussion here is necessarily general considering there are few absolute rules in the process.

THE PARTIES

As mentioned in the introduction to this book, to the extent distressed investing can be compared to chess, it requires an expansion of the "one-against-one" chess framework to reflect the reality of many different constituencies essentially playing against each other as well as the distressed firm. One of the most important processes that occurs at the beginning of a chapter 11 case is an effort to convert this free-for-all into a more or less one-on-one affair through the appointment of the official committee of unsecured creditors (the committee). While the appointment of the committee certainly does not end the moves that various parties, even unsecured creditors, can make, for purposes of the formal restructuring process before the bankruptcy court, the key parties can be reduced to the distressed firm, which will now be referred to by the more common bankruptcy label *debtor*; the debtor's legal counsel and financial advisors; the committee and its counsel and advisors; the secured creditors (which can be one or many depending on a firm's capital structure); and the judge. Depending on the case, there are many other parties that may be involved including the U.S. Trustee,[1] potential representatives for the equity, governmental authorities, etc., but typically those first outlined are the primary players in a chapter 11 case.

The Debtor

Outside of situations involving particularly egregious incompetence or fraud, management of the debtor will remain in control of the enterprise, which for certain purposes will be deemed to have been transferred into a new "fictitious" entity called the *debtor in possession* or DIP. Management, however, will be charged with a new set of fiduciary obligations[2] that requires it to operate the business for the benefit of both creditors and equity holders. In addition, management must generally seek court approval for all acts out of the ordinary course of business, which gives the committee, or any other claimant or party to the case, the right to potentially object. Within those constraints, however, management is allowed to continue in day-to-day control of the business and make important decisions such as staffing, product development, marketing choices, and the assumption or rejection of contracts.[3] Management and its advisors will also, in most cases, have primary control of the shape of the proposed plan of reorganization and the proposed valuation of various assets in the DIP estate, as well as the postreorganization entity. In particular, under the important right of plan exclusivity, which will be discussed in more detail below, the debtor is given exclusive control of the preparation and presentation of the proposed plan for the first 120 days following the filing of the petition. If this is not sufficient time, which is usually the case unless the reorganization is a simple financial reorganization that has been largely prenegotiated, the debtor can request extensions that, even if opposed by creditors, are typically granted in the initial stages of the case for most large chapter 11 reorganizations.

Debtor's Bankruptcy Counsel

In most cases, the debtor will have retained bankruptcy counsel well in advance of the chapter 11 process to help assess alternatives and prepare. Debtor's counsel may be the distressed firm's normal outside commercial counsel, but it is generally considered better to employ different counsel for the chapter 11 process to avoid potential conflicts of interest and bring an objective party into what is undoubtedly a very trying atmosphere. Debtor's counsel typically plays a very significant role because, in most cases, the board and management will have no experience in a chapter 11 and will, therefore, rely heavily on the advice of counsel. In addition, debtor's counsel often will have established contacts with many of the other specialized personnel or services that the debtor may need, such as financial advisors, forensic accountants, turnaround consultants, etc.

Debtor's Financial Advisor

If the debtor has not already retained a restructuring financial advisor, this will be one of the first recommendations of debtor's counsel. Typically, the financial advisor will be retained well ahead of the chapter 11 filing to assess the potential of resolving the financial distress outside of a chapter 11 process and, if it cannot be resolved, work with the debtor during the process. Primary responsibilities of the debtor's financial advisor are to (a) analyze the debtor's businesses and assets with a view to what can be done to maximize value (which may mean sales or closures of business units, rejections of contracts and leases, etc.); (b) complete detailed valuations (including both liquidation and going-concern approaches) so that the financial trade-offs of different strategies are clearly understood; and (c) act as a conduit for information about the debtor with creditors and the unsecured creditors committee so that management's limited time is focused on fixing the business, not responding to repetitive questions about what went wrong, what the various assets and liabilities are, when a plan of reorganization will be proposed, and so on.

The Committee

In most cases where firms are approaching financial distress, there likely will have been some organization of bondholders into an unofficial bondholder committee. Where a debtor has proactively encouraged this, which will happen in many situations where a debtor is attempting a consensual reorganization outside of chapter 11, the unofficial committee will often be given authority to retain legal counsel, and oftentimes even financial advisors, at the debtor's expense.

When a debtor files for chapter 11 protection, the official committee of unsecured creditors must be formed as authorized under the Bankruptcy Code.[4] The committee is selected by the U.S. Trustee and, per BRC §1102, is to be comprised of the seven largest unsecured creditors willing to serve. Procedurally, the U.S. Trustee will often review the schedule of the 20 largest unsecured creditors, which is required to be filed by the debtor at the beginning of the case, and send questionnaires to some or all of those listed to indicate their willingness to serve. Usually the largest creditor schedule will list as the creditors only the indenture trustee for any bond issues, even though the indenture trustee probably will not actually own any bonds. The indenture trustee, however, usually will be able to ascertain the largest actual holders of the bonds, and these holders will then be contacted regarding their interest in serving. Increasingly, many of the largest investors may decline to serve, as previously mentioned, because they do not want to receive nonpublic information distributed to committee members, which would cause them to become restricted in trading their investment position.

In practice, the U.S. Trustee has a fair amount of discretion and usually will attempt to construct an official committee of unsecured creditors that is representative of the different creditor constituencies. For example, if trade creditors are an important source of working capital to a firm, the U.S. Trustee may appoint one or more trade creditors to the committee, even if their claims at the time of the petition were not among the seven largest. Similarly, where a firm employs a significant amount of organized labor, the U.S. Trustee may include a union representative on the committee, even though the union itself may not be a creditor at all. Finally, the U.S. Trustee almost always appoints the indenture trustee to the committee even though, technically, the indenture trustee is unlikely to be a direct creditor.

Note that secured creditors cannot be members of the official committee of unsecured creditors, at least with respect to their secured claims. Secured claims are always in a different voting class than unsecured claims, and there is usually a significant conflict of interest between the two classes. Often, secured creditors may be undersecured, in which case the under- or unsecured portion of their claim technically is part of the unsecured class and thus makes the creditor eligible for the committee. While nothing in the Bankruptcy Code precludes a secured creditor from serving on the committee to represent its unsecured claim, in practice it is rarely allowed because the inherent conflict of interest makes it questionable that such a creditor could serve as a fiduciary for the unsecured creditors.[5]

A major point of contention in many cases involving complex capital structures is whether there should be separate committees for different classes of claims, such as senior and subordinated debt. The situation can also arise when the plan of reorganization proposes to substantively consolidate various entities, which often tends to be detrimental to the trade creditors at the often debt-free operating-company level. Once again, the decision is largely in the discretion of the U.S. Trustee, who ideally weighs the interests of the parties against the expense and administrative complexity entailed in authorizing multiple committees. As a general rule, different unsecured classes tend to be combined into one official committee of unsecured creditors in order to expedite the dialogue between the two groups and lead to a negotiated resolution of the conflict, but there are certainly many cases where the balance of interests has led to the formation of multiple committees.

Another procedural issue involves the continuity between any unofficial bondholder committee that may have been formed prepetition and the composition of the official committee of unsecured creditors. This usually will depend on the circumstances. Again, the general rule is that the committee should be made up of the seven largest holders, with the practical consideration that it may be more effective if it is representative of the more significant constituencies. Prepetition bondholder committees typically include only bondholders (usually only of one class) and thus tend not to be adequately representative. Thus, usually the prepetition committee will not en masse become the official committee; however, in the exceptional situation where a chapter 11 filing has been made solely to help effect or implement a restructuring largely agreed to prepetition that is not expected to impair any other claim holder, then the U.S. Trustee may overlook the traditional rules is favor of maintaining a continuity which will facilitate an expeditious process.

Committee Legal Counsel

The official committee of unsecured creditors first will select its legal counsel. The selection process usually involves various members of the committee essentially nominating candidates. The merits of the different law firms either will be discussed internally or the committee may request representatives of the various proposed law firms to make presentations to the committee, generally known as a "beauty contest." Following whatever deliberation approach has been chosen, the committee will then make a selection by internal vote. Where a prepetition unofficial committee has already retained counsel, which is therefore familiar with the case and the parties, that law firm likely will be appointed committee counsel out of expedience. The law firm chosen by the committee must submit an application to the bankruptcy court and the U.S. Trustee for approval (usually pro forma), and its reasonable fees and costs will be paid as an administrative claim from the estate.

The committee legal counsel plays a very important role in advising the committee and representing it before the bankruptcy court. Committee counsel will be responsible for (a) legal due diligence on the debtor to determine the rights of the unsecured holders and identify any claims the committee or the debtor may bring against other claim and interest holders (particularly challenges to secured claims), management, and others; (b) a strategic analysis of how the committee can maximize recoveries and different sources of leverage which may be available to negotiate a plan or reorganization; (c) assisting with the negotiation of a plan of reorganization; and (d) perhaps most importantly, helping forge a consensus among the various creditor constituencies so that a plan of reorganization, when supported by the committee, has the best possible chance of support. The committee's counsel also helps analyze the debtor's activities during the case and advises the committee on what to support and oppose.

Committee Financial Advisor

After choosing legal counsel, the committee's next act likely will be to select a financial advisor. The process is fairly similar to that used for selecting counsel, except that a "beauty contest" among various potential candidates is almost always held, except in a situation where an unofficial prepetition committee has already retained an advisor.

The primary obligations of the committee's financial advisor are to (a) complete extensive financial due diligence on the debtor's business to determine what can be done to maximize its value; (b) complete detailed valuations (including both liquidation and going-concern approaches) so that the financial trade-offs of different strategies are clearly understood; and (c) represent the committee in negotiations relating to the financial aspects of any proposed plan of reorganization. However, it should be noted that as institutional investors have become increasingly experienced in the reorganization process, a subcommittee of the committee, comprised of the most experienced member, may be appointed as lead negotiator of the financial aspects of the plan.

The Secured Creditors

Depending on the magnitude of secured debt relative to enterprise value, the secured creditor may be the most powerful player in the restructuring game.

Interestingly, however, the scheme envisioned by the Bankruptcy Code does not particularly make the secured creditor a pivotal, proactive player in the reorganization process as much as a potentially powerful party with whom the debtor and the committee must deal. The primary source of the secured creditor's power rests in its liens on the debtor's assets and the requirement, under the Bankruptcy Code, that those assets cannot be used unless the creditor is provided with adequate protection. It should be noted that from the secured creditor's perspective, once a chapter 11 petition has been filed, the debtor is using the secured creditor's "property" without the creditor's consent. This view is based on the fact that at the filing of the petition, if not well before, the secured creditor most likely had the right under the lending agreements and state law to foreclose on the collateral securing the loan, but is barred from exercising this right due to the imposition of the automatic stay at the beginning of the case.

As mentioned above, secured creditors do not join the official committee of unsecured creditors, nor, if there is more than one secured creditor, is there generally any type of committee for secured creditors. Where there are multiple secured creditors, they will be grouped into voting classes on the basis of collateral securing the claim on the theory that the difference in collateral is a material difference in the nature of the claim. In the case of large syndicated bank loans, the agent bank usually will form a steering committee from among the loan participants. This steering committee will almost always seek to have legal and financial advisor expenses paid out of adequate protection payments.

The Bankruptcy Judge

Although typically not an active participant in any aspect of the restructuring negotiation, the particular bankruptcy judge overseeing a case can have a fair amount of influence on a number of critical aspects, including the pace of the case and assessments of critical issues such as plan of reorganization exclusivity, claim allowance, adequate protection, and valuation. As mentioned in Chapter 4, the debtor often will consider the potential judge it will receive when selecting the jurisdiction in which to file the bankruptcy case. Currently, the two most common jurisdictions in which to file are Delaware and the Southern District of New York. Both are favored because there is considerable case law precedent that allows counsel to better anticipate how various issues will be decided. Delaware, however, faced with a tremendous caseload, has adopted the practice of using visiting judges from other areas. This practice has made it more difficult to predict which judge is likely to preside over any particular case, and thus counsels who prefer to work with judges with whom they have substantial experience may, where the debtor has the choice, recommend the Southern District of New York. Perhaps not coincidently, New York is also the home location for many of the law firms most involved in bankruptcy practice.

TYPES OF CHAPTER 11 CASES

Technically, there is only one type of chapter 11 case under the Bankruptcy Code. However, in practice, the nature of a case will vary greatly depending on the degree of preplanning with the creditors, as well as the type of operational restructuring that may be required. Three of the more common types of cases are prepackaged or prenegotiated restructurings, preplanned sales leading to either liquidation or reorganization, and free-fall or contested restructurings. Those who associate corporate liquidations with chapter 7 of the Bankruptcy Code may be surprised by the notion of a liquidation under chapter 11. Liquidation can be done under both. The difference is that under chapter 7, management is removed and a liquidating trustee is appointed to oversee the process. The practical issue is which approach will result in the highest net recoveries — after taking into consideration expenses, which are typically lower in the chapter 7 approach. Usually, if a debtor has operations that can be sold as integrated "going-concern" units, recoveries should be higher, and the higher expenses (management salaries, potential incurrence of negative operating cash flow and higher professional fees) can be economically justified. In this section, each of these will be discussed in more detail, together with the implications for investment return.

Before discussing how the reorganization process can vary, it may be helpful to review (since Chapter 4 may seem like a long time ago) the basics of what procedurally must be accomplished in a chapter 11. There are essentially four significant steps: (1) the restructuring of the debtor's operations by asset sales and contract assumptions and rejections, (2) the development and dissemination of a proposed plan, (3) a vote on the plan by the claim and interest holders, and (4) confirmation of the plan by the bankruptcy court. The development of a proposed plan generally will take the longest period because it may require a lengthy analysis of the best way to maximize the value of a business, estimate the value of the enterprise, and develop an appropriate and acceptable capital structure. After the proposed plan is developed, the disclosure statement is prepared. The disclosure statement discusses the debtor, the chapter 11 process, any organizational changes the debtor has undertaken, an estimate of the debtor's future value, and most importantly, the terms of the plan, which will determine creditor recoveries. The plan cannot be distributed to creditors for their vote until the bankruptcy court approves the adequacy of the disclosure statement.[6] Lawyers whose clients want to delay the process or force some change in the plan will, like good parliamentarians seeking to delay a vote through endless procedural bickering, find ways to challenge the documentation and delay the process. Court approval of the disclosure statement (which should be thought of as approval of form only and not as any type of endorsement) is a very significant step because it means that of the almost limitless scenarios that could have been conceived, for the time being, there is only one option on the table for consideration (occasionally, the bankruptcy court may approve competing plans, and while this provides a choice, the alternatives are reasonably finite).

Once the approved disclosure statement and plan are disseminated to the creditors, the voting begins. The voting rules are, at least on their face, fairly simple: if a class is impaired, it is entitled to vote. In order to approve the plan, class members with at least 67% in amount and more than 50% in number (based on who actually voted) must vote in favor. The concept of an impairment entitling a claim to vote is extremely broad. If there is virtually any change[7] in the nature or a claim, even if the change arguably makes the claim better, it is deemed impaired and the class is entitled to vote. If the class votes to approve the plan, the proposed treatment of the class will, assuming confirmation, be imposed on all class members regardless of whether they voted against the plan or did not vote at all.

As the penultimate step, voting is important, but not necessarily decisive since there are ways (the cram-down provisions) of implementing the plan of reorganization even if a class objects. From the perspective of the plan proponent, the ability to bind dissenting creditors and even entire classes is an extremely valuable power afforded under the Bankruptcy Code. In contrast, as discussed in Chapter 4, a class minority can effectively defeat the wishes of the majority to effect an out-of-court restructuring. In bankruptcy, minority rights are significantly reduced.

Once the plan is voted on, it must then go through the process of confirmation.[8] Confirmation is the ultimate or decisive step because the bankruptcy court's confirmation order, which can include the satisfaction of a variety of conditions, is what paves the way for a plan to be implemented or become effective. Confirmation entails the bankruptcy court deciding whether the plan conforms to a lengthy list of requirements set forth in BRC §1129. As will be discussed later, several of the requirements under this provision are subjective, which means that many different kinds of issues can be raised to derail the process. While typically the confirmability of a plan of reorganization can be reasonably assessed on the basis of the formal objections that are filed, occasionally the outcome is uncertain right up to the crack of the gavel.

Preplanned Restructuring

Generally, the goal of advanced planning in a chapter 11 case, when it is feasible, is to shorten the time the debtor is in bankruptcy. Minimizing the debtor's time in bankruptcy is usually in everyone's best interest, because it reduces costs, limits the risk to the business, and accelerates payouts to creditors. However, three constituencies that might have an interest in a protracted process are management, the equity, and any classes of "out-of-the-money" creditors. Both equity holders and out-of-the-money creditors might hope that a protracted process will allow a fundamental change in the economy or the debtor's market to occur, which could substantially improve enterprise value and hence the potential value of their claim. Management, which might own a lot of equity and thus generally have the same view as any stockholder, could have an independent interest in delaying if those in management feel this maximizes their job tenure.

When the source of financial distress is primarily related to capital structure issues (absolute amount of debt, ability to pay principal and/or interest, violation of lending covenants, etc.), often the debtor and a bondholder group will attempt to negotiate a consensual restructuring. As a matter of economic reality, both parties recognize that, in a worst-case bankruptcy scenario, the creditors are likely to ultimately control the debtor's equity. This essentially widens the range of scenarios that both parties, particularly the debtor and/or management, should find acceptable, including some type of debt for equity swap that may significantly dilute existing equity. Usually, if there is sufficient time and the appearance of bondholder amenability, the proposal will form the basis for a voluntary exchange offer, as discussed in Chapters 4 and 9. The preplanned chapter 11, which varies in form depending on the formality of creditor support, is what follows when the exchange offer or restructuring proposal fails to garner sufficient participation.

Full Prepack

Full prepacks, presumably derived from "a full prepackaged filing," involve the most coordination and the best prospect of an expedited trip through chapter 11. In a full prepack, when the petition is filed it is accompanied by a complete disclosure statement and proposed plan of reorganization, together with an agreement to support the plan that is binding on a sufficient number of the class to satisfy the applicable voting tests. Under BRC §1126(b), votes can be solicited prepetition if the soliciting materials comply with applicable law (typical Securities and Exchange Commission rules relating to tender or exchange offers in the case of public companies) and the normal requirements for a disclosure statement. If the bankruptcy court determines that the solicitation process used in soliciting the votes was appropriate, an expedited hearing to consider both the adequacy of the disclosure statement and confirmation can take place in less than 45 days.

Full prepacks are not common. To be able to garner sufficient votes prepetition means, practically speaking, having a very limited number of classes (usually only a bond class and perhaps a bank class) entitled to vote; otherwise, obtaining the voting commitments is unwieldy. Usually this means that the impaired consenting class (e.g., the bonds) must be willing to leave pari passu trade creditors intact. For example, the plan of reorganization may provide that the bondholders will exchange their claim for 90% of the equity and all other creditor claims will remain intact. Whether bondholders will be willing to accept such discriminatory treatment will depend upon their perception of the value of the equity. If they perceive the consideration offered as being worth as much as, or more than, their claim or the recovery they would likely receive in a non-prepack chapter 11, then the prepack may be feasible. On the other hand, if 90% of the equity is worth less than an alternative recovery, it would be unlikely that the bondholders would be willing to reduce their claim in a manner that benefits the other creditors. The rational decision should be based not on the relative treatment between the claims (impaired versus unimpaired), but on whether at the end of the contemplated reorganization (including costs, potential disruption to the business, delays in receipt of funds, etc.) the bondholders determine they are better off. This dynamic is what makes true prepacks feasible in only a select set of situations. Table 12-1 presents data on completed prepacks, which in the 1998–2002 period represented less than 7% of cases. Even when the prerequisites for a prepack are present, there are a variety of issues, such as the adequacy of the disclosure statement and the nature of the solicitation process, which can cause delays. In the example above, it could be anticipated that the equity holders, which are being substantially diluted, might raise objections during the confirmation process.

A variation on the full prepack occasionally is found in conjunction with voluntary exchange offers. In an exchange offer, the debtor and the unofficial bondholder committee will negotiate a mutually acceptable restructuring proposal that the debtor will then formally circulate to all bondholders. The terms of the exchange offer will clearly state that if the exchange offer is not successful, which is always challenging when a fairly high participation rate (e.g., 85–90%) is required, the company will file chapter 11 and propose a plan of reorganization similar to (or less favorable than) the exchange proposal. Bondholders that vote for the exchange may also bind themselves to support, if the exchange fails, the subsequent plan. Combination exchange offers such as this

Table 12-1.   Trends in Prepackaged Chapter 11 Reorganizations

Year	Number of Prepackaged Plans	% of All Chapter 11s
1986	1	0.7%
1987	1	0.9%
1988	2	1.6%
1989	2	1.5%
1990	2	1.7%
1991	7	5.7%
1992	12	13.2%
1993	18	20.9%
1994	12	17.1%
1995	6	7.1%
1996	9	10.5%
1997	6	7.2%
1998	6	4.9%
1999	10	6.9%
2000	12	6.8%
2001	8	3.1%
2002	12	6.2%

Source: *2003 Bankruptcy Yearbook & Almanac*

are effective at both soliciting plan votes and conveying a "do this voluntarily or we'll shove it down your throat" threat to potential holdouts.

Prenegotiated Filings

Further down the continuum are prenegotiated filings. These can vary widely in the degree of prenegotiation and prefiling commitment of creditor support. In the context of a prefiling exchange offer that failed, it may be that the ultimate plan of reorganization will need to leave several classes impaired or will envision certain operational changes that make a prepack infeasible. However, to expedite the plan process and provide momentum and a sense of support, bond creditors will often sign a *plan support agreement* that obligates those creditors that sign it to vote for a plan consistent with the terms outlined in the agreement. Other times, when it is difficult to foresee what changes will be required to gain sufficient creditor support, perhaps only a term sheet or memorandum of understanding will have been arrived at with financial creditors, although even this is likely to accelerate the process depending on the position and proposed treatment of the nonfinancial creditors. For example, a term sheet with bondholders that outlines leverage reductions, terms of new securities, a proposed valuation, etc. normally would greatly expedite the process, but if it is based on substantive consolidation, it could be a "nonstarter" with trade creditors.

Only a limited number of situations are conducive to meaningful advanced preparation. Where many constituencies of the debtor will be negatively impacted by a reorganization process, it is very difficult to have an effective dialogue before the actual bankruptcy filing. Trade creditors, in particular, usually are very opposed to voluntarily compromising their claims. In contrast, pari passu bond investors likely will have incurred a mark-to-market loss on their distressed position that essentially gives them more flexibility. Similarly, where a credit facility that will be compromised is involved, banks that own the facility likely will have taken reserves or write-downs and be prepared to negotiate, whereas collateralized debt obligation (CDO) holders may want to postpone a filing for as long as possible.[9] Once a filing occurs, there tends to be a "reality check," and creditors, especially unsecured creditors, recognize that some loss is inevitable, which shifts the focus to how to minimize that loss. Financial creditors, such as distressed debt investors, will tend to be very focused on what maximizes recoveries in the near term. Business creditors, union constituencies, and management likely will have a bias toward preserving as much future potential value as possible, even if that entails a longer process. Thus, financial creditors might prefer to break up the debtor and sell pieces to various buyers as a way of maximizing short-term cash returns. However, if this means management people lose their jobs or trade creditors might no longer be suppliers, these constituencies might oppose the proposed strategy.

From the distressed investor's perspective, all preplanning efforts generally should be viewed as favorable for returns. The worst enemies of the investor are delay and uncertainty. To the extent that preplanning signals that management is committed to a faster process, it can only help with the outlook for expense minimization and an earlier realization horizon.

Asset Sales

For many financially distressed entities, an important tool for resolving the distress may be the sale of the entire enterprise or severable business units or assets. As discussed in Chapter 9, asset sales can be an effective way to increase liquidity and perhaps reduce leverage. If completed early enough, they may effectively resolve a firm's financial distress. However, as a debtor's financial distress becomes more acute, the negotiating dynamic with prospective purchasers becomes clouded with issues that either make a prepetition sale impossible or reduce the price a prospective purchaser is willing to pay.

It is difficult to generalize about the implications of asset sales in the chapter 11 context for distressed investors because investors may have completely conflicting interests. On the one hand, a general unsecured creditor likely will be positively disposed toward a process that maximizes the estate's value and hence creditors' expected recoveries. This has been the general perspective of this book. On the other hand, it is conceivable that a distressed investor's strategy may be to acquire the debtor, or a particular asset, at a discount to fair value, which may enhance that investor's returns at the expense of other creditors. In the latter case, it is a zero-sum game where one player's gain is only at another's expense.

Sales Intended to Enhance Recoveries by Maximizing Estate Value

As mentioned, the clearer it is that a firm is in such distress that a bankruptcy is possible, the more reluctant a purchaser may be to consummate any type of transaction for fear, among other things, that it will be unwound after the fact as a fraudulent conveyance. This is a double-edged sword, of sorts, for the prospective purchaser, because he or she likely will also perceive the seller's distress as "desperate." Therefore, the buyer, especially a cash buyer, may have significant negotiating leverage. This is precisely the type of scenario against which fraudulent conveyance laws are intended to protect. In these cases, the logical course may be to prenegotiate a sale that is then consummated within a chapter 11 process. Of course, once the debtor files, creditors, even unsecured, have a natural tendency to look at the estate as "their property." From this perspective, the inherent conflict between the asset buyer seeking a bargain and the seller wanting to make a "killing" broadens to include the creditor, which also sees its interests affected by the sale.

How a distressed investor views asset sales will depend on where the investor is positioned in the capital structure. An investor that holds secured debt and will receive the proceeds of the sale likely will be very supportive. An investor that holds the fulcrum security which likely will receive a significant portion of the reorganized firm's equity may oppose the sale because it could diminish long-term enterprise value. Other investors may be relatively indifferent as long as they feel the sale process will extract "fair" value for the asset. This is a major tension that exists between secured and unsecured creditors. The secured creditor, as long as its claim is recovered, is more interested in the speed of the process than maximization of proceeds. The primary concern of the unsecured creditor will be to have a thorough process that maximizes value, even if it takes a little longer. However, unsecured creditors should be realistic in recognizing that the debtor is a "motivated" seller and that the alternatives

Table 12-2. Information on Selected BRC §363 Asset Sales in 2002

Debtor	Assets Sold	Purchaser	Cash Paid ($ Million)*
Acme Metals	Riverdale Strip Mill	AK Steel	65.0
Big V Supermarkets	27 Stores and Other Assets	Wakefern Food	185.2
Borden Chemicals	Addis Plant and Equipment	Shintech	38.0
Budget Group	Substantially All Operations	Cendent	107.5
Burlington Industries	Substantially All Operations	Berkshire Hathaway	579.0
Casual Male	Big & Tall Operations	Charlesbank Capital	137.0
Casual Male	Casual Male Operations	Designs, Inc.	170.0
Comdisco	Availability Solutions Unit	Hewlett-Packard	750.0
Comdisco	Healthcare Leasing Assets	GE Capital	165.0
Conseco	Conseco Finance	GE Capital	1100.0
Exodus	Substantially All Operations	Cable & Wireless PLC	575.0
Fitzgerald Gaming	Three Casinos	Majestic Investors	149.0
Fruit of the Loom	Apparel Operations	Berkshire Hathaway	840.0
Genuity	Substantially All Operations	Level 3 Communications	60.0
Global Telesystems	Substantially All Operations	KPNQuest NV	568.0
IT Group	Substantially All Operations	Shaw Group	105.0
Learnout Hauspie	Speech Technology Unit	ScanSoft	53.8
Peregrine Systems	Remedy Unit	BMC Software	335.0
Polaroid	Identification System Unit	Digimarc	56.5
Rhythms NetConnections	DSL Assets	WorldCom	31.0
Trans World Airlines	Substantially all Operations	AMR Corp (American Airlines)	742.0

* Consideration often includes the assumption of certain liabilities, which may be more significant than the cash amount paid.

Source: *2003 Bankruptcy Yearbook & Almanac*

are letting management continue to run the business or, in the worst case, a liquidation. Accordingly, alternatives that maximize near-term cash recoveries are generally viewed positively. In addition, sales tend to reduce the number of issues that must be considered in the rest of the reorganization and thus generally expedite the process.

BRC §363 is a powerful tool for buyers and sellers that want to effect asset sales in a financially distressed context. Among the important advantages to the buyer is the ability to purchase the asset free and clear of virtually all liens and claims, with little or no risk of the transaction being subsequently unwound. Asset buyers want to get a good deal, but they also value a visible time line and certainty, both of which BRC §363 can provide. Table 12-2 provides information on a selected group of significant BRC §363 sales that occurred in 2002 to give an indication of the level of such activity.

Procedurally, only the debtor can propose to sell assets pursuant to a BRC §363 process. The process envisioned by the Bankruptcy Code is an open outcry auction conducted either in court or such place as may be approved, often the offices of debtor's legal counsel. This is a rather stark contrast to the typical process of a corporate sale, which can involve multiple rounds of essentially sealed bids.

There are generally two ways a BRC §363 sale develops in the large public company context: (1) sale negotiations begin prepetition, but it is decided the sale can only be completed within a BRC §363 context or (2) the debtor decides postpetition that an asset divestiture is an important part of the reorganization process and proposes a sale. The key issue for the debtor is to avoid a worst-case scenario where only one bidder shows up at the auction and submits a deeply discounted bid. Strategically, this typically requires that the debtor arrange to have a prominent, acceptable "stalking horse" bid in place at the beginning of the auction. When the context is a prepetition sale being completed under BRC §363, the prepetition purchaser fills this role. When there is no bidder in hand, the customary practice is for the debtor's financial advisor to conduct a marketing process for the asset designed to, at the very least, develop an acceptable starting bid.

For the acquirer, playing the stalking horse role entails various trade-offs. One significant disadvantage is that the amount and terms of the initial bid must be disclosed well in advance, giving prospective competitors time for detailed review. On the other hand, the stalking horse bidder typically has the best opportunity to learn about the assets being auctioned and shape the composition of the assets and liabilities involved in the sale to his or her preference. In addition, the stalking horse can negotiate the terms of the sales procedures including break up fees and minimum overbid provisions. These fees and structuring advantages can act as an inducement for third parties to play this valuable role.

For example, assume Acme Foods, a consumer product company, has filed chapter 11 and decides that it wants to sell its canned fruit division (CFD) as part of its reorganization. This type of sale is outside of the ordinary course of business and thus subject to bankruptcy court and committee oversight. The debtor's financial advisor determines, after some inquiries, there are 8 potential strategic buyers and up to 20 potential financial buyers, at the right price, for the CFD. The financial advisor begins the marketing process and identifies Biscuit Partners, a financial buyer, as interested in CFD. After thorough due diligence, Biscuit indicates it will bid $75 million for the CFD in the §363 auction, but wants a breakup fee of $3 million if someone else wins the auction and a minimum first-bid increment of $5 million. The committee in the Acme case may be pleased with the decision to sell the CFD and view the $75 million bid, though naturally somewhat low, as acceptable, but believe that the breakup fee and bid increment each should be $2 million.

Auction terms are typically heavily negotiated. With respect to breakup fees, the initial bidder, or stalking horse, wants to be compensated for its due diligence efforts (which include out-of-pocket costs for lawyers and accountants), the credibility its bid brings to the process, and the fact that by voluntarily submitting to an auction process it is potentially setting itself up to pay a higher price (Biscuit presumably would like to purchase the CFD but prefers to only pay $75 million). Creditors recognize the value of the stalking horse, but view breakup fees as erosion of estate value that should be minimized. The dynamics of minimum bid negotiations go back to standard game theory issues. If it could, Biscuit likely would prefer a minimum bid increment of $15 million, which would mean that the next bidder would have to bid $90 million, a possibly uneconomic price. The seller wants the increment low enough that multiple bidders can potentially get involved, but still needs to have the first increase be at least equal to the amount of the breakup fee to ensure that the estate would receive at least as much as from the stalking horse bid. Negotiations usually will lead to a consensual decision on the auction terms; otherwise the bankruptcy court will make a final determination.

A final point to note about asset sales, in particular where essentially the entire business is being sold, is the role and interests of management. Executives want job security and/or money. These can be threatened by the prospect of selling "their" firm. Where the buyer is a financial buyer, especially a buyer they have helped cultivate, executives may have an expectation of favorable compensation arrangements and be positively disposed toward the transaction. What managers generally do not want is for the firm to be sold to a strategic buyer that, almost by definition, has its own senior management and no need for the distressed firm's executives. However, BRC §363 auctions are open to any party. Accordingly, management often will attempt to incorporate bidding procedure rules that make it very difficult for strategic buyers to participate. Examples of such devices include confidentiality agreements that would effectively force a prospective buyer to discontinue any competing business it may have in order to conduct due diligence on the distressed firm. Another common tactic is to require a prospective strategic buyer to submit onerous and expensive competitive market studies to establish in advance that if it were to prevail in the auction, the purchase would not run afoul of antitrust prohibitions. This is not to say that, in particular with respect to confidential information or trade secrets, a distressed firm should not be careful to protect its franchise. However, unsecured creditors' committees need to be vigilant about the details of the bidding rules in order to make sure they foster as much participation in the auction as feasible.

Sales Designed to Maximize Creditor Recoveries

As mentioned, the distressed investor's strategy in an investment may involve using a firm's financial distress as a way to acquire assets at attractive prices. For the most part, this book has assumed that the path to this outcome is for the investor to purchase debt that likely would end up controlling the equity. However, there are many other scenarios that are also possible. Returning to the CFD example, assume that the secured lender in the $80 million claim scenario decided to sell the loan at a discount following the determination that the collateral was worth only $50 million and the lender was $30 million undersecured. This sale, in which FruitCake investors purchased the loan for $55 million, was completed before the possibility of a BRC §363 sale had been raised. When the subsequent BRC §363 auction occurs, FruitCake, after a BRC §1111(b) election, could make what is known as a *credit bid,* which allows the credit bidder to use part or all of the secured claim (measured at face value) as currency in the auction. Other parties generally would be required to pay cash and to win the auction would have to pay above $80 million. If FruitCake wins the auction with a "credit bid," it obviously will have purchased the CFD at an attractive net price of $55 million.

Free-Fall and Contested Chapter 11 Reorganizations

When the source of financial distress comes from a sudden economic event, for example an adverse court judgment of liability, or operational issues as opposed to simply excessive leverage, then the debtor's chapter 11 filing may come with little preplanning with creditors, other than its banks. The term *free-fall* will be used here to mean any non-prenegotiated chapter 11, including cases driven by sudden events (the classic free-fall context) and those where the complexity of the debtor's circumstances made preplanning difficult. Free-fall chapter 11s can be especially risky for distressed debt investors, particularly in unsecured paper, because they are shrouded in significant uncertainty and the prospect of substantial costs. Free-falls also can be fairly contentious, as when, for example, the debtor, in order to build a war chest of liquidity, draws down on a revolving credit line immediately before filing.

A significant concern in an unplanned chapter 11, from the distressed investor's perspective, is the uncertainty surrounding management's failure to attempt to initiate a restructuring dialogue. There are numerous things that can be read into this type of omission: Is management just incompetent? Did management, perhaps understandably, not see it as in its commercial best interest, given vendor relationships and other factors, to risk a dialogue that might exacerbate the financial distress? Or, worst case, is management planning to use the chapter 11 process as a way, not withstanding theoretical or legal fiduciary obligations, to advance its own interests? This last scenario often can lead to contentious, drawn out, and expensive chapter 11 processes that can hurt distressed debt recoveries. If the chapter 11 process becomes a hotly contested battle between management and the creditors, or among the creditors, significant uncertainty can enter the investment outlook.

Sources of Leverage in the Chapter 11 Process

If the coiner of the phrase "all is fair in love and war"[10] had been on the losing end of a distressed debt investment, the phrase never might have been as memorable. Bankruptcies can be nasty and mean-spirited. They are extremely complicated negotiations because they are a perfect setting for brinkmanship: One facing the prospect of losing everything may perceive only upside from certain extreme acts. Even parties that are not facing complete losses may decide to take actions to punish other parties in the case either out of vindictiveness or to establish the credibility of their threats in future matters.

Although it may sound simplistic, all most investors care about is money and time: How much will they get and when will they get it? For typical institutional investors, the two are very intertwined because these investors will generally have given their clients a target return expectation of between 15 and 25% per year, depending on the market environment and the risk profile of the fund. When performance is measured by the particular rate of return, the timely receipt of recovery can be almost as important as the amount. For a $100 investment to achieve a 20% rate of return, it must realize $120, $144, and $173 by the end of years one, two and three, respectively.

In a negotiation, it is often considered advantageous not to let the other party know your primary objective. The distressed debt investor's objectives are usually unambiguous, which means other parties know exactly how to apply leverage. Since most investors perceive the value of the debtor as declining the more protracted the chapter 11 is (because of strained customer relations, declining employee morale, and mounting administrative expenses), it is usually viewed as critical to keep the restructuring process moving. The amount and kind of recoveries, of course, are also important, and while an investor may have forecast what these were likely to be at the time of investment, significant events can occur within the reorganization process, particularly free-falls, that result in the best estimations going awry. Although time and recovery are the ultimate sources of leverage in the chapter 11 negotiation, the specific tools or weapons, depending on one's perspective, are delay, priority, and valuation, each of which is discussed in more detail below.

Table 12-3.   Trends in Time to Complete Chapter 11 Reorganizations

Year	No. of Completed Reorganizations	Months in Chapter 11		
		Minimum	**Maximum**	**Average**
1990	43	2	69	19.1
1991	34	1	36	12.6
1992	55	1	44	14.0
1993	64	1	83	16.8
1994	54	1	71	18.1
1995	25	1	63	17.1
1996	30	1	71	14.4
1997	39	1	49	15.2
1998	37	1	81	14.8
1999	48	1	44	11.5
2000	68	1	138	14.0
2001	61	2	34	13.5
2002	54	2	50	13.8

Source: *2003 Bankruptcy Yearbook & Almanac*

Delay

Outside of the paid-by-the-hour lawyers and financial advisors on monthly retainers, generally speaking everyone should be better off with a speedy chapter 11 process.[11] Some cases, simply by the nature of the business complexities (e.g., airlines, large retailers, etc.) will require a significant amount of time to resolve, even in the best of circumstances. As shown in Table 12-3, the average time in bankruptcy has stayed fairly constant in the 1999–2002 period. This is somewhat surprising given that the sheer increase in the number of bankruptcies during this period (see Table 2-1) has strained the resources of the bankruptcy courts and professionals. Perhaps offsetting the workload is the fact that professionals and creditor constituencies have gained considerable experience and thus, when potentially complex issues are confronted, have a recent experience to reference. One could easily envision an unsecured creditors' committee discussion to the effect: "This problem is sort of like what happened in Case Y. Should we think about doing it the way they did?" At this point, very few situations represent a case of first impression.

Since the motivations for a speedy chapter 11 process are fairly clear (lower administrative expenses, faster payouts, less risk to the business enterprise), when delays occur, or are threatened, it is a signal that something about the process is working against some party's interests and that party is willing to potentially hurt other claims in an effort to improve its position. Two constituencies that frequently can be counted on to delay the process are management, when executives are losing their jobs, and/or the junior interest holders (both debt and equity) that are expecting to recover nothing or only a *de minimus* amount under the plan of reorganization.

Management and the Right of Exclusivity

A powerful weapon wielded by management in the battle with creditors is the right of exclusivity. Under BRC §1121(b), the debtor has the exclusive right to propose a plan of reorganization for 120 days following the filing of the petition and then an additional 60 days to solicit acceptances of the plan. Prior to the 120-day period lapsing, management can petition the bankruptcy court for an extension, which, as a practical matter, is almost always granted — at least in the initial stages. As a generalization, as long as management appears to be acting in good faith to further the restructuring process, bankruptcy courts tend to give the debtor the benefit of the doubt.

Exclusivity tends to work against creditor interests because management may not have the same incentives for a speedy resolution as creditors, particularly unsecured creditors. During the exclusivity period, while creditors may be receiving little or nothing, those in management continue to receive salaries — often at inflated levels — and can sit back and wait for a better economic environment to help their core business. In the meantime, management basically has the benefit of all the capital, which unsecured creditors have provided the debtor, as an interest-free loan (secured creditors likely are collecting some compensation through adequate protection payments). Exclusivity can even protect debtors that are incurring negative cash flows which threaten creditor recoveries. To the extent a debtor is generating positive cash flow, the longer management does not have to pay interest expense allows it to accumulate cash either to minimize the need for exit financing or to build a pot to get creditors to accept discount payoff proposals. Management can attempt to put itself in the position of being able to offer a choice between $Y in cash now or 2x $Y in new paper — knowing many creditors would elect the former, which leaves the going-forward business significantly less burdened.

In contrast, if there were no right of exclusivity, one could envision that after making an operational assessment, creditors would move quickly to identify a strategy to maximize recoveries (which in many cases likely would involve selling the debtor outright or in going-concern pieces) and then attempt to negotiate an acceptable allocation among themselves. The potential rights of equity would, at best, be a fleeting consideration. Management would enter into the equation only to the extent it was truly viewed as integral to the success of the business — and it is the unusual case that management is not viewed as fungible. This tension between management and creditors on the exclusivity issue is significant, but it seems fairly clear that the framers of the Bankruptcy

Code had a bias for wanting to rehabilitate the debtor, even if this meant some disadvantages to the creditors.

There often is very little that creditor constituencies can do to force a management team to come forward with a proposed plan of reorganization while the umbrella of exclusivity protects it. As mentioned above, bankruptcy courts usually will have a predisposition toward allowing the debtor time to present a plan and then lobby creditors for support. Thus, as long as management is reasonably politic about appearing to be diligent and cooperative, the creditor's options are limited.

Among the few tools of the creditors is to ask the bankruptcy court to appoint either a chapter 11 trustee or an examiner under BRC §1104. The request to appoint a chapter 11 trustee is effectively an effort to oust management. The appointment of an examiner, in contrast, allows management to remain in day-to-day control, but inserts an independent party (typically a consultant, accountant, or lawyer) to review management's supervision of the business. Requests to appoint chapter 11 trustees and examiners are infrequent and only occasionally granted. For the situation to be compelling, the proponent of the motion (which can be virtually any party to the case including the U.S. Trustee, the official committee of unsecured creditors, or an individual with an equity interest) typically requires evidence of exceptional misconduct or self-dealing. Table 12-4 summarizes some selected situations where there were either motions for or appointments of either chapter 11 trustees or examiners.

The appointment of an examiner does not, by itself, impact the right of exclusivity, but what it puts in place is a party (the examiner) that the bankruptcy court will accord with particular credibility. Thus, if an examiner is appointed and is critical of management, creditors will have much stronger grounds for arguing that exclusivity be terminated. As a tactical matter, the creditors proposing a chapter 11 trustee (or even the less invasive examiner) is a fairly hostile move and must be considered carefully. It definitely signals that, from the creditors' perspective, management has no role in the future enterprise. Thus, since management still has control of the business, creditors will probably only want to do this when they think there is very little downside.

An alternative to the "stick" approach of a trustee or examiner, of course, is the "carrot." Since creditors benefit from an expedited process, it might be in their best interest to share some of that benefit with others to make sure everyone has equal incentives. For example, it is fairly typical in the structure of the financial advisor to the official committee of unsecured creditors to structure bonus payments that give incentives for a timely resolution of the case. Giving explicit incentives to management can be difficult. Management's compensation is determined by the board of directors, which has fiduciary duties to others besides the financial creditors. However, the concept of incentives can

Table 12-4. Selected Cases Involving at Least a Request for Chapter 11 Trustee or Examiner

Company Case	Event Relating to Chapter 11 Trustee or Examiner	Party Requesting
AppOnline.com	Chapter 11 Trustee Appointed	U.S. Trustee
County Seat Stores	Chapter 11 Trustee Appointed	U.S. Trustee
Covanta Energy	Motion for Examiner	Various Trade Creditors
Decora Industries	Motion for Examiner and Chapter 11 Trustee	By Equity Holder Against Committee Objection
Enron	Motion for Examiner	U.S. Trustee
Flag Telecom	Motion for Examiner and Chapter 11 Trustee	Individual Financial Creditors
Fruit of the Loom	Motion for BRC Section 2004 Examination	Individual Financial Creditors
General DataComm	Motion for Examiner	Official Committee
Global Crossing	Motion for Examiner and Chapter 11 Trustee	By Official Equity Committee Against Committee Objection
Grand Court Lifestyles	Motion for Examiner	U.S. Trustee
Halo Industries	Motion for Examiner	By Equity Holder Against Committee Objection
IT Group	Motion for Examiner	Official Committee
Kitty Hawk	Chapter 11 Trustee	Official Committee
Learnout & Hauspie	Motion for Examiner	Individual Financial Creditors
NewCare Healthcare	Motion for Examiner	Official Committee
NewPower Holdings	Motion for Examiner	U.S. Trustee
Planet Hollywood	Motion for Examiner	Official Committee
Polaroid	Motion for Examiner	NA
Sun Healthcare	Motion for Examiner	By Equity Holder Against Committee Objection
Tower Air	Chapter 11 Trustee	U.S. Trustee
UniDigital	Motion for Examiner	U.S. Trustee
WorldCom	Motion for Examiner	U.S. Trustee

Source: *2003 Bankruptcy Yearbook & Almanac*

be raised during the course of negotiations in an effort get the process moving. There is a fine line, of course, between a "bribe" and being the victim of extortion. As will be discussed next, constituencies often will use delay tactics in an effort to extract some benefit from other parties.

Creditors and the Threat of Litigation

A common source of delay is litigation during the chapter 11 process. Litigation in this sense means not only lawsuits between various parties in the case, but also challenges to different aspects of the proceeding, particularly at the point where the bankruptcy court is asked to rule on the adequacy of the disclosure statement or at the point of plan of reorganization confirmation. Litigation, once commenced, can be very expensive and time consuming. For example, lawyers can request time to obtain and review all sorts of documents and records, then request interrogatories from people about the documents, then request depositions about the interrogatories, etc.

Thus, a common strategy for a creditor that wants to gain negotiating leverage, primarily with other creditors (though certainly creditor versus debtor actions or at least contests are also common), during the course of the reorganization is to threaten to sue someone or contest something. Since lawsuits can be brought by just about anyone for anything, the leverage accorded the threat will turn on the other parties' assessment of the potential "aggravation" or expense of the threatened action. The first factor to assess is the merits of the issue. Sometimes this may hinge on a legal ambiguity (e.g., what the appropriate interest accrual rate is for an unimpaired, unsecured creditor), and the task of the committee's counsel will be to develop a risk analysis. Other times it may involve a factual ambiguity (e.g., whether or not a particular process was followed to perfect a security interest). In addition to the merits, the ability of the party making the threat to fund the litigation or action will be considered. In particular, if the party raising the issue must fund any litigation itself, rather than at the expense of the debtor's estate, then the claim must be fairly credible and substantial for the other parties to feel threatened. If the threatening party is not perceived as having the wherewithal to fund the litigation, the other parties may conclude they could outspend the threatening party even if the claim has merit. This is not to say that some concessions will not be made to get rid of a potential irritant, but no party in a negotiation wants to appear easily bluffed. The most common sources of conflict leading to actual or threatened litigation are the issues of priority and valuation, discussed next.

Priority

The relative priority of one claim versus another will, in many cases, be the single most important determinant of recovery or investment return. Figure 12-1 draws upon some of the legal and structural priority concepts developed in Chapters 3 and 7 to present an example that should help reinforce the importance of these issues.

On the left, Boxco is shown in its constituent parts: an operating company, with secured bank and trade credit, and a holding company, with unsecured, unguaranteed senior notes. On the right, Boxco is shown as a consolidated unit with the claims arranged in the normal or expected order of priority. The reorganized value, which will be discussed later under valuation, is just enough

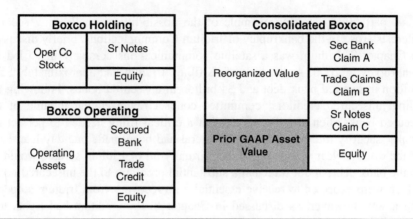

Figure 12-1. Illustration of Importance of Priorities

to cover claims A and B, with a partial recovery to claim C. If the reorganized value changes (and it is important to remember that the real reorganization value likely will not change; only the amount calculated in the plan valuation), some claims may be allocated more or less recovery. However, the importance of priority must be considered. All too often in analyzing a distressed debt investment, assumptions will be made about the relative priority of claims based on security interests, contractual provisions, etc. Most of the time, these assumptions will prove valid. In the restructuring negotiation, however, nothing will be assumed. A, the secured debt, may seem to be entitled to the first-priority position, but what if the validity of its liens can be attacked and it becomes pari passu with B? Or worse, at least for A, what if it is equitably subordinated and falls below C? That would suggest that C gets a full recovery and the equity, which may now include A, is entitled to a partial recovery. Or perhaps Boxco should be substantively consolidated, which could make B and C pari passu. The payout matrix would again shift.

Most of the grounds for challenging priorities were discussed in Chapter 11 under legal due diligence and will not be fully reviewed here. In general, unsecured creditors will always seek to attack the status of the secured creditor if they can. The primary sources of attack[12] are:

- Technical defects in the "perfection" process
- Challenges on voidable preference theories
- Valuation of the collateral
- Equitable subordination due to lender misconduct

A particularly striking example of the possibility of challenging security interests arose in the bankruptcy of Iridium Communications, briefly discussed in Chapter 8. Iridium was a satellite communications company that filed for bankruptcy in 2000. At the time of its filing, Iridium had approximately $500 million in secured bank debt and $4 billion in unsecured bonds. Following the filing, unsecured creditors' committee counsel reviewed the minutia of the secured banks' lien and discovered that a critical filing needed to perfect the banks' security interest in certain collateral had been made one day late. Prior to the discovery, it was assumed that virtually all of Iridium's value would go to the bank debt, and it traded at a substantial premium to the unsecured notes, which were expected to receive essentially no recovery from Iridium's operating assets; however, as discussed in Chapter 8, the creditors had rights to a potentially valuable litigation claim. When news of the possible challenge to the banks' security interest circulated, the bank debt quickly dropped in value and the notes appreciated. Ultimately, the senior notes and bank debt reached a settlement concerning the claim; however, it was very clear that the possible challenge to the banks' secured status gave the unsecured creditors significant negotiating leverage.

Unsecured creditors can also challenge the rights and status of other unsecured creditors. Potential sources of challenge include:

- Invalidity of guarantees
- Substantive consolidation
- Critical creditor/vendor status
- Interpretation of contractual subordination language
- Violations of covenants
- Transfers that might be deemed fraudulent conveyances

As mentioned, oftentimes the issue is not so much the outright merits of the challenge, although clearly it cannot be completely specious, as much as the credibility of the proponent in bringing the charge. This illustrates an important reason why creditors of different standing attempt to get their own committee with a separate, debtor-funded counsel. Challenges offered by a funded committee typically result in more negotiating leverage and the actual commencement of litigation than an objection raised by a minority member of a single committee. That is not to say that it is impossible for claims to be asserted and litigated by a minority member of a single committee, but the dynamic of the committee process, as a practical matter, makes it more difficult. This dynamic is one of the reasons why there may be a bias for combining different classes on the official committee of unsecured creditors; it tends to result in more negotiated, rather than litigated, resolutions.

Secured Creditors

Under the Bankruptcy Code, there are two primary protections for the secured creditor: the adequate protection provisions, mentioned above, and the confirmation requirements. The notion of adequate protection, which is loosely grounded in the U.S. Constitution's Fifth Amendment prohibition against "takings" without due process, means that the secured creditor must be protected against the diminution in the value of the collateral due to the debtor's continued sale or use or from general erosion.

Adequate protection is a fairly vague term under the Bankruptcy Code, which, in addition to stating the concept, provides for three ways in which adequate protection can be provided: (1) a lien on additional property, (2) cash payments, or (3) other relief amounting to the "indubitable equivalent"[13] of the creditor's liens; however, these are not to be viewed as exclusive. The requirement to demonstrate and provide adequate protection arises from three situations: (1) the debtor's request to use, sell, or lease the collateral; (2) the debtor's request to grant a lien of equal or superior status in favor of another creditor, as is common when securing postpetition DIP financing; and (3) the secured creditor's request to have the automatic stay lifted by the bankruptcy court, so that it can repossess the collateral, is denied.[14] As a practical matter, prior to or immediately following the filing, debtor's counsel will conduct negotiations with secured creditors on the subject of adequate protection in an effort to develop a mutually acceptable scheme. In the absence of such an agreement, one of the first moves the secured creditor will make at the beginning of a case is to request that the stay be lifted on all collateral, immediately putting the burden on the debtor to establish "adequate protection." If the parties cannot reach an agreement, then the matter will be argued in the bankruptcy court and the judge will decide. If the scheme of adequate protection agreed to by the creditor or approved by the bankruptcy court over the creditor's objection proves, after the fact, to be inadequate, the secured creditor is allowed a priority administrative claim that is senior to other administrative claims. This priority recovery right provides an incentive to make sure the adequate protection requirement is met; however, it also gives incentives to attack the valuation of the collateral because the lower the collateral's established value, the easier it will be to adequately protect.

This final point raises the all-important issue of collateral valuation. The value of the secured creditor's collateral is critical for at least two reasons. One is the adequate protection issue just mentioned. The other is that the secured creditor is allowed to accrue interest and costs postpetition only to the extent that the value of the collateral exceeds the allowed claim.[15] Thus, if a secured creditor had extended $70 in credit against collateral valued at $100, the creditor would be entitled to accrue and recover at least $30 in such interest and costs (as long as the creditor is legally entitled to under its lending agreement). Given the importance of the valuation issue, one might assume the Bankruptcy Code would provide clear guidance on how to determine the value of collateral, but it is silent both as to the timing (whether the value should be fixed as of the beginning, middle, or end of the case) and methodology, other than the "guidance" in BRC §506(a) that the purpose of the valuation and proposed use or disposition of the collateral should be considered. This presumably prevents a debtor from proposing a "fire-sale" liquidation value when it intends to continue using the collateral in the going concern, but the lack of clear guidance has left the matter to often conflicting case law precedent.[16] Although a low collateral valuation may not entitle the secured creditor to accrue interest under BRC §506, the creditor may be able to extract adequate protection payments that are similar to postpetition interest.

The second source of protection afforded a secured creditor is the confirmation provisions of the Bankruptcy Code. Specifically, BRC §1129 relates to confirming a plan of reorganization over the objection of a creditor class — the so-called "cram-down" provisions ("cram-down" refers to the imposition of the plan over objecting classes and will be discussed in more detail later in this chapter). The cram-down provisions basically provide the "minimum" that a secured class that "objects" to its proposed treatment under the plan must be given.

Valuation

Another inevitable battleground, particularly in complex capital structures, is valuation of the postreorganization enterprise. As illustrated in Figure 12-2,

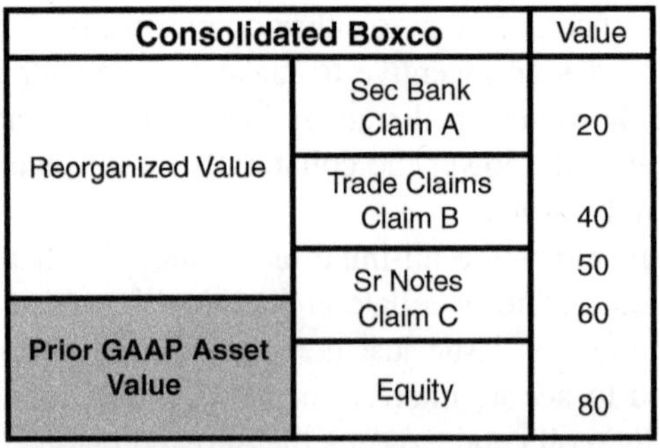

Consolidated Boxco		Value
Reorganized Value	Sec Bank Claim A	20
	Trade Claims Claim B	40
	Sr Notes Claim C	50
		60
Prior GAAP Asset Value	Equity	80

Figure 12-2. Boxco Recoveries with Values

which is the same as Figure 12-1 with values added, valuation is critical because it defines the size of the pie that gets split up. In this illustration, the implied valuation is 50, with claims through B of 40. Accordingly, if the plan of reorganization does not provide for some recovery to C, that class will have a strong objection (depending on expenses and other value deductions) because it appears to be "in the money." Similarly, if the plan of reorganization allocates no recovery to the equity but that class wants to challenge the treatment as unfair, at confirmation the equity class will have to try and convince the bankruptcy court that Boxco is worth more than 60.

It is worth reiterating that the valuation used in the chapter 11 process and the "true" value of a firm may not necessarily be the same, and senior classes will always have an incentive to argue for a "conservative" valuation because it can be used to justify excluding or limiting the participation of other creditors in the recovery. Returning to the example, if the valuation had been 40 instead of 50, theoretically no part of reorganized Boxco would need to be shared with C, which at the 50 valuation would have received a 50% recovery. If after confirmation in the open trading market it turned out that Boxco was worth 60, B would have received a windfall and C would feel justly mistreated.

From Figure 12-2 it is fairly easy to see some of the basic tensions that arise in the valuation process. The following are some generalizations about the biases certain classes may have in the valuation of a reorganized entity:[17]

- **Debtor**: Debtor's constituents, especially the equity (which may include management), are typically served by a relatively higher valuation that implies that value should be allocated to the lowest classes.
- **Management**: Management generally prefers a low valuation because most plans of reorganization provide equity incentive compensation (e.g., options or warrants) to management, which are priced in conjunction with the plan valuation. Thus, if the plan valuation turns out to be conservative, management's incentive compensation will immediately appreciate. An exception to this general proposition may be merited when management owns a significant share of the equity. In this case, management interests are likely more aligned with the debtor, and a higher valuation would be preferred to allow management to retain some of its prior equity. Management may also have an incentive to argue for a low valuation (especially if the executives are relatively new to the debtor) in order to be able to demonstrate large improvements in the company's performance after emergence from bankruptcy, due, no doubt, to the executives' skill.
- **Secured creditors**: The valuation interests of the secured creditors will have a bias toward low valuations, but the extent of the bias will depend

on the objectives of the then secured debt holder. If the secured debt is primarily held by the original bank lending syndicate, then the lenders' general desire for a low valuation may be tempered by a desire for the value to be sufficient to justify that some amount of secured debt be reinstated in the capital structure (and given to the secured creditors) so that the entire recovery is not in a volatile, nonearning asset such as equity. On the other hand, if a distressed debt investor whose strategy is to control the postreorganization equity has purchased the secured debt, then there will be a strong bias for as conservative a valuation as possible.

- **Senior unsecured creditors**: It is difficult to generalize about the bias of the senior unsecured creditors, which are likely to control the committee and strongly influence the selection of the financial advisor. If there is a significant amount of secured debt, then the unsecured creditors will want a higher valuation that dictates they will share in the recovery. If there is no or minimal secured debt, then the unsecured creditors will be in a very similar position as the secured debt. If mutual funds and insurance companies largely still hold the unsecured bonds, then there may be a bias for a low valuation, but with some recovery in the form of debt. However, if equity-oriented distressed debt investors have accumulated a significant stake, the bias may be toward receiving mainly equity.
- **Subordinated unsecured creditors**: Like the equity, if there is any meaningful amount of senior debt relative to enterprise value, the subordinated creditors are very vulnerable to getting squeezed out in the valuation process and, accordingly, usually will have a bias toward a high value, except in the rare cases where that could lead to value being distributed to the equity. If there is no senior debt, as was fairly common in late 1990s technology companies whose only debt was subordinated convertible debt, then the subordinated debt effectively becomes the senior debt and should have a bias back toward a low valuation.

The initial process of developing the valuation used in the plan of reorganization is the responsibility of the debtor's financial advisor. Depending on how contentious the relationship with the unsecured creditors' committee is, the preliminary valuation likely will be shared with the committee as part of the process of trying to negotiate an acceptable plan. Of course, if the secured debt is a large part of the capital structure and it is likely that it will be impaired under the plan, it also should be included in the negotiation of the plan.

When the relationship between the debtor and the unsecured creditors' committee is contentious or where the secured debt is a significant factor in the negotiation, then a valuation that is deemed inaccurate by the committee (which could be either low because of the secured debt influence or high out of a desire to provide for the equity) may result in a valuation battle. In a full-fledged valuation contest, creditors or equity interest holders that believe the treatment of various claims is illegal or unfair will challenge, at the confirmation hearing, the valuation contained in the disclosure statement and upon which the plan of reorganization is premised. The bankruptcy court, which in almost all cases would prefer the parties to come to some type of consensus, will hear the conflicting testimony of the debtor's and committee's or other challenger's financial advisors. Often, in the process or brinkmanship involved in the hearing, the parties will come to a compromise. Otherwise, they will force the bankruptcy court to decide the debtor's value for them and have to live with a decision they may not like.[18]

VOTING AND CONFIRMATION

Following the bankruptcy court's approval of a disclosure statement, the proponent of the plan, typically the debtor, distributes the plan, disclosure statement, and ballots to impaired creditors and equity holders of record and begins the process of trying to elicit support for the plan. As a practical matter, most of the lobbying, which is usually done by the debtor's financial advisor, needs to be done up front because making minor modifications to gain the support of different creditors can require an amendment, another disclosure statement hearing, a second bankruptcy court approval, and a recirculation of voting materials — all of which take time and cost money. However, the debtor (typically the proponent of the plan) must continue to attempt to hold together support as different creditor factions may be working to build opposition against the plan.

Voting

The complexity of the voting process largely will be driven by the relative complexity of the capital structure. The plan, within the constraints of the Bankruptcy Code, can propose the segregation of claims and interests into various classes. The plan then will state whether the class is impaired and has the right to vote. Unimpaired classes are not entitled to vote. As mentioned before, the notion of impairment is very broad; effectively, a claim must be either paid off in full or reinstated under identical terms to be unimpaired. Any other treatment (even improvements) likely will be judged as an impairment. For a class to approve a plan, 66.7% of those voting in amount and more than 50.0% in number must approve. If a class does not approve the plan, then the proposed plan will fail unless the cram-down provisions can be satisfied.

While fairly simple on its face, there are many intricacies to the voting process. Many of the nuances come into play only in exceptional cases and are difficult, if not impossible, to anticipate. Accordingly, they are of limited use on a prospective basis by a distressed investor attempting to analyze a situation. For example, sometimes a plan proponent may attempt to gerrymander classes in a way most likely to garner approval. Other times, either plan proponents or opponents will challenge votes, alleging they were cast in bad faith (consider a situation where a competitor of the debtor purchases claims at a discount and then votes against a plan of reorganization because the creditor/competitor would prefer the debtor be liquidated). These issues[19] may be critically important when they in fact arise, but the risks are seldom understood well enough before then to affect the valuation of securities, particularly at any point prior to the proposal of a plan, and most distressed investing is done at much earlier stages of the process.

Often the process of building support for a plan among diverse constituencies will appear similar to getting a bill through Congress. Since legislation requires majority approval to pass, legislators may be able to negotiate certain modifications to satisfy one or another special interests in exchange for their vote. Sometimes provisions will be added that, objectively speaking, are extraneous to the original scheme of the legislation. This is inherent to the democratic process. Similarly, as a plan is being fashioned, especially in situations where there is a constructive dialogue between the debtor and the committee, a certain amount of "horse trading" will occur. Returning to Figure 12-2, the senior notes of Boxco, claim C, might be threatening to litigate the issue of substantive consolidation because they want more than a 50% recovery. To help keep the process moving, perhaps B will give up some of its recovery, say some of the equity, in return for a partial cash payout under the plan. Or perhaps the equity, which appears to be getting shut out, is threatening to litigate the valuation, claiming that Boxco is worth 60. This time, perhaps both B and C agree to give the equity some warrants, with a strike price based on a value of 60, in order to build consensus. This process, which in particular gives value to claims that would appear to be out-of-the-money, is called *tipping*. In the congressional context, it might be called "pork barrel." A layman would just call it buying votes. Regardless of the characterization, it is a part of the bankruptcy scheme and was a process that the legislators who framed and voted on the modern Bankruptcy Code understood and condoned.

One voting issue that the distressed investor needs to understand clearly is the negotiating implications of the blocking position. The two-pronged voting requirement — 66.7% in amount and more than 50% in number — was designed to prevent one large holder from imposing its will on a class where the majority (in number) objects to the proposed treatment. However, the 66.7% in amount test implies that any investor (or group thereof) that accumulates a 33.4% position in the claims of a class can prevent approval by voting no. This is a blocking position; the investor cannot enforce its will, but can stymie the process. A blocking position is strategically very significant because it provides considerable leverage. From the standpoint of the plan proponent, it means they either have to give the blocking position what it wants (which may not necessarily be what everyone else in the class ideally wants) or be prepared to struggle through a cram-down. Since a cram-down, as will be discussed, often is challenging and prevents certain claim settlement options, this gives the owner of the blocking position significant power. If the blocking position is in a critical piece of secured debt that will be impaired, it can be even more powerful.

One strategy a debtor will use to minimize the effect of a potential blocking position is to include the claim in a class with other claims so that the holder's position no longer exceeds 33.4% of the class. For example, assume, going back to Figure 12-2, that Boxco should be substantively consolidated, which makes claim B (the operating company trade debt) and claim C (the holding company senior notes) pari passu. Block Partners, a distressed investor, has acquired 45% of claim C. The debtor may have been considering putting the bond issue and the trade claims in separate unsecured classes in order to tailor its payout to its preferences. For example, the debtor may have been considering giving the bonds some new paper and equity, while offering the trade claims a discounted payoff in cash (funded either out of accumulated cash reserves or exit financing). However, if Block Partners has indicated that it wants its Class C to receive 100% of the equity, management, which may believe its days are numbered under Block Partners' ownership, may combine the bonds and trade claims together in one class so that Block Partners' bond stake does not represent a blocking position for the combined class. Of course, if Block Partners had accumulated its position in claim A, a secured claim, this strategy would not work since secured claims are required to be segregated into classes in accordance with the underlying collateral.

Confirmation

Following the voting, the final event of the chapter 11 process is confirmation. Confirmation is an affirmative ruling by the bankruptcy court that approves the plan of reorganization and sets the stage for it to become effective. Even if all impaired classes have approved a plan, it still requires bankruptcy court review to be confirmed. If the notion that creditors get to vote to accept a proposed bankruptcy is likened to democracy, then the confirmation provisions of BRC §1129 should be viewed as tempering the process into one of limited democracy. The confirmation step was essentially designed to ensure that certain minimal creditor protections enshrined in the Bankruptcy Code are always observed — a bill of rights. For example, imagine Boxco management and claims A and B go into a smoke-filled back room and hammer out a deal among themselves. The next day, a plan is proposed with an indicated valuation of 35, which proposes that all claims will be paid in equity, with A, B and management receiving 45, 45, and 10%, respectively. C and the existing equity will be wiped out. In the subsequent vote, the plan is approved by A and B and objected to by C. Confirmation is essentially C's "due process" protection that its minimum rights will be considered. This due process requires the court to independently conclude that certain confirmation standards have been satisfied. It also allows individual creditors to raise objections to confirmation, even if they are part of a class that has voted to approve the plan.

BRC §1129 charges the bankruptcy court with the obligation to find that a plan satisfies a lengthy list of specific requirements before it can be confirmed. These were discussed in Chapter 4, where the requirements were split and characterized as largely procedural in nature or requiring a subjective assessment by the bankruptcy court. Although objections relating to confirmability occasionally are raised with respect to the procedural items (e.g., was the U.S. Trustee paid, were requisite governmental approvals obtained, were postconfirmation officers and directors disclosed, etc.), the primary battleground is usually on the more subjective tests: Is the plan feasible, was it proposed in good faith, and is it in the best interests of the creditors? While these are inherently subjective, in practice, the case law that has developed under these provisions tends to limit the scope of allegations that can be raised successfully. The basic premise appears to be that so long as the various classes are voting to accept a plan, the procedural safeguards only need to go so far.

Additional safeguards, however, arise when a class rejects a plan and the proponent of the plan nonetheless requests that the plan be imposed on the objecting class. This is the essence of a cram-down. For a plan to be crammed down on an objecting class, there are three requirements: (1) at least one impaired class must vote in favor of the plan, without counting the votes of insiders; (2) the plan may not unfairly discriminate against the objecting class; and (3) the plan must be fair and equitable with respect to the objecting class.

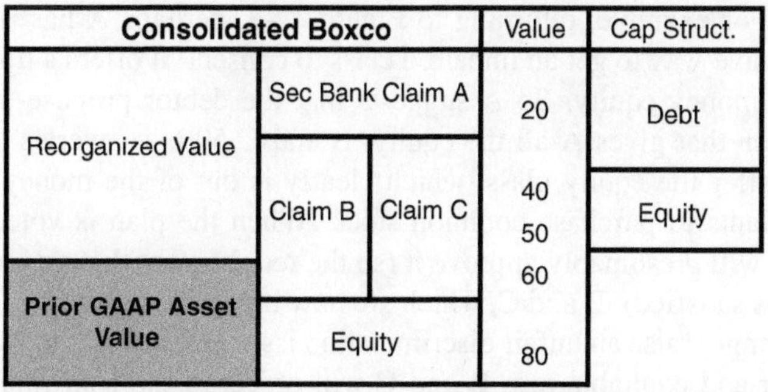

Consolidated Boxco			Value	Cap Struct.
Reorganized Value	Sec Bank Claim A		20	Debt
	Claim B	Claim C	40	Equity
			50	
			60	
Prior GAAP Asset Value	Equity		80	

Figure 12-3. Boxco Recoveries in Substantive Consolidation Scenario

The unfair discrimination test requires that any differences in treatment afforded to different classes must be fair. Since all claims within a class must be accorded identical treatment, the main purpose of creating separate classes of claims with similar priority is to give them different treatment. Thus, a degree of discrimination is okay, as long as it is not "unfair." Consider Figure 12-3, which essentially is Figure 12-2 with the assumption that, for purposes of the plan, Boxco was substantively consolidated, which effectively makes claims B and C pari passu unsecured claims. Earlier it was suggested that either the debtor or the creditors themselves might have an interest in the B and C claims being in separate classes so that treatment could be shaped to their preferences; the trade claims (B) might prefer cash, while the notes (C) might prefer new paper and equity. If the trade creditors are not being paid off in full, both classes are clearly impaired and entitled to vote. Assume that the trade creditors are negotiating for a higher payout; perhaps they were originally offered 70%, but they want 75%. If their demand is not met, they will be able to credibly threaten to reject the plan by raising classification issues or, in the event the plan reaches a cram-down process, argue that the plan unfairly discriminated because they did not get any equity, whereas the pari passu notes (C) did.

The second test under the cram-down provisions is the fair and equitable test. This test has very different rules depending on whether the objecting claim is secured or unsecured. One main effect of this test in the case of unsecured debt is fairly simple: No claim junior to the objecting class can receive any recovery unless the objecting class's claims are paid in full — essentially, strict enforcement of the absolute priority rule. The reasons for this structure are presumably grounded in fairness, but also serve to cut off an obvious source of abuse. For example, returning to Figure 12-3, perhaps A has figured out a less expensive way to get an impaired class to consent: it offers a tip to the well-out-of-the-money equity. So A suggests that the debtor propose a plan of re-organization that gives A all the equity, B and C 50% recoveries in new debt, and then offer the equity class, which clearly is out of the money, a "gift" of some warrants to purchase common stock. When the plan is voted on, A and the equity will presumably approve it (so the requirement that an impaired class approves is satisfied). B and C, which are now being treated equally, may object but they cannot raise an unfair discrimination issue. However, they are protected by the fair and equitable test. B and C will object to the confirmability of the plan because they are impaired and a junior class (the equity) is receiving a recovery.[20]

This seems very reasonable when that which is being prevented is clearly abusive or manipulative. But what if the reason for the tip to the equity class was because that class was raising various litigation issues that could be expensive and require significant time to resolve — comparable to a filibuster within the legislative context? If the plan was unconfirmable because of the tip, when it is amended to eliminate the tip, the equity class may follow through with its litigation and cause significant delays. There is nothing wrong, per se, in this outcome; it just once again forces all the constituencies to come up with a mutually acceptable plan.

There are at least two lessons here. First, if the plan employs various tips to garner the support or at least acquiescence of various constituencies, then the proponent must count votes accurately because such plans can only be confirmed where all impaired classes are supportive; if one class objects, it can force the entire confirmation strategy to be rethought.

Second, since "tipping" is a very common, if not expected, part of the plan consensus-building process, investors in more senior claims may want to budget in potential "tip giving" that could reduce their expected recovery. Conversely, out-of-the-money junior claims often are a bet on how big a tip can be extracted. Besides the perceived strength of the class's negotiating leverage or nuisance value, in gauging the magnitude of the tip that might be feasible to extract it is important to bear in mind the relative size of the "tip-giving" and "tip-receiving" classes. The larger the tip-giving class is relative to the tip-receiving class, the lower the cost of the tip will appear on a relative basis. For example, if a $250 senior note class is trying to induce the cooperation of a $50 preferred stock class, a 2-point give up by the senior would result in a 10-point improvement to the preferred holders — a substantial windfall if they are arguably out-of-the-money.

The protection given to prepetition secured creditors under the cram-down provisions is also significant, although the applicability of this protection usually is limited since typically prepetition secured creditors, particularly those secured by working capital, will have been either paid off or converted into postpetition secured debt because of the debtor's need to use the collateral. Postpetition creditors, of course, have administrative claim status that requires complete satisfaction (i.e., payment in cash or the creditor's consent) as a requirement of confirmation.[21] Thus, an unsecured creditor is extremely vulnerable when the debtor's circumstances are such that exit financing cannot be obtained in an amount sufficient to pay off all administrative claims; frequently this is a reason why a rights offering to raise new cash from creditors is included in plans of reorganization.

In those minority of cases that involve an effort to confirm a plan over the objection of an impaired prepetition secured creditor,[22] which usually are limited to situations involving liens or mortgages on fixed assets, the minimum requirement, absent a BRC §1111(b) election (discussed next), is (a) if the collateral is sold, that the lien attach to the proceeds or (b) if the collateral is used, the creditor be allowed to retain the lien to the extent of the allowed claim[23] and receive a stream of payments with a present value equal to the lesser of the value of the collateral or the allowed claim.[24] In the event of the BRC §1111(b) election, the creditor waives its right to an unsecured claim for the amount it is undersecured in exchange for (1) a lien equal to the face amount of the claim and (2) a stream of payments with a gross amount equal to the face amount of the claim but a present value[25] equal to the lesser of the value of the collateral or the allowed claim.

Working through to the essence of these provisions, and avoiding the issue of whether present value is appropriately determined, the spirit of the cram-down provisions is that the secured claim must, at a minimum, receive a new secured piece of paper with a present value equal to the secured portion of the allowed claim, although, absent a BRC §1111(b) election, whatever overcollateralization the creditor may have had can be eliminated by stripping down the lien to the amount of the allowed claim. Accordingly, if a plan of reorganization proposes to, for example, partially equitize a secured claim, either because the secured claim is high relative to enterprise value or in light of other contemplated postconfirmation secured financing, the plan likely will need to be acceptable to the secured class (i.e., affirmatively voted upon) or it will have strong grounds to challenge confirmability of the plan.[26] Thus, anytime the debtor and the committee face a situation where in order to make a postconfirmation capital structure viable they must ask the secured class to accept equity or an unsecured claim as partial compensation, the secured creditor has significant bargaining leverage.

SUMMARY

The process of developing a confirmable plan of reorganization is a fairly complex exercise in democratic process. The fact that the Bankruptcy Code envisions a system where the disadvantaged creditors are given a right to vote on their treatment basically creates a system where the bankruptcy court is not deciding who gets what as much as it is playing referee in a process. Thus, developing a confirmable plan of reorganization requires not only careful compliance with myriad legal requirements, but, in most cases, the negotiated support of many constituencies as well. The process of piecing together this support is somewhat analogous to the process of trying to win bipartisan support for a piece of legislation; concessions often will be made to this or that special interest to garner sufficient support. The distressed investor, as a creditor, is part of this process. He or she can attempt to use his or her position to win concessions from others and must recognize that other constituencies will use whatever leverage they have to win concessions from the distressed investor. It is often a messy process.

The plan of reorganization approval process is generally the "endgame" of the investment process. The investment will typically be made well ahead of the filing, let alone the plan negotiation process. The investor's analysis, depending on the investment strategy, will have led to assumptions about how the reorganization process will evolve. The primary drivers of return expectation will be valuation and priority. Both of these are pivotal issues in the formal reorganization process. But there are also many other issues that, at the margin, can affect the timing and form of recoveries. Accordingly, unless an investor has amassed a significant position such that he or she is a proactive participant in the process, most of the analysis of the potential dynamics is needed before the investment. Oftentimes many unforeseeable events will arise; this is just part of the risk profile of distressed investing.

The final chapter of the book addresses a few of the considerations the distressed investor must bear in mind even after a plan of reorganization has been implemented and remains effective. The confirmation of a plan of reorganization will determine the form of the recovery, but absent situations involving cash, the value of that recovery will be a function of events and trading markets following the confirmation of the plan of reorganization. The investor needs to be aware of these dynamics to best manage the last step. Investments begin with dollars and they must ultimately end in dollars, but the final conversion typically happens after the chapter 11 process is concluded.

> **This Chapter's Chess Moves**
> 26. Qc2, Bxa4
> **White Resigns**

13

POSTREORGANIZATION CONSIDERATIONS

A common element of virtually all investments, distressed or otherwise, is that at some point they need to be returned to cash. Clients give investment managers cash to manage with the expectation that at some point they will receive cash back. The nature of the investment strategy and the evolution of market events will dictate the appropriate time and method to close out or conclude those investments. If it is an investment premised on a short-term market misvaluation, then the point at which the market appropriately adjusts may be the correct time to close out the investment. Depending on the volatility and responsiveness of the markets, the investment could be a day, a week, a month, or longer. In most of these strategies, the investment will come to a close by selling the identical security that was purchased — but hopefully at a price that results in the investor making a profit. Bonds, unlike stocks, have a finite life, and thus another possible outcome is that a bond matures or is optionally redeemed (i.e., called by the issuer) or mandatorily redeemed (i.e., put by the investor). In these cases, the investor simply has his or her principal returned, potentially with a premium. This is essentially the same as selling at 100[1] and thus presumably is profitable if the security was purchased at a discount.

In many distressed debt investment scenarios, however, the strategy may be to hold the debt investment through the completion of a restructuring and then realize an investment return through securities received following the reorganization. The classic scenario is to own a company's postreorganization equity through an earlier investment in its distressed debt. Bonds or bank debt are purchased at a discount on the expectation that, in the reorganization, those claims will receive equity in the reorganized entity that will be worth substantially more. As has been explained in the previous chapters, care must go into the identification of both the proper company and the security that must be purchased in order for the investment strategy to be successful. However, to maximize this success, care must also be taken in the last step — the disposition of those securities. That is, appropriately, the subject of this final chapter.

Generally speaking, there are several types of securities that can be realized at the conclusion of a reorganization. The most common types include new equity instruments, debt instruments, and interests in liquidating trusts. Each of these general categories will be reviewed and considered from the perspective of maximizing investment return.

POSTREORGANIZATION EQUITIES

In virtually all chapter 11 reorganizations, with the possible exception of those in which the filing was caused by a near-term liquidity event, some portion of the capital structure will be transmuted from a liability or debt to equity. This makes the distribution of new equity, which is commonly referred to as "back-end" equity, a fairly common feature of plans of reorganization (plans). During the preconfirmation phase of a restructuring, much attention will be given to how much equity is created (i.e., the relative debt versus equity composition of the postreorganization capital structure) and to which creditors it will be distributed. Both of these determinations can have significant ramifications for how the new stock is valued after the entity emerges and thus should be considered during the formulation of the plan of reorganization.

At first blush, the amount and distribution of equity would seem irrelevant to valuation.[2] As a general matter of finance theory, this may be correct, although many academic studies have debated whether or not leverage can impact valuation. However, there do appear to be a variety of issues that, from a technical market perspective, can impact valuation. Two of the more prominent issues are the size of the expected market capitalization and the magnitude of share float.

Size of Expected or Probable Market Capitalization

Basic economic supply/demand principles suggest that the more potential buyers of a stock, the better the chance that demand for a fixed supply of shares will lead to the stock's maximum potential valuation. Stock issued pursuant to a bankruptcy is freely tradable[3] and thus theoretically can be purchased by anyone from the creditors to whom is it distributed. As a practical matter, however, significant portions of the institutional investor marketplace, which commands the vast majority of investment capital, may not invest in stocks of small-capitalization companies. There are two reasons for this phenomenon. First, institutional investors generally want to be able to commit a significant amount of investment dollars to any particular situation. Like the distressed investor, a portfolio manager who is going to commit the resources to analyze a situation will want to know that he or she can invest enough to make it worth the time and expense. Second, public equity investors tend to prize liquidity, as measured by the average amount (in both dollars and shares) of stock trading on a daily basis. The portfolio manager will generally want to know that he or she can accumulate a meaningful stake in a relatively short period of time without putting undue price pressure on the market and — just as important — exit a position as efficiently as possible. Accordingly, the minimum market capitalization generally required by small- and micro-cap funds is $500 million and $50 million, respectively.[4] In other words, these important categories of potential back-end equity investors, which in aggregate represent over $160 billion in assets,[5] will tend to avoid, or may be precluded from, investing in firms with equity capitalizations below these thresholds.

The notion that small-capitalization companies often are undervalued has been the subject of many academic studies.[6] These studies have generally approached the question from the perspective of trying to prove or disprove the so-called "small-cap effect." The small-cap effect is basically the proposition that small-cap managers can outperform larger cap managers because the latter have an inherently smaller universe of securities in which to invest. Early studies suggested that there was strong empirical support for the proposition.[7] However, more recent studies argue that once relatively higher management fees and costs are factored in, there is no statistically significant advantage.[8] What is implicit in the theory is that smaller capitalization companies have a greater likelihood of being undervalued, which is why investors in these securities potentially can outperform their larger cap peers. The fact that recent studies suggest that professional investors cannot exploit this misvaluation due to transaction costs does not dispute the premise that small-cap securities may, in certain instances, be undervalued. This will be called the "small-cap penalty."

The practical implication of this observation is that postconfirmation capitalization should, where possible, be formulated to avoid incurring the potential small-cap penalty.[9] Where the enterprise value of the debtor is small, there may be little that can be done. However, for debtors with an enterprise value in excess of $500 million, the standard small-cap equity threshold, thoughtful planning can minimize the risk of incurring the small-cap penalty. In many cases, the key issue will be the amount of leverage that is placed on the postreorganization enterprise. If enterprise value is, for example, $700 million and only a $100 million working capital exit financing is put in place, the implied market equity capitalization is a comfortable $600 million. However, if creditor constituencies that prefer recoveries in the form of debt lobby for $300 million of debt in the capital structure,[10] then the implied equity capitalization is a below-threshold $400 million.

Sometimes a distressed investor's strategic objectives — for example, to control a significant percentage of the postreorganization equity — may complicate the postconfirmation equity decision. This strategy could drive an investor with sufficient negotiating leverage to insist on a plan that allocates recoveries to other creditors in the form of debt, so that the control investor's class retains the equity. In these situations, the investor must weigh the potential trade-offs between control and optimum valuation technicals.

Postreorganization Trading Float

Valuation may also be affected by trading liquidity. As mentioned before, most institutional investment managers prize liquidity. Thus, in addition to market capitalization, a second technical factor they will consider is market float. Returning to the previous example, even if the firm emerges from chapter 11 with an implied equity capitalization of $600 million, if it is clear that control-type investors will hold 50% of the equity, the portfolio manager may again avoid investment, recognizing that the "effective" or "investable" market capitalization is only $300 million. So both the absolute and effectively available market capitalization are technical factors that can affect the relative interest of institutional investors.

Unless a distressed investor is activist-oriented and has a significant stake, in most situations he or she will have very little influence on the postreorganization capital structure. In these situations, the investor will want to carefully analyze the plan of reorganization's implied postconfirmation equity capitalization and likely composition of the holders. If because of the size of the equity capitalization or the composition of its expected holders the investor feels a valuation penalty may be applied, he or she will want to weigh this in considering his or her exit strategy. Usually during the period between when a plan is proposed and confirmed, the market trading prices of the prepetition securities begin to reflect, albeit typically at some discount, expected postreorganization values. Often these expected values will be significantly influenced by the valuation set forth in the disclosure statement. If the investor is concerned that technical or other factors may cause the reorganized equity to trade at values that are lower than what the investor considers "fair value," he or she needs to weigh the discount incurred by selling early against that potentially incurred later. Depending on the situation, an investor may reach the conclusion that the highest return (particularly when the time value of money is taken into consideration) may be realized by selling his or her prepetition securities before the confirmation and purchasing the equity after it has started trading. If the equity trades poorly, but the investor still has conviction concerning the firm's ultimate value, the sell-off may allow for investment at an even more attractive valuation. Particularly if the investor can sell the securities before confirmation for a gain, the market risk on emergence is greatly mitigated.

When the investor retains his or her prepetition claims through confirmation and subsequently receives equity, he or she still faces the decision of when and how to sell his or her shares. In developing an exit strategy, a number of factors should be considered. However, regardless of this forethought, once the stock begins trading, actual market behavior may dictate the decision. It is important to note that when plans are confirmed and it is, therefore, highly likely that the debtor will emerge from bankruptcy with the capital structure proposed in the plan, a "when-issued" market will often develop for the postreorganization stock. A when-issued market is an over-the-counter market that trades the right to receive a share of stock at the moment it is technically available for delivery.[11] The when-issued market can be used by holders to manage their holding risk during the period between confirmation and the effective date of the plan, which is when an investor will technically possess the new security provided for under the plan.

Forced Sellers

Banks and collateralized debt obligations (CDOs) are not natural holders of equity securities.[12] The business model of these entities causes them to significantly prefer income earning assets as opposed to equities. Over and above the business model considerations, these entities may face regulatory or contractual restrictions on holding equities. For example, banks that take equity in exchange for debt, whether through in-court or out-of-court restructurings, generally are required to dispose of that equity within two years after receipt[13] and the security receives unfavorable capital treatment[14] during the period it is held. Similarly, CDOs usually have contractual limitations on the absolute amount of and length of time they are allowed to hold equity. The limitations placed on banks and CDOs are typically designed to discourage holding equities, but not to make the entities hostages of the market. Hence they provide some holding period flexibility so as not to make them immediate, known forced sellers. Nonetheless, when such entities are known to be large holders of the postreorganization equity, other market participants will certainly consider their net sell disposition.

To address this problem, plans sometimes will be structured to provide CDOs with an alternative, nonequity form of recovery. For example, assume that in a particular reorganization, the secured lenders were going to receive their recovery, estimated at 40%, in the form of equity. If much of the secured debt had been purchased in the secondary market by hedge funds, this might not present a problem since these types of investors generally can hold equity securities indefinitely. However, if 20% was held by CDOs, the equity recovery would be less desirable. The plan of reorganization could provide these holders with the option of receiving an economically equivalent recovery in the form of attractively structured debt.[15]

Company Profile

Another factor affecting postconfirmation equity valuation can be the relative lack of market awareness of a company. When a company files for bankruptcy, it often is faced with the daunting task of developing an entirely new market constituency and "persona." Stock analysts who followed the firm before it became financially distressed likely will have dropped their equity coverage, recognizing that the investment outlook for the prepetition equity holders was poor. Institutional equity investors that lost money in the stock the first time may be reluctant to immediately reinvest a second time. Thus, particularly in the case of smaller market capitalization debtors that emerge, it can be challenging for them to attract market awareness and sponsorship. These considerations can have significant implications for exit or postconfirmation financing strategies. For example, a debtor may want to consider various options for exit financing. Typically, most exit financing is in the form of a bank facility of some type. While bank facilities are likely the easiest to arrange and potentially the lowest cost, the arrangement of these facilities often will involve a relatively few institutions, most of which have little or anything to do with equity.

In contrast, a debtor might consider a bond offering, which could significantly enhance institutional investors' market awareness of the firm. The typical marketing process for a bond offering involves what is known as a "road show." A road show is a marketing tour, generally arranged by the underwriter or placement agent,[16] in which management of the issuer discusses the issuer's business outlook with investors. Road shows usually stop at most of the major financial centers (New York, Boston, Chicago, San Francisco, and Los Angeles for U.S. domestic offerings) and can include breakfast and/or lunch presentations, where multiple institutional investors are invited, and one-on-one visits with the largest institutions in the area. While a bond road show will be targeted to fixed income investors, the sponsor also likely will encourage equity investors to attend (for example, if a mutual fund's high-yield analyst will attend the road show, the sponsor may invite the fund's small-cap equity analyst) to get a better understanding of the reorganized company's outlook.[17] Compared to a traditional bank-provided exit facility, the bond offering involves more risk since it is difficult to predict ahead of time whether the offering will be feasible and what its cost will be, but it has the definite advantage of creating a marketing opportunity to institutions.[18]

Apart from the exit financing, a debtor may also want to plan on making a public securities offering of some type following the company's emergence. Sometimes attempting a public offering in conjunction with exit financing may be difficult or inappropriate because of the firm's most recent operating performance. Bankruptcy is obviously not a period when a firm tends to post outstanding financial results. A business tends to operate at below peak efficiency, restructuring expenses reduce free cash flow, and the future outlook may be very uncertain. In these cases, which is probably the majority, a firm likely will be better served by emerging, recording several quarters of financial performance in its postreorganized form, and then approaching the capital markets with, it is hoped, positive operating momentum. The goal and process still will be the same: to use the process of a security offering to focus institutional investor and sell-side analyst interest on the reorganized company. To the extent that this strategy is either expressed or reasonably foreseeable, the distressed investor may want to factor this into his or her strategy of when to sell.

Postconfirmation Lockups

In cases where the investors that likely will be in control of the postreorganization equity have the ability to hold the securities and they perceive that the equity may trade poorly (because of the technical factors reviewed above), it may be in their interest to prevent or limit trading in the equity following confirmation. This can be true for at least two reasons. First, the investors may want to avoid the risk of potentially taking a severe mark-to-market loss on their positions (which often will be initially valued at the plan of reorganization valuation) due to the poor initial trading. Second, once a stock trades down, it tends to affect investor perception and can result in technical issues that can make it more difficult to attain its "true" valuation. For example, if a stock trades down to $2 a share, investors will always associate $2 as being the potential downside. Thus, the stock's perceived risk profile can increase. Also, if the stock starts trading up, investors that bought at lower levels may become sellers, creating resistance points on the rebound. For these reasons, the controlling investors may be better off foregoing liquidity for a period of time. This can be accomplished by voluntarily entering into a restricted stock agreement[19] among themselves, although there may be other approaches as well.[20] In sum, it may be desirable to initially take the emerged company private and then, once the company's postbankruptcy operating performance is fully demonstrated, provide for registration rights or plan a stock offering or other security in which an underwriter will be used to help raise investor awareness of the firm.[21]

Tax-Based Trading Restrictions

Another potential impediment to a stock's trading is restrictions imposed due to tax considerations. The most common of these is to preserve net operating loss (NOL) carryforwards. As discussed in Chapter 11, under IRC §382 a firm's ability to use previously incurred NOLs to shield future income may be limited if a change in ownership is deemed to occur. The test for determining whether or not a change of ownership has occurred, although complex, basically relates to changes in the holdings of shareholders with more than 5% of the stock. Accordingly, when firms emerge from bankruptcy with substantial unrestricted NOLs, the plan of reorganization or the firm's revised articles of incorporation may preclude shareholders from making purchases that would cause them to become 5% holders.[22] While tax-oriented restrictions on balance serve to maximize the value of a firm, they can limit the purchase activity of certain holders and thus inherently limit the potential demand for shares.

Warrants

While shares of a reorganized entity's common stock likely will be the most common and plentiful form of equity distributed under a plan of reorganization, oftentimes plans provide for different constituencies to receive various types of warrants to purchase equity. As discussed in Chapter 12, warrants can be a very useful tool to try to orchestrate support for a plan of reorganization. Warrants give the holder an economic interest in a firm, but also require the holder to pay cash upon exercise (i.e. the strike price of the warrant) to purchase a share of its stock. Investors presumably are better off because they generally would not exercise warrants unless the stock was higher than the exercise price. On the other hand, where the strike price is above the plan of reorganization's projected value, the firm is effectively, relative to the plan, receiving a premium. Warrants are typically freely tradable when issued but generally are less liquid than the underlying stock simply because a much smaller number will be issued.

Trading Performance of Back-End Equities

It is difficult to generalize about the trading performance of back-end equities. The conventional wisdom is that back-end equities should perform relatively well both because of the conservative valuation bias in most plans of reorga-

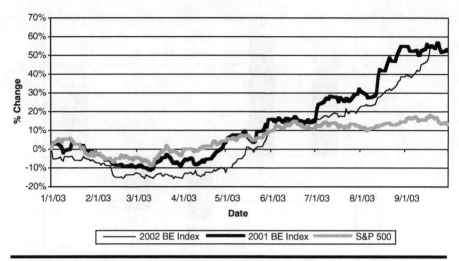

Figure 13-1. 2003 Performance of Back-End Equities Versus S&P 500 (Source: Imperial Capital and Bloomberg)

nization[23] and because usually it is feasible for the newly emerged entity to post strong results relative to the periods when it was in bankruptcy, thus making it appear to grow faster than its industry peers. However, these factors can easily be offset by technical factors such as significant stock overhang from technical sellers and an absence of market data about and/or sponsorship for a firm. During 2003, back-end equities that emerged during the most recent cycle posted a remarkable performance and significantly outperformed the S&P 500.[24] Interestingly, as shown in Figure 13-1, this occurred regardless of whether the stock emerged in 2001, and therefore should have been relatively well "seasoned" by the beginning of 2003, or in 2002.[25]

More generally, academic studies have tended to find empirical support for the proposition that back-end equities outperform market averages.[26] A 1998 study concluded that outperformance is most pronounced during the first 200 days after a stock emerges and in those situations where institutional investors demanded to receive only equity in the restructuring.[27] The latter, of course, suggests that knowledgeable insiders had a strong view that the equity was undervalued.[28] A more recent study, which was based on an analysis of 117 significant postreorganization equities that emerged between 1986 and 2003, also suggested that back-end equities outperform market averages.[29] This study made a number of interesting observations. For example, unlike the case with "hot" initial public offerings that often trade up significantly during the first days after the offering, price action in the early days did not exhibit significantly

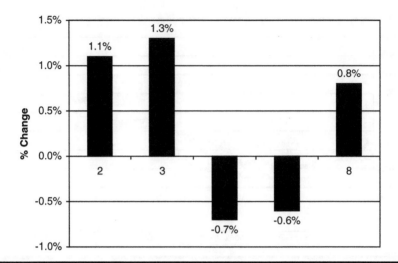

Figure 13-2.   Back-End Equity Trading Performance Immediately After Emergence (Source: J.P. Morgan)

abnormal volatility. As shown in Figure 13-2, the study found that, on average, the trading pattern over the first several days following emergence exhibited no consistent directional pattern; thus there appears to be no need to either sell quickly or, conversely, rush in to buy.

The study also found that although much of the overall outperformance was in the first month following emergence, it was, as shown in Figure 13-3, generally spread out across the entire first 12-month period.

Although on average the first month had the best performance, consistent with the random walk observed by efficient market theory advocates, the prob-

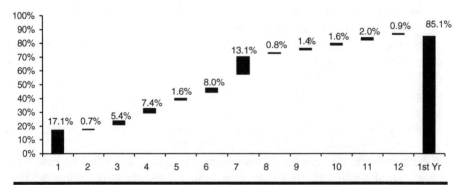

Figure 13-3.   Back-End Equity Trading Performance in First 12 Months of Emergence (Source: J.P. Morgan)

Table 13-1.   First-Month Performance as Indicator of 12-Month Performance*

Up in First Month	
Number of Companies Up	57
Percent of Companies Up	49%
Number of Companies Up in First Month and Up in Months 2–12	24
Percent of Companies Up in First Month and Up in Months 2–12	42%
Down in First Month	
Number of Companies Down	60
Percent of Companies Down	51%
Number of Companies Down in First Month and Down in Months 2–12	27
Percent of Companies Down in First Month and Down in Months 2–12	45%

* Based on 117 company sample set of significant post reorganization equities from 1986 to 2003.

Source: J.P. Morgan

ability that the stock would go up or down in the first month was approximately equal. Furthermore, as shown in Table 13-1, regardless of whether the stock went up or down in the first month, the study found there was an approximately equal likelihood that it would rise over the next 11 months.

As with many statistical studies, it is difficult to discern which factors — inaccurate investor expectations, the small-cap penalty, poor market liquidity, lack of market following, forced selling — most heavily influence the results observed.

POSTREORGANIZATION DEBT SECURITIES

Next to back-end equity, the next most common security that a distressed investor might receive under a plan of reorganization is new postconfirmation debt. As with back-end equities, it is very hard to generalize about the postconfirmation trading characteristics of postreorganization debt. Much will depend on whether it is secured or unsecured and the relative leverage contemplated by the plan. Secured debt, depending on its lien status vis-à-vis any exit financing that may be put in place, will have a reasonable likelihood of trading close to par. Unsecured debt can take virtually any form and may have been created for a variety of purposes. In most cases, it likely will be designed to trade at par. However, there are other situations where debt securities are designed largely as tips to minor creditors, in which case they may have odd structural features (for example, zero coupon or deferrable coupon features) that cause them to trade at a discount. One element that tends to act as a check on the inclusion of high-principal amount/low-value debt in the postreorganization capital structures is the desire for the new entity to have a clean, low-leverage balance sheet.

The factors that should be used to assess the likely trading characteristics of the postconfirmation debt securities are similar to those for any other fixed income investment. Will it be large enough to have acceptable trading liquidity? What are its basic credit characteristics? If it were rated (usually postreorganization debt securities are not initially rated), what might its rating be? How does the coupon compare to the yield on other bonds in the same industry with similar credit characteristics?

LIQUIDATING TRUSTS

As mentioned in Chapter 12, one feature that has been adopted with increasing frequency in chapter 11 reorganizations is postconfirmation liquidating trusts. The basic purpose of these trusts is to allow for the complete resolution of issues of interest to creditors in a way that does not impede the emergence of the postreorganization entity. Essentially, as soon as the basic restructuring details of the debtor's plan of reorganization can be completed, the plan should be implemented and the reorganized firm should move on. How much the creditors will ultimately recover often is simply a matter of "splitting the pie," which should not impede the process. To the extent that creditors have not yet resolved everything that should be in the pie and who should share in the pie, these issues should be settled separately without risking further damage to the debtor's enterprise.

There are two common situations in which postconfirmation trusts are used to expedite the chapter 11 process. The first is when there are lawsuits that the creditors want to pursue against third parties to increase overall recoveries. This can be viewed as increasing the size of the pie to be shared. Common actions include lawsuits against former officers or directors of the debtor, various professionals involved in financings (including accountants, lawyers, and investment bankers), and third parties that may have dealt with the debtor, especially alleged perpetrators of fraudulent conveyances. Any "deep pocket" within reach certainly will be considered. Such actions, if contested, can take years to prosecute to completion. To hold up confirmation until these are settled would unduly prolong the process and expose the debtor to continuing risk of business deterioration. Furthermore, these lawsuits often will have little to do with improving the debtor per se; they are just about improving the recoveries of the creditors.

An excellent example of a litigation intended exclusively to benefit creditors arose in the Iridium case, briefly reviewed in Chapter 8.[30] Iridium was a satellite communications company that filed for chapter 11 when its business failed to develop as expected. The operating business assets were liquidated, but the asset deemed potentially the most valuable, from the perspective of creditor recoveries, was a lawsuit that sought damages of between $2 and $3 billion from Motorola, Inc.,[31] a previous business partner and financier of Iridium. To fund the litigation, $40 million from the proceeds of the operating assets, which could have been distributed to the unsecured creditors, was deposited in a trust. The litigation could take years to resolve if fully litigated. As of this writing, the litigation continues, with changes in bond prices typically attributed to changes in the outlook for different settlements.

A second situation where postconfirmation trusts can be helpful involves the resolution of claims against an estate.[32] These situations involve reducing the number of pieces of the pie, so that everyone's share is bigger. It is not uncommon at the beginning of a bankruptcy for a large number of claims to be filed against the debtor's estate. Claims should not be filed in bad faith, but if there is any basis for a claim, and a creditor is aware that the debtor has filed for bankruptcy, there is a good chance one will be filed.[33] For a claim to be entitled to share in recoveries from the debtor estate, it must be deemed "allowed."[34] To be allowed, a claim either must be listed as an obligation on the debtor's schedule of liabilities or a creditor must file a proof of claim that is uncontested or allowed. Often, even creditors that appear on the debtor's schedule of liabilities will contest the amount of the claim listed on the schedule and will file a proof of claim to demand a different, naturally higher, amount. When a proof of claim is filed and disputed, it usually will be settled via negotiation; otherwise it will require a decision by the bankruptcy court.[35] For large debtors, the number of claims asserted and requiring review can be staggering. The numbers can easily run into the thousands and the amounts into the billions of dollars, particularly in cases involving mass torts.[36] Most such claims fall into the general unsecured class (secured claims, because of the additional formalities involved in obtaining and perfecting a security interest, are generally more easily resolved) and thus are pari passu, absent structural priority issues, with unsecured financial creditors. If a claim becomes an allowed claim, then it gets to share in the pie of assets that are allocated to that class. The more claims that are allowed, the less everyone recovers. Accordingly, because many claims may be contingent or unliquidated, legitimate creditors have a significant financial incentive to make sure illegitimate or questionable claims are not allowed.[37]

Another common area for the use of a postconfirmation trust is mass liability claims, such as for injuries from asbestos. The basic challenge with tort claims is that not all potential claimants may even know they have been injured by the debtor at the claim bar date. Accordingly, these cases usually have been resolved,[38] through the creation of a trust into which the debtor contributes stock (at least 51% of postreorganization equity) and potentially a note providing for periodic cash contributions in exchange for discharge of all past and future liability.[39]

Procedurally, the creation of a postconfirmation trust is the same, with the exception of BRC §524(g) trusts established to manage potential future claims, regardless of the purpose of the trust — and trusts can have multiple purposes. A trust will be described in, and its governing documents included as exhibits to, a disclosure statement. When a plan of reorganization becomes effective, the trust will come into existence pursuant to the provisions of the plan. Beneficial interests in the trust will be aspects of the debtor's estate that will be distributed to creditors or claimholders just like new bonds, shares of common stock, or warrants. For example, a plan of reorganization might provide that certain litigation and recovery rights, together with a specified amount of stock, will be transferred to a trust for the benefit of the Class 6 creditors. Then a plan distribution provision could specify that Class 6 creditors will receive an aggregate of one million shares of common stock and 100% of the interests in the trust.

Where the primary purpose of a trust is to resolve disputed claims related to the size of a class, then there likely will be no distribution other than interests in the trust. In that case, the plan may specify that a trust for the benefit of the Class 6 claims will be created and the debtor will transfer to the trust, for example, a specified amount of cash plus 10 million shares of the debtor's new common stock. The distribution provisions will provide that all allowed claims as of the confirmation will receive one beneficial interest for each dollar of allowed claim. As the trust resolves which asserted claims are genuine and will be "allowed," trust interests will be awarded in the same ratio.

This does not necessarily mean that creditors will be deprived of distributions of stock or other trust assets until all claims are finally resolved — a process that could take years. Typically, the trustee (no relationship to the U.S. Trustee) who administers the trust, with the oversight of trust board members,[40] will make an estimate of class assets and make such interim distributions as are feasible without jeopardizing the interests of unresolved claims. For example, assume, as illustrated in Table 13-2, that a trust's sole assets are 10 million shares of new stock and $10 million in cash to fund the trust. The allowed claims total $100 million and there is another $100 million of contested claims, although the trustee estimates that only $20 million of these ultimately will be allowed. The trustee, in order to give trust beneficiaries some liquidity, could distribute 5 million shares (50 per allowed $1000 claim) to the existing allowed

Table 13-2. Analysis of Recoveries and Trust Distributions

	Claims Allowed	Claims Disallowed	Shares Distributed	Shares in Reserve	Per $1000
Shares Deposited in Trust				10,000,000	
Allowed Claims in Trust	100,000,000				
Asserted Claims in Trust	100,000,000				
Initial Distribution to Allowed Claims ($100 Million)	100,000,000		5,000,000		50.0
Adjusted Reserve				5,000,000	
Initial Distribution to New Allowed Claims ($15 Million)	15,000,000		750,000		50.0
Adjusted Reserve				4,250,000	
Claims Disallowed		80,000,000			
Distribution to All Allowed Claims ($115 Million)			3,833,333		33.3
Holdback for Unresolved Claims ($5 Million)					
Adjusted Reserve				416,667	
Claims Disallowed		5,000,000			
			416,667		3.6
Adjusted Reserve				0.0	
Total	**115,000,000**	**85,000,000**	**10,000,000**	**0.0**	**87.0**

claims and reserve 5 million until the claim pool is better resolved. As claims are allowed, they will receive a pro rata allocation of shares from those that have been held in reserve. Assume that one year following confirmation, the trustee has found that $15 million of the asserted claims are legitimate and should be allowed and has successfully discharged $80 million of the asserted claims as having no foundation. Five million dollars in asserted claims are still unresolved. Assuming the newly allowed claims have been given shares in proportion to the initial distribution, the trustee could then make a separate distribution related to shares reserved for claims that have been discharged. This would represent 4 million shares (80/200 × 10 million). Those 4 million shares would be allocated against the $120 million in allowed ($115 million) and potential ($5 million still unresolved) claims. This would imply that an additional 33.3 (4/120) shares (per $1000 claim) could be distributed to each of the $115 million of allowed claims. The trust would still be holding 416,667 shares (5/120 × 10 million) in reserve relating to the potential $5 million in asserted, but as yet unresolved, claims. If they are allowed, those shares will go to the newly allowed claims. If they are all discharged, then the 416,667 shares will be allocated among the $115 million in allowed claims. The final pool of allowed claims would also receive a proportional share of any cash remaining in the trust that had not been used for administration. Assuming the final $5 million in asserted claims are discharged, the total allowed claims then would share the remaining reserve shares for a total recovery of 87 shares per $1000 claim as illustrated in Table 13-2. Note that if $85 million in claims had not been disallowed, the recovery would only have been 50 shares.

When postconfirmation trusts will be included as part of a plan of reorganization, there are several factors that creditors should consider as it is being formulated, including funding and liquidity. First, as a practical matter, the trust needs to have a mechanism to fund its operations. After the plan of reorganization is confirmed and the debtor exits chapter 11, the cost of administration of the trust typically is no longer the responsibility of the debtor. The trust is for the benefit of the creditors, which become its beneficiaries, and they bear the burden of the associated costs. Trust operating expenses (for trustee, legal, and accounting fees) usually are funded by an initial holdback of cash, which otherwise would be distributable to the creditors/trust beneficiaries, or self-funded from the proceeds of recoveries made by the trustee. For example, sometimes there will be a variety of small nonessential assets of the debtor that as of the time of the confirmation have not been monetized. These could be physical assets that need to be sold and liquidated or accounts or notes receivable that either must be collected or, if not voluntarily paid, litigated and recovered. As these are liquidated, collected, or otherwise reduced to cash, they can help fund the administration of the trust. As mentioned above, when the Iridium litigation trust was formed, it was funded with $40 million in held-back cash to fund the litigation. This is an inordinately large amount, but the creditors felt it important, since the defendant, Motorola, had relatively unlimited resources, to convey that the trust had staying power to fund the litigation through any number of appeals or other eventualities. The cash not consumed by legal fees remains the property of the trust beneficiaries. Accordingly, when the case is decided or settled, these funds also will be distributed to creditors.

A second planning consideration is the liquidity of trust interests. Creditors generally prefer to have the right to trade investments (i.e., immediately realize cash) rather than be forced to hold them. Thus, as a trust is being formulated, it is desirable that the trust interests be made as freely tradable as possible. If nothing else, the ability of the trust interests to trade allows the investors to have an independent assessment of value (i.e., the trading price), which can help with future portfolio valuation requirements. In some cases, however, there may be tax and/or securities law issues that may make trading restrictions appropriate. Postconfirmation trading could jeopardize the value of certain, potentially valuable, tax attributes. Also, depending on the number of trust interest holders, if the interests were freely tradable registration and periodic reporting could be required under various securities laws.[41] In such situations, there may be a debate about whether the cost and administrative burden associated with allowing transfers of trust interests are a good use of trust resources. The ability to trade does clearly impose some incremental expenses on an estate; however, where a trust is likely to have significant value for more than six to nine months, investors usually will view the benefits of having liquidity as more than worth the incremental decline in recovery resulting from the attendant costs.

SUMMARY

This chapter considered the final step of the distressed investment cycle — the monetization of postreorganization securities. While most of a distressed investor's energy naturally will be devoted to the early stages of an investment when a distressed firm is analyzed and the specific securities to invest in are decided upon, the last step cannot be overlooked.

The three most common securities issued pursuant to plans of reorganization are new equity interests, new debt, and postconfirmation trust interests. Plans can, of course, also distribute cash to investors, but this requires no particular consideration on an investor's part. When an investor is likely to receive equity, which may have been the primary investment goal, the investor needs to consider how that equity will trade postconfirmation. If as the plan of reorganization is proposed an investor feels the equity component is poorly designed from the standpoint of size, or that the other holders of securities likely to receive the equity will be rapid sellers regardless of price, the investor may be better off selling his or her prepetition claim prior to confirmation and then deciding to reinvest in the equity postconfirmation depending on its trading level. Alternatively, the equity may trade strongly following confirmation, and an investor will have an immediate opportunity to sell and realize his or her investment strategy. In other cases, more patience may be required.

Postreorganization senior debt securities are more likely to trade at par, and an investor's decision to hold or sell likely will be driven more by the ongoing investment objective (whether the investor wants to continue credit exposure to the restructured firm or just be an equity holder) than strategic disposition issues.

Postconfirmation trusts can be interesting speculative plays. Oftentimes they will be conservatively valued when distributed because of the inherent uncertainties in their ultimate value. Where a trust is intended primarily to recover asset values for the estate (i.e., increase the size of the pie), the ultimate amount to be recovered may be difficult to estimate. Similarly, where a trust is designed to resolve claims, these can fluctuate. To the extent an investor can influence the process, he or she will want to make sure the trust is adequately funded and created in such a way that its interests can be traded.

Reviewing how to conclude the distressed investment is the appropriate point to conclude this book. It is hoped that the reader has a sounder understanding of the elements and strategies of distressed debt investing. Although recent default rate trends may suggest that the halcyon days of the 2000–2002 cycle have passed, if history is any guide, many equally profitable opportunities will continue to present themselves.

Good luck, sweat the details, and always think three moves ahead.

This Chapter's Chess Moves

Potential Moves to Checkmate[42]

27. Qxa4, Qxe4

28. Kf2, Nd3+

29. Kg3, Qh4+

30. Kf3, Qf4+

31. Ke2, Nc1 Checkmate

ENDNOTES

Chapter 1

1. All data from McHugh (2003).
2. See Credit Suisse First Boston (2003).
3. All figures are only rough estimates provided as background. Magellan does not disclose either its average contract rate or its cost to provide service.
4. Shinkle (2000).
5. SEC filings also disclosed that by 2000 Blum Capital had increased its holdings to almost 15%, but indicated it only intended to be a passive investor.
6. Shinkle (2002a).
7. Shinkle (2002b).
8. Shinkle (2002c).
9. Gleacher Partners.
10. Shinkle (2002d).
11. Shinkle (2003a).
12. Shinkle (2003c).
13. Shinkle (2003d).
14. Shinkle (2003e).
15. Share amounts and prices reflect a 2.3:1 share split announced on the effective date.
16. If you bought the subs at 67 on the first bad news and sold at 22 feint of heart, then you definitely need to read this book!
17. Martin Fridson, currently CEO of Fridson Vision LLC, was the long-time director of high yield research at Merrill Lynch.
18. See Fridson and Jonsson (1994, 1995). A basic measure of credit risk is the difference between the yield to maturity (YTM) or expected return of the security being analyzed compared to the treasury or risk-free rate yield of the comparable maturity U.S. Treasury note or bill — which is generally referred to as the "risk-free" rate. Thus, if the distressed bond being analyzed had a three-year maturity and a YTM based on its discount price of 15%, and the YTM of a three-year treasury note was 3%, the risk premium or credit spread would be 12% (15–3) or 1200 basis points. But see also Fridson and Cherry (1991a) for a critique of this methodology.

19. Speculative grade as captured by the DLJ High Yield Index. See Credit Suisse First Boston (2002).
20. The appropriateness of viewing many preferred stocks as debt was recently given support by the Financial Accounting Standards Board (FASB), which recently acted to force various kinds of preferred stock to be classified as liabilities, as opposed to a component of equity, on corporate balance sheets. See FASB 150: "Accounting for Certain Financial Instruments with Characteristics of Both Liabilities and Equity" (2003).
21. Based on CSFB Lower Tier High Yield Index Returns. The lower tier category includes CCC, split-CCC, and default securities. See Credit Suisse First Boston (2004).
22. For example, during the reorganization of MCI Communications (formerly, WorldCom), several of its competitors, which apparently would have preferred to see MCI liquidated rather than emerge from bankruptcy as a potentially strong competitor, petitioned the courts and lobbied through Congress to block the reorganization process. See Braine (2003b).

Chapter 2

1. See National Bureau of Economic Research (2003).
2. Because different sources were used to compile these data and those sources use slightly different definitions of default or scope of applicable market, the exact numbers may not always be consistent, but the major trends are unmistakable.
3. See Hamilton et al. (2004). Other Moody's-related data credited herein can be found in Hamilton et al. (2002, 2003) and Sherwin et al. (2004).
4. Hamilton et al. (2004).
5. A good example of this occurred with Orbital Sciences in the second quarter of 2002. During most of 2001 and the first half of 2002, Orbital's bonds traded at a discount because there was a risk the firm would default on a maturing bond. As it turned out, these bonds were refinanced and investors who purchased at a discount enjoyed handsome returns; however, there was never a default, technical or otherwise. See the discussion in Chapter 8.
6. Altman (2003).
7. Leveraged buyouts during this period had an aggregate transaction value in excess of $225 billion. M&A Database, *Mergers and Acquisitions* (1997).
8. See Figure 2-12.
9. National Bureau of Economic Research (2003).
10. 12 U.S.C. §3331 et seq.
11. See White (1991).
12. Depending on the subject matter of the statistic, different universes of bonds (such as only speculative grade or all corporate bonds including investment grade) may form the base or denominator for this calculation.
13 The spike in 1970 is not particularly relevant because it was primarily due to the default of the Penn Central Railroad, which failed for a variety of economic and noneconomic reasons. See Daughen and Binzen (1993).
14. Investment-grade corporations, such as Banco de Montevideo, that defaulted on rated obligations other than bonds (e.g., bank notes or bank deposits) are listed here as defaulters, but are not included in Moody's cohort-based bond default rate statistics. Bond amounts may include bank debt and commercial paper in certain cases.

15. See McDermott (2002).
16. The challenges of the cable TV sector were completely different. Cable has always been a fairly predictable generator of cash flow. The issue, apart from cases like Adelphia, which apparently involves fraud, mismanagement, or both, has generally been valuation and whether valuations were premised on an unreasonable expectation of cash flow growth.
17. Data for 1990 exclude retail industry defaults. Data for 2000–2002 exclude media/ telecom defaults. Most of the Credit Suisse data presented graphically is drawn from Credit Suisse First Boston (2004).
18. The word "related" is being used here purposefully to connote the nonstatistically rigorous nature of the analysis. No statistical assertions relating to the causality are made; it is left to other researchers to attempt such studies. The intent is to note and summarize those factors that appear to have some nexus with defaults.
19. Calculated from data in Credit Suisse First Boston (2003). See Altman et al. (2000) and Fons et al. (1994).
20. Data from Fitch Ratings.
21. There is no requirement that a rating be obtained in order to issue a bond. Usually the time and expense of obtaining a rating are incurred because it is perceived that investors will respect the independent assessment of the rating agency and the cost of borrowing will, all things being equal, be lower. When a bond is sold not rated (NR), there is an inevitable "negative pregnant" of why a rating was not obtained; the usual suspicion is that the issuer did not like the rating that the rating agency indicated it would place on the issue. The default rates suggest that investor skepticism of not-rated issues may be justified. See additional discussion of the rating process in Chapter 8.
22. The notion is that even if expected loss rates are, for example, 200 basis points higher, if the average yield on the portfolio is increased 200 basis points or more to compensate for this risk, the investor is, putting aside the issue of volatility of returns, theoretically, indifferent. However, default rates should not be confused with loss rates. The loss rate measures the financial loss incurred for those bonds that have defaulted. The loss rate will therefore be higher than the default rate. The "average" amount of price improvement needed to make an investor indifferent relative to loss rate is not a simple matter to calculate and needs to reflect the expected loss rate over the life of a broad portfolio of issues.
23. It is very difficult to ascribe causality to any particular factor in a dynamic market. Here it is suggested that a withdrawal of funds caused prices to decline. At one level, this is a defensible supposition, but it does not ask the related question of why funds were withdrawn. Was it (1) because prices were declining or (2) due to a separate independent variable or catalyst such as an economic slowdown that fundamentally changed investor expectations on default and recovery rates?
24. See Fridson and Garman (1998a).
25. Although the basis of this theory can be traced back to Louis Bachelier's "Theory of Speculation" published in 1900 (see Cootner [1964]), it was formalized as the EMT by Eugene Fama in 1965. See Fama (1965).
26. Fama (1970).
27. The bankruptcy courts of this state do not yet participate in the on-line PACER docket access system; thus it is often necessary to either directly work with the clerk of the court or find the relevant lawyers who are involved in the case.

28. From July 16, 2002 (the day WorldCom/MCI filed for chapter 11 bankruptcy protection) to June 30, 2003, there were approximately 490 unique news stories posted on Bloomberg (www.bloomberg.com) relating to AT&T. In comparison, during the same period, there were approximately 350 unique stories related to WorldCom posted on Bloomberg and there were 9,686 filings totaling over 100,000 pages filed on the bankruptcy docket.

29. As discussed in detail in Chapters 4 and 11, investors with restricted information are, in most cases, allowed to continue to trade securities as long as they disclose to the counter-party that they have such information. This is usually done through the process of obtaining what is known as a "big-boy" letter.

30. While anyone can access SEC filed documents for free on the Internet through the EDGAR system, bankruptcy documents obtained on-line through the PACER system have per-page charges.

31. See Shefrin (2002) and Shiller (2000).

32. The Shared National Credit (SNC) program is jointly administered by the Federal Reserve Board, the Federal Deposit Insurance Corporation, and the Office of the Comptroller of Currency. The primary objective of the SNC (often pronounced "snik") rating is to avoid duplicative analyses of the same loan credit by various agencies so that the review process will be more efficient and consistent.

33. The SNC program has essentially five ratings categories: pass, and then four categories of "classified" loans — special mention, substandard, doubtful, and loss.

34. This is not to say that the sale is not rational from the perspective of the portfolio manager maximizing his or her compensation or retaining his or her job.

35. Although only a one-time historical event, it should be noted that a significant factor impacting the severity of the 1990 high-yield sell-off was the previously mentioned Financial Institutions Reform, Recovery and Enforcement Act (FIRREA) legislation. This legislation, ostensibly intended to improve the portfolio quality of savings and loan institutions, effectively required the S&Ls to, within a fairly short time frame, liquidate their high-yield bond portfolios. Whatever the long-term wisdom of this regulatory initiative, over the short term it forced these institutions to become irrational sellers (from the perspective of perceived value) and paved the way for the near-record high-yield return performance in the 1992 and 1993 time frame. The FIRREA-induced forced selling appeared to cause a fairly straightforward wealth transfer from one investor group (savings and loan equity holders) to another (distressed security investors). See White (1991).

36. When a loan is "written down," it essentially means that some or all of the loan balance has been charged off, and the allowance for loan losses reduced, effectively reducing the carrying value of the loan on the bank's balance sheet.

37. CDO was initially used to describe structured finance vehicles that held both high-yield bonds and leveraged loans. Now it has become a generic term. The collateral used in backing structures has broadened over the years and now includes such instruments as trust preferred stock, synthetic securities, and low-rated tranches of asset-backed securities (which are, in turn, backed by mortgages, car loans, and credit-card receivables). See Goodman and Fabozzi (2002).

38. See Goodman and Fabozzi (2002).

39. Negative arbitrage essentially means that the cost of the financing (750 basis points) is greater than the income from the collateral (535 basis points), which would suggest a "loss." However, the BB/B tranche will still make economic sense to the equity

tranche holder as long as the expected return to equity (which will be derived by the 535-basis-point earning rate less the 110-basis-point weighed average funding cost) is greater than 750 basis points.

40. Not surprisingly, according to data from Credit Suisse First Boston, peak arbitrage spreads (which CSFB measures net of any required interest rate swap costs) often coincide with those periods of greatest dislocation in the high-yield/distressed market. For example, in the most recent period, the peak arbitrage was approximately 850 basis points in October 2002. In the 1990 period, it was approximately 900 basis points in the third quarter of 1990. As of November 2003, the arbitrage spread had dropped to 335 basis points, which was below the historical average since 1990 of 448 basis points. Consequently, in the 1999–2002 period, in aggregate over $75 billion in CDOs was issued, while in 2003 less than $1 billion was formed. See Credit Suisse First Boston (2004).

41. According to data from Credit Suisse First Boston, from 1995 to 2003 the average portion of new CDO structures rated single-A or better varied between 77 and 85%. See Credit Suisse First Boston (2004).

42. CDO-ORs are typically fairly CDO specific, so it is difficult to generalize about their exact provisions. See Goodman and Fabozzi (2002).

43. As a fine point, the investor may rationally stop purchasing because his or her optimal portfolio allocation had been satisfied.

44. The transaction fee, sometimes also called the "ticket charge," will be a nominal amount designed simply to cover the costs associated with the processing of a transaction but not generate any substantial profit. Typically, the biggest fee associated with a securities transaction is the sales commission. In the case of shares of common stock, this fee will usually be an agreed to amount per share (e.g. $0.02–0.05 per share). However, in the typical corporate bond transaction, the dealer will pay this fee to its sales staff out of the difference between the dealer's purchase and resale price, often referred to as the spread. In most instances, the investor involved in the transaction will not know the exact spread.

Chapter 3

1. See the discussion in Chapter 2.

2. For an exhaustive discussion on valuation, see Copeland et al. (2000).

3. Such a business strategy is evocative of Global Crossing, which filed for bankruptcy in 2002.

4. For more detailed discussion on the treatment of purchase cost in excess of assets acquired, see Keiso et al. (2003).

5. DJIA peak value on January 14, 2000 of 11722.9 versus low of 7286.3 on October 9, 2002. NASDAQ peak on March 10, 2000 of 5048.6 versus low of 1114.1 on October 9, 2002.

6. A good example is Enron stock. Despite management having declared publicly that the stock had no value, it continued to be traded at positive values in large volumes well after the company filed for bankruptcy. On some days, inexplicably, it would actually increase in value. See Emshwiller (2002). For academic studies, see Altman (1983), Bonnier and Bruner (1985), Clark and Weisenstein (1983), Morse and Shaw (1988), and Shane (1994).

7. An interesting example of option value in a distressed equity was arguably present in the Seitel case. An investor purchased all of the bonds of Seitel at distressed levels. Seitel filed for chapter 11 protection and proposed a plan of reorganization (plan) under which the bondholder would receive all of the equity and stockholders would receive a nominal per-share cash payment if they voted to support the plan — otherwise they would receive nothing. The plan did not garner approval of the equity class, and the proponents of the plan moved to have the plan confirmed over the equity's objection. One week before confirmation, the stock was trading at $1.45 share (November 26, 2003). If the plan was confirmed, purchasers of the stock would receive nothing; if it was not confirmed, the potential equity recovery was unclear. As it turned out, the equity class prevented confirmation of the original plan and ultimately paid off the once distressed bonds using the proceeds of new debt and equity offerings.

8. One important restriction is the "down tick" rule. See Short Sale Rule §3350, Conduct Rules — National Association of Securities Dealers Manual (2003).

9. Based on the author's 15 years of experience.

10. Although GAAP generally uses historical cost for the valuation of most assets, market prices are considered relevant for items such as marketable securities. See Financial Accounting Standards Board Statement of Financial Accounting Standards No. 115: "Accounting for Certain Investments in Debt and Equity Securities" (1993). In general, see Keiso et al. (2003).

11. Once again, the problem of how to interpret market price information is presented. To acknowledge that the sub debt has any value arguably implies that the senior debt must first recover its full $500 face value. In fact, in most instances, if the author were calculating leverage ratios through the sub debt, he would value the senior debt at full face value. Here, just the market values of each security are being used on the rationale that if all the debt could be purchased at existing market levels, following a restructuring the assets would effectively have been purchased for $290. As discussed more fully below, however, a distressed debt investor would likely attempt a direct valuation of the firm or assets rather than make inferences of value from securities prices.

12. True asset value is, of course, merely a concept. The notion is what a firm would be sold for in a competitive auction or how the assets would be valued relative to peers in a normalized environment.

13. To state this in a manner that an EMT adherent might accept: the firm's incremental capital cost exceeded the expected return on assets, implying that the risk-adjusted present value of the investment would be negative.

14. See Bibeault (1999), Gaughan (2002), Gertner and Scharfstein (1991), Gilson (2001), Jensen (1989), John (1993), Levine (1991), Platt (1997), and Wruck (1990).

Chapter 4

1. The author would like to acknowledge in particular the thorough and insightful contribution made by David Hollander of Tennenbaum Capital Partners, LLC to Chapters 4, 11, 12, and 13.

2. As commenced by a filing pursuant to BRC §301; Federal Rules of Bankruptcy Procedure 1002.

3. This should not be forgotten. The tone of this book is, intentionally, clinical. Also, the process has been analogized to chess — a game in which the opponents rarely

speak and it is gauche to show emotion. The reality of financial restructurings is that some investors will incur substantial losses and potentially be at risk of losing their jobs or even their careers. It is usually a zero-sum game, where the loser leaves with hands in pockets he or she feels have been picked. At the extreme, it can even be a negative-sum game, where one party takes a scorched earth policy, either out of spite or to establish the credibility of his or her threats for the next restructuring.

4. For a discussion of the direct and indirect costs of bankruptcy, see, among many, Altman (1984), Andrade and Kaplan (1998), Ang et al. (1982), Betker (1997), Lawless and Ferris (1997, 1999), Luben (2000), Opler and Titman (1994), and Weiss (1990).

5. For a more detailed discussion of out-of-court restructurings, see, among many, Brown et al. (1993), Franks and Torous (1989a), Gilson (1991), and James (1995, 1996).

6. To name just two, Atmel and Internet Capital Group used significant cash balances to significantly deleverage their balance sheets. See Moyer and Laufman (2003a) and Moyer and Cray (2002).

7. If the exchange is not completed with an effective registration statement, or if it is completed pursuant to a Securities Act §3(a)(9) exemption and the security being exchanged is unregistered, it might be possible to sell the stock only under SEC Rule 144.

8. The choice will depend on the holder's expectation of the value of the new common stock (which currently appears worthless) and the trading value of the new bonds. Note that the existence of the option complicates the analysis since the amount of cash potentially used for the "cash-out" option could potentially affect the firm's outlook and liquidity.

9. The term bondholder committee will be used here to refer to informal groups of financial creditors that generally are formed before a bankruptcy. This type of group should not be confused with the official unsecured creditor committee formed at the beginning of a chapter 11 case.

10. Participation on an informal committee typically does not impose any special legal duties, other than duties under securities laws resulting from the receipt of material nonpublic information. In contrast, members of the official unsecured creditors' committee appointed under BRC §1102(a) in a chapter 11 owe a fiduciary duty to all unsecured creditors.

11. In general, under BRC §1102, the United States Trustee is required to appoint the official unsecured creditors' committee from the seven largest creditors willing to serve, although in practice other creditors and persons will be appointed to represent constituencies deemed necessary to develop a confirmable plan of reorganization.

12. In periods of less political correctness, these were originally referred to as "Chinese walls."

13. There are a variety of "devices" or "blocking procedures" that can be used, including physical barriers to prevent access by unrestricted personnel to the work area of restricted persons, computer security measures, etc. See Pozen and Mencher (1993). The disadvantage of becoming restricted can also arise in a chapter 11 context for official unsecured creditor committee members. In that case, to backstop internal processes, official unsecured creditors' committee members may also seek a bankruptcy court order to the effect that trading by the committee member's firm will not constitute a breach of fiduciary duty so long as appropriate blocking procedures are followed. See Weil, Gotshal & Manges (2003), Chapter 19. It should also be noted

that restricted status can also arise when a bond investor purchases bank debt and receives nonpublic information in conjunction with that holding.

14. See Weil, Gotshal & Manges (2003), Chapter 19. Primarily Exchange Act §10(b) and rule 10(b)(5) thereunder and Securities Act §17(a).

15. Thus, if a restricted holder sold bonds to a new investor without disclosing that the holder had nonpublic information and the bonds subsequently declined in value, the new investor (trade counter-party) could effectively demand that the restricted holder repurchase the bonds at the original transaction price. This would effectively transfer the loss to the restricted holder, which is presumably the risk the holder wanted to avoid by selling the bonds. See Weil, Gotshal & Manges (2003), Chapter 19.

16. The etymology of the term "big-boy" letter is unclear. The obvious meaning of the expression is that the party to the disclosure is a knowledgeable, experienced investor capable of protecting his or her own interests.

17. While the on-point decided case law is minimal, many lawyers and investors are skeptical that a big-boy letter would be sufficient to shield an investor from trading on highly material information (e.g., knowledge that the firm lost its biggest customer or was about to disclose an accounting scandal). There is no statutorily recognized "carve-out" for such agreements. In fact, Exchange Act §29(a) essentially nullifies any effort by one party to have another party waive its rights under the Exchange Act. However, courts have found that when parties of equal bargaining power negotiate restrictive contracts, they are enforceable. *Herco v. Segui* 91 F. 3d 337 (2d Cir. 1997). See Weil, Gotshal & Manges (2003), Section 19-24. Investors in possession of information that could be reasonably expected to materially affect trading prices when it becomes known should recognize that a big-boy letter may not provide complete insurance. Because of these various risks, broker-dealers often insist that the counter-parties directly exchange letters with each other.

18. The author is unaware of any study that analyzes the market impact, if any, of the disclosure that one of the parties to the transaction has nonpublic information. The lack of analysis is probably due to the nonreported nature of such transactions and the difficulty of obtaining reliable market price information. The author's anecdotal experience is that the effect is asymmetrical: it does not matter much to sellers if the buyer has insider information, but it can cause reluctance by buyers if the seller is an insider.

19. MatlinPatterson Asset Management apparently pursued such a strategy with regard to WorldCom bonds. As of January 2003, MatlinPatterson had potentially purchased as much as 20% of certain of WorldCom's debt, but apparently declined to become involved in the official unsecured creditors' committee because it might impede the firm's future trading flexibility. Zuckerman (2003).

20. However, it should be noted that bank debt itself is not deemed a security under U.S. securities laws, and thus the trading restrictions/liabilities thereunder previously mentioned for bonds do not apply to the trading of bank debt. However, bankruptcy courts have used different equitable theories and Bankruptcy Code provisions to limit the rights of purchasers of nonsecurities claims. See Fortgang and Mayer (1990) and Weil, Gotshal & Manges (2003), Chapter 19.

21. It should be noted that there are instances where some members of an informal bondholder committee remain unrestricted throughout the process, although it can make certain aspects of the committee's work awkward.

22. A possible exception to this generalization is where the entire enterprise value is effectively being given to creditors. If management is sufficiently realistic to understand that this is the inevitable outcome, the delay and expense associated with a contentious negotiation can be limited or avoided.

23. Readers interested in a fictional account of the beginning stages of the negotiation of a bank restructuring should read the Chapter titled "Saddlebags" in Wolfe (1993).

24. See Pacelle and Frank (2002).

25. See discussion relating to *Credit Lyonnais* case in Chapter 11.

26. A tender offer consists of an offer by the debtor to purchase the securities for cash. An exchange offer involves swapping or exchanging the securities for other securities or a package of consideration, which can include new securities and cash.

27. Financial advisors to distressed firms may engage in informal conversations with significant holders in a way that does not divulge nonpublic information (since the firm has presumably not made any firm decisions) and does not bind or restrict the investor.

28. As a practical, real-world matter, the nondilution of the existing equity is likely to be temporary. Under the stated assumptions, Boxco needs more capital to finance operating losses and build out its network. Under the circumstances, it is highly unlikely it could borrow this money, so its only practical option to raise capital is to sell equity. However, the debt repurchase could end up benefiting existing equity holders if, for example, it made Boxco a more attractive acquisition target.

29. For example, any internal projection that tended to show the risk of insolvency would be very valuable to a creditor seeking to bring an action on the theory that the firm is operating within the zone of insolvency. See discussion of *Credit Lyonnais* case in Chapter 11.

30. For example, Aames Financial completed an exchange offer for its subordinated notes that was contested by holders of Aames' senior notes. Since the challenge by the senior note holders was reasonably foreseeable, it would have made little strategic sense for Aames to attempt a consensual process. See Moyer (2002a).

31. The numerous considerations involved in complying with the Exchange Act are beyond the scope of this book. For a general discussion, see Bienenstock (1987) or Weil, Gotshal & Manges (2003).

32. The "prisoner's dilemma" is a nonzero-sum game used in game theory to analyze cooperation. In the game, two players have the opportunity to either "cooperate" or "defect." If both cooperate, their gains are greater than if both defect, but if only one defects, his or her gains would be much higher. Although both know the outcome matrix, neither knows the other's action with certainty. See Axelrod (1984).

33. BRC §1129(b).

34. In a chapter 11, if a plan of reorganization is confirmed, all members of a class are bound by the terms, even if they were part of a minority that voted against the plan, so 100% participation is assured. See the discussion of voting and confirming a plan of reorganization later in Chapter 4.

35. The 90% figure was randomly chosen, but is representative of the high participation rates typically required. Some exchanges will require as high as 95% participation.

36. Although often daunting in complexity, exchange offers in complex, multitier capital structures are not unprecedented. Two prominent examples include Foster Wheeler (see Cray [2004]) and Qwest Communications (see Oldfield [2004]).

37. This estimate excludes restructurings consisting of amendments to bank loan agreements.

38. In many cases, the debtor openly discloses the need for and timing of the eventual filing beforehand. As a result, the filing seldom significantly impacts prices of distressed debt and sometimes debt will actually trade up slightly in price (perhaps because an uncertainty has been eliminated). See, generally, Betker (1998), Clark and Weisenstein (1983), Dawkins and Bamber (1999), and Lawless et al. (1996). However, on those occasions when the filing does surprise the market, price declines can be significant. See, for example, Theodoros (1999).

39. This is particularly true in preplanned chapter 11 filings. Some studies suggest that the price impact of the filing will depend on the purpose of the reorganization. Rose-Green and Dawkins (2002). There are certainly many instances where the chapter 11 filing will significantly impact prices. For example, in the case of ICO Global Communications Ltd., bond prices fell over 60% following its bankruptcy filing. Theodoros (1999).

40. Among many, see Salerno and Hansen (2001), Weil, Gotshal & Manges (2003), LoPucki and Mirick (2003), Bienenstock (1987), and Epstein et al. (1993).

41. If an investor becomes heavily involved and is appointed to the official unsecured creditors' committee, he or she will, of course, have access to significantly more information as well as committee counsel for advice on specific issues.

42. BRC §301.

43. BRC §303. In certain cases, only one creditor may suffice. See Bienenstock (1987), Chapter 4.

44. As a procedural matter, an involuntary petition is basically a complaint filed by creditors alleging the debtor's insolvency; the voluntary petition of the debtor includes an admission of insolvency, which clearly gives the bankruptcy court in which it is filed jurisdiction. As a practical matter, while the petitioning creditors might have grounds to make a jurisdictional challenge, they will usually be content with the fact that the objective of their petition, putting the debtor under bankruptcy court supervision, has been achieved. Of course, it is not always true that the debtor prevails in its choice of forum. In the Iridium case, creditors filed an involuntary petition in the Southern District of New York, which was followed several hours later by Iridium filing a voluntary petition in Delaware. After almost two weeks of negotiation, Iridium consented to move the case to New York for the convenience of the parties. Jelisavcic (1999).

45. Increasingly, chapter 11 is chosen even when the reorganization strategy is a sale or liquidation of the business. And while it may be counterintuitive that a management team that "caused" the failure should be left in control, in practice new crisis turnaround managers will have been added to or replaced the original executives. The installation of turnaround managers is often required by creditors, particularly bank creditors, as a condition to waiving a previously incurred breach of the lending documents.

46. For a discussion of strategic considerations, see Eisenberg and LoPucki (1999) and LoPucki and Whitford (1991). For an interesting analysis of how "competition" among bankruptcy courts may affect the reorganization process, see LoPucki and Kalin (2000) and LoPucki and Doherty (2002).

47. Technical default should be distinguished from payment default. When a borrower fails to make a required payment on a bank loan (a payment default), the lender will

typically have to classify the loan as nonperforming (even if it is likely that all amounts due under the loan will likely be recovered from collateral), which can have financial and nonfinancial (e.g., regulatory reporting) implications for the bank. Thus a payment default is always a significant event. A technical default, in contrast, means the borrower is not in compliance with some term of the lending agreement (see the discussion in Chapter 7 relating to covenants), but still paying. Technical default gives the lender significant leverage over the borrower, including, in certain circumstances, the right to demand immediate repayment. However, since acceleration of the debt would likely only lead to a payment default (and probably a bankruptcy filing), which would then cause the loan to be characterized as nonperforming, the lender will usually work with the borrower to amend the agreement (for a fee, of course) and "cure" the default.

48. This is particularly true when the debt in question is subordinated debt. Blockage provisions do not uniformly entitle the bank lender to block payments on senior unsecured debt.

49. In particular, where it is generally recognized that the debtor's financial circumstances are such that a reorganization is inevitable and the recovery to unsecured creditors will be significantly discounted, then the payment of a coupon can be viewed as "irrational" from the debtor's perspective. Of course, from the distressed investor's perspective, every interest payment received can significantly enhance returns, particularly if the bonds were purchased at steeply discounted prices. For example, if the investor bought a 10% coupon bond at 20 and received one interest payment of 5, this would be a 25% recovery of the amount invested (depending on how much, if any, accrued interest was paid at the time of purchase). In contrast, if the coupon is not paid and the cash is left in the estate, then it must be shared with other creditors. Viewed from this perspective, the payment of a coupon essentially favors certain creditors relative to others. More practically, if cash is limited, withholding the coupon and then filing for chapter 11 protection allows the debtor to retain valuable working capital.

50. See Nitzberg (1999).

51. See Fortgang and Mayer (1985).

52. The notion of a debtor in possession can be thought of as substituting management, subject to a new fiduciary role, for a court-appointed trustee. BRC §1107.

53. BRC §§363, 1108.

54. BRC §1104(a).

55. BRC §1104(a).

56. BRC §1102.

57. BRC §1103.

58. BRC §506(b). See LoPucki and Mirick (2003), Chapter 12.

59. Equity interests include shares of stock in a corporation or rights to purchase such shares (e.g., warrants or options) or general or limited partnership interests. BRC §101(16). When equity holders are not receiving any recovery under a plan of reorganization, they will usually be deemed to reject the plan without the formality of voting. In other instances, however, they may be entitled to vote.

60. The required content of a plan of reorganization is proscribed by BRC §1123.

61. BRC §1123.

62. BRC §1125.

63. The solicitation processes are similar in that voting on an action (either approval of the plan of reorganization in the bankruptcy context or the subject of the proxy solicitation in the securities context) is legally permissible only through an "approved" solicitation document. Technically, filings required to be made under the Exchange Act, such as proxy statements with the SEC, are not affirmatively "approved." The SEC has a predetermined time period to review the filing and comment on whether it will or will not challenge the document if it is used for solicitation. In contrast, under the Bankruptcy Code, the bankruptcy court must affirmatively approve (which involves a finding only on the adequacy of the disclosure, not the appropriateness of the plan) the disclosure statement. BRC §1125.

64. BRC §1125.

65. Under BRC §1129, even if creditors accept a plan of reorganization, the bankruptcy court must make an independent determination that the plan is, among other things, feasible, proposed in good faith, and complies with the Bankruptcy Code.

66. BRC §1141(d)(1).

67. BRC §1121(b).

68. BRC §1121(c). In the majority of cases, however, exclusivity never lapses and the debtor's proposed plan is the only one ever considered.

69. See, for example, *In re Allegheny International, Inc.* 18 B.R. 282 (Bankr. W.D. Pa. 1990).

70. For elaboration on some of the issues that result from the Bankruptcy Code's bias to allow debtors to retain exclusivity, see Kerkman (1987) and LoPucki (1983, 1993).

71. In a prenegotiated plan, holders participating on the bondholder committee will often bind themselves to vote in favor of a formally proposed plan of reorganization which is consistent with the prepetition agreement via a "lockup" agreement.

72. In a formal prepackaged plan, formal solicitation of and voting by the impaired class occurs before the filing and is enforceable afterward. As a practical matter, this usually requires that the proposed plan only impairs the financial creditors and reinstates trade and other creditors that would be too difficult to solicit. For additional information, see Betker (1995) and Tashijian et al. (1996).

73. For example, in Knology's chapter 11 reorganization, the prepackaged plan of reorganization was confirmed and declared effective in approximately 60 days.

74. BRC §1123(a) requires the plan of reorganization to address seven specific topics, but not all of these are "operative." Structurally, the typical plan will usually contain sections such as definitions, treatment of classified claims, description and classification of claims and equity interests, means of implementation, description of securities to be issued in connection with the plan, treatment of executory contracts, conditions precedent, claims objection process, retention of jurisdiction of the bankruptcy court, effect of discharge, and miscellaneous provisions and exhibits. See Salerno et al. (2001).

75. BRC §362.

76. The length of time a debtor can use a secured lender's collateral or a leasehold without making payments to the creditor will vary depending on the circumstances and the nature of the asset in question. See Weil, Gotshal & Manges (2003).

77. BRC §361. See LoPucki and Mirick (2003), Chapter 12 relating to "adequate protection."

78. BRC §364.

79. Access to liquidity can be particularly complicated if the debtor has granted a broad "floating" lien on its assets. A floating lien is a fairly standard feature of working capital loans under which the lender is granted a security interest in all accounts receivable, inventory and other property, and "proceeds thereof." The floating lien essentially means that the cash proceeds from collateral (e.g., the collection of an account receivable or the sale of an item of inventory) become the creditor's collateral. Although the automatic stay prevents the creditor from seizing the collateral (which may just be a bookkeeping entry when the creditor requires all accounts to be maintained with the creditor bank), the Bankruptcy Code does give the creditor the right to object to the debtor using the creditor's "property" and to demand that the secured creditor's collateral interest be adequately protected. BRC §361.

80. Debtors generally will plan the timing of their bankruptcy filing at a point where they have sufficient cash resources to fund near-term operations. Sometimes this "planning" can involve borrowing all amounts available on lending facilities immediately prior to filing to try and maximize cash on hand. See, generally, Salerno et al. (1997).

81. In general, most interest payments on debt cease upon the filing of a petition. On unsecured debt, interest ceases to accrue on the creditor's claim (although in unusual cases the unsecured creditor may be entitled to postpetition interest when there are sufficient assets to pay the claim in full). On secured debt, interest will continue to accrue to the extent that the debt is oversecured. Payment of postpetition interest on secured debt is often agreed to by the debtor in negotiated adequate protection agreements. See Weil, Gotshal & Manges (2003).

82. Under BRC §547(b), there are five elements that must be established to avoid a transfer: (1) the transfer was to or for the benefit of a creditor, (2) relating to an antecedent debt, (3) while the debtor was insolvent, (4) which took place within 90 days of the bankruptcy filing (one year if the creditor is an "insider"), and (5) as a result the creditor was better off than it would be if the debtor was liquidated. See Epstein et al. (1993).

83. Under BRC §101(31) "insiders" include, among others, officers and directors of the debtor.

84. BRC §547(c) provides a variety of "defenses" that can be raised by the creditor, including that the transfer was (a) for new value, (b) made in the ordinary course of business, and/or (c) related to the perfection of a purchase money security interest. See Epstein et al. (1993) and LoPucki and Mirick (2003).

85. Prior to the Bankruptcy Code, fraudulent conveyance was a general tort emanating from the equitable principles of fraud. In many states, those principles were codified by the adoption of either the Uniform Fraudulent Conveyance Act (approved in 1918) or the more recent Uniform Fraudulent Transfer Act. BRC §548 created a Bankruptcy Code–based cause of action. See Epstein et al. (1993).

86. See Salomon (1988). Another common context for potential fraudulent conveyances involves the spin-off of subsidiaries.

87. While a fairness opinion can be thought of as good insurance, it is not a guaranty. Almost all fraudulent conveyance actions are brought in the face of a fairness opinion on the premise that the opinion can be contested and that the trier of fact will find the plaintiff's opinion more credible.

88. Debtors have the power within chapter 11 to bring a broad range of recovery actions. In certain circumstances, particularly where the debtor may have a conflict of interest, a creditor or the official committee of unsecured creditors will have derivative standing to bring an action for the benefit of the estate. See Epstein (1993), *In re The Gibson Group, Inc.* 6 F.3d 1936 (6th Cir. 1995).

89. For example, certain allegations in Iridium's lawsuit against Motorola, discussed in more detail in Chapter 13, effectively make this claim. See Gill and Levin (2000).

90. For example, in the Conseco reorganization, substantial lawsuits were brought against the former CEO and CFO. Hallinan and Pacelle (2003).

91. While few auditors have escaped such suits, among the most widely publicized were actions brought against the now-defunct Arthur Andersen in the Global Crossing and WorldCom cases.

92. BRC §365.

93. See Countryman (1973). While this is perhaps the most widely employed definition, the U.S. Supreme Court has adopted a broader definition requiring only that "*performance is due to some extent on both sides.*" *NLRB v Bildisco & Bildisco,* 465 U.S. 513 (1984). This approach eliminates the requirement that the remaining performance be sufficient that nonperformance would constitute a material breach. To complicate matters further, there is also the "result-oriented" definition under which the pivotal issue is whether treating the contract as executory results in an outcome that is more consistent with the policies underlying the Bankruptcy Code. See Bienenstock (1987), Chapter 14.

94. Under BRC §502(b)(6), the damage formula for real property leases is the prepetition arrearage plus the greater of (a) one year's rent or (b) 15% of the remaining term rent (subject to a three-year cap).

95. Under this standard, the test is not whether the debtor is losing money under the contract, but rather whether it would be more profitable to utilize resources differently. See Bienenstock (1987), Chapter 14.

96. BRC §365.

97. In considering the totality of the circumstances, an important consideration the bankruptcy court will weigh is whether the probable magnitude of the damage claim the rejected party may assert against the estate will outweigh the benefit to be realized. See Bienenstock (1987), Chapter 14.

98. Rejection of collective bargaining agreements is governed by BRC §1113 and retiree benefits by BRC §1114. Several other types of contracts are subject to special treatment under the Bankruptcy Code, including, among others, shopping center leases, airport landing slots, intellectual property licenses, and time share agreements. In addition, judicial decisions have created other types of contracts that are difficult or impossible to reject. See Salerno et al. (2001). It should also be noted that there is currently a significant jurisdictional battle taking place between bankruptcy courts and the Federal Energy Regulatory Commission (FERC) over the ability of electricity generators to reject uneconomic supply agreements. For example, assume an electricity generator is obligated under a long-term supply agreement to sell electricity to a utility for $35 per megawatt hour (MWh). The generator subsequently files for chapter 11 protection and seeks to reject the supply contract either because it now costs more than $35 per MWh to produce the electricity (so it is losing money) or the prevailing

market rate is $45 per MWh (so it could make more money). Under bankruptcy principles, the decision to reject would appear to be a valid exercise of business judgment and would likely be approved by the bankruptcy court depending on the totality of the circumstances. However, the FERC has asserted jurisdiction in several cases and demanded that the contract be honored for as long as possible by the debtor on the grounds that the economic burden should not fall on the utility's ratepayers. This is the so-called Mobile-Sierra Doctrine established by the U.S. Supreme Court in *Federal Power Commission v. Sierra Pacific Power Co.,* 350 U.S. 348 (1956). These conflicting approaches, which directly pit the interests of creditors against the interests of ratepayers, will likely result in either a high-stakes, potentially winner-take-all U.S. Supreme Court case or a legislative solution. See Siegel (2003).

99. Murray and Kranhold (2003).
100. BRC §524(g).
101. Technically, BRC §1125(b) permits a bankruptcy court to approve a disclosure statement without a valuation or appraisal, but within the context of reorganizations of significant enterprises, valuations are generally provided. As a practical matter, without a valuation, it will be very difficult for the typical creditor to estimate the value of a claim.
102. BRC §1129(a)(7).
103. See Fortgang and Mayer (1985).
104. See Chapter 10 for a more detailed discussion of the implications of valuation on creditor recoveries.
105. In some situations, even where a creditor ostensibly has the right to vote on the plan of reorganization, its actual voting power may be constrained by provisions of the indenture or an intercreditor agreement.
106. BRC §1125(b).
107. BRC §1129(a).

Chapter 5

1. This statement is generally valid for those situations in which the source of financial distress is primarily overleverage. The bankruptcy process provides important tools to allow firms to potentially increase enterprise value in addition to simply changing the capital structure.
2. See Brealy and Myers (2000), Chew (1998), Copeland et al. (2000), Cornell (1993), Gaughan (2002), Keown et al. (2002), Pratt (2001), Reilly and Scheins (2000), and Stickney (1996).
3. See Bierman and Smidt (1984), Copeland et al. (2000), Francis (1988), and Van Horne (2001).
4. When the decision is made to discontinue part of a firm's operations, the income and expense attributable to these operations and assets are shown as a separate line item on the income statement, generally titled "Income, Gains, and Losses from Discontinued Operations," and are presented net of tax. See Accounting Principle Board Opinion No. 30: "Reporting Results of Operations" (1973) and Keiso et al. (2003).
5. Under recent SEC rules generally referred to as Reg FD (Full Disclosure), companies are now prohibited from selectively disseminating material information about their

business. Thus many managements take the view that disclosing anything beyond what is discussed or disclosed in SEC filings or public forums (such as quarterly earnings calls or formal analyst presentations) is a violation of Reg FD.

6. For a more detailed explanation, see Damodaran (2002).

7. Depreciation represents the periodic expensing of a previously capitalized investment. It represents the allocation of the cost of an asset to the periods that benefited from its use. Keiso et al. (2003).

8. It is beyond the scope of this book to comment on the ethics of choosing the location of manufacturing facilities on the basis of the ability to pollute without direct cost to the polluter.

9. Initially, the intangible asset created by the excess of cost over value of assets acquired (i.e., goodwill) was required to be amortized over a period of not more than 40 years. Accounting Principle Board Opinion No. 17: "Intangible Assets" (1970). However, this treatment was superceded by Statement of Financial Accounting Standard 131, which now requires that an annual valuation of the intangible asset be made, with a charge to income required if the intangible asset is deemed to have declined in value.

10. Costs associated with the issuance of debt securities, which are primarily made up of the legal, printing, and underwriting fees, are typically treated as a deferred charge and amortized over the life of the debt. See Accounting Principle Board Opinion No. 21: "Interest on Receivables and Payables" (1971) and Keiso et al. (2003).

11. The deductibility of goodwill amortization for tax purposes has also been the subject of much debate. For acquisitions completed before August 10, 1993, goodwill was not tax deductible; for acquisitions completed after that date, it can be amortized over a 15-year period. See Morris (1995).

12. See Statement of Financial Accounting Standard No. 109: "Accounting for Income Taxes" (1992) and Keiso et al. (2003).

13. For a critique on the overreliance on EBITDA, see Fridson (1998).

14. For a more comprehensive discussion of the limitations of EBITDA as a measure of cash flow, see Stumpp et al. (2000).

15. See Gaughan (2002). The concept has also been referred to as "entity value." See Copeland et al. (2000).

16. See Keiso et al. (2003).

17. For example, if there were warrants to purchase one million shares at $10 per share and the current share price was $12, it would be appropriate to adjust the share count to reflect what is issuable under the warrants because they are "in the money." Under the "treasury stock" dilution accounting method, which is GAAP as per Accounting Principle Board No. 15: "Earnings per Share," the number of CSEs added to the share count would reflect an assumption that the firm used all cash received on the warrant exercise (i.e., $10/share) to repurchase stock at the then market price (i.e., $12 per share). Thus, the CSE figure is effectively [1 − (exercise price/market price) × number of warrants]. Alternatively, financial analysts, recognizing that the treasury stock method is not representative of what a firm is likely to actually do, will add the full number of shares issuable under the warrants to the share figure and then add the aggregate exercise proceeds to cash.

18. Under American Institute of Certified Public Accountants Statement of Position 90-7: "Financial Reporting by Entities in Reorganization Under Bankruptcy Code" (1990), liabilities of the postreorganized entity are carried on the balance sheet at estimated fair

market value, with any discount (from face value) amortized as additional interest expense using the effective interest method.

19. Very often, primarily due to the market's historical convention of structuring bond coupon rates in 1/8% increments, bonds will be sold at slight discounts. For example, if a bond carries a 10.50% coupon but the appropriate rate in the market for a comparable credit is deemed to be 10.58%, then the bond will be issued at a discount such that the expected yield to maturity will be 10.58%; this might mean a price of 98 depending on the maturity. Although for accounting purposes such bonds are classified as discount securities, these are not what bond market professionals usually mean when referring to a discount bond. As used here, a discount bond is a bond structured to sell at a substantial discount (i.e., 20 points or more) such that the interest payments effectively are being deferred to the maturity of the bond.

20. A common variation of such a bond structure developed by Merrill Lynch is called Liquid Yield Option Notes (LYONs™).

21. Accounting Principle Board Opinion No. 21: "Interest on Receivables and Payables" (1971).

22. Finally, we note that the recent change to ameliorate the "double taxation" of corporate profits by allowing individuals to exclude dividends from income has brought renewed attention to corporate cash management strategies. This policy change resurrected the debate on whether the policy of taxing individuals for the receipt of interest and dividends, but only allowing corporations to deduct interest (but not dividends) as an expense, promotes a strategic bias for corporations to hoard cash rather than pay it out to shareholders as dividends. This debate is outside the scope of this work but tends to validate the view that cash balances often may not be needed in core operations and thus need to be excluded when attempting to value those core operations.

23. These included well-known firms such as Kohlberg Kravis Roberts & Co.; Texas Pacific Group; Freeman Spogli & Co.; and Hicks, Muse, Tate & Furst Inc. to name but a few.

24. Notable private equity firms include Silver Point Capital; Golder, Thoma, Cressey, Rauner LP; Castle Harlan; AEA Investors; Veritas Capital; Hibernia Capital Partners; Carlyle Group; Madison Dearborn Partners; and Warburg Pincus.

25. In simple terms, the rationale for such a thought process is that as long as the IRR is greater than the cost of capital, the economic value of the transaction (and hence benefit to equity holders) is positive. See Francis (1988) and Van Horne (2001).

26. To cite a recent example, buyout fund Freeman Spogli purchased Century Maintenance in 1998 for a net investment of $67.5 million. Four years later, after significantly improving EBITDA and with the benefit of an improved valuation multiple, it sold Century to Hughes Supply, Inc. (a strategic buyer) for approximately $140 million. See Holman and Carey (2003).

27. Outside of the context of readily marketable assets, GAAP has a strong bias toward carrying assets on a historical cost basis. Keiso et al. (2003).

28. The author has not seen an academic study supporting or disproving this proposition, which he posits on the basis of significant anecdotal market observation.

Chapter 6

1. Under the given facts, it would seem unlikely that any collateral would be available to offer as security, but perhaps at the time the loan was obtained the firm had substantial

means or the collateral consists of stock of subsidiaries that previously had significant market value but went bust.

2. The approach to credit analysis used in this chapter is somewhat different than the classic approach, which proceeds from the analysis of the "3 Cs" of lending: credit, capacity, and collateral. In the classic context, credit essentially refers to the borrower's prior repayment experience, capacity to the notion of income to repay the loan, and collateral to the value of the hard assets pledged.

3. It should be noted that within in the context of construction lending, it is fairly typical to capitalize interest (i.e., effectively increase the size of the loan) until such time that the property begins to generate cash or can be refinanced.

4. Bank loans are not necessarily structured on the expectation they can be fully repaid from internally generated operating cash flow. Sometimes only a partial repayment will be expected or required by the terms of the loan, particularly in junior tranches of multiclass term loans. In other cases, amortization schedules may be structured on the expectation that proceeds from asset sales will be used to pay down debt.

5. Term loans are typically amortized over the life of the loan, whereas a revolving loan may be structured with annual reductions in availability or an annual 30-day $0 balance cleanup feature designed to demonstrate that the revolver is needed only for seasonal working capital.

6. Periodic amortization features in corporate bonds are unusual, but certainly not unheard of. In contrast, many municipal bonds amortize principal over the life of the bond through a sinking fund.

7. The author believes this to be the case based on anecdotal evidence gathered from professionals in the field and not based on any compensation study comparing the two. In general, bond fund managers are compensated on the performance of their fund relative to a benchmark index. Thus, in a severe recession, many bonds in the portfolio may default, but as long as this amount is relatively less than what was experienced in the index, the fund manager may still receive significant performance bonuses. On the other hand, when bank loan portfolio managers experience defaults, their compensation typically suffers regardless of the economy or their "relative" performance.

8. Based on an analysis of data on the developed by the Federal Deposit Insurance Corporation, the average charge-off rate for all commercial banks from 1992 to 2002 was approximately 0.63% of assets.

9. For an excellent discussion of the inherency of economic cycles, see Kindleberger (2001).

10. When confronted with cyclical credits, credit capacity measures can vary widely and may be based on metrics such as minimum or average expected EBITDA.

11. It would, of course, be desirable to lend with no risk — to expect that in any foreseeable and even unforeseeable circumstance or scenario that the loan would be repaid. But lending is a competitive business, and any lender that attempts to compete on an absolutely risk-averse basis will be at a competitive disadvantage compared to lenders that will accept some level of risk. For example, nuclear holocaust is a foreseeable risk (hopefully a very, very small risk, but nuclear weapons do exist). If one only made loans in situations where even in the event of a nuclear holocaust one would expect to get repaid, very few lending opportunities would present themselves. Whether rightly or wrongly, many credit officers and investors tend to dismiss the impact of devastating,

but low-probability, risks with the rationalization that should such a disaster happen, they would not be around to be fired anyway.

12. A few of the many possible examples include Nextel, Internet Capital Group, EMCORE, Priceline, Finisar, Sepracor, and Elan Pharmaceutical.

13. Rhetorical restraint will be used; otherwise, an allusion to seasickness readily comes to mind.

14. It should be noted that when interest payments consume all of EBITDA, firms generally have minimal taxable income.

15. The making of secured loans in high-default-risk contexts has become a popular strategy with many distressed investors and asset-based lenders. Returns on such loans, which will generally be structured with a combination of high upfront fees, high interest rates, and equity warrants, often will have expected returns of 30% or more.

16. The basic impetus for these instruments was both balance sheet and tax motivated. Part of the theory of creating these instruments was to allow the issuer, which at the time of issuance may have had negative taxable income (thus the nondeductibility of the preferred stock dividend would have had little opportunity cost) to convert or exchange the preferred stock into a bond that paid tax-deductible interest.

17. It is beyond the scope of this book to discuss in detail the structural characteristics of convertible bonds. While the referenced conversion premium is fairly representative of a broad range of offerings, when the volatility of the equity security underlying the convertible bond is high, the conversion premium can be 40% or more. For additional information, see Calamos (2003), Connolly (1999), and Nelken (2001).

Chapter 7

1. There are no "rules" governing how securities are titled or described or the typical provisions required for a security of a particular name.

2. See Sharpe (1970).

3. This also applies to Articles of Rights and Preferences that define the rights of preferred stock.

4. The Uniform Commercial Code (UCC) is a model law drafted for the purpose of having consistent laws among the many state jurisdictions. Each state has adopted the UCC, generally with only minor variations. The determination of many issues relevant to creditor rights is determined by state law or the UCC. For example, while the Bankruptcy Code establishes the rights of a secured creditor, it is the relevant state UCC provision that will determine if the creditor is, in fact, secured.

5. Within the context of describing the price volatility of a bond, the term "duration" has a meaning different than the normal usage of a period of time. Mathematically, duration is a weighted average term to maturity of a security's cash flows. The measure allows the price volatility of bonds with different terms to be compared using a single parameter. A bond with a calculated duration of 6.2 will have more price volatility to a given change in interest rates than a bond with a duration of 4.7. See Fabozzi (1995).

6. See Barnhill et al. (1999) and Fons (1994).

7. For high-grade issuers, the decision on the term of a bond will be based on a variety of internal capital structure considerations as well as the shape of the yield curve and the structure of credit spreads. See Van Horne (2001).

8. This is a fairly pessimistic characterization. During periods of economic growth, when the issuer expects its credit quality to improve, it may view shorter maturities as preferable on the assumption that when such obligations mature, its cost of capital will be lower. An "in-between" alternative is to structure the obligation with a long final maturity but give the issuer the right to redeem or call the bond early.

9. This will be true in any interest rate environment in which the typical positively sloped yield curve is present.

10. In the mid-90s, several highly rated companies, such as IBM and Disney, issued 100-year bonds (century bonds). In the case of IBM, its 7.125% senior bond due in 2096 was issued at a yield that was only 80 basis points higher than the yield on the 30-year U.S. Treasury bond at that time. Given how few of the prominent businesses of the 1890s were still prosperous in the 1990s, one wonders if the market is properly pricing the risk associated with bonds of this length.

11. The bank recovery would be 33.3. Note that in the real world, there likely would be covenant provisions in the bank debt to prevent the repayment of sub debt under these circumstances.

12. The risk of certain creditors unduly benefiting from early payoff is the primary reason for the voidable preference provisions (BRC §547) discussed in Chapter 4. In the previous example, the hypothesized debt payoff appears to have been made in the ordinary course of business and was made more than 90 days before the filing of the bankruptcy petition; thus the voidable preference provisions should not apply.

13. A real-world illustration of this arose in November 2002 with Amkor Corp. Amkor had subordinated bond issues that matured in 2006 and 2007, well before a senior note issue that matured in 2008. On February 24, 2003, the 2007 sub note traded at 58, while the 2008 senior note traded at 92. On May 23, 2003, approximately three months later, during which Amkor's fundamentals improved and the capital markets became more accessible, the 2007 and 2008 bonds were trading at 80 and 104, respectively. Investors in the 2007 bonds enjoyed a total return of over 35% over this period. See Moyer and Laufman (2003b, 2003d).

14. Adding the required subordination language would theoretically be possible, but it would require the agreement of a majority of the holders of the senior notes, which, as a practical matter, would be difficult to obtain and would certainly cost something in the form of consent fees. Intercreditor agreements are another mechanism besides indenture provisions to control or specify payment priorities in complex capital structures.

15. By operation of law, the $90 left in Holding Corp. after the payoff of the $100 in senior notes would be the property of Holding Corp.'s equity holders. Absent a guaranty or extenuating circumstances, shareholders (i.e., Holding Corp.) are generally not liable for the corporation's (i.e., Sub-1 Corp.) debts.

16. This should not be construed to imply that all laws can be overridden by contractual provisions. For example, a contractual provision in a secured lending agreement that provided "Notwithstanding anything in the Bankruptcy Code to the contrary, in the event the borrower files for bankruptcy protection, the lender shall have the right to immediately take possession of the collateral" would not be effective at overriding the provisions of the automatic stay.

17. See Financial Accounting Standards Board Interpretation No. 46: "Consolidation of Variable Interest Entities" (2003) and Statement of Financial Accounting Standards No.

140: "Accounting for Transfers and Servicing of Financial Assets and Extinguishments of Liabilities" (2001).

18. Investment-grade bond issues will typically only have general operating covenants relating to continuation of the business, maintenance of certain offices, etc.

19. See Petersen and Rajan (1995).

20. And at least one recovering lawyer, the author.

21. This is particularly true in the case of international subsidiaries.

22. A good example is Ireland, which provides relocation incentives to companies in manufacturing and other sectors in the form of grants, relief from municipal taxes, tax allowances, certain income exemptions, and caps on corporate tax rates. See KPMG (2003).

23. Most bond indentures provide that the failure to pay any interest payment does not constitute a default unless the borrower fails to "cure" within 30 days. This is referred to as the grace period.

24. For example, see the restricted payment provisions in the covenants example available for download at www.jrosspub.com. The author is unaware of any published studies attempting to ascertain the most typical structure of such provisions.

25. Such covenants are generally limited to the bank context because of the relative ease (compared to the amendment of an indenture for publicly issued notes) of the lender to renegotiate the terms of the loan if the borrower does not meet performance milestones.

26. A put option is a contract that gives the holder the right to sell a certain quantity of an underlying security to the writer of the option at a specified price (strike price) up to a specified period (expiration).

27. The most common example is a security structure created by Merrill Lynch called the Liquid Yield Option Note or LYON™.

28. See, for example, the terms of a security developed by Credit Suisse First Boston called Remarketable Term Income Deferrable Equity Securities (High TIDES℠).

29. See Stumpp (2001).

Chapter 8

1. This policy is essentially mandated by the recently enacted Regulation FD, which prohibits selective disclosure of material nonpublic information and requires issuers that inadvertently make such disclosures to promptly make them public through the filing of a Form 8-K. Rule 100, 65 FR 51716, 51738, August 24, 2000.

2. The bond issuance rating fee is generally 3.65 basis points of the amount issued, subject to a minimum fee of $37,000 and a rate step-down to 2.30 basis points on amounts above $500 million. The annual rating maintenance fee is $37,000 for companies with $1 billion or less in outstanding issues, with gradual step-ups as the outstandings increase. These prices are based on Standard & Poor's U.S. Industrial Corporations credit rating fee schedule as of January 2004.

3. Sometimes these "beliefs" will be based on the judgment of professionals at the underwriter. Investment banks will often hire ex-rating-agency personnel to advise potential issuers on what their rating would likely be and what they can do to improve it. In other cases, the rating agencies will actually provide the underwriter or issuer with an informal verbal indication of a rating, which the issuer will consider in deciding whether or not to obtain an official published rating.

4. The rating process and goals of the various agencies differ and, to a certain extent, are ambiguous. S&P generally assigns a D rating any time a default has occurred, regardless of risk of loss. Moody's attempts to use its C ratings to indicate severity of ultimate loss. Thus, a Caa rating implies a full or nearly full recovery, a Ca rating implies a partial recovery, and a C rating implies little to no recovery.

5. See Baker and Mansi (2002).

6. Moyer and Gubner (2001).

7. See, for example, Form 8-K filed by Southern California Edison Company dated January 10, 2001.

8. It should be noted that in the PG&E and Southern California Edison case, the rating agencies were in a very conflicted position. Much of the debt of both utilities contained provisions requiring the companies to redeem the debt should their ratings fall below investment grade. Thus, there may have been concern by the agencies that had they downgraded the entities prior to the default, their actions could have been perceived as forcing the entities to file for bankruptcy — undoubtedly a less than desirable political position. Nonetheless, at the end of the day, the fact remains that despite very obvious warnings that the financial situation of the utilities had deteriorated materially, the agencies waited for an actual payment default (the imminence of which had been well publicized) before lowering the ratings of the utilities to below investment grade. See Moyer and Gubner (2001). Other examples where rating agency actions might be criticized as not offering investors sufficient advance warning include Enron, which was rated investment grade by Moody's and Standard & Poor's four days before its chapter 11 filing; WorldCom, which was investment grade three months before its default; and Global Crossing, which was investment grade five months before its default. See comment letter dated November 10, 2002 to J. Katz, Secretary of the Securities and Exchange Commission, from S. Egan and B. Jones, available at www.egan-jones.com/sec.letter.aspx. See also Stumpp (2001) for a discussion of the consequences of ratings triggers from the perspective of a rating agency.

9. See Hickman (1958), Beaver (1966), and Altman (1993).

10. Dr. Edward I. Altman, Max L. Heine Professor of Finance, Leonard N. Stern School of Business, New York University.

11. Professor Altman developed the "Z-score" model in 1968. Altman (1968). This was subsequently revised to allow the application of the model to certain situations not originally included in the original sample set. Altman (1993).

12. See Shefrin (2002) and the many studies cited therein.

13. Although not as numerous as in the case of equities, there have been studies of the information content of bond price movements. See Brown and Mooradian (1993), Eberhart and Sweeney (1992), and Ketz (1978).

14. For example, in the first quarter of 2001, Covad Communications had a market cap in excess of $500 million and yet most of its bonds were trading below 80, suggesting that bond investors perceived a significant risk of default. However, this observation should not be interpreted to imply that the equity market was oblivious to Covad's circumstances, as its equity had traded down from much higher levels. See also Kwan (1996).

15. For a general discussion of why businesses fail, see Platt (1997).

16. The fact pattern in this hypothetical is arguably what happened to Flooring America and Color Tile, both of which went bankrupt and liquidated.

17. Based on the author's general observations and discussions with investors, the recovery experience of unsecured creditors of retailers in liquidations is usually fairly unfavorable. In the Flooring America and Color Tile cases cited above, recoveries to unsecured creditors were under 10%. According to Credit Suisse First Boston, for the period 1980–2001, out of 20 sectors analyzed, the retail sector had the second highest default loss rate, after food and tobacco. Credit Suisse First Boston (2003).

18. At the time, the choice between holding company and operating company obligations had the opposite implications from a credit perspective than one would normally expect. The operating utilities were the entities which had incurred material operating deficits that led to an escalation in liabilities. The utility holding companies, in contrast, often held interests in other more financially sound subsidiaries and maintained relatively strong credit fundamentals. Later, when the market fundamentals changed, many of the holding company's previously valuable subsidiaries, particularly those which housed nonregulated merchant power operations, became financially distressed.

19. Such fundamentals included a wide variety of factors ranging from future precipitation in the Pacific Northwest, which had implications for the potential supply of hydroelectric power, to economic growth trends in the Silicon Valley to the future price and availability of natural gas.

20. See Kindleberger (2001).

21. The reasons for this relate to the general operation of securitization trusts, the details of which are beyond the scope of this book but well explained in AmeriCredit's 2002 Securities and Exchange Commission filings.

22. See Lyle (1999).

23. Estimate. Cash was $208.2 million as of the September 30, 1999 operating statement.

24. See Glovin (2000). It should be noted that while the final sale price for Iridium's assets was quite low, in the early stages of the bankruptcy there were indications of interest from such notable parties as Craig McCaw (the billionaire founder of McCaw Cellular) and ICO Global, which led many to speculate that values could be considerably higher.

25. Even this low price did not represent the value of the firm's physical assets, which was actually less. However, Iridium's bondholders had brought a multibillion-dollar lawsuit against Motorola, Iridium's development partner and influential shareholder, and this lawsuit, as discussed in more detail in Chapter 13, had speculative recovery value. See Gill and Levin (2000).

26. This example is generically based on the history of the various so-called "Sprint affiliates" (e.g., Alamosa, Airgate, Horizon, Ubiquitel). It should not be taken as a discussion of every issue or any particular situation.

27. See, for example, Kaplan (1989), Jensen (1989), Easterwood and Seth (1993), Garvey and Hanka (1999), and Kane et al. (1984). The seminal work on how capital structure decisions are biased by taxes is Modigliani and Miller (1958). Jensen and Meckling (1976) were among the first to explore the agency issue.

28. See McDermott (2002) and Darby et al. (2002).

29. For a good summary of Wendt's challenge at Conseco, see Hornaday (2002). More generally, see Khurana (2002).

30. For a general discussion of effective management practices, see Drucker (1985, 2002, 2003).

31. For example, if a retailer had a weak Internet service capability.

32. Lender liability arises when a lender exerts inappropriate influence, which results in the breech of a common-law duty or a violation of a statutory provision, that results in damage to either the borrower or another creditor. An offending lender may be held liable for damages or have its claim equitably subordinated or even entirely voided. See Weil, Gotshal & Manges (2003), Chapter 18.

33. As discussed in Chapter 10, a variant of this scenario is a firm that has no bank debt, but two pari passu bond issues with different maturities (e.g., one that matures in three months and the other in three years). Assuming the firm is experiencing distress, the later-maturing bond may be trading at a substantial discount, say 60. However, the bond that matures in three months, if there is a plausible chance it can be refinanced, might be trading significantly higher, perhaps 85. Those investors willing to pay 85 (or not sell at 85) are betting that the refinancing will occur and their bond will be paid off shortly at 100. This would represent a 15-point cash profit and an annualized rate of return of well over 50%. On the other hand, if the bond cannot be refinanced, it is likely to force a bankruptcy or restructuring, and the early-maturing bond should trade down to the same level as the longer pari passu bond, or 60. So the downside is 25. Those with a penchant for probabilities will discern that if the upside/downside ratio is 15/25, the implicit expected probability that the refinancing will occur is better than 50/50 (62.5%, to be exact). In an efficient market, the probability-weighted value of each outcome should be equal: $15 \times 0.625 = 25 \times 0.375$.

34. See Moyer (2002c).

35. Orbital Sciences stock traded in a range between $5.42 and $7.70 in May 2002.

36. See Moyer (2002d).

37. Although this discussion of tort liability occasionally will use fairly pejorative language, this should not be interpreted to suggest that the author does not believe that firms should not be responsible for foreseeable damage caused by their willful or negligent acts. However, the author does believe that the current system for adjudicating these claims could and should be made significantly more efficient.

38. See the Fairness in Asbestos Injury Resolution Act of 2003. Senate Bill 1125, May 22, 2003.

39. BRC §524(g). See additional discussion in Chapter 4 and Weil, Gotshal & Manges (2003).

40. There were six intermediate holding companies between GAF and BMCA. See Curley (2001).

41. Even with respect to companies directly associated with the tort liability it is possible that some may be able to survive. In particular, those that were not direct manufacturers but only involved with the installation may survive if their prior installation activity was relatively minor, they have adequate insurance, and they retained good records of the personnel associated with the installation. For example, Foster Wheeler is the subject of numerous asbestos liability suits, but as of this writing the company's insurance has paid all costs and claims and its strong internal record keeping allows it to enjoy a fairly high dismissal rate. See Kellstrom and Cray (2002).

42. Disclosure relating to firms' activities in and exposure to derivatives has only recently been required by Finance Accounting Standards Board 133: "Accounting for Derivative Instruments and Hedging Activities" (2000).

43. See Gubner (2002).

44. See Berman (2002).

45. See Ryan (2002).
46. See Hubbard (2001).
47. See Voreacos (2003).
48. Learnout & Hauspie was a Dutch concern involved in, among other things, the development of sophisticated voice-recognition software. The company engaged in a series of complicated transactions with various related parties that were formed to apply Learnout's technologies or methods to various languages. The company allegedly recognized noncash "investments" in these affiliated entities as revenues. Learnout itself had very little debt, but in 2000 acquired Dictaphone Corp., which had $158.5 million in senior subordinated notes maturing in 2005. As the accounting scandal developed, Learnout sought bankruptcy protection in Delaware. In its bankruptcy, the company was essentially liquidated through a series of asset sales.
49. See Maremont et al. (2000).
50. On the basis of the facts as known when the accounting issue was revealed in June 2002, it appeared that operating expenses were "shifted" or characterized as capital expenditures (CAPX). Thus EBITDA was overstated by the same amount as CAPX. Therefore, EBITDA-CAPX was potentially unchanged.
51. See Ronson (2003b).
52. It is arguable that since virtually all shareholder value had been wiped out (the stock fell to $0.03 per share, down 99.8% from its 2002 high of $14.82 per share) and WorldCom faced a relatively weak economic environment, which could present challenges in any case, management made the strategic decision to use the occasion to reorganize so that the company might have a competitive advantage later. WorldCom's competitors actually began lobbying to stop the company from reorganizing, arguing that this essentially would allow the company to benefit from its wrongful act (the competitors conveniently overlooked that WorldCom's existing shareholders were virtually certain to lose everything). The competitors appeared to prefer that WorldCom's operations be liquidated in an auction where they could purchase the spoils at attractive levels and go forward in a less competitive environment. See Young and Berman (2003).
53. The Sarbanes-Oxley Act of 2002 (SEC Release No. 33-8180) January 24, 2003. Section 302 of the act requires the CEO and CFO of the issuer to personally attest to the "fairness" of financial statements and attaches civil and criminal penalties for willful violations.
54. See Shinkle (2003b).

Chapter 9

1. For a general discussion of the firm's options from a legal perspective, see Miller (1999).
2. Note holders would not be allowed to recover more than their claim, so this would imply, depending on the magnitude of the claims and expenses, that the equity would have a recovery (which is only fair since they invested $1000).
3. A prospective equity investor's analysis will be as follows: if they have $225 in cash and plan to spend $150 for CAPX and burn another $20 in operations, in a worst-case scenario that leaves $50 when the notes mature. So if I contribute any equity junior to

the notes, it will just be to the notes' benefit. However, if the note holders could be induced to make a full or partial tender of their notes for repurchase at a significant discount, then it potentially would be feasible to raise additional equity to fund such repurchases in the form of either new equity or a contribution from existing equity holders via a rights offering.

4. This could be the case because in this scenario Webco's only noncash collateral will be interests in or assets of Internet companies that are difficult to value.
5. Arguably, another option would be to sell Webco. But if Webco's valuation at that point materially exceeded debt such that there was a return to equity, the managers' selfish interest in retaining their positions (a risk in most sale scenarios) might lead them to attempt a rights offering that would be used to pay off debt.
6. This example is based in significant part on the facts of Internet Capital Group, as present in the second quarter of 2002. It should be noted that a year later, the company's notes had approximately doubled in price. See Moyer and Cray (2002).
7. This means a covenant violation not related to nonpayment.
8. In which case one would wonder why the bonds are trading at only 50.
9. A good example of a situation where an equity sponsor continued to support a troubled situation is WKI Holdings. WKI was a vehicle used by Kohlberg Kravis Roberts & Co. (KKR) to purchase certain branded consumer products businesses from Corning (these included Pyrex™, EKCO™, Revere Ware™, and Corningware™). KKR, the 96% equity holder, purchased portions of WKI's bonds and bank debt at a discount and caused an affiliate to extend loans to WKI all in an effort to keep WKI afloat. Ultimately, however, WKI went through a chapter 11 reorganization. See Gilbert (2002, 2003).
10. The WCI Steel reorganization is a good example. WCI was owned and controlled by The Renco Group, Inc. Shortly following WCI's chapter 11 filing, Renco committed to extending $10 million in new capital through a debtor-in-possession facility. See Farricielli (2003).
11. Equitable subordination refers to the power of the bankruptcy court to, in appropriate circumstances, subordinate the status of one claim to another. The merits of an equitable subordination challenge would turn on the thinness of the company's capitalization, the owner's general fairness (absence of bad acts) toward the firm, and whether a third party would have been willing to make the loan. See Chapter 11. For a more extensive discussion, see Bienenstock (1987).
12. The coupon in two weeks does not count because if the bond trades with accrued interest, the investor will have effectively prepaid this coupon. So the best the investor can collect is the coupon due in another six months (which would be six months before maturity). This coupon payment is by no means certain and would essentially represent another focal point to trigger a restructuring or bankruptcy filing. If a bankruptcy is expected when the notes mature, it is highly unlikely the final coupon will be paid (although the accrued interest would become part of the note holders' prepetition claim and thus might be partially recouped in the restructuring).
13. Over 40 companies in the steel industry filed bankruptcy during this time frame. See Steelnews.com (2003).
14. The word "appear" is used because it is unclear what the actual market value of the exchange consideration will be relative to 50.
15. To simplify the illustration, other claims have been ignored, although in the typical steel company reorganization these claims would likely be quite substantial.

16. If Steelbox filed for chapter 11 protection within 90 days of the exchange, an action, which would have a reasonable chance of success, might be brought under BRC §549(b) to challenge the transfer of the second lien as a voidable preference.
17. Even though paying the coupon would buy time, it would only increase the amount of secured debt, which at the margin would be a disadvantage to the equity holder.
18. There potentially could also be some cash recovery depending on the cash build during the chapter 11 case.
19. See Chapter 2 for a discussion of the investment preferences of CDOs.
20. See the discussion of BRC §363 sales in Chapter 12 and Hotchkiss and Mooradian (1997, 1998), Pulvino (1999), Stromberg (2000), and Thorburn (2002).
21. This is often the case when the loan is structured with significant pay-downs over time. The loan structure may have been designed assuming the pay-downs would be financed from internally generated funds or asset sale proceeds. When the borrower fails to comply with the preset pay-down schedule, the lender has leverage to effectively force an asset sale.
22. The unsecured debt might be happier if the sale proceeds were used to buy back bonds at a discount, but this will likely be barred by the terms of the bank credit facility.
23. Whether this is true will depend on the circumstances. If a chapter 11 filing is a reasonably foreseeable risk, then a sale within the context of chapter 11 may generate the best price. See the discussion of BRC §363 sales in Chapter 12.
24. It is conceivable, although unlikely, that there is no such provision, but the presumption should be that one exists.
25. See CapitalEyes (2003) and Davenport (2004). It should also be noted that, conversely, second-lien loans can be an attractive vehicle for the distressed investor to make a potentially attractive direct investment into a distressed situation.
26. The sunk-cost fallacy is economic jargon for the proposition that the amount of money already invested and lost is irrelevant to the decision to make an additional investment.
27. It should be noted that loans made in such circumstances risk being equitably subordinated. See Chapter 12 and endnote 11 above.
28. Many "real-life" examples of this phenomenon could be cited. For example, in the case of Encompass Services, Apollo Partners, its largest stakeholder, astutely decided not to make a follow-on investment (which would have been in equity and thus also at risk) in 2002 because it was reasonably apparent that the underlying business was in trouble and the original stake would be lost. See Moyer 2002b. In contrast, in the case of Metris Companies, Thomas H. Lee Partners, the primary equity holder, made a $125 million secured loan in 2003 to bolster liquidity in the face of regulatory scrutiny and a $250 million bond maturity requirement in 2004. See 10-Q dated March 31, 2003. At the time of the investment/loan, Metris's bonds were trading at 50, implying substantial doubt as to the value of the equity, but Metris's primary asset, a credit card bank, had sufficient excess capital to fund the bond maturity.
29. Companies often choose to conduct repurchase programs through the underwriter that issued the bonds on the grounds that the underwriter likely has the best knowledge of who holds the bonds.
30. Normally, one would suspect that if the fact that the firm was the purchaser would trigger a price movement, then a disclosure obligation would arise. However, usually a firm's Securities and Exchange Commission filings will be careful to preannounce the possibility of such market activities.

31. Investors should carefully review the footnotes to the balance sheet for such disclosures.
32. Sometimes a firm's activities become known due to a market "leak." More benignly, a firm's activities will become known when the firm is in effect forced to disclose the purchases in its quarterly regulatory earnings reports. For the issuer to initiate the process by contacting and soliciting the holder could be construed as a violation of the 1934 act which prohibits tender offers except pursuant to an approved offering statement.
33. As discussed in Chapter 5, since the market values the debt at only $120 and the firm has $200 in cash, the market does not appear to have a very positive view of the firm's basic business.
34. For example, such a prohibition was contained in the terms of the Transwitch Corp. exchange offer dated May 16, 2003. See Moyer and Laufman (2003d).
35. As mentioned in endnote 16, the granting of a security interest in an exchange offer could be challenged as a voidable preference under BRC §547(b). However, here it can still be a valuable inducement because the transfer may be outside the relevant look-back periods and therefore withstand challenge. Further, even if the liens are voided, the new notes still may benefit from contractual seniority depending on the subordination language of the original subnotes. For example, Avondale has successfully induced holders of senior subordinated notes to exchange into a discounted amount of senior notes. See Gilbert and Whitesell (2004).
36. For a more complete discussion of the HealthSouth situation, see Chapter 8 and Shinkle (2003b).
37. See Nitzberg (1999).

Chapter 10

1. Certain hedge funds will use the strategy of employing leverage (i.e., invest using borrowed funds) to increase the return potential of their portfolios. In these cases, the portfolio manager may prefer lower returning but less speculative investment options and then use fund leverage to increase returns. Conceptually, such hedge funds are very similar to collateralized debt obligations discussed in Chapter 2.
2. For example, in 2003 low-rated bonds enjoyed a total return of 50.8% versus a 28.7% return for the S&P 500. See Credit Suisse First Boston (2004).
3. See Fabozzi (1995).
4. Even investors willing to become involved in chapter 11 workouts will want to do so only when the expected returns justify the incremental risk and time delay.
5. For purposes of this example, it will be assumed that the conversion price is substantially above the current market value and thus there is little or no option value.
6. As discussed in Chapter 7, as a due diligence matter, the investor would want to examine closely the restricted payment provisions of the '09 seniors. The stricter these provisions are on refinancing subordinated debt (e.g., requiring that it be refinanced only with subordinated securities or equity), the more weight the investor should accord future refinancing risk.
7. In small closely held issues, the market effectively may be limited to holders already involved.
8. If the fund prenegotiated a purchase, it is highly unlikely it would do so without performing due diligence involving nonpublic information.

9. BRC §547. See discussion in Chapter 4.

10. Of course, if there was an argument that the exchange would result in the '09 senior trading to a higher level, an exchange might be feasible, but there would be a considerable incentive to hold out.

11. It may be possible to offer second lien bonds, but the exchange could, if Chipco filed for bankruptcy shortly thereafter, be deemed a preferential transfer and unwound. However, as long as the '04 seniors do not reduce their claim amount (i.e., exchange at less than face amount), it is hard to see how they would be any worse off in this event.

12. In the event of a chapter 11, there should be a slight difference in price level to reflect the difference in claim amount between the two bonds caused by differences in accrued interest at the time of filing.

13. There is nothing, per se, in the reorganization process that requires an allocation of postconfirmation debt on the basis of claim priority. It is quite possible that the plan could contemplate allocating some amount of debt to the junior creditors. Alternatively, sometimes the plan will contemplate that the postconfirmation debt will be issued to raise fresh cash and that this will be used to pay junior creditors in cash. For example, in the Laidlaw reorganization, it issued $400 million in senior notes as part of its exit financing and used the proceeds to pay certain prepetition creditors cash. See Shinkle (2003f).

14. See Chapter 6.

15. As previously mentioned, true value is an abstract concept which is intended here to represent what a firm might sell for in an undistressed context in a competitive auction or what value might be suggested in a peer multiple analysis with no valuation discounts.

16. In the rare case where a firm filing for chapter 11 is deemed not to have been insolvent, unsecured prepetition claims may be able to recover postpetition interest. See Bienenstock (1987).

17. See, for example, the discussion of HealthSouth in Chapter 8.

18. In a "participation agreement," the legal title to the investment stays with the seller, but the purchaser essentially purchases all of the economic interest as well as the right to direct the voting of the interest. A standard participation agreement is available for download at www.jrosspub.com.

19. The Securities and Exchange Commission has begun to examine the need and appropriateness of more regulation of hedge funds. See Securities and Exchange Commission (2003) and Cadwalader, Wickersham & Taft (2003).

20. A discussion of the use of credit default swaps in hedging is beyond the scope of this book but well covered elsewhere. See Nelken (1999) and Tavakoli (2002).

21. "Higher positive volatility" is used to mean that the upside (37%)/downside (–24%) expected price movements of the sub note are net positive.

22. The conversation with a person at the bank arguably is not material inside information since it is indicated that no decision has in fact been made. However, were it deemed material nonpublic information, the investor should not trade on the basis of this information.

23. The expected return would be calculated as $50\% \times (15.66) + 50\% \times 39.34 = 11.84$.

24. See, for example, the Metamor case, where it is alleged that PSI (Metamor's parent following an acquisition) made a loan to Metamor, but no note was ever created or executed. See Martin (2003).

25. In the PSI Net bankruptcy, initially the notes of Metamor, an acquired subsidiary, arguably were misvalued. In the Global Crossing situation, the claims against Frontier Vision, an acquired subsidiary, also were initially misvalued.
26. Ideally, these notes should be issued by the same entity that is the obligor of the trade claim. Investors should bear in mind that the cost of carry in these hedges is higher than in the typical bond versus bond case because trade claims generally do not accrue interest.
27. See Rule 3350: Short Sale Rule, Conduct Rules: National Association of Securities Dealers (2003).

Chapter 11

1. An expression favored by political commentator John McLaughlin.
2. Analysis performed by Imperial Capital.
3. This contrarian strategy is followed at the investor's peril. After all, there probably are fairly good reasons why most other investors are avoiding the situation.
4. Examples of such due diligence checklists can be found in Sahakian (1998).
5. Absent a court or other regulatory order to compel disclosure, a firm's nonpublic information is its property, and its officers typically will be bound by contractual and fiduciary duties to not disclose such information outside of the appropriate circumstances. Within the acquisition context mentioned above, such information is provided under the protection of a confidentiality agreement within the context of a voluntarily entered into negotiation with the other party.
6. In a distressed context where an informal committee has been formed, there may be three levels since the committee members may negotiate for access to a more limited amount of nonpublic information so as to limit the period they will be restricted.
7. In circumstances where a firm has issued securities pursuant to a registration exemption such as Rule 144 and has never subsequently registered securities with the SEC, investors may be forced to sign confidentiality agreements simply to obtain information comparable to SEC filings.
8. For simplicity, the potential issue of structural seniority will be assumed away.
9. The rules relating to the proper perfection of a security interest are governed by complex state laws. Even when creditors diligently attempt to comply with such provisions, it can and often will be argued they did so improperly. Typically, however, it will be very difficult for an investor to make such a determination.
10. Under BRC §502(b), damages for lease rejections, which for real estate leases are capped under BRC §502(b)(6), are prepetition claims of the lessor/creditor. Accordingly, analyzing the recovery of such a claim would be similar to that of a general unsecured claim.
11. Typically, the trading value of the debt is not admissible for purposes of establishing valuation. The assumption here is that there is strong independent evidence on the valuation issue, which the market is reflecting in the trading value.
12. As discussed in Chapters 4 and 10, allocating the value of a bankruptcy estate among creditors and interest holders is typically a zero-sum game: more to one claim means less to another. Thus, even if there is a colorable argument that the value of a firm is in excess of the creditor claims, it is in the creditors' interest to argue that the value of the firm is lower so as not to have to share any value with junior creditors or

preferred or common equity holders. If later it turns out that the firm is worth significantly more, the creditors may receive a recovery greater than that estimated in the disclosure statement.

13. BRC §§503 and 1102.

14. Some of the better known services include Bloomberg, FactSet, and Capital IQ.

15. Readers seeking more background on basic financial statement analysis should consult any of several excellent texts on the subject including Fridson and Alverez (2002) and White et al. (2003).

16. Federal Rules of Bankruptcy Procedure 1007 and 2015 govern the initial and periodic, respectively, reporting requirements of the debtor. See Bienenstock (1987), Chapter 10.

17. This should not be construed as suggesting that such contacts cannot be informative and valuable. Many investor relations officers are experienced professionals who are extremely conversant about their firm's operations and industry trends. However, even in situations where such a professional is involved, investors typically still prefer some regular contact with senior officers if for no other reason than to form a personal impression of their competence, goals, and integrity.

18. 17 CFR 243.100–243.103.

19. See Blake and Williams (2002).

20. The usual reason for the decision to discontinue Exchange Act §15(d) periodic requirements is that the issuer's/debtor's operating circumstances are so uncertain that reliable financial information cannot be prepared.

21. Although not technically a situation in reorganization, when i2 technologies entered a period of financial uncertainty due to the disclosure of certain accounting changes that would lead to material earnings restatements, it suffered a severe decline in new contract wins. See Moyer and Laufman (2003b).

22. For example, Orbital Imaging sells satellite-generated images to various parties, including the U.S. government. During the course of its chapter 11 reorganization in 2002 and 2003, it was not able to enter into new contracts with the U.S. government because of its bankrupt status. When it emerged, in January 2004, it was able to enter into such contracts and materially increase its firm backlog. Orbital Imaging is another standout example of the investment returns possible in distressed investing. At the beginning of 2003, its 11.625% senior notes traded at under 10. When it emerged at the end of that year, those notes were trading for 65. See Martin (2003).

23. It is, of course, difficult to gauge the state of mind of individuals and the author has not seen credible surveys (although many may exist) studying the impact of bankruptcy on consumer purchase decisions. Consumer product and service firms often will experience a decline in sales during a chapter 11 process, but it is hard to know whether this should be attributed to consumer aversion or simply a decline in business execution and/or marketing by the distressed firm. A consumer purchasing a durable good, such as a motor vehicle which might require ongoing repair or where the value of a future warranty is important, likely would consider the financial stability of the manufacturer, if aware of it, in the purchase decision. On the other hand, consumers, including the author, often flock to bankrupt retailers in the hopes of finding attractive values in liquidation sales.

24. The power to assume or reject an executory contract or lease is conferred by BRC §365 but is subject to bankruptcy court approval. In deciding whether to approve such actions, bankruptcy courts can be asked to weigh a variety of equitable factors, which tends to

limit the debtor's discretion. See Chapter 4 for additional discussion and Bienenstock (1987), Chapter 14.

25. If it is entitled to adequate protection. See Chapter 4.

26. See Braine (2003a).

27. This type of review would have helped an investor considering an investment in United Airlines. Based on the precedents in other airline reorganizations, the investor could have anticipated that holders of frequent-flier mileage claims would receive preferred status, a result which one might not find intuitively obvious.

28. The author gratefully acknowledges that this tax section benefited from review and comments by Menasche Nass and Andrew Bernknopf of De Castro, West, Chodorow, Glickfeld & Nass.

29. For a more detailed discussion of tax issues, see Aeder (1999) and Henderson and Goldring (1998).

30. For example, a key issue in determining eligibility for the "bankruptcy" exception to IRC §382 is the holding periods of certain debt holders prior to the filing of a bankruptcy petition. Many debtors often have little data on this issue at any given time.

31. With the special exception that losses incurred in 2001 or 2002 can be carried back five years.

32. The effective tax rate of the firm often will be disclosed in SEC filings.

33. In Penton's 10-Q for the September 30, 2002 period, it disclosed an operating loss of $233.8 million. See Moyer and Laufman (2002).

34. Investor caution likely was also fueled by the ill fortunes of Key3 Media, a company that had a trade show business that was arguably comparable to Penton's. In November 2001, Key3 was facing an uncertain liquidity outlook and its bonds were trading at under 10, down 40–50 points over the prior six months.

35. It is difficult to attribute securities price movements to one particular event. With hindsight, the U.S. economy clearly rebounded in 2003, but the magnitude of rebound arguably was not completely clear during the first quarter of that year and Penton's own operating result did not improve materially. See Moyer and Laufman (2003c).

36. IRC §382(f). This is an interest rate published monthly by the IRS that generally is developed with reference to tax-exempt bond yields. The applicable rate is that which is in effect during the month in which the change of ownership occurs.

37. IRC §382(b)(1).

38. See Aeder (1999).

39. IRC§382(c).

40. IRC §382(l)(5)(A), (E), (H).

41. IRC §382(l)(6).

42. However, the valuation, if any, contained in the disclosure statement is not controlling for IRC §382 purposes. Generally, if the IRC §382 limitation applies despite application of the bankruptcy exception, the limitation is based on the lesser of (a) the value of the corporation's stock immediately after the COO (valuing any stock issued in connection with the COO at an amount not exceeding cash and property received for the issuance of the stock) or (b) the value of the corporation's assets before the COO (determined without regard to liabilities). Reg. §1.382-9(j), (k)(7).

43. See Bromley et al. (2004) for a discussion of a proposed model order to prevent trading which would jeopardize NOL usability.

44. For a more detailed discussion of this topic, see Bienenstock (1987) Chapter 16.
45. This hypothetical example is inspired by Global Crossing's acquisition of Frontier Vision.
46. See Bienenstock (1987), Chapter 16.
47. See Bienenstock (1987), Chapter 16.
48. See Bienenstock (1987), Chapter 16 and Weil, Gotshal & Manges (2003), Chapter 18.
49. 33 Del Ch. 215, December 30, 1991.
50. See Weil, Gotshal & Manges (2003).
51. See UCC §3-104. Fortgang and Mayer (1981).
52. See UCC §3-302. Fortgang and Mayer (1981).
53. It should be noted that debtors can amend filed schedules of claims rendering a previously admitted claim challengeable.
54. Federal Rules of Bankruptcy Procedure 3001(e). See Sabin et al. (1991).
55. See Sabin et al. (1991).
56. Sarbanes-Oxley Act of 2002, 107 P.L. 204 §1 et sec., 116 Stat. 745, July 30, 2002.
57. See Cimilluca (2003).
58. Broker-dealers active in the U.S. primary high-yield market and secondary high-yield and distressed debt market include Banc of America Securities, Banc One Securities, Bear Stearns, CIBC, Credit Suisse First Boston, Deutsche Banc, Citigroup Securities, Dresdner Kleinwort Wasserstein, Goldman Sachs, Jefferies, JP Morgan Chase, Lehman Brothers, Merrill Lynch, Morgan Stanley, TD Securities, UBS Securities, and Wachovia Securities. Other broker-dealers active in the U.S. high-yield and distressed secondary market include CBA Securities, Credit Research & Trading, Debt Traders, Fieldstone Capital, Friedman Billings Ramsey, Imperial Capital, Maxcor Financial, Miller Tabak Roberts, M.J. Whitman, Morgan Joseph, Seaport Securities, and Tejas Securities.
59. For example, Bloomberg under the holders function.
60. Unless the investor is Warren Buffett, Carl Icahn, or someone of comparable repute.
61. The author wants to disclose that although he believes this to be an objective appraisal of the trade-offs, he is a partner of a specialty broker-dealer and therefore potentially biased.
62. The National Association of Securities Dealers requires that trades in specified bonds, usually larger issue sizes or of large capitalization firms, be electronically recorded by broker-dealers into the Trade Reporting and Comparison Entry Source (TRACE[SM]). However, most of the securities required to be posted do not constitute distressed securities.
63. Dissemination occurs in many ways, including the dealer's salespeople mentioning the trade in conversations with customers or including it in written market briefings to clients.
64. An acronym for Committee on Uniform Security Identification Procedures. Every security is issued a unique CUSIP number to establish its identity. The system is operated by Standard & Poor's for the American Bankers Association.

Chapter 12

1. Which should not be confused with a trustee that may, in certain circumstances, be appointed to operate the debtor. BRC §1104.

2. As discussed in Chapter 11 in the section on zone of insolvency, the broadening of management's fiduciary obligations actually begins at the point of insolvency, not the formal filing of a bankruptcy petition. See Weil, Gotshal & Manges (2003).
3. The assumption or rejection of executory contracts requires bankruptcy court approval and thus is not a unilateral decision which management can make. BRC §365.
4. BRC §1102(a).
5. See Kurtz et al. (1999).
6. BRC §1125(b).
7. Under BRC §1124, for a claim to avoid being deemed impaired, it essentially must be either paid off or reinstated. See Bienenstock (1987), Chapter 16.
8. As a legal matter, for a plan of reorganization involving an impaired class to be confirmed, at least one impaired class must vote in favor, without counting the votes of insiders. BRC §1129(a)(10). As a practical matter, if the debtor did not have an expectation of some minimum level of support, it would be unlikely to propose a plan.
9. Depending on the terms of the collateralized debt obligation (CDO) and the trading level of the credit facility, the bankruptcy filing may be an event that triggers loss recognition that hurts the CDO's apparent performance. CDOs essentially would have the same issue if they hold bonds, although loss recognition is more likely to have been triggered through declines in the trading values of the bonds. A common provision in a CDO is that the asset is essentially "written off" when the trading price falls below 50. See Goodman and Fabozzi (2002).
10. Generally attributed to Francis Edward Smedly's "Frank Fairleigh: Or, Scenes from the Life of a Private Pupil" published in *London Magazine* (circa 1850). Interestingly, according to the *1911 Encyclopedia*, Smedly may have had debt problems and spent part of his life as a recluse in an effort to evade creditors.
11. It should be noted that many financial advisor compensation agreements include bonus compensation if the case is concluded before a specified date in order to provide some incentive to expedite the process. Often, however, such advisor agreements simply provide for a success fee (in addition to monthly payment) tied to a resolution of the case, regardless of timing.
12. For a comprehensive list of strategies to attack security interests, see LoPucki and Mirick (2003).
13. This phrase was first coined by Judge Learned Hand in *In re Murel Holding Corp.* 75 F.2d 941 (2d Cir. 1935) and then subsequently included in the language of BRC §§361(3) and 1129(b)(2)(A)(iii).
14. See Fortgang et al. (1999).
15. BRC §505(b).
16. See Fortgang and Mayer (1985).
17. These observations should not be construed as suggesting that any professional in the position of a financial advisor or valuation consultant ever does anything other than render an impartial and objective opinion on value.
18. Courts, no less than financial advisors, have to struggle to determine with any precision the value of ongoing businesses, and creditors insist on court valuations at their peril. Faced with the problem of reconciling conflicting testimony on the value of an oil drilling company with properties in the Canadian Arctic, one bankruptcy judge concluded:

With all of these things, to say that you can forecast — that you can appraise the values in the Canadian Arctic is to say that you can attend the County Fair with your crystal ball, because that is absolutely the only possible way you can come up with a result....My final conclusion...is that it is worth somewhere between $90 million and $100 million as a going concern, and to satisfy the people who want precision on the value, I fix the exact value of the Company at $96,856,850, which is of course a total absurdity that anyone could fix a value with that degree of precision, but for the lawyers who want me to make that fool estimate, I have just made it.

Citibank v Baer, 651 F2d 1341, 1347 (10th Cir. 1908) (quoting district court opinion). More recently, in the chapter 11 reorganization of Exide, the original valuation proffered with the plan of reorganization was $1 billion, just enough to cover the secured debt but leaving little for the unsecured debt. At the confirmation hearing, the unsecured creditors convincingly argued that the valuation was closer to $1.8 billion. The judge determined that the valuation would be $1.4 billion and directed the parties to renegotiate the plan. See Ronson (2004).

19. For a more detailed discussion of some of the issues that can arise in the voting process, see Epstein et al. (1993), Klee (1990), LoPucki and Mirick (2003), and Weil, Gotshal & Manges (2003).
20. As a strategy to avoid this objection, there have been cases where the tip was "given" out of A's recovery, although this is an unsettled practice that may not be permissible in all jurisdictions. See *Unsecured Creditors' Committee v Stern* (In re SPM Manufacturing), 984 F2d 1305 (1st Cir. 1993).
21. BRC §364.
22. BRC §1129(a)(9).
23. BRC §1129(b)(2)(A)(i)(I).
24. BRC §1129(b)(2)(A)(i)(I). The code is silent on the process for determining the appropriate discount rate for this calculation. It should also be noted that BRC §1129(b)(2)(A)(iii) also adds the option of providing the vague "indubitable equivalent" of either option. See Fortgang and Mayer (1985).
25. Again, the appropriate process for determining present value is not specified. Case law varies on the proper approach, but some cases do articulate the financially sound approach of an appropriate risk-adjusted discount rate. See Fortgang and Mayer (1985).
26. As previously noted, the "indubitable equivalent" provision of BRC §1129(b)(2)(A)(iii) may allow a bankruptcy court to find that the fair and equitable test has been satisfied, but the plan proponent likely would face a vigorously contested and uncertain confirmation hearing.

Chapter 13

1. The payment actually could be greater than 100 in the case of certain redemptions.
2. See Leibowitz (2002).
3. BRC §1145.
4. These capitalization limits are not fixed and can vary widely from fund to fund. As of May 30, 2003, the average capitalization of the Russell 2000® Index, the general bench-

mark for small-cap investment funds, was $443.5 million (www.russell.com/us/indexes/us/2000.asp).

5. Based on data from Lipper Analytical Services.

6. See Banz (1981), Barry and Brown (1984), and Pradhuman (2000).

7. See Pradhuman (2000) and Damodaran (2003).

8. See Horowitz et al. (1996).

9. Obviously, there is only so much that can be done in the plan of reorganization formulation process to facilitate an optimal market capitalization. Once a security freely trades in the market, it is out of the "planner's" hands, and market forces could cause a stock price to fall well below expected or planned levels, thus causing a stock expected to be a small- or micro-cap to no longer qualify.

10. This is foreseeable when, for example, a secured bank term loan is still being held by the original lenders.

11. When-issued stocks trade with a "v" at the end of the standard trading ticker to distinguish their status. The regulation of when-issued securities is governed by Section 4, National Association of Securities Dealers Uniform Practice Code.

12. See discussion of collateralized debt obligations in Chapter 2 and Goodman and Fabozzi (2002).

13. Banks can, in special circumstances, request extensions from the normal requirement. The usual context for such a request is an equity security that has very little market liquidity or where the bank may have legal or contractual restrictions on its ability to sell.

14. In general, the regulatory capital treatment of assets held by FDIC-insured institutions is governed by the risk-based capital guidelines specified in 12 C.F.R. Part 325. These rules generally limit the relative amount of equity in nonfinancial subsidiaries an insured institution can hold and provides for increasing capital "penalties" the higher that percentage is relative to regulatory capital. Although not yet directly applicable, most major banks are also managing their balance sheets in anticipation of the probable implementation of international risk-based capital standards as set forth in the Basel II accords. See Basel II: International Convergence of Capital Measurement and Capital Standards: A Revised Framework, available at http://www.bis.org/publ/bcbs107.htm.

15. Such an option was provided for in the GenTek plan of reorganization. Depending on how the plan is structured, a provision of this nature would need to be accepted by the relevant class; to take otherwise pari passu claims and offer one equity and the other debt clearly would give rise to an issue under the unfair discrimination requirement of BRC §1129. In the GenTek plan, this problem was avoided by offering all of the pari passu claims both options. As it turned out in that case, however, the options were not perceived as having economically equivalent value, and creditors predominantly chose the equity-based option. See Ronson (2003a).

16. The technical distinction between underwriter or placement agent will turn on the nature of the offering (e.g., an underwritten offering of registered securities versus a Rule 144 placement), but the marketing role effectively is the same.

17. An example of one firm that used this approach is Laidlaw. Laidlaw issued and sold $400 million in bonds as part of its exit financing plan. The marketing effort for the bond issue included a standard road show that gave many equity investors the opportunity to see management and hear the reorganized company's new strategy. See Shinkle (2003f).

18. There could be other strategic reasons for preferring exit financing to be in the form of a bond, including the ability to have a longer maturity than is typical with bank facilities.

19. A restricted stock agreement is a form of contract often entered into by shareholders of closely held corporations which will control, among other matters, sales voting and requests for registration.

20. Other approaches to going private include filing with the SEC to discontinue periodic reporting under Exchange Act §15(d) by reason of having fewer than 300 holders. However, these approaches must comply with Exchange Act Rule 13e-3. See Weil, Gotshal & Manges (2003), Chapter 17.

21. An example of this approach, although it is not possible to know the precise strategy, appears to be present in the Acterna case. As Acterna emerged from chapter 11, its operating turnaround was not yet evident in financial results. In addition, the equity was being distributed to a relatively small number of holders of the bank debt, potentially creating a situation with very limited trading liquidity. Upon emergence, Acterna discontinued periodic reporting under the Exchange Act (i.e., went private) and granted the new equity holders (i.e., former bank creditors) demand registration rights that could be exercised after two years.

22. In many cases, to reduce the risk that this could unintentionally occur through inadvertence or through a reduction in the number of shares outstanding, the ownership cap may be set at 4.75%.

23. It has been discussed above that certain creditor constituencies often will have a bias toward conservative valuations in the disclosure statement. However, the projections of future performance in the disclosure statement are primarily the province of management and these can be fairly optimistic. See Betker et al. (1999).

24. See Lee and Cunney (2004).

25. The 2002 BE Index and 2001 BE Index were constructed by Imperial Capital from a population of the largest capitalization back-end equities to emerge during the respective index years. The companies included in the 2001 BE Index were Covad Communications, Genesis Healthcare, Kindred Healthcare, Stage Stores, Crimi Mae, and Imperial Sugar. The companies included in the 2002 BE Index were Arch Wireless, ITC Deltacom, ACC Corp., Mcleod USA, Rotech Healthcare, Washington Group, Chiquita Brands, WilTel Communications, and Regal Entertainment. The indexes measured the relative price appreciation of these baskets of securities through calendar year 2003. All pricing from Bloomberg.

26. See Eberhart et al. (1999) and Hotchkiss (1995).

27. See Eberhart et al. (1999).

28. See Brown et al. (1993).

29. See Lee and Cunney (2004).

30. The litigation trust in the Iridium case is chosen as an example because of its size and notoriety. It technically is not an example of a postconfirmation litigation trust because it was formed and the litigation is being prosecuted during the pendency of Iridium's chapter 11 case.

31. The various litigation theories in the lawsuit are fairly complex. Some of the theories were more appropriately actions by Iridium against Motorola, not the creditors directly. However, the creditors argued that due to Motorola's extensive involvement in the

financing and management of Iridium, Iridium had a significant conflict of interest and, essentially, the creditors were the more appropriate parties to pursue such actions. See Gill and Levin (2000).

32. The determination of the validity of a claim can be extremely complex. For a more complete discussion, see Epstein et al. (1993), Section 11-A.

33. BRC §501. The form and filing of claim is governed by FRBP 3001 and 3002.

34. BRC §502.

35. BRC §502(b). It should be noted that under this provision, bankruptcy courts will be asked to value claims, including contingent and unliquidated claims, for differing purposes such as voting and distribution. See Epstein et al. (1993), Section 11-4.

36. To illustrate the potential extremes, in the Safety Kleen and Laidlaw bankruptcy cases, the two parties asserted over $20 billion in claims against each other.

37. The Washington Group restructuring, reviewed in Chapter 8, is a good example of how a postconfirmation trust can expedite the confirmation process. Washington Group filed for chapter 11 with virtually no preplanning in May 2001. The company proposed a plan of reorganization in September 2001, only four months later. The plan contemplated that at confirmation, there likely would be over $2 billion in asserted, but not allowed, claims on the effective date and proposed that those claims be transferred to a liquidation trust until they could be resolved. Anticipating that many of the claims would not be allowed, the recovery estimates contained in the disclosure statement assumed that the allowed claims would total between $525 and $975 million, less than 50% of the amount initially asserted. See Gubner (2002).

38. As noted in Chapter 8, the historical practice of using BRC §524(g) trusts to resolve such cases may change pursuant to recent legislative developments.

39. BRC §524(g).

40. The board members usually will be elected or appointed by the creditor class.

41. If there are over 300 holders, compliance with the Exchange Act may be required. In addition, depending on the postconfirmation trust's assets and operation, compliance with the Investment Company Act of 1940 could also be required.

42. White (Spassky) resigned following Black's (Fischer) 27th move. The moves listed are a potential mating scenario foreseen by National Master Bruce Pandofini. See Pandofini (1993).

LITERATURE SURVEY AND SELECTED REFERENCES

Aeder, M. R. 1999. Tax planning in corporate reorganizations. In *Workouts and turnarounds II*. ed. D. DiNapoli. Hoboken, NJ: John Wiley & Sons.

Aghion, P., O. Hart, and J. Moore. 1992. The economics of bankruptcy reform. *Journal of Law, Economics and Organization* 8:523–546.

Aharony, J., C. Jones, and I. Swary. 1980. An analysis of risk and return characteristics of corporate bankruptcy using capital market data. *Journal of Finance* 35(2):1001–1016.

Alderson, M. J. and B. L. Betker. 1995. Liquidation costs and capital structure. *Journal of Financial Economics* 39:45–69.

Alderson, M. and B. L. Betker. 1999. Assessing post bankruptcy performance: An analysis of reorganized firms' cash flows. *Financial Management* 28:68.

Altman, E. I. 1968. Financial ratios, discriminant analysis and the prediction of corporate bankruptcy. *Journal of Finance* 23:589–609.

———. 1983. The behavior of common stock of bankrupt firms. *Journal of Finance* 38(2):517–522.

———. 1984. A further empirical investigation of the bankruptcy cost question. *Journal of Finance* 39(3):1067–1099.

———. 1989. Measuring corporate bond mortality and performance. *Journal of Finance* (September):909–922.

———. 1990a. *Distressed securities: Analyzing and evaluating market potential and investment risk*. Chicago: Probus Publishing.

———. 1990b. How 1989 changed the hierarchy of fixed income security performance. *Financial Analysts Journal* (May–June):9–20.

———. 1990c. Setting the record straight on junk bonds: A review of research on default rates and returns. *Journal of Applied Corporate Finance* 3(2):82–95.

———. 1993. *Corporate financial distress and bankruptcy*. 2nd ed. Hoboken, NJ: John Wiley & Sons.

————. 1996. *The high-yield debt market: Investment performance and economic impact.* Washington, D.C.: Beard Books.

————, ed. 1999a. *Bankruptcy and distressed securities: Analytical issues and investment opportunities.* Washington, D.C.: Beard Books.

————. 1999b. Market dynamics and investment performance of distressed and defaulted debt securities. In *Workouts and turnarounds II.* ed. D. DiNapoli. Hoboken, NJ: John Wiley & Sons.

————. 2003. The importance of corporate default prediction in a turbulent regulatory and economic environment. Warszawski Instytut Bankowosci Presentation. May 27.

Altman, E. I. and J. C. Bencivenga. 1995. A yield premium model for the high yield market. *Financial Analysts Journal* (September–October):49–56.

Altman, E. I. and A. C. Eberhart. 1994. Do priority provisions protect a bondholder's investment? *Journal of Economic Theory* 20:67.

Altman, E. I. and V. M. Kishore. 1996. Almost everything you wanted to know about recoveries on defaulted bonds. *Financial Analysts Journal* (November–December):57–64.

————. 1997. *Defaults and returns on high-yield bonds.* New York: Salomon Center.

Altman, E. I. and S. A. Nammacher. 1987. *Investing in junk bonds: Inside the high yield debt market.* Hoboken, NJ: John Wiley & Sons.

Altman, E. I., N. Hukkawala, and V. Kishore. 2000. Defaults and returns on high-yield bonds: Lessons from 1999 and outlook for 2000–2002. *Business Economics* 35(2): 27–38.

Altman, E. I., A. C. Eberhart, and R. Aggarwal. 1999. The equity performance of firms emerging from bankruptcy. *Journal of Finance* 54(5):1855–1868.

Amihud, Y. and H. Mendleson. 1988. Liquidity and asset prices: Financial management implications. *Financial Management* 17:5–15.

————. 2000. The liquidity route to a lower cost of capital. *Journal of Applied Corporate Finance* 12(4):8–25.

Anderson, R. W. and S. Sundaresan. 1996. Design and valuation of debt contracts. *Review of Financial Economics* 9:37–68.

Andrade, G. and S. Kaplan. 1998. How costly is financial (not economic) distress? Evidence from highly leveraged transactions that became distressed. *Journal of Finance* 53:1443–1493.

Ang, J. S. and J. H. Chua. 1980. Coalitions, the me-first rule, and the liquidation decision. *Bell Journal of Economics* (Spring):355–359.

————. 1981. Corporate bankruptcy and job losses among top-level managers. *Financial Management* (Winter):70–74.

Ang, J. S., J. H. Chua, and J. J. McConnell. 1982. The administrative costs of corporate bankruptcy: A note. *Journal of Finance* 37:219–226.

Aron, D. 1991. Using the capital market as a monitor: Corporate spin-offs in an agency framework. *RAND Journal of Economics* 22(Winter):505–518.

Asquith, P., D. Mullins, Jr., and E. Wolff. 1989. Original issue high yield bonds: Aging analysis of defaults, exchanges and calls. *Journal of Finance* (September):923–952.

Asquith, P., R. Gertner, and D, Scharfstein. 1994. Anatomy of financial distress: An examination of junk bond issuers. *Quarterly Journal of Economics* 109:625–658.

Atkinson, T. R. 1967. *Trends in corporate bond quality.* New York: Columbia University Press.

Aumann, R. J. and M. Maschler. 1985. Game theoretic analysis of a bankruptcy problem from the Talmud. *Journal of Economic Theory* 36:195–213.

Axelrod, R. 1984. *Evolution of cooperation.* New York: Basic Books.

Baker, H. K. and S. A. Mansi. 2002. Assessing credit rating agencies by bond issuers and institutional investors. *Journal of Business Finance & Accounting* (November/December):1367–1398.

Baird, D. G. 1986. The uneasy case for corporate reorganizations. *Journal of Legal Studies* 15:127–147.

––––––. 2002. *Elements of bankruptcy.* Chicago: Foundation Press.

Baird, J. and T. H. Jackson. 1985. Fraudulent conveyance law and its proper domain. *Vanderbilt Law Review* 38:829.

––––––. 1988. Bargaining after the fall and the contours of the absolute priority rule. *University of Chicago Law Review* 55:738–789.

Bandopadhyaya, A. 1994. An estimation of the hazard rate of firms in Chapter 11 protection. *Review of Economics and Statistics* (May):346–350.

Banz, R. W. 1981. The relationship between return and market value of common stock. *Journal of Financial Economics* 9:3–18.

Barclay, M. J. and C. W. Smith, Jr. 1996. On financial architecture: Leverage, maturity, and priority. *Journal of Applied Corporate Finance* 8(4):4–29.

––––––. 1999. The capital structure puzzle: Another look at the evidence. *Journal of Applied Corporate Finance* 12(1):8–20.

Barnhill, T. M., Jr., W. F. Maxwell, and M. R. Shenkman, eds. 1999. *High yield bonds: Market structure, portfolio management, and credit risk modeling.* New York: McGraw–Hill.

Barry, C.D. and S. J. Brown. 1984. Differential information and the small firm effect. *Journal of Financial Economics* 13:283–294.

Barth, J., D. Brumbaugh, and G. Yago, eds. 2001. *Restructuring regulation and financial institutions.* Boston: Kluwer Academic Press.

Beaver, W. H. 1966. Financial ratios as predictors of failure. *Journal of Accounting Research* (Supplement):77–111.

Beaver, W. H., P. Kettler, and M. S. Scholes. 1970. The association between market determined and accounting determined risk measures. *Accounting Review* 45:654–682.

Bebchuck, L. A. 1988. A new approach to corporate reorganization. *Harvard Law Review* 101:775–804.

Bebchuck, L. A. and H. F. Chang. 1992. Bargaining and the division of value in corporate reorganization. *Journal of Law, Economics & Organization* 8:253–279.

Bebchuck, L. A. and J. Fried. 1996. The uneasy case for the priority of secured claims in bankruptcy. *Yale Law Journal* 105:857–891.

Beck, T. and R. Levine. 2002. Industry growth and capital allocation: Does having a market- or bank-based system matter? *Journal of Financial Economics* 64:147–180.

Becketti, S. 1990. The truth about junk bonds. *Economic Review, Federal Reserve Bank of Kansas City* (July–August):45–54.

Bencivenga, J., R. Cheung, and F. J. Fabozzi. 1992. Original issue high-yield bonds: Historical return and default experience, 1977–1989. *Journal of Fixed Income* (September):58–75.

Ben-Horim, M. and H. Levy. 1981. *Statistics: Decisions and applications III: Business and economics.* New York: Random House.

Bennett, P. and J. Kelleher. 1988. The international transmission of stock price disruption in October 1987. *Federal Reserve Bank of New York Quarterly Review* 13:17–33.

Benveniste, L. M., M. Singh, and W. J. Wilhelm, Jr. 1993. The failure of Drexel Burnham Lambert: Evidence on the implications for commercial banks. *Journal of Financial Intermediation* 3:104–137.

Bergman, Y. Z. and J. L. Callen. 1991. Opportunistic underinvestment in debt renegotiation and capital structure. *Journal of Financial Economics* 29:137–171.

Berkovitch, E., R. Israel, and J. F. Zender. 1997. An optimal bankruptcy law and firm-specific investments. *European Economic Review* 41:487–497.

Berman, D. K. 2002. Global Crossing's capacity swaps were of little value, study says. *Wall Street Journal* (February 19).

Bernanke, B. 1983. Non-monetary effects of the financial crisis in propagation of the Great Depression. *American Economic Review* 73(3):257–276.

Bernanke, B. and C. S. Lown. 1991. The credit crunch. *Brookings Papers on Economic Activity* 2:205–247.

Bernanke, B., M. Gertler, and S. Gilchrist. 1996. The financial accelerator and the flight to quality. *Review of Economics and Statistics* 78:1–15.

Bernstein, A. 1996. *Grounded: Frank Lorenzo and the destruction of Eastern Airlines.* Washington, D.C.: Beard Books.

Besanko, D. and G. Kanatas. 1993. Credit market equilibrium with bank monitoring and moral hazard. *Review of Financial Studies* 6(1):213–232.

Betker, B. L. 1995a. An empirical examination of prepackaged bankruptcy. *Financial Management* 24:3–18.

———. 1995b. Management's incentives, equity's bargaining power, and deviations from absolute priority in Chapter 11 bankruptcies. *Journal of Business* 68:161.

———. 1997. The administrative costs of debt restructurings: Some recent evidence. *Financial Management* 26:56–68.

———. 1998. The security price effects of public debt defaults. *Journal of Financial Research* 21:17.

Betker, B. L., S. P. Ferris, and R. M. Lawless. 1999. Warm and sunny skies: Disclosure statement forecasts. *American Bankruptcy Law Journal* 73:809.

Bibeault, D. B. 1999. *Corporate turnaround: How managers turn losers into winners.* Washington, D.C.: Beard Books.

Bienenstock, M. J. 1987. *Bankruptcy reorganization.* New York: Practicing Law Institute.

———. 1992. Conflicts between management and the debtor-in-possession's fiduciary duties. *Cincinnati Law Review* 61:543.

Bierman, H. and S. Smidt. 1984. *The capital investment decision.* New York: McMillan Publishing.

Black, F. 1972. Capital market equilibrium with restricted borrowing. *Journal of Business* 45(3):444–455.

Black, F. and J. C. Cox. 1976. Valuing corporate securities: Some effects of bond indenture provisions. *Journal of Finance* 31:351–367.

Black, F. and M. Scholes. 1973. The pricing of options and corporate liabilities. *Journal of Political Economy* 81(3):637–654.

Black, F., M. C. Jensen, and M. Scholes. 1972. The capital asset pricing model: Some empirical tests. In *Studies in the theory of capital markets.* ed. M. C. Jensen. New York: Praeger.

Blackwell, D., W. Marr, and M. Spivey. 1990. Plant-closing decisions and the market value of the firm. *Journal of Financial Economics* 26:277–288.

Blake, C. R. and P. A. Williams. 2002. Does Reg FD have a "chilling effect" on the quantity and quality of corporate information? Working paper available at www.bnet.fordham.edu/public/finance/cblake/RegFD111602a.pdf.

Blum, W. J. 1980. The fair and equitable standard for conforming reorganizations under the new bankruptcy code. *American Bankruptcy Law Journal* 54:165–172.

Blum, W. and S. Kaplan. 1976. *Corporate readjustments and reorganizations.* Mineola, NY: The Foundation Press.

Blume, M. E. and D. B. Keim. 1991a. Realized returns and defaults on low-grade bonds: The cohort of 1977 and 1978. *Financial Analysts Journal* (March–April):63–72.

———. 1991b. The risk and return of low-grade bonds: An update. *Financial Analysts Journal* (September–October):85–89.

Blume, M. E., D. B. Keim, and S. A. Patel. 1991. Return and volatility of low-grade bonds, 1977–1989. *Journal of Finance* 46(1):49–74.

Blume, M. E., F. Lim, and A. C. MacKinlay. 1998. The declining credit quality of U.S. corporate debt: Myth or reality? *Journal of Finance* 53(4):1389–1413.

Bolton, P. and X. Freixas. 2000. Equity, bonds and bank debt: Capital structure and financial market equilibrium under asymmetric information. *Journal of Political Economy* 108:324–349.

Bonnier, K. A. and R. Bruner. 1985. An analysis of stock price reaction to management change in distressed firms. *Journal of Accounting and Economics* 11:95–106.

Bookstaber, R. and D. P. Jacob. 1986. The composite hedge: Controlling the credit risk of high-yield bonds. *Financial Analysts Journal* (March–April):25–36.

Bouhuvs, H. and S. Yeager. 1999. Recent developments in the high yield market. *Journal of Applied Corporate Finance* 12(1):70–77.

Bowen, R., L. Daley, and C. Huber, Jr. 1982. Evidence on the existence and determinants of inter-industry differences in leverage. *Financial Management* 11:10–20.

Bradley, M. and N. Seyhun. 1997. Corporate bankruptcy and insider trading. *Journal of Business* 70(April):189–216.

Braine, R. 2003a. November in bankruptcy by the numbers. *Daily Bankruptcy Review* (December 1):8.

———. 2003b. MCI won't be the only star during this fall season. *Daily Bankruptcy Review* (September 4):3.

Branch, B. and H. Ray. 1997. *Bankruptcy investing: How to profit from distressed companies.* Washington, D.C.: Beard Books.

Brealy, R. A. and S. C. Myers. 2000. *Principles of corporate finance.* 6th ed. New York: Irwin McGraw-Hill.

Brennan, M. J. and E. S. Schwartz. 1977. Convertible bonds: Valuation and optimal strategies for call and conversion. *Journal of Finance* 32:1699–1715.

———. 1984. Optimal financial policy and firm valuation. *Journal of Finance* 39:593–607.

Brodsky, M. D. and J. B. Zweibel. 1990. Chapter 11 acquisitions: Payoffs for patience. *Mergers and Acquisitions* (September–October):47–53.

Bromley. J., J. Lamport, and K. Hess. 2004. *All yell "stop trading."* New York: Cleary Gottlieb. August.

Brown, D. T. 1989. Claimholder incentive conflicts in reorganization: The role of bankruptcy law. *Review of Financial Studies* 2:109–123.

Brown, D., C. James, and R. Mooradian. 1993. The information content of distressed restructurings involving public and private debt claims. *Journal of Financial Economics* 33:93–118.

Brys, E. and F. Varenne. 1997. Valuing risky fixed rate debt: An extension. *Journal of Financial and Quantitative Analysis* 32:239–248.

Buell, S. G. 1992. The accuracy of the initial pricing of junk bonds. *Journal of Fixed Income* (September):77–83.

Bulow, J. L. and J. B. Shoven. 1978. The bankruptcy decision. *Bell Journal of Economics* (Autumn):437–456.

Bygrave, W. and J. Timmons. 1991. *Venture capital at the crossroads.* Cambridge, MA: Harvard University Press.

Cadwalader, Wickersham & Taft. 2003. *Proposed fund of fund and developments in the regulation of hedge funds.* Memorandum to Clients & Friends. November 10. Available at http://www.cadwalader.com/assets/client_friend/11-10-03PropRulesHedgeFunds.pdf.

Calamos, N. P. 2003. *Convertible arbitrage: Insights and techniques for successful hedging.* Hoboken, NJ: John Wiley & Sons.

Callas, J. 1990. DIP financing helps troubled LBOs. *The Secured Lender* (July–August):18.

Calomiris, C. W. and B. Wilson. 1998. Bank capital and portfolio management: The 1930s capital crunch and scramble to shed risk. Working Paper No. 6649. Cambridge, MA: National Bureau of Economic Research.

Campbell, J. Y. 2000. Asset-pricing at the millennium. *Journal of Finance* 55:1515–1567.

CapitalEyes. 2003. Completing the capital structure with a second lien loan (www.fleetcapital.com/resources/capeyes/a04-03-158.html).

Carey, M., S. Prowse, J. Rea, and G. Udell. 1993. *The economics of the private placement market.* Federal Reserve Board of Governors Staff Study 166. Washington, D.C.: Federal Reserve.

Carpenter, R. E., S. M. Fazzari, and B. C. Petersen. 1994. Inventory (dis)investment, internal finance fluctuations and the business cycle. *Brookings Papers on Economic Activity* 2:75–138.

Casey, C., V. McGee, and C. Stickney. 1986. Discriminating between reorganized and liquidated firms in bankruptcy. *Accounting Review* (April):249–262.

Castinias, R. 1983. Bankruptcy risk and optimal capital structure. *Journal of Finance* 38(4):1617–1684.

Castle, G. 1980. Term lending: A guide to negotiating term loan covenants and other financial restrictions. *Journal of Commercial Bank Lending* (November):26–39.

Chatterjee, S., V. S. Dhillon, and G. G. Ramirez. 1996. Resolution of financial distress: Debt restructuring via chapter 11, prepackaged bankruptcies, and workouts. *Financial Management* 25:5–18.

Chemmanur, T. J. and P. Fulghieri. 1994. Reputation, renegotiation and the choice between bank loans and publicly traded debt. *Review of Financial Studies* 7:475–506.

Chen, G. 1993. Minority business development: Where do we go from here? *Journal of Black Political Economy* 22(2):5–16.

Chew, D. 1998. *The new corporate finance: Where theory meets practice.* New York: McGraw-Hill.

Christensen, D. G. and H. J. Faria. 1994. A note on the shareholder wealth effects of high-yield bonds. *Financial Management* (Spring):10.

Cimilluca, D. 2003. WorldCom agrees to pay $500 million to settle SEC Charges. *Bloomberg News* (May 19).

Clark, T. A. and M. I. Weisenstein. 1983. The behavior of common stock of bankrupt firms. *Journal of Finance* 38(2):489–504.

Coleman, P. J. 1999. *Debtors and creditors in America: Insolvency, imprisonment for debt and bankruptcy, 1607–1900*. Washington, D.C.: Beard Books.

Colin-Dufresne, P. and R. Goldstein. 2001. Do credit spreads reflect stationary leverage ratios? *Journal of Finance* 56:1929–1957.

Connolly, K. B. 1999. *Pricing convertible bonds*. Hoboken, NJ: John Wiley & Sons.

Cooper, R. A. and J. M. Shulman. 1994. The year-end effect in junk bond prices. *Financial Analysts Journal* (September–October):61–65.

Cootner, P., ed. 1964. *The random character of stock market prices*. Cambridge, MA: MIT Press.

Copeland, J., T. Koller, and J. Murrin. 2000. *Valuation: Measuring and managing the value of companies*. Hoboken, NJ: John Wiley & Sons.

Corcoran, P. J. 1994. The double-b private placement market. *Journal of Fixed Income* (June):42–51.

Cornell, B. 1992. Liquidity and the pricing of low-grade bonds. *Financial Analysts Journal* (January–February):63–67.

———. 1993. *Corporate valuation: Tools for effective appraisal and decision making*. Burr Ridge, IL: Irwin Professional Publishing.

Cornell, B. and K. Green. 1991. The investment performance of low-grade bond funds. *Journal of Finance* (March):29–48.

Countryman, V. 1973. Executory contracts in bankruptcy: Part I. *Minnesota Law Review* 57:439–460.

Cramton, P. C. 1995. Money out of thin air: The nationwide narrowband PCS auction. *Journal of Economics and Management Strategy* 4:267–343.

Cray, A. 2004. *Foster Wheeler Ltd: Exchange terms out — Securities still discounted*. Beverly Hills, CA: Imperial Capital. April 13.

Credit Suisse First Boston. 2002. *2001 leveraged finance outlook*. New York: Credit Suisse First Boston.

———. 2003. *2002 Leveraged finance outlook*. New York: Credit Suisse First Boston.

———. 2004. *2003 Leveraged finance outlook*. New York: Credit Suisse First Boston.

Curley, S. F. 2001. *Building Materials Corp. of America: Situation update*. Beverly Hills, CA: Imperial Capital. January 30.

Cutler, D. and L. Summers. 1988. The costs of conflict resolution and financial distress: Evidence from Texaco-Pennzoil litigation. *Rand Journal of Economics* 19:157–172.

Dagget, S. 1991. *Railroad reorganizations*. Washington, D.C.: Beard Books.

Damodaran, A. 2002. *Investment valuation*. Hoboken, NJ: John Wiley & Sons.

———. 2003. *Investment philosophies: Successful strategies and the investors who made them work*. Hoboken, NJ: John Wiley & Sons.

Darby, L. F., J. A. Eisenach, and J. S. Kraemer. 2002. *The CLEC experiment: Anatomy of a meltdown*. Progress on point 9.23. Washington, D.C.: The Progress & Freedom Foundation.

Datta, S., M. Iskandar-Datta, and A. Patel. 1997. The pricing of initial public offers of corporate straight debt. *Journal of Finance* (March):379–396.

————. 1999. The market's pricing of debt IPOs. *Journal of Applied Corporate Finance* 12(1):86–91.

Daughen, J. R. and P. Binzen. 1993. *The wreck of the Penn Central*. Washington, D.C.: Beard Books.

————. 1996. *Ling: The rise, fall and return of a Texas titan*. Washington, D.C.: Beard Books.

Davenport, K. A. 1999. *Public vs. private markets: A review of high yield financing techniques*. Los Angeles: Latham and Watkins.

————. 2004. The silence of the liens. *New York Law Journal* July 9.

Dawkins, M. C. and L. S. Bamber. 1999. Does the medium matter?: The relations among bankruptcy petition filings, broadtape disclosure, and the timing of price reactions. *Journal of Finance* 53:1149.

DeNatale, A. 1981. The creditors' committee under the bankruptcy code: A primer. *American Bankruptcy Law Journal* 55:43–62.

Denis, D. and T. Kruse. 2000. Managerial discipline and corporate restructuring following performance declines. *Journal of Financial Economics* 55:391–424.

DeRosa-Farag, S., J. Blau, P. Matousek, and I. Chandra. 1999. Default rates in the high yield market. *Journal of Fixed Income* (June):7–31.

De Soto, H. 2000. *The mystery of capital: Why capitalism succeeds in the West and fails everywhere else*. New York: Basic Books.

Diamond, D. W. 1994. Corporate capital structure: The control roles of bank and public debt with taxes and costly bankruptcy. *Federal Reserve Bank Richmond Economic Quarterly* 80:11–37.

Dichev, I. D. 1998. Is the risk of bankruptcy a systematic risk? *Journal of Finance* 53:1131–1147.

DiNapoli, D., ed. 1999. *Workouts and turnarounds II*. Hoboken, NJ: John Wiley & Sons.

DiNapoli, D. and E. Fuhr. 1999. Trouble spotting: Assessing the likelihood of a turnaround. In *Workouts and turnarounds II*. Hoboken, NJ: John Wiley & Sons.

Douglas-Hamilton, M. 1975. Creditor liabilities resulting from improper interference with the management of a financially troubled debtor. *Business Lawyer* 31:343–365.

Drucker, P. F. 1985. *Management: Tasks, responsibilities, practices*. New York: HarperCollins.

————. 2002. *The effective executive*. New York: HarperCollins.

————. 2003. *On the profession of management*. Cambridge, MA: Harvard Business School Publishing.

Dunne. 1997. The revlon duties and the sale of companies in Chapter 11. *The Business Lawyer* 52:1333–1357.

Easterbrook, F. 1991. Is corporate bankruptcy efficient? A comment. *Journal of Financial Economics* 27(2):411–417.

Easterwood, J. and A. Seth. 1993. Strategic restructuring in large management buyouts. *Strategic Management Journal* 13(2):25–37.

Eberhart, A. C. and R. J. Sweeney. 1992. Does the bond market predict bankruptcy settlements? *Journal of Finance* 47(3):943–980.

Eberhart, A. C., W. T. Moore, and R. L. Roenfeldt. 1990. Security pricing and deviations from the absolute priority rule in bankruptcy proceedings. *Journal of Finance* 45(5):1457–1469.

Eberhart, A.C., E. I. Altman, and R. Aggarwal. 1999. The equity performance of firms emerging from bankruptcy. *Journal of Finance* 54–5:1855–1868.

Eisenberg, T. and L. M. LoPucki. 1999. Shopping for judges: An empirical analysis of venue choice in the bankruptcy reorganization of large, publicly held companies. *Cornell Law Review* 83:1771–1810.

Emshwiller, J. R. 2002. No accounting for logic: Enron lives as penny stock. *Wall Street Journal* (November 27).

Eppling, D. J. 1993. Fun with non-voting stock. *Bankruptcy* 10:17.

Epstein, D., S. Nickles, and J. White. 1993. *Bankruptcy*. St. Paul, MN: West Publishing Company.

Evans, C. 1991. The investment banker's role in the workout process. In *Workouts and turnarounds*. eds. D. DiNapoli, S. Sigoloff, and R. Cushman. Homewood, IL: Business One Irwin.

Fabozzi, F. J., ed. 1989. *Advances and innovations in the bond and mortgage markets.* Chicago: Probus.

———, ed. 1990. *The new high-yield debt market: A handbook for portfolio managers and analysts.* New York: HarperCollins.

———, ed. 1995. *The handbook of fixed income securities.* 4th ed. Chicago: Irwin.

Fabozzi, F. J. and J. H. Carlson, eds. 1992. *The trading and securitization of senior bank loans.* Chicago: Probus.

Fama, E. F. 1965. The behavior of stock-market prices. *Journal of Business* 38(1):34–105.

———. 1970. Efficient capital markets: A review of theory and empirical work. *Journal of Finance* 25(2):383–417.

Fama, E. F. and M. Jensen. 1983. Separation of ownership and control. *Journal of Law and Economics* 26:301–325.

Fama, E. F. and M. H. Miller. 1972. *The theory of finance.* New York: Holt, Rinehart and Winston.

Farricielli, J. J. 2003. *WCI Steel: Pension payments could erode bondholder value.* Beverly Hills, CA: Imperial Capital. December 1.

Fenn, G. W. 2000. Speed of issuance and the adequacy of disclosure in the 144A high-yield debt market. *Journal of Financial Economics* 56(3):383–406.

Finnerty, J. D. 1992. An overview of corporate securities innovation. *Journal of Applied Corporate Finance* 4(4):23–39.

Fischer, E. O., R. Heinkel, and J. Zechner. 1989. Dynamic capital structure choice: Theory and tests. *Journal of Finance* 44:19–40.

Fitzpatrick, J. D. and J. T. Severiens. 1978. Hickman revisited: The case for junk bonds. *Journal of Portfolio Management* (Summer):53–57.

Fons, J. S. 1987. The default premium and corporate bond experience. *Journal of Finance* (March):81–97.

———. 1991. *An approach to forecasting default rates.* New York: Moody's Investors Service.

———. 1994. Using default rates to model the term structure of credit risk. *Financial Analysts Journal* (September–October):25–32.

Fons, J. S. and A. E. Kimball. 1991. Corporate bond defaults and default rates, 1970–1990. *Journal of Fixed Income* (June):36–47.

Fons, J. S., L. Carty, and J. Kaufman. 1994. *Corporate bond defaults and default rates, 1970–1993.* New York: Moody's Investors Service.

Fortgang, C. J. and T. M. Mayer. 1990. Trading claims and taking control of corporations in chapter 11. *Cardozo Law Review* 12:1–115.

————. 1991. Developments in trading claims and taking control of corporations in chapter 11. *Cardozo Law Review* 13:1–67.

————. 1985. Valuation in bankruptcy. *UCLA Law Review* (August):1061–1107.

Fortgang, C. J., S. Gardner and D. Caro. 1999. At the front of the line: The secured creditor. In *Workouts and turnarounds II.* ed. D. DiNapoli. Hoboken, NJ: John Wiley & Sons.

Fraine, H. G. and R. H. Mills. 1961. Effects of defaults and credit deterioration on yields of corporate bonds. *Journal of Finance* (September):423–434.

Francis, J. C. 1988. *Investments.* New York: McGraw Hill.

Franks, J. and W. Torous. 1989a. A comparison of financial recontracting in distressed exchanges and Chapter 11 reorganization. *Journal of Financial Economics* 35:349–370.

————. 1989b. An empirical investigation of U.S. firms in reorganization. *Journal of Finance* 44:747–769.

Fridson, M. S. 1989a. The economics of liquidity. *Extra Credit: The Journal of High Yield Bond Research* (December):4–13.

————. 1989b. *High yield bonds: Identifying value and assessing risk of speculative grade securities.* Chicago: Probus.

————. 1991a. Everything you ever wanted to know about default rates. *Extra Credit: The Journal of High Yield Bond Research* (July–August):414.

————. 1991b. This year in high yield. *Extra Credit: The Journal of High Yield Bond Research* (February):4–15.

————. 1991c. What went wrong with the highly leveraged deals? *Journal of Applied Corporate Finance* (Fall):5767.

————. 1992a. High yield indexes and benchmark portfolios. *Journal of Portfolio Management* (Winter):77–83.

————. 1992b. Modeling the credit risk of non-rated high yield bonds. *Risks and Rewards: The Newsletter of the Investment Sector of the Society of Actuaries* (March):6–11.

————. 1994a. Do high-yield bonds have an equity component? *Financial Management* (Summer):76–78.

————. 1994b. The state of the high yield bond market: Overshooting or return to normalcy? *Journal of Applied Corporate Finance* (Spring):85–97.

————. 1995. Loads, flows, and performance in high-yield bond mutual funds. *Journal of Fixed Income* (December):70–78.

————. 1998. EBITDA is not king. *Journal of Financial Statement Analysis* (Spring):59–62.

Fridson M. S. and F. Alvarez. 2002. *Financial statement analysis: A practitioner's guide.* 3rd ed. Hoboken, NJ: John Wiley & Sons.

Fridson, M. S. and J. A. Bersh. 1994. Spread versus treasuries as a market timing tool for high-yield investors. *Journal of Fixed Income* (June):63–69.

Fridson, M. S. and M. A. Cherry. 1990. Initial pricing as a predictor of subsequent performance of high yield bonds. *Financial Analysts Journal* (July–August):61–67.

————. 1991a. A critique of the spread-versus treasuries concept. *Extra Credit: The Journal of High Yield Bond Research* (July–August):41–45.

————. 1991b. Explaining the variance in high yield managers' returns. *Financial Analysts Journal* (May–June):64–72.

Fridson, M. S. and A. de Candia. 1991. Trends: Follow, buck or ignore? *Journal of Portfolio Management* (Winter):50–55.

Fridson, M. S. and Gao, Y. (1996). Primary versus secondary pricing of high yield bonds. *Financial Analysts Journal* (May/June):20–27.

Fridson, M. S. and M. C. Garman. 1997. Valuing like-rated senior and subordinated debt. *Journal of Fixed Income* (December):83–93.

———. 1998a. Determinants of spreads on new high-yield bonds. *Financial Analysts Journal* (March–April):28–39.

———. 1998b. Erosion of principal and the rebasing of illusion. *Journal of Fixed Income* (December):85–98.

Fridson, M. S. and J. G. Jonsson. 1994. *Spread versus treasuries and the riskiness of high-yield bonds.* New York: Merrill Lynch.

———. 1995. Spread versus treasuries and the riskiness of high-yield bonds. *Journal of Fixed Income* (December):79–88.

Fridson, M. S., M. A. Cherry, J. A. Kim, and S. W. Weiss. 1992. What drives the flows of high yield mutual funds? *Journal of Fixed Income* (December):47–59.

Fridson, M. S., M. C. Garman, and S. Wu. 1997. Real interest rates and the default rate on high-yield bonds. *Journal of Fixed Income* (September):29–34.

Friend, I. and L. Lang. 1988. An empirical test of the impact of managerial self-interest on corporate capital structure. *Journal of Finance* 43:271–281.

Frierman, M. and P. V. Viswanath. 1994. Agency problems of debt, convertible securities, and deviations from absolute priority in bankruptcy. *Journal of Law & Economics* 37:455.

Fries, S. M., M. Miller, and W. R. M. Perraudin. 1997. Debt pricing in industry equilibrium. *Review of Financial Studies* 10:39–68.

Froot, K. A. 1989. Buybacks, exit bonds and the optimality of debt and liquidity relief. *International Economic Review* 30:49–70.

Fudenberg, D. and J. Tirole. 1991. *Game theory.* Cambridge, MA: MIT Press.

Garman, M. C. and M. S. Fridson. 1996. *Monetary influences on the high-yield spread versus treasuries.* New York: Merrill Lynch.

Garvey, G. T. and G. Hanka. 1999. Capital structure and corporate control: The effect of antitakeover statutes on firm leverage. *Journal of Finance* 54(2):519–546.

Gaughan. P.A. 2002. *Mergers, acquisitions and corporate restructurings.* Hoboken, NJ: John Wiley & Sons.

General Accounting Office. 1988. *High yield bonds: Nature of the market and effect on federally insured institutions.* Washington, D.C.: U.S. General Accounting Office.

Gertler, M. and C. S. Lown. 1999. *The information in the high yield bond spread for the business cycle: Evidence and some implications.* Prepared for the Conference on Financial Instability, Oxford University.

Gertner, R. and D. Scharfstein. 1991. A theory of workouts and the effects of reorganization law. *Journal of Finance* 46:1189–1222.

Giammarino, R. 1989. The resolution of financial distress. *Review of Financial Studies* 2:25–47.

Gilbert, J. S. 1990. Substantive consolidation in bankruptcy: A primer. *Vanderbilt Law Review* 43:207–245.

Gilbert, M. R. 2002. *WKI Holding Company: Initiating coverage.* Beverly Hills, CA: Imperial Capital. March 5.

———. 2003. *WKI Holding Company: Post bankruptcy review — Weakened retail climate impacts EBITDA.* Beverly Hills, CA: Imperial Capital. May 28.

Gilbert, M. R. and R. P. Whitesell. 2004. *Avondale: EBITDA off over 50%, but liquidity still adequate.* Beverly Hills, CA: Imperial Capital. August 24.

Gill, L. and M. Levin. 2000. *Iridium Operating LLC — Situation update*. Beverly Hills, CA: Imperial Capital. May 9.

Gilson, S. C. 1989. Management turnover and financial distress. *Journal of Financial Economics* 25:241–262.

———. 1990. Bankruptcy, boards, banks and blockholders: Evidence on changes in corporate ownership and control when firms default. *Journal of Financial Economics* 27:355–387.

———. 1991. Managing default: Some evidence on how firms choose between workouts and Chapter 11. *Journal of Applied Corporate Finance* 4:62.

———. 1997. Transactions costs and capital structure choice: Evidence from financially distressed firms. *Journal of Finance* 52(1):161–196.

———. 2001. *Creating value through corporate restructuring*. Hoboken, NJ: John Wiley & Sons.

Gilson, S., E. Hotchkiss, and R. Ruback. 2000. Valuation of bankrupt firms. *Review of Financial Studies* 13:43.

Gilson, S. C., J. Kose, and L. Lang. 1990. Troubled debt restructurings: An empirical study of private reorganization of companies in default. *Journal of Financial Economics* 27(2):315–353.

Glovin, D. 2000. Iridium judge says he will approve asset sale to Colussy group. *Bloomberg News* (November 15).

Goldstein R. N. and H. Leland 2001. An EBIT-based model of dynamic capital structure. *Journal of Business* 74:483–512.

Goodman, L. S. 1990. High-yield default rates: Is there cause for concern. *Journal of Portfolio Management* (Winter):54–59.

Goodman, L. S. and J. F. Fabozzi. 2002. *Collateralized debt obligations: Structures and analysis*. Hoboken, NJ: John Wiley & Sons.

Gosnell, T., A. Keown, and J. Pinkerton. 1992. Bankruptcy and insider trading: Difference between exchange listed and OTC firms. *Journal of Finance* 47(March):349–362.

Graham, B. 1959. *The intelligent investor: A book of practical counsel*. 3rd ed. New York: Harper & Brothers.

Grossman, S. J. and O. D. Hart. 1982. Corporate financial structure and managerial incentives. In *The economics of information and uncertainty*. ed. J. McCall. Chicago: University of Chicago Press.

Gubner, A. 2002. *Washington Group International: Conservative valuation provides attractive opportunity*. Beverly Hills, CA: Imperial Capital. January 17.

Gudikunst, A. and J. McCarthy. 1997. High-yield bond mutual funds: Performance, January effects, and other surprises. *Journal of Fixed Income* (September):35–46.

Hagedorn, R. B. 1980. The survival and enforcement of the secured claim under the Bankruptcy Reform Act of 1978. *American Bankruptcy Law Journal* 54:1–28.

Hallinan, J. T. and M. Pacelle. 2003. In collection battle, Conseco ex-CEO is fighting back. *Wall Street Journal* (December 5).

Hamilton, D. T., R. Cantor, and S. Ou. 2002. *Default & recovery rates of corporate bond issuers: A statistical review of moody's rating performance 1970–2001*. New York: Moody's Investors Service. February.

Hamilton, D. T., P. Varma, S. Ou, and R. Cantor. 2003. *Default & recovery rates of corporate bond issuers: A statistical review of Moody's rating performance 1920–2002*. New York: Moody's Investors Service. February.

———. 2004. *Default & recovery rates of corporate bond issuers: A statistical review of Moody's rating performance 1920–2003.* New York: Moody's Investors Service. January.

Hansen, C. D., T. J. Solerno, and B. L. Brown. 1990. Technology licenses under section 365(n) of the bankruptcy code: The protections afforded the technology user. *Commercial Law Journal* 95:170.

Hart, O. and J. Moore. 1998. Default and renegotiation: A dynamic model of debt. *Quarterly Journal of Economics* 113:1–41.

Haugen, R. and L. Senbet. 1978. The insignificance of bankruptcy costs to the theory of optimal capital structure. *Journal of Finance* 33:383–393.

———. 1988. Bankruptcy and agency costs: Their significance to the theory of optimal capital structure. *Journal of Financial and Quantitative Analysis* 1(March):27–38.

Hawley, D. D. and M. M. Walker. 1992. An empirical test of investment restrictions of efficiency in the high yield debt market. *Financial Review* (May):273–287.

———. 1993. Speculative grade ratings and the investment decision process: A survey of institutional money managers. *Financial Practice and Education* (Fall):39–46.

Healy, P., K. Palepu, and R. Ruback. 1992. Does corporate performance improve after mergers? *Journal of Financial Economics* 31:135–175.

Heller, R. H. and M. S. Khan. 1979. The demand for money and the term structure of interest rates. *Journal of Political Economy* 87:109–129.

Helwege, J. 1999. How long do junk bonds spend in default? *Journal of Finance* 54:341–357.

Helwege, J. and K. Kleiman. 1997. Understanding aggregate default rates of high yield bonds. *Journal of Fixed Income* (June):55–61.

———. 1998. The pricing of high-yield debt IPOs. *Journal of Fixed Income* (September):61–68.

Henderson, G. D. and S. J. Goldring. 1998. *Failing and failed businesses.* New York: Panel Publishers.

Hickman, W. B. 1958. *Corporate bond quality and investor experience.* Princeton, NJ: Princeton University Press.

Higgins, R. C. 2001. *Analysis of financial management.* 6th ed. New York: McGraw Hill.

Higgins, R. C. and L. D. Schall. 1975. Corporate bankruptcy and conglomerate merger. *Journal of Finance* 30:93–113.

Hogan, S. D. and M. C. Huie. 1992. Bigness, junk, and bust-ups: End of the fourth merger wave? *Antitrust Bulletin* 37(4):881–956.

Holman, K. and D. Carey. 2003. Hughes buys century maintenance. *The Daily Deal* (November 19):1.

Holtz-Eakin, D., D. Joulfaian, and H. S. Rosen. 1994. Sticking it out: Entrepreneurial decisions and liquidity constraints. *Journal of Political Economy* 102:53–75.

Hornaday, B. W. 2002. Conseco CEO Wendt resigns. *Indianapolis Star* (October 4).

Horowitz, J., N. E. Savin, and T. Loughran. 1996. A spline analysis of the small-firm effect: Does size really matter? Working paper available at http://econwpa.wustl.edu:80/eps/em/papers/9608/9608001.pdf.

Hoshi, T., A. Kashyap, and D. Scharfstein. 1990. Troubled debt restructurings. *Journal of Financial Economics* 27:67–88.

Hotchkiss, E. S. 1995. The post-emergence performance of firms emerging from chapter 11. *Journal of Finance* 50:3–21.

Hotchkiss, E. and R. Mooradian. 1998. Acquisitions as a means of restructuring firms in Chapter 11. *Journal of Financial Intermediation* 7:240.

————. 1997. Vulture investors and the market for control of distressed firms. *Journal of Financial Economics* 43:401.

Houlihan, Lokey, Howard & Zukin. 1999. *1998 transaction termination fee study.* Los Angeles, CA: Houlihan, Lokey, Howard & Zukin. July.

Houston, J. and C. James. 1996. Bank information monopolies and the mix of private and public debt claims. *Journal of Finance* 51:1863–1889.

Howe, J. 1988. *Junk bonds analysis and portfolio strategies.* Chicago: Probus.

Hradsky, G. T. and R. Long. 1989. High yield losses and the return performance of bankrupt debt. *Financial Analysts Journal* (July–August):38–49.

Hubbard, R. 2001. Enron shares fall on concern over CFO's partnerships. *Bloomberg News* (October 19).

Jackson, T. 1986. *The logic and limits of bankruptcy law.* Cambridge, MA: Harvard University Press.

James, C. 1987. Some evidence on the uniqueness of bank loans. *Journal of Financial Economics* 19:217–235.

————. 1995. When do banks take equity in debt restructuring. *Review of Financial Studies* 8:1209–1234.

————. 1996. Bank debt restructurings and the composition of exchange offers in financial distress. *Journal of Finance* 51:711–727.

Jarrow, R. A. and S. Turnbull. 1995. Pricing derivatives on financial securities subject to default risk. *Journal of Finance* 50:53–86.

Jelisavcic, B. 1999. Iridium bankruptcy court proceedings move to New York. *Bloomberg News* September 13.

Jensen, M. C. 1986. Agency costs of free cash flow, corporate finance and takeovers. *American Economic Review* 76:323–329.

————. 1989. Active investors, LBOs and the privatization of bankruptcy. *Journal of Applied Corporate Finance* 2:35–44.

————. 1991. Corporate control and the politics of finance. *Journal of Applied Corporate Finance* 4(2):13–33.

————. 1993. Presidential address: The modern industrial revolution, exit, and the failure of internal control systems. *Journal of Finance* 48:831–880.

Jensen, M. C. and W. Meckling. 1976. Theory of the firm: Managerial behavior, agency costs, and capital structure. *Journal of Financial Economics* 3:305–360.

Jensen, M. C., S. Kaplan, and L. Stiglin. 1989. The effects of LBOs on the tax revenues of the U.S. Treasury. *Tax Notes* 42(6):727–733.

Jensen-Conklin, S. 1992. Do confirmed Chapter 11 plans consummate? The results of a study and analysis of the law. *Commercial Law Journal* 97:297–317.

John, K. 1993. Managing financial distress and valuing distressed securities: A survey and research agenda. *Financial Management* 2:60–78.

John, K. and B. Mishra. 1990. Information content of insider trading around corporate announcements: The case of capital expenditures. *Journal of Finance* 45(July):835–855.

John, K., L. Lang, and J. Netter. 1992. The voluntary restructuring of large firms in response to performance decline. *Journal of Finance* 47:891–918.

Johnson, D. J. 1989. The risk behavior of firms approaching bankruptcy. *Journal of Financial Research* 12:33–50.

Jones, P. E., S. P. Mason, and E. Rosenfield. 1984. Contingent claims analysis of corporate capital structures: An empirical analysis. *Journal of Finance* 39:611–625.

Jonsson, J. G. and M. S. Fridson. 1996. Forecasting default rates on high yield bonds. *Journal of Fixed Income* (June):69–77.

J.P. Morgan Securities. 2002. *CDO handbook.* New York: J.P. Morgan Securities.

Kahan, M. and B. Tuckman. 1993. Do bondholders lose from junk bond covenant changes? *Journal of Business* (October):499–516.

Kalbfleisch, J. and R. Prentice. 1980. *The statistical analysis of failure time data.* Hoboken, NJ: John Wiley & Sons.

Kanda, H. and S. Levmore. 1994. Explaining creditor priorities. *Virginia Law Review* 80:2103–2111.

Kane, A., A. Marcus, and E. Rosenfeld. 1984. How big is the tax advantage to debt? *Journal of Finance* 39:841–852.

Kao, D. 1993. Illiquid securities: Issues of pricing and performance measurement. *Financial Analysts Journal* 77:28–35.

Kaplan, S. 1989. The effects of management buyouts on operations and value. *Journal of Financial Economics* 24:217–254.

———. 1991. The staying power of leveraged buyouts. *Journal of Financial Economics* 29:287–314.

———. 1997. The evolution of U.S. corporate governance: We are all Henry Kravis now. *Journal of Private Equity* (Fall):7–14.

Kaplan, S. and J. Stein. 1993. The evolution of buyout pricing and financial structure. Working Paper No. 3695. Cambridge, MA: National Bureau of Economic Research.

Keegan, S. C., J. Sobehart, and D. T. Hamilton. 1999. Predicting default rates: A forecasting model for Moody's issuer-based default rates. *Moody's special comment.* New York: Moody's Investors Service.

Keiso, D. E., J. J. Weygandt, and T. D. Warfield. 2003. *Intermediate accounting.* 12th ed. Hoboken, NJ: John Wiley & Sons.

Kellstrom, M. W. and A. Cray. 2002. *Foster Wheeler Ltd.: 3Q02 results.* Beverly Hills, CA: Imperial Capital. November 18.

Keown, A. J., J. D. Martin, J. W. Petty, and D. F. Scott. 2002. *Financial management principles and applications.* 9th ed. Englewood Cliffs, N.J.: Prentice Hall.

Kerkman, J. R. 1987. The debtor in full control: A case for adoption of the trustee system. *Marquette Law Review* 70:159.

Kester, C. 1991. Japanese corporate governance and the conservation of value in financial distress. *Journal of Applied Corporate Finance* 4(2):98–104.

Ketz, F. J. 1978. The effect of general price level adjustments on the predictive ability of financial ratios. *Journal of Accounting Research* Supplement:273–284.

Khurana, R. 2002. *Searching for a corporate savior: The irrational quest for charismatic CEOs.* Princeton, NJ: Princeton University Press.

Kihn, J. 1994. Unraveling the low-grade bond risk/reward puzzle. *Financial Analysts Journal* (July–August):32–42.

Kim, E. H. 1978. A mean-variance theory of optimal capital structure and corporate debt capacity. *Journal of Finance* 33:45–63.

Kim, E. H. and, J. D. Schatzberg. 1987. Voluntary corporate liquidations. *Journal of Financial Economics* 19:311–328.

Kim, E. H., J. J. McConnell, and P. R. Greenwood. 1977. Capital structure rearrangements and me-first rules in an efficient capital market. *Journal of Finance* 32:789–810.

Kim, I. J., K. Ramaswamy, and S. Sundaresan. 1993. Does default risk in coupons affect the valuation of corporate bonds? A contingent claims model. *Financial Management* (Autumn):117–131.

Kindleberger, C. P. 2001. *Manias, panics and crashes: A history of financial crisis.* Hoboken, NJ: John Wiley & Sons.

King, L. 1979. Chapter 11 of the 1978 Bankruptcy Code. *American Bankruptcy Law Journal* 53:107–131.

Klee, K. 1979. All you ever wanted to know about cram-down under the new bankruptcy code. *American Bankruptcy Law Journal* 53:133–171.

———. 1990. Cram down II. *American Bankruptcy Law Journal* 64:229–244.

———. 1995. Adjusting Chapter 11: Fine tuning the plan process. *American Banker Law Journal* 69:551.

Kleiman, R. 1992. Debtor-in-possession. *Business Credit* 94(8):13–15.

Klein, W. A. 1997. High yield ("junk") bonds as investments and as financial tools. *Cardozo Law Review* 19(2):505–510.

Kohn, R., A. Solow, and D. Taber, 1995. Pure debtor-in-possession financing. *Secured Lender* 51:6–10.

KPMG. 2003. Doing business in Ireland — Tax incentives. KPMG. May. Available at http://www.kpmg.ie/inv_irl/Pubs/DB_IRL/Tax_Incentives.pdf.

Kurtz, D. S., J. W. Linstrom, and T. R. Pohl. 1999. Representing the unsecured creditors' committee in insolvency restructurings. In *Workouts and turnarounds II.* ed. D. DiNapoli. Hoboken, NJ: John Wiley & Sons.

Kwan, S. H. 1996. Firm-specific information and the correlation between individual stocks and bonds. *Journal of Financial Economics* 40:63–80.

Lamoureux, C. G. and J. W. Wansley. 1989. The pricing of when-issued securities. *Financial Review* 24:183–198.

Lawless, R. M. and S. P. Ferris. 2000. The expenses of financial distress: The direct costs of Chapter 11. *University of Pittsburgh Law Review* 61:629-656.

———. 1997. Professional fees and other direct costs in Chapter 7 bankruptcies. *Washington University Law Quarterly* 75:1207.

Lawless, R. M., S. P. Ferris, N. Jayaraman, and A. K. Makhija. 1996. Industry wide effects of corporate bankruptcy announcements. *Bankruptcy Developments Journal* 12:293.

Lederman, J. and M. P. Sullivan, eds. 1993. *The new high yield bond market: Investment opportunities, strategies and analysis.* Chicago: Probus.

Lee, T. J. and J. Cunney. 2004. *The chapter after Chapter 11: A strategic guide to investing in post-bankruptcies.* New York: J.P. Morgan. January 9.

Leibowitz, M. L. 2002. The leveraged p/e ratio. *Financial Analysts Journal* (November/December):68–77.

Leland, H. E. 1994. Corporate debt value, bond covenants and optimal capital structure. *Journal of Finance* 49:1213–1252.

Leland, H. E. and K. B. Toft. 1996. Optimal capital structure, endogenous bankruptcy and the term structure of credit spreads. *Journal of Finance* 51:987–1019.

Levine, S. N., ed. 1991. *Investing in bankruptcies and turnarounds: Spotting investment values in distressed businesses.* New York: Harper Business.

Lichtenberg, F. R. 1992. *Corporate takeovers and productivity.* Cambridge, MA: MIT Press.

Livingston, M., H. Pratt, and C. Mann. 1995. Drexel Burnham Lambert's debt issues. *Journal of Fixed Income* (March):58–75.

Loderer, C. and D. Sheehan. 1989. Corporate bankruptcy and manager's self-serving behavior. *Journal of Finance* 44:1059–1075.

Loeys, J. 1986. Low-grade Bonds: A growing source of corporate funding. *Business Review, Federal Reserve Bank of Philadelphia* (November–December):3–12.

Longstaff, F. A. and E. S. Schwartz. 1995. A simple approach to valuing risky fixed and floating rate debt. *Journal of Finance* 50:789–819.

LoPucki, L. M. 1983. The debtor in full control — Systems failure under Chapter 11 of the Bankruptcy Code. *American Bankruptcy Law Journal* 57:247.

———. 1993. The trouble with Chapter 11. *Wisconsin Law Review* 1993:729.

LoPucki, L. M. and J. W. Doherty. 2002. The failure of public company bankruptcies in Delaware and New York revisited. *Vanderbilt Law Review* 54:331–356.

LoPucki, L. M. and S. D. Kalin. 2000. The failure of public company bankruptcies in Delaware and New York: Empirical evidence of a 'race to the bottom.' *Vanderbilt Law Review* 54:231–282.

LoPucki, L. M. and C. R. Mirick. 2003. *Strategies for creditors in bankruptcy proceedings.* 4th ed. New York: Aspen Law & Business.

LoPucki, L. M. and W. C. Whitford. 1990. Bargaining over equity's share in the bankruptcy reorganization of large, publicly held companies. *University of Pennsylvania Law Review* 139:125–196.

———. 1991. Venue choice and forum shopping in the bankruptcy reorganization of large, publicly held companies. *Wisconsin Law Review* 1:1–63.

———. 1993. Corporate governance in the bankruptcy reorganization of large, publicly held companies. *Pennsylvania Law Review* 141:669–800.

Lorie, J. H. and M. T. Hamilton. 1973. *The stock market: Theories and evidence.* Homewood, IL: Richard D. Irwin.

Lown, C. S., D. P. Morgan, and S. Rohatgi. 2000. Listening to loan officers: The impact of commercial credit standards on lending and output. *Economic Policy/Review* 6(2):1–16.

Luben, S. J. 2000. The direct costs of corporate reorganization: An empirical examination of professional fees in large Chapter 11 cases. *American Bankruptcy Law Journal* 74:509.

Lummer, S. L. and J. J. McConnell. 1989. Further evidence to the bank lending process and the capital market response to bank loan agreements. *Journal of Financial Economics* 25:99–122.

Lyle, M. 1999. Iridium unveils new strategy; announces lower phone and service pricing. *Bloomberg News* (June 21).

Ma, C. K., R. Rao, and R. L. Peterson. 1989. The resiliency of the high yield bond market: The LTV default. *Journal of Finance* 44(4):1085–1097.

Maksimovic, V. and G. Philips. 1998. Efficiency of bankrupt firms and industry conditions: Theory and evidence. *Journal of Finance* 53:1495–1532.

Maremont, M., J. Eisinger, and M. Song. 2000. Lernout & Hauspie surges in Korea, raising questions. *Wall Street Journal* (August 8).

Martin, D. 2003. *Orbital Imaging Corporation.* Beverly Hills, CA: Imperial Capital. December 15.

Mason, S., R. C. Merton, A. Perold, and P. Tufano. 1995. *Cases in financial engineering: Applied studies of financial innovation.* New York: Prentice-Hall.

Masulis, R. 1988. *The debt/equity choice.* Cambridge, MA: Ballinger Publishing Company.

Maxwell, W. F. 1998. The January effect in the corporate bond market. *Financial Management* (Summer):18–30.

McConnel, J. and H. Servaes. 1991. The economics of pre-packaged bankruptcy. *Journal of Applied Corporate Finance* 4(2):93–97.

McDaniel, M. 1986. Bondholders and corporate governance. *Business Lawyer* 41:413–460.

McDermott, M. F. 2002. *CLEC: Telecom Act 1996, An insider's look and the rise and fall of local exchange competition.* Rockport, ME: Penobscot Press.

McHugh, C. M. ed. 2003. *The 2003 bankruptcy yearbook and almanac.* Boston: New Generation Research.

McQueen, C. R. and J. Crestol. 1990. *Federal tax aspects of bankruptcy.* New York: McGraw-Hill.

Meakin, T. K. 1990. Junk bond hysteria hits insurer stocks. *National Underwriter* 7:61–66.

Mella-Barral, P. and W. R. M. Perraudin. 1997. Strategic debt service. *Journal of Finance* 52:531–556.

Mello, A. S. and J. E. Parsons. 1992. The agency costs of debt. *Journal of Finance* 47:1887–1904.

Merton, R. C. 1974. On the pricing of corporate debt. *Journal of Finance* 29:449–470.

———. 1990. The financial system and economic performance. *Journal of Financial Services Research* 4:263–300.

———. 1992a. *Continuous time finance.* Malden, MA: Blackwell.

———. 1992b. Financial innovation and economic performance. *Journal of Applied Corporate Finance* 4(4):12–22.

Michel, A. and I. Shaked. 1990. The LBO nightmare: Fraudulent conveyance risk. *Financial Analysts Journal* (March–April):41–50.

Milken, M. R. 1999. Prosperity and social capital. *Wall Street Journal* (June 23):26.

———. 2000. The democratization of capital. *California Lawyer* (July):57–60.

———. 2003. The corporate financing cube: Matching capital structure to business risk. In *Business encyclopedia.* ed. J. Kurtzman. New York: Crown Books.

Miller, H. R. 1999. Looming financial or business failure: Fix or file — A legal perspective. In *Workouts and turnarounds II.* ed. D. DiNapoli. Hoboken, NJ: John Wiley & Sons.

Miller, M. H. 1988. Financial innovation: The last twenty years and the next. *Journal of Financial and Quantitative Analysis* 21(4):459–471.

———. 1992. Financial markets and economic growth. *Journal of Applied Corporate Finance* 11(3):8–14.

———. 1996. Financial innovation: Achievements and prospects. *Journal of Applied Corporate Finance* 4:4–11.

———. 1997. Debt and taxes. *Journal of Finance* 32:261–275.

Miller, M. H. and F. Modigliani. 1958. The cost of capital, corporation finance and the theory of investment. *American Economic Review* 48:261–297.

———. 1961. Dividend policy, growth and the valuation of shares. *Journal of Business* 34:411–433.

———. 1963. Corporate income taxes and the cost of capital: A correction. *American Economic Review* 53:433–443.

Miller, S. C. 1990. The emerging market for distressed senior bank loans. *Loan Pricing Corporation* (November):3.

Millon, T .J. and S. P. Pratt. 1999. Valuation of companies within workout and turnaround situations. In *Workouts and turnarounds II.* ed. D. DiNapoli. Hoboken, NJ: John Wiley & Sons.

Mishkin, F. 1991. Asymmetric information and financial crises: A historical perspective. In *Financial markets and financial crises*. ed. R. G. Hubbard. Chicago: University of Chicago Press.

Mitchell, M. L. and J. H. Mulherin. 1996. The impact of industry shocks on takeover and restructuring activity. *Journal of Financial Economics* 41:193–229.

Mitchell, M. L. and J. M. Netter. 1989. *Triggering the 1987 stock-market crash: Anti-takeover provisions in the proposed House Ways and Means Tax Bill*. Washington, D.C.: Office of Economic Analysis, U.S. Securities and Exchange Commission.

Modigliani, F. and M. H. Miller. 1958. The cost of capital, corporation finance and the theory of investment. *American Economic Review* 48(3):261–297.

Moore, D. 1990. How to finance a debtor-in-possession. *Commercial Lending Review* 4:3–12.

Moore, T. F. and E. Simendinger. 1998. *Hospital turnarounds: Lessons in leadership*. Washington, D.C.: Beard Books.

Morellec, E. 2001. Asset liquidity, capital structure and secured debt. *Journal of Financial Economics* 61:173–206.

Morris, J. 1995. *Merger and acquisitions: Strategies for accountants*. Hoboken, NJ: John Wiley & Sons.

Morrison, C. J. and D. Siegel. 1998. Knowledge capital and cost structure in the U.S. food and fiber industries. *American Journal of Agricultural Economics* 80(1):30–45.

Morrison, R. W. 1985. *Business opportunities from corporate bankruptcies*. Hoboken, NJ: John Wiley & Sons.

Morse, D. and W. Shaw. 1988. Investing in bankrupt firms. *Journal of Finance* 5(December):1193–1206.

Moyer, S. G. 2002a. *Aames Financial: Situation update*. Beverly Hills, CA: Imperial Capital. May 1.

———. 2002b. *Encompass Services: 2Q02 update*. Beverly Hills, CA: Imperial Capital. August 20.

———. 2002c. *Orbital Sciences: Situation update*. Beverly Hills, CA: Imperial Capital. February 5.

———. 2002d. *Orbital Sciences: 2Q on track — Expect exchange offer proposal in July*. Beverly Hills, CA: Imperial Capital. May 31.

———. 2002e. *Orbital Sciences: Refinancing update*. Beverly Hills, CA: Imperial Capital. August 9.

———. 2004. *Magellan Health Services, Inc.: Deleveraged company well positioned to remain as leader of MBH*. Beverly Hills, CA: Imperial Capital. January 9.

Moyer, S. G. and A. Cray. 2002. *Internet Capital Group: Situation summary*. Beverly Hills, CA: Imperial Capital. December 13.

Moyer, S. G. and A. Gubner. 2001. *Southern California Edison and Pacific Gas & Electric: Situation summary*. Beverly Hills, CA: Imperial Capital. February 5.

Moyer, S. G. and R. Laufman. 2002. *Penton Media: 3Q02 update*. Beverly Hills, CA: Imperial Capital. November 12.

———. 2003a. *Atmel Corp.: 4Q02 update*. Beverly Hills, CA: Imperial Capital. January 31.

———. 2003b. *Amkor Technology, Inc.: Situation update*. Beverly Hills, CA: Imperial Capital. February 24.

———. 2003c. *Penton Media: 4Q02 update*. Beverly Hills, CA: Imperial Capital. March 20.

———. 2003d. *TransSwitch Corporation: Offers discount exchange offer with cash put feature*. Beverly Hills, CA: Imperial Capital. May 19.

————. 2003e. *Amkor Technology, Inc.: 1Q03 update.* Beverly Hills, CA: Imperial Capital. May 23.

————. 2003f. *i2 Technologies, Inc.: Accounting restatement completed, cash position solid.* Beverly Hills, CA: Imperial Capital. July 28.

Murdoch, D., L. Sartin, and R. Zudek. 1987. Fraudulent conveyances and leveraged buyouts. *Business Lawyer* 43:1–26.

Murray, S. and K. Kranhold. 2003. Asbestos factions still struggle to settle their 30-year war. *Daily Bankruptcy Review* (October 16):1.

Myers, S. 1977. Determinants of corporate borrowing. *Journal of Financial Economics* 4:147–176.

————. 1984. The capital structure puzzle. *Journal of Finance* 39:575–592.

Myers, S. and N. S. Majluf. 1984. Corporate financing and investment decisions: When firms have information that investors do not have. *Journal of Financial Economics* 13:187–221.

National Bureau of Economic Research (NBER). 2003. *Business cycle expansions and contractions.* NBER (www.nber.org/cycles.html).

Nelken, I. 1999. *Implementing credit derivatives.* New York: McGraw-Hill.

————. ed. 2001. *Handbook of hybrid instruments.* Hoboken, NJ: John Wiley & Sons.

Nitzberg, J. 1999. Preparing for bankruptcy: Building the war chest. In *Workouts and turnarounds II.* ed. D. DiNapoli. Hoboken, NJ: John Wiley & Sons.

Ohlson, J. A. 1980. Financial ratios and the probabilistic prediction of Bankruptcy. *Journal of Accounting Research* 18:109–131.

Oldfield, G. S. (2004) Bond games. *Financial Analysts Journal* (May–June):52–65.

Opler, T. C., M. Saron, and S. Titman. 1994. Financial distress and corporate performance. *Journal of Finance* 49:1015–1040.

————. 1997. Designing capital structure to create shareholder value. *Journal of Applied Corporate Finance* 10(1):21–32.

Osbourne, M. F. M. 1964. Brownian motion in the stock market. In *The random character of stock market prices.* ed. P. Cootner. Cambridge, MA: MIT Press.

Pacelle, M. and R. Frank. 2002. Michael Douglas learns a new line: Grim is good. *Wall Street Journal* (December 12).

Pandofini, B. 1993. *Bobby Fischer's outrageous chess moves.* New York: Fireside.

Paulus, J. D. and S. R. Waite. 1990. High-yield bonds, corporate control, and innovation. In *The new high-yield debt market: A handbook for portfolio managers and analysts.* ed. F. J. Fabozzi. New York: HarperCollins.

Penman, S. H. 2001. *Financial statement analysis and security valuation.* New York: Irwin McGraw-Hill.

Penman, S. H. and T. Sougiannia. 1998. A comparison of dividend, cash flow, and earnings approaches to valuation. *Contemporary Accounting Research* (Fall):343–384.

Peters, E. E. 1996. *Chaos and order in the capital markets.* 2nd ed. Hoboken, NJ: John Wiley & Sons.

————. 1999. *Complexity, risk and financial markets.* Hoboken, NJ: John Wiley & Sons.

Petersen, M. A. and R. G. Rajan. 1995. The effect of credit market competition on lending relationships. *Quarterly Journal of Economics* 110:407–443.

Pindyck, R. S. 1988. Irreversible investment, capacity choice and the value of a firm. *American Economic Review* 79:969–985.

Platt, H. D. 1993. Underwriter effects and the riskiness of original-issue high yield bonds. *Journal of Applied Corporate Finance* 6(1):89–94.

———. 1994. *The first junk bond: A story of corporate boom and bust.* Armonk, NY: M.E. Sharpe.

———. 1997. *Why companies fail: Strategies for detecting, avoiding and profiting from bankruptcy.* Washington, D.C.: Beard Books.

Platt, H. D. and M. Platt. 1991. A linear programming approach to bond portfolio selection. *Economic and Financial Computing* (Spring):71–84.

Pozen, R. and J. Mencher. 1993. Chinese walls for creditor's committees. *Business Lawyer* 48:747.

Pradhuman, S. D. 2000. *Small cap dynamics.* New York: Bloomberg.

Pratt, S. 2001. *The market approach to valuing businesses.* Hoboken, NJ: John Wiley & Sons.

Pulvino, T. C. 1999. Effect of bankruptcy court protection on asset sales. *Journal of Financial Economics* 52:151.

Queenan, J. F. 1989. The collapsed leveraged buyout and the trustee in bankruptcy. *Cardozo Law Review* 11:1.

Rajan, R. and L. Zingales. 1995. Is there an optimal capital structure? Some evidence from international data. *Journal of Finance* 50:1421–1460.

———. 1998. Financial dependence and growth. *American Economic Review* 88 (3):559–586.

Ramaswami, M. 1991. Hedging the equity risk of high yield bonds. *Financial Analysts Journal* (September–October):41–50.

Ravenscraft, D. J. and F. M. Scherer. 1987. *Mergers, sell-offs, and economic efficiency.* Washington, D.C.: Brookings Institution.

Reehl, W. F. 1993. Plan feasibility: A quantitative approach. *California Bankruptcy Journal* 21(2):29.

Regan, P. J. 1990. Junk bonds — opportunity knocks? *Financial Analysts Journal* (May–June):13–16.

Reilly, F. K., ed. 1990. *High yield bonds: Analysis and risk assessment.* Charlottesville, VA: Institute of Chartered Financial Analysts.

Reilly, F. K. and D. J. Wright. 1994. An analysis of high-yield bond benchmarks. *Journal of Fixed Income* (March):6–25.

Reilly, R. F. and R. P. Scheins. 2000. *The handbook of advanced business valuation.* New York: McGraw-Hill.

Roache, J. T. 1993. The fiduciary obligations of a debtor-in-possession. *University of Illinois Law Review* 133:1–56.

Roberts, M. 1993. The conundrum of directors' duties of nearly insolvent corporations. *Memphis State University Law Review* 23:273–292.

Roe, M. 1983. Bankruptcy and debt: A new model for corporate reorganizations. *Columbia Law Review* 83(3):527–602.

———. 1987. The voting prohibition in bond workouts. *Yale Law Journal* 97:232–279.

———. 1993. Takeover politics. In *The deal decade: What takeovers and leveraged buyouts mean for corporate buyouts.* ed. M. M. Blair. Washington, D.C.: The Brookings Institution.

Rohman, M. 1990. Financing Chapter 11 companies in the 1990s. *Journal of Applied Corporate Finance* 5(2):96–101.

Roll, R. 1977. A critique of the asset pricing theory's tests, part I: On past and potential testability of the theory. *Journal of Financial Economics* 4:129–176.

Roll, R. and S. A. Ross. An empirical investigation of the arbitrage pricing theory. *Journal of Finance* 35(5):1073–1103.

Romer, P. 1986. Increasing returns and long run growth. *Journal of Political Economy* 94:1002–1037.

Ronson, C. R. 2003a. *Gentek*. Beverly Hills, CA: Imperial Capital. September 26.

———. 2003b. Global Crossing, Ltd. *Bankruptcy reorganization monitor*. Beverly Hills, CA: Imperial Capital. November.

———. 2004. *Exide Technologies: Deleveraged company with strong projections*. Beverly Hills, CA: Imperial Capital. April 27.

Rose-Green, E. and M. Dawkins. 2002. Strategic bankruptcies and price reactions to bankruptcy filings. *Journal of Business Finance & Accounting* (November/December):39–55.

Ross, S. A. 1976. The arbitrage theory of capital asset pricing. *Journal of Economic Theory* 13:341–360.

———. 1977. The determination of financial structure: The incentive signalling approach. *Bell Journal of Economics* 8:23–40.

Ross, S. 1989. Institutional markets, financial marketing, and financial innovation. *Journal of Finance* 44:541–556.

Rutberg, S. 1999. *Ten cents on the dollar — or the bankruptcy game*. Washington, D.C.: Beard Books.

Ryan, J. 2002. WorldCom bonds plummet after falsely reporting expenses. *Bloomberg News* (June 26).

Sabin, J., M. Neporent, and C. Weiner. 1991. Legal considerations of purchasing securities. In *Workouts & turnarounds: The handbook of restructuring & investing in distressed companies*. eds. D. DiNapoli, S. Sigoloff, and R. Cushman. Homewood IL: Business 1 Irwin.

Saggese, N. P. and A. Ranney-Martinelli. 1993. *A practical guide to out-of-court restructurings and plans of reorganization*. New York: Matthew Bender.

Sahakian, C. E. 1998. *Sahakian's due diligence checklists*. Chicago: The Corporate Partnering Institute.

Salerno, T. J. 1992. Seventh circuit sounds a death bell for reorganization of toxic polluters. *American Bankruptcy Institute Journal* (September):8.

———. 1993. And the beat goes on: The Seventh Circuit espouses the "greater fool" theory as a solution for environment contamination problems. *American Bankruptcy Institute Journal* (April):8.

———. 1994. Future claimants in mass tort bankruptcy cases — good news and bad news for debtors and reorganization cases from the southern district of Florida. *American Bankruptcy Institute Journal* (September):8.

Salerno, T. J. and C. Hansen. 1991. A prepackaged bankruptcy strategy. *Journal of Business Strategy* (January–February):36.

Salerno, T. J. and J. A. Kroop. 2000. *Bankruptcy litigation and practice: A practitioner's guide*. 3rd ed. New York: Aspen Law Publishers.

Salerno, T. J., S. Ferland, and C. Hansen. 1990. Environmental law and its impact on bankruptcy law: The saga of toxins-R-US. *Real Property Probate and Trust Journal* 25:261.

Salerno, T. J., C. Hansen, J. Haydon, and C. Owens. 1996. The 111(b)(2) election: A primer. *Bankruptcy Development Journal* (Winter):99.

Salerno, T. J., C. Hansen, and R. Meyer. 1997. *Advanced Chapter 11 bankruptcy practice.* 2nd ed. Aspen Law and Business.

Salerno, T. J., J. A. Kroop, and C. Hansen. 2001. *The executive guide to corporate bankruptcy.* Washington, D.C.: Beard Books.

Salomon Bros. Inc. 1988. *Leveraged buyouts and leveraged restructurings: Risks and rewards for pre-existing bondholders.* New York: Salomon Bros. November 2.

Sandler, L. 1981. Post-bankruptcy shares: Next big play? *Wall Street Journal* (May 16).

Schwartz, A. 1981. Security interests and bankruptcy priorities: A review of current theories. *Journal of Legal Studies* 10:1–38.

Schwartz, S. 1997. The easy case for the priority of secured claims in bankruptcy. *Duke Law Journal* 47:428–489.

Scott, J. H. 1977. Bankruptcy, secured debt and optimal capital structure. *Journal of Finance* 32:1–19.

Securities and Exchange Commission (SEC). 1990. *Recent developments in the high yield market.* Washington, D.C.: Securities and Exchange Commission.

———. 1991. *Transparency in the market for high yield debt securities.* Washington, D.C.: Securities and Exchange Commission.

———. 1996. *Capital formation and regulatory processes.* Washington, D.C.: Securities and Exchange Commission.

———. 2003. *Implications of the growth of hedge funds.* Washington, D.C.: Securities and Exchange Commission. September.

Shane, H. 1994. Co-movements of low-grade debt and equity returns of highly leveraged firms. *Journal of Fixed Income* (March):79–89.

Sharpe, S. 1994. Financial market imperfections, firm leverage, and the cyclicality of employment. *American Economic Review* 84:1060–1074.

Sharpe, W. F. 1964. Capital asset prices: A theory of market equilibrium under conditions of risk. *Journal of Finance* 19 (3):425–442.

———. 1970. *Portfolio theory and capital markets.* New York: McGraw-Hill.

Shefrin, H. 2002. *Beyond greed and fear: Understanding behavioral finance and the psychology of investing.* Cambridge, MA: Harvard Business School Press.

Sherwin, H., D. Hamilton, and R. Cantor. 2004. *Moody's rating actions, reviews and outlooks — quarterly update.* New York: Moody's Investors Service. January.

Shiller, R. 2000. *Irrational exuberance.* Princeton, NJ.: Princeton University Press.

Shinkle, T. H. 2000. *Magellan Health Services: Initiating coverage with buy recommendation.* Imperial Capital. August 18.

———. 2002a. *Magellan Health Services: Situation update.* Beverly Hills, CA: Imperial Capital. March 22.

———. 2002b. *Magellan Health Services: 2Q02 results: Missed guidance depresses securities.* Beverly Hills, CA: Imperial Capital. May 15.

———. 2002c. *Magellan Health Services: 3Q03 update — Down quarter depresses bonds.* Beverly Hills, CA: Imperial Capital. August 16.

———. 2002d. *Magellan Health Services: Potential restructuring announced.* Beverly Hills, CA: Imperial Capital. October 1.

———. 2003a. *Magellan Health Services: 1Q03 update — Operations improving; restructuring proposal expected soon.* Beverly Hills, CA: Imperial Capital. February 24.

———. 2003b. *HealthSouth Corp.: Substantial asset value present — Fraud uncertainty creates buying opportunity.* Beverly Hills, CA: Imperial Capital. March 24

———. 2003c. *Magellan Health Services: Bankruptcy plan filed — Summary of terms and valuation of securities*. Beverly Hills, CA: Imperial Capital. March 25.

———. 2003d. *Magellan Health Services: Onex commits to $200MM MGL investment — sr sub valuation revisited*. Beverly Hills, CA: Imperial Capital. May 30.

———. 2003e. *Magellan Health Services: Onex revamps offer at $28.50/share — sr sub recoveries 20% higher*. Beverly Hills, CA: Imperial Capital. July 1.

———. 2003f. *Laidlaw: Company out of bankruptcy; new management seeks efficiencies*. Beverly Hills, CA: Imperial Capital. July 21.

Shleifer, A. and R. Vishny. 1992. Liquidation values and debt capacity: A market equilibrium approach. *Journal of Finance* 47:1343–1365.

Shulman, J., V. Bayless, and K. Price. 1993. The influence of marketability on the yield premium of speculative grade debt. *Financial Management* (Autumn):132–141.

Shumway, T. 2001. Forecasting bankruptcy more accurately: A simple hazard model. *Journal of Business* 74:101–124.

Siegel, H. L. 2003. Bankruptcy courts vs. FERC: Smackdown. *Public Utilities Fortnightly* (September 1):62–65.

Smith, C. W., Jr. 2001. Organizational architecture and corporate finance. *Journal of Financial Research* 24(1):1–13.

Smith C. W. and J. Warner. 1979. On financial contracting: An analysis of bond covenants. *Journal of Financial Economics* 7:117–161.

Smith, C. W. and R. Watts. 1992. The investment opportunity set and corporate financing, dividend, and compensation policies. *Journal of Financial Economics* 32(3):263–292.

Smythe, W. 1989. Insurer investigations in junk or below-investment grade bonds: Some questions and answers for regulators. *Journal of Insurance Regulation* (September):4–15.

Spero, J. E. 1990. *The failure of the Franklin National Bank: Challenge to the international banking system*. Washington, D.C.: Beard Books.

Steelnews.com. 2003. Steel industry bankruptcies. October 28. Available at http://www.steelnews.com/companies/steel_bankruptcies.htm.

Stein, S. 1999. *A feast for lawyers*. Washington, D.C.: Beard Books.

Stickney, C. P. 1996. *Financial reporting and statement analysis*. 3rd ed. Orlando, FL: Dryden Press.

Stigliz, J. E. 1972. Some aspects of the pure theory of corporate finance: Bankruptcies and takeovers. *Bell Journal of Economics and Management Science* 3(Autumn):458–482.

Stromberg, P. 2000. Conflicts of interest and market illiquidity in bankruptcy auctions: Theory and tests. *Journal of Finance* 55:2641.

Stulz, R. M. 1990. Managerial discretion and optimal financial policies. *Journal of Financial Economics* 26:3–26.

———. 1999. Globalization, corporate finance and the cost of capital. *Journal of Applied Corporate Finance* 12(3):8–25.

Stumpp, P. M. 2001. *The unintended consequences of ratings triggers*. New York: Moody's Investors Service. December.

Stumpp, P. M., T. Marshella, M. Rowan, R. McCreary, and M. Coppola. 2000. *Putting EBITDA in perspective: Ten critical failings of EBITDA as the principal determinant of cash flow*. New York: Moody's Investors Service. June.

Sullivan, T. A., J. L. Westbrook, and E. Warren. 1998. *As we forgive our debtors: Bankruptcy and consumer credit in America*. Washington, D.C.: Beard Books.

Sutton, R. and A. Callahan. 1987. The stigma of bankruptcy: Spoiled organizational image and its management. *Academy of Management Journal* 30:405–436.

Taggart, R. A., Jr. 1990. Corporate leverage and the restructuring movement of the 1980s. *Business Economics* 25(2):12–18.

Taleb, N. N. 2001. *Fooled by randomness.* New York: Taxere.

Tashijian, E., R. Lease, and J. McConnell. 1996. Prepacks: An empirical analysis of prepackaged bankruptcies. *Journal of Financial Economics* 40:135–162.

Tavakoli, J. M. 2001. *Credit derivatives & synthetic structures.* New York: John Wiley & Sons.

Thaler, R. H., ed. 1993. *Advances in behavioral finance.* New York: Russell Sage Foundation.

Theodoros, L. 1999. ICO Global bonds plunge after bankruptcy filing. *Bloomberg News* (August 27).

Thorburn, K. S. 2000. Bankruptcy auctions: Costs, debt recovery, and firm survival. *Journal of Financial Economics* 58:337.

Titman, S. 1984. The effect of capital structure on a firm's liquidation decision. *Journal of Financial Economics* 13:137–151.

Titman, S. and R. Wessels. 1988. The determinants of capital structure choice. *Journal of Finance* 43:1–19.

Treister, G. M., J. R. Trost, L. S. Forman, K. N. Klee, and R. B. Levin. 1988. *Fundamentals of bankruptcy law.* 2nd ed. Philadelphia: American Law Institute.

Triantis, G. 1993. A theory of the regulation of debtor-in-possession financing. *Vanderbilt Law Review* 46:901–935.

Trifts, J. W. 1991. Corporate takeover bids, methods of payment and the effects of leverage. *Quarterly Journal of Business & Economics* 30(3):33–47.

Trost, J. R. 1979. Business reorganizations under Chapter 11 of the new bankruptcy code. *Business Lawyer* (April):1309–1346.

Tufano, P. 1989. Financial innovation and first-mover advantages. *Journal of Economics* 25:213–240.

Tversky, A. 1990. The psychology of risk. In *Quantifying the market risk premium phenomena for investment decision making.* Charlottesville, VA: Institute of Chartered Financial Analysts.

Vanderhoof, I. T., F. S. Albert, A. Tenenbein, and R. F. Verni. 1990. The risk of asset default: Report of the Society of Actuaries' C-1 Risk Task Force of the Committee on Valuation and Related Areas. *Transactions* 41:547–582.

Van Horne, J. C. 2001. *Fundamentals of financial management and policy.* 12th ed. Englewood Cliffs, NJ: Prentice Hall.

Voreacos, D. 2003. HealthSouth workers talking to U.S. fraud prosecutors. *Bloomberg News* (March 24).

Wagner, H. and M. Van De Voorde. 1985. Post bankruptcy performance of new equity securities issued in exchange for pre-petition debt. *Journal of Fixed Income* 4:49–59.

Waite, S. R. 1991. The eclipse of growth capital. *Journal of Applied Corporate Finance* 4(1):77–85.

Warner, J. 1977a. Bankruptcy, absolute priority and the pricing of risky debt claims. *Journal of Financial Economics* 4:239–276.

———. 1977b. Bankruptcy costs: Some evidence. *Journal of Finance* 32(2).

Warren, C. 1999. *Bankruptcy in United States history.* Washington, D.C.: Beard Books.

Weil, Gotshal & Manges. 2003. *Reorganizing failing businesses: A comprehensive review and analysis of financial restructuring and business reorganization.* New York: American Bar Association.

Weinstein, M. I. 1987. A curmudgeon's view of junk bonds. *Journal of Portfolio Management* (Spring):76–80.

Weintraub, B. and A. N. Resnick. 1990. Bankruptcy trustee's strong arm power balked by constructive trust. *U.C.C. Law Journal* 22:367–370.

Weiss, L. A. 1990. Bankruptcy resolution: Direct costs and violation of priority of claims. *Journal of Financial Economics* 27(2):285–314.

White, G. I., A. C. Sondhi, and H. D. Fried. 2003. *The analysis and use of financial statements.* 3rd ed. Hoboken, NJ: John Wiley & Sons.

White, L. J. 1991. *The S&L debacle: Public policy lessons for bank and thrift regulation.* New York: Oxford University Press.

White, M. J. 1979. Bankruptcy costs and the new bankruptcy code. *Journal of Finance* 38:477–504.

———. 1980a. Bankruptcy and reorganization. Working Paper, New York University, Graduate School of Business Administration.

———. 1980b. Public policy toward bankruptcy: Me-first and other priority rules. *Bell Journal of Economics* (Autumn).

———. 1989. The corporate bankruptcy decision. *Journal of Economic Perspectives* 3(Spring):129–151.

———. 1996. The costs of corporate bankruptcy: A US-European comparison. In *Corporate bankruptcy: Economic and legal perspectives.* eds. J. Bhandari and L. Weiss. Cambridge, U.K.: Cambridge University Press.

Whitney, J. O. 1999. *Taking charge: Management guide to troubled companies and turnarounds.* Washington, D.C.: Beard Books.

Wigmore, B. A. 1990. The decline in credit quality of new-issue junk bonds. *Financial Analysts Journal* (September–October):53–62.

Winch, K. F. 1990. *High yield bond market.* Washington, D.C.: Congressional Research Service.

Wolfe, T. 1993. *A man in full.* New York: Bantam.

Wright, M., N. Wilson, and K. Robbie. 1997. The longer term performance of management buy-outs. *Frontiers of Entrepreneurship Research* (Spring):555–569.

———. 1998. The longer term effects of management-led buy-outs. *Journal of Entrepreneurial and Small Business Finance* 5(3):213–234.

Wruck, K. H. 1990. Financial distress, reorganization and organizational efficiency. *Journal of Financial Economics* 27:419–444.

Yago, G. 1990. Corporate restructuring in the United States. In *Corporate restructuring.* ed. M. Smith. London: Euromoney Publications.

———. 1991a. The credit crunch: A regulatory squeeze on growth capital. *Journal of Applied Corporate Finance* 4(1):96–100.

———. 1991b. *Junk bonds: How high yield securities restructured corporate America.* New York: Oxford University Press.

———. 1993. Financial repression and the capital crunch recession. In *Economic policy, financial markets and economic growth.* eds. B. Zycher and L. Solmon. Boulder, CO: Westview Press.

————. 2001. Financing global environmental futures: Using financial market and instruments to advance environmental goals. *Milken Institute Policy Brief* (March 20).

Yago, G. and L. Ramesh. 1999. *Raising regulatory costs of growth capital: Implications of the proposal to amend Rule 144.A.* Santa Monica, CA: Milken Institute.

Yago, G. and D. Siegel. 1994. Triggering high yield market decline: Regulatory barriers in financial markets. *Extra Credit: The Journal of High Yield Bond Research* 21:11–24.

Yago, G. and S. Trimbath. 2003. *Beyond junk bonds: Expanding high yield markets.* New York: Oxford.

Young, S. and D. K. Berman. 2003. MCI's re-emergence portends tougher telecom competition. *Daily Bankruptcy Review* (November 4).

Zuckerman, G. 2003. Matlin's Strategy hits bumps as bonds of WorldCom rally. *Wall Street Journal* (January 23).

Zycher, B. 1993. Bank capitalization standards, the credit crunch, and resource allocation under regulation. In *Economic policy, financial markets and economic growth.* eds. B. Zycher and L. Solmon. Boulder, CO: Westview Press.

APPENDIX: CHESS NOTATION AND GAME MOVES

INTRODUCTION TO CHESS NOTATION*

A chessboard can be thought of as an 8×8 grid map with the vertical rows designated with letters a–h and the horizontal lines designated with numbers 1–8. Each square is named by its intersecting coordinates, with the southwest corner serving as the origin. In addition to the coordinates for each square, other symbols are used in following the moves in a chess game:

Piece Symbols

K = King
Q = Queen
R = Rook
B = Bishop
N = Knight
P = Pawn

Move Symbols

X = captures piece
+ = check
0-0 = castle-Kingside
0-0-0 = castle-Queenside

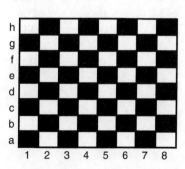

---

* Prepared in consultation with Pandofini (1993).

433

It is assumed that the ending location of a piece is sufficient to indicate which piece must have been moved. White pieces are on the bottom half of the board. Thus, 1. Pd4 indicates that the pawn that was at b4 was moved to d4. Captures are noted by the square of the capture. Thus, 7. Pxc3 indicates that a pawn captured whatever was on c3 (the type of piece making the capture is needed because often several pieces may be involved).

BORIS SPASSKY (W) VERSUS BOBBY FISCHER (B)
GAME 5 OF 1972 WORLD CHAMPIONSHIP
REYKJAVIK, ICELAND

Move	Spassky White	Fischer Black	Move	Spassky White	Fischer Black
1.	Pd4	Nf6	18.	Rb2	Rb8
2.	Pc4	Pe6	19.	Rbf2	Qe7
3.	Nc3	Bb4	20.	Bc2	Pg5
4.	Nf3	Pc5	21.	Bd2	Qe8
5.	Pe3	Nc6	22.	Be1	Qg6
6.	Bd3	Bxc3+	23.	Qd3	Nh5
7.	Pxc3	Pd6	24.	Rxf8+	Rxf8
8.	Pe4	Pe5	25.	Rxf8+	Kxf8
9.	Pd5	Ne7	26.	Bd1	Nf4
10.	Nh4	Ph6	27.	Qc2	Bxa4
11.	Pf4	Ng6	White resigns — Moves leading to mate		
12.	Nxg6	Pxg6	28	Qxa4	Qxe4
13.	Pxe5	Pxe5	29.	Kf2	Nd3+
14.	Be3	Pb6	30.	Kg3	Qh4+
15.	0-0	0-0	31.	Kf3	Qf4+
16.	Pa4	Pa5	32.	Ke2	Nc1 — Checkmate
17.	Rb1	Bd7			

DISCLOSURE OF POSSIBLE CONFLICTS OF INTEREST OF THE AUTHOR AND/OR HIS EMPLOYER WITH CERTAIN OF THE COMPANIES MENTIONED OR REFERRED TO IN THIS BOOK AS OF SEPTEMBER 1, 2004

Company	Ticker	Disclosure	Company	Ticker	Disclosure
Airgate	PCSA	None	ICO Global	ICOHA	None
Alamosa	APCS	None	Internet Capital Group	ICGE	None
AmeriCredit	ACF	None	Iridium	NA	2, 4
Amkor	AMKR	None	Johns Manville	N/A	None
Armstrong	YRM	2	Kmart	KMRT	None
Building Materials	N/A	None	Lernout Hauspie	NA	None
Color Tile	N/A	None	Loral	LRLSQ	None
Conseco	CNO	None	Lowe's	LOW	None
Covad	N/A	2, 3	Motorola	MOT	None
Dow Corning	N/A	None	Orbital Sciences	NA	None
Edison	EIX	None	Penton Media	PTON	None
Enron	ENRNQ	None	PG&E	PCG	None
Flooring America	NA	None	Raytheon	RTN	None
Foster Wheeler	FWC	2, 3	Safety Kleen	N/A	4
GAF	N/A	None	Transwitch	TXCC	None
Global Crossing	GBLCF	4	UbiquiTel	UPCS	None
Halliburton	HAL	None	USG	USG	None
HealthSouth	HLSH	None	Washington Group	WGII	2
Home Depot	HD	None	WCI	N/A	2
Horizon	N/A	None	WKI	N/A	4
i2	ITWO	7	WorldCom	MCIAV	2, 3

1 As of September 1, 2004, the author (or a member of his household) has a financial interest in the securities of this entity.

2 Imperial Capital LLC (IC), a firm in which the author is a partner and the Director of Research, makes markets in the debt securities of this entity.

3 IC makes markets in the equity securities of this entity.

4 As of the date hereof, IC or persons associated with it own securities of this entity.

5 In the past 12 months, IC has managed or co-managed a public offering of securities or received compensation for investment banking services for this entity.

6 IC has received compensation for investment banking services from this entity within the 12 months prior to the date hereof.

7 IC expects to receive or intends to seek compensation for investment banking services from this entity within three months from the date hereof.

8 An employee of IC serves on the board of directors of this entity.

INDEX